ACCLAIM FOR THE REVISED EDITION

"I'm so happy to see this significant book back in print. The revised edition of this important history will now be available for a new generation who missed it earlier. As the issues of monastic life and history only become more and more complex, Sister Ann Kessler is one of the foundational voices we need to hear. Without this wide-ranging and inclusive chronicle, the history of fifteen centuries of monasticism is left with a very valuable missing piece."

Joan Chittister, O.S.B.

Benedictine Sister of Erie, Pennsylvania, best-selling author of over 50 books, including *The Monastery of the Heart: An Invitation to a Meaningful Life* and *Wisdom Distilled from the Daily: Living the Rule of St. Benedict Today*

"I'm so gratified to know that this work is no longer out of print. So many of the monasteries of our St. Ottilien Congregation, world-wide, have benefited from its use and may need more copies for their monks and associates."

Abbot Fidelis Ruppert, O.S.B. (Retired 2006)

Münsterschwarzach Abbey, Germany, co-author with Anselm Grün, O.S.B., *Christ in the Brother: According to the Rule of St. Benedict and in Everyday Life*

"This is an appealing and unique history of the Order of St. Benedict because it is an account of Benedictines both male and female. Ann Kessler tells the whole story and she does it very well."

Benet Tvedten, O.S.B.

Assumption Abbey, Richardton, North Dakota, author of *How to Be a Monastic and Not Leave Your Day Job* and *The Motley Crew: Monastic Lives*

"Sister Ann Kessler tells the story of monasticism like no one else. Anyone interested in history will enjoy this book."

Antonio Linage Conde
Spanish medievalist, lawyer, poet, and historian, University of Salamanca and Universidad CEU San Pablo, author of *San Benito y Los Benedictinos* in 7 volumes, *Religión y Sociedad Medieval: El catecismo de Pedro de Cuéllar (1325)* and *El Monacato en España e Hispanoamérica*

"Shortly after my election to the United States Senate, a wise farmer in my home state of South Dakota gave me the best advice I have ever received. Though simple, his words have stuck with me all these years: *Never forget where you came from. Come home. Remember us.* I could not help but see this charge through the lens of my Catholic upbringing, understanding my political service as a true calling to something far beyond myself. Every day in Washington, I embraced the call never to forget those I served while remembering I was a privileged participant in a remarkable chain of history. Like the sacred calling of monastic men and women traced in this book, I found myself grounded in a living tradition. No matter what I faced, I could never be uprooted from all those who had walked into the Senate chamber in both good and troubled times.

"Sister Ann Kessler knows this calling to a centuries-old tradition well. Her descriptions of the changing events of Benedictine history show how monasteries have left a profound imprint, not only on Christianity, but on the development of the world. Monastics actively contributed to education, health care, community welfare, agriculture, and even the ever-changing politics of governments that supported, suppressed, or dissolved their institutions. This book's story provides a purposeful touchstone, helping all of us to remember how religious communities fare well under some governments but tragically suffer under others."

Tom Daschle
Former U.S. Senator, Author of *Like No Other Time: The 107th Congress and the Two Years That Changed America Forever* and *The U.S. Senate: Fundamentals of American Government*

"We are fortunate that Ann Kessler's invaluable and detailed study of fifteen centuries of Benedictine life is being reprinted. This book is not only a vast treasury of Benedictine history, but has also been a valuable source for scholars interested in social, intellectual, cultural and gender studies. Sister Ann Kessler, a former fellow graduate student of mine at Notre Dame, has always been known as a superb scholar whose wide ranging research and writing have enriched academic and religious communities for more than four decades."

L. S. Domonkos, Ph.D.
Professor Emeritus of Medieval and Renaissance History, Youngstown State University, co-author and editor of *Studium Generale: Studies*, University of Notre Dame; *Louis the Great King of Hungary*, Columbia University; and *The Laws of the Medieval Kingdom of Hungary*, Vol. I and III

"It is so good that many more persons will have access to this comprehensive work by Ann Kessler. This book has been a valuable reference tool for me as a long-term monastic researcher and historian. I am not aware of any one volume that contains as much historical Benedictine background. For several decades I have been aware of Ann Kessler's vast store of knowledge concerning the Benedictine monastic scene. I was so pleased when Ann agreed to do the chapter on Elena Coronaro—the first woman ever to receive a university degree in 1678—in *Benedict in the World*, a book I edited with Roberta Bondi."

Linda Kulzer, O.S.B.
St. Benedict's Monastery at St. Joseph, Minnesota, author and co-editor of *Medieval Women Monastics: Wisdom's Wellsprings* and *Purity of Heart in Early Ascetic and Monastic Literature*

BENEDICTINE MEN AND WOMEN OF COURAGE

BENEDICTINE
MEN AND WOMEN OF COURAGE

Roots and History

REVISED EDITION

ANN KESSLER, O.S.B.
WITH NEVILLE ANN KELLY

LEAN SCHOLAR
Seattle, Washington

Lean Scholar Press, an imprint of Lean Scholar Initiative. Seattle 98125
© 1996 Sacred Heart Monastery
© 2014 Neville Ann Kelly and Sacred Heart Monastery

First edition originally published 1996. Revised edition 2014.

ISBN 978-0-9904497-0-6 (paper)
ISBN 978-0-9904497-1-3 (hardcover)

Cover image "Benedict and Scholastica"
by Fr. Maur van Doorslaer, O.S.B. (1925–2013),
Sint-Andriesabdij, Zevenkerken, Belgium.
Used with permission of Saint Andrew's Abbey, Valyermo, California, USA.

Edited by Neville Ann Kelly and Joseph Fruscione
Revisions by Neville Ann Kelly

Cover design by Cheryl Finbow

Publisher's Cataloging-in-Publication

Kessler, Ann.
    Benedictine men and women of courage : roots and
history/ Ann Kessler, O.S.B. ; with Neville Ann Kelly.
-- Revised edition.
    pages cm
    Includes bibliographical references and index.
    LCCN 2014942002
    ISBN 978-0-9904497-0-6 (pbk.)
    ISBN 978-0-9904497-1-3 (hardcover)

    1. Benedictines--History. 2. Benedictine nuns--
History. I. Kelly, Neville Ann. II. Title.

BX3006.3.K47 2014   271'.1
                QBI14-600137

For the thousands of Benedictine monks, nuns, oblates, academic colleagues, college students, and others interested in monasticism throughout the world, and for those whose lives have touched mine, especially my Benedictine community in Yankton, South Dakota.

To the memory of my deceased parents, George and Elizabeth Kessler, and brothers, Bob and Ken.

History suggests that we tend to be overconfident about what we know, and that we never know as much as we think we do. Some Victorians believed that they had brought science to an end by discovering all there was to know, but they were wrong. In fact they were on the verge of a scientific revolution. Whatever age we live in, our perspective is always much more limited than we believe, and even as we progress in our understanding, blind spots remain that astonish and appall those who come after us. Yet it is also true that we have learned enough, over thousands of years, to have developed some idea of what helps us to live more fully and compassionately, and to recognize what hinders us.

—Kathleen Norris
Acedia & Me: A Marriage, Monks, and a Writer's Life

CONTENTS

CHAPTER 3

Carolingian and Cluniac Reforms
Ninth through Twelfth Centuries

CHAPTER 4

European Reform and Mysticism
Tenth through Thirteenth Centuries

CHAPTER 5

Rise and Fall of English Benedictines
Tenth through Fourteenth Centuries

CHAPTER 6

Autumn and Winter of Monasticism: Decline and Suppression
Twelfth through Sixteenth Centuries

CHAPTER 7

Benedictine Spring: The Catholic Counter-Reformation
Sixteenth and Seventeenth Centuries   155

CHAPTER 8

The French Revolution and Benedictine Monasticism
Eighteenth Century   187

CHAPTER 9

Benedictine Restoration, Renewal, Expulsions, and Expansion
Nineteenth and Early Twentieth Centuries

CHAPTER 10

Benedictine Roots in North America
Nineteenth Century

CHAPTER 11

North American Expansion and Indian Missions
Nineteenth Century

CHAPTER 14

Continuing Change and Contemporary Perspectives
Mid-Twentieth Century and Beyond

FOREWORD TO THE REVISED EDITION

*Let Us Prefer Absolutely Nothing to Christ, and May Christ Lead Us
All Together to Everlasting Life.*

Benedictines have long looked to our past to guide us in our present moment and into our future. Our long history allows us to explore "what worked" and "what did not work" when faced with challenges and opportunities. Forgetting our past limits our ability to listen with discernment to our present questions.

The twentieth century unfortunately endured endless, bloody war. Human life seemed endlessly devalued. Monasteries, like the rest of civilization, were devastated. Whole countries were ransacked for their natural resources. Countries were created for the benefit of colonizers and their corporations. Cultural sensibilities were violated. An authentic peace and reconciliation, grounded in just relationships, became an imperative. Once the enormity of the Shoah became known, Catholic and Jewish leaders reached out to one another, seeking understanding and meaningful cooperation. Benedictine monastic communities began to respond to the imperative of sharing the contemplative life in the midst of violence and social chaos.

In 1926 American Benedictine Women regained the "right"—taken from them in the late 1800s—to pray the Divine Office. Energies and resources were dedicated to train the Sisters in Latin and in chant with high levels of competency, thus returning the sisters to a deeply valued tradition. Benedictines also were involved in the American Liturgical Movement, which deepened our capacity to internalize "all things liturgical" for our daily monastic observance.

In 1950, Pope Pius XII invited some of the prioresses of American Benedictine communities to Rome as part of his effort to support Women Religious in our way of life. We were encouraged to improve our level of professional education. The pontiff firmly believed that a higher level of education was foundational to the contemplative life and much needed in a broken world. Out of this discussion the Sister Formation

Conference was established in 1954. The Benedictine Institute of Sacred Theology was begun at St. Benedict Convent, St. Joseph, Minnesota, in 1958, which provided the opportunity for Benedictine Women to deepen their exposure to theology, and particularly to monastic theology. American Benedictine women were actively reclaiming our heritage.

With the opening of the Second Vatican Council in 1962 and yet another call for renewal in religious life with *Perfectae Caritatis*, Benedictines again pursued studies of our charism as monastics (and not as apostolic religious), renewing our understanding of the essentials of monastic life. The influence of the vision and life work of Benedictine Bede Griffiths (Swami Dayananda) and Benedictine Henri Le Saux (Abhishiktananda) in India, as well as the work renewing our contacts with Buddhist and Hindu monastics and leaders (and the establishment of DIMMID), was given a certain fame in the United States by the involvement of Trappist Thomas Merton (Father Louis). Benedictines were encouraged to consider the complex ways the Holy Spirit shapes monastic life, especially as a life lived on behalf of the People of God and in service of the Gospel. I see the involvement of Benedictine women in the American Civil Rights Movement along with their endeavors in peacemaking in the 1960s and onward as giving life to our monastic communities in new ways. We grew (again) in our understanding of balancing the contemplative life with the demands of an active life, living both from a fundamentally contemplative stance.

With the impetus of the impending Sesquicentennial in 1980, Benedictines—and especially monastic women—began a renewed search for the narrative of our founding stories in North America as well as for the global contributions of Benedictine women to this monastic endeavor. Benedictine communities have been blessed with oblates, many of whom have taken an active interest in preserving and sharing monastic spirituality with the people in their lives. Oblates are involved in the ministries of the monastery and have shared their experiences in scholarship around spirituality, justice, and the Rule of Benedict.

After the Second World War, new monasteries were established in Southeast Asia and Africa. With the monumental events in 1989 that initiated the demise of Communism, monastic communities that had lived, at best, in hostile environments or literally underground began emerging and making contact with monastics elsewhere. Relationships grew. New monasteries in Eastern Europe were established, and old ones were given resources, both financial and educational, to help them flourish. Women's monasteries, having survived in hostile countries and frequently living in poverty, established relationships with their western sisters. We were as enriched as they were by these new relationships.

Benedictines continue our work of religious understanding and peacemaking as connections with women across the globe expand and deepen. The challenges to the rhetoric of hatred, particularly since the events of 9/11 and the subsequent round of wars, invite us to deepen our connections and commitments to the People of God.

Scholars of monasticism, as with other disciplines, have been exploring anew the many contexts—anthropological, cultural, economic, political, and social—that both shaped and were shaped by monasticism. Scholars of literary criticism have been examining the texts produced by monastics to better understand the constructs, intents, and influences of these texts. How were the voices of women silenced? Women's leadership undermined or denied? How did the story of Benedictine women get subsumed into the narrative of Benedictine men? And as always, we strive to understand the Rule of Benedict in the midst of many other monastics rules. Why this one among the many other rules? How might this Rule both nurture our monastic calling and challenge us out of our complacency? We are all in context: of our broader international culture and within politics and societies. These insights help us discern our call into the future.

People are looking anew at the possibilities of Benedictine spirituality and the monastic way of life. Intentional communities based on the Gospel, a Rule of Life, and with a commitment to works of justice continue to emerge. These new *and* traditional monastic communities are connecting. Families are basing their lives and the raising of children on the Rule of Benedict. Increasing numbers of people are becoming oblates, bringing the wisdom of Benedict to their communities.

Sister Ann Kessler took on an admirable task decades ago when she attempted an inclusive history of Benedictines—not only that of restoring women to the story, but also of the emergence of the global Benedictine community. She was working with an unwieldy amount of information needing synthesis. Neville Ann Kelly brought her keen mind and compassionate insight into supporting Sister Ann in this new edition: sharpened writing, cleaner narrative, and updated information. Her bibliography is impressive.

Benedictine Men and Women of Courage: Roots and History provides an excellent resource for those beginning their journey with this ancient tradition—those in formation as oblates, "new monastics," and traditional monastics. Readers simply interested in some aspect of Benedictine history will find this book a useful resource.

That In All Things, God May Be Glorified!

Laura Swan, O.S.B.
St. Placid Priory, Lacey, Washington

FOREWORD TO THE FIRST EDITION

Teilhard de Chardin, in *The Future of Man*, states that, "Everything is the sum of the past and nothing is comprehensible except through its history." To date, however, there is no single Benedictine history available that includes monks, nuns, Europeans, Australian, Asians, Africans, and Americans. Benedictine history has been neglected in many monasteries where there was no one prepared to share the rich history and traditions of the way of life undertaken by the monks and nuns.

Benedictinism, mistakenly, has become identified with monks only—as indicated in a recent edition of the *Columbia Encyclopedia* that defines Benedictines as "monks of the Roman Catholic Church following the Rule of St. Benedict." Nuns were almost totally neglected, or relegated to a few token pages. All kinds of rationalizations have been used to excuse this discrimination. Dom Stephanus Hilpisch, for example, introduces his brief edition of the nuns' history stating that women have not written their story because *"Das ist nicht Aufgabe der Frau"* (that is not woman's work).

Nuns have published many monographs about Benedictines but, up to this point, the world has lacked a Benedictine history text usable by all the men and women in formation in monastic communities studying the Order's general history, or for those readers who are interested in learning more about monasticism in a single volume. Almost 19,000 nuns and about 9,000 monks claim affiliation to the International Confederation of St. Benedict. It is of, and especially for, these that this book is written. The author also offers this book with the hope that all who study monasticism in their monasteries and those Benedictine oblates, relatives, colleagues, and students of monks and nuns who are intellectually inclined to learn more about Benedictines find that this history more than adequately fills the gap in publications about monastic men and women. The general public has been exposed to numerous myths about monastics. Knowing the historical truth is a way to demythologize those misconceptions.

The "Black Benedictines," the focus of this study, and some "White Benedictines" as well (with special reference to the Olivetans), include most of the followers of the Rule of Benedict with the major exception of the Cistercians and Trappists, who have published their own medieval and modern histories. Benedictines of the Church of England (Anglican) also receive only general reference. They, too, have a story of their own.

Even a general survey, let alone a comprehensive view, cannot be included in a volume of this length, but the most significant events and people who influenced the Benedictine way of life before and after the time of Benedict are treated here in a manner that will inspire the reader to delve into more detailed history of a certain event or era, or the biography of an outstanding individual who influenced the course of his or her century because he or she had the courage to do so.

This work has been written for readers, teachers, and students of all faiths who are interested in learning about the rich, important influence of monasticism in world and Christian history during the past fifteen centuries. Monastics spread and preserved Christianity as well as, and sometimes better than, others solely dedicated to the apostolate.

Readers interested in Christian theology also will find something to intrigue them in this work. In his brilliant *Followers of Christ: The Religious Life and the Church*, Johannes B. Metz maintains that, "when the history of the religious life is understood as a collective biography, as the family chronicle of a community engaged in the following of Christ, then this history itself has a theological status." I trust, then, that those who read these stories of the lives of Benedictine men and women and their institutions will find them both historical and theological.

Abbot Fidelis Ruppert, O.S.B. (retired 2006)
Münsterschwarzach Abbey, Germany

PREFACE TO THE REVISED EDITION

The history of the Order of Saint Benedict is one of human experience marked with contradictory alternations of transforming wisdom and devastating folly. Fifteen centuries of change, adaptation, decline, restoration, and renewal continue to disclose the extraordinary resilience of the simple but life-encompassing Rule of Benedict that unites divergent men and women—monks, nuns, oblates, "new" monastics, and others (Catholic or non-Catholic, Christian or non-Christian)—across the globe. The story of this worldwide movement accompanies and often mirrors the development of Christianity as a whole within the varied cultures, states, and situational contexts where it has taken root.

Benedictine history reflects humanity's undulating course, promising untold hope at times yet wielding abysmal despair at others. Made humbly and poignantly aware of our personal and cultural limitations, we can nonetheless follow Benedict's injunction to eagerly "race along the way" (RB Prologue 49), knowing that the history of the ground one stands upon evokes the present's power to affect the future. In this light, this revised edition of Sister Ann Kessler's *Benedictine Men and Women of Courage: Roots and History* seeks to expand our vision of ourselves— whether Benedictine or non-monastic—and invites our response as collective co-creators of the future.

Sister Ann Kessler's research and teaching spans over five decades of deepening her and many others' knowledge of Benedictine history's intrigue, controversy, commitment, and inspiration. Throughout her graduate work, and as her later teaching responsibilities allowed, Sister Ann traversed several continents visiting men's and women's monasteries where she performed personal interviews, mined archival records, and amassed substantive documentation of primary and otherwise unavailable sources.

Ultimately, a number of her students, monastic formation directors, and other academics persuaded her to collate the varied manuscripts, lecture notes, and handouts that accompanied her courses and seminars into a single accessible volume. Published in 1996, the first edition of this book presented a description of the development of the order for both monks and nuns, making an inclusive and comprehensive history finally available for its eager readers. By 2000, the publication had long sold out and was no longer in print despite its demand. This new edition responds to that need as *Benedictine Men and Women of Courage: Roots and History* nears the twentieth year of its first publication.

While the first edition included an expansive collection of Sister Ann's detailed archival research, this revised edition has maintained the original passages' intent while shortening some detail and clarifying their aim. Honoring contemporary methods and linguistic sensibilities, I have judiciously repositioned some content and updated the book's language and terminology. With Sister Ann's input, sources and endnotes have been amended and updated for readers' ease of reference; readers will also find a new index. While much has been simplified and shortened from the first edition, this revision hopes to stimulate further inquiry for those interested in more extensive detail.

This volume invites Benedictines and non-monastics to comprehend our present through the lens of both favorable and tragic past events, personalities, and contexts that continue to ground our present and shape our future. Sister Ann's tireless zeal for monastic history and its implications for life within both the monastery and the world make this book a timely outpouring of love, caution, and possibility. As I have pored over the intricacies of this manuscript, I have often felt present at a refectory table, listening to the story unfold like any disciple of old. Seated there, I join a wide-ranging lineage of Benedictine men and women who—as Benedict and Scholastica discovered during that rainstorm vigil so long ago—find their love and its potential far exceeding their limitations.

Neville Ann (Nev) Kelly

ACKNOWLEDGEMENTS

Numerous monastic formation directors, both men and women, convinced me (Sister Ann Kessler) of the need for the first and revised editions of this book, and I find no adequate words to thank those who have inspired and assisted in their publication. I remain deeply grateful to the hundreds who have influenced my writing and have made significant contributions to my research for many decades. Though space limitations prevent my naming them all, I express my deepest and sincerest gratitude.

I am especially indebted to the Kessler family—my parents, brothers, nephews, and nieces who supported me with financial assistance—as well as to the support and companionship on monastic excursions abroad. I am profoundly grateful to my Benedictine community of Sacred Heart Monastery, Yankton, South Dakota. The prioresses—especially Sisters Kathryn Easley, Jacquelyn Ernster, and Penny Bingham—formation directors (notably Sister Leonette Hoesing, my novitiate director), and nuns have been first and foremost in the recognition of the value of this study. Their invaluable gifts of time, affirmation, encouragement, and financial support throughout my decades of research and writing have made this work possible.

I also offer deep appreciation to the superiors and archivists of almost two hundred monasteries of men and women that I have visited in the Americas and overseas. These monastics have been most gracious with their time and resources, as well as with their unparalleled Benedictine hospitality. Special mention must be made of several monastic readers, notably Luke Dysinger of Valyermo, Jane Klimisch of my own monastery in Yankton, Joel Rippinger of Aurora, and Judith Sutera of Atchison, who shared wisdom after critical perusal of manuscripts leading to the first edition.

Archivists and librarians of many non-monastic institutions who were also very generous with their time and efforts are also too numerous to list, though I must mention those at the National Archives and National Library in Paris, the University of Notre Dame, and St. John's University,

Collegeville, Minnesota. Gratitude is also due to my graduate school advisors, Arthur Umscheid at Creighton University and Leon Bernard at Notre Dame, for their affirmation of my writing.

I am also grateful for the inspiration of Mount Marty College's administration, faculty, and students, with whom I worked for almost forty years, for encouraging me to compile the manuscripts from my graduate research and monastic history lecture materials into a single volume. College librarians have been more than helpful in obtaining resources. Publication of the first edition would not have been possible without the research sabbaticals granted me by the college and the editing and design assistance I received there from Jennifer Hostler, Karen and Christina Bloomquist, and Frank Tudor, as well as Sisters Cynthia Binder, Kathleen Hickenbotham, Wilma Lyle, Mary Kay Panowicz, Victorine Stoltz, and Louise Marie Goettertz.

I also wish to express gratitude to all who have made contributions to this revised edition, especially to the monks of St. Andrew's Abbey in Valyermo for granting permission for the cover image, our vigilant copy editor Joe Fruscione, and brilliant graphic designer Cheryl Finbow. Above all, my gratitude goes to my colleague and former student Dr. Neville Kelly. Without her determination, revisions, and dedication, this new edition would never have reached those now reading these pages.

BENEDICTINE MEN AND WOMEN OF COURAGE

CHAPTER 1

Benedict and Scholastica:
Their Predecessors and Contemporaries

First through Seventh Centuries

Like Christianity, the monastic way of life originated in the austere deserts of the Middle East, spreading to Africa, Asia, Europe, Oceania, and the Americas. Christian monasticism began in response to universal spiritual aspirations and grew into a multifaceted spiritual movement. Its unifying distinction would be the Rule of Benedict, written by one of the most significant founders of Western monasticism: Benedict of Norcia. His Rule and the global monastic tradition following its instruction began from the simple beginnings of this sixth-century Italian monk's experience and wisdom. The following pages tell the remarkable story of the origins, development, expansion, and continuing challenges of fifteen centuries of the Benedictine way of life.

Benedict was not the first Christian monastic founder, nor was he writer of the first monastic rule. Several centuries of monastic developments—in both East and West—preceded him. Early Indian, Chinese, Tibetan, and Japanese Hinduism and Buddhism fostered a diversity of monastic lifestyles, communities, and teachings.[1] In the Greek era, the term *cenobite* described the common life of the Pythagorean community. Vowed or quasi-monastic Jewish movements such as the Nazirites, Rechabites, and Essenes preceded Christian monasticism, and were active during Jesus of Nazareth's lifetime. While this is speculative, John the Baptist, Jesus of Nazareth's mother Mary, or Jesus himself may have had some contact with this Essene community.[2] These Middle Eastern movements, among others, framed the religious environment surrounding early development of Eastern Christian monasticism and its founder Basil of Caesarea (330–379), who structured many Mediterranean Christian communities under his monastic rule. Theological writers like John Cassian (360–435) and the bishop-monk Augustine of Hippo (354–430) then brought monastic ideals to Western Europe. In the sixth century, the Italian monk Benedict of Norcia complemented earlier monastic documents—most notably, the *Rule of the Master*[3]—with the Hebrew and Christian scriptures as he formed his Rule, recommending study of the earlier monastic sources in Chapter 73.[4] As we will discuss throughout this book, Benedict's Rule continues to guide many Christian monastics in both hemispheres.[5]

The Desert Origins of Christian Monasticism

The term *monastic* originally comes from the Greek word *monos*, which eventually denoted one who lived alone—first in the Palestinian, Egyptian, and Syrian deserts—as a celibate solitary or anchorite. Initially applied to male hermits, the term *monachos* applied to monks, celibate men who lived alone or in a community separated from the world and its values. The term also implied asceticism, or *asketes*, a term meaning solitary, austere, and self-denying. Both terms implied a lifestyle dedicated to contemplation, prayer, fasting, and spiritual values, often in solitude, a state called eremitism. Most monks lived as celibates though they often lived in separate lodgings in large communities. Interestingly, these single abodes were originally called cells, a term later adopted by prisons to distinguish their small rooms from large dormitories.

Monasticism was not limited to men in the pre-Benedictine period. Women dedicated to the solitary life joined others under a common leader in several desert regions, initiating the earliest models of monastic communities. The elders of these groups gathered younger women, accounting for the Greek *nonna* (elder) which became the French *nonnes* and English "nun."[6] Later, the term *moniales* referred to those more commonly known in Christian literature as virgins. When large numbers of women began to take up the eremitical life, teachings of several notable Desert Mother *ammas*, such as Syncletica,

Sarah, and Theodora, among many others, were circulated and mentioned in important historical sources.[7] Men and women sometimes lived in close proximity within single communities as they voluntarily submitted to the direction of the closest elder. These early desert solitaries shared Saturday or Sunday prayer, liturgy, and meals with one another in their regions.

Eventually, the fame of these men and women drew many visitors to the desert communities. Welcomed to the communal liturgies and individual hermitages, visitors sought counsel and spiritual instruction from the elders. At times, followers became so numerous that anchorites were often compelled to organize a separate community, or cenobium, where they shared their lives in common. A mother or abbess (*amma*) or Father (*abba*) led and taught those choosing to follow their practical and spiritual guidance. Written manuscripts preserved some of these teachings.[8]

Renowned Early Fathers and Mothers

Numerous monastic rules arose in the early Christian centuries. [9] Among their writers was Antony of Egypt (c. 251–356), the founder of Eastern monasticism and most famous of the Egyptian desert abbas. According to legend, he determined to leave all and follow Christ after the death of his prosperous peasant farmer parents. He sold his inherited land, provided for his sister, and then gave his possessions to the poor. For twenty years (c. 271–290) he placed himself under the direction of several anchorites. He lived in a cave near his native village where he dedicated himself to prayer, manual labor, and rigorous austerity. Around 290 he went to the desert to occupy a small hermitage for fifteen years. After 305 he was forced to modify his eremitical lifestyle when numerous disciples intruded upon his solitude. Antony subsequently guided small communities of men as an eremitical ascetic, traveling to Alexandria offering pastoral support to workers and prisoners. His last urban apostolate consisted of theological disputes with Alexandrian Arians.[10] Antony died at age 105 in 356. His teaching and example spread rapidly to legendary proportions as his Greek biography and sermons were translated into Latin, Syriac,

Ethiopian, Armenian, and Arabic and disseminated throughout the Roman Empire.[11]

One of Antony's younger contemporaries, the Palestinian Hilarion (291–371), grew up near Gaza and was educated in Alexandria. He discovered Antony's desert abode and lived near him for three months. By the time he returned to Palestine with the insights gained from his mentor, his parents had died and left him with possessions he distributed to his family and the poor. Only fifteen at the time, he chose to lead a solitary life southeast of Gaza where he lived for forty-five years. His reputation attracted numerous visitors as he became known as a healer, counselor, and exorcist.

While Antony was gathering numerous disciples in Lower Egypt, the Coptic Pachomius (c. 292–348) was organizing the first monasteries of men and women in the Egyptian Thebaid. Born in the region of modern Esneh about 292, a non-Christian Theban family raised Pachomius. While serving with the Roman military, he was inspired by Christian charity and baptized around 307. He lived under the spiritual direction of Palemon, a Theban anchorite, organizing a precisely structured community of hermits in Tabennesi by 315. Pachomius established another monastery for monks at Pbow, eventually founding seven more as his membership increased. New foundations followed closely upon his death in 346, with Pachomian monks in Alexandria numbering over 2,000. Pachomius also founded a monastery for nuns at Tabennesi in 330, appointing his sister Mary as its first superior. After more than 400 women had joined the community, he established another. The popularity of these monasteries for women grew; by the end of the third century, there were several in the Nile valley as the model soon spread to Asia Minor, Syria, and Palestine.[12]

Pachomius wrote the first cenobitic rule including detailed descriptions of daily life. In the Pachomian monasteries, each monk had an individual cell, though they shared work, income, and meals.[13] Monks' two daily meals were exceptionally frugal, allowing no meat, wine, or oil. Sleep was brief; monks slept fully clothed in a low chair and were instructed to leave their doors open all night.[14] Clergy originally came from nearby villages to preside at the Sunday

Eucharist, though records indicate some monks were ordained by the 480s. The monks and nuns assembled in their respective chapels for common prayer three times a day, with a final prayer near midnight that included psalms, scripture readings, and litanies. Intellectual work was not preeminent, and most monastics were unable to read but memorized scripture taught to them orally.

Eucharist was celebrated only on Sundays in a larger church around which the small community houses had been built. Manual labor such as textile weaving, tailoring, carpentry, cooking, baking, basket weaving, and other occupations occurred in strict silence, and skilled laborers lived together in distinct groups. A village-monastery numbered from 600 to over 2000 people who engaged in outside trade of surplus goods. Led by a superior and coadjutor, these communities were not autonomous with ultimate authority resting in the hands of Pachomius and his successors. Two annual plenary assemblies reunited all the Pachomian monks at Pbow. At these meetings, the local superiors rendered their accounts of the economic and spiritual life of the members.

Eastern Monastic Influences and Founders

Basil (329–379), his sister Macrina (c. 327–380), and his two brothers, Gregory of Nyssa (c. 335–c. 395) and Peter, were members of a prosperous Cappadocian family. Basil completed his studies at Constantinople and Athens where he befriended Gregory of Nazianzus (c. 329–390). He traveled to Egypt, Palestine, Syria, and Mesopotamia to acquaint himself with monastic life. Upon his return, he divested himself of his possessions in favor of the poor and joined, for a time, the monastery his brother Peter and sister Macrina had organized on the family's estate in Pontus. After some years as a councilor of Eusebius, Bishop of Caesarea, he was named to replace him as bishop. His nostalgia for the monastic life prompted him to establish a community near his cathedral, where he visited daily.

The *Rule of Basil* is a collection of conferences on various aspects of the religious life, some explaining difficult scriptural passages, others describing obstacles to the spiritual life (and how they might be avoided).[15] Basil, like Pachomius, emphasized asceticism and community over the solitary life. Basil's monks established a strong urban ministry that gave rise to a vast village surrounding his episcopal residence. Their complex contained a monastery, inn, hospital, and workshops all in service to the needy. Ordination of some of Basil's monks led to their appointments as superiors of new foundations and several became bishops, establishing a precedent of monastic clerics accepting appointments to pastoral and episcopal ministries.[16]

Ordained by Basil and Gregory of Nazianzen, Evagrius (345–399) influenced Western monasticism significantly through his influence on John Cassian, and through Cassian, Benedict of Norcia. At one point he resided on the Mount of Olives in desert mother Melania's monastery. A founder of monastic mysticism, Evagrius had a notable influence that came to greater light in the twentieth century as charges against him as proponent of the Origenist heresy often caused disguise of his work under other theologians' names.[17] Evagrius lived for a time in the Nitrian Desert and later in the Cellia in Egypt, where he died in 399. His writings, according to annotations to the *Lausiac History* of his student Palladius, provided textbooks for the ascetics of both East and West.[18] Along with numerous shorter treatises, Evagrius's works include the profoundly influential spiritual trilogy on prayer, the *Praktikos, Gnostikos, and Kephalaia Gnostica*.[19] The theological nature of the intriguing controversy surrounding his thought, while outside the scope of this book, warrants attentive study by the student of monastic history.[20]

Byzantine and Roman Nuns

Like many of the early Church Fathers, Basil the Great and his brother, Gregory of Nyssa, were supported and very often deeply influenced by their mothers and sisters. Gregory of Nyssa's biography credits his sister Macrina the Younger with inspiring Basil's preference for the monastic life. This woman persuaded her widowed mother, Emmelia, to establish an ascetic community of women on the family estate at Annessi. When Emmelia died, Macrina became the head of this group, known for its contemplative life and acts of mercy. She rescued women dying of starvation from the roads, nursed them back to health, and often welcomed them into the community. She established a hospital for the poor at Annesi and her community always attempted to feed the hungry, while also engaging in spinning, weaving, and copying. Although nothing she wrote has survived time, Macrina's voice is heard in the writings of her famous brothers. She died in 380, not long after Basil.[21]

About 340 in Rome, the daughter of Constantine established a community of women near the basilica constructed over the tomb of St. Agnes. At the same time, Athanasius (c. 296–373), Antony of the Desert's biographer and former bishop of Alexandria, was in Rome introducing the ideals and stories from the desert communities. Inspired by these legends, lower-class women joined monasteries while some members of the nobility began to model the ascetic life while remaining in their homes. The monastic movement quickly spread to Bologna, Florence, Ravenna, Milan, and Verona and throughout the Italian peninsula.[22]

Double monasteries of men and women were also firmly rooted in Jerusalem. Former Roman aristocrats Melania the Elder (341–410) and her granddaughter Melania the Younger (c. 383–439) governed double monasteries established in 375 on the Mount of Olives. Although Melania the Elder had only originally governed the house of nuns, the Younger Melania assumed the governance of both after her death.[23] Paula, a wealthy Roman, visited Melania's monasteries in 385 accompanied by the Latin father Jerome (c. 347–420). Jerome and Paula used the latter's wealth to establish two monasteries at a short distance from one another, one of women guided by Paula, the other of men guided by Jerome. In keeping with its time, the nuns' monastery separated the nuns according to their social rank in three different buildings. Much later—as we will see—a similar stratification of classes among nuns became commonplace in European distinctions between choir, lay, and extern nuns.

Nuns in early monastic communities were not yet wearing distinctive attire. By the third century, most had donned veils to distinguish themselves from young women destined to be offered to men in marriage by their fathers or brothers. Veils identified the nuns with married women who wore them to indicate their unavailability. Thus, monastic and eremitical women were set apart in society with their married counterparts. In the fourth century, Augustine only recommended that nuns keep their dress simple to avoid attracting attention. Special garb would come only later when, in some cases, medieval ladies' costumes would be adopted and retained.

Augustinian Monasticism

During the early Christian centuries, episcopal dignitaries such as Ambrose (c. 340–397), bishop of Milan, commonly established monasteries in or near their residences. One of the most preeminent Christian theologians, Augustine (354–430), followed this pattern when he became bishop of the North African city of Hippo around 395. After his conversion and baptism in 387 by Ambrose in Rome, Augustine eventually returned to his familial home in current-day Algeria and began a small monastic community with a group of friends. When he became bishop, he continued his monastic lifestyle and established a monastery near the cathedral that soon became a flourishing seminary. Priests ordained in Hippo sustained the pattern as they constructed monasteries in their cities.

In Hippo, Augustine's clerical monastic community coexisted with the seminarians and non-clerical monks, otherwise known as brothers. He also founded a monastery for women placed under the leadership of his widowed sister, Perpetua, who was abbess for twenty-five years (396–420). When the new superior faced a revolt after her death, Augustine wrote a letter in 423 offering a general code of conduct for the nuns. This document and one similarly written for monks became his rule for monastic life.[24] This Rule, dated near the late fifth or early sixth century, advocated firm guidelines applied with moderation and included many monastic traditions practiced during that era.

Augustine's writings deeply influenced several subsequent monastic rules including those of Caesarius, Aurelian of Arles, Isidore of Seville, Benedict of Norcia, and Chrodegang, Bishop of Metz. It also continued to provide the basis for many religious orders' constitutions in later centuries. St. Norbert gave the Rule of Augustine to his Premonstratentian Canons in the twelfth century, and St. Dominic included it in his Constitutions of 1216. During that same century, the Servants of Mary, or Servites, used its adaptation as their guide, as did the Order of the Hermits of Saint Augustine in 1256.

French and Spanish Monasticism

The works of Antony and Pachomius were carried to the region of Gaul, or current-day France. Gallic patricians, soldiers, artisans, peasants, and slaves were inspired to form ascetic cenobitic communities after listening to the renowned Athanasius, exiled to Treves from 335 to 337. Permanent leadership, however, was lacking in these communities until the imposing figure of Martin of Tours (316–397) responded to the need.

Martin of Tours and Early French Foundations

Born about 316 in what is now Szombathely, Hungary, Martin spent his childhood in northern Italy where his father worked as Roman Tribune to the military garrison. By the time he was seventeen he, too, was assigned to a military station at Amiens, the setting of the legendary story of his conversion. Convinced that it was Christ who appeared in a dream—clothed in the half of his military cloak that he had given a freezing beggar—Martin asked for baptism. He secured his release from the Roman army in 356 and soon joined Bishop Hilary at Poitiers. When the Bishop was sent into exile during the Arian Controversy, Martin took up the eremitical life near Milan, then on the island of Gallinaria on the Ligurian coast. When Hilary returned from exile, he gave Martin a hermitage at Ligugé near Poitiers in 363. Aspirants to the community soon joined him and Gallic monasticism began.[25] In addition to original monastic foundations, many French pilgrimage shrines became significant monasteries that endured from the early sixth century to their suppression in the middle eighteenth century. More will be said about these French monasteries in the pages that follow.

Another woman founder was Radegund (c. 520–586), a Thuringian princess who became one of the seven recognized wives of Clothaire, son and successor of Clovis. Eventually her husband acceded to her wishes and built her a monastery in Poitiers, where she was ordained a deaconess. Radegund assigned another nun as abbess over the community of two hundred women. Despite overtones of a double monastery, a city wall separated the house of nuns from that of the monks, also established by Radegund. The name of the abbey was changed from Notre Dame to Sainte-Croix after an alleged relic of the cross was acquired. The hymnodist Venantius Fortunatus, a member of the men's priory, wrote processional verse in honor of the reception of the relic. These hymns ultimately became the marching songs of the crusaders sung in Latin and English even today; for instance, "Pange lingua gloriosi" and "Vexilla Regis prodeunt" are often sung during Holy Week.[26]

Under the leadership of the solitary Honoratus, a hermitage had developed a monastery on the island Lérins, about four or five miles off the southeastern coast of France near Cannes. Its famous bishops included Hilary of Arles (c. 403–449) and Caesarius of Arles (c. 468–542). The latter, a Burgundian from Chalons, was sent from Lérins to Arles for apparent health reasons. After being aggregated to the local clergy, he was elected bishop of Arles in 502. A decade later he established a monastery of nuns, St. Jean, which he organized under the leadership of his sister, Caesarea. By 550 this monastery had 220 members. Caesarius wrote the *Regula sanctarum virginum*, an outline for the ascetic life based on Augustine's rule, for his sister's community.[27] It became one of the most popular rules in monasteries of women, advocating a strict walled-in area that no one was to leave, symbolizing complete renunciation of the world. A provisor, generally a monk, was to assist the abbess in external business affairs. Even though these women relied on monks to assist them in such matters, mid-twentieth century Benedictine historian Stephanus Hilpisch noted that historically "the nuns were just as much interested in books as the monks were."[28] The rule written by Caesarius' successor Aurelian required nuns to nourish their intellects as well as their spirits, prescribing equal devotion to prayer and reading as well as handwork and manuscript copying.

In addition to these foundations, many French pilgrimage shrines became significant monastic sites that endured from the early sixth century to their suppression in the mid-eighteenth century. In Spain, the cenobitic life was firmly rooted prior to 384 when some monasteries had already fallen into ruin, apparently the result of the Gothic invasions. North African monks, fleeing the invasions of the Vandals, often fled to Spain. After the Arian Visigoths had become Christian under Bishop Ulfilas, monasticism flourished. Most prevalent were the traditions of the primitive Egyptian monastics probably introduced in the late sixth century by a contemporary of Benedict, Martin of Braga (d. 580).

John Cassian

John Cassian (c. 360–435), another monastic founder, established houses of men and women at Marseille for whom he wrote his instructions, *The Institutes* and *The Conferences*. As a youth, Cassian had received a strong classical education, then journeyed to Palestine with the future bishop of Auxerre, Germain, to learn of the monks' lives and practices. The two men lived the ascetic life for two years in Bethlehem and then proceeded to Egypt. During the Origenist controversy, they sought refuge in Constantinople where Patriarch John Chrysostom ordained Germain to the priesthood and Cassian to the diaconate. After Chrysostom's expulsion, Germain and Cassian proceeded to Rome where Cassian was ordained to the priesthood by the bishop who later became Pope Leo the Great. Cassian traveled to Provence about 415 where he began a reform at Lérins. Influenced by Evagrius and the Egyptian monastics, he prescribed stricter observances and deepened spiritual practice modeled on desert asceticism.[29]

Early Irish Monasticism

Irish monasticism is associated with the island's most famous saints, Patrick (c. 387–461) and Brigid (c. 453–c. 524). Patrick, the great Apostle of Ireland, was born in Roman Britain, preceding

Benedict's birth by about sixty years. Patrick was close to sixteen when he was seized by Irish raiders on a British shore and sold into slavery on the island where he would spend most of his later life. After six years as a shepherd, the twenty-two-year-old Patrick escaped aboard a ship and eventually reached his home. Though he was already a nominal Christian, his Irish captivity was a spiritual experience. According to legend, he felt that he would have to return to Ireland to try to convert the Celts to Christianity, whom he heard in a dream calling him back to the island.

Patrick traveled to France to study for the priesthood and probably stayed some time as a disciple of Germain at Auxerre. Pope Celestine had sent Palladius to the Irish as their first bishop in 431, appointing Patrick his successor. He concentrated on western and northern Ireland where no one had yet preached the Christian gospel. Wherever he established an episcopal see, he added a quasi-monastic chapter of clerics modeled after those he had found as standard on the European Continent.[30] The communities Patrick established varied from traditional monasteries because their members were groupings of ascetic apostolic missionaries. Four centuries later, the Apostle of Germany, Boniface, called these missionaries monks and nuns, and those evangelizing England in the sixth century and Scandinavia and Eastern Europe in the High Middle Ages would also use these terms. Like Augustine, these missionary monastics emphasized that action in service to the world must accompany spiritual experience and contemplation.[31]

According to extensive legends, Brigid was born to a slave in Ireland. The child's father finally acknowledged her and gave the infant Brigid to a foster mother who instructed her in reading, writing, embroidery, and household duties. In time, she was sought by a suitor whom she rejected because she had vowed her virginity to God. After overcoming paternal objections, she had a church erected at Cill Dara (Kildare), the Church of the Oak in the province of Leinster (now County Kildare). She soon realized that she was the most important Christian personage in the area and could thus convince the bishop, Conlaed, to leave his hermitage to take up residence in a house beside the monastery of women she had built adjacent to the church. Soon other monks arrived, and a double monastery developed.

With the approval of the bishops in Armagh, Brigid and her successors continued to exercise jurisdiction over the faithful of the region. Her life stories have become a mélange of fact and fiction. Purportedly at one time she helped the needy by changing water into beer—no doubt a favorite miracle.[32] Brigid is also credited with the expansion of the monastic ideal throughout Ireland when she personally traveled coast to coast by chariot to raise and supervise communities. Her death occurred around 528, about the time Benedict began writing his Rule. Like many women monastics, Brigid has frequently been omitted in historical scholarship, but her influence has nonetheless flourished.

Other Irish abbeys under prominent founders emerged in the sixth century. Kieran (c. 516–544) is credited with Clonmacnois (545) and another Kieran (c. 501–c. 530) founded the complex at Saigir, where his and his mother's monasteries stood near each other. Two Irish saints named Finian (one died in 549, the other in 552) established Clonard and Moville. Clonfort was the abbey to which Brendan the Navigator (c. 484–c. 577) belonged. Comgall (c. 510–520–597/602) founded the famous Ulster abbey of Bangor about 555. Columban (543–615) left there about 570 to spread the Irish monastic traditions on the Continent. His influence on women's monastic rules is discussed later in this chapter.

Columban and Columba (521–597), contemporary Celtic saints, are often confused. Columba was under the tutelage of St. Finnian, the founder of the Irish abbey of Clonard. He, too, founded several monasteries including Durrow and Derry. As the result of a bloody battle that he had provoked to end a quarrel with the king, Columba was condemned to a penitential exile. With a dozen disciples, he embarked for Iona where he spent the next thirty-four years as missionary and head of a monastic congregation. Under his leadership, over 150 monks on this desolate island celebrated liturgical prayer, copied manuscripts, worked the fields, and evangelized the neighboring islands. After the abbot's death, Iona became a widely known pilgrimage site. Eventually, Columba's body was transferred to the monastery of Down in Ulster to be buried near Saints Brigid and Patrick. Later Irish abbeys of note were also founded in Cork, Lismore, and Carlow (Lasarian). Aidan (d. 751) was the founder of Clonemore, Melrose (Scotland), Lindisfarne, and many others.[33] Irish monasticism, which was separated from the European continent, developed customs and practices that continued into later centuries. The divergence between Celtic and Roman monasticism became significant later in history, as we will discuss below.

Benedict of Norcia

Christian monasticism, predominantly influenced by its Eastern origins, appeared in many forms throughout the first six centuries. One man would confirm it in the Christian West, Benedict of Norcia (c. 480–543/547). At the time Benedict was born in the Italian city of Norcia (Nursia), the Roman Empire was entirely subjected to the occupation and rule of northern Teutonic tribes who had gradually conquered its regions. Sacked in Benedict's century, a Germanic Emperor ruled in Rome after 476. Nevertheless, Benedict was sent to Rome to complete his education while still in his teens. The chief source of St. Benedict's life is St. Gregory's *Dialogues*.[34] Although apparent that Gregory wrote the biography of the great founder for edification and instruction rather than to record historical facts, the legend and symbolism are easily culled. Throughout the main outline, a truly historical, rather than a solely legendary Benedict, emerges.

Benedict's Background

Gregory relates that Benedict, scandalized by the Roman culture, felt that he had to withdraw from its influence. He had a brief sojourn in a village determined to be Enfide (modern Affile) where an incident with a sieve borrowed by his housekeeper made him so popular that he had to send her back to Norcia and seek solitude near a lake, in a cave at Subiacum ("by the lake" equated with modern Subiaco).[35] Romanus, a neighboring monk, secretly brought food there to the young hermit and gave him the simple garb of the ascetics of the time to replace his patrician attire. He probably also shaved his head in the anchorites' style of the tonsure, leaving a circular rim only around the edge of the hairline, a custom that endured for centuries among monastic men and also among some of the nuns who wore this crown with or without veils.

Eventually, Benedict found himself instructing the shepherds of the neighborhood who had discovered his hiding place. In turn, they supplied his material needs and spread the good news of their find; his fame traveled some distance. A community of rather extreme monks, who practiced asceticism chiefly for competition's sake, requested that he be abbot of their fledgling community. Although Gregory did not name this so-called monastery, it is presumed to be Vico Varo. Benedict was too firm, too much of a reformer, and too confirmed in his values for real acceptance from this group; soon they used various means to rid themselves of him so they could go back to their accustomed lifestyle. When they even resorted to poisoning (a contaminated wine goblet broke as he blessed it), Benedict, aware he was no longer wanted, returned to his cave at Subiaco. Disciples hastened there as well.

To provide for those gathering in great numbers near his hermitage, Benedict eventually founded his first communities—a group of monastic houses centered on his cave. He appointed deans over these twelve small groups of men, usually numbered about twelve each, and began his experience as the leader of a cenobitic institution. His initial experiences would serve him well when he wrote his Rule for Monte Cassino. Florentius, a neighboring priest, jealous of the abbot's popularity again shattered peace, causing several incidents prompting Benedict—aiming to preserve order and avoid further contrived temptations of his monks—to leave the area. He headed for a mountaintop above Cassino, a village nestled in a valley midway between Rome and Naples along the old Appian Way. To this day, the abbey of Monte Cassino, atop a peak reached by five miles of hairpin roads to an altitude of 1700 feet, is considered the cradle of the Benedictine Order of monks and nuns—where Benedict wrote his rule, governed his monks, and was buried.[36]

The Rule of Benedict

Benedict's Rule, modern monastic scholars agree, not only owed much influence of Basil, Cassian, Caesarius, Aurelian, and Augustine, but even more to the anonymous author of the *Regula Magistri* or *The Rule of the Master* that also relied on earlier sources.[37] He makes no mention of the anonymous *Regula*, which continues to be studied and debated by different schools of thought. Most schools agree that *The Rule of the Master* preceded Benedict's writing, but no agreement about its authorship remains. Throughout my monastic research and experience, I have often wondered if *The Rule of the Master* could have been written early in the Subiaco period, then rewritten and revised at Monte Cassino. After leading a community of monks for decades, Benedict may have seen the need for change, concluding that his guidelines should be altered, more concise, less detailed and interpretive, and more adaptable to the lives of the men and women he may have foreseen living under that Rule for centuries. Experience in monasticism may have prompted the changes. A survey of the expansion of monasticism in the East and the West indicates how Benedict could, with comparatively less difficulty than if he were the first to devise a certain way of life, construct the final version of a very viable Rule.

Speculation aside, Benedict succeeded in composing an opus that provided for a change in environment and membership. The Rule is so adaptable and highly revered that it has provided the basis for almost all subsequent rules of most of the founders of the religious orders of Christian men and women throughout the Middle Ages and thereafter. Volumes of commentary on and about Benedict's Rule by monastic and other scholars have not yet exhausted its riches. Beginning at the mountaintop abbey, monks and nuns traveled to the first daughterhouse at Terracina and to thousands of later foundations, interpreting and reinterpreting that same Rule for fifteen hundred years into its current twenty-first century adaptations.[38]

The Rule is essentially a guide for seeking God. The monastery, Benedict points out, is a school of the Lord's service where one pursues personal and communal peace by living the Benedictine way of life. Moderation is the key, and the Rule lists few specifics. If prayer is prescribed in detail, wide latitude is permitted for the abbot to change whatever he sees fit in regard to the *Opus Dei*, or communal prayer, and almost all other circumstances including food, drink, and discipline in general. In Chapter Four, Benedict uses scriptural values to encourage communal charity while serving others outside the monastery. Providing a model for hospitality, the "tools of good works" extend the monastery to the world outside its walls. Other chapters discuss the monastic promises of obedience, stability, and conversion of life. Practically, Benedict prescribes no special garb, except that it should fit, be simple, and be obtainable in the region. Monks were to have all their needs supplied by the monastery. The Abbot was to lead every member of the community lovingly and without preference.

The *ora et labora* (pray and work) chapters go into some detail describing who is to do manual labor and who is excused. Above all, the author's sensitivity to the monks' needs and his compassion for the weak and the sick stand out as most reflective of his gospel values. Scriptural quotes and paraphrases abound, indicating Benedict's deep familiarity with the teachings and principles grounding his communities. In Benedict's Rule Eucharist was celebrated only on Sundays, as ordination of monks or admission of priests was rare in the early communities. Although hours were to be dedicated to *lectio divina* (holy reading), no definite period of what later came to be known as meditation was prescribed. It appears that Benedict integrated *oratio* (prayer) with *lectio* (reading) giving no specific directives regarding *contemplatio* (contemplation) or *meditatio* (meditation).

Benedict had no illusions about the heroic temperament of his monks.[39] He wrote for both the strong and the weak, calling his Rule one for beginners. Honored in Pope Pius XII's 1947 encyclical, *Fulgens Radiatur*,[40] Benedict was proclaimed Patron of Europe in 1964 by Pope Paul VI during consecration of the reconstructed abbey of Monte Cassino following its destruction in World War II. Benedict was not aloof from the crises in the world and church of his day.[41] His portrait is painted with "brushstrokes dipped in the oils of the sixth century, particularly the Italian culture, monastic tradition and ecclesiastical backdrop of which Benedict was so much a part."[42] A man of profound vision, he designed a masterpiece for all ages. Benedict's Rule has been successfully adopted by and adapted to every nation, ethnicity, and Christian tradition in every century.[43]

Scholastica, Benedict's Sister and Women's Monastic Model

Although volumes of written works exist about Benedict's life and work by monk historians and lay scholars, his sister Scholastica has frequently been ignored.[44] Even if the ninth-century tradition that began to claim her as Benedict's twin may be pious fabrication, Gregory the Great was not likely to have invented her. His sources for the two saints' lives were the two successors of Benedict at Monte Cassino as well as the Abbots of the Lateran and Subiaco, men not that far removed from the incidents Gregory recalls.

Gregory's Legend

Despite Scholastica's absence in many monastic sources, Gregory describes the last conference of Benedict and his sister in Book Two, Chapter 33 of his *Dialogues*.[45] They met at a small shelter belonging to the abbey, some distance down the mountain path. After spending an entire day in prayer and spiritual conversation, they shared a meal as darkness fell. Scholastica, reluctant to say goodbye to her beloved brother, asked him for a favor: to remain with her for the rest of the night, sharing each other's thoughts until dawn. Benedict, shocked by her petition, stated that her request was impossible since he could not remain outside his monastery all night. Persistent, Scholastica appealed to a higher authority for a favorable response. She placed her folded hands upon the table, bowed her head upon them, and asked God for the favor her brother refused to grant. It had been a perfectly cloudless day, but while sorrowfully rising from prayer, lightning flashed, thunder roared, and torrential rainfall prevented everyone from leaving the shelter. After Benedict's perturbed reproach—"God forgive you, sister, what have you done?"—Scholastica succeeded and the brother and sister talked until dawn.

Gregory attributed her power to change the weather to the fact that her love was great. De Vogüé interprets the story's significance as "observance of the Rule is not everything" and that "love in certain cases makes little of observance." He maintains that "the love she hoped for was personal rather than regular, and in the judgment of God it was greater."[46] Scholastica appeared to know when to bend the Rule from its letter to its spirit. In the same passage, Gregory reports that three days after their meeting, Benedict saw his sister's soul departing her body and wending its way in the form of a dove to heaven. He informed his brothers of her death and then sent monks to bring her body back to the abbey for burial in the tomb prepared for him. "The bodies of these two were now to share a common resting place, just as in life their souls had always been one in God," Gregory wrote as he called down the curtain on the only scene which included both founders.

Scholastica's Influence

Benedict and Scholastica were siblings but probably not twins as popular legend proposes. A medieval misinterpretation of Gregory's reference to their being one in life and death may have led to the erroneous assumption that they were twins. Another controversy surrounds the extent of Scholastica's religious commitment. Although it may be hard to prove, one may presume that she was a nun or at least lived as a professed religious in a home at the base of Monte Cassino or nearby at Polumbario. Gregory in his *Dialogues* uses the words *monasterium* and *cellam* when describing the home to which Benedict was to return after the dialogue with his sister. He uses *cellam* when referring to Scholastica's abode.[47] Translators use various words—*convent, abbey, house, home*—for both. It is also possible that she may have been a virgin in her own home rather than a community leader. She may have been a member of a community as these were common for virgins by this time.

Scholastica obviously enjoyed some liberty of movement, yet that would have been possible had she been a hermit, elder, or leader of a group of women. Gregory speaks of "her own place" or "own cell" (*cella propria*) near Monte Cassino. Perhaps she lived in a house where she had followed the example of Benedict and gathered nuns under one roof, following his Rule—or she could have preceded Benedict to the foot of the mountain and recommended that to him when he felt that he had to leave Subiaco. Why Gregory mentioned Benedict's companions at the meeting—but not hers—remains a mystery, as does her freedom to stay out while Benedict felt compelled to return (or was it just a priority of love over regulation?). In this regard, some writers question the assumption that she followed his or another monastic rule.[48] A monastery of nuns (St. Scholastica's), located at the foot of the mountain in Cassino, claims to date back to the sixth century.

It is possible that only after Benedict's death nuns adapted his Rule, although there is no evidence to establish or deny that Scholastica used the Rule to guide her nuns. Even the monastery Gregory established for nuns in Sicily may not have used the Rule immediately. An unknown, edited Rule, dating from the seventh or eighth century, alters all the masculine terms to feminine (e.g., *fraters* [brothers] to *sororess*, *abba* to *abbatissa*, and *filii* to *filia*). There were later feminine versions, however, which are still extant. These include the manuscript of the Rule for women written for the French nuns of Notre Dame de Saintes and the Altenburg Rule (1505) for the Benedictine women at Göttweig.[49] The majority of the nuns in the first Benedictine centuries, however, continued to be spiritual eclectics. Their rules were often mixtures of those of Caesarius, Leander, Aurelian, Augustine, Cassian, Pachomius, Macarius, and Fructuosus, but they leaned most heavily upon someone probably born about the same time, or just after the death of Benedict: Columban.

Columban's Monasticism

Columban (543–615) was born during the last years of Benedict's life. He was Celtic (Gaelic) a member of a rich and noble family of the province of Leinster, one of the five kingdoms of sixth-century Ireland. At fifteen he renounced a brilliant future and entered the monastery of Cluaninis in Ulster where the Abbot, Sinneill, was renowned for his knowledge and piety. He left there for Bangor (near present Belfast) where Comball, the founder, had organized a complete monastic city. After a long ascetic preparation he received authorization from his abbot to leave for the continent. First he inhabited wilderness solitude in Gaul (France) in the Vosges Mountains near Annegray, where he began his first monastic community. After about 590, he occupied the ruins of a deserted resort, Loxovium, which had been evacuated by the Huns. Here he established the famous monastery of Luxeuil and another, about nine miles distant, at Fontaines. Columban directed all three abbeys in their liturgical prayer, study, and manual labor. Obedience, humility, and severe austerity characterized the monks' lives.

About 610, King Thierry of Burgundy—pressured by his mother and the bishops who reproached the abbot of Luxeuil for his criticism and independence—arrested Columban and his monks. They were brought as prisoners to Nantes; yet as the ship was to leave, it was thrown back on the coast. Columban and his companions escaped and eventually went up the Rhine where they installed themselves near what is now Bregenz, southeast of the Lake of Constance. Here they preached the gospel to the not-yet evangelized Teutonic peoples. When King Thierry also conquered that area, the seventy-year-old Columban hastened to cross the Alps into Milan. Because his disciple, Gall, was ill with fever, he had to be left behind. This monk's tomb later became the site of the grand Swiss abbey of Saint Gall.[50] In Italy he founded the monastery of Bobbio with the exiled monks from Luxeuil. He died there peacefully in 615.

Columban had written a rule for monks (*Regula Monachorum*) at Luxeuil.[51] It was also a type of penal code for violations with sanctions for infractions, and a codification of current Irish penitential usages. The Rule was very severe, but it was often, even before the ninth century, combined with the Rule of Benedict and was followed by both nuns and monks. A seventh-century monastic document blending the two rules was adopted all over the continent where it was known as the *Regula cujusdam patris ad virgines*.[52] One-fourth Columban and three-fourths Benedictine, its author is presumed to be Walderbert, a monk of Luxeuil, whose abbot had assigned him to teach monastic life to the women of the monastery, later known as

Faremoutier. In 629, Walderbert himself became abbot of Luxeuil and adopted the Rule of Benedict for his monastery.

Early Double Monasteries of Both Men and Women

Monastery complexes that housed both men and women were common in early Christian monasticism. Double monasteries were such a frequent phenomenon in the sixth century that Justinian's Code mandated certain restrictions be observed within the walls. Conversation was limited between the sexes and all other communication that might excite suspicion was to be avoided. Separate buildings were to be provided for men and women, and monks were not to be buried in monasteries of women. When burial of nuns required the services of men, only the gatekeeper and abbess were to be present at the ceremony if they wished. The commemorative feast following the burial was not to be an occasion for the meeting of monks and nuns.[53]

A combination of rules governed many of these double monasteries. Jouarre, the famous royal abbey in the Marne valley founded by Adon about 630, was a double monastery, in which the mixed rule of Columban and Benedict guided the men and women. The abbess was Telchilde (d. c. 665), and her brother Agilbert—the future bishop of Paris—was one of the monks. They lived in separate houses, but the two communities were under the same rule and authority, comprising a single juridical entity. Jouarre made foundations of double houses in France and present-day Belgium in rapid succession at Soissons, Nivelle, and Chelles. The Bishop of Soissons prescribed the Rule of Saint Benedict for the nuns "in the mode of the monastery of Luxeuil," or Columban's house.[54]

Double monasteries could accommodate married couples or brothers and sisters, so the Mayor of the Palace of Neustria, Ebroin, and his wife both became members of the Soissons community. In 678, St. Leodegar and his wife, Sigrada, also retired there. The monastery had an attached hospital treating the sick poor *gratis* (a common practice of communities in the Middle Ages). Until the thirteenth century, the staff consisted of sisters and non-clerical monks from both houses. The abbey was known for its intellectual life and library, and the nuns also had an educational program for young men. Later, the Abbot of Corbei composed a treatise, *De partu virginis*, addressed to the abbess and nuns of Soissons in which he spoke of his student days and how much he loved his teachers, the nuns. Soissons and Nivelles each had two churches where monks and nuns celebrated Eucharist together, although nuns often chanted their psalmody and the prayers of the Divine Office alone in the church of St. Mary. There are indications that all wore the tonsure (the haircut allowing only a circular ring of varied widths), attended chapter together, and were all at the bedside of their dying abbess, who was buried in the monk's church. From her deathbed in 658, Abbess Gertrude (c. 621–659) commended temporal affairs to the care of the brothers and the care of domestic matters within the walls of the house to the nuns. She appointed her niece, Wulftrude (d. 663), abbess with the advice and consent of the monks and nuns. Her twenty-year-old nephew, raised at Nivelle, was named cellarer, or business manager.[55]

Chelles was established ten miles from Paris, also on the River Marne, as the third foundation of Jouarre. In 662, Queen Balthilde (639–685) restored a sixth-century ruin of an abbey that Queen Clothilde (475–545) had founded for the new double monastery. Saxon kings of England used Chelles as a source of monks and nuns to begin the establishment of monasteries in their jurisdiction. English monastics, in turn, came to Chelles to learn from that double monastery's disciples. Theodoric IV, King of Neustria (Burgundy), was raised in the abbey. Other famous members included Hereswitha and Mildred of Kent. Salaberga (d. c. 665), the abbess at Laon, headed another double monastery. She ruled over a group of monks and more than three hundred nuns, who worked and prayed side by side. The abbess was also responsible for the establishment of seven churches.

Double monasteries continued to dot the European landscape. Columban and Benedictine abbeys of men and women abounded, particularly in sixth- and seventh-century Gaul. Ireland could boast only one—Kildare. English double monasteries occurred in the seventh century but almost ceased to exist in the eighth. However, there were still many in the German-speaking areas of the Holy Roman

Empire in the eighth century. Spanish double monasteries following the Rule of St. Fructuosus existed already in the seventh, but in Iberia (later Spain and Portugal) the fullest development of double monasteries occurred only in the ninth century.

In France's Faremoutier, seventh-century Abbess Fara was the sole authority of the double monastery. The monks and nuns were both obliged to confess to her three times daily. She also had the power to excommunicate. Discipline became so severe that some of the new entrants attempted to escape by ladders out of the dormitories. Before Fara's death in 660, the Benedictine Rule was combined with that of Columban as the monastic guide for this house. When she wrote her will in 632, she could dispose of her private property as she wished, which was apparently acceptable under the general interpretation of Columban's rule.

Another French double foundation was Remiremont in the Vosges Mountains, founded by a monk of Luxeuil in 620. He converted his family property into a monastery, then a common occurrence. The monks had an abbot, Amatus, and the abbess, Mactefled, ruled the nuns. The abbot, however, had some disciplinary authority over the nuns and decreed practical matters such as which vessels should be used for mill, where to put the honey bees, and other details requiring obedience by both men and women. A nun who ate an apple without the leave of the senior who had the power to grant that authority found herself in great difficulty. Yet Abbot Amatus, despite administrative obligations, principally led a hermit's life. He would leave his cell only on Sundays to read the scriptures with either the monks or nuns. At his deathbed, both monks and nuns were present. For reasons unknown, the nuns later moved from the hill to the banks of the Moselle.

The largest group of double monasteries was in northeast Gaul, now modern Belgium. Amand, Abbot of Elnon and Bishop of Maastricht, founded the double monastery of Marchiennes on the river Scarp near Ghent. The monks there were under the government of Jonatus. He then recruited both monks and nuns and, in 646, placed the widow, Rictrude, as the nuns' guide. Her mother-in-law also headed a double monastery at Hamay, and all of Rictrude's family became monastics. Marchiennes remained a double monastery throughout the next century. The most significant monasteries of men and women appeared in England and the Holy Roman Empire.

From its origin in the desert, monastic life flourished as men and women sought to live a way of life that reflected the teachings of Jesus. Large numbers of these monks and nuns required organization structures that embodied their values in practical life. These guidelines, shaped and modified with time and observance, eventually became the earliest monastic rules. Benedict of Norcia established his Rule on this venerable tradition, moderating the original desert monasticism's austerity with a new approach toward moderation. Benedict's Rule—also adapted to varied times and places—will continue to guide men and women throughout the following centuries. ✸

CHAPTER 2

Early Benedictines in Europe

Seventh through Ninth Centuries

Benedictine monks and nuns continued monastic lives of prayer and work for centuries after the deaths of Benedict and Scholastica. Increasing awareness of non-Christian peoples throughout continental Europe and the British Isles impelled many monastics to preach and establish communities of men and women throughout these regions. While the characteristics of these missions varied, they shared the rapid spread of Benedictinism from the sixth-through ninth-century European world.

Early Medieval Britain

Venerable Bede (672–735), long titled the "Father of English History," was a monk of Wearmouth-Jarrow in present-day northeast England. When only seven, he was committed to the care of Abbot Benedict at Wearmouth. Later he transferred to Jarrow where he remained for the rest of his life. As a scholarly priest-monk, he reveled in the rich libraries of these monasteries, becoming the first famous English historian.[21] He was the mentor of Egbert, successor of Abbot Benedict Bishop and later Bishop of York. Under Egbert's jurisdiction the school at York became the intellectual center of Northumbria. Among its principal students was Alcuin, who eventually organized and administered the palace school at the court of Charlemagne.

Bede's widely copied and distributed *Ecclesiastical History of the English People* remains a significant source of his era's cultural and religious context. Though demonstrating his ethnic bias, Bede's social analysis offers a demographic summary of diversity in the Britain of his day.[1] Interested in establishing missions among the Angles, British, Scots, and Picts of Bede's account, Pope Gregory I (c. 540–604) commissioned Augustine (d. 604)—the future Archbishop of Canterbury—and forty monks to evangelize the Anglo-Saxons in Britain.

Augustine and the monks landed on the island of Thanet in Kent in 597. King Ethelbert and his Christian wife eventually welcomed them, and the missionaries baptized many of his subjects at Pentecost. While some uncertainty about the king's baptism remains, Bede reports that he gave his palatial complex at Canterbury for use as a monastery and cathedral and later constructed another monastery—dedicated to Saints Peter and Paul—that thrived as Saint Augustine's Abbey from around 598 until the English Reformation. After his 597 consecration as Bishop of Canterbury, Augustine and his monks baptized thousands of English people and installed monastic bishops in London and York. Within two decades, both Canterbury and York boasted archbishoprics that remain high-ranking episcopal seats to this day.[2] The well known Westminster Abbey, later built by Edward I, began as Canterbury monks occupied its London area site in 610.

Due to the influence of Augustine's monasticism in England, Northumbria—the region of present-day southeast Scotland—and Ireland became centers of early Christian controversy. Bishop Aidan (d. 651), a monk of Iona, founded the abbey of Melrose following Celtic Christian rites rather than those practiced by the Roman monastics in England.[3] Most controversial between the two rites were external observances such as the date for the celebration of Easter—a Celtic Christian would be celebrating Easter while a Roman Christian might be still observing the Lenten fast—baptismal rituals, and the monk's tonsure. In the latter's regard, Celtic monks shaved the front of their heads from ear to ear, leaving the hair long in the back while the Romans shaved everything except a ring encircling the head. Such a practical concern was important to the monks on both sides since their shaving patterns reflected deeply held theological statements. Other differences were more organizational. Roman Christianity emphasized a hierarchical structure and strict conformity in thought and ritual, while the Irish preferred fostering independence of thought and much less centralization. As would often occur in subsequent Christian ages, a woman would actively participate in the resolution of the conflict. The founding abbess of Whitby, installed by Aidan, would help bring a measure of unity—at least for a time—to Christianity in the British Isles.[4]

Hilda of Whitby

Considered the most learned woman of her time in England, Hilda of Whitby (c. 614–680) was born a princess, grandniece of the great King Edwin of Northumbria, and future aunt of the King of East Anglia.[5] Paulinus of York (d. 644), who had accompanied Augustine to England, baptized her when she was thirteen. As part of a royal family, she had engaged in the management of affairs of the kingdom before becoming a monastic leader. Her parents had died, likely sparing her an arranged marriage. She was thirty-three when asked by Bishop Aidan for assistance to bring Celtic monasticism's practice and scholarship to what is now northern England. Hilda's first monastery of women occupied a piece of land by the River Wear. A year later, Aidan asked Hilda to head Hartlepool Abbey on the North Sea coast when its foundress died. There her administrative brilliance perfected the abbey's discipline and organization. Hilda quickly gained the respect of ecclesial leaders and secular dignitaries; she also gained a steady following of men and women of every station of life. All seeking her counsel soon found their way to her monastery.

As Hilda's reputation grew, King Oswy of Northumbria entrusted care of his daughter Elfleda (654–713) to Hilda's monastery. Elfleda's dowry consisted of some dozen estates, one of which was about thirty miles down the coast from Hartlepool, named Streaneshalch ("Lighthouse Bay") but commonly known as Whitby. In 657, Hilda supervised building a double monastery there, and the monks and nuns elected her as their abbess.[6] During her tenure, she established regular study of the liberal arts including music, and monastics of both genders were expected to be able to play the harp or another instrument. Bede records the story of the musician Caedmon—England's first identifiable Old English speaking Christian poet—whom Hilda persuaded to join her monastery to study Scripture and "sacred history."[7] Along with managing the menial tasks of community life, Hilda directed the manual copying of Scripture and the classics, and of translating and illuminating manuscripts in the scriptorium. Unlike early monastic life in Jerome and Paula's Jerusalem, no distinction between the social classes existed at Whitby, and all shared equally in domestic labor.[8] Early twentieth-century monastic historian Philibert Schmitz summarized her auspicious character as "one of the most curious figures of the Anglo-Saxon church; she is the type of the great abbess of England, whose power and influence appears to be very considerable and whom one must take into account."[9]

The Synod of Whitby, summoned in 664, was held at the double monastery headed by this remarkable abbess. As the synod progressed, the intellectual vigor of Hilda and her nuns most likely kept them energetic participants, attuned to and appraising the arguments presented by their own Celtic advocates and the opposing Roman visitors. After much discussion between both sides, King Oswy and Hilda were convinced by the advocates of the Roman rites that unity depended upon their acquiescence. According to the accounts, both consented reluctantly, but, achieving some semblance of peace among the Christians of Britain, eventually became wholehearted supporters of the Roman traditions including Benedictine monastic practice.

Hilda sent some of her monks to Canterbury to learn about monasticism according to the Rule of Benedict, which Whitby ultimately adopted. Over time, several monks of Hilda's monastery, such as John of Beverly, became bishops in the prominent sees of York, Dorchester, and Hexham. Aidan's Lindisfarne Abbey, also Celtic in observance, followed Hilda's lead in adopting the Benedictine Rule, spreading Benedict's legacy northward.[10] The renowned Hilda of Whitby lived until age 66, succeeded by King Oswy's daughter, Elfleda. While peace between Celts and Romans seemed secure, Elfleda and her brother, King Egfrid, continued addressing unresolved controversies related to the Romanization of Northumbria, particularly regarding Bishop Wilfrid.[11] Hilda's Whitby relics disappeared after the Vikings destroyed the abbey in 875. The stark abbey ruins still dominate the Whitby skyline, a short distance south of the Scottish border.

English Abbesses with Quasi-Episcopal Powers

The abbesses of Whitby were not alone in notable power and influence in the early Christian centuries in Britain. One contemporary of Hilda's was Ebba (d. 679)—aunt of Elfleda, sister of Kings Oswy and Oswald, and the abbess of the double monastery of Coldingham. Called *sacerdos maxima* in historical annals, this abbess—along with many royal-princess abbess contemporaries—were likely to have held quasi-episcopal powers.[12] These abbesses' stature and rank entitled them to do almost everything a bishop could, and contemporarily historical arguments—far outside the scope of this book—abound about the possible ordination of such women. Regardless, abbesses of this era were significant leaders with elevated episcopal statures.[13]

Etheldreda (d. 679), also known as Audrey, made her profession at Coldingham on the southeast coast of Scotland. She later became *sacerdos maxima* of Ely, founding the double monastery around 672. Daughter of King Anna of East Anglia, she was first married to Prince Tonbert. After the prince's untimely death before their marriage consummation, she married King Egfrid. Bede discloses some intimate details of their marriage to emphasize Etheldreda's twelve-year insistence on sustaining a non-sexual marriage with the king. Wanting to ensure the accuracy of Etheldreda's perpetual virginity, Bede relates he confirmed the rumor as fact rather than mere gossip with Bishop Wilfrid. Wilfrid—apparently aware of the couple's arrangement—confirmed it, verifying the platonic nature of their marriage.

The bishop, according to Bede, stated that Egfrid had promised a prize of a wealthy landholding to anyone who could persuade the queen finally to grace his marriage bed. Apparently, no one could convince Etheldreda to do so, and she finally received Egfrid's reluctant permission to join Coldingham after pleading for years to be allowed to enter a monastery. As the first year of her monastic vow culminated, she became abbess of Ely, founded on an island her first husband Prince Tonbert had bequeathed her. She lived austerely as the monastery's abbess for seven years until her death in 679. According to Bede, her body was incorrupt when exhumed seventeen years later.[14] Evidence suggests Ely remained a double monastery under her successor and sister, Sexburga (d. 680), widow of the King of Kent. Bede's chronicle notes that during Etheldreda's gravesite exhumation, "the whole community stood around it chanting, the brothers on one side, and the sisters on the other."[15] While the early legends emphasize these legendary abbesses' sanctity, they also demonstrate that they exercised substantial authority.

From as early as the seventh century, Benedictine houses of men and women were exempted from episcopal jurisdiction by Pope Gregory I.[16] Many legal documents of the time corroborate this independent status of monasteries. For example, King Withred of Kent (d. 725) granted episcopal exemption to all the monasteries following any of the traditional Rules at the 694 Council of Beccanceld. At this Council, the notoriety of the exempt abbesses overshadowed that of ordinary bishops and clergy: archbishops first affixed their signatures to the conciliar decrees, then the five abbesses of the monasteries of Thanet, Dover, Folkeston, Lyming, and Sheppy, with bishops and clergy signing last.[17] Official exemption from episcopal control was the norm the prominent abbeys of women in the early medieval period, and abbesses clearly held far-reaching authority and influence regularly exceeding that of their local bishops. Famous legends of women such as the daughter of King Merwald of Mercia, Mildred, Abbess of Thanet (d. c. 700), among many others, often eclipsed their male counterparts as popular piety extolled their beauty, virtue, and administrative competence.

Powerful nuns such as Hilda, Etheldreda, and their successors, as well as many others, continued to influence—and provoke—the continued development of Benedictine monasticism and Christianity as a whole. Often partners in their efforts, many monastic men also exerted a notable influence in early medieval Britain. Among the most significant monastic men in the seventh century was Benedict Biscop (629–690) whose disciples included Venerable Bede. Biscop was a Northumbrian noble who repeatedly made pilgrimages to Rome, eventually becoming a monk at Lérins in southern France. He returned to Britain, founding the abbey of Saint Peter at Wearmouth in 673. When he received a second donation of land in 682, he constructed St. Paul's at Jarrow.[18]

Originally a minor monastic school founded by Maidulf in 650, Malmesbury in southern England became famous through the efforts of the Saxon, Aldhelm (c. 639–709). A Hebrew, Greek, and Latin scholar who had studied at Canterbury, Aldhelm became the first Saxon to write instructions to the common people in the vernacular. After thirty years as Abbot of Malmesbury, he became Bishop of Sherborne in Wessex and died shortly thereafter in 709.[19] Many other monastic men impacted the continuing contemplative and active work of Benedictine monasticism throughout the British Isles.

Often, the monastic men and women of early medieval Britain were cultivated litterateurs. Nuns and monks often quoted Virgil and the other classics, Scripture, and the Fathers of the Church. They usually read Greek and composed Latin verses. As noted above, highly educated abbesses assisted at ecclesiastical synods with kings and bishops, and at times they signed synodal documents. Also persons of deep prayer and spirituality, many of these men and women were later venerated as saints and are listed in the traditional roster of the great luminaries of the Order of Saint Benedict.[20]

However, despite the brilliance of some, not all monastics were admirable. In many of the familial abbeys—and especially in the case of nuns' monasteries—the leadership was often dynastic, associated with royal families' gifts of vast land holdings and luxurious abbeys. For women, monastic life potentially appeared to be a field of vast activity compared to the restricted, patriarch-dominated life led by their sisters whose arranged marriages and lack of educational opportunities considerably controlled their daily lives. In this context, the choice of monastic life allowed some women to ensure greater and freedom and independence. Not all English nuns followed the expected enclosure within their cloisters, and some bishops complained that the nuns wore overly costly colored garments, ribbons, and no veils. Many abbesses were often powerful and prestigious enough to be invited to join the great lords, bishops, and abbots in the parliamentary King's Council. Empowered by their religious and secular influence, these women of the early Middle Ages were unparalleled leaders of their time, setting a high and rarely reached standard for the monasticism to follow.

Early Medieval English Double Monasteries

Often headed by abbesses of great renown, England's early medieval countryside was dotted with double monasteries from the seventh to tenth centuries. Like their abbesses, some of these gained a great deal of prominence. Cuthburga (d. c. 720), sister of King Ina of Wessex, founded Wimborne, where she "ruled with an iron hand."[21] She was succeeded by her sister Tetta (d. c. 760), who eventually authorized the establishment of Benedictine missions in the German lands.[22] Barking, another English double monastery, was founded by Bishop of London Erconwald (d. c. 693) for his sister Ethelburga (d. 664), whom he appointed as its first abbess. The Abbey of Barking, renowned for its intellectual activity, maintained a hospital and school admitting children as young as three. An alumnus, Bishop Aldhelm of Sherborne (640–709), wrote a celebrated treatise on virginity for the nuns of Barking, addressing Ethelberga's successor Hildelithas as "Abbess Maxima." Like many other monastic houses, Barking was burned to the ground by the Danes in 870.[23]

Regulated and gradually suppressed by the Second Council of Nicaea in 787, the men's and women's areas were scrupulously separated in these double monasteries. According to the Council,

> From now on no more double monasteries are to be started because this becomes a cause of scandal and a stumbling block for ordinary folk. If there are persons who wish to renounce the world and follow the monastic life along with their relatives, the men should go off to a male monastery and their wives enter a female monastery, for God is surely pleased with this.
>
> The double monasteries that have existed up to now should continue to exist.... Monks and nuns should not live in one monastic building, because adultery takes advantage of such cohabitation. No monk should...speak in private with a nun, nor any nun with a monk. A monk should not sleep in a female monastery, nor should he eat alone with a nun. When the necessary nourishment is being carried from the male area for the nuns, the female superior, accompanied

by one of the older nuns, should receive it outside the door. And if it should happen that a monk wishes to pay a visit to one of his female relatives, let him speak with her in the presence of the female superior, but briefly and rapidly, and let him leave her quickly.[24]

In compliance, the abbess often spoke to the monks and outsiders through a window, and only the priest offering sacraments was allowed in the nuns' chapel. Each gender often had its own church, and usually had a separate own choir area for the chanting of psalms. Later, some monasteries erected a thick wall through the middle of the church between the monks and nuns, though it was low enough for the nuns to hear the officiating cleric. Often their austere mode of life seems to have lacked the moderation Benedict advised. The Rule was interpreted literally, allowing little flexibility. Red meat was banned at meals, though fish was allowed. Wine, mead, or beer—depending on the area's traditional drink—was permitted at the table. Dress between men and women in these monasteries was initially quite similar, and nuns wore a black habit, cowl, or hooded cloak like the monks.[25] Also, men and women usually shared their burial ground, though an epidemic among the monks at Barking caused the nuns to prepare a separate gravesite for themselves to avoid contagion. While sustained for several centuries, English double monasteries gradually disappeared until their later revival in the twentieth century.

Spread of Monasticism to the German Lands

Irish, English, and Scottish monks and nuns were inspired to spread the Christian Gospel and their way of life throughout the British Isles. However, Benedictine monastics did not confine their ministry to Britain and France but expanded into the northern areas of Europe later known as the Holy Roman Empire. Although Saint Boniface (672–754) has long been described as "Apostle of the Germans," other missionaries to the Teutons preceded him in the seventh and eighth centuries. Fridolin (d. c. 540), former abbot of St. Hilaire in Poitiers, was evangelizing the Germanic areas in the seventh century. He was buried at the abbey of Sackingen on an island in the Rhine near present Basle. Pirmin (700–753) founded Reichenau in 724 on an island in the Lake of Constance on the Rhine, which later founded a daughter-house at Niederalteich in Bavaria. Pirmin also founded Murbach in Alsace in 727 and several other monasteries in the German-speaking lands. Rupert (c. 660–710) later founded the Viennese monastery of Saint Peter's at Salzburg. Martyred in Wurtzburg, the Irish Kilian (640–689) labored in Thuringia. Emmeran (d. 652) preached in Ratisbon where admirers erected a monastery named for him over his tomb.[26]

In the seventh century, both Bishop Wilfrid of York (c. 633–709) and Egbert (d. 729) preached Christianity to the inhabitants of Friesland (now Netherlands). Willibrord (658–739), however, had the most notable early success evangelizing the Frisians. Placed in the monastery of Ripon in England when seven years old, he joined Egbert in Ireland at twenty, remaining a student for twelve years. Willibrord and eleven Benedictine monk companions left England for Frisia in 690. Five years later, Willibrord was appointed Archbishop of Utrecht, where he established a Benedictine monastery at his cathedral. When he died at Echternach, he was revered as the principal apostle to the Flemish areas of present-day France, Belgium, the Netherlands, and Luxembourg.[27] Germanic Benedictinism was not only influenced by these monks, but was particularly influenced by a pair of English collaborators, Boniface and Lioba.

Boniface and Lioba

Boniface (c. 675–754) solidified the Benedictine influence in the German-speaking lands. His childhood was spent first at Exeter Abbey in England and later at Nurstling in the diocese of Winchester. Ordained a priest in 710, he travelled to Rome where he sought the Pope's blessing on his intended mission to Germany. Nine years later on May 14, 719, Pope Gregory II assigned him the task of evangelizing the non-Christian Germanic peoples. Since the papal audience took place on the feast day of a fourth-century martyr, his name was changed from his baptismal Winfred to Boniface in honor of the saint.

Thereafter, he journeyed to Bavaria and Thuringia and established his first monastic community at Amoneburg. In 722, he was appointed bishop and given letters of recommendation to Charles Martel, the powerful Duke of the Franks. When Martel halted the Muslim advance at Poitiers, Gregory III appointed Boniface to the Archbishopric of Mainz in 732.

After 738, Boniface concentrated his efforts on the Bavarian lands of southern Germany. He also founded the bishoprics of Salzburg, Regensberg, Freisling, Passau, and Eichstätt, founding a monastery at each cathedral.[28] In 744, Boniface founded Fulda, eventually noted for its scholars and library. After being named Apostolic Delegate to the Franks by the papacy, Boniface used that mandate and the authority it gave him to reform the church in the Frankish lands (France), which had laid early claim to its entitlement as eldest daughter of the Church in Europe. Despite opposition from French clergy hostile to reforms promoted by an Anglo-Saxon, Boniface convened several national synods.

Boniface did not accomplish the mission to the Alemanni, Thuringians, Bavarians, Hessians, and Franks alone. In addition to his monks, he was greatly assisted by distinguished monastic women also from England, less celebrated but nonetheless also "Apostles of Germany."[29] He petitioned Abbess Tetta of Wimborne Abbey to send missionary nuns across the English Channel. Outstanding among the thirty collaborators who responded were Lioba, Walburga, and Thecla of Kitzingen, all relatives of Boniface. These English nuns and their companions were eventually most influential in the initiation and formation of early German monasticism for women.

Monks and nuns in the early Germanic monasteries did not live in the massive stone buildings that later replaced the first humble wood shelters. The original monastic houses were often no better than straw-thatched huts located near a stream or spring. Community members tilled the land, taught those in the area how to farm, and schooled the children in their primitive monasteries. While monks preached and baptized, the nuns educated the young and old, dispensed medicines, food, and clothing and maintained hospices and inns for travelers and guests.

Lioba (710–782), sent as a child to Wimborne Abbey, immersed herself in religious studies. She did not, however, neglect the liberal arts including art, literature, grammar, arithmetic, astronomy, and music of the medieval trivium and quadrivium. Eventually, Lioba received parental permission to become a nun, and was soon reputed for her holiness and learning.[30] She was—according to some of the earliest sources—angelically beautiful, intelligent, discreet, moderate in her expectations and open in her affections. During their joint missionary endeavors, Lioba favorably impressed Boniface who often sought her counsel and gave her a great deal of authority over other monastics. She freely visited each of the abbeys she established and frequently met with princes, bishops, and nobles who deeply admired her. She was a friend of Charlemagne's Queen Hildegard, who often summoned her to court. Boniface granted Lioba the unique privilege (given to no other woman) of joining his monks in choir for the Liturgy of the Hours and the right to participate in their spiritual conferences.

Rudolf, the Fulda monk commissioned to write Lioba's biography three decades after her death, recalled the last encounter between Boniface and Lioba at Fulda. According to the account, Boniface commended her to the senior monks, admonishing them in case of his death to care for her with reverence and respect. He reaffirmed his earlier testament that after his death her bones should be placed next to his in the tomb, so they who had served God together during their lifetime with equal sincerity and zeal should await together the day of resurrection. After expressing his wishes, he gave Lioba his cowl and pleaded with her never to leave her adopted land for her native England. Shortly thereafter, Boniface left for Frisia, where he was ambushed by bandits and killed as he prepared for a confirmation ceremony.[31] After his death and burial at Fulda, the monks neglected to follow Boniface's final mandate regarding Lioba. Though they did transport her body to Fulda three years after she died, they buried her on the north side of the altar instead of placing her in the tomb occupied by Boniface. After the church's expansion during the reign of Abbot Eigil, her bones were transferred to the west porch.

Boniface had given Bischofsheim ("bishop's house") to Lioba as a monastery. Thecla (d. 790), her relative and collaborator at that site,

later became abbess of Ochsenfurt and finally foundress of Kitzen-
gen. Another of Lioba's companions, Walburga (c. 710–777 or 779)
is often overshadowed by her brothers Willibald (c. 700–c. 787) and
Wunibald (d. 768), who travelled to Palestine with their father—
Richard, a minor Saxon king—around 720. Two years later, after
their father's death in Lucca, the two brothers arrived in Rome. Wunibald remained there, probably at St. Paul's, while Willibald proceeded
to the Holy Land.[32] Seven years later Boniface, then Archbishop of
Mainz, consecrated Willibald Bishop of Eichstatt. There, Willibald
built a cathedral and a monastery. At Heidenheim, he established
a double monastery under the leadership of his brother, Wunibald.
Walburga later governed the nuns there. After her brother's death, she
became abbess of the monks as well. She wrote her brother Wunibald's biography including an account of the journey to the Holy
Land, becoming one of England and Germany's first women authors.

Walburga

Walburga, Heidenheim's abbess, was reputedly a mystic; legends
about her supernatural powers and care for the needy abound. Walburga
died in 777 or 779, but when some of her bones were translated to Eichstätt in 870 a phenomenon began. A flow of odorless, colorless oil has
flowed from Walburga's relics at certain times of the year for eleven
centuries except during a few times of war and other crises when its
flow has temporarily ceased. The abbey remains a shrine and place of
pilgrimage where "Walburga's Oil" is sought for healing. Some of her
relics are also preserved—or claimed as such—at Cologne in the Jesuit
church, at Saints Cosmas and Damian in Munich, at Rheims, and at
Wittenberg.[33] In their abbeys, German nuns educated young and old,
dispensed food, clothing, and healing herbs while maintaining centers
of hospitality for travelers and others in need.

The successors of Boniface opened other monastic houses. Archbishop Lullus (c. 710–786) founded Hersfeld. Tegernsee was erected in
757 and twenty years later, Kremsmunster. At St. Gall's in Switzerland,
the Rule of Benedict replaced that of St. Columban around 750.
Metten—the monastery Boniface Wimmer left in the nineteenth

century to found North American missions—was founded in 766 and shortly later, nearby Benediktbeuren. The French abbey of Corbei in Picardy established a daughter house at Korvey (Corvey) about 823. These monasteries functioned as schools for secular and religious instruction and were seminaries for clergy. As bases of evangelistic outreach to the surrounding areas, they offered monastic missionaries places of refreshment and rest while opening their doors and resources to those in spiritual or material need. These monastic houses were thus the heart of Christianity in the early German Middle Ages. The Benedictine tradition had begun to flourish in Britain and continental Europe, especially in what would become modern-day France, Belgium, the Netherlands, Luxembourg, Austria, and Germany.

Expansion on the Iberian Peninsula

Monasticism in Spain seems to date from the sixth century, but its actual origins are obscure. Some eremitical communities, following John Cassian's earliest Eastern Christian tradition, appear to have been present on the Iberian Peninsula. Many of the Spanish ascetics apparently followed the Rule of Basil, but most of their monasteries were destroyed by the invasions of the Goths and Vandals in the fourth and fifth centuries. Later, Martin of Braga (c. 520–580), Abbot of Duma and later Archbishop, founded several monasteries based using the Cassian observance. The abbey Servistan near Valence was founded in the mid-sixth century by Abbot Donatus (d. 550). Biclar in the province of Terragona, founded by a monk named John, had a number of disciples by the end of the sixth century. Saint Julian de Pedrenales must have been a double monastery in the sixth century as an Abbess Hositia is named in a community charter as the "abbess of a flock of monks."[34] Early in the seventh century, Leander (c. 534–c. 600) and Isidore (c. 560–636), brothers who succeeded each other as bishops of Seville, wrote monastic rules. Leander's was an instruction on the spiritual life for his sister Florentine at Astizi. Influenced by pre-Benedictine rules, Isidore wrote one for monks. The monastic customaries composed later by Saint Benedict of Aniane and used at Cluny show traces of Isidore's rule.

Though the exact time of introduction of the Benedictine ideal within Spanish monastic life is unclear, the controversial rule of the seventh-century monastic bishop, Fructuosus of Braga (d. 665), seems to demonstrate familiarity with the Rule of Benedict. Fructuosus, the youngest son of a noble family of royal Visigothic blood, began monastic life at Valencia, where he may have encountered the Benedictine Rule. Returning to his native Asturia, he founded a monastery on his family's property, writing an original rule for the monks there called the *Regula monachorum,* predominantly based on Cassian's *Conferences.*[35] After several years as a hermit, he made a second foundation, Saint Felix at Visuna, and subsequently travelled to Galicia. Seeking to reform the region's monks, he wrote another rule for communities of married men and women known as the *Regula communis.* This rule may have been based on that of Benedict, but it differed in significant ways.[36]

Observed for eight centuries, Fructuosus' rule allowed for the organization of families—men and women with children under age seven. Although confined to the Iberian peninsula, this rule rapidly diffused throughout what is now Spain and Portugal. Fructuosus was later made bishop of Duma, becoming Archbishop of Braga in 656. He died at San Salvador de Montelios in 665. Despite his distinct approach to monastic life, Fructuosus is included the early twentieth century *Benedictine Martyrology.*[37]

Spanish family monasteries existed prior to Fructuosus' rule, as is evidenced by his intervention at a monastery located between Seville and Cadiz. Assuming leadership, Fructuosus immediately separated the sexes and may have written this rule to counter previously established communities of extended monastic families' organization. Discovering such communities, usually residing on a member's family estate, he immediately set to their comprehensive reform, providing strict guidelines and structure. An abbot governed the men, women, and children, and their attention was directed to spiritual practice rather than the mundane affairs of the monastery, which would care for all their needs.

The strict rule of Fructuosus appears harsh to contemporary sensibilities. Spouses were forbidden to live together and had to seek the superior's permission to speak to each other. If a monk were to speak alone illicitly with a nun, he was subject to a hundred lashes. Only in certain circumstances was greeting by kissing of hands permitted between monks and nuns. Even the abbot was not to offer a kiss to the abbess, and no one was to "lay his head on a sister's bosom as if by agreement nor may the nuns touch with their hands the head or barb of the monk."[38] Fructuosus was concerned that the sexes dwell together in chastity in his rule; while permitting monks and nuns to pray the psalmody together, he dictated that their choir stalls were to remain strictly separated. Children were confined to separate quarters with a supervisor to care for them, and could not visit their parents any time they wished. Care of the children was thus incumbent upon the general membership of the monastery, but serious efforts were made to develop in the child a desire for a monastic vocation.

Family monasteries observing Fructuosus' *Regula communis* endured for almost eight centuries until they disappeared during Moorish conquests. Interestingly, similar types of familial communities existed in other regions, officially banned during the fifteenth century by Catholic monarchs on the charge that families organized as monastics to evade taxes. The traditional Benedictine rule eventually replaced—or at least took priority over—other rules in most of the communities of monks and nuns in Spain and Portugal.

Expanding Italian Monasticism

Italy, home of Benedict, had sustained monastic life after his death, and the Benedictine Rule was disseminated widely despite numerous political and other crises. Most of the abbeys also continued to follow a model developed at the monastery at Vivarium by Cassiodorus (c. 485–c. 585) whose *Institutiones* prescribed cenobitic monks' predominant occupation the copying and illuminating of manuscripts while balancing their scholarly work with the prayer and manual labor mandated by Benedict.[39]

Lombard invasions from the mid-sixth to the mid-seventh centuries continued to wreak havoc with monasteries of Italy, and monastic communities ceased to exist in all but the city center of Rome and at Spoleto. Monte Cassino's monks fled to Rome after its destruction by the Lombards in 581, taking refuge at the monastery of St. Pancratia near the Lateran. Only Bobbio, founded by Columban (c. 543–615) in 613, was added to the monastic rolls until after 688 when a period of peace allowed establishment of several more monasteries. Farfa in the Sabines was founded as an imperial abbey, and St. Vincent of Vulturno near Naples was subsequently founded by the Farfa monks. A sizable number of Franks, with the aid of several local hermits, joined this community and assisted Petronax of Brescia (c. 670–c. 747) in the restoration of Monte Cassino. During the early eighth century, Monte Cassino became the center of Benedictine expansion in Italy and eventually across the Alps. In Sicily, where Pope Gregory I had overseen the foundation of six monasteries, Latin monasticism prevailed until the end of the seventh century when Saracen invasions destroyed the buildings and exiled the monks. Benedictine monasticism was restored there under the Normans in the late eleventh century.[40]

There were also Italian foundations for nuns: a royal abbey at Brescia, two monasteries at Pavia, and others at Milan, Venice, Turin, Asti, Naples, Ferarra, and smaller towns. As in the case of the men's monasteries, many abbeys for women were founded by families for their own family members. Although the patrons maintained that they were seeking eternal reward by their patronage of houses for monks and nuns in general, they often stipulated that their daughters, mothers, sisters, or eventually their widows would be abbess.

At the beginning of the ninth century, Rome numbered more than a dozen Benedictine monasteries of women. Due to early medieval economic and social circumstances in Italy, these nuns never exercised the influence that their sisters had in Gaul, England, and Germany. Rather than exercising political and ecclesial power, they led very quiet lives of prayer and work simply striving to sustain their monasteries. Education was never held in the high esteem prevalent in abbeys of northern Europe, and fewer Italian foundations gained the prestige of the women's monasteries elsewhere.

Chrodegang's Rule and Canons and Canonesses

Another type of religious life was considered less demanding and became popular in the mid-eighth century. Canons and canonesses existed under the jurisdiction and followed the canons (rules) of the bishops whom they generally assisted in the Church's work. Although many communities were exempt from episcopal control, they were not closely supervised until the ninth century. Between 740 and 750, Chrodegang (d. 766) the bishop of Metz wrote the *Regula Canonicorum* for these men and women, and the Council of Verneuil gave official recognition to the institution in 755.[42] As the nobility sought to procure peace and security for their sons and daughters, bishops often favored this rule because canons and canonesses could better respond to the period's social and economic preoccupations. The movement spread rapidly into Germany, Lorraine, Belgium, Italy, and France but was less common in England. Benedictines and canons and canonesses had much in common, and it could be difficult to distinguish between them. Canons and canonesses also lived in communities, and kept some of the spirit and prescriptions of the Rule of Benedict, although they did not have the same obligations of prayer. They did not commit to separation from the outside world in an enclosure, nor did they profess poverty. Nonetheless, their houses were still known as abbeys and monasteries, and were commonly called a *stift* in Germany. Later, they became known as the Chapter of Canons or Canonesses.

The leader of the canonesses resembled an abbess in authority and especially in the form of her consecration. The bishop used the words *consecratio* and *ordinatio* and the phrase *"sacer ordo, in officium divinum, in opus ministeri Dei"* during the celebration, and this liturgy was essentially the same as the ordination of deacons or monastic abbess, only slightly modified from ordination to the priesthood.[43] The newly consecrated superiors of the canonesses were, as the canons, to take part in the meetings of the cathedral chapter and diocesan synods. They likewise held power to discipline community members and, to a certain degree, the clerics attached to their churches. They distributed communion, baptized, and cared for the sick and needy. In general parlance, the superiors were addressed as deaconesses. Like the abbesses, these privileged women often wore vestments including the stole and occasionally the maniple, though use of the crosier—the quasi-episcopal symbol—was confined to the monastic cloistered abbesses who also had the privilege of the bishop's mitre in same areas. Certain councils after the fifth century forbade conferring the diaconate on women but rarely enforced the prohibition. Even in Rome, there were several such ordinations in the ninth and tenth centuries.[44]

The norms of Aix-la-Chapelle in 816 demanded that the canons and canonesses be regulated more strictly by observance of either the Rule of Benedict or Chrodegang's guidelines for regular canons in particular. They were also required to promise chastity and obedience, but were excused from committing themselves to poverty. They were allowed to eat meat and have servants, were non-cloistered, and continued to occupy themselves primarily with the education of young girls and the care of the sick and poor. Dormitories and common dining rooms were also part of the lifestyle for some. However, the canonesses tended to become more clerical, especially in comparison with the strictly cloistered Benedictine nuns. Since their churches were usually parish places of ordinary peoples' prayer and worship, the canonesses collaborated with the canons in parochial duties, essentially functioning as medieval pastoral ministers.[45]

Over time, many canons and canonesses often relaxed their lifestyles and no longer lived in community but in private residences. They were allowed to take vacations and ordinarily did not wear a distinctive habit, and they came to the church only to chant the Liturgy of the Hours in common morning, evening, and possibly at noon. Sustained to the present in France, Vespers at Chartres Cathedral is still chanted by the Cathedral canons from various parts of the city. After the eleventh century, some of the canonesses were no longer committed to perpetual celibacy and could marry.[46]

Throughout the next centuries, Benedictine abbeys were often advised to adopt the mode of life of the canons or canonesses. Especially in Germany, many celebrated Benedictine monasteries became houses of canonesses, not least among these Gandersheim, Essen,

Quedlinburg, Lindau, and Fischbeck. Belgian houses like Nivelles, Maubeuge, Mons, and their sister monasteries also became houses of canonesses. French Benedictines at Metz and Epinal, members of the great abbey of Remiremont, and a number of other prominent monasteries became canonesses. Italian monastics at Saint-Victor in Pavia, Sainte-Marie in Cremona, and Sainte-Marie in Rome also gave up the monastic life. Not all these institutions prospered and a number of them were driven to this choice by the more restrictive regulations introduced by Benedict of Aniane in the late eighth century, whose interpretation of Benedict of Norcia's Rule influenced and changed Benedictine monasticism for centuries to come. ❊

CHAPTER 3

Carolingian and Cluniac Reforms

Ninth through Twelfth Centuries

A s the ninth century opened in Europe with the formal crowning of Charlemagne as Holy Roman Emperor, all was not well in monastic circles. Before the close of the eighth century, Boniface (the "Apostle to the Germans") had complained that the bishops' not holding regular synods and the over-involvement of the episcopate in feudal political battles relaxed church discipline. He deplored that the Church was generally in a state of decadence, especially the monasteries.[1]

Boniface had a point. The patronage of the wealthy founder— bishop, king, or prince, who had donated the land or the buildings and endowed the monastic estate with fields, forests, and villas— brought with it many problems. Not only did the donor expect to name the abbot or abbess (who might have little concern or ability to administer temporal goods or exert spiritual leadership) but also the individual too often did not even feel called to the monastic vocation. It was the day of the *commende*, the naming of commendatory monastic leaders as well as bishops and cardinals for personal gain to the donor or the individual named. Unfortunately, the commendatory abbot or abbess was often a lay person who seldom, if ever, resided at the monastery but claimed a major portion of its revenues. A prior or prioress was assigned to see to the temporal and spiritual welfare of the monks and nuns. The men and women in the monastery's ranks often lost control of their own destiny, contrary to the Rule of Benedict which provided for elected superiors. The Rule also required consultation and counsel from the whole community before acting on major decisions.

The Era of Charlemagne

Charles Martel, grandfather of Charlemagne, was guilty of granting multiple benefices (offering a church office or a monastery), and his successors continued the disastrous practice even after the Reformation. After Charlemagne (d. 814) was crowned in 800, the new emperor became one of the leading caesaropapists, in effect leading church and state simultaneously. Although the emperor was considered a great patron of monastics (his statue in Monte Cassino's courtyard holds the same prominence as those of Benedict's parents), he was most interested in promoting political unity through uniformity. Emperors saw control in the hands of the leader under "one rule, one faith, one monarch." They felt strict law and order were the best means of maintaining their power.

To this end—uniformity above all—Charlemagne imposed the Rule of Benedict on all houses leading monastic community life unless those attached to basilicas or cathedrals chose to follow Chrodegang's Rule for Canons.[2] The emperor ordered the Abbot of Monte Cassino to send an approved copy of the Rule to all other monastic houses, further demanding the assurance that the monks and nuns were keeping all their vows and studying only what he considered conformed to their monastic profession. He sent each house scales to weigh the allotted daily pound of bread and a container to limit the various measures each monastery adopted as conforming to the daily "hemina of wine" permitted by Benedict. This uniform adaptation of Benedict's Rule represented Charlemagne's interpretation more than Benedict's intent.

Instituting vast educational reforms, Charlemagne required each monastery and cathedral to open a school. Favoring religious houses like Chelles known for their intellectual bent, the emperor also used monasteries for personal reasons. When his sister Gisela (757–810) and his daughter Rotrude (775–810) needed a retirement home, he sent them to Chelles, where the former eventually became abbess.[3] He also insisted that the monasteries be not only centers of agricultural cultivation and learning with extensive library holdings, but also sites of constant intercessory prayer for the empire and its leaders. He consistently named monastic abbesses and abbots from the episcopal royalty's offspring and princely ranks. For example, the Archbishop of Sens received the Abbey of Echternach and one of the emperor's noble counts was named Abbot of Saint-Maixent. This practice led to many abuses of power in some monasteries, with more devastating policies to follow.[4]

Feudalism of this period also impacted monasticism. Men and women of nobility, who received fiefs at the hands of the monarchs or minor princes, were classed as vassals with consequent privileges and obligations. Because monasteries were usually wealthy and owned property, these communities of monks and nuns were also considered vassals that owed the emperor something in return for his leadership and protection. Military service was among these obligations. Monasteries were required to provide a stipulated number of mercenary knights, usually younger sons of the nobles, to be available on demand. Exchanges of gifts between monasteries and monarchs were common, with more specified precious metals or produce often given to monarchs and the ruling authorities by abbeys than the reverse. Throughout the feudal period, civil rulers dominated the monastic institutions just as they dominated European Christianity as a whole.

Alcuin

Alcuin (c. 735–804) was an imperial scholar and liturgist under Charlemagne, accorded a saint reluctantly appointed to the king's court by some popular traditions. Uncertainty remains about his background though it was likely he was a deacon and could have been a secular priest or Benedictine monk. Assuredly, he was a notable educator and ultimately was made an abbot. The Emperor rewarded his life's work with several monasteries: Saint Loup at Troyes, Saint Joseph in Flavigny, FerrièresAbbey, Saint Josse in Boulogne, and Saint Martin at Tours' Abbey of Marmoutier, where he retired for the last eight years of his life.

Alcuin was born in England, probably in the vicinity of York. He spent his childhood and youth at the York Cathedral School then under the leadership of Benedictine Archbishop Egbert (a disciple of Bede). Alcuin was only thirty-two when he was put in charge of his alma mater and forty-six when Charlemagne met him at Parma while on a Roman tour. At Parma, Charlemagne urged Alcuin to come to his capital at Aix-la-Chapelle to conduct the Palace School. Charlemagne, lacking the barest academic rudiments, would often attend this school, which often travelled with the court when it changed residence. In the course of his duties, Alcuin exerted no little influence in the political and academic spheres. He also participated in a significant measure of liturgical reform and wrote several commentaries. Alcuin dedicated his energies to the Saint Martin of Tours' abbey school, adding volumes to the library and otherwise enhancing the monastery's prestige during the final years of his life.[5] Buried at the Abbey of Saint Martin, the value of his contribution to the Carolingian Renaissance is undisputed.[6]

The Reforms of Benedict of Aniane

Benedict (c. 747–821), son of the Count of Maguelone, was born near Aniane. Baptized Witiza, he was sent as an adolescent to the royal court of Pepin and remained to serve Charlemagne and his son, Louis the Pious. An incident from his youth about 774 compelled him to reflect on the course of his life. According to his biographer, Ardo Smaragdus (d. 843), Witiza and his brother were fording a river when the force of the water carried his brother away. At great personal risk, Witiza rescued him. This near-death experience determined him to dedicate his life to God after such a narrow escape. He joined the community at the Abbey of St. Seine in Burgundy, where he imposed upon himself the most severe penances and other ascetical practices.

Self-driven to interpret the Rule of Benedict literally, he refused to bathe (Benedict of Norcia had decried the use of the public baths but not private bathing) and endured strict fasts. He ignored his abbot's attempts to moderate his lifestyle. After that abbot died, the monk Witiza, now known as Benedict, was unanimously elected to replace him, but he refused the honor. He left the abbey for his own familial estate at Aniane, where he built himself a cell close to the residential chapel.[7]

The young recluse soon attracted a group of companions. Around 780 he organized monastic life at Aniane where he enforced the Rule with vigor. From 782–787 he erected a monastery with a grand church and spacious library. With personal authorization from Char-lemagne to reform monasticism in certain French houses, he visited monasteries of southern France to introduce his reforms. When his abbey at Aniane had over three hundred monks, in anticipation of even greater influx of monastic candidates, he expanded the buildings to accommodate a thousand of them.[8]

At the request of diocesan bishops, Benedict sent monks from his own monastery to found or reform others in Touraine, Berry, Auvergne, Albi, and at Saint-Savin, among others. Although the Benedictine Rule established autonomous houses, the ninth-century Benedict kept all monastic houses under his sole jurisdiction, trans-ferring monks from one monastery to another. In essence, he devised a small federation of monastic congregations, eventually serving as a model for the tenth-century Cluniac reforms. The emperor Louis the Pious (814–840) charged Benedict to instruct the strict interpretation of the Rule to monks in Aquitaine, immediately affecting about twenty-six houses. The monarch also presented him with the monastery of Inde (later Kornelimunster) near the capital. Benedict then reformed Marmoutier in Alsace, and after the synod of Aix-la-Chapelle in 817, and in most cases assumed the role of legis-lator superior of most Benedictine monasteries in the western part of the Holy Roman Empire.

Benedict's conviction that each literal detail of the Rule should be interpreted strictly enforced adherence to the letter over the more moderate spirit Benedict of Norcia had emphasized. His belief that monastics had no place in evangelization—for him, the Great Com-mission to preach the Gospel to every nation was now fulfilled—so he turned monks and nuns to exclusive study and contemplation rather than to works of mercy that had so characterized monasticism's early generations. Benedict of Aniane's study of pre-Benedictine monasticism probably contributed to the rigorous discipline he enforced, deemphasizing the traditional Cassinese interpretation of the Rule in favor of older, more literal observances. In attempting reform, he often appeared to model the Fathers of the Desert and Pachomius more than Benedict of Norcia.[9] He collected all the older monastic rules into a *Codex Regularum* which he edited. In another work, the *Concordia*, he noted the concordance between the Rule of Benedict and parallel passages from other monastic literature. He maintained that these more ancient monastic practices culminated in the "one rule" of Benedict of Norcia, or at least the Rule as he interpreted it.[10] When the monks and abbots met in synod, the famous capitularies of Aachen reflected his penchant for a strict interpretation.[11] Later, in many areas of Europe, particularly the Continent, Benedictinism reflected not the original spirit of Benedict of Cassino but the exacting innovations of Benedict of Aniane.

Benedict of Aniane often departed from the prescriptions of the original Benedict's Cassinese Rule. He regarded work in the fields as occupation for serfs, not monks. Though he forbade monastics to teach any children but those given by their parents as cloister oblates, he did allow Fleury-sur-Loire to open a school for boys outside the monastic walls while still insisting that other monasteries had to close their educational institutions. An even greater innovation was his restructuring of the Liturgy of the Hours, extending the psalmody and readings required by Benedict. He added the daily recitation of the Office of the Dead and multiple series of psalms and prayers. Since most of the monks were now ordained clerics, he maintained that they were to be preoccupied with religious studies in solemn Eucharistic liturgies, and in long hours of prayer in the choir stalls of the church. Benedict of Aniane, the reforming revolutionary, changed the balance and neglected to preserve the moderation so characteristic of the original spirit of the Cassinese Rule. Though Benedict of Aniane's influence was extensive, he often quashed what autonomy still remained in monasteries, trying to centralize them while enforcing uniformity of custom and prayer. His departure from the traditional practice of the Benedictine Rule was not always questioned, gradually becoming part of the monastic tradition. Though his interpretation differed profoundly from the preceding centuries of Benedictine monasticism, Benedict of Aniane remains one of the most influential monastic personages after Benedict of Norcia.[12]

Following Charlemagne's example of scrutinizing enforcement of his civil *missi dominici*, Benedict of Aniane dispatched emissaries to see if the monastics were sufficiently observant. Every monastery compelled or voluntarily committed to his reform had to follow the model at Kornelimünster Abbey at Inde. Monks from different abbeys traveled there to learn the approved implementation of the customary. However, full implementation of Benedict of Aniane's reform could not yet come. The Saracen and Viking invasions soon followed his premature death in 821, completely destroying some monasteries and temporarily devastating others. The uniform adoption of Aniane's reforms was, thus, delayed. It was not until the tenth-century rise of Cluny that the stamp of the ninth-century Benedict was indelibly impressed upon the Benedictine way of life.

Monastic Literature, Art, and Architecture

Despite the challenges of the ninth century, great literary figures continued to abound in the monasteries. Among the monks venerated as scholars of that time are two literateurs from Corbie, Paschasius Radbertus (785–865) and Ratramnus (d. c. 870). Fulda, then considered the greatest intellectual center of the Germanic peoples, boasted Candidus Bruun (d. 845). His fame was superseded only by his abbot, Rabanus Maurus Magnentius (c. 780–d. 856), later to be named Archbishop of Mainz. In addition to commentaries on the Scriptures, Rabanus composed an encyclopedia collating what he considered all the significant facts to date. He also composed religious poetry and compiled a textbook for the education of clerics.

The Swiss monastery of St. Gall also boasted several writers, notably Notker the Stammerer (c. 840) and Ratpert (c. 855–911), author of a picturesque history of his monastery. However, the woman Wiborada (d. 926)—a recluse who lived in a cell near St. Gall's—was, because of her passion for books, chosen as patron saint of librarians and bibliophiles. Legends report that as the invading Hungarians advanced into the area near the monastery, Wiborada admonished the Abbot to save first the books, then the sacred vessels and other monastery possessions.[13] The architecture of St. Gall Abbey is splendidly representative of the emerging architectural plans of the new monastic builders. Typically, the monastery complex was a large quadrangle including dining and store rooms, library, scriptorium, and chapter room, all dominated by the cruciform church. This architectural pattern resembled that of the old Roman villas and the ancient military camps.[14]

Medieval monastics immersed themselves in practice of the fine arts of Western culture. Products of ordinary monks' daily labor, European churches still contain the most celebrated of the medieval sculptures, painting, goldsmithing, and woodcarving. European national archives and museums house myriad illuminated manuscripts from the medieval period, acquired from abbeys subjected to dissolution during the Reformation and French Revolution. Most of the large abbey's monks and nuns were calligraphers, miniaturists, and illuminators. The nuns also added embroidery and design of church vestments and tapestries.[15]

Ansgar in Denmark and Sweden

Though Benedict of Aniane had discouraged Benedictine missionary efforts during the ninth century, the labors of some were not entirely thwarted. Ansgar (801–865), an educated Frankish nobleman from the northern French Abbey of Corbie, became known as "Apostle of Scandinavia." Sent southward to the newly founded German Korvey in 826, he educated youth while participating in the monastery's efforts to evangelize the Saxons. Harold, rival to the Danish throne, solicited political support from Emperor Louis the Pious in 826. After baptism of the would-be King at Mainz, he requested that someone go to Denmark and evangelize the Danes. Walla, Abbot of Corbie and uncle of the Emperor, designated Ansgar to fulfill this request. Since the Danish king's rival supported this mission, Ansgar was compelled to leave Denmark in 827 after Harold failed to secure the throne. Three years later, the King of Sweden, Bjorn, also asked for Christian missionaries, and Ansgar again responded with several monks to the region of present-day Bjorko, the political and commercial center of Sweden at that time.

A year later, Ansgar was appointed Abbot of Korvey by Louis the Pious, who created an independent bishopric near the Scandinavian countries at Hamburg in northern Germany. Pope Gregory IV commissioned Ansgar its new Archbishop and made him papal legate for Scandinavia. When the Viking raids threatened the Frankish coastal areas, Ansgar used the Flemish monastery of Thouront as a seminary for young Danes. When the Vikings burned Hamburg in 845, the Archbishop sought refuge in Bremen. Seven years later Ansgar was again in Sweden to confer with King Olaf, who finally accorded Ansgar and his followers freedom to evangelize his country. In addition to his work among the Scandinavians, Ansgar founded three monasteries before his death in 865: Ramelsloh near Hamburg, a community in Bremen, and a monastery of nuns at Bassum near Hanover. Ansgar and his monastic companions' evangelization of Denmark and Sweden, like Charlemagne and Benedict of Aniane, made a lasting imprint on ninth-century Christianity.

The Cluniac Reforms

Benedict of Aniane's influence on the Western monastic tradition was sustained centuries after his death through the strict Cluny reforms of the tenth century.[16] Begun in the lineage of an abbey founded by Aniane—from Saint-Savin to Saint Martin in Autun to Baume and to Cluny—the reform gave subsequent monasticism a particular tradition that endured for more than eight centuries. Even after its demise in the eighteenth, those who restored monasticism in France in the nineteenth century tried to revive some of the same power and influence, spirit, and triumphalism of the Cluniac tenth.[17]

The elderly and heirless Duke William of Aquitaine (875–918), seeking reparation for a murder he had committed, wished to erect a new monastery. In common practice, wealthy nobility would often make monastic foundations to repent for sin while having their names perpetually included in the community's prayers. The Duke had inherited an estate at Cluny in the Burgundian valley of the Saone, not far from Macon, and called Berno of Baume (850–927) to be abbot in 909. Departing from ordinary practice of the Duke's *and* bishop's jurisdictions, the abbey was uniquely granted full autonomy. Also departing from the Rule of Benedict's norms for election of an abbot, Duke William left abbatial succession in the sole hands of his predecessor. Each of the first four Cluniac abbots independently named his own successor, whether or not they possessed suitable qualifications.[18]

Cluny's influence spread rapidly, with the monasteries in Berry and Bresse first confided to Abbot Berno. There, Berno supervised the strict observance of Benedict of Aniane's Kornelimunster traditions. The Cluniacs became known as professional "pray-ers" in this early feudal age of professional warriors. Intercessors were valued, and Cluny and other reputable monasteries became recipients of gifts from rich and poor alike, gifts designed to propitiate a feared God and ensuring constant prayer for sinners and their loved ones. The monastic liturgies reflected the seriousness of this task, and the length, rigor, and solemnity of common prayer in choir impressed and inspired donors. Cluny and its affiliated houses adopted schedules whose severity left little or no space for study or other work and "precious little time for anything at all"; it was a schedule that small monasteries could not adhere to for long, as "sheer fatigue would ensure that."[19]

Abbot Berno resided at Cluny only at intervals. In his will, he disposed of the monasteries as if they were personal properties, leaving the abbeys of Baume, Gigny, and Mouthier in Bresse to his nephew, Guy, and giving Cluny, Déols, and Massay in Berry to his favorite disciple, Odo. Odo's famous successors expanded Cluny's domain as five great abbot saints of Cluny ruled for 157 years (927–1109), making it unrivaled in wealth and influence.

Noteworthy Abbots of Cluny

Berno's immediate successor Odo (c. 878–942) reigned as abbot at Cluny only fifteen years, a relatively short time compared to some of his successors' tenures. Formerly one of the canons at Saint Martin of Tours, he joined Berno at Baume Abbey where his reputation and concern for reform, organization, and sanctity prompted others desiring renewal to invite him to introduce the Cluniac reforms in their monasteries. Princess Adelaide (931–999), confiding the imperial abbey of Romainmôtier to him in 929, began Odo's friendly relations with the imperial house henceforth favoring the Cluniac spirit even amidst pervasive conflicts between the state and Christian church. Also maintaining the papal confidence, Odo gained favor with princes, feudal lords, and bishops who began adding their ruined or decadent houses to the Cluniac reform. Such prominent monasteries as Limoges, St. Julien at Tours, Fleury-sur-Loire in France, and Saint Paul Outside the Walls and St. Mary's on the Aventine in Rome all became associated with the charismatic abbot. Cluny was soon recognized in the capital of Christendom as the standard-bearer of strict observance in Benedictine renewal.[20]

Odo's successor, Aymard (c. 910–965), was not so influential though, during his short reign (943–948), Cluny's land holdings expanded by at least 278 charters of donation with landed estates of various sizes and values added to the monastery. Aymard resigned in 948 in favor of Mayeul (c. 910–994), his picked successor, who governed the house for the next forty-six years. Born into an aristocratic family of Provence, Mayeul was archdeacon of Macon when he joined Cluny to avoid being appointed Bishop of Besançon. He had been a man of the world—lettered, eloquent, diplomatic, and trusted counselor of princes and emperors while remaining charitable and saintly. When Princess Adelaide became empress, he had a strong advocate in the highest circles. The Ottonian rulers of the Holy Roman Empire commissioned him to make voyages to Italy to reform monasteries or secure peaceful resolutions to conflicts in the civil or ecclesiastical realms. Adelaide gave him abbeys in Rome, Pavia, and Ravenna, and Pope Benedict VIII requested he restore Lerins. The noble proprietors of Marmoutier, Auxerre, and Saint-Maure-de-Fosse entrusted monasteries to him. While en route to St. Denis in 994, Mayeul died at the Priory of Souvigny near Moulins.

Odilo (c. 962–c. 1048), whom Mayeul favored as his successor, governed Cluny for the next fifty-five years. He too had been a Canon—at St. Julian in Brioude. Reportedly short in stature, he was known for his sweet disposition and determination coupled with his deep humility and faith. He exerted administrative ability, increasing from thirty-seven to sixty-five the number of houses restored or founded by Cluny while leading his monasteries in significant charitable work among the poor, even selling church vessels to finance his social ministry. Odilo introduced the annual commemoration of the dead on November 2 known as All Souls' Day, which was adopted universally by the Church. He introduced innovative military practices such as the Truce of God, limiting the time of fighting in the constant feudal battles, and designated certain cease-fire intervals known as the Peace of God. It prohibited warfare on holy days and weekends, and all of Lent and Advent. Eventually, it was mandated in most of the conciliar decrees of the Church and was honored by the majority of the French, German, and Italian feudal lords. Odilo declined the Archbishopric of Lyons that was offered to him in 1031. He died in 1049.

The zenith of Cluny's power and prosperity came during the sixty-year reign of Odilo's successor, Hugh (1024–1109). A member of one of the first families of Burgundy, he was appointed by Odilo at age twenty and had ministered to the community in that position until the death of his predecessor. Being a consummate diplomat, the new abbot brought to Cluny favors and beneficence of the kings of France and England and their great lords, while maintaining the traditional Cluniac attachment to the imperial house of the Empire. It was not long before popes and emperors solicited Hugh's participation in diplomatic missions. Two popes, Nicholas II and Gregory VII, named him papal legate for Aquitaine. He convened two councils at Vienne and Toulouse that addressed the abuse of simony, the prevalent practice of buying coveted positions in the church. He acted as a conciliator in one of the most famous medieval church-state conflicts, the controversy between Emperor Henry II and Pope Gregory VII over lay investiture wherein civil liege lords had vested bishops with both feudal and ecclesiastical symbols.

Throughout Hugh's reign "a vast and complex network of relationships began to emerge between Cluny and its dependencies which has baffled the descriptive powers of modern historians."[21] Some abbeys were reduced to the state of priories while others like Vézelay and Moissac were allowed to keep their abbatial status but remained subject to the Abbot of Cluny. Upon the acquisition of authority of La Charité, for example, Cluny also gained its far-flung family of some seventy dependencies including five foundations in post–Norman Conquest England. Other monasteries could adopt Cluniac observances without surrendering any autonomy.

In England—despite Hugh's reluctance—the first draft of the Congregation of Cluny's provincial structure began to be formulated at the insistence of William the Conqueror. Concurrently, dependent monasteries arose in England, France, Spain, Italy, and throughout the Empire, with an annual tax paid to Cluny affiliate's most obvious mark.[22] Hugh also had time to build, completely reconstructing the cloistered areas at Cluny and renovating the refectory and infirmary. He also constructed the great church whose ruins still reflect Cluny's splendor, magnificence, and power. He is considered the greatest of the abbots, reputedly combining prudence, piety, moderation, and a talent for conciliation. At Hugh's death in 1009, Cluny had jurisdiction of 1184 monasteries in Europe, of which 880 were French. Pope Calixtus II canonized Hugh at Cluny in 1120,[23] and several future popes sustain the Cluniac spirit throughout their reigns, notably: Stephen IX, former abbot of Monte Cassino (d. 1058); Gregory VII (d. 1085), author the controversial Gregorian Reforms; Urban II, the Benedictine who preached the First Crusade at Clermont: as well as Victor III (d. 1099), Pascal II (d. 1118), and Gelasius II (d. 1119).[24]

Cluniac Nuns

The Cluniac reform also included women.[25] Abbess Ava of St. Maur at Verdun traveled to several houses desiring to institute the strict regular observance. The chronicle of Hugh of Flavigny records that she was received by St. Odilo at Cluny, where—despite prohibitions of a woman's presence in the church cloister—he introduced her at the monastic chapter meeting. The juridical relationship between monks and nuns in the congregation, however, was never clearly defined.[26]

Hugh of Cluny founded Marcigny-sur-Loire in 1055 and appointed his sister, Ermengarde, first prioress. Other great women— Hugh's mother, several princesses, the mother of Peter the Venerable, the sister of St. Anselm of Canterbury, and many other notables— also joined that community, making Marcigny the leader of the other fifteen Cluniac houses then existing. Despite women's presence in the monasteries, an anecdote of Marcigny emphasizes the strictness of medieval women's enclosure. According to the legend, when a fire ignited close to the priory's thatched roof, the Bishop of Lyons—present on the scene—begged the nuns to evacuate the building. They refused, declaring they preferred to die rather than leave the cloister. Perhaps appealing to a convenient *deus ex machina*, Schmitz remarks that "moved by such fidelity, the bishop obtained through prayer the cessation of the flames."[27] Although Marcigny was subject to Cluny, it was, in reality, a double monastery. Hugh established a small community of about a dozen of his monks near the nuns, ostensibly charged with the nuns' temporal and spiritual direction. Like the monks, the nuns made their profession of vows before the Abbot of Cluny or his delegate. For each house it founded, Cluny named both a prioress and a monk as another superior. Marcigny, like many other French abbeys and priories, endured until the French Revolution.

Essence of the Cluniac Reform

The Cluniac reform and the council of abbots at Aix-la-Chapelle, rooted in the Cassinese Rule as implemented by Benedict of Aniane, particularly emphasized silence, work, stability in the monastic enclosure, and the practice of virtue. Liturgical prayer—considered the principal and, at times, only task of the Cluniac monk and nun—was given priority over all other activities. While the nuns were required to pray only 100 psalms daily, the monks prayed a regular 138. The numbers of these requisite psalms increased in ratio to the number of benefactors. At the night office before Lent, the entire books of Genesis and Exodus were read as lessons, and on Good Friday all 150 psalms were recited. Restriction of nourishment also occurred in the Cluniac monasteries. Though the monks had the choice of a variety of fish that regularly arrived from subject priories, no red meat was allowed until the fourteenth century. Some eggs and cheese were also available and wine was permitted in moderation. The administrative structure included general chapters where delegates represented monasteries. They modified their communities' varied decrees, leading to an official text of the Cluniac Customary ultimately issued around 1063. Bernard of Marseille made a further revision of this customary about 1080 and was adapted for the Germanic monastic houses by William of Hirsau.[28]

Since choir duties consumed most of the monastics' time, Cluny was never known for its intellectual activity. Yet, libraries existed in each house where members read Scripture, the Fathers, and other spiritual writers. Conferences took place on the spiritual life and Scripture. Only about a dozen boys or girls, however, were permitted in the monastery schools, and the instructors did little writing. Illumination of manuscripts continued, and the monasteries produced chalices, censers, chandeliers, processional crosses, reliquaries, and other items of silver, gold, and ivory to enhance the splendor of the sanctuary.

The Cluniac influence was most evident in the field of architecture. Cluny diffused Roman architectural design and principles, favoring enormity of size. When the final touches were put on the church at Cluny in 1250, it became the largest Christian church in the world. Its structure and style were imitated to some degree throughout France, England, Spain, and Poland. Medieval sculpture was also valued, and Cluny played a preponderant role in its development. Images of the saints and Christ and his mother adorned all the columns and doors, and instructive and allegorical frescoes abounded.[29]

Monks of the Italian Peninsula

During Cluny's dominance of European monasticism, men's monasteries in Italy opened and closed in an undulating fashion. After the 720 restoration of Benedict of Norcia's Monte Cassino, the cradle of Benedictine monasticism had not yet resumed its former primacy among Italian monasteries before it was destroyed (again) by the Saracens in 883. Late in the eleventh century, Subiaco reached its apogee under Abbot John. Farfa, affiliated with Cluny, prospered and its daughter houses dotted central Italy. St. Michael of Cluse, founded about 985 in the Piedmont, was known not only for its riches and hospitality to pilgrims, but also for its 160 dependent priories.

The monastery at Cava made the greatest Cluniac impact in Italy. Favored by Pope Gregory VII (c. 1015/1028–1085), all the monasteries of the region were subjected to this abbey. Founded by the hermit Alferio Pappacarbona (930–1050), a nephew of the prince of Salerno, attracted former monks of Cluny as disciples. Among them was his nephew Pierre (1038–1123), who organized the community into a monastery with Cluniac observances. Eventually forty abbeys, thirty-five priories, and sixty-five churches were given to Abbot Pierre by princes, lords, and bishops. Ultimately numbering seventy-seven subject abbeys, a hundred priories, and four hundred churches, Cava dominated the southern peninsula and Sicily. Some distance east of Cava, another monastery, Monte Vergine, dominated a flourishing congregation during the twelfth and following centuries, lasting even to this day.

During the eleventh-century Norman retrieval of Sicily from its Saracen conquerors, monks Christianized the serfs on the immense land-holdings they were given by the Norman monarchs, and augmented the Saracen and Byzantine population with imported Latin peasants. Greek monasteries at Messina and Calabria had daughter-houses subject to them, but Sardinian monasteries were less numerous. A few Tuscan monasteries with small dependent houses existed on the island of Corsica. In addition to the Cluniac monastery of St. Mary on the Aventine in Rome, two monastic communities were founded about 980 by the metropolitan patriarch of Damascus. The abbeys of St. Boniface and Alexis were foyers of Eastern monasticism, and the community boasted both Greek and Roman monks. Members of this community included Adalbert of Prague (c. 956–997) and his brother Gaudence, both massacred at the beginning of the eleventh century near Lublin in Poland. By the end of that century, the Vatican and Lateran communities in Rome had replaced the Benedictine observance with the Rule for Canons.

English Benedictines

Monastic life in tenth-century England was chaotic, and most monks and nuns were living more like secular canons and canonesses than vowed monastics. Times called for a reformer—Dunstan (c. 909–988)—who received his early schooling at Glastonbury Abbey, which still had a good library and dedicated clerics. After ordination he became chaplain of the Bishop of Winchester then counselor of King Edmund. His enemies at court persuaded the new king to exile him, which the monarch soon regretted after a close call with death. He named Dunstan Abbot of Glastonbury where the Rule of Benedict was immediately reintroduced. Ethelwold (c. 904/909–984), one of Dunstan's monk-disciples at Glastonbury and later Bishop of Winchester, was charged to reform the monastery at Abingdon. When Edwig became King, he again banished Dunstan, who fled to the reformed monastery of Blandinium in Ghent. There, Dunstan came into contact with Cluniac customs. Recalled by King Edgar in 967, Dunstan was appointed Archbishop of Canterbury in 959. Oswald (d. 992), a monk who had spent eight years at Fleury, was given the See of Worcester and sent for his Fleury companion Germanus (d. c. 1013), settling him with some followers from Worcester in a small monastery at Westbury. Ramsey Abbey, founded by Oswald about 971, soon overshadowed Westbury and it soon had famous daughter-houses at Winchcombe. In Scotland, Benedictine monasticism owed its introduction to the eleventh century Queen Margaret (c. 1045–1093), wife of King Malcolm Canmore, and her sons continued its patronage. She sent her daughter Mathilda to her aunt, Abbess Cristina of Romsey, who later also headed Wilton.[30]

About thirty monasteries of men and six of women soon sprang up under the guidance of Glastonbury, Abingdon, and Westbury. Romsey, founded earlier for monks in 907, was turned over to nuns in 967. The three monastic bishops decided that a uniform way of monastic life benefited all the monasteries and placed them under the direct protection of the crown, a radical departure from the Cluniac practice. The English bishops, abbots, and abbesses met at Winchester in 970 to devise a comprehensive code for English monasticism based on Aniane's *Concordia*. Known as the *Regularis Concordia Anglicae Nationis Monachorum Santimonialiumque*, it was to be observed in all monasteries in England. The document detailed the horarium, the liturgical functions of the day and year, and even some job

descriptions of certain monastic offices. It included elaborate prescriptions for the ceremonials, prayers, and Masses at the death of one
of its members, as well as added a postscript freeing the monasteries
from the "heriot" (a type of inheritance tax due the king at the death
of a property-owner). Though not named, Ethelwold is given credit
for compiling the prescriptions.[31]

In addition to Aniane's document, the English customary
showed some dependence on the Chrodegang rule for canons. It
also incorporated the Isidorian Rule with some practices traceable to
letters of Pope Gregory I to Augustine of Canterbury that had been
preserved by Bede. The customary's emphasis remained liturgical
and claustral with no attempt to eliminate the accretions of psalmody
and vocal prayers. Especially significant was the document's exhorta-
tion to daily communion. Time outside choir was spent in teaching,
writing, illuminating, and craftwork, although the *Concordia* of the
English does not explicitly mention these works. There were some
nationalistic concessions—more fires in winter than prescribed on
the continent, sheltered work areas, and the recognition as *ex officio*
patrons the King and Queen—with special prayers mandated after
certain hours of the daily office for these monarchical guardians of
monasticism. This tradition may explain why French nuns, exiled
from Solesmes early in the twentieth century, welcomed the King and
Queen into their refectory at the Isle of Wight when no other lay or
clerical individual could "violate" the cloister.[32]

The abbatial election was subject to royal approval, but when the
monastic community was also a cathedral abbey of clerics it selected
the bishop, someone who would wholly conform to the monastic rules,
from its own membership. The *Concordia* assumed that the cathedral
chapter would be a thoroughly organized monastic community with
the right to elect its own superior. This affected, in a remarkable way, the
Church of England. It was a determination to continue the practices of
Augustine of Canterbury and his early successors, often leading to the
imposition of the monastic lifestyle on diocesan clerics as more monks
returned to the episcopal leadership roles. The English monarchs
held the abbots, abbesses, monks, and nuns in such high esteem that
they were often invited to participate in various important gatherings.

Dunstan had early encouraged this participation to cement national unity, and abbots, abbesses, monks, and nuns attended the king's coronation ceremonies when at Bath Abbey in 973. As guests of the queen, they also participated in the coronation banquet. Abbots and abbesses were influential members of parliamentary councils like the Witan, in person or through their delegates until the Norman Conquest of 1066.

Non-Cluniac Communities of Women in Palestine and Europe

Benedictine nuns were present in Palestine during the eleventh century. Before the Crusades, they could already be found in Jerusalem at Saint-Mary-la-Petite, and later appeared in Bethany and at the church of Saint Ann. When the Arabs reconquered Jerusalem in 1187 Christian nuns sought refuge in Acre. At Antioch, there were nuns in Carpathia and at Saint-Lazare.[33] In Europe, monasteries of women flourished in the Lowlands from the middle of the eleventh century to that of the twelfth. In 890, the monks' house at Susteren had already become an abbey for women. Thorn was founded about 992. Monks, however, replaced the Marchiennes nuns when the women were deemed "unreformable."[34]

In the eleventh century, there was scarcely a region in the Italian peninsula that did not claim a new foundation of Benedictine nuns. Even small villages like Cremona had three monasteries, and Florence boasted several. In 1003, however, the nuns of St. Savior at Siena were replaced by monks at the instigation of the royal Normans then ruling Sicily. It would be the richest, most privileged of the monasteries in the new realm. In Spain, the Benedictine Rule was followed in the abbey of nuns at San Pedro de las Puellas at Barcelona and several other cities. Around 1055 the Council of Coyanza imposed the Rule of Benedict on all monasteries in the Iberian Peninsula. In 1103, the Abbot of Sahagun, at Pope Pascal II's request, assembled all the nuns from double monasteries subject to his jurisdiction to San Pedro Abbey. In the Portuguese territory, the oldest abbey was the tenth-century double monastery of Arouca.[35]

Benedictine traditions also found their way into Eastern Europe. Near 970, nuns received the Church of Saint George of Hradcin at Prague where the body of Saint Ludmilla reposed. The first abbess, Princess Milada, was the daughter and sister of two kings, Boleslas I and II, respectively. Blessed by the pope at Rome, she received the title of princess-abbess and the perpetual right of co-coronation of the Queen of Bohemia. There were nuns in Dalmatia in the eleventh century, first at Cherso then at Arfbe (Rabb), Trau, and Zara. Nevertheless, nuns' monasteries never totaled more than a dozen. Some nuns are mentioned in Bishop Brunon's writings in the early eleventh century, and historians seem aware of some Benedictine sanctimoniales then in the region.

The Cistercian and Trappist Reforms

During the Middle Ages, several distinct groups followed the Rule of Benedict. The Camaldolese, Vallambrosians, and the unique Congregation of Fontevrault with their double monasteries— always headed by an abbess—began in the eleventh century. The Carthusians were founded in the twelfth century, with others making later appearances: Sylvestrines in the thirteenth, Olivetans in the fourteenth, and the Armenian Benedictines—the Mechitarists—in the eighteenth century. Despite their importance and influence, none of these groups would have the momentum or enduring influence of the Cistercian and Trappist reforms.[36]

The Congregation of Cluny had become centralized and so rich and powerful that its compliance with the Rule was questioned. Robert, Abbot of Molesmes (1024–1111) sparked a new movement. With a fervent group of twenty-one monks, including the pious and zealous Alberic (d. 1109), Abbot Robert left in 1098 to found a new community at Citeaux in Burgundy, about twenty miles south of Dijon. It was a solitary site, a clearing in an immense forest between the Shone River and the surrounding hills. Here the community found their longed-for solitude, as well as the Rule's characteristic poverty.

The monks at Molesmes, however, petitioned Urban II to order the abbot to return. Robert complied, leading the community for twelve more years of material and spiritual growth. At Citeaux the monk Alberic was elected to replace Robert, whereupon he led significant departures from the traditional Cluniac observances. Citeaux was juridically placed under the direct protection of the Roman pontiff; the customaries were revised and strict regulations concerning poverty, hospitality, amalgamation of lay brothers, and new foundations were legislated. There was a considerable shortening of choir duty as the lengthening of the Liturgy of the Hours had consumed almost all of the Cluniacs' time. There was now time for private prayer and as well as the *labora* legislated by Benedict necessary for the new foundation's sustenance.

Stephen Harding (d. 1134), Alberic's successor, headed Citeaux from 1109–1133. He completed the reorganization, accomplished the liturgical reform, and revised the regulations in 1114 with constitutions. This document, known as the *Carta Caritas* (Charter of Charity) received pontifical approval in 1119.[37] The future Order of Citeaux, known in the English-speaking world as Cistercian (from the Latin *Cisterciensis*), was assured. With the arrival of Bernard (1090–1153) and thirty of his relatives and friends whom he had personally recruited, Citeaux could look to a long future. Bernard was only twenty-four when he was sent to make the foundation at Clairvaux and to become its first abbot. By the sheer power of his ability and personality, he soon overshadowed the earlier founders, and his name is inextricably woven with the early success of the new Congregation. They were later called the White Benedictines because their garb's color (Benedict's Rule recommended that clothes be made from what could be obtained in the area, regardless of color). Despite many vicissitudes the Cistercians have endured to this day, although Citeaux itself did not outlast the French Revolution.

The new Congregation included nuns. Molesmes had established a feminine branch eventually located at Juilly, and Bernard sent women he had won to the Cistercian observance to that monastery. The first prioress was Elizabeth, wife of Bernard's eldest brother, and the second was Humbeline, Bernard's sister. About 1132, these women left Jully to establish the first Cistercian abbey of nuns at Tart, in the diocese of Langres.[38] Juilly itself remained under the jurisdiction of the Abbot of Molesmes. He admitted candidates to the habit, approved the profession of vows, and sent several monks to minister to the women's spiritual needs. These monks' superior, known as prior by the nuns, represented the nuns at the General Chapters of Cluny. The Abbess of Crisenon, another foundation, was permitted to attend the annual chapter at Molesmes .[39]

By the time Bernard died in 1153 he had founded, restored, or reformed sixty-six monasteries. Centuries later, the French Cistercian abbey La Trappe's commendatory abbot, Armand de Rancé (1626–1700) established stricter norms and began a significant reform of the Cistercians, who had become somewhat lax in their observances. Known as the Cistercians of Strict Observance (OCSO), these Trappists carved out their own history based on the earlier Benedictine traditions. Most contemporary Cistercians now follow a modified Trappist regimen and are almost indistinguishable from those still known as Cistercians of the Common Observance. New Orders continued to arise; many of them reinterpreting Benedict and developing their own traditions and observances. As time progressed, further reform movements and monastic expansion demonstrated the remarkable adaptability of the Benedictine Rule. ✳

CHAPTER 4

European Reform and Mysticism

Tenth through Thirteenth Centuries

Many monasteries in tenth- and eleventh-century Europe needed varied measures of change and spiritual reinvigoration. Unless affiliated with the Cluniac, Cistercian, or other reform congregations, monastic men and women could not determine their own monastery's policies as outlined in the Rule of Benedict. Commendatory abbots and abbesses, appointed by royalty, or cardinal protectors ordinarily regulated what happened within the monasteries under their patronage. Few could elect their own superiors while popes, kings, bishops, and ruling families continued to ensure that abbatial leaders would be compatible with their political policies. Thus, monastic leaders' values did not always coincide with those of the monastery's members, and income for a favorite or a family monk or nun superseded concern for the monastic life as a whole. Many monasteries suffered as an abbot or abbess appointed relatives as successors, often naming a co-adjutor during his or her lifetime to assure the succession of the individual's choice. Reform and renewal would respond in varied ways to these challenges.

Non-Cluniac or Cistercian Reform Movements and Congregations

During the Cluniac centuries, other reform congregations distinct from Cistercians and Trappists were reexamining, restructuring, and renewing their Benedictine lifestyles.

Flemish Reforms

Flemish changes began at Brogne when Count Gerard (c. 895–959), bent on reform, founded an abbey there in 919 and became its first abbot. Other abbeys that introduced the Brogne observances included the monastery of St. Ghislain in Hainaut, two monasteries in Ghent (St. Pierre and St. Bavon), and the abbeys of St. Bertin and St. Amand. At the Duke of Normandy's request, the abbatial Count's disciple, Maynard, reformed Mont St. Michel, St. Ouen, and St. Wandrille at Fontanelle that had been founded by its namesake in 649, later restored in the 960s after the Viking invasions. The reform was modest; Gerard never became a professed monk although he was the abbot. The Brogne Reform never exercised the great or lasting influence of some of the other renewals.[1]

The efforts under the leadership of Jean de Venders in 959 at Gorze Abbey near Metz were more successful than the Brogne Reform. The Bishop of Metz, encouraged by the numbers of admissions and the abbey's monastic discipline, supported the manner of its reform in other monasteries in his diocese including Saint Arnoul, Senones, and Saint Trond. These monasteries followed a common observance and were directed by deans, but they remained autonomous.[2]

The Vannist Reform

The Vannist reform was even more influential and significant. Richard of Verdun (970–1046), Dean of the Chapter at Rheims, became abbot of Saint Vanne in the French Lorraine region in 1005. Twenty other monasteries were soon confided to his leadership. Among these were St. Mihiel, Chalons and Liège Another renewal attempt ended in the assassination of Abbo of Fleury (c. 945–1004). A distinguished scholar and canonist, Abbo had been an instructor in the abbey school of Saint-Benoît at Fleury-sur-Loire, becoming abbot just as the monastery reached the peak of its prestige. Abbo was firm in regulating the discipline and zeal necessary to spread monastic reforms. He had allied himself with Odilo in the battle against certain bishops when the issue was monastic autonomy. In 988, he was called to initiate changes at the priory of La Reole, where he met his violent death in 1004.[3]

Other Reformed Monasteries

The Abbey of Bec, in the province of Normandy, founded by Herluin in 1035, became the most famous in the region because of its renown as a great intellectual center. After William the Conqueror, Duke of Normandy, conquered England, he appointed two Bec abbots to succeed each other as the first two Archbishops of Canterbury. Although the English Norman kings traditionally installed the archbishops, William appointed Lanfranc who was succeeded by Anselm, both former leaders of the Norman Bec Abbey. Anselm, attracted to the Bec Abbey by Lanfranc, had been abbot of the ducal monastery, St. Etienne at Caen. This abbey had been founded by Duke William in 1063 in reparation for his neglecting to secure papal dispensation to marry within forbidden bloodlines. Duke William's wife, later Queen Matilda of England, had an abbey for nuns also built at Caen.[4] Fond of the monks' Caen abbey, William mandated his burial at Saint Etienne, although he had been King of England from 1066 to his death in 1087.[5]

Chaise-Dieu Abbey, an eleventh-century foundation of Robert of Turlande (1001–1067), had reformed itself by the thirteenth century. Its observance spread to 186 priories throughout France and 17 outside its borders. The Benedictine abbey of Saint Victor at Marseilles was the base of operations for pontifical politics in Castille and Provence between 1064 and 1079. Led by Abbot Bernard, a confidant of Pope Gregory VII, the Roman liturgy regionally displaced the Castillian. After his death, Saint Victor monastery became affiliated with Saint Paul's in Rome and daughter houses were located in Provence, Languedoc, Catalonia, and Italy.[6]

Life within Medieval Monastic Walls

During the early medieval period, no minimum age was required for community leadership. A nun could be—and occasionally was—named abbess at age twelve. Abbots were often only in their twenties when appointed, and both abbots and abbesses were usually elected or appointed for life. Even the great Cluniac abbots and Cistercians such as Bernard were youthful, resulting in long reigns wherein leading monastics often influenced selection of their successors. The Gratian Decretals later set thirty as a minimum age for superiors and also required public profession of religious commitment. Unenforced, the decrees were usually ignored. After the Reformation, the Council of Trent tried again, mandating that the superiors be at least forty.

Some abbesses continued to use certain pontifical symbols usually associated with the rank of bishop, including the pectoral cross, crosier, and, at times, mitre. A few abbesses also wore the stole, conventionally reserved to men in major orders. Abbesses, like abbots, occupied abbatial thrones in their churches or chapels. Some limitations to these privileges remained, however, and some abbesses were granted them only much later. For example, the Abbess of Goss was not permitted to wear a pectoral cross in public until after 1751. The Abbess of Eichstätt was accorded the same privilege only in 1743. Called an "abbess nullius," a superior with quasi-episcopal status was accorded the privilege of all the pontificals: gloves, sandals, and mitre, although the mitre was often placed near her on the throne with her crosier. Occasionally the abbess wore a crown resembling the head-dress of the Oriental Rite prelates. French monastic historian Schmitz notes that in one monastery, use of mitre and crosier by the abbess of San Michele of Champagne "greatly disturbed the bishops."[8]

Abbesses were ordinarily accorded a special place in the sanctuary with the bishops and abbots who were not celebrating the Eucharist. In the absence of the bishop they often occupied the episcopal throne. There were complaints that some of the abbesses even arrogated to themselves the right to chant the Gospel, preside at the consecration of virgins, and hear the confessions of their nuns.[9] Several abbesses published decrees, consecrated churches, installed curates and vicars, and presided over tribunals. The Abbess of Montivilliers, not atypically, exercised quasiepiscopal jurisdiction over a dozen parishes and seven chapels.

In the late medieval period, abbots and abbesses tended to withdraw more frequently from the communal life of their monasteries. They often resided in a special abbatial apartment or house within the monastic walls to enjoy their own culinary services or share meals in their private residence with guests and favored monks or nuns of their communities. They attended community prayers only on Sundays or days of special feasts, privately reciting the psalmody in their own oratory at other times. The prioress and prior—appointed to assist the abbatial leaders—often had the most direct contact with the members of the community and served them in lieu of a committed and concerned abbot or abbess.

Monks and nuns solemnly professed the three Benedictine vows: obedience to the superior; conversion of life as a promise to live according to the monastic Rule's spiritual and ascetic values; and stability, binding the monk or nun to one community or congregation. Poverty and chastity were implied but not expressly stated as direct mandates within the Benedictine Rule. Canon Law later stipulated that profession of poverty and chastity be made by monastic women whose canonical promises, in many cases, were called simple rather than solemn vows. This purely juridical policy, mandated because of their non-papal claustral enclosure, was later reversed in the late-twentieth century canonical reforms.

Clericalism dominated the abbeys of men after monks' ordination became a general norm, although brother monks in simple vows had become a usual part of the medieval monastic culture. In the tenth century, 75 percent of the monks at Salzburg were ordained priests; at Saint Gall, almost 50 percent were clerics. Customarily, brothers and priests held rank according to the time of their profession rather than by their clerical status. Perhaps the Cistercian practice of hiring peasants for farm labor, intending to free the monks to chant in choir, influenced the later mandate separating clerics from brothers. Regardless, all choir monks eventually ranked above their non-ordained brothers.

Social class distinction also prevailed in monasteries of nuns. Some houses were even categorized as monasteries reserved for noble women. Other houses became known for their admission of non-nobles, sometimes exclusively admitted to those places. Many French abbeys of women, more often than not, limited their entrants to the aristocracy. Those who admitted both classes separated choir nuns from "lay sisters" within the walls. As rules became stricter regarding cloister, a third group—the extern sisters—was organized to serve guests, do the external business, and take care of whatever could not be accomplished through the use of the grille, an iron grate to separate the nuns from the visitors, family, friends, or even clerical and episcopal confreres.

Almost all abbesses were from royalty or of the noble caste although some were the illegitimate daughters of high-ranking nobles, clerics, or monarchs. Historians and biographers can mistakenly assume that nuns of renown certainly were abbesses as well, since abbatial leaders generally were the only ones who became famous in the literature of their time. Contrarily, Gertrude the Great of Helfta— discussed below—was a famous mystic but never an abbess. Easily confused with her abbess, Gertrude of Hackeborn who belonged to the nobility, Gertrude of Helfta did not. Statuary and paintings of Gertrude the Great with an abbatial crosier and references to her as an abbess have dominated devotional art, though she never was abbess of her community.

Most medieval abbeys of men and women also admitted lay men and women. Claustral oblates lived and prayed with the monks and nuns in monasteries of their gender. Laypersons were not perpetually committed, but they wore the religious habit and had certain rights and obligations. Some married men and women, and single-celibate individuals living outside the monastery within their own family circles became affiliated with abbeys of men and women not necessarily of their own gender. These oblates were occasionally the clerics or priests who assisted in abbey services at times. This tradition of affiliating claustral and lay oblates persists to the present day at many Benedictine monasteries across the world.[10]

Monastics engaged various ministries throughout the Middle Ages. Some monasteries had hospices and hospitals on or near their grounds. Others administered large landed estates that had been acquired or donated to the monastery. Some of these were so vast and productive that during the zenith of two English royal abbeys, a witticism claimed that if the Abbess of Shaftsbury married the Abbot of Glastonbury their heir could claim more personal land than the King of England. Monasteries also cultivated acres of vineyards, had wine distilleries, raised hops, and brewed beer. Even the nuns' communities at Frauenchiemsee, Hohenwart, and Kühbach had breweries. While other kinds of industry and commerce flourished in some abbeys, poverty reigned supreme in others. In the fifteenth century, for example, the Montmartre nuns had a royal commissar imposed upon them to administer their finances so that the abbey's debtors could be compensated.[11]

The Need for Reform in Some Women's Monasteries

Some medieval monasteries were considered in definite need of reform. Canonical visitation reports occasionally revealed that lax morals, prevalent during the High Middle Ages, had served as corrupting influences in some communities of women. A significant number of interventions by the Holy See suppressed entire communities in response to their reportedly dissolute lifestyles. Houses of nuns were seemingly suppressed more than those of monks; men, even of different orders, were often given the houses from which the nuns had been evicted. In the twelfth century, Canons Regular replaced the nuns at Charenton and Steinfeld, Augustinians those at Mairie de Laon and Schöningen. Monks from Chaise-Dieu occupied Faverney after the nuns were required to evacuate that monastery. Those of St. Jean at Verdon were also replaced by monks, as were the nuns of Donauwörth and Liesborn. Men also replaced the nuns at the Italian abbey of St. Sixtus at Plaisance and dozens of other monasteries.

Since women were generally not free to choose their spouse or their religious vocation, less committed lifestyles may have been inevitable. Some houses of nuns, in contrast, could not survive because of economics. Nuns often lacked basic finances needed for necessities. Corrupt hired lay employees deprived several monasteries of much of their income. These men, while overseeing the monastic landholdings—the primary source of the nuns' income—pocketed more than their share. Similarly, tenants took advantage of the women, knowing they would not treat them harshly or take them to the courts if they did not pay their rents or give them their fair share of the crops. Many houses were in such miserable condition financially that, according to one monk-historian, "poverty had ruined the practice of the vow of poverty!"[12]

Women's Cloister and Policies of Enclosure

During and after the High Middle Ages, the greatest dissimilarity between monks and nuns was policy and practice concerning the strictness of the enclosure, or cloister.[13] Benedict's Rule speaks of the monks' laboring in the enclosure of the monastery (*operemur claustra*). Chapter sixty-seven states that monastics may not leave the monastery environs without express permission of the superior. Elsewhere, the Rule legislates the time and place for prayer and meals when monastics perform tasks outside the monastic walls or are on a journey. Monks traditionally addressed these regulations with more latitude than did the nuns, though the nuns went out frequently at times, taking part in religious processions, going on pilgrimages, attending funerals of bishops and abbots, and sharing in special celebrations such as the dedication of a church or coronation of a monarch. Individuals often left for health reasons, to visit their parents, or for other authorized sojourns. Sometimes nuns exited their monasteries to confer with spiritual directors. Furthermore, most nuns were not only allowed to select their confessors but also their monastic chaplains, a privilege seldom granted after the Catholic Counter-Reformation's Council of Trent in 1563.

English nuns at times ignored enclosure completely. The Council of Trent tried to enforce it strictly, but until the final dissolution of monastic life in England during the reigns of Henry VIII and Queen Elizabeth I, English nuns tended to disregard its observance. When exiled nuns returned to England from France in the nineteenth century, they reinvigorated the tradition of strict enclosure by bringing their practice back to England. However, this return to strict enclosure was short-lived; the Second Vatican Council's mid-twentieth century sweeping reforms mitigated the practice.

During the sixth century, the rule of Caesarius of Arles stipulated that nuns be safeguarded from harm by never leaving the monastery until death.[14] This practical rationale continued with variations in dioceses and monastic communities, but eventually became equated with a monastic vow in itself. Thus, enclosure—mandated earlier for security reasons—assumed the role of virtue. Myriad anecdotes abound which extol the "heroism" of those who preferred death by fire, violence, or self-mutilation rather than violate the seclusion of their cloister. Such overzealous commitment to the monastic cloister, though not prevalent, nonetheless dominated the lives of many nuns.

Though monastic women were predominantly cloistered, visitors could easily come and go from the most enclosed areas of the monasteries. Earlier monastic tradition attests that Boniface, for example, shared meals in the refectory with the nuns in Trier, though this was usually not permitted clerics or guests before the mid-twentieth century. On her deathbed, Austreberta, abbess of Pavilly (630–704), welcomed clergy and monks into the most sacrosanct of the monastic confines—the dormitories—to make her farewells. During the Middle Ages, the public had some access to monasteries of women to visit or receive their spiritual direction—often in public parlors and through iron grilles—but guests could occasionally remain for days for these kinds of conferences or special pilgrimages.

Throughout monastic history, young boys and girls traditionally resided and were educated within the confines of nuns' monasteries. Often, rich and noble elderly women retired to live with the nuns as boarders paying for the cost of their keep. After leaving their thrones to their sons, or wishing to retire from public life, some kings, queens, emperors and empresses, and widows and widowers came to live in or near monasteries. In the sixteenth century, Emperor Charles V retired with his retinue to a palatial annex of the Spanish monastery at Escorial allowing him peace, quiet, and the proximity of a community with whom he conversed and prayed. Certain royal guests eventually made monastic profession at the monastery. Others, like the famous Eleanor of Aquitaine, first a French then an English Queen, were buried in nuns' habits as she was at Fontevrault.[15]

By the twelfth and thirteenth centuries, devotion to cloister was waning, and only those forced by their bishops were inclined to adhere to it strictly. Before the thirteenth century ended, the hierarchy felt so strongly that nuns' monasteries were in need of reform regarding enclosure Pope Boniface VIII responded to these clerical concerns. In 1298, he promulgated the decree *Periculoso* written "wishing to provide for the dangerous and abominable situation of certain nuns."[16] The only universal regulation of cloister until Trent, all women members of religious orders were required to observe perpetual cloister. They were to go to the outside world only if suffering from a contagious disease or with special permission of the bishop, even if a member of an exempt order.

Superiors, including abbesses, were to be represented by a male procurator when required by civic feudal authorities. No one, moreover, was to enter the cloistered areas except for grave causes and only with permission of the proper authority, generally the bishop. Medieval cynics, not lacking a certain malice, bruited about the phrase *"aut virum aut murum oportet mulierem habere"* (women must be guarded by either a husband or a wall).[17] Women of the Middle Ages seemed limited to being married or enclosed for life behind monastery walls.

During the fifteenth century, the architecture of the nuns' monasteries was altered to make all entrances and exits through one single door, danger of fire notwithstanding. Furthermore, this door had to be locked with two different keys, one from inside by the abbess, the other from the outside by the designated monk or abbot. Turnstiles to convey packages and mail from inside to the outside, or from behind the grille to someone in front, were installed. Iron grilles became ever more prevalent.[18]

At times the nuns rebelled as some stories attested. For example, when the Archbishop of Paris had grilles erected at Yerres, the nuns took them down and threw them into the river. On the other hand, some isolated communities took a special vow of cloister. As a general rule, Benedictine nuns ordinarily respected or tolerated strict enclosure, but seldom if ever committed themselves to keeping it entirely. Some bishops, especially among the English, gave up trying to impose it and just severely limited sojourns outside the cloister walls.

Sizes of Monasteries

Strict observance of the monastic rule, however, was not usually in proportion to strictness of cloister. There was seemingly some correlation between the number of monks or nuns in an individual abbey and the quality of observance—the smaller the community, the better the observance. Some monks' monasteries were numbering in the hundreds between the seventh and ninth centuries. Several, like Corbie, had over 300 members. Saint Wandrille was largest at 900. After the ninth century, however, communities with more than a hundred monks were considered very large. These included Saint Vaast, Reichenau, and Saint Gall. After the Viking raids, the monasteries again recouped and increased their membership. At the beginning of the twelfth century, Cluny had 400 monks but Christ Church at Canterbury only 150.

Sometimes the numbers were fixed in proportion to the monastic revenues. The Council of Aix-la-Chapelle in 817 stipulated that abbesses could not receive more novices than they could feed. They were not allowed without special dispensation to exceed the maximum number of nuns stipulated in the foundation charter. The Count of Siena limited his foundation at Saint-Sauveur to twenty nuns. Chelles was allowed only eighty. If the number reached the maximum, a candidate for the community had to await the death of a member before she could enter.[19] Numbers were no longer a concern after the Hundred Years War (1337–1453), fought primarily in France, resulted in a marked decrease in the membership of Benedictine monasteries of men and women there.

Notable Germanic Nuns and Their Monasteries

Scores of significant Germanic monasteries of nuns gained a great deal of renown during the High Middle Ages. Most prominent among these were Herford in Westphalia, Quedlinburg, Gandersheim, and Helfta. They exerted an incalculable social and intellectual influence. The nuns and their students studied the classical and religious writers, as well as civil and canon law. As was true of most communities of women, the nuns also mastered the arts of spinning, weaving, and embroidery. Nuns' monasteries in the German-speaking Empire ordinarily had a scriptorium where the members copied and illuminated classical and scriptural manuscripts.

Gandersheim

Gandersheim, founded by Duke Luidolf in 852, returned to the Benedictine observance in the twelfth century after some time as a *Stift* of Canonesses. Two centuries earlier, Emperor Otto I had invested the abbess with all the privileges and authority of royal vassal. The monastery not only kept a mercenary army in case its liege lord needed it, but it also had the right to mint coinage and conduct its own court, to which the abbess could summon violators, though a proctor usually made judgment. The abbess was also summoned to the Emperor's parliament, the Imperial Diet, attending in person until the sixteenth century when a delegate began representing her. The abbey was responsible directly to the pope, exempt from episcopal interference.

Abbess Hathumod of Gandersheim (c. 840–874) spent a great deal of time at the royal court of the monarchs, remaining so much in touch with imperial life and politics that she could supply her most famous subject, the dramatist and historian Roswitha (Hrotsvitha), with materials for her classic poetic history of Otto the Great. Often lauded as "the outstanding female author of the early Middle Ages,"[20] this noble nun—Gandersheim was limited to members of the nobility—wrote metrical legends, composed seven dramas in the style of Terence, and composed histories in metrical form.[21]

Another German abbey, Quedlinburg, had been established by Matilda, mother of Emperor Otto the Great. After the death of her husband, King Henry the Fowler, Matilda affiliated Nordhausen and several others to Quedlinburg. The Abbess was titled Imperial Princess, and lands, privileges, and immunities richly endowed the monastery. It was also renowned for its intellectual activities and as a center for the creative arts. Quedlinburg survived the German political and religious upheavals until the nineteenth-century dissolutions.

Elizabeth of Schönau

The greatest of the twelfth-century mystics were two German nuns, Elizabeth of Schönau (1126–1165) and Hildegard of Bingen (1098-1179), both known as the precursors of the German mysticism movement. After centuries of popularity, Hildegard was finally canonized as a Doctor of the Church in 2012, and Elizabeth has long been listed in the Roman martyrology. Elizabeth joined the double monastery of Schönau in the Rhineland, not far from modern Bonn, when she was twelve.[22] According to legend, she showed an insatiable desire for self-mortification early in life, inflicting many austerities upon herself. When she was about twenty-three, she began to have visions, insights, and dreams that she and her associates judged supernatural. So overcome during an ecstasy for long periods at a time, she became oblivious to everything around her. These visions most often occurred during the Liturgy of the Hours or a Eucharistic celebration.

Elizabeth believed that Christ intimately initiated her into the mysteries of his life, death, and resurrection during these mystical episodes. At other times she felt in direct communication with the Blessed Virgin, angels, and saints. Her mysticism was not self-absorbed, however, and she was not without concern about abuses in the medieval Church, especially the corruption rampant among its leaders. Elizabeth was also an inspired prophet who was instrumental in numerous conversions. Only 148 documents remain of the voluminous quantity she wrote about her revelations. She had given her notes to her brother, Egbert—disciple of Hugh of Saint Victor and later abbot at Schönau—who later published three volumes about her mystical experiences.[23]

Hildegard of Bingen

Not far from Schönau, on Rupertsberg Mountain overlooking the Rhine, one of Elizabeth's correspondents, Hildegard of Bingen, eventually overshadowed her contemporary. An outstanding woman of many gifts and talents, Hildegard of Bingen—consecrated to God by her parents at birth—was confided at age eight to Blessed Jutta von Sponheim, a recluse in a hermitage attached to the Benedictine Abbey at Disibodenberg. By the time Hildegard made her profession at age fourteen, the hermitage had become a monastery. She was thirty-eight when Jutta, her mentor, died there in 1136.[24] During this formative and educational period in her life, Hildegard, fluent in Latin, gained extensive knowledge and love of Scriptures and the writings of the Church Fathers, later completing a commentary on the Athanasian Creed. She excelled in arranging liturgical music, eventually composing volumes of sacred music that remain in print and are regularly performed.[25]

Hildegard attained remarkable achievements in philosophy, science, and medicine as well as music. Having cared for the sick in the Disibodenberg infirmary, Hildegard knew the healing power of herbs and later wrote several books detailing their medicinal as well as noxious properties. Many hailed her as a physician. Hildegard built her life upon the Rule of Benedict, eventually writing her own commentary and frequently referred to the Rule in her writings.[26] Her most influential works, however, were the records of her mystical experiences. From age fifteen, as she reported, Hildegard experienced in "a wonderful way the power of the mysteries of secret and wonderful visions."[27]

After Jutta had died, Hildegard became abbess. Within seven years, she completed most of the volumes explaining why she felt called to commit to writing the secret mysteries her visions disclosed. Intending to inspire humanity with compassion, she dictated the three volumes—*Scivias Domini* (Know the Ways of the Lord), *Liber vitae meritorum*, and *Liber divinorum operum*—detailing her mystical experiences. *Scivias* contains the detailed, lengthy accounts of twenty-six visions. Written in stirring prose, she relates the final vision in more detail and portrays the kingdom of the saints as they celebrate the exaltation of the Blessed Virgin.[28]

Another work created for the use of her nuns, the *Ordo*, is a short drama in three scenes that speaks of the love of God for humankind.[29] Throughout her works, Hildegard interprets her visions as a series of theological allegories spanning the entire history of the cosmos from creation to its culmination in Christ's mystical union. During the Synod of Trier in 1147, the abbot of Disibodenberg submitted *Scivias* to Pope Eugenius III for his approval, which was given within the year. Subsequently, Hildegard received laudatory letters from both the Pope and Abbot Bernard of Clairvaux, also present for the Trier Synod's discussions of her writing. With the papal confirmation of the credibility of her experiences and written works the abbess became widely celebrated.[30]

To gain more independence for her community of nuns, Abbess Hildegard soon realized that it was necessary to relocate her monastery. When she proposed that the nuns move to Rupertsberg, a high bluff above the town of Bingen nestled against the Rhine, Abbot Kuno and his monks vehemently opposed their leaving. Conflict arose as the monks were reluctant to see the community transferred because the site of Abbess Jutta's life and death had become a shrine. Furthermore, the men's community would also have to forgo the benefits accruing from the nun's substantive dowries and Hildegard's fame were they to depart. When the monks refused to let the nuns go, Hildegard became seriously ill. Fearing that the suffering was a divine punishment, the abbot finally capitulated. With the aid of the monks, the nuns undertook the construction of an abbey designed to house fifty women. Eighteen monastics made the move to their new residence in 1150.

The Rhine, highway of communication in Hildegard's day, kept Hildegard in touch with the world. It also provided her with ferry service when she crossed it later to visit the Bingen daughter-house at Eibingen that was erected directly across the river from Rupertsberg. Hildegard entertained visitors frequently and often journeyed to Cologne, Trier, Wurzberg and Bamberg. This oracle of the Rhine also kept up a voluminous correspondence with popes, princes, bishops and others who sought her counsel.[31] Hildegard's resourcefulness and determination were often put to the test, most notably in a bitter experience that occurred near the end of her life. A protracted controversy with authorities in Mainz over the burial of a nobleman in the nuns' cemetery at Rupertsberg escalated into a serious crisis. At one time, the archbishop had excommunicated the young nobleman, but he had received the sacraments and been reconciled with the church before his death. In the absence of the archbishop, the Mainz church authorities ordered Hildegard to have the corpse exhumed and reburied in unconsecrated ground.

The abbess refused to obey, fully aware that the penalty for refusal would be her own and her nuns' excommunication. Reportedly, she personally reconsecrated the grave site by signing the cross over it with her abbatial staff, and then wiped away all traces of identification from the grave and disguised its location. In a letter pleading for an end to the interdict of worship services placed upon her and her community as punishment for her refusal to comply, Hildegard expressed the reason for her defiance of the episcopal order: she had received a revelation of conscience, an insight convincing her that she had divine approval of her actions.

Hildegard was particularly pained when the interdict forbade her and her community to participate in the celebration of the Eucharist, receive communion, or chant the Liturgy of the Hours. After many appeals and letters from Hildegard, the Archbishop of Cologne temporarily lifted the interdict, a surcease that was abrogated once word reached Archbishop Christian in his Italian refuge. Finally in March 1179, the Archbishop of Mainz responded to further appeals and ended the interdict and excommunications. Free at last of the bitter experience, Hildegard made the most of the short time she had left.

Eight hundred years after her 1179 death, Pope John Paul II described Hildegard as "an outstanding saint." He praised her highly, calling her "a light to her people and her time...shin[ing] out more brightly today."[32] Canonized and made a Doctor of the Church in 2012, Hildegard has finally gained the universal recognition she deserved centuries earlier. Other mystics followed—especially those who joined another German house a century later.

Thirteenth-Century Helfta Mystics

The fame of the Bingen abbey, located in the western area of the medieval Germanic lands, was equaled a century after Hildegard by the monastery at Helfta near Eileen in Saxony. Helfta had four known mystics, all contemporaries. Uncertainty remains whether this abbey was Cistercian or Benedictine, though some evidence suggests it was not accepted at any time as Cistercian by the General Chapter of that Order.[33] Although some Cistercian usages had been adopted, the schedule and liturgical rites were not those of Citeaux, and Helfta Abbey designated itself as Benedictine.[34]

The four mystics all gained prominence even in their own day. Abbess Gertrude of Hackeborn (1232–1292), who governed the abbey from 1251 to 1291, wrote least about her revelations, and little is known about them. Her sister, Mechthild of Hackeborn (c. 1241–1299), was also a mystic. The most outstanding among them were Gertrude the Great (1256–c. 1302) and Mechthild of Magdeburg (c. 1207–1282/1294). The latter entered Helfta in 1290 after living some years as a Beguine, most likely beginning her written revelations before entering the Helfta community. Like Elizabeth and Hildegard, she felt that she had received the mission to instruct and correct those church leaders who erred.[35] Mechthild castigated those whose vices dishonored the church and reproached ecclesiastics and monks who came to seek her counsel; this display of courage made her more than a few enemies. She lived only a dozen years at Helfta after—at age sixty—she made her monastic profession. Mechthild had written of devotion to the Sacred Heart already in her pre-Helfta days. Gertrude the Great and the other Mechthild of Hackeborn developed many of her themes jointly with their own records of revelations and insights. Mechthild of Magdeburg's revelations, recorded in *The Book of Divine Grace*, eclipsed Gertrude the Great's reputation as a mystic and writer in the two following centuries.[36]

It was only in the late sixteenth century that Gertrude the Great became better known—primarily because of her concentration on the love of Christ as symbolized by his Sacred Heart. Mechtilde's sister mystic, Gertrude the Great, left her humble bourgeois household in 1261 at age five to be educated at Helfta. She admitted that she was rather lukewarm of heart until age twenty-five when, after having concentrated on mastering the liberal arts, she had a spiritual revelation. She then focused her studies on Scripture and the Fathers, translating large sections of both from Latin to German. Her mystical visions developed a theology of the Sacred Heart. The two Mechtilds and Gertrude the Great shared mystic experiences with each other and served as counselors and spiritual guides within the monastery and to those clergy, Dominicans, Franciscans, and laity who sought their counsel. All three had similar mystical experiences.[37]

Advent of the printing press made publication of the works of the Helfta nuns possible. Early in the sixteenth century they were admired and disseminated by the venerable Abbot of Liessies, Louis de Blois. Later their writings would gain more readership when the devotion to the Sacred Heart became universal, although few realize these Helfta mystics were initiators of the devotion. Gertrude's *Spiritual Exercises* were readily available throughout the centuries.[38] Abbot Cisneros of Monsterrat, centuries after Gertrude, may have used her as his model when he wrote his *Exercises*. St. Ignatius of Loyola, founder of the Jesuits, may have been inspired to write his own after perusing both of the earlier *Exercises*, which he become familiar with during his prolonged sojourn at Montserrat. In the nineteenth and early twentieth centuries, rhymed verses drawn from Gertrude's *Exercises* were used at times of communal prayer by some German, Swiss, and American Benedictine women.

Abelard and Heloise: A Spiritual Drama of Twelfth-Century Intellectuals

The history of the achievements and relationship of two promi-nent Benedictines, at one time an abbot and abbess, bears telling in this context. Although some may consider their life histories more dramatic than inspirational, they played a prominent part on the stage of history during their lives. The study of medieval monasticism often includes Abelard, but Heloise's life and gifts are seldom related or assessed, certainly not sufficiently valued. The lives of Abelard and Heloise have been used to produce a number of novels and dramas, usually a mélange of history and legend, but accounts of their dramatic love affair often subsumes the actual substance of their contributions.[39] Over-emphasizing their relationship risks neglect of their significant achievements, successes, and failures as they lived out their lives as monastics.[40]

Peter Abelard

Although Thomas Aquinas, a thirteenth-century Dominican, would eventually dwarf all other medieval philosophers, the Benedictine Abelard was among the more notable of the early figures who strengthened the dialectic method, so it became the preferred form of reasoning used by the Scholastics.[41] Aquinas had Benedictine connections himself, having received his early childhood education at Monte Cassino. His family destined him to succeed his uncle in the abbacy after University, a destiny he changed with no little opposition. Eventually, Aquinas became the great light of the Dominican Order and the leading Scholastic philosopher of his and later times.

Peter Abelard (1079–1142) gained renown as a teacher, philosopher, master of dialectic, and leader in the art of disputation, particularly regarding the philosophical problem of universals. Although a contemporary of other great thinkers like Peter Lombard and Gratian, Abelard was exceptional in his gifts as well as his life. As a youth of fifteen and son of the Lord of Pallet in Brittany, he replaced the pursuits and privileges of the knightly class with the pursuit of learning. After acquiring mastery of logic, rhetoric, and theology, he confounded many of the great scholars of the day even in their own lecture halls. He settled in Paris where he taught at the Cathedral School of Notre Dame. Later he would be acknowledged as one of the founders of the University of Paris.

His was not a life of fame and ease. Abelard's fame rests on his literary works, some condemned by the French bishops and religious leaders at the Councils of Soissons and Sens. His first significant work, the *Dialectics*, was followed by his most famous treatise, *Sic et Non* (Yes and No), both published before 1122.[42] His major theological writings included *Scito te ipsum* and an unfinished manuscript, *Dialogus inter philoso phum, Judaeum et Christianum*, written after the Council of Sens. In these, Abelard presented himself as a sincere Christian seeking a rational basis for his faith. He reportedly stated that he did not wish to be known as a philosopher if it meant rejecting Saint Paul or an Aristotelian if it meant separating himself from Christ.

In *Sic et Non*, Abelard coined the rules for the reconciliation of conflicting statements from biblical and patristic authorities. He called for textual criticism, for checking the authenticity of the texts while at the same time questioning the accuracy of certain

translations. He advised evaluation of the circumstances and precise reasons for statements. He maintained that etymology—the
meaning of the syntax in the culture of its composition—must be
explored, reminding scholars that language was fallible. Gratian and
Peter Lombard further expounded his call for textual criticism in
their writings.

Abelard's *Scito te ipsum* outlines his ethical theories. He insisted
that intent was a major factor in sin; no one could judge the intent of
another; sin was personal rather than original; and contrition alone
could obtain absolution for the sinner. Later, when he recorded
his personal history of the last years of his life—and wrote of his
calamitous fall in *Historia calamitatum*—he was ultimately writing a commentary on both the intellectual and affective aspects
of the twelfth century.[43] His biography is psychological as well as
theological in nature, perhaps unconsciously written for its own
therapeutic value.[44]

Despite his brilliance, Abelard had significant shortcomings.
Reportedly, he was arrogant, highly opinionated, and egotistical. He
had difficulty relating to his peers wherever he went, perhaps because
he regarded himself as superior in wisdom and knowledge. He
arguably came off well *if* the measurement of a man is by his enemies'
prestige. The only philosopher-theologian, however, who could check
him (at least for a time) was Bernard of Clairvaux, who convinced
the Councils at Soissons and Sens to censure Abelard and charge
him with heresy. Only shortly before their deaths were they reconciled. Abelard's dialectics never died, however, becoming part of the
substance of early Scholasticism.[45]

Heloise

Abelard's name has always been inextricably bound with that
of his one-time mistress and later wife, Heloise.[46] Their association
produced the most remarkable love letters of the twelfth—perhaps of
any—century, though truth and legend are confused in their history.
What is certain is that Abelard was teaching in Paris in 1115 when
Canon Fulbert of the Notre Dame Cathedral chapter engaged him

to tutor his brilliant protégé, Heloise, in return for room and board at the Canon's home. Abelard was thirty-six, Heloise about seventeen.[47] He may have been a deacon although there is doubt that he was, for that reason, committed to celibacy. Rather, as a philosopher-theologian and lecturer, he was expected to remain celibate.

Heloise (1090–1164), in modern parlance, had both beauty and brains.[48] Niece of Canon Fulbert, she knew the classics, was fluent in Greek and Latin, and could dispute with the best—especially in philosophical and theological matters. Eventually, the tutoring sessions evolved into a clandestine love affair. When Heloise became pregnant, Abelard secretly married her and then took her to stay with his family in Brittany for her own and the child's safety. On Abelard's return to Paris, he confined Heloise to nuns at Argenteuil, infuriating Canon Fulbert. He resented Abelard's treatment of his niece, leaving her with the nuns instead of keeping her by him. Fulbert hired some ruffians to castrate him.

When this news reached Heloise, she temporarily returned to Paris to care for the wounded Abelard. Their son, Astrolabe, remained with Abelard's family in Brittany. Concluding that the criminal violation of his body had been God's retribution for his sin, Abelard sought refuge in monastic life. He joined the Benedictine community at Saint Denis, located in what is presently a Paris suburb, while searching for similar security for Heloise. At his bidding, she initially made monastic profession with the Benedictines at Argenteuil where she soon became prioress. Abelard then resumed his teaching in Paris until 1121, when the Soissons Council condemned his writings on the Trinity. Four years later he was Abbot of Saint Gildas in Brittany, his home province.

The Paraclete Monastery

Disaffected with the community there, he began construction of a monastery for himself and several of monks in the diocese of Troyes. When Argenteuil closed in 1128, Prioress Heloise and her nuns needed shelter. Abelard turned over his almost completed monastic building to her. They had called it the Paraclete—the first monastery named for the Holy Spirit—a name the nuns retained. Abelard helped her organize monastic life there. She was about thirty but more mature in wisdom and common sense, always admitting that she knew herself incapable of forgetting her early love.

Monastic historians who discuss these two influential persons usually give Abelard most of the credit for the highly commended spiritual life at the Paraclete. Abbess Heloise, however, generally proposed the policies that Abelard ratified. She mastered Hebrew to study Scripture in the original. Ironically, the outstanding characteristic of the mature Abbess Heloise was prudence, perhaps a virtue she had lacked earlier. The observances she set for her nuns were eminently practical. She governed sagely, seeking to diminish the occasions of temptation without breaking the spirit of the women who flocked to live under her leadership. Heloise adopted some flexibility and tolerated some deviations from the traditional fasts in the amount and kinds of food, as well as in clothing and bedding. The lifestyle that she designed was practical, yet human. Her erudition and spiritual leadership made her famous. Cluny's Abbot Peter the Venerable, one of her admirers, never tired of singing her praises and invited her to travel to his Cluniac monastery of nuns at Marcigny to recommend ways to raise the quality of the intellectual and spiritual life there.

Although she and Abelard continued to exchange letters, eventually their correspondence was wholly dedicated to commentaries on the Paraclete's monastic practices.[49] Abelard's responses to her discussions were veritable treatises on the organization of monasteries of women and how to implement the Rule. He stressed poverty and detachment from secular values. The nuns were to keep what was necessary for the annual sustenance; the rest was to be given to the poor. They were to observe strict silence and keep the monastery's solitude as inviolate as possible.[50] The nuns ate meat three times a week, but the ill were to have all they needed. Nuns were not allowed to fast unless they had proper approval, and they could drink wine if they diluted it with water. Abelard prescribed less luxurious and ostentatious habits than were customary in great abbeys. The church was to be simple, with no gold or silver objects except the chalices. A wooden cross on the altar was the only thing necessary—no statuary or paintings—and two bells were sufficient. Neither Abelard nor Heloise made mention of cloister.

Abelard prioritized the study of Scripture, and the Paraclete nuns became even better known not only for their knowledge of the Old and New Testament but also for their knowledge of the early Fathers.[51] Unlike other abbeys of that time, the Paraclete Abbess shared the refectory and dormitory with her nuns. Abelard did admonish her not to add indiscreetly to the number of monastics to the detriment of those already there. The 150 psalms of the psalter were to be recited in a week, as Benedict prescribed, not in a day as at some monasteries, and the entire Bible was to be read annually during the Liturgy of the Hours.

Abbess Heloise ultimately became highly regarded. Over a dozen commendatory papal decrees accorded numerous privileges to the Paraclete community that would receive an exemption from episcopal control. By the time Heloise died in 1164, her monastery headed a number of others, including a small congregation of six houses of women; Pommeraie, which later transferred to Sens; the priories of Noëfort, Saint Flavit, Saint Martin of Boran, Saint Madeleine of Traînel, and Laval, with many affiliated granges. Later other monasteries of women adopted the Paraclete customary. By 1616, however, the statutes had been revised and made much more rigorous.

Abelard died in 1142 at the Cluniac house at Chalons-sur-Saône where he was in the good graces of the Congregation of Cluny. Peter the Venerable, lifelong friend of the two monastics, informed Heloise of his death. Most writers claim that after his body had been secretly exhumed, she received it for reburial at the Paraclete. The body reposed at the Paraclete for the twenty-two years Heloise outlived Abelard. After her death and the transfer of both bodies to several locations, some of their remains were brought to Paris in 1817 where they are enshrined side-by-side. They rest in abbatial garb beneath sculptured effigies at Père-Lachaise cemetery, one of the most famous French burial grounds for those who had achieved renown during their lifetime. Sidney Packard, who discusses the two at length in his *12th Century Europe: An Interpretative Essay*, concludes with this comment: "The twelfth century without Abelard and Heloise would have been a much duller place, but it is perhaps easily true that the whole of European history would be far more prosaic without them."[52] Twelfth-century monasticism—and the world—was enriched by their presence.

The European reform movements of the tenth through thirteenth centuries renewed monastic life by their distinct adaptations of the Benedictine Rule. While many monasteries continued in need of reform, many mystics of the period inspired a deepening commitment to the observance of the Rule's spirit. The theological contributions of monks and nuns furthered the pursuit of faith seeking understanding, setting the stage not only for the emergence of Scholasticism, but also for the coming centuries of further alternations of decline, reform, renewal, and adaptation that will continue to characterize the Benedictine future. ✱

CHAPTER 5

Rise and Fall of English Benedictines

Tenth through Fourteenth Centuries

As the monastic reform movements initiated change throughout Europe, English monasticism presented a variegated palette before the Norman Conquest of England in 1066. The *Regularis Concordia*, a document seeking to unify monastic practice, had introduced continental practices to English monasticism about 970, though some customs remained distinctly English.[1]

Anglo-Saxon monasteries like Fleury, Canterbury, Evesham, and Worcester—influential in later reforms at Durham and Yorkshire—showed unparalleled vitality, with simplicity and austerity their norm. Some smaller English monasteries, however, were in serious decline; two or three had become scandalously relaxed. As on the European continent, political change and reform would impact tenth- through thirteenth-century English monasticism significantly.

English traditions and culture were often different from those on the European continent, and monastic observance was no exception. Often in England, monks and nuns had failed to enforce strict enclosure in their monasteries, and they were less scrupulous about private relationships with the laity. Consequently, some Norman monastic chroniclers—most notably Eadmer of Canterbury, William of Malmesbury, and Ordericus Vitalis of St. Evroul—made sweeping condemnations of life in pre-Norman monasteries.

According to the *Domesday Book*, the greatest abuse was how monks inherited and disposed of family land holdings.[2] In most cases the abbey received the income and final ownership, and it had been allowed. The English monastic historian David Knowles maintains there was no serious moral decadence in this customary arrangement.[3]

Regardless, William the Conqueror's invasion brought sweeping change to England's way of life, including among monastics.[4]

Reception and Effects of William the Conquerer

Duke William did not begin as a favorite of the English monastics; many continued their hostility long after the English Conquest. A number of the leaders of the abbeys belonged either to the former royal family of the Saxons or to the nobility. Several houses took part in the resistance to the Duke of Normandy's claim to the throne. Aethelsig, Abbot of St. Augustine's Canterbury, died on the battlefield at Hastings, although it is uncertain if he was a hostile combatant fighting William's troops. Among those conspicuous for their loyalty to Harold (William's opponent) was Leofric of Peterborough, who was stricken with a fatal illness while serving in Harold's retinue. Because of their unwillingness to accept William as their king, many notable churchmen and monastics, including Aethelnoth of Glastonbury, were exiled within a year after William completed his conquest. Others sought voluntary exile; Aethelsig of St. Augustine's went to Denmark and Fritheric of St. Albans transferred to Ely. Some less fortunate monastics became political prisoners.

During the first decade of his reign, William dealt with many monastics' opposition. Sithric of Tavistock became a pirate, joining the sons of Harold in the Irish Sea after the revolt of the West. Ealdred of Abingdon was imprisoned first at Wallingford castle and later with Walkelin at Winchester after allegedly conspiring with the Danes. Turstan, the abbot of Ely who had been a nominee of Harold and a friend of the Danish royal house, courted disaster by hosting a Danish fleet in 1069. The revolt of the Earls in 1075 involved several abbots. One of these, Wulfketel of Croyland, was deposed in 1086 by Lanfranc and sent to Glastonbury to be kept in custody. During the political storms, the abbey of Peterborough suffered most. The Danes sacked the abbey, took the church treasures and spoils, set fire to the monastery buildings, and then took the non-resisting monks with them to Ely. When Turold, William's appointee, arrived at Peterborough he found only ashes and one ill monk. Those who had fled the Danes eventually returned. The monks who had been taken to Ely also returned to Peterborough after the pirates left the city.[5]

Demonstrating King William the Conqueror's eleventh-century triumph, he founded what became known as Battle Abbey (St. Martin de Bello) at Hastings on the very spot where the last Anglo-Saxon king had fallen. The Conqueror brought monks from a non-Norman abbey—Marmoutier in France—to populate Battle Abbey, and then granted it autonomy and endowed it with broad civil and ecclesiastical exemptions.[6] As resistance to William's conquest ebbed, other significant foundations appeared in England during the eleventh century: Selby, Shrewsbury, Chester, Spalding, and Colchester, Chester, Shrewsbury, and a new foundation at Tewkesbury, a distant property located at the confluence of the Avon and Severn Rivers in Gloucestershire.[7]

Norman Influence on English Monastic Life

Across the English Channel, monasticism in Normandy had become a composite of Cluniac influence including the Italian reform of William of Dijon (962–1031) and the flourishing revitalized monasteries of Fécamp, Jumièges, St. Wandrille, Mont St. Michel, and St. Ouen at Rouen with its nine daughter-houses. Over twenty-one new foundations had been made in Normandy between 1030 and 1066. Duke William, who encouraged his barons to make and endow numerous foundations, used monasticism as the most powerful instrument in reforming the Norman Church. Unfortunately, this meant the monasteries were very much a part of the feudal organization that regarded the Duke as the liege lord. Duke William granted authorization for their establishment, appointed the abbots and abbesses, and took custody of the abbeys during interregnums. Many houses rendered the traditional feudal obligations to him, including the supplying of knights and mercenaries.

The Italian reformer, William of Dijon, made Norman monasteries centers of intellectual revival in contrast to those of Cluny whose *raison d'être* had become that of choir duty and constant communal prayer solely.[8] The Norman monks, perhaps because of their Viking heritage and culture, had particular characteristics (including vitality, enterprise, and administrative ability) that helped them excel in constructing mammoth architectural monuments and in governing numerous great estates. In the fine arts, however, the sculptors of southern France and the English artists and craftsmen surpassed them. The Norman monastics that Duke William exported to his new English lands indelibly stamped the 500-year-old island monasticism with a continental and Norman cast.

Influential Monks from the Norman Abbey of Bec

The Norman abbey of Bec, the main conductor of the Anglo-Norman current, refined and handed on all that was best of the eleventh- and twelfth-century world around it. Inspiring saints and impressive intellectuals found their way to this abbey, and Bec was so significant in English ecclesiastical history that no abbey or individual to the Protestant Reformation—with the possible exception of Augustine, the first Archbishop of Canterbury—was similarly consequential.[9] Bec's founder and subsequent patron saint, Herluin (d. 1078), resolved to turn from the world and seek God at age thirty-seven, apparently after some dangerous adventure when he was in the military retinue of the Count of Brionne. After two years of prayer and a futile search for the right abbey, Herluin was ordained a priest and began monastic life with two companions on his family estate. Here, he emphasized poverty and seclusion, and the monks worked all day clearing land, farming, gardening, and building. Herluin's mother, living in a house nearby, relieved them of the task of doing laundry. Over time, the expanding membership at Bec challenged Herluin's administrative and intellectual capabilities, but Providence intervened about 1042 with the admission of Lanfranc, perhaps viewed as the answer to the founder's prayer.[10]

Lanfranc

Lanfranc (d. 1080), a former instructor of law and letters in Lombardy, had crossed the Alps to teach briefly in France, turning to Bec in search of a life of solitude and obscurity. He found that peace—at least for a few years—after he joined the community's thirty-four monks. To assist in providing some of the financial support needed by the rapidly growing community, he began to tutor lay students.

Fifteen years after Lanfranc's arrival, Anselm (1033–1109)—destined to eclipse Lanfranc—joined Bec. Anselm, also an intellectual, was attracted to the monastery by Lanfranc's presence and leadership as the community's prior. By this time, Bec had become a very influential center and Lanfranc the trusted counselor of Duke William, naming him abbot of St. Etienne at Caen in 1066. Anselm's life and writings reflected the culture and spirituality of Bec, exerting a pervasive influence over the following centuries.[11] When Hugh of Cluny refused the request of King William for French monks to govern the English abbeys, William summoned Lanfranc from Caen to Christ Church Abbey and to the position of Archbishop of Canterbury.

Until his death in 1089, Lanfranc was essentially *the* influence in English monasticism. He was a skillful leader, yet he was widely known for his compassion and care; even the parents of the monks never suffered want. Lanfranc's community would be his legacy, as would the general reform of the English Church. Although he could be the ultimate statesman, the Archbishop and Abbot's heart remained in the monastery. His policy as Archbishop and Primate of England was to develop monasteries into great centers for the reorganization of the Church's spiritual life. He continued to use Normans for the revitalization, constantly appealing to the monasteries at Bec and Caen when he needed men for bishoprics or abbacies, or wanted to increase membership in Christ Church Abbey itself. Some of Lanfranc's greatest contributions remain in print.[12]

The tone of Lanfranc's *Monastic Constitutions* suggests the culture he sought to build:

> Surely no reader can travel through Lanfranc's regulations without gaining the impression that they were composed for a flourishing and self-confident monasticism. There is no sense of strain nor any hint that the writer is fighting a losing battle against relaxation or decay, or that he is preoccupied

with the restraint of abuses. Lanfranc is clearly writing for those who are willing to live a life of strict claustral exercises as a way of devoting themselves to God.[13]

Although the constitutions were originally written at Canterbury, at least a dozen or more of the principal cathedrals and abbeys of England followed them.[14]

Lanfranc incorporated some aspects of the Cluniac horarium, or daily schedule, for English use. The monks were to pray the day's Matins and Lauds in chapel and the Office of the Dead before dawn for probably three hours, thereafter returning to bed. To the psalms prescribed by the Rule for Prime were added the seven penitential psalms, the miserere, and the litany of the saints. Eucharist, at which they received communion, was celebrated after Terce in winter and followed by it in summer. Speaking was allowed between the Liturgy of the Hours to outline the day's tasks. While seated in the cloister between prayer hours, the monks were required to do holy reading— namely the *lectio* mandated by Benedict's Rule. Another Mass—a "High Mass"—was scheduled daily between Sext and None. A siesta was permitted in summer after the noon meal but in winter, reading was prescribed. During the summer months, an extra drink in the refectory was to be provided after the afternoon siesta and the liturgical Hour of None. Vespers was later in the day. Prayer consumed most of the monks' time, leaving only short intervals for work. There are no traces of the English *Regularis Concordia* in Lanfranc's constitutions, and most of the traditions he followed were of French or Italian origin.[15] Lanfranc's monastic schedule—like Benedict of Aniane's— deviated from the integration of the *ora et labora* prescribed by Benedict find its emphasis on community prayer.

Lanfranc permitted child oblation—allowing young children to be dedicated at an early age by their parents—as Benedict had prescribed. Although this practice declined some fifty years after Lanfranc's death between the seventh and twelfth centuries, it was the traditional way to assure that future monks, ecclesiastical dignitaries, and civil rulers had good primary educations. Lanfranc allowed some corporal punishment of boys and monks, to be used only in cases of great moral lapses. He also designed a customary to implement the Rule and the constitutions. Not only did he prescribe how distinguished visitors were to be received but he also included the job description of the abbot, prior, claustral prior, cantor, sacristan, and other officials. He directed how the monks were to shave and to be bled. He dedicated a chapter to the "priest of the week" and described how promotion was secured in the monastery. He explicitly detailed treatment of the wayward, novices, and children. He showed great concern for the care of the sick and prescribed the rituals for monks' wakes and funerals. In his culturally situated customary and its detailed application to English daily life, Lanfranc demonstrated astute adaptation of the Benedictine rule for eleventh-century England.[16]

In Archbishop Lanfranc's perception there was no substitute for the example and influence of the monks in the regeneration of the Christian Church in England. Nor did he establish a collegial system of rule; he promoted, rather, a strong hierarchy under a powerful primate and an absolute king. Although the king traditionally appointed men and women to vacant abbacies, as the leading ecclesiastic of the Witan (the English King's Council), the Archbishop had a great deal of influence in these appointments. Nonetheless, he made no clean sweep of the leadership of the abbeys, and most abbots were replaced only by attrition. When the William the Conqueror died, however, only three non-Norman abbots remained: Bath, Ramsey, and Holme.[17]

The most apparent immediate result of Lanfranc's influence in England's monasteries was a great and rapid growth in those aspiring to live as Benedictines. Some abbeys' memberships doubled or tripled. In thirty years, for instance, Gloucester increased from ten to one hundred members. Many new monastics came from the families of the Norman invaders although others, like Worcester and Peterborough, remained predominantly Anglo-Saxon long after the Conquest.

Anselm of Canterbury

Lanfranc died in 1080 as one of the most significant English monastics of his age, having adapted the Benedictine Rule as a man of his time. Four years following his death at Canterbury he was succeeded by a man seemingly for *all* times, Anselm—a thinker, genius, and spiritual guide *par excellence*—perhaps "the most luminous and penetrating intellect between Augustine and Aquinas."[18] Anselm was born into a noble family of Aosta in 1033. As a youth, he matriculated at Avranches in France. Fifteen years after Lanfranc's arrival at Bec, Anselm joined the community succeeding the founder Herluin in 1078. A thorough and influential teacher, he was a man whom his students admired and loved. At Bec, Lanfranc had been his mentor, and William Rufus—the Conqueror's son and heir—appointed Anselm to succeed him. In 1095 he received the archbishop's pallium from Rome.

Anselm also gained fame as a writer of seminal treatises that did not deny the value of logic but attempted to integrate reason with faith. His contribution to the development of scholasticism rested in his integrative synthesis of theology with reasoned dialectic.[19] Anselm demonstrates his combined intellect, humanity, and spirituality in his correspondence with English abbesses and nuns. He was the spiritual guide of Eulalia of Shaftesbury and Alice of Wilton. At one point, his attention to devotional detail comes into view as he rebuked the nuns of Romsey for venerating an uncanonized person as a saint. He wrote aesthetic and sensitive letters to monastic women; one of his most poetic recalls a nun return to her former, better self.[20]

As Archbishop of Canterbury, Anselm inherited Lanfranc's successes but was also heir to the church-state conflicts of the Conqueror's heirs. During King Henry I's reign, monasticism enjoyed peace and prosperity. The prestige of the monasteries was unchallenged, and their solidarity was not yet seriously undermined by the *esprit de corps* of individual houses or rivalry with the new orders. According to Knowles, the Anglo-Norman monasteries were still "the main spiritual and intellectual reservoirs of the country."[21] Vast structures in the new architectural styles replaced old Anglo-Saxon churches at many monasteries, notably at Durham, Ely, and Canterbury. The monks accumulated great treasuries of vestments, utensils, and illuminated manuscripts, and monastic libraries were constantly expanded.

Of the two abbeys at Canterbury, the Archbishop's monastery Christ Church not only had more members than Saint Augustine's but also was more involved in the public life of the English Church. Christ Church was often in the middle of the century's many heated controversies, and it consistently took a leading role in supporting successive archbishops in their struggles with the monarch. Canterbury abbey also endeavored to obtain professions of obedience from the archbishops of York and the abbots of Saint Augustine's, which agitated for papal exemption from episcopal jurisdiction. The abbey also hosted distinguished canonists and men of letters from whose presence the monks benefited.

Other Influential Monasteries: Rochester, Glastonbury, and Malmesbury

Rochester was another noteworthy abbey with remarkable leaders including the saintly Gundulf, Ralph (former Abbot of Seez and later Archbishop of Canterbury), and former monk of Beauvais, Ernulf. Prior Ralph, who had been a monk of both Bec and Caen, became Abbot of Battle Abbey in 1107. Under his leadership, he and Battle Abbey gained a high reputation for their quality of observance and care for the needy. Glastonbury, the wealthiest abbey in England at the time of the Conquest, had flourished since the tenth century when the Anglo-Saxon Saint Dunstan—later Archbishop of Canterbury—restored monastic life and structures, introduced the Rule of Benedict, and ruled as its abbot during its zenith.

A series of devastations, alienations of lands, financial mismanagement, and general chaos impacted Glastonbury following the Norman Conquest. During the forty-year abbacy of Henry of Blois its economic situation finally stabilized. Henry, an excellent administrator and generous benefactor, at times was so preoccupied with external matters that he could not always exercise his abbatial duties fully.[22]

From 1081 to 1105 Malmesbury was led by Abbot Godfrey, who had been a monk of Jumièges in his youth and developed an appreciation for learning. He founded the abbey library of which a prominent historian, William of Malmesbury (c. 1095–c. 1143), would later take charge. Many scholarly monks still resided at the abbey when it was seized in 1117 by Roger, Bishop of Salisbury, whose political ambition paralyzed its development for over 20 years.[23] After Roger of Salisbury's death, the mercenary Robert Fitz Hubert attacked the castle near Malmesbury and, plundering the region, entered the chapter room of the monastery and threatened more violence.[24] During this tumultuous era, Malmesbury was not the only monastery struggling to survive. Wilton was also ravaged by Robert Fitzwalter in 1140 and later turned into a fortress by King Stephen. Fire-bearing arrows, employed by the Bishop of Winchester, set fire to Hyde Abbey and the women's monastery at Winchester. William of Ypres had the nuns' house at Wherwell burned down because it had supported the Empress against the King.[25]

The cultural impact of the Middle Ages set unfortunate precedents for women's place in the church, particularly in monasticism. Women and lay brothers in the new congregations, especially of the White Monks but also in some of the Black Monk groups, found papal and abbatial conferences and general chapters of congregations averse to including non-clerical monastics. In some cases in the thirteenth century, they seemed indifferent to any but priest-monastics. After the Conquest, women could no longer hold property by law, so even monastic houses of women were required to have their property subjected to nominal ownership or an abbot or abbey of monks.[26] Despite such challenges, aspects of women's spirituality thrived as luminaries such as eleventh-century Christina of Markyate and thirteenth-century Julian of Norwich gave light to their own—and succeeding—generations.

Monks of Saint Albans and Christina of Markyate, Mystic

Saint Albans was already a prominent abbey in the twelfth century, fortunate in that it had a series of great abbots, most of whom had been selected from the abbey's membership. The abbots were overly careful in screening new members: one person they rejected would later occupy the papal throne. The only English pope, Adrian IV (c. 1100–1159), was born on an estate belonging to St. Albans. He became an Austin Canon under the *Rule of St. Augustine* after he was advised by the monastic administration to wait several years until he would be mature enough to be accepted at the Benedictine monastery.[27]

Matthew Paris (1200–1259), a monk of Saint Albans, was both an artist and historian.[28] King Henry III (1207–1272) was so impressed with the monk that on a visit to St. Albans, he sought him out personally. Many times the King singled him out of a crowd and bade him write about what he was witnessing. King Haakon IV (c. 1204–1263) of Norway, a patron of English artists, also highly esteemed Matthew for his artistic ability; there are still pieces of artwork in Norway today that are attributed to the monk's sojourn in that country. Paris chronicled events of the time as he saw them, usually interested in persons and events rather than in principles and movements, and he was often criticized for his ethnocentric conservatism by later writers.[29] Nonetheless, this monk-historian used some innovations such as interviews and extracts from original documents, now modern techniques, in his work.

The exceptional abbot of Saint Albans was mathematician and inventor Richard of Wallingford (1292–1336), a noble Norman friend of Saint Anselm's. In 1115, in the presence of the king, queen, and many bishops and barons, Abbot Richard dedicated the new church his predecessor had built. His immediate successor, Abbot Geoffrey de Gorham (d. 1146), author of a series of liturgical and dietary regulations, built a London Road hospital for lepers. He also established a community of enclosed nuns at Sopwell. Other persons, reputed as saints, deeply affected life in twelfth-century Saint Albans. One was a woman, Christina of Markyate (c. 1096–c. 1155), who became a recluse and mystic at the Markyate hermitage, about seven miles from the monastery.[30]

Originally named Theodora, Christina was a noble young girl of wealth and position from Huntingdon. Legends tell of her vow of chastity during a visit to Saint Albans. Afterwards, she resisted the advances of a lecherous bishop who, after he was rebuffed, convinced her father she should accept a marriage to his acquaintance. To escape both bishop and husband, Christina mounted a horse and escaped to the monastery cell at Flamstead where she was hidden by an anchoress for two years. Moving to Markyate, the anchorite Roger hid her in a closet-like cell walled off from his hermitage for another four years. After her marriage to the bishop's acquaintance had been annulled, Christina endured another interval of exile after her protector Roger's death, returning to Markyate where several companions joined her.[31]

She made profession of vows at Saint Albans and became a close friend and counselor of Abbot Geoffrey, who had jurisdiction over her priory and had built a new monastery with a chapel for Prioress Christina and the nuns. As her notoriety as a saintly healer and miracle worker spread, her priory grew rapidly in membership until her death (c. 1155–1166).[32] Knowles suggests that the monks of Saint Albans profited spiritually from having a mystic and several hermitages in its neighborhood when he wrote that "the existence of such types of sanctity in the vicinity, and the encouragement of them by Saint Albans and its great abbot, are a sure proof that the things of the spirit had a real value within its walls."[33] Saint Albans' rich spiritual and liturgical legacy—including its renowned Psalter—resulted, in part, Christina of Markyate's presence and determination.

While the plague and other calamities besieged Saint Albans during the thirteenth century, one youthful abbot, Thomas de la Mare (1309–1396), assumed leadership when the preceding abbot, prior, sub-prior, and fifty monks died during the Black Death epidemic. Politically active as friend of notable dignitaries, he also became the president of what was being organized as the English Congregation of Black Monks. Thomas was a dedicated ascetic who banned popular pastimes like hunting and hawking, but he often stayed at the holiday resort—Redburn—with his men, ringing the bells for prayer when others failed to do so and smilingly denying wine to latecomers to dinner. Thomas, known for his willingness to assist in the monastery's menial labor in the efforts of rebuilding he ordered, died after nine years of a debilitating illness at the age of eighty-seven in 1396. Serving Saint Albans forty-seven years as abbot and seventy-one as a monk, he exemplified dedication that sustained the abbey through one of its darkest periods.[34]

Julian of Norwich

The first Bishop of Norwich, Herbert Losinga (d. 1119), founded Norwich Abbey near the end of the eleventh century. From an initial twenty monks under his leadership, abbey membership rapidly increased as the monastery became known for its quality of observance and hospitality. A monastery of women was built nearby on Carrow Hill, and among the nuns' holdings was the church where the celebrated fourteenth-century mystic Julian of Norwich (c. 1342–c. 1416) lived as a recluse. Julian spent her life less than a mile from the Carrow Benedictines in a small cell attached to the church. Rediscovered in the seventeenth century, Julian's mystical writings have become widely available.[35]

Uncertainty—and considerable debate—remains about whether Julian was a Benedictine nun. In the post–World War II reconstructed Norwich cathedral, she is pictured in a massive stained glass window depicting an array of Benedictine saints.[36] Julian is garbed in monastic dress, surrounded by such famous monastics as Benedict, Gregory, and Bede. Local tradition claims that she was Benedictine, though no clear documentation exists.[37] Julian's writings show familiarity with the Benedictine Rule and she indisputably had some connection with the Carrow Priory where she may have spent part of her youth as a boarding student or even a professed nun who first resided there. After a time in the monastery, she may have moved to Carrow's parish church in Norwich, seeking greater solitude, prayer and a more accessible place to counsel the many who sought her advice.[38] According to Schmitz, a hermitage that belonged to a medieval England religious order was usually occupied only by those professed in the community, and recluses were common in Benedictine monasteries.[39] As the Carrow community's prioress had the authority to choose who inhabited the cell where Julian was allowed to reside, it is likely she was a nun or at least affiliated with the Benedictines.[40]

Writing as a mystic, Julian's *Showings*, also entitled *Revelations of Divine Love*, reflect a profound theological depth.[41] Twentieth-century monastic theologian Jean Leclercq attributed her popularity to her "feminine model" of theology and spirituality needed by the contemporary world.[42] Similarly, French monastic historian Schmitz admired Julian for her mysticism's major theme, God's love shown in his "maternal mercy." More recently, Julian has been recognized as a significant systematic theologian, advancing complex developments in soteriology (the study of salvation) from her personal mystical experiences.[43] She wrote a great deal on the concept of the Trinity, wherein God is mother as well as father, divining that the motherhood of God was not opposed to or distant from the fatherhood, but complementary. Leclercq writes of the expansive nature of Julian's insight:

> She works for an integration of all that is best of what we conceive and experience of God. This theological synthesis is the result of her own psychological, spiritual and mystical integration. Through her experience and her understanding, she grasps the total mystery of God as far as this is possible in this life, and she want to communicate to us a glimpse of it.[44]

Though Julian's themes are cosmic in proportion, her style is memorable for its simplicity. One of her most-quoted passages reveals the nature of her prayer and the simple optimism evoked by its answer:

> And thus our good Lord answered to all the questions and doubts that I might make, saying full comfortably: "I make all things well, I can make all things well, I will make all things well, and I shall make all things well, and thou shalt see thyself that all manner of things shall be well."[45]

The consideration of nature and grace, good and evil, assertions of divine love, and identification with Christ, as well as universal salvation, in Julian of Norwich's *Showings* are at once theological and devotional. These Benedictine-influenced, fourteenth-century writings deserve our full twenty-first century attention.

Effects of the English Church-State Controversies

Shortly following Julian's era, King Stephen's troubled reign (1135–1154) affected monastic life. The abbeys were demoralized by the constant hostilities and lawsuits related to the issue of jurisdiction and subordination, phenomena prevalent in most of medieval Europe.[46] Battling on every level took its toll then as it continued to do throughout all of the Christian centuries. Thomas Becket's murder in the Cathedral became one of the most dramatic church vs. state events in the High Middle Ages, widely involving monastics and affecting monasteries.

Throughout the mid-twelfth century, controversy raged between King Henry II and the former Chancellor Thomas Becket—also the Archbishop of Canterbury—over the jurisdiction of church and civil courts. Canterbury's Christ Church Abbey had continued to support its archbishop, the non-Benedictine Becket after his assassination in 1170.[47] With Becket immediately canonized in 1172 and considered a martyr for the rights of the church, Henry II—directly implicated— left some abbeys without leadership for years and made only a few abbatial appointments. Finally in 1175, Henry II's Great Council at Woodstock filled the vacancies, and another period of hope was hailed by the English Black Benedictines.[48]

From the time of Dunstan in the tenth century through the early decades of the thirteenth, English monasticism grew, developed, and expanded. It was a golden age for the Black Monks who occupied over a hundred large monasteries and for the Black Nuns, who, however, had fewer houses. Knowles estimates 4000–5000 Black Monks and almost as many White Monks—though considerably fewer nuns—in late twelfth-century England.[49] As newer mendicant orders such as the Franciscans and Dominicans crossed the Channel to England, Benedictine land holdings and ecclesiastical influence seemed to have reached a saturation point. Even before the Conquest in 1066, Black Monks owned about one-sixth of the cultivated land and actual rents of southern England. These increased after the Conquest as wastelands were cultivated and sheep farming developed. The monks' share of the wealth in lands, rents, and dues amounted to between a quarter and a third of the total by 1170. Benedictine monastics were owners or patrons of about 25 percent of the churches of England. Monasteries of men and women housed the finest fabrics, precious objects of all kinds, and almost all the books and artistic treasures of the British Isles.

Monasteries began to decline rapidly after 1215; by mid-century, the significance of the Benedictines and Cistercians had dwindled considerably. Monasticism had all but ceased to have any formative or directive influence over the spiritual and intellectual life of church and state in England. It was a drastic plunge from the 950–1000 era when the monks and nuns had been "the very core and kernel of the nation, and by their achievement in the transmission of the heritage of the past and in the execution of works of literature and art they had placed all succeeding generations in their debt."[50] After the Conquest, abbeys had been the most refining and enlightening power in the land, but feudalism took its toll—eroding the former influence and prestige of monastics. There was, as well, a new and well-educated hierarchy and a vast increase in universities—especially of theology and canon and civil law—that ultimately replaced the domination of education previously enjoyed by the English monastics.

Although the monastic influence on ecclesiastical renewal had been substantial, the days of monastic supremacy died in 1153 with the demise of both Pope Eugene III (c. 1080s–1153), the Cistercian Bernard of Pisa, and his former abbot and mentor Bernard of Clairvaux. Although the monastics in England retained some importance until the reign of Henry VIII and the Protestant Reformation, they were certainly not the spiritual or intellectual force they once had been. Before the beginning of the thirteenth century, it seems that all of what was specifically monastic influence upon the policies of the church at large dwindled to a relative insignificance.[51]

As the originally counter-cultural monastics resorted to the same Machiavellian tactics prevalent in the feudal government and society, the gradual decline of monastic communities ensued. The feudal noble families who supplied commendatory abbots and abbesses and bled the monasteries financially for their own gain are also responsible for their decay. Too often, abbeys and priories became safe havens for men and women without personal interest in religious life. Nepotism set noble sons and daughters as heads of communities, and unruly members—some of them psychologically challenged and abandoned by their families—left many monasteries floundering. The *labora* inside monastic walls—study, writing, and manuscript illumination—also proved less satisfactory and economically feasible. Commercial enterprises took over much of this work and some aspects of manual labor stopped. Further, there was the resentment of the rank and file over the separation of the life of the leaders from those who were often destitute while the abbots and abbesses enjoyed lives of luxury.

After 1215, a new era of renewal of discipline followed the memorable signing of the Magna Carta by King John and the meeting of the Roman Lateran Council called by Innocent III. After King John died in 1216 the English monks and nuns attained a healthier milieu in which to live according to the Rule. There were great Gothic architectural achievements in the expansion of Westminster and York and some of the other monasteries, but the spiritual life inside most monasteries was especially affected by papal decrees on how life was to be organized and supervised. Throughout the thirteenth century, eminent monastic individuals were few in England's annals though some communities, such as Saint Albans and the monastic college at Oxford, could be counted as great lights of their time.

Conciliar and Synodal Impact on English and Other Monastics

Decrees emanating from the Fourth Lateran of 1215 directly affected monastics, especially in regard to general chapter meetings and visitations by authorities commissioned to evaluate and assess whether certain monasteries were living in accordance with law. The Council ordered the Black Monks to organize into provinces and meet in general chapter every three years. Cistercian abbots were to attend the first conferences to instruct the Benedictines on procedures.

This mandate was implemented at Canterbury when the Cistercian abbots of Thelma and Warden attended the Canterbury meetings under the presidency of William of Saint Albans and Hugh of Bury in 1218 and 1219. The abbot participants returned to put their own houses in order in compliance with the chapter's decrees. Special targets of reformers included the peculium, a particular money amount allotted to individual monks and nuns to purchase general necessities. Reforms addressed abbatial expenses and liberties and others deplored some monks' excessive travel. Some of the decrees caused a great deal of furor, especially those prescribing dietary changes relating to the use of meat and certain other foods. Ultimately, however, the decrees were lifted, often dropped, and mostly ignored leaving the monks largely unaffected.[52]

Two more attempts to gather the monks in general chapters in 1222 and again in 1225 were fiascoes. At the latter, in Northampton, only fifteen superiors of the sixty summoned came, and none of the presiders arrived; this did not daunt the remnant, who proceeded to pass a number of ordinances governing visitations. Later chapters were slightly more regular, but complete records of them are missing. Although women were not present at any of the chapters in these centuries, communities of nuns were expected to accept and put into effect all mandated decrees, and they usually complied.

Ecclesiastical Visitations Address Problems

During the thirteenth century, the nuns and often the monks received no fewer than four and sometimes five different visitations by an ecclesiastical legate: monastic, episcopal, archiepiscopal, and occasionally, papal. While their own superiors ruled Benedictine monks and nuns, Franciscan Archbishop of Canterbury John Peckham (c. 1230–1292) visited houses of monks and nuns in nearly every diocese of southern England and Wales. He was not the only member of the mendicant orders who initiated movements for change in houses of monastics. Some houses still had episcopal exemption, but even these were visited on occasion. Pope Gregory IX (d. 1241), who reigned from 1227 until his death, appointed three men to visit exempt houses. The major problems addressed in these visitations were lack of adherence to the dietary regulations, notably who might be exempted from the Rule's mandate of a meatless diet. The monastics used all kinds of subterfuges, and the visitors attacked these with vigor. They often discovered how hard it was to govern the meals monks took during their vacations at the monastery's country homes where they went during intervals for relaxation. Yet chapters and superiors had broad dispensing powers in the matter of consumption of meat, which they used rather freely.[53]

The visitors and other reformers also checked the observance of silence. At one point, the English language was banned in the cloisters in favor of Latin or French to prevent excess speaking. The quantity of beverages, however, prompted the most interesting statutory regulations. A single meal was the norm in monasteries for almost half a year, and monastics needed addition of a refreshing drink. Since neither tea nor coffee had yet found its way to England, beer, mead, or wine was the drink of choice. As sharing an evening drink had been such a long tradition, even Archbishop Peckham accepted the rationale for this *and* a late afternoon libation in summer. There was, especially among the monks, a tendency for one refreshing drink to follow another, so the reformers were kept busy trying to stem the abuse. Even after the canonical hour of Compline, in supposedly absolute silence, a beverage was often shared when one of the monastery's officials returned from his travels. With refreshments came violation of silence as the latest news from the outside world regaled the official's companions. Visitation reports repeatedly showed that, despite all attempts at regulation of drink and silence times, "ineradicable human weakness was at odds with the law."[54]

Another matter that dominated chapter discussions and preoccupied visitors was the daily schedule of work and prayer. The Chapter gradually called for more abandonment of the liturgical accretions and elaborations, such as additional prayers, litanies, and psalmody added to the Liturgy of the Hours. Monastics were directed to spend more time studying theology. Manual labor was still done, for the most part, by serfs and servants. Division of the communities into clerical and brother monks and choir and lay nuns became commonplace. Petitions against these reforms flowed into Rome demanding the status quo in liturgical prayers and ceremonies, a phenomenon sustained to the present day when change in monastic practice occurs.

Other changes in traditional practices gradually appeared in English monasteries. Even before the thirteenth century, the acceptance of very young children had ceased. The Black Monks eventually decreed eighteen the minimum age for entrance to the novitiate. Women entering communities of nuns no longer required dowries. The sum of five English pounds became a fixed fee for the monastic clothing the novice received although some houses varied these fees. Art and music—especially Gregorian chant—also changed. The chant accompanying the liturgy had been greatly rearranged across the centuries, but by the thirteenth century it had been stripped of accretions almost to the simplicity of two to four centuries earlier. By the fifteenth century, descant and polyphony of every kind, as well as motets, were more in vogue than Gregorian chant.[55]

Monasticism Enters the Era of the University

The opening of a common house of studies at Oxford also brought inter-monastery controversy. Scholasticism and the greater demand for educated church authorities sent monks to the great universities. Black Benedictine enrollment lagged behind the Franciscans, Dominicans, and Cistercians, already instructors and students at the universities by mid-century. In 1277, the Benedictine monks' General Chapter resolved to send men to Oxford, paying for the house of studies by a prorated tax on all the monasteries. The two dependencies of Bec and other foreign-dependent priories protested.[56] Archbishop Peckham decided in their favor and forbade the tax levy, an act the chapter considered outside his jurisdiction. Overruled by monastics, the Franciscan Archbishop retaliated with pejoratives, calling the monks boors, dunces, and dullards.[57]

Finances to support monks at priories near universities remained a serious problem until 1283 when a benefactor gave a site to the Benedictines at Oxford. There, a small house of study was established under the auspices of Gloucester Abbey. The house, eventually called Gloucester College, was overseen by varied Benedictine chapters that governed their novices, but was owned by Malmesbury Abbey. A prior had direct administration of the house, but various houses were responsible for the rooms and staircases occupied by the monks from their respective monasteries. The public dining room and chapel were maintained by general funds contributed by all the monasteries. Nuns, of course, were always denied entrance to the universities, as were most other women until the seventeenth century when Elena Cornaro Piscopia graduated from the University of Padua—having been educated by tutors, not with the men in the classrooms.

While the thirteenth century has often been romanticized as the greatest of the medieval period, fourteenth-century Christianity and monasticism both reached their nadir.[58] It was the century of the Black Death, the beginning of the Hundred Years War between France and England, and the era of the Western Schism or "Babylonian Captivity" of the popes at Avignon.[59] These all affected monasticism, but the most devastating was the plague. The British Isles and Continental Europe lost almost a third of their populations, and monasteries of men and women suffered even higher ratios and often lost their superiors. Though some young members called to fill their positions—like Thomas de la Mare of Saint Albans—were outstanding luminaries, many monasteries were further compromised by lack of experienced leadership.

Nuns' Survival: Supervision and the Black Death

Nuns had more difficulty rebounding after the ravages of the Black Death than did the monks. Most women's monasteries were economically poorer than the men's, so the plague ruined some of the smaller houses and reduced others to bankruptcy. Nuns were seen on the streets openly begging. Many houses never recovered membership or finances. Nuns, moreover, were not in full control of their destiny and continued to sustain further blows when more regulatory exactions were made on them than those levied on the monks.[60]

Nuns were also more closely supervised than monks, but under the Franciscan Archbishop of Canterbury Peckham, their burdens became even more onerous. At one point, he ordered the Abbess of Romsey to select for herself a suitable companion, a feminine chaplain whose additional duties included accompanying the abbess whenever she traveled outside the monastery grounds. Later these same chaplains were ordered to be frequently changed —often annually—to prevent favoritism and keep the Abbess honest. It was also customary and often mandatory that this nun be the roommate of the abbess if they were sleeping outside the dormitory rooms at the monastery or were on a journey.

Some bishops mandated that if the abbesses were outside the monastery, the feminine chaplain must also share her bed, contrary to the traditional requirement that all nuns occupy separate beds in the monastic dormitories. At some houses, the Archbishop appointed a male *custos* as chaplain and business manager, overseeing the monastery's spiritual and temporal welfare. In many nuns' communities the male "prior," as he was often named, exerted an inordinate amount of power. He was considered the only one trustworthy enough to do the reporting tasks required by the male ecclesiastical superior who was suspicious of the nuns' ability to maintain good observance and efficient fiscal management. In 1284, Peckham ordered the nuns of Usk to obtain a priest to be "master of all your goods, internal and external, temporal and spiritual."[61] After a visitation at one monastery he left the nuns the following injunction:

> For the purpose of obtaining a surer witness to chastity, we ordain that nuns shall not leave the precincts of the monastery, save for necessary business which cannot be performed by any other persons. Hence we condemn forever...those sojourns which were wont to be made in the houses of friends, for the sake of pleasure and of escaping from discipline, and when it shall befall any to go out for any necessity, we strictly order these...to be observed. First that they be permitted to go out only in safe and mature company as well of nuns as of secular persons helping them. Secondly, that having at once performed their business, so far as it can be by them performed, they return to their house; and if the performance of the business demand a delay of several days, after the first or second day it shall be left to proctors to finish it. Thirdly that they never lodge in the precincts of men of religion or in the houses of clergy, or in other suspected habitations. Fourthly that no one absent herself from the sight of her companion or companions, in any place where human conversation might be held, nor listen to any secret whispering, except in

the presence of the nuns her companions, unless perchance
father or mother, brother or sister have something private to
say to her.[62]

There seems to be no record of like injunctions given to monks.
Peckham told the nuns of the abbey at Barking that the only cause
sufficient for leaving the monastery was the imminent death of a
parent. His efforts at nuns' protection extended to their would-be
seducers, and in 1281 he published a decree excommunicating all
who attempted or succeeded in seduction. Absolution for such sins
was reserved for bishops or the pope, unless the perpetrator was on
point of death. He added, of course, that it was a violation of enclosure
by nuns and their wandering about in the world that gave the opportunity for such crimes.

The archbishop made some allowances, including one that certain
groups of nuns could go out for three days for recreation, six days for
business (more if needed for illness), and carte-blanche if they went
out to beg the necessities of life. (Apparently they were not subject to
nor the object of temptation while begging.) He insisted nuns stay
at monasteries of women when out of their own, that they avoid the
"haunts of men," and that they refrain from all food and drink if they
were able to return home the same day. He mandated monastic dress
for all those who left the house, which indicates the nuns sometimes
left their ordinary wear back at their monasteries when they ventured out.[63] Any nun leaving the monastery to resume the lay state
was immediately excommunicated.

Peckham was very alarmed when he received rumors that the
nuns of Romsey "enter houses of laymen and even of clerics in the
town, eating and drinking with them."[64] However, when some scandal concerning the morals of the subprioress of Godstow came to his
ears, he announced that he did not believe it. The Archbishop probably never recovered from the consequences of the Wylton-Giffard
kidnap and rape scandal of 1286. It appears that Juliana Giffard was
abbess of a community in which a young relative—Alice Giffard,
sister of the Bishop of Salisbury—was a member. Another relative,
Sir Osbert Giffard, was excommunicated when he "with sacrilegious
hand ravished and abducted in the silence of the night sisters Alice

Russel and Alice Giffard, professed according to the rule of Saint Benedict in the monastery of Wylton."[65] Sir Osbert was absolved but had to do penance, including bringing back the two nuns and all their goods. His sin was to be published in the church of Salisbury. After corporal punishment and public humiliation there and in the marketplace, he was sentenced to go to Wylton church and the city market for the same treatment and then to serve in the Holy Land for three years. No one has recorded if he turned up for the beatings or if he ever went to the Holy Land.

We do know that the seducer of a nun of Harrold in 1298 was excommunicated again when he refused to take the marketplace beatings. Some violators of nuns got off quite easily by appealing to the bishop's compassion. For example, Richard Gray—a married boarder at Stamford—fathered a child by the nun Elizabeth Willoughby in the fifteenth century. After the imposition of a similar penance as Gifford, Gray made appeal to Bishop Alnwick, who commuted the penance of beatings to a fine of twenty shillings to be paid to the nuns within a month, and another twenty to the cathedral church—not the nuns' monastery—to be remitted within six weeks. When other publicly embarrassing sections of his sentence were not mitigated, Gray appealed to the court at Canterbury. When he pleaded illness, judicial hearing was postponed but finally, because no penance was performed, he was again excommunicated. After that, he disappears from history.

Exacting penance from the nun, Elizabeth, whom Gray had seduced, was simpler. She was excommunicated until she had done penance at her monastery or was sent to perform it at another monastery of women. Such punishment of penitents was not popular with the nuns since its implementation would cause too much disturbance in the lives of the other monastics. Most often, however, those seduced generally remained at their own monastery but were, at times, imprisoned there. They were put on fasts of bread and water on Fridays, bread and vegetables on Wednesdays; they were also shackled or beaten and forbidden to wear the veil. More rarely the sentence consisted of being present at longer, more demanding hours of prayer, the recitation of penitential psalms and litanies, and prostrations in the chapel.[66] Sometimes the guilty nun, if she were an abbess or prioress—despite policy demanding her resignation from office—could circumvent the penalty. The Prioress of Markyate, who had added perjury to her violation of chastity, retained her office for nine more years. Abbess Elizabeth Broke of Romsey, convicted of perjury and adultery, was reelected and continued in her abbatial role.

Contrasted with the extent of these English nuns' supervision, their education was almost wholly neglected. There is no monastery comparable to the German Gandersheim or Helfta in England before the modern day. In fact, many nuns were illiterate. Some were incapable of memorizing readings or praying the Divine Office, so they were restricted to reciting the Lord's Prayer and the Hail Mary. Abbot de la Mare once decreed that only literate women were to be received at the nuns' monastery at Saint Albans (St. Mary de Pré). To assure him of that the requirement was met, all novices were required to write their own vow formula when professed.[67]

At Oxford and Cambridge, the nuns did come into contact with educated men—the monk-students at the two universities. At one point the nuns were instructed to refuse the students' admittance to the monasteries and even to the parlors because this practice, according to the hierarchy, was leading to abuse and possible scandal. Archbishop Peckham added even more restrictions. The Godstow nuns, who resided within visiting distance of the Oxford students at Gloucester College, were known willingly to converse with the young monks, so they were forbidden to speak to them without the explicit permission of the abbess. The Archbishop decreed that only if the scholar were "of kin to her, in the third grade of consanguinity at least" could he be admitted to the parlor. Peckham added an admonition to the monks: "nor shall you desire to be united in any special tie of familiarity with them, for such affection often excites unclean thoughts."[68]

When William the Conqueror arrived in England in the eleventh century, there were about a dozen abbeys of nuns. In the course of the twelfth century sixty new foundations were made. By the middle of the fourteenth century there were eighty monasteries of women, two of which were Cluniac. The number declined drastically before the Dissolution, however. When the Reformation began there were sixty-seven Benedictine houses of nuns; only twelve had abbatial rank. Schmitz claims that monasteries of monks at the time of the suppression still numbered 164 (including 27 Cluniac communities), 63 fewer than the 227 of earlier days.[69]

Nuns and monks remained a great social force despite their decline during the fourteenth century, considered the nadir of their existence. Through the plague, epidemics, war, and schisms, the nuns and monks maintained a very high quality of intellectual and spiritual life. Some monasteries were pockets of great spiritual activity, apostolic ministry, and eminent men and women. In fifteenth-century England, growth replaced decline until the Dissolution displaced all the English monks and nuns for centuries to come. Even then, they would be destined to return. ❋

CHAPTER 6

Autumn and Winter of Monasticism: Decline and Suppression

Twelfth through Sixteenth Centuries

E ven as reform movements had deeply affected Benedictine monasteries, European monasticism began a gradual decline from the twelfth to the sixteenth century. The spirit and practice of many of monasticism's earlier ideals diminished while sporadic reforms unsuccessfully attempted their restoration. Large congregations dwindled in size, and many small monastic houses occupied vast properties under absentee abbots.

Many new reform movements arose in response to monastics' deepening need for renewal, occasionally spurring extensive debate and skepticism about their orthodoxy.[1] While leaders and legislation tried to enforce a predictable uniformity, new forms of spirituality—popular even beyond monastic walls—led to monasticism's continuing evolution even as politically imposed dissolution threatened its existence in England.

The Gradual Decline of European Monasticism

The French Congregation of Cluny experienced peaks and valleys, going from its zenith to nadir under one abbot, then reviving somewhat under another famous leader, only to stagnate just before political forces mandated its demise. When Pons de Melgueil succeeded Saint

Hugh as abbot in 1109, the motherhouse at Cluny began a perceptible decline, culminating in the abbot's forced resignation for squandering the monastery's goods. A cultivated charitable leader with administrative capabilities, Pons was altogether too fond of the pomp and circumstance that twelfth–century medieval culture expected of its baronial vassals. By the time Pons' successor, Peter the Venerable (c. 1092–1156) called a General Chapter in 1132, the mother abbey's financial situation was almost irredeemable.[2] Though prior Matthew of Albano (d. 1134) worked tirelessly to remedy the situation there and in the other Cluniac houses, attempts at reform generally failed. As the congregation simplified its observance to a near Cistercian model, it focused its attention on the formation of clerics, neglecting young monks' education. Only six out of the three hundred monks at the motherhouse attended universities, and the torch of learning passed from the Benedictines to the Franciscans and Dominicans.[3]

Most attempts of thirteenth-century popes to reform the Cluniacs and other Black Benedictines failed. The Lateran decrees of 1215 mandated the holding of provincial chapters, and Popes Honorius III and Gregory IX doubled the numbers of canonical and extraordinary visitations to stimulate reform.[4] Replacing triennial with annual chapters, Gregory gave new powers to the visitators and placed more emphasis upon community life. Benedictines were encouraged to become better witnesses of the vow of poverty and to have more respect for the sanctity of the monastic enclosure. The papal pleas to strengthen the common life, compel abbots and abbesses to live in their monasteries, and eradicate the scandalous luxury the abbots and abbesses enjoyed were all approved in essence by the Chapters. Unfortunately, the effects were minimal.

The prescriptions concerning provincial chapters exempted the congregations and major houses that already convened general chapters or that belonged to priories subject to a major monastery. Thus, Cluny, Chaise-Dieu, Molesmes, Bec, Saint-Victor at Marseille, and other small communities were exempt. The provincial general chapters were ineffective partly because they lacked cohesion: the superiors were not representing houses with the same customs; the houses were not of the same importance; and insufficient research preceded the policy-making. The monastics resented what they considered interference in their affairs by bishops and visitors as interventions by episcopal and other non-monastic visitors threatened the Benedictines' collective self-esteem. Monastics balked, understandably, when Cistercians, Dominicans, and Franciscans presided over their chapter meetings. These met less frequently after the pontificate of Pope Innocent IV (d. 1254). During his financially strapped pontificate, "donations" secured all kinds of privileges and dispensations. The most deplorable abuse—the naming of commendatory abbots and abbesses—accelerated at this time. Lay men and women, and Dominicans and Franciscans, could be named head of an abbey provided only that they professed adherence to the spirit of the Rule.[5]

The *Benedictina* Attempts to Confront Abuses

A Cistercian, Benedict XII—who occupied the papal throne from 1334 to 1342—determined to do something, even if it meant closing some monastic houses. This austere pope imposed a program of reform upon all religious orders. In 1336, he issued a *bullum* affecting the Benedictines, known popularly as the *Benedictina* (officially titled the *Summi magistri dignatio*). Its thirty-nine articles were dedicated to reforming the governance of monasteries, management of material affairs, educational opportunities, and issued a call to monastic ideals. Restructuring monasteries into provinces, the *Benedictina* reimposed the triennial chapters that were to examine the visitors' reports and seek remedies to the abuses recorded therein.[6] To ensure the raising of intellectual tenor in the monks' monasteries (this part of the mandate did not include nuns) the decree legislated that the monks master grammar, logic, and philosophy. The document stipulated that one in twenty monks were to be university educated. Six capable Benedictine abbot-consultants were to assist an in-depth inquiry into the economic situation of the individual monasteries. These were also to assure more domestic peace and better adherence to the prescriptions of the Rule by checking the impact of the presence of numerous friars who took to residing for brief or long periods in the

Benedictine or Cistercian monasteries where they often disturbed regular observance.

Even these reform efforts proved unsuccessful. Again, there was no single responsible authority on the provincial level. The detailed prescriptions with their rigorous sanctions attempted to impose the same customs on hundreds of different monasteries with very diverse national cultures and traditions. The civic leaders, kings, and princes of all sorts were also opposed to the implementation of the bull that threatened their very lucrative exploitation of monastic revenues. Greed continued to undermine reform. The *Benedictina* remained in force less than ten years. Following the decimation of the monastic communities by the Black Death, monastic revenues plummeted. Exploited serfs on the landholdings rebelled, and the tenant farmers and domestic servants stoked the flames that would erupt in the next century and spell the doom of many Benedictine monasteries.[7]

The French and English monks and nuns had the added disruptive burden of the Hundred Years War (1337–1453) that sometimes resulted in burning or pillage of monasteries.[8] The monastics were often reduced to abject misery, yet kings and their retinues continued to strain monastic hospitality. King Saint Louis IX held court at Cluny in 1245 and 1248, Philip IV in 1304, and Philip VI in 1330. The early tradition that no Cluniacs accept bishoprics was set aside when monks were appointed to head the dioceses of Saint-Flour and Valence. Consequently they were numbered among the distinguished courtiers and often acquired personal fortunes that helped assure their Congregation a certain temporal prosperity. It made possible the founding of the College of Cluny in Paris in 1270 where the student monks lived during their years of philosophy at the University.[9]

The Cluny Abbot from 1351–1361, Androin de la Roche, used his diplomatic status to fund the priory-college of Saint Martial at Avignon and endow it with his considerable fortune. During the last half of the fourteenth century, however, the Congregation of Cluny began to disintegrate. The monasteries in the Italian Lombardy province ceased to have any rapport with the Burgundian mother-abbey. The English priories severed their relations with Cluny during the Hundred Years War, choosing nationalism over congregational affiliation.

The Spanish monasteries were already financial disasters before the dawning of the fourteenth century, and Cluny found itself on a course leading to ruin.[10]

New Reform Congregations and Contemplative Movements

The Council of Constance (1414–1418) charged the hundred-plus Benedictine abbots in attendance to undertake monastic reform.[11] To fulfill this mandate, the abbots of Mainz and Bamberg held a meeting at the Abbey of Petershausen in 1417. The monasteries of men responded—126 of the 133 invited sent delegates. The conference reaffirmed the prescriptions of the *Benedictina* of 1336, confirming the obligations of community life and stigmatizing those abbeys that still restricted admission to those of noble rank. The abbots swore to carry out the mandated statutes within the year. They provided for a revised Customary that spelled out 105 detailed observances. Visitators were appointed, which brought obstinate resistance from certain abbeys. Given that there was no sole responsible authority, too much diversity in observance, and hostility from bishops (because it limited their control), the movement generally failed.[12]

Spanish and Italian Reforms

Although the fourteenth century might be considered the deepest of winters for the Benedictines, the fifteenth blossomed with many major attempts at reform. Augustinian Canon and Venetian noble appointed abbot of Saint Justina in Padua in 1408, Ludovico Barbo (1381–1443), made one of the earliest. Assigned to reform the life of the decadent old Clunisian abbey, he worked vigorously to fulfill his commission. After his profession as a Benedictine and the abbatial installation, he organized regular observance—with no little opposition from the monks. In 1421, when the Padua house numbered over 200 members, communities at Verona, Bassano, Pavia, and Genoa fused with Padua to form the nucleus of the new Congregation of Saint Justina (Giustina). Eighteen years later the Congregation numbered sixteen monasteries. The new Congregation emphasized poverty, stability, and the common life, and eventually reversed the autocracy established by Barbo and restored authority to the community's General Chapter. To eradicate abuses, especially that of commendatory abbacies, the times demanded this kind of radical initiative. The popes were quite willing to approve an aristocratic, feudally modeled congregation—somewhat parliamentarian—of centralized, yet collegial, governance.

The Cassinese

The new Congregation of Saint Justina saved Italian monasticism. After the Abbey of Monte Cassino joined the Saint Justina Congregation in 1505, the name was changed to Cassinese. A year later, the Sicilian Benedictines joined. By 1521, when the first effects of the German Reformation was being felt in Italy, the Congregation had peaked in numbers, monasteries, and wealth and reputation.[13] Eugene IV (1431–1447), its great protector, in order to guard its cohesion, decreed that the Congregation be confined to Italian Benedictine monasteries. The abbey of Lérins in Provence was temporarily permitted to aggregate with the Cassinese in 1516, but it left the Congregation in 1756. By 1995 there were only ten Italian monasteries remaining—with fewer than 150 monks.[14]

At first, nuns were not welcome in the new Cassinese Congregation and the monks opposed the aggregation of women's monasteries.[15] In 1436, the Chapter expressly forbade nuns to join, rationalizing that they wished to spare themselves the burdens associated with acceptance of women's monasteries. Nevertheless, some nuns were accepted in 1505 thanks to the intervention of Pope Julius II, who charged the congregation to accept their spiritual and material direction, though the congregation rejected a third of the nuns' monasteries recommended. Once incorporated, the nuns lost their autonomy to the General Chapter, and no novice could be received without the approval of the Abbot President and the Visitors. The nuns' union with the Cassinese was short-lived. Julius II, reneging on his threat, eventually acceded to the request of the abbots who did not care for the "inconvenience" of being responsible for nuns. He granted their request to deny affiliation to women's' monasteries.[16] The Cassinese include no nuns—to this day.

The Celestines

The Celestines also appeared in the thirteenth century. Celestine V, the earlier Pietro del Morrone, preferred his hermitage to the papacy and resigned less than six months after his election as Pope in 1294 at age eighty-five. He had founded the group that eventually took his name some time before 1264, the date of its approval by Urban IV. The Congregation's leadership was transferred to the Abbey of Sulmona in the Abruzzi in 1293. Their constitutions were eclectic, a blend of Benedictine and Cistercian traditions with some penitential practices of the Camaldolese and Franciscan tenets regarding poverty. Popular in Italy with one hundred houses, the Congregation was introduced in France by King Philip IV (1285–1314). Twenty houses dotted the French landscape by the end of the fifteenth century.

The Olivetans

Bernardo Tolomei (1272–1348) founded the Olivetan Benedictine Congregation in the fourteenth century. A noble from Siena, Tolemei took two companions with him into solitude on Monte Oliveto, a forested promontory twenty-two miles south of his home. The growing community, while attempting a return to the eremitic life, soon adopted a modified version of the cenobitic Benedictine Rule. Olivetans became distinguished by their austerity as they observed a meatless diet, continual silence, and a return to manual labor. Like the Cluny model, the daughter houses were not allowed to be autonomous and remained dependent priories subject to the Olievetan motherhouse that strictly supervised their observances. To prevent the abuse of commendatory appointments, abbots were elected for a term not exceeding four years.

By 1400, the congregation had eighty-three houses in Italy. The Olivetans likely inspired other reforms in the next century, including that under the leadership of the abbey of Saint Justina of Padua.[17] The General Chapter of that new Congregation appointed priors and other officials, and also had a fixed, three year term for abbots. The Olivetan Congregation continued to prosper and soon spread to a few areas outside Italy, and the constitutions were completely revised after the French Revolution. During the twentieth century, Olivetans numbered about thirty monasteries of men and women, some double, including Our Lady of Guadalupe in Pecos, New Mexico, Holy Trinity Monastery in St. David, Arizona in the United States, Abbaye de Notre-Dame du Bec in France, and Abu Gosh in Jerusalem.

The Silvestrines

The Cistercian Order was one of several Benedictine branches, and other new congregations emerged in the late medieval period. Pope Innocent IV approved the Silvestrines, named for founder Sylvester Gozzolini d'Osimo (1177–1267), in 1247. Its beginnings were in the Italian Marches region in a semi-eremitic community at Monte-Fano. Influenced by hermit-founder of the Carthusians, Romuald (c. 951–1027), the monks practiced prayer, preaching, hearing confessions, and austere poverty. The order had grown to eleven houses when the founder died, fifty-six at its peak. The number of houses dwindled by the later twentieth century to five: one each in Sri Lanka, India, Australia, and the United States and two in Italy including the Generalate at St. Stephan Protomartyr in Rome, with about 200 monks residing in the five priories and fourteen dependent houses.

Other European Movements and Reforms

Other Italian congregations arose during this period. The Congregation of Montevergine, founded about 1120 by the pilgrim-hermit William de Verceil (1085–1142), grew from its original foundation on Monte Vergine near Naples to ninety houses. The congregation declined by the mid-fourteenth century but survived until 1872 when it became part of the Congregation of Subiaco in the Benedictine Confederation. Another founder, the celebrated mystic-theologian Joachim de Flore (c. 1135–1202), lived in a series of Cistercian monasteries before establishing an abbey at Flore in 1189. His movement, approved by Celestine III in 1198, spread so rapidly throughout central Italy, thirty-eight monasteries owed submission to the head of the congregation, the Abbot of Flore, by the thirteenth century. A later decline in membership and finances, caused in part by the system of commendatory abbots, weakened the congregation so much that the Cistercians absorbed it by the end of the sixteenth century. Joachim's mystical theology, particularly regarding the New Testament book of Revelation, ignited considerable debate among subsequent centuries.[18]

In Germany, another reform similar to Barbo's Cassinese occurred in the Bavarian diocese of Eichstätt. Abbot Otto Nortwiener opened a new monastic community at Kastel about 1380 where he adopted Cluniac observance. Within a century, twenty houses united with Kastel, including Saint Gall, Saint Emmeran in Ratisbon, and Ottobeuren. When Melk and Bursfeld began similar reforms after 1450, the Kastel union ceased to expand to any degree.

Reform and Influence of the Austrian Abbey of Melk

Austrian reforms were also successful. In 1415, during the sessions of the Council of Constance, the Polish bishop of Poznan had asked the Austrian, Nicholas Seyringer—leader of a group of Germanic monks who had joined Subiaco Abbey—to meet at Constance at the end of November with several of his confreres. The Duke of Austria, Albert V, who was interested in reforming his duchy's monastic life, intercepted their journey and retained them in Austria to begin reform there. The group chose as its headquarters the Abbey of Melk with papal approval, situated on a cliff overlooking the Danube. There, Nicholas was elected abbot to head the renewal. He and he and his companions and several more volunteers established the Subiaco observance at Melk. Their initiative spread rapidly, first to the Celtic monasteries at Vienna, Kremsmünster, Seitenstetten, and then elsewhere. Thanks to Peter of Rosenheim (c. 1380–1443), the reform was also introduced in Tegernsee in Bavaria, Saint Ulrich in Augsburg, and Wiblingen in Swabia. During the fifteenth century, Melk hosted 120 monks from other monasteries who came to live there to reclaim the renewal customary to their own monastic communities.[19]

The Melk reform insisted on rigorous observation of the Rule, including its meatless diet. It reorganized the institution of lay brothers that had almost disappeared. It substituted some Roman usages that somewhat simplified the Cluny customs that had come via Hirsau.[20] This reform lasted until the Reformation but lacked precise organization. The bond that united the monasteries to Melk was too fragile; the houses simply imitated the leading abbey in customs and rites. Because there was no formalized Congregation, the Melk reform had no perceptible lasting effects outside its scholarship, including an innovative technique using alphabetized couplets for memorizing the Gospels.[21]

As Melk was the child of Constance, Bursfeld was the daughter of Basel (1431–1440), another Council that included many abbots interested in overall reform.[22] Monasteries again subscribed to the regulations of the *Benedictina*, and Bursfeld attempted in the northern German houses what Melk had attempted in the Austrian area and Barbo in Italy. John Dederoth, a monk of Northeim, assumed leadership of the movement and by 1449 it numbered thirty-six houses.[23] The Bursfeld Union reformed monasteries while allowing them to preserve their autonomy, though the Abbey of Bursfeld's abbot always headed the Congregation, which sent delegates to the annual chapter.

The Congregation spread rapidly throughout northern and western Germany and in Denmark, Holland, and Belgium. At its apogee it included 180 monasteries, with a few nuns' houses. Renaissance Cardinal and mystical theologian Nicholas of Cusa (1404–1464), pontifical legate in Germany from 1451–1452, favored Bursfeld and vigorously promoted the reform.[24] Popes also energetically supported the Union. Pius II (1458–1464) ratified the constitutions and accorded Bursfeld the same privileges held by Saint Justina. Three attempts to unite the reforms of Melk and Kastel under Bursfeld failed in the late fifteenth century; most of the monasteries preferred the status quo. The Bursfeld Congregation endured until the German secularizations of the nineteenth century.

Effects of Germanic Reforms on Nuns

Melk and Kastel had repercussions in some women's communities. Living outside the monastery, even on the farms, was forbidden. The monastic life was to be one of common residence as well as ownership. Stricter enclosure for nuns was again to be enforced.[25] The mandates of Cardinal Nicholas of Cusa were binding on houses of monks and nuns, though the reforms met a great deal of hostility to reform in some houses in the Empire. For example, the Cardinal at Sonnenburg in the diocese of Brixen deposed and excommunicated one abbess and installed another who was also unsuccessful in reform attempts. Then, interference from Duke Sigismund of Austria, the diocesan chanceries of Vienna and Brixen, and the Roman Curia threw Sonnenberg and the whole area into an uproar. Other monasteries also denied the need for renewal, some much more dramatically than others.

Strict Conformity's Attempts and Resistance

Reform attempts in Württemberg set the stage for more than one drama. Margaret of Freiburg went to the monastery of Heggbach to acquaint herself with the new reform so she could introduce it at Urspring. She had the support of the monastery's ecclesiastical superior, the Abbot of Saint George, and the assistance of Duchess Mechthild, a descendant of the land-holding family of Urspring. Several nuns of the reformed monastery at St. Walburg were also willing to accede to Mechthild's request to assist in transmitting the renewal to Urspring. When the Duchess appeared at the monastery with the nuns to introduce them personally to the Urspring community, a dramatic scenario ensued:

> One day she appeared with them at the convent entrance together with some abbots, several preaching friars and a number of noblemen to assist her in case she met opposition from the nuns. Some noblemen of the opposite party also appeared. Under the direction of Barbara van Stein, the group of obstinate nuns who refused the reform had withdrawn into the isolated infirmary in the convent garden and

fortified themselves by barricading the doors with tables, benches, blocks of wood and stones. They themselves occupied the upper floor and appeared at the windows, showing their weapons: stones, sticks, whips and spears. The duchess gave her people the command to attack the house. But the noblemen objected, explaining that it would always remain a disgrace if they fought against women. Besides, they did not wish to make enemies with their equals; after all, these were noblewomen....The Duchess then had the alarm sounded from the nearby bell tower. This brought the common people. The simple townsmen and peasants prepared to attack and stormed the house. Those nuns who resisted were bound and put under arrest.[26]

The nuns from St. Walburg then entered the monastery confines. Those who did not wish to accept the reform were allowed to go home to relatives or join other communities of nuns. Many who left later returned contritely to Urspring. Peace and quiet were gradually restored, and Urspring became a model of reformed observance.

Other congregations of German nuns were easily convinced of the value of affiliation with the Bursfeld Congregation and exacted strict conformity. If an Abbess refused to accept the tenets of reform, she was obliged to resign. A reformed monastery would recruit a new abbess and several nuns who would assure compliance with strict observance. Abbesses, elected for life, promised under oath to preserve the Bursfeld observance and to support the Chapter decrees. Those who failed to do so were deposed on recommendation of the visitators.

Characteristics of the German Reforms

The Bursfeld reforms still permitted child oblates, though they had to freely decide to leave or stay when they reached maturity. Novices had to be at least twelve years old, and profession of vows was made only after age sixteen. Although she made a vow of stability, the novice was also required to promise that she would accept a transfer to another community in the interest of reform. Nuns spent much of their day at prayer in choir, but they also assumed the major domestic duties in the monastery's kitchen, garden, and common rooms.

The nuns' spiritual life was well regulated. Although they received the Sacrament of Penance weekly, they could receive the Eucharist only monthly. Congregational Decrees prescribed points of personal hygiene as well. Although the nuns could wash their hair every two weeks, baths were limited to six and eight weeks apart depending on the season. Enclosure was very strictly enforced, but abbesses had more freedom. They could travel to pay homage to the barons or monarchs or to attend the General Chapter. The rank and file traveled only when it was in the Congregation's interest. Every nun was expected to do some handiwork: sewing, weaving, embroidery, bookbinding, preparing parchment, or copying and illuminating manuscripts. The art of calligraphy was recultivated and preserved.[28]

Bursfeld promoted the education of nuns. Novices were to be well versed in Latin; they were advised to speak it among themselves and with others. Those monasteries without schools for new members were mandated to find teachers from outside the community if necessary. German nuns maintained contact with the leading scholars of the fifteenth century.

Correspondence between men and women religious was prolific. Some of these scholars, such as early cryptographer and historian Abbot John Trithemius (1462–1516), were moved to leave literary monuments to their nun-friends.[29] John Butzbach (1477–1516) lauded the nuns' scholarship in his *De illustribus mulieribus*, noting as the ideal intellectual nun the highly educated Aleidis of Rolandswerth.[30]

The Union required all applicants be admitted without discrimination as to class, though three social classes within the walls still prevailed in many of the nuns' monasteries. Choir nuns were usually in the majority, daughters from noble or wealthy bourgeois families. The lay Sisters were not obligated to choir or to know Latin. They recited prayers elsewhere when their domestic duties permitted. Noble ladies were often permitted to hire maids if no lay Sisters were present to do the menial labor. In some houses, nobility received no partiality. In most monasteries of nuns, extern Sisters did the material work outside the enclosure, wearing gray dress in contrast to the black worn by the choir and lay nuns.

Reform and Spirituality

Not only legislative, reforms also arose from new forms of spirituality. Devotional currents of the fourteenth through sixteenth centuries took a new turn from traditional practices as predominantly lay or semi-monastic Beguine, Beghard, and *devotio moderna* movements spread throughout northern Europe and the Low Countries. These new spiritualities emphasized living one's life in imitation of Christ through voluntary poverty and charitable works while nurturing deep prayer and mysticism.

Gerard Groote (1340–1384), a Dutch deacon, initiated the mode of contemplative silence later illustrated by Thomas à Kempis' *Imitation of Christ*.[31] One new community reflecting this teaching became known as Brothers and Sisters of the Common Life. Under the leadership of Groote's disciple Florens Radewyns (1350–1400), they sought to both reform and inspire lay and religious life through its simplicity, reflecting in the *devotio moderna*'s mode of spirituality. Their influence became widespread through their many educational institutions, use of the printing press, and such notable associates as Pope Adrian VI (1459–1523) and the Reformer Martin Luther (1483–1546).[32]

The Exercises of the Benedictine Abbot of Montserrat, Garcia Cisneros (1455–1510), integrated this new spirituality with that of the more traditional Gertrude the Great.[33] In turn, Ignatius of Loyola (1491–1556)—founder of the Society of Jesus, popularly known as the Jesuits—reflected the spirituality of Cisneros in his own *Spiritual Exercises*, composed after spending time with the Abbot at Montserrat in 1522.[34] Jesuits often served as chaplains to Benedictine nuns, and the new devotional spiritually took root there as well.

Swiss, French, and Portuguese Monks

Monasteries of monks were in a critical state in fourteenth-century Switzerland. Saint Gall and Einsiedeln were at their nadir with only one or two monks in each of these vast abbey complexes. At the end of the fifteenth century, Saint Gall began slowly to regain stature and membership as its economic situation stabilized, but Einsiedeln still had only one monk in 1513.

In the same period, French monasteries were attempting to recover from the Hundred Years War and the Great Western Schism, during which they had suffered more than any other Benedictine nationals. An additional curse, the Pragmatic Sanction of Bourges (1438), gave the French king, not the pontiff or bishops, the right to approve abbatial elections. Abrogated temporarily, it was reinstated and lasted until the Concordat of Bologna in 1516—like the Pragmatic Sanction—negotiated an agreement between the monarch and the papacy.

Portuguese monasteries began a reform mandated in 1436 by the king and Florentine Abbot Gomez.[35] In 1566 Pope Pius V finally united all the reformed monasteries of Portugal, abolishing the *commende* though the king—renouncing his patronage—still retained the right for ten more years to name the monastic visitators.[36]

Monks and Nuns in Spain

Fourteenth-century Spanish monks still suffered from the *commende*, and lack of stability was pervasive as monks wandered between monasteries until they wore out their welcome. Juan I, King of Castile and León, reacted against these problems, founding San Benito monastery at Valladolid in 1390. Among the monstery's firmly established practices were strict enclosure, stability, and constant observance of the Rule.

By the mid-fifteenth century another congregation, partially modeled after Saint Justina in Padua, emerged and prospered with the support of Ferdinand and Isabella. Abbots had four-year terms and exerted a great deal of power in the congregation's autonomous abbeys. Novices made vows of stability to the house, not the Valladolid Union. Forty-five monasteries eventually joined the congregation including the great Catalan abbey of Montserrat, which had earlier asserted its independence. Unfortunately for Montserrat and Spanish monasticism, the celebrated Abbot Cisneros died prematurely in 1510.[37]

The *commende* continued to affect monasteries in Spain through the fifteenth century. King Henry IV (1454–1474) appointed his former mistress Catherine de Sandoval as abbess of San Pedro de las Duenas and, with due cynicism, charged her to reform the morals of the community. In general, the court of Castile during Henry's reign exercised an undesirable influence on the religious who came from that milieu into Benedictine communities. Nuns' houses perceptibly declined in the fourteenth and fifteen centuries. Some houses maintained a modicum of regularity and a small number of foundations were made, including Santa Cruz in Burgos. The nuns' royal abbey of El Moral, founded in the twelfth century by Alfonso VIII, had become a veritable city-state. Civil and criminal jurisdiction over a large number of estates rested in the hands of the abbess who ruled as a baroness over vast manorial holdings.[38] After the Black Death decimated the membership in the Spanish monasteries, applicants were hastily admitted. Since, according to Spanish law, kings' widows could not remarry, queens often retired to the monastery. At their favorite retreat, San Pelayo el Real in Oviedo, it was customary that these former queens, in deference to their rank and position, to receive the abbatial office, often to the detriment of the community.

After 1390, six monasteries of women, including two at Oviedo and one in Madrid, joined the Congregation of Valladolid and adopted the monks' constitutions. When the celebrated Abbey of El Moral began its renewal, other houses of nuns followed but still remained under episcopal jurisdiction. Despite these reforms, some of the nuns' monasteries had only two or three nuns in residence in the late fifteenth century. Valladolid monks acted as visitators at the nuns' monasteries that were experiencing troubles. Subsequently, by virtue of the authority granted her, Queen Isabella deposed several abbesses and suppressed a number of houses. When some houses still rejected renewal efforts, Ferdinand and Isabella appealed to Rome. Innocent VIII's pleas were also ineffectual. When, in 1505, Ferdinand appealed to Julius II, the pope put the Benedictine nuns of Castile and León under the jurisdiction of the Abbot General of the Valladolid Congregation. This abbot delegated his powers to various abbots who were to visit the monasteries and implement renewal by mandate.[39]

An earlier union of nuns called the Congregation of the Claustrales remained intact. The Catalan Abbey of San Pedro de las Puellas in Barcelona, a member since 1330, remained the most celebrated in the area and retained its exemption from episcopal control. The life-term abbess was confirmed directly by the papacy and received the blessing from a delegate of the pope. She enjoyed the pontifical privilege and the stole of the diaconate. She possessed civil and spiritual jurisdiction over the parish, conferred benefices, and made canonical visits. Two other Catalan monasteries of women in the Claustrales were Saint Daniel of Girona and Saint Claire of Barcelona. The latter, founded by the Poor Clares, petitioned Rome for Benedictine status in 1406.[40]

Hungarian and Italian Monks and Nuns

Hungarian monasteries—also subject to the *commende*—were also in critical condition. Civil strife—including dynastic quarrels, the Turkish threat, and battles with neighboring states—did nothing for monastic stability. Hungary's reformer came in the person of Matthew Tolnai, appointed Abbot of Pannonhalma (1500–1535) and commissioned by the king to reform the Benedictines, a move supported by Pope Julius II. The Cassinese observances were strictly followed; shortly thereafter the community increased from four to forty members.

Within a decade, about ten monasteries followed the lead of Pannonhalma. In 1514 Pope Leo X named Tolnai archabbot and perpetual president of the Hungarian Congregation. Shortly all Benedictines in Hungary were aggregated to the congregation, and commendatory abbacies disappeared. The reform did not last, and Pannonhalma was back in the hands of the civil authorities, to be extinguished by 1560. It would be three hundred years later, 1802, before its restoration, destined to survive even the Communist era through 2000 when the abbey and its four dependent priories numbered almost a hundred monks.[41]

Francis of Rome's Benedictine Oblates

Throughout the Italian peninsula—divided into Papal States, several city-states, duchies, and a kingdom or two—the Cassinese Congregation continued its renewal efforts. Frances of Rome founded Benedictine women oblates, an apostolic group, in the early fifteenth century. Although living in community, they made private profession of vows. They were not cloistered, dedicating their lives to works of mercy and caring for the sick and the underprivileged.[42]

Benedictine monasteries of nuns dotted the Italian Peninsula. Many did not belong to the Cassinese Congregation—including dozens of small houses in Rome, eleven in Perugia, ten in Padua, seven in Milan, and six in Venice. Every small Italian village could boast a house of nuns. Sicily included seven monasteries of nuns in Palermo, five in Syracuse, and many more in the other Sicilian towns. As these houses proliferated, the nuns attempted to cooperate in the categorization of new candidates—limiting certain houses to one or more social classes. In Brescia, for example, the exempt abbey of Saint Julia's admitted only women from the nobility while Saints Cosmos and Damian accepted the bourgeois and the peasants.

The Santuccia Congregation of the Servants of Mary

One of the first Benedictine congregations controlled by women was Italian. Santuccia of Gubbio (d. 1305), a woman of considerable wealth, erected a nuns' monastery in 1258. Her spiritual director, the Abbot Sperandes of Saint Pierre at Gubbio, interpreted the Rule in constitutions for the nuns. Shortly thereafter twenty-five more monasteries adopted them and formed the Congregation of the Servants of Mary. The Abbess General was elected by the Chapter composed only of women, abbess definitors, and community delegates. The Chapter held jurisdiction over all the affiliated houses of nuns with the privilege of visitation and correction. The Abbess General named all the superiors, and Gubbio remained the head of the Congregation until 1306 when that prerogative passed to Santa Maria in Rome (renamed Sant'Anna de Funari in 1500). The Holy See exempted the congregation and later extended to the women all the Cassinese privileges as well. Eight more houses joined in the early fourteenth century. The nuns were usually called the "Santuzze" or "Santuccia" in honor of their foundress.

Mendicant Women and the Benedictine Tradition

Franciscan women also depended a great deal on the Benedictine traditions. Cardinal Hugolino, patron and protector of the Franciscans, imposed the Rule of Benedict as observed by the Cassinese on Clare and her community at San Damiano in Assisi. She had first been sent to learn community life from the Benedictine nuns, but neither she nor her counterpart Francis anticipated that the Cardinal would impose strict enclosure on her community. Thus, the Poor Clares became an enclosed Order of the traditional type.[43] The Dominican Sisters eventually experienced the same enforced legislation although they, too, had been founded primarily as an apostolic, not a solely contemplative community, then attracting many from the rural areas.[44]

Changing Cultural Morals and Monasteries of Women

In this era of reform and renewed spirituality, some observances in nuns' monasteries reportedly had—quite contrarily—become so lax and the nuns' reputations so tainted that one legate charged that some nuns seemed more dedicated to Venus than to God. Even the civil authority in Milan complained to Pope Paul II in 1538 that he needed to intervene at Ranchate where, he claimed, the nuns had fallen so far that one could no longer call them virgins.[45]

In Italian Liguria, complainants recommended closer surveillance of some nuns because too many local young men were making sport of the "conquest" of the nuns' chastity. Venice had had similar problems in the fourteenth century. In 1349 the Council issued a decree against those who committed fornication in monasteries of nuns. At the Italian carnivals in the next century, the singers chanted bawdy songs about nuns who had left their monasteries to join their lovers. At this point, as Schmitz was writing his report of these events, he sighed, "What good is there in continuing?"[46]

This was the period of the Renaissance and Avignon popes who openly legitimized their mistresses' children by giving them power and political office. It was the time when the notorious Pope Alexander VI and his equally depraved son, Cesare Borgia, used the papacy for self-aggrandizement, and the della Rovere popes put Renaissance art above spiritual concerns.[47] It was also the era of the Medici popes who were enjoying, but not enhancing, the papacy. The monks and nuns throughout Europe —and their leaders—often reflected the moral culture of the Renaissance as it moved north and west, ceasing their originating, counter-cultural mission. Still many committed individuals and observant communities remained among the Benedictines. When the Protestant Reformation soon changed the religious landscape of Western Europe, monasticism—and Christianity—would become vastly different territory.

The Lutheran Reformation Begins in Germany

Italian, French, and Spanish monks and nuns would be spared the deprivation and, more often, dissolution that Germanic and English monasteries had to endure during the Reformation, though they would also face a number of repercussions. During and after the Protestant Reformation, sixteenth-century monasticism was challenged with a series of mass persecutions and dissolutions. The Holy Roman Empire was earliest and most affected by Lutheranism while both Calvinism and Lutheranism affected the other European countries. Regardless, monasticism was not favored by any of the Protestant reformers, so Benedictines suffered irreparable damage under the Reformation, although this also brought about a needed purification.

Martin Luther, Augustinian Monk

The German Reformation leader Martin Luther (1483–1546) was an Augustinian monk, though he renounced his monastic vows in 1521, four years after his posting the ninety-five theses on the door of the Wittenberg Cathedral. The same year, Luther wrote a treatise on monastic vows, *De votes monasticism*, that he later considered the most powerful and irrefutable of all his written works.[48] It had an immediate and lasting influence, although the arguments he expressed were a mélange of Lollard and Hussite thought.

Luther maintained that monks relied on practices and rules, thus imitating the Jews and Manichees. He called the vow of poverty a sham and argued that the profession of chastity was unnecessary for the preservation of virtue. The life of a Christian, he maintained, was dedicated to performance of acts of mercy, not in wearing a cowl, shaving one's head, scourging oneself, fasting, or repeating a series of prayers. He was quite convincing. Within a year everyone in the Augustinian priory at Wittenberg, with the exception of the prior, had renounced his vows.[49]

Political and Religious Repercussions

Political, not only religious, upheaval characterized the early Reformation era. The 1555 Peace of Augsburg finally quelled the storm by allowing political leaders to determine the religion of their subjects. Every ruler in the Empire—whether Duke, Elector, King of Bavaria or petty kingdom—could legally retain his Catholic or Lutheran faith and require all under his jurisdiction to subject themselves to his creed. Nevertheless, monasteries outside Bavaria and a few other small states were subjected to legal persecution and, more often, dissolution. About half the monasteries of Black Benedictine monks, some 800 of the 1550 in Europe and England in 1517 disappeared before 1590.

Effects were less systematic in the German-speaking lands, and sometimes it was just a matter of encouraging monastic men and women to exercise their freedom by renouncing their vows and leaving the community. Often, the property was confiscated, and dwindling membership in the face of the chaos led inevitably to dissolution. Most of the monasteries in northern Germany gradually disappeared.

Bursfeld and fifty of its houses, more than a hundred other abbeys, and at least forty priories of monks—as well as seventy-six abbeys and seven priories of nuns—were all forbidden to admit novices, forcing them to close when the last monk or nun died. Thus, attrition brought demise. Some houses of nuns became Lutheran. When aging Abbess Behr of Walrode could no longer perform her official duties in 1538, a Lutheran nun took her place.[50]

One of the largest in membership, the German monastery at Lune went down fighting. Although in 1486 it had professed thirty-six novices in one day, in 1526 it still had eighty-seven choir nuns. The Duke ordered the community to listen to the sermons of a Dominican-turned-Lutheran, who preached why there were only two sacraments. Scarcely had he began when the Abbess got up and left the chapel followed by all her nuns. To get rid of the unwanted preacher, they then burned old furs and rags in the sacristy and smoked him out. In 1562, after the death of the last Catholic nun, the civil authorities confiscated the house.

Many monasteries of monks and nuns were destroyed or plundered beyond repair during the German Peasants' War. This tragic era sorted out Christian factions—when Luther first sided with the peasants against their wealthier neighbors, nobles, and houses of religious alike, then with the nobles against the peasants. The nuns' monasteries that were unable to weather those storms included Allendorf, Helfta, two in the Fulda area, Walbeck, and several others. Many monasteries were abandoned before the Lutheran civil authorities suppressed them. About eighty-five monasteries of Benedictine nuns never recovered from the Protestant Revolution in the Empire. Nuns often chose to leave their monastic homes when their vows were implicitly or explicitly nullified.[51]

Communities of nuns that chose voluntarily to follow Luther included Eschwege, Gernrode, Kornberg, Neuburg, and Sandau. The nuns of Überwasser at Münster joined the Anabaptist movement. Catholic and Lutheran nuns often prayed and lived together in their communities until the Thirty Years War (1618–1648). In the Lutheran monasteries the Hour of Matins (2 a.m. vigils) was eliminated, and devotions honoring the saints and the Virgin Mary were forbidden.

The Reformation Affects Swiss, Scandinavian, and Dutch Monasticism

John Calvin (1509–1564), neither priest nor monk, led the Swiss reform after the priest Huldrych Zwingli's (1484–1531) death. The impact of the Zwingli reform and Calvinism in Switzerland, which followed closely on the heels of German Lutheranism, was immediate on Swiss monasticism. In 1524, the council of Zurich dissolved the religious houses within the confines of its jurisdiction and allocated the revenues to poor relief and education.

In Basel, the leaders had expelled all the monastics and confiscated their homes and properties in 1529, all by legal mandate. A year later Geneva terminated all monastic life.[52] In 1531, during an abbatial vacancy at Saint Gall, the council that had designated itself as the monastery's protector confiscated the property of the prestigious, thousand-year-old Benedictine community. Calvinist brigands scattered many of the library holdings of precious books and manuscripts. In 1530 Abbot Diethelm Blarer of Wartensee (1530–1564) could rebuild much of the library. The Swiss Congregation, formed in 1602, initiated Saint Gall's precedence. Some decades later a printing press at the monastery became one of Switzerland's most prestigious. In 1712 pillage by the Swiss took place, again scattering the library holdings. In 1805 the abbey suffered its final dissolution by the Swiss government. Eventually, the church became a diocesan Cathedral, and the monastic buildings were converted into an episcopal residence and cantonal bureaucrats' offices.[53]

Scandinavian Monasticism

Scandinavian monasticism fared similarly. In Denmark, King Christian II and his successor, Frederick I, severed links between the Danish Church and Rome simply by the 1534 Ecclesiastical Appointments Act that implicitly—but not formally—repudiated papal authority. Freedom of conscience had been proclaimed in 1527, followed by the call of the Danish Diet to all priests and monastics to choose freely between celibacy and marriage. Norway and southern

Sweden (Scandia), then under Danish rule, had the same history somewhat. Monastics were encouraged to leave so their homes could be confiscated by the Crown. Some monks and nuns remained with their communities until the beginning of the seventeenth century. In the twentieth, attempts were made to revive monasticism, but the ruins of most abbeys and priories of monks and nuns remain on the "sights to see" flyers for tourists interested in viewing historical ruins— although one Danish house of nuns reopened in 1939.[54]

Monasteries were not as numerous in Sweden as in England or France, and some prominent houses owned a disproportionate share of the national wealth. The monasteries had marshaled great social and economic power. Monastics had acted as baronial feudal magnates in Sweden just as they had in France and the Empire, so civic authorities coveted their holdings. Initially, the monarch approved the marriage of priests; then he started harassing monasteries by billeting troops upon them, taking over their affairs and finding legal pretexts for reclaiming lands his predecessors had donated to them. In 1527, the King manipulated the Diet (legislature) to decree all anti-Catholic legislation he desired, much of which touched religious orders.

The Crown claimed all Swedish property the king deemed superfluous to the needs of the religious. All tax-exempt land given to monastics after 1454 was returned to the families of the donors. All taxable land was returned as well, regardless of the date of the legacy. Monks were subject to the surveillance of civil authority. Consequently, monastic communities that were deprived of their property, almost without exception, eventually ceased to exist.

The Netherlands' history is also diverse. Most of the Dutch monasteries of nuns had been converted to houses of canonesses in the fourteenth and fifteenth centuries. The nuns at Rijnsburg, the most renowned abbey that had remained Catholic and Benedictine, were no longer living in strict observance. The monastery and its neighboring village were pillaged in 1574. The community survivors retired to live in the town on the abbey revenues, and most became Protestant. Only four nuns remained at Frisian Mariendael in 1529, and authorities suppressed the nuns' abbey of Kikninge in 1603. Monasteries were often converted into hospitals or schools. Utrecht had two nuns' monasteries—Saint Laurent and Saint Mary's, both suppressed in 1584. Zwartewater disappeared at the end of the sixteenth century; Claarwater was pillaged in 1572 and abandoned in 1600. Thesinge, sacked in 1581, was finally suppressed by the state in 1629. Local authorities usually dispersed revenues and properties.

Belgian and Dutch Monasticism

In the Spanish Netherlands (later Flemish Belgium and Holland) most monasteries were originally affiliated to the Congregation of Bursfeld, but language and cultural differences soon strained community bonds. During the last half of the sixteenth century St. Trond and St. Peter at Ghent were pillaged and burned by the Lutheran and Calvinist soldiers of William of Orange, the Stadtholder who was in revolt against Rome and Philip II, King of Spain and the Spanish Low Countries. During the conflicts, monks sought refuge in the cities. Furthering the destruction, William of Orange left no monastery standing where his revolt succeeded in occupying the territory. By 1580 most Belgian houses had disappeared.[55] Due to the Reformation, monasticism in the Netherlands was suspended for the time.

The Dissolution of English and Irish Monasteries

Although there were some reports of scandal in a few English monasteries of monks and nuns, there was no general decadence in the years just preceding the English dissolution. Visitors to some monasteries noted lack of membership, too-free access to monastic corridors by some women of questionable repute, inconsistent attendance at choir, and in one (Humberstone, where there were only three monks) the abbot complained that the monks were in the village playing tennis when they should have been praying in the chapel. The monks had serious complaints about their abbot also. Another report came after a visitation to Peterborough, one of the largest, though not richest, abbey in the Lincoln diocese. The communities of fifty monks were unfortunate in their abbot, Edmund Kirton. He was disregarding his community financially and neglecting his monks while he sought solace in the tavern owned and managed by the abbey. However, only the sacristan was accused of living unchastely.[56]

Romsey was rich but in the worst shape of all. Doors remained unlocked all night; the prior was a bad-tempered alcoholic, and no one instructed the young monks. Only eight or ten monks attended Matins; just two or three of the forty who should have been there participated in the conventual's Mass. The senior monks apparently spent much time gambling. Thirteen years later, things seemed to have improved, but the same abbot was in charge. The Romsey nuns also had a checkered history toward the end of the fifteenth century when successive abbesses living rather scandalous lives prompted visitations. These also revealed a general neglect of buildings, financial irregularities, inadequate provision of food, neglect of religious duties, and even amorous liaisons.

Richard Fox

Bishop Richard Fox (1448–1528) attempted reform and issued severe disciplinary injunctions regarding the abbess of Romsey in 1507. When informed that one of the problems in the abbeys of English nuns was that they did not understand the Latin Rule which was read to them daily, he undertook to translate it for them—with commentary—and had it printed in 1517, the year Luther posted his ninety-five theses at Wittenberg.

Bishop Fox used the feminine forms and pronouns in his translation and the term "minchin" or "mynchin" for "nun." He also loosely interpolated what he felt should be added for that time and place, for example, when the Rule mentions wine, he added ale and beer. His main concentration, however, was on the second chapter of the Rule, the kind of person the Abbess ought to be.[57] But the measures were too late, and within two decades, these monasteries were all suppressed.

Richard Kidderminster

Winchcombe had the good fortune to have, for forty years, the most distinguished English abbot of the period, Richard Kidderminster

(1488–1527). He had studied at Gloucester College, Oxford, and initiated a full-fledged program of monastic studies, something found only at the largest monasteries such as Durham and Canterbury.

The abbot was delighted when the increase in novices gave him twenty-eight monks total. Likewise, he was pleased with the regularity of observance, the practice of monastic charity, and that the cloister at Winchcombe had all the appearances of a young university, minute though it was. Even Henry VIII had high regard for Kidderminster. When the king petitioned Rome concerning his annulment, he recommended that the judges be Archbishop Warham of Canterbury and Kidderminster, who had resigned his abbatial duties when he reached sixty-five. Before he had to make a decision on the King's Test Oath, he died in early 1532.[58]

John Islip

John Islip (1464–1532) of Westminster was another notable English abbot. Remembered as one of the last of the great monastic builders, he was responsible for much expansion at Westminster Abbey including the construction of the Lady Chapel that had been commissioned by Henry VIII.[59] King Henry invited Abbot Islip to join the Privy Council in 1513. His signature was on the petition to the pope concerning the king's annulment in 1530, and Islip was also mentioned as Warham's alternate for the English annulment trial. His death at Chelsea in 1532 saved him, like Kidderminster, from taking sides in the controversial marriage of the king to Anne Boleyn in 1533. On the day before Islip's funeral, Convocation made submission to the king and acknowledged the monarch as head of the Church in England. On the day of the funeral, Sir Thomas More resigned the chancellorship, executed in 1535 for defying Henry in the matters of his second marriage and his declaration as Supreme Head of the Church in England.[60]

Thomas Wolsey

Cardinal Thomas Wolsey (c. 1473–1530), More's predecessor in the Chancellorship, holds responsibility for much of the fate of monasticism in England: he initiated its termination and gave Henry the idea of using monastic properties to augment the bankrupt national treasury. Thomas Cromwell, More's successor, and Archbishop Cranmer completed the temporary burial of Benedictinism in England, though it would rise again centuries later. Even before the deaths of Kidderminster and Islip, there had been some dissolution by bishops interested in endowing colleges at Oxford or Cambridge with the revenues of decaying or derelict priories. They found sources of funds for their pet projects by assigning leases or revenues from the sale of the monastic landholdings to whatever they considered more useful purposes.[61] Henry VIII followed their example. He obtained papal bulls suppressing Mottisfont for the benefit of Windsor Castle. By uniting the monks of Luffield Priory with Westminster Abbey, he could add Luffield's revenues to Windsor.

Wolsey particularly favored the suppression of small houses to benefit the favorite foundations of the church's and state's powerful leaders. As Cardinal Archbishop of York, Papal Legate, and England's Chancellor, Wolsey often used his power for his private ends. In 1524, he obtained a papal bull giving him authority to visit and "reform" even the exempt houses of men and women in England's religious orders. After issuing a book of regulations designed to suffocate the monasteries and prevent further admissions to monastic houses, he sent commissaries to make sporadic visitations to see if his privately devised constitutions were enforced, despite the monks' objections to the imposed austerities. He compelled certain abbots and priors to resign; others he arbitrarily replaced. When an abbatial vacancy occurred, the cardinal could convince the community that he should be entrusted with the appointment of the successor. The favored candidate was expected to make a handsome contribution toward Wolsey's new college or his private coffers. In 1522, Wolsey appointed himself commendatory Abbot of St. Albans, then one of the wealthiest houses in England. All the large, financially secure houses received periodic demands for contributions toward the cardinal's expenses.[62]

Between 1514 and 1529, Wolsey dissolved twenty-nine houses of monks, canons, and nuns on grounds that they had fewer than twelve members or that their income was below sustenance level. At Oxford,

Saint Frideswide monastery was suppressed to make way for Christ Church College, Wolsey's pet project. Twenty more houses went to Thomas More, who admired most monastics and was an oblate of London's Carthusian monastery, agreed that some houses needed reform. Yet, he had earlier passed on to Wolsey some of the complaints against Wolsey's chief agent, Dr. Allen, and against Thomas Cromwell, then a minion of Wolsey's, both of whom were guilty of abusing their authority. The Cardinal ignored More's report of the injustices of the unscrupulous agents. When Wolsey needed financing again, this time for a college at Ipswich, he proceeded against seven more small houses. This set the stage for all houses of religious men and women being wrenched away from the Church by the State.

The English Oath

In May 1533, the bishops and abbots were required to take an oath repudiating the promise of obedience to the pope that they had made at their installation and to recognize the king as head of the Church. On June 1, they were required to be present at Westminster Abbey for the royal coronation of Anne Boleyn. The community's priest-monks were all present, attired in copes. After the passage of the Act of Succession in 1534 placing Anne's daughter (Elizabeth) and any other children she might have in line for the throne of England before the former Queen Catherine's daughter Mary, each individual in every religious house was required to choose between loyalty to Queen Catherine and Mary, or to Henry and Anne. Most chose the safer path and survived. Some refused and suffered the consequences.

Twenty-six Black Monk Abbots and the Cathedral Prior of Coventry were members of the House of Lords in Parliament. All prelates, abbots, and priors were members of Convocation, the king's ecclesiastical council. Nuns were no longer represented in these national political assemblies. During summer and fall 1534 the king's commissioners toured the country demanding adherence from members of chapters, monastic communities, colleges, and hospitals—from all men and women in religious orders. Most did not refuse—or at least the lists (often written in the same hand) reported that they acquiesced. A monk of Woburn successfully evaded the issue and replied to the question of how he "took the king" by saying "I take him as God and the Holy Church take him; and I am sure he taketh himself none otherwise." That satisfied the civil visitators.[63]

Political Mysticism: Elizabeth Barton, the Maid of Kent

The involvement of one nun had extensive ramifications. Elizabeth Barton (c. 1506–1534), popularly known as the Holy Maid of Kent, resided at the Benedictine Monastery of Saint Sepulcher at Canterbury. Before her novitiate, she had been a teenage servant-maid of the steward of the archiepiscopal estates near Aldington in Kent. During an illness at Eastertime in 1525, she seemed to be in ecstasy, correctly predicting such events as her own cure at the chapel of Court-at-Street. Archbishop Warham selected a Benedictine monk, Dr. Edward Bocking (then cellarer of the Cathedral Monastery of Christ Church at Canterbury) as his agent to investigate the phenomena. Bocking, soon convinced of Elizabeth's authenticity as a mystic, later became her confessor, ultimately joining her at the execution block.[64]

Relentless in denouncing the age's corruption, Elizabeth berated civil and church officials for their laxity and spoke openly against Henry's annulment attempts. The king personally interviewed her, and she predicted that a catastrophe would overtake him if he persevered in his chosen path. Henry feared that the reputed saint and visionary were too influential with leaders like More, Fisher, Friars, and the Carthusians, so she had to be silenced. Historians are still arguing about whether the Holy Maid was an authentic mystic, prompting David Knowles to comment that after hundreds of years they have not yet succeeded in reaching an agreement never achieved by contemporaries. Dr. Bocking, the Canterbury monk, was quickly convinced and went so far as to publish some of her prophecies and to assist others to do the same. He may have, at least in one historian's opinion, entered waters "too deep for him."[65] When her final challenge came, Sister Elizabeth, the Maid of Kent, had already won the esteem of many during her eight years as Benedictine. Warham was dead, and the king was married to Anne Boleyn.

Cromwell and Cranmer were leading Church and State on an irrevocable course when in 1533 Archbishop Cranmer ordered the prioress of Saint Sepulchre to bring the "Barton nun" to him for an interview. He was determined to diminish her influence. Following the conference with him, she was also required to appear before the judicial Star Chamber. That assembly unjustly charged her with treason, of having perniciously influenced Archbishop Warham, Wolsey, and even Pope Clement VII against the king's annulment and remarriage. Her companions in the Tower included the monk, Bocking, and another monk of Canterbury, John Dering.

Like Joan of Arc earlier and the Jesuit Edmund Campion later, Elizabeth succumbed to intolerable pressure and temporarily recanted, agreeing that her revelations were figments of her imagination. However, she made no confession of guilt, holding that all her admonitions were based on what she believed was true. It was a failure of constancy, not an admission of fraud, and in the sequel, again like Joan of Arc, she endeavored to prevent its consequences. But, her credibility had been destroyed. Further, she was publicly denounced by Anne's protégés, a number that included the Abbot of Hyde. She was finally defeated by a commonly practiced Bill of Attainder that convicted, sentenced, and executed her without benefit of trial by jury in 1534. Thomas More and John Fisher were first implicated with her and her other companions, but More's defense was so strong that the king begrudgingly agreed not to charge him then (he would be executed later for refusing to take the Oath). Fisher was later condemned and executed in 1535.

The 1536 Act of Suppression of Monasteries

The Irish monastics were not spared, and dissolution was recommended as early as 1536. As the agents listed the monasteries in the Pale of Ireland, they surmised that if the king moved against the monks and nuns without warning he could realize a large sum of money. Henry continued to rationalize that the dissolution was justified because money spent on "untruth and beastly living" could be better used for matters of state.[66] In 1535, he advised his nephew

James V of Scotland to emulate him in this efficient manner of increasing state revenues. James died too soon to implement the King's Counsel.[67] The second round of visitators were commissioned to find incidents of scandal as the rationale for the confiscation of monastic property.

The Act of Suppression of Monasteries in 1536 set minimum viability standards at twelve residents and a certain annual income. Word of impending dissolutions leaked to the public and petitions reached the king from courtiers and other nobility asking for the gift of their favorite estates.[68] At first the smaller houses were attacked, allowing the members to go to one of the larger monasteries or leave with a dispensation from the Church of England Archbishop and a small gratuity. Approximately 40 percent of the monks chose to leave, but only 10 percent of the nuns agreed to be dispensed by Cranmer. About half of the ordained monks opted to become Anglican diocesan priests. At first the monks and nuns who left were not allowed to marry despite the dispensation of the other vows. For ordained monks, parish work was an alternative. Some old and debilitated nuns retired to homes of friends; young nuns often went home to their families.

The Pilgrimage of Grace

The northern England insurrection known as the Pilgrimage of Grace demanded the suppression of no more abbeys. The laymen who originated the uprising had mixed religious, social, and economic grievances. Another group of Lincolnshire men rioted for about three weeks. At rare times, some rebels demanded that the abbots and monks join them. As they succeeded, some captured monasteries were temporarily restored to the monks by the rebels who felt that the poor and needy would be deprived of their main source of assistance if all the monasteries were eliminated.

When leader of the abortive Pilgrimage Robert Aske (1500–1537) later wrote his Apologia for the revolt in prison, he noted that the spiritual and material solace the monasteries gave was sorely missed when the houses were closed. He maintained that the preaching apostolate of some monasteries, the spiritual thrust they provided, architectural beauty, and education of the poor and rich all justified continuing the monastic institution. Aske never regarded them as harbors for those living scandalous lives. Henry and his ministers paid no heed to this attitude and continued their suppressions and executions. Some of the canons, several monks, and two abbots were eventually charged with treason and executed for their alleged part in the insurrection led by Aske.

Final Dissolution

At England's general dissolution in 1539, there were about 140 monasteries of women, half of which were Benedictine. About half of those were suppressed earlier because of small numbers or inadequate income. Scandals had been dredged up or exaggerated to justify the closures, but some fifty houses remained to fall under the final Act of 1539.[69] About 850 Benedictine nuns lost the right to remain part of the religious community in which they made vows, and the monks outnumbered them. Fifty-four monasteries numbering over 1300 men were dissolved.

Generally the men's houses gave up more wealth to the looters than the women's, yet there were exceptions. Barking Abbey (nationalized in 1539) had precious metal plates weighing over 3000 ounces, a monstrance of sixty-five ounces of gold, and such costly priests' vestments of gold cloth that they were to be reserved for the king's use.[70] Some abbesses fared quite well if they had the right connections. Archbishop's Cranmer's sister was the prioress of the Benedictine house in Sheppey.

Wolsey's illegitimate daughter was a nun at Shaftesbury. She was willing to give up the life her father had compelled her to lead for lack of a better place to dispose of his misalliance. Under her alias, Dorothy Clansey, she received a small annual pension where she was still listed in 1556. Gabrielle Shelton from the Abbey at Barking lived out her days in the Carrow Priory at Norwich. Although marriage was forbidden for former monastics, it was contracted and seldom punished. Edward VI lifted his father's ban against it, legalizing even the marriages contracted during Henry's reign.[71]

Outside Adaptation of Monks and Nuns

The evicted monks and nuns had to adapt. Unless imprisoned on some trumped-up charge, most monks received a fair annual pension which varied according to age and the wealth of the suppressed monastery of their profession. Some abbots and priors received bishoprics in the King's church; some drew rather princely sums as pensions and joined the landed gentry.

The nuns usually received just over half that allotted to the monks, as women were customarily considered of less worth. It may also have been considered a supplement to other income, assuming that women found other means of support. Purchasing power was soon seriously eroded, so many of these nuns lived on the sustenance level unless some unexpected expenditure sent them into penury. Some monks and nuns married, but seldom to each other—although this was profitable because it meant two pensions. More monks than nuns married.

One aged monk of Evesham, William Lyttleton, lived until 1603. Before he died, he was reconciled to the church and his monastic profession by Dom Augustine Bradshaw, a member of the English community at Douai Monastery in France, who was in the underground mission in England. The last pensioner died about 1607 or 1608. Some evicted Benedictines also remained in English underground, but others fled abroad. There was a brief respite when Mary Tudor followed Edward VI to the throne, but when Elizabeth succeeded her any public attempts to revive Catholicism were immediately terminated. Most of the nuns and monks who had resurfaced during Mary's reign left for the Continent.[72]

Disposition of Monastic Property

The monastic property, vast holdings, and great expanses of land became assets of the Crown. Many abbey buildings were converted into schools, such as at Ely and Saint Albans. Tavistock Abbey in Devon was granted to the Russells; a descendant, the present Duke of Bedford, is its owner. Evesham Abbey remains a private residence. The Anglican Benedictine monks' community of Nashdom first occupied the abbey site at Pershsore but left there in 1926. The largest abbey churches that had also been sees of bishops became great Anglican cathedrals. Westminster Abbey and Bath Abbey retained the monastic names but lacked a monastic community. Durham, Worcester, Gloucester, Peterborough, Ely, Chester, and many others still retain their monastic architecture, but the Anglican church ritual predominates, not the Benedictine Liturgy of the Hours.

After Cromwell had "feathered his nest very comfortably," other properties were auctioned at the "greatest land-sale in English history."[73] The total net income to the Crown was considerably below what Henry had anticipated, but they did receive about £149,000 for the real estate that had been confiscated in his name from all the houses of religious that included the Benedictines. This boon effectively more than doubled the royal income.

The monastic movable articles were sold, in Dickinson's opinion, "with immense haste and immense waste."[74] Artistic and literary losses that included invaluable ancient manuscripts and centuries of monastic library collections would be considered one of the greatest catastrophes in the history of English learning. Only about 3600 of the several hundred thousand manuscripts remain. The Anglican Bishop Matthew Parker, during Elizabeth's reign, acquired a magnificent library of manuscripts, including the Canterbury Gospels that he left to Corpus Christi College, Cambridge. An Ipswich citizen gave Pembroke College at Cambridge a large collection from Bury Saint Edmunds. Durham and Worcester Cathedrals retained some abbey manuscripts. Some discoveries were poignant but rare. A manuscript from Glastonbury was discovered by an Oxford antiquary in 1722 when he received some tobacco sent to him on a leaf of it. Only a few of the monastic archives remained intact.

Irish and Scottish Closures

All the Irish and Scottish monasteries were closed as well. Scotland was still a separate realm, and its primary creed was Calvinist, rather than Anglican. The Scottish Benedictines traced their traditions to three roots—those daughter-houses of old English abbeys of Canterbury, Durham, or Reading; those considered "offshoots" of the Abbey of Tiron in Picardy; and those once affiliated with Cluny. The royal abbey of Dunfermline with its dependent priories at Coldingham, Urquhart, Pluscarden, and the Reading daughterhouse on the Isle of May were outstanding abbeys that traced their roots to England. Dunfermline had been intended by King Malcolm III as the burial place of the Scottish royalty as his Queen was entombed there. Subsequently his three sons—Kings Edgar, Alexander, and David—and Prince Edward were all buried there, as was King David's successor, his grandson Malcolm IV.

Dunfermline was destroyed by order of the Presbyterian Lords of the Congregation in 1560. The choir was reduced to ruins, the organ broken into fragments, the bells and bell tower nearly demolished. The twenty-six monks were dispersed, but some returned to keep vigil "with doors bolted and barred kept watch in their choir by the shrines of Saint Margaret and Saint David, the sepulchers of Bruce and Randolph."[75] Coldingham Priory was the most important of the Dunfermline dependencies. After the dissolution the property was owned by the Home family (who were former bailiffs). Oliver Cromwell, the Puritan Protector, completed the monastery's destruction in 1648. Nothing remains but a few foundations, portions of some walls now part of the modern parish church, and one gate.

The Clunisian house of Crossraguel was finally taken when the Lords of the Secret Council passed an Act "that all places and monuments of idolatry should be destroyed."[76] Subsequently the Earls of Arran, Argyll, and Glenmcaire—accompanied by the Presbyterians of the western region who had burnt the Cluniac monastery, Paisley Abbey—attacked and demolished at least part of the Crossraguel properties. Today the remains are walls, gables, traces of the refectory, and the chapter house. Much of the abbot's house and tower still stands. There is no monastic community that can claim the five neighboring churches, or the coal pits, mills, and forests. Crossraguel and Paisley are only memories.[77]

Thus passed from the scene monastic houses, many of which would never rise again. Lost for the most part were the great and little monasteries of Benedictine men and women in the British Empire, Scandinavia, the Netherlands, England, Ireland, and Scotland. Yet, the Benedictine spirit remained, and some nations would later see a restoration of monastic community life. As autumn and winter passed, a long-awaited spring would arrive in the sixteenth and seventeenth centuries. ✻

CHAPTER 7

Benedictine Spring: The Catholic Counter-Reformation

Sixteenth and Seventeenth Centuries

T he gradual decline of monastic life during the twelfth through sixteenth centuries culminated in devastating effects from the Protestant Reformation. The autumn of this decline—often tempered by reforms and heightened spirituality—turned to full winter with the 1536 English Acts of Suppression. As the storm raged, an official Catholic response to the Protestantism began with the Council of Trent (1545–1563).

The theologically defensive posture of Trent not only anathematized Protestant doctrine but also necessitated some self-assessment and house cleaning. By the day preceding the final adjournment, the Council Fathers had addressed their concerns about monasticism's state of affairs, finally pronouncing decrees intended to remedy a number of abuses. Attempting to stem the decline of the monasteries begun in the pre-Reformation period, the Council finally saw the beginning of an early spring.

Monastic Effects: The Council of Trent

The Council of Trent focused its reform on monastics' choice of vocation, nuns' enclosure, episcopal exemption, the need for union of congregations, and the *commende*.[1]

Choice of Vocation

First, the Council forbade the acceptance of any candidates not freely choosing to be monastics. To ensure compliance, the bishops were to interview postulants and novices to ascertain if they had been forced into monastic life. Anyone exerting undue pressure or forcing a woman to accept monastic life was subject to excommunication. Moreover, no woman could be prevented from entering a religious order if she so desired, a counter-cultural option at a time when families were still very patriarchal, and fathers or brothers determined whether and whom their daughters and sisters might marry. The outcome of this legislation varied in its effectiveness, and many women were constrained to enter monasteries by their lack of social options.[2]

Nun's Enclosure

Although the Council forbade force regarding entrance to the monastery, it was permitted when needed to keep nuns in strict enclosure. The Bishop was obligated to employ censure and resort to civil enforcement to ensure that nuns remained in strict enclosure. Trent called upon the princes of the states to assist the bishops in the implementation of this decree. Furthermore, under threat of excommunication no man or woman was to enter the enclosure of any monastery of nuns without the express permission of the bishop.

The bishops were also urged to move the monasteries of nuns to towns so that within the city walls their virtue and security, persons, and property would be more secure. The rural isolation, the Council Fathers feared, might be a source of physical danger to their person or property or lead them or others into scandal.[3] The church leaders at Trent did not address the monks' or nuns' modes of the dress with any specificity, suggesting only that professed men and women should observe the daily life, dietary regulations, and dress common to their specific communities.[4]

Union of Congregations

Unaffiliated houses exempt from episcopal jurisdiction were required to join other congregations, submit to their respective bishops, or organize their own confederacies, which many of them did. The Council stipulated that monastic congregations hold triennial chapters. If they failed to do so, the metropolitan bishop of the ecclesiastical province was to call the heads of the monasteries concerned to report to a general chapter meeting. Hence, implementation and enforcement of the decrees often depended exclusively on the bishops. Monasteries of women were either to be under the jurisdiction of the Holy See or the local bishop. Universally, female candidates could not be accepted under age twelve, and women could make perpetual profession only after they reached twenty-one. Men could make profession at sixteen after a year of probation in the novitiate. For both genders, transfer to different religious orders with less rigorous rules was forbidden. According to Trent, monastic superiors, abbots, and abbesses were to be elected by secret ballot. The monk or nun elected to lead a community was to be selected from those who had professed vows for at least eight years and had achieved the mature age of forty.

The Council also addressed sacramental life. Nuns were to confess and communicate at least monthly, and a highly ranking confessor was to be sent to houses of nuns at least two or three times a year to ensure compliance. No members of religious orders could enter the service of any prelate, church official, or prince without the permission of the superior. The Council reaffirmed the policy that, although religious individuals could not hold property, individual monasteries were generally communal religious communities that could own immovable property. All material things were to be held in common, and personal landholdings were explicitly forbidden.

The Commende

The *commende* was addressed but not eradicated. During the sessions, the Cardinal of Lorraine informed the Council that in France alone 1040 monastic houses were governed by commendatory superiors who reaped the benefits of the revenues, often leaving the monks and nuns almost destitute. Furthermore, only thirty or forty French monasteries had superiors who lived at the monasteries they governed. This intervention of the Cardinal led certain pessimists among the prelates to consider the complete suppression of the monastic orders instead of trying to remedy the abuses, but the detrimental practice continued. Among many examples, Cardinal Richelieu rewarded a teenage violinist with a monastery in the seventeenth century; moreover, he appointed himself head of Cluny. The abuse persisted, and a seven-year-old received revenues of Saint Mihiel in the following century. Even Protestants received abbacies, and French finance minister Maximilien de Béthune, Duke of Sully under Louis XIV, reaped the benefits of four houses. Another Revolution would eliminate all the monastic houses from France before the nineteenth century.[5]

Post-Conciliar Congregations

After the Council closed in 1563, unaffiliated monasteries immediately joined a congregation or formed a new union. Despite the Tridentine decrees, some bishops refused to let the monasteries escape their jurisdiction. Bishop of Augsburg Jean Christopher prevented exemption in Lower Swabia in 1665 by organizing the houses in his diocese into a congregation under his jurisdiction. Eight monasteries joined this Congregation of the Holy Spirit. After 1699, with more liberal statutes revised by the Abbot of Ottobeuren and approved by the new bishop, the Congregation prospered.[6] Celestine Vogl, the Abbot of St. Emmeran in Ratisbon, formed another congregation in 1684 when he established the Bavarian Congregation of the Holy Angels, eventually including nineteen communities. This community observed an unusual practice by electing a liaison between the monks and the abbot, who also had charge of informing the president of the Congregation concerning the material and spiritual tenor of the monastery.

Monasteries in Austria were almost ruined by the Peasant Wars, the religious-economic conflicts following the Reformation, and the Ottoman-Hungarian invasions. Further governmental intervention and creation of a "Klosterrat" did not prevent several valorous abbots from meeting to restore the Congregation of Melk in 1617, and the emperor and Pope Urban VIII approved the new statutes in 1625.

Regardless, obstinate opposition of the Bishop of Passau impeded, at least temporarily, the actual functioning of the Congregation.[7] At Salzburg, the archbishop insured the viability of his city's university by confiding it to the Benedictines in 1617, and then, in 1636, the Abbot of St. Peter established the new Benedictine Congregation of the Diocese of Salzburg in 1641, including seven monasteries. Elsewhere in Germany, the Bursfeld Congregation claimed 142 affiliated monasteries in 1629 but had only 41 that were truly aggregated. Discipline was good and the union boasted several outstanding presidents. A prosperous seminary was soon functioning at Cologne for the clerics who frequented the university. Attempts to unite all German monasteries under Fulda—originally encouraged by the emperor, pope, and nuncio—never succeeded.[8]

The Abbey of Einsiedeln took the leadership in Switzerland. Abbot Joachim Eichhorn (1544–1569) had restored the abbey, and it was prospering. In 1602, the Swiss (Helvetian) Congregation was founded, exempted from episcopal jurisdiction by Pope Gregory XV's 1622 approval of their constitutions. Einsiedeln retained its leadership of the union. In Poland, the monarch and commendatory abbots stopped all attempts to organize congregations. Congregations in Bohemia-Moravia were more successful. The abbots of Brevnov-Braunau headed the restoration movement with some success later in the seventeenth century.[9]

Montserrat monks came from Spain in 1635 to revive the abbey of Emmaus at Prague. The Bohemian monks eventually adopted the spirit of the Congregation of Valladolid and organized an autonomous union. Monks from that congregation were also sent to Vienna in response to the invitation of Emperor Ferdinand II in 1632. Nuns in the area saw reform prompted by Madeline Morteska (1556–1632) of Culm. When the Ottoman Turks passed through on their way to Vienna near the end of the seventeenth century, they burned the restored abbey of Pannonhalma.

The Congregation of Claustrals in Spain, after some radical changes by Pope Clement VIII in 1592, finally revised its own constitutions and met papal approval in 1662. Meanwhile, the Italian Congregation of Monte Cassino continued to grow, aggregating fourteen more monasteries in the sixteenth and seventeenth centuries. They were solidly organized and witnessed significant prosperity. Several prominent bishops, cardinals, and reformers came from this abbey, influencing other monasteries in France, the Iberian Peninsula, Poland, and the Dalmatian Islands.[10]

Restoration of the English Congregation

After the Protestant Reformation, seminaries were established in Douai, Flanders; St. Peter's, Rome; and Valladolid, Spain. Here, English seminarians were instructed to return to the underground mission in England after ordination. Several alumni of these schools joined various Benedictine monasteries on the continent.[11] Augustine Bradshawe, a Valladolid seminarian, became a monk at Compostella, John Roberts and four other Englishmen soon followed. Soon afterward the Holy See authorized the English Benedictines in Italy and Spain to return to their native land to assist the clergy in the underground mission. In December 1602, Dom Bradshawe set out for England and was followed shortly thereafter by Thomas Preston and Anselm Beach who left Italy to join him.[12]

Paul V recognized the restored English Congregation, aggregating to it the English monks who transferred from the Valladolid union in 1619. In 1633, Urban VIII granted the rights and privileges of the ancient congregation. Its members were permitted to add to the usual profession promises that of consecration to the English mission. In 1642, the English monks took possession of the monastery of Lamspring in Germany, a former house of canonesses that had been suppressed in 1542. Located in the diocese of Hildesheim in Westphalia, it gave them a site for recruiting and training English monks. It served as a safe house until 1803, when most of the monks returned openly to England. After the restoration of the Stuarts in 1646, English anti-Catholicism was somewhat subdued. Some monks momentarily returned to England in the seventeenth century with royal permission founding a Benedictine community at the royal chapel at Somerset House, London, and at St. John's, Clerkenwell.[13]

An English Spiritual Drama: Dom Baker, Lady Abbess Gascoigne, and Dame Gertrude More

English mystic and writer Augustine Baker (1575–1641) became one of the most well-known members of the newly restored English Benedictine Congregation. Enduring decades of controversy, his teaching held widespread influence.

Augustine Baker

Baker, a convert from atheism, made his novitiate at Saint Justina in Padua. After meeting English Benedictines affiliated the Cassinese, he went to England in 1607, made his profession, and then returned to the continent. Ordained at Rheims in 1610 and then returned to the English mission. Baker was first affiliated with the priory at Dieulouard, although he never resided there. In 1670, he went to Devonshire as Philip Fursden's domestic chaplain where he developed deep mental prayer while teaching others how to do the same. An aspiring scholar eager to convert many to Catholicism, Baker gave free legal counsel to all who sought it.[14]

Baker left the Fursden household to take up residence at Gray's Inn, the lawyers' house of studies, in London. His superiors charged him with investigating the pre-Reformation history of the English Benedictines, particularly to disprove a 1622 claim published by a former member that the Congregation had once been a dependency of Cluny. Baker also refuted the opinions of Baronius that Saints Gregory I and Augustine of Canterbury were not Benedictines. These scholarly pursuits soon brought him into the circle of Sir Robert Cotton, whose distinguished library provided the nucleus of the British Museum.

Baker's research culminated in a volume entitled *Apostolate Benedictinorum in Anglia* (*Benedictine Apostolate in England*). Though written in collaboration with Fathers Jones and Reyner, the 1626 Douai publication listed Baker as the sole author. The manuscript—originally intended as the first part of a more elaborate historical work—was later exploited by the historian Cressy for his *Church*

History of Brittany from the Beginning of Christianity to the Norman Conquest, published at Rouen in 1668.[15] When persecution of Catholics again escalated in 1624, Baker left for the Continent, where he was appointed auxiliary confessor for the French monastery of nuns at Cambrai, Our Lady of Comfort, for their spiritual direction.[16] He remained there until 1633, nine years after his arrival. A number of the treatises written for these nuns appear in Serenus Cressy's later compilation, *Sancta Sophia (Holy Wisdom)* though some of the nuns' superiors often opposed his approach to spirituality. Abbess Catherine Gascoigne (1600–1676), fought many battles to ensure Baker's mystical teaching would reach later generations.[17]

Dame Catherine Gascoigne and Dame Gertrude More

Lady Abbess Gascoigne claimed descent from several prominent men of the same surname. Catherine, who retained her given name after her monastic profession, was a native of Yorkshire. The family was steeped in the tradition of that York county where, for almost a century, the fight to keep the faith had persisted and "whose castle walls had seen more famous confessors and martyrs than any other prison in England."[18] Despite the family's attempts to detain her longer at home, Catherine applied to the Bishop of London for permission to leave the country when she was nineteen, but she was refused. Attributing her beauty to the Bishop's decision, she prayed to have the offending gift altered and was stricken with a case of smallpox that radically changed her facial appearance. She made a private vow of virginity resolving, if all else failed, to live as a holy virgin at home. Four years later she set out for Flanders with the necessary approval, entering the Abbey of Paix (Peace) in Douai and founding a small community of eight young Englishwomen under the leadership of Dame Gertrude More, great-granddaughter of the martyred Saint Thomas More. They were housed in the town then, waiting to proceed to Cambrai to open a monastery for women under the jurisdiction of the monks, Catherine was invited to join the Cambrai contingent.[19]

Dames Gertrude More, Catherine Gascoigne, and seven other women received the Benedictine habit from Archbishop Vanderburch,

Duke of Cambrai.[20] For the first three years three nuns sent from Brussels governed the monastery, introducing the Ignatian system of meditation learned from their Jesuit chaplains. When Dom Baker arrived as spiritual director, his innovative approach to spirituality caused more than a little tension. Dame Catherine supported Baker, but Dame Gertrude opposed him. The struggle waged on throughout 1625. Four years later, the Holy See appointed Catherine, six years Dame Gertrude's senior, as abbess. She held this office from 1629 to 1641 and again from 1645 to 1673, three years before she died at age 76.[21] Dame Gertrude's masterly exposition of the contemplative life inspired by Dom Baker was later printed in 1658 in an edition of her *Spiritual Exercises*.[22]

Catherine and Gertrude eventually resolved their differences and became Baker's most devoted disciples. A considerable number of the nuns who sought him as their confessor over their appointed chaplain joined them. This monk, Francis Hull, had arrived five years after Baker and apparently resented the nuns' adherence to what was being called Father Baker's Way—later referred to as the "Mystic Way" or the "Way of Affection." Temperamentally, the two monks were opposites. Baker emphasized the love of God and others while the chaplain resorted to preaching violent and terrifying sermons to the nuns on the penalties attached their Christian duty and especially to disobedience to lawful authority. What the nuns needed, he apparently concluded, "was good, solid meditation on Death, Judgment, Hell and Heaven."[23]

Challenge and Polarization

The English Congregation President called the two monks to the General Chapter in 1633 where the orthodoxy of Father Baker's doctrine could be challenged. However, his teaching adhered to the standard teaching of the mystical writers of all ages, such as Gregory the Great and John of the Cross. When Dame Catherine was called to defend Baker, she did so in terms of the Rule of Benedict.[24] Baker emphasized the inner guidance of the spirit, together with a corresponding de-emphasis of formalities and externalities of worship.

Two theologians present at the Council, Leander Jones and Rudisind Barlow, drew attention to the similarity of his teaching to that of the Desert Fathers and finally approved his work. The Chapter labeled the charges against Augustine Baker "misunderstandings" and recommended that nuns' chaplains refrain in the future from treating them to "offensive sermons." On the day following Baker's vindication, Dame Gertrude, then twenty-seven, became critically ill and died two weeks later.[25]

Neither of the two monks was sent back to Cambrai. Francis Hull was transferred to Paris where he soon became ill, dying at St. Malo in 1645. Baker went to the monastery of his choice, Saint Gregory's at Douai, where he lived in seclusion, dispensed from choir duty and seldom departing his cell except to attend chapel and share meals. Because of his renown as a spiritual guide, Baker was increasingly sought by the monks, laypersons, clerics, and other religious. He was also socially affable; many people sought his pleasant company, but he was still not safe from controversy. It was destined to become more acrimonious than before, and the outcome more devastating.

The Douai abbey was affected by the polarization of the active and contemplative life, threaded throughout Benedictine history. In this case, the two camps were composed of those who sought designation as missionaries to the homeland, and those who regarded the conventual observance of the monastery as their proper and only way of life. Baker was a partisan of the latter group. For him, missionary work was an occupation to be obediently endured, rather than enthusiastically sought. Dom Barlow shared those views.[26] The two parted company when Baker, resenting Barlow's "endorsement," circulated a satirical portrait of him. Barlow succeeded in convincing the Prior to removing Baker, who was dispatched to England even though he was sixty-three and in very poor health. After the failure of attempts to have his assignment rescinded, he sailed for England in 1638, accompanied by two fellow exiles, his later biographers, Leander Prichard and Salvin.[27]

Unable to be an active missionary, Baker continued to be faithful to contemplative prayer, living as a semi-invalid during the three remaining years of his life spent in and around London. He was pursued during the renewed outbreak of persecution of Roman Catholics in 1640, finding his last refuge at the house of a Mrs. Watson, mother of one of the Cambrai nuns. As he seemed ill with a contagious disease, his pursuers were deterred from entering the home where, unattended, he died on August 9, 1641. The site of his grave is unknown.

Dom Baker's Censure and Legacy

Dom Baker's death, instead of diminishing his influence, seems to have augmented it. A cult sprang up among the English people who soon styled him as "Venerable." The General Chapter of the Congregation in 1653 delegated Dom Cressy to edit Baker's works, and two years later the Cambrai nuns were ordered to surrender to every autographed manuscript of Baker's in their possession to the English Congregation's president, Claude White, and his assistants. Dame Catherine felt this request was devious, "that he meant not to alienate anything from our convent but to purge the books that we might not feed upon poisonous doctrine."[28] The real motives are difficult to discern. The nuns' chaplain, Dom William Walgrave, maintained that Dom Barlow was behind the request, charging him with not having given up seeking vindication. The Stanbrook nuns later assessed jealousy as the cause of the seizure.[29]

In 1653 when the Congregation's Chapter authorized the publication of Baker's works that were still in manuscript, Dom Barlow seemingly feared that the non-flattering portrait of him would reach posterity. He may have prompted the desperate movement to seize all manuscripts so—under the pretext of expurgating dangerous or offensive doctrine—the pages of Baker's *Treatise of the English Mission* denigrating Barlow could be destroyed.[30] The nuns unanimously signed and forwarded a petition to Dom White asserting their rights to the manuscripts and requesting deferment of any examination of Baker's manuscripts. Subsequently White arrived in person, determined to enforce his mandate of surrender of all Baker's writings. He first summoned the abbess and ordered her to hold a meeting of her Council, during which the Councilors were to declare in writing if they would give up the manuscripts.

A dramatic scenario ensued. The Abbess and all the Councilors first prostrated before him while humbly petitioning deferment of the matter. The document they submitted was a model of tact, deference, and unshaken resolution. It closed with the statement, "We humbly beseech your V. R. Paternity to pardon us that we do not answer you in the simple word of I [aye] or No, we having given your Paternity many reasons why we feared it might carry a show of disrespect to your V. R. Paternity to whom we owe and desire to perform all dutiful obedience and respect."[31] This obsequiousness did not deter the President's wrath. At the conclusion of the conventual Mass, he convened the entire community in the choir stalls and in a violent peroration made sweeping indictments of the abbess, nuns, and chaplain while declaring Baker's works to contain poisonous, pernicious, and diabolical doctrine. The abbess was running to perdition and the chaplain was maintaining a faction, the irate President scolded. He constantly interrupted any intervention by Dame Christina Brent, whom the abbess had designated as spokeswoman. White then required each nun to come forth individually to swear concurrence of difference with the petition submitted by the abbess and councilors. Most, despite their names being recorded as they responded *sotto voce*, supported the petition.

Dom White then resorted to blackmail. After dinner, he sent for the abbess to whom he announced that he would not proceed with the profession of three novices until his demands were met. Dame Catherine stood her ground. She countered with her own threat: she would, to preserve the manuscripts intact, withdraw from the English Congregation and place the community under the jurisdiction of the Archbishop of Cambrai. The next morning, the third Sunday of Lent, the President again summoned the community to the chapel in one final effort to force their surrender. Abbess Gascoigne met the attack with her usual quiet courtesy. Defeated, White returned to Paris threatening to darken their door again at Easter. That would not happen, and his death that autumn was followed by that of Dom Barlow's the next year. *Sancta Sophia* was published in 1657, thus ending the thirty years war over the teachings of Father Baker.[32]

When Catherine Gascoigne celebrated the fiftieth anniversary of her profession of vows in 1673, the General Chapter accepted her resignation. On her deathbed three years later, Dame Catherine pleaded with the new Abbot President, her nephew Dom Benedict Stapylton, to seek another confirmation of the nuns' rights to Baker's writings, which were "the greatest treasure that belongs to this poor community."[33] Despite her petition, all the originals, so dear to the abbess and the community, have subsequently perished. Baker's published works live on, however, read and revered by modern contemplatives and others seeking to enrich the spiritual in their everyday life.[34]

English and Irish Nuns Outside England

Many English and Irish families sent or allowed daughters and sisters to go to the Continent to join Benedictine communities. The Cambrai nuns were well known, but there were other prominent individuals and communities—among them the mystic Dame Lucy Knatchbull (1584–1629). She joined the community at Brussels when she was twenty and professed vows in 1609. She founded another monastic community at Ghent in 1624 where she was elected abbess. Holding this position until her death five years later, she wrote spiritual treatises and had her sisters copy other mystical writings to read to the community, including a spiritual tract by the abbess of Elpidia in Saxony.

In the act of copying, sisters were instructed to engage the task as a spiritual practice, each person becoming "a co-labourer with the author or the divine word, reproducing, but also experiencing, the formative force the text."[35] She was favored with mystical graces most of her life, and knew the works of the Carmelite Saint Teresa of Avila (1515–1582) well. Like most of her contemporaries, Dame Lucy was also influenced by Jesuit spirituality and Vincentian spirituality. She wrote that she was personally "greatly assisted in this undertaking" by help from Monsieur Vincent de Paul.[36]

Most of the English nuns in Belgian and Dutch communities were from the landed gentry. The Ghent community also opened a monastery at Dunkirk in 1662 where the nuns operated a school. In 1785, this community absorbed that of Pontoise, a Ghent foundation no longer viable. Pontoise also boasted a mystic, Dame Claire Vaughan

(1656–1687), who was enriching her community by her contemplative experience. During the French Revolution, after eighteen months imprisonment at Gravelines, the Ghent nuns traveled to England where they first occupied the historic Mary Ward Convent at Hammersmith. In 1862, they moved to Teignmouth, closed their school and began the devotion of Perpetual Adoration of the Blessed Sacrament at their monastery. They were permitted to make solemn vows in 1953, but for lack of new members, the community's doors were closed in the 1990s.

The Irish nuns fared much better. They left Ghent for Ypres in 1665 and were soon known as the "Irish Dames of Ypres."[37] Apparently, this congregation was not forced to evacuate until World War I when bombs destroyed their abbey. They took refuge in England in 1914 but in 1916 transferred the community to Wexford, Ireland. In 1922, they occupied Kylemore Castle in County Galway where the community is still flourishing. They staff a secondary school for girls.[38]

Continental Developments

Not many new foundations of women's communities were made on the Continent in the aftermath of the Reformation, yet there were some exceptions. In Switzerland, the nuns from Engelberg moved to Sarnen in 1615.[39] Klosterwald and Lilienberg were new Bavarian foundations. The Austrian government, under the so-called enlightened monarch Joseph II, caused much suffering for the nuns in the late eighteenth century. No woman was allowed to make profession until she was twenty-five, and then only with government approval. In 1782, all but the communities involved in teaching and nursing were dissolved by statute. In France, however, as new congregations were formed, there was an unprecedented monastic renaissance, more brilliant and consequential than elsewhere in Europe.[40]

The Vannists

Pope Gregory XIV charged Cardinal Charles of Lorraine to reform the monasteries of Lorraine and Barrois. After some fruitless efforts, several abbots proposed a foundation at St. Vanne in Verdun.

The commendatory abbot there, Bishop Eric de Vaudèmont, placed his energy and authority behind the task and in 1598 recognized the new prior chosen by the community, Didier de la Cour (1550–1623), who adopted the Cassinese constitutions. Novices soon arrived at the abbey, and the prior soon sent monks to the abbey of Moyenmoutier to introduce the reform there. Pope Clement VIII approved the two monasteries as the Congregation of St. Vanne and St. Hidulphe in 1604; within six years the congregation included twelve monasteries and eventually grew to over fifty. Vannist practice and thought spread as the College of Cluny in Paris obtained Vannist professors and a common scholasticate was based at Pont-à-Mousson near the university, and then transferred to Breuil near Commerçy.

The Constitutions of St. Vanne were certainly those of Monte Cassino: an annual General Chapter with president, visitators, superiors, and a delegate from each monastery. They examined the spiritual and temporal state of the communities and took appropriate disciplinary measures. The Chapter named the superior general for one year, the local priors for five years (six abbeys had elected abbots). The monks professed stability in the Congregation and so could change monasteries. Study, pastoral ministry, and teaching were all undertaken with fervor during the major part of the seventeenth century. St. Vanne also could boast some published historical works of value such as the work of Dom Jean François, who researched and published a bibliography of Benedictine writers, *Bibliothèque générale des écrivains de l'Ordre de Saint Benoit.*[41] Vannist theologians were fewer than Maurists, but—among other writers' contributions— Chardon's six-volume *Histoire des sacrements* was published in 1745.[42]

The Maurists

The most renowned Benedictine scholars of the pre-Revolution era in France were members of the Maurist Congregation organized to unite non-Vannist French houses. The Vannists released Dom Bénard to set up the Congregation, but the real organizer was Dom Grégoire Tarisse, elected the first Superior General at the General Chapter at the monastery of Blancs-Manteaux in Paris in 1618.

Tarisse was commissioned to draw up the constitutions that finally gained the approval of the monks after several revisions. These statutes were successful because they were being lived as they were being revised, making them relevant to monks' daily lives. This capacity for adaptation helped the Maurists endure longer than the Vannists.[43] Dom Bénard died a year before the publication of the papal bulls establishing the Congregation of Saint Maur in 1621. With the favor of King Louis XIII and his Queen, Anne of Austria, as well as that of the Court and the French Parlement, the Congregation prospered.

In 1622, François de La Rochefoucauld was nominated by King Louis XIII and named by Pope Paul V as visitator and apostolic reformer of the Augustinians, Benedictines, Cluniacs, and Cistercians. He organized a task force of monks that eventually favored the promotion of the Vannist and Maurist reforms. The Brittany monasteries and those of the Congregation of Chézal-Benoît likewise affiliated with the Maurists.

The Maurist Congregation numbered 180 monasteries by 1685, including such famous houses as St. Germain in Paris, Blancs Manteaux, Fleury, Fécamp, Marmoutier, Flavigny, and Corbeil. The Congregation of St. Maur reached its zenith at the end of the seventeenth century during the generalates of Dom Marsolle (1672–1682), Dom Brachet (1682–1687), and Dom Boistard (1687–1705). At the beginning of the eighteenth century 191 Benedictine monasteries were Maurist. The Maurist movement contributed most significantly to monasticism and the civil societies with which they interacted.[44]

Monastic historian David Knowles designated the Maurist's century (1630–1730) the "Golden Age of Scholarship":

> The work of the Maurists remains, and may well remain for centuries to come, the most impressive achievement of cooperative—or at least coordinated—scholarship in the modern world. Unlike in the boldness and the wisdom of its planning, the skill and success of its organization, the industry and long perseverance of its execution, and the high technical and intellectual quality of its content, the

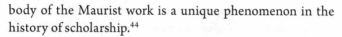

body of the Maurist work is a unique phenomenon in the history of scholarship.[44]

Contributing to their achievements, Maurist monks were to be thoroughly grounded in the classics and church history. They were also constantly being directed to explore a personal interest in some aspect of patristic or historical research. Most of the talent and intellectual activity of the Maurists took place at the Abbey of Saint-Germain. Those monks, whom the leaders considered had promise, were sent to that abbey where the library was continually being expanded to fill the individuals' research needs.[45] The greatest works were generally conceived and executed by an individual scholar who selected one or two younger monk-colleagues as research assistants, one of whom often completed projects if the scholar's death predated their completion. The scholars had access to the resources of the whole congregation in the copying of manuscripts, proofreading, indexing, and the like. Although the Congregation at different times numbered between three and four thousand monks, only about forty were committed full time to research and writing.[46]

Non-monastic historians are also very generous in their praise of the Maurist scholars. G. P. Gooch, in *History and Historians in the Nineteenth Century*, notes that the French Benedictine Maurists maintained supremacy "in the storage of erudition" in the seventeenth *and* eighteenth centuries. He commends them for their works that threw light on almost every province of ecclesiastical history.[47] But Maurist writers did not remain confined to their monastic libraries. They carried on a voluminous correspondence and traveled extensively in France and elsewhere, sharing their knowledge with others.

Gatherings for oral exchange among scholars—monastic and lay—were planned occasions at Saint-Germain. Consequently the abbey entertained a procession of the brilliant, the talented, and the powerful. Among these were Fleury, Fènelon, and Bossuet of the French hierarchy, Colbert, Le Tellier, Chevreuse, Abbé Louvois (son of the famous Council Minister), and other renowned men who resided in or visited Paris.[48]

Dom Jean Mabillon

The contributions of Dom Jean Mabillon set him distinctly apart from his contemporaries and later Maurist scholars. Despite this destiny, his origin was inauspicious; he was born in 1632 to a peasant family in the province of Champagne. A priest-uncle in a neighboring parish supervised his elementary education, the usual mode for poor families. Eventually, he spent six years studying humanities at the University of Rheims, entering the diocesan seminary there in 1650. His monastic vocation seems to have been prompted by a scrape with death when the brothers of his priest-uncle's young mistress physically assaulted him. The emotional trauma following this event, especially the discovery of his uncle's sexual immorality, prompted his leaving the diocesan seminary.[49]

Mabillon subsequently entered the novitiate at the ancient Benedictine Abbey of Saint-Remy near Rheims, which had been Maurist since 1627. He was immediately assigned to instruct the novices, but because of chronic ill health he was sent to Nogent, a small, desolate abbey located between Laon and Soissons. To console himself during his periods of homesickness for Remy, he took up historical research, including an archaeological dig in hopes of finding the tomb of Guibert, the celebrated former abbot of Nogent.

He was later sent to Corbie in the diocese of Amiens, an abbey that—though shorn of its former splendor—still commanded considerable renown. The monastery claimed one of the finest libraries in France. At Corbie, Mabillon was assigned the respective offices of porter, procurator, and cellarer, positions allegedly to prevent need for the excessive mental application so deleterious to his health. In 1660, he was ordained to the priesthood in Amiens and then sent to Saint-Denis near Paris to resume his studies. Apparently his health had improved enough to enable him to make the almost forty mile journey to that abbey on foot during one July day in 1663.

The prior at St. Denis, aware of Mabillon's taste for antiquity, placed him in charge of the abbey museum where many priceless treasures were preserved. Soon, however, the aged and infirm Dom Luc d'Archery, then residing at Saint-Germain-des-Prés, sought a capable assistant who could succeed him. In 1664, Mabillon was sent to the abbey where he would fulfill the goal and ambition of those who preceded him and become the universal Maurist exemplar. Over the years, he produced one after another monumental publication from the vastly researched erudition of his celebrated fame.[50]

On his arrival at Saint-Germain, Mabillon found a great quantity of material sent by monasteries of the congregation or gathered by other Maurists on research ventures. After editing the works of Saint Bernard, Mabillon assisted and then completed the work of d'Archery in the production of six outsize volumes containing the lives of the monastic saints arranged chronologically: the massive *Acta Sanctorum O.S.B.* (1689). All of Mabillon's publications were received with great enthusiasm by the learned of Europe. The true quality of his genius, however, had already become known eight years before the *Acta* appeared, when what is generally regarded as his masterpiece—the *De re Diplomatica*—was published. Initially a response to a challenge, it became the most significant work in the newly arising modern historical method.[51]

The challenge came from Jesuit Bollandist scholar Daniel Papebroch (1628–1714) in his introduction to one of the volumes of his publication on the saints. There, Papebroch propounded myriad rules for discerning what was genuine and fraudulent in certain documents. He condemned as spurious a series of early monastic charters, among them those of Saint-Denis and Corbie. Mabillon saw that the authenticity of a whole class of records was being questioned and set out to extract from all the charters and documents available to him their characteristics of writing, style, form, dating, signature, sealing, and so on. He formulated rules for authenticating various types of records.

Six years later, without abandoning his other commitments, he finished a work that methodically and patiently, and with admirable lucidity and economy, had processed the whole fields of paleography, linguistics, and chronology. Providing abundant examples and facsimiles, he then passed with ease from the broadest principles to the minutest deails.[52] After a celebrated exchange of letters, labeled the Maurist-Bollandist debates by historiographers, Papebroch finally accepted Mabillon's conclusions and the Jesuit begged to be considered the Benedictine's student. Great paleographers of the past and present have proclaimed Mabillon's eminence.

Mabillon was not, however, without other opponents. He had a famous altercation with the most famous of the Trappists, Armand de Rancé (1626–1700). Mabillon's treatise on monastic studies, in which he defended monasticism against the charge that monastic life should be one of most rigorous asceticism, was prompted by the Abbot of La Trappe's condemnation of study as the greatest obstacle to a life of abnegation and renunciation. De Rancé contended that only private prayer, communal chanting of the psalms, manual labor, and perpetual silence made a monastic. He considered pursuit of the scholarly life directly contrary to the spirit of Benedict.[53]

In addition to this theological conviction, de Rancé filled his response to Mabillon with personal accusations. Mabillon refrained from doing the same when he went public with his "Réflexions sur la Réponse," and the verbal battle raged on. A year later, at the instigation of the Duchess of Guise, Mabillon traveled to La Trappe where he and de Rancé were reconciled and affectionately embraced with every indication of mutual cordiality and esteem. In a letter to a friend after the reconciliation, de Rancé commented that only with difficulty could one find together "more humility and more erudition than in this good Father."[54]

Mabillon eclipsed all other Maurists and probably all his scholarly contemporaries. One of his biographers points out the enduring significance and influence of his work, stating, "the present state of organized and scientific historical method traces its origin to the work of Dom Jean Mabillon."[55] Mabillon's celebrated six-volume treatise, *De re diplomatica* (*The Study of Documents*) created the science of diplomatic criticism, contributing to the technique for determining the authenticity of historical documents.[56]

He not only made great contributions to hagiography but also to archaeology. Further, he advanced liturgical studies with the publication of his discoveries during his research tours in Germany and Italy, especially his *Museum Italicum* and *De liturgica Gallica* that included the Luxeuil lectionary and the Bobbio missal, setting him, in the opinion of modern liturgists, in the vanguard of their liturgical predecessors. His publications remain as works of inestimable value.[57]

Mabillon died at age seventy-six in 1707, about six years after the publication of the last volume of the *Acta Sanctorum O.S.B.* and three years before the printing of the *Gallia Christiana*, multi-volume tomes detailing the history of bishoprics and abbeys in France. He had completed the fourth volume of the *Annales*; the two unfinished volumes detailing the history of the Benedictines to the middle of the twelfth century were not completed until thirty years after his death. Subsequent writers of these volumes used Mabillon's research documentation, but progress was slowed due to unexpected deaths of several Maurists engaged in completing the work.

Mabillon has been celebrated posthumously up to and including the present century, but he was also recognized for his erudition during his lifetime. Besides his correspondence with most of the era's literary greats, Mabillon received a request from Pope Alexander VIII to write to him weekly. King Louis XIV named him an honorary academician of the Royal Academy of Inscriptions.

Mabillon's fame has never diminished. In 1907, on the second centenary of death, the coadjutor Bishop of Paris presided over a commemoration ceremony at the ancient abbatial, now parish church of Saint Germain where Mabillon's body rests in a side chapel. Scholars from throughout the world attended the event, followed by a year of scholarly discussion, conferences, and recognition in the press. The Benedictines of Ligugé published in his honor a mélange of Mabillon's works and a series of archival documents, now in the fifth volume of the learned Archives de la France Monastique series.[58]

A scholarly periodical, *Revue Mabillon*, carries continues to publish articles for students of history and modern historical criticism.[59] David Knowles comments on Mabillon's pioneering insight; he possessed "appreciation of the greatness and melancholy of human things and a sense, rare in his age, of the development of institutions and of the movement of cause and effect." His writings, Knowles claims further, still retain their power to move the imagination and enlighten the mind. He "stands next to the Venerable Bede, whom he resembles so closely in mind and character, as an embodiment of the ideal monk-scholar."[60]

Edmond Martène and Bernard Montfaucon

After Mabillon's death, other eighteenth-century Maurist scholars furthered his intellectual legacy. Edmond Martène (1654–1739) and Bernard Montfaucon (1655–1741) succeeded Mabillon's gifted disciple and biographer, Thierry Ruinart (1657–1709).[61] Dom Martène edited two large collections of texts in five volumes and another in nine volumes that were all published by 1733. He finished the final volumes of the *Annales* as well as the authoritative history of the Congregation of Saint Maur.[62]

Montfaucon was an aristocrat who had worn a sword before exchanging it for the Benedictine habit. He succeeded Mabillon in Paris and throughout the world as the chief example of Maurist erudition. A vivacious, high-spirited monk with a commanding presence, he authored many publications, including a fifteen-volume study of the social and art history of the modern era, but he left unfinished a five-volume series on the French monarchy.[63]

With Dom Martin Bouquet (d. 1745) Montfaucon, Martène, and their contemporaries were the last of the great age in which Maurist monks produced an overwhelming number of canonical scholarly works. Most often their publications are the best—frequently the only—source of the type of information they relayed though many still await translation from Latin into major modern languages. Because of the Maurists' exceptional reputation, intellectual Europe began to attach the designation "learned" to all Benedictine monks of the eighteenth century. David Knowles, who can be said to have been describing himself, wrote, "no higher praise can be given to a monastic scholar than to call him a Maurist of today."[64]

Elena Cornaro Piscopia: A Would-Be Maurist

During the Maurist century, a contemporary of Mabillon, who had she been born male and become a monk, might also have been on the roster of great intellectuals of that congregation. On June 25, 1678, nobles, knights, civic officials, scholars, the vicar general, and all members of the University of Padua's College of Philosophers and Physicians assembled at the Cathedral of the Virgin to witness a young woman, the first ever accorded this privilege to stand for her oral doctoral examination.[65] She was an oblate of the Venetian Abbey of San Giorgio and destined to be buried in a Benedictine habit in the famous Paduan St. Justina Abbey.

Elena Cornaro Piscopia (1646–1684), a native of Venice, had a distinguished lineage of noblemen and -women. She is finally being recognized as a pioneering barrier breaker; she was the first woman ever to receive a degree of any kind from a college or university. Born in 1646 to one of the highest Venetian officials, Giovanni Battista Cornaro—the Piscopia name added when his ancestor gained an estate in Cyprus in return for a loan—was the Procurator of St. Mark's. Elena was a child prodigy yet humble young lady who, although she had command of seven languages, is best known as a philosopher and theologian. She was also more than proficient in mathematics, music, literature, and the arts. Having been tutored by the most renowned scholars in Venice and Padua, she had no desire to break the gender barrier at the University of Padua. She agreed to apply for a degree only to make recompense to her father who had, after several attempts to arrange her marriage, submitted to her wish to honor her private vow of chastity. The family had lacked a famous individual for two generations, so he counted on her, the most outstanding among her siblings (who included brothers).

From an early age, she had treasured her association with Benedictines. She and her family rejected the idea of her becoming Benedictine as the Venetian nuns were strictly cloistered, usually unschooled, and not held in high esteem by her family, who had selected another convent for her. Elena, disillusioned by the lack of deep spirituality she found at the convent, treasured the Benedictine life. She was known for truly exemplifying the values of the Rule throughout her life, especially Benedict's call in Chapter Four to aid those needing assistance.[66]

Although she qualified and could initially apply for a doctorate in theology, certain cardinals feared that it would prompt a quest for her ordination. They thus countered that only ordained men could receive theology doctorates; the powers-that-be convinced her father to be satisfied with Elena's achieving a doctorate in philosophy. She was thirty-two when she was acclaimed and unanimously praised for her responses to two complex Aristotelian theories and other questions. That Elena was cheered and applauded spontaneously for the learning shown in her scholarly dissertation, and its astute defense, compelled the judges to declare that the doctorate of philosophy was hardly an adequate honor for so towering an intellect. At the close of the convocation, she was clothed with the professor's ermine cape, the doctoral ring, and poet's laurel crown, titled master and doctor of philosophy as the whole assembly rose to chant the *Te Deum*.[67]

The scholarly world knew of Elena Cornaro Piscopia's fame and erudition so well her oral examination known became one of the most outstanding events in the University's history. A life-sized, seated marble statue now commands the lower end of the staircase near a main door in the old University building. Hers is the only feminine memorial, distinctive among those of Galileo, Albertus Magnus, and others of similar renown. In the Basilica of St. Anthony, a bust remains on the wall to commemorate this extraordinary young woman. Her achievement is also commemorated in the United States with a monumental stained-glass window at Vassar College in New York, and her portrait hangs in the Italian Room at the University of Pittsburgh.

Two centuries following her death, Abbess Mathilde Pynsent exhumed Elena's remains and added a biographical description to her tomb. The abbess later published the first English biography of Elena in 1896.[68] Relatively unknown until the mid-twentieth century, she continues to be honored by American scholars through the efforts of Ruth Crawford Mitchell at the University of Pittsburgh, who organized Elena's Tercentenary celebration in 1978, commemorating her reception of her degree.[69] The marble stone at her grave has again been replaced, and a definitive, lengthy, and well-researched biography published for the occasion by a monk of St. Justina, Francesco Maschietto, was translated and published in 2007. Unfortunately, most of what she wrote was destroyed according to her wishes or has been lost during the past three centuries.[70]

Women Saints, Scholars, and Founders

As evidenced by Elena Cornaro Piscopia, there were outstanding individuals and houses of scholarly Benedictine women. Though many nuns lacked opportunities for the development of scholarship, numerous outstanding scholars and learned women monastic founders emerged during the seventeenth and eighteenth centuries.

The Feuillantine Scholars

One of these scholars belonged to a branch of Cistercians who had received approval in 1630 as the Feuillant Congregation.[71] The feminine monastic branch, the Feuillantines, had already organized in 1588. Their first house was at Montesquieu; another was opened in Toulouse and a third in Paris. A Feuillantine nun, Joanna de l'Estonnac (d. 1640) established another congregation of Benedictine women at Bordeaux, whom she called Daughters of Our Lady. This group, which Pope Paul approved in 1617, spread rapidly throughout France and Spain.

The nuns were dedicated to educating young women, a work they continued until the Revolution. Another Feuillantine, the Duchess Antoinette d'Orléans-Longueville (1572–1618), known as Sister Antoinette of Saint Scholastica became the foundress of the Benedictine Congregation of Our Lady of Calvary in cooperation with the Grey Eminence, Capuchin Père Joseph du Tremblay (1577–1638), mentor of the king's principal minister Cardinal Richelieu. This congregation would ultimately weather the Revolution and survive into the twenty-first century.[72]

Women Reformers and Mystics

Jansenism was somewhat prevalent in the nuns' and monks' monasteries. About 1563 at Saint-Pierre-des-Chases in Auvergne, Madeleine de Foix-Caraman, although a professed nun, was an adherent of the Huguenots' Calvinism and tried to dissolve the community and create a private barony with the monastic dependencies. She failed to achieve this, so she left the abbey to marry. At the Paraclete

Abbey, Abbess Jeanne de Chabot, a sixteenth-century successor of the famous medieval Abbess Heloise, openly professed alliance with the Huguenot movement. The authorities expelled her in 1592. At St. Laurent in Bourges, Abbess René de Lévy accepted the Calvinist gospel also. Before her death in 1564, she recommended that her community elect a nun as her successor, who was known to favor Protestantism. In the diocese of Paris, at Yerres, Marie Pisseleu was appointed abbess by the king but was more than open to the new teachings of the Calvinists. The nuns found this unacceptable and forced her to leave their monastery.[73]

Regardless of personal convictions, many nuns saw the need to join a reform congregation when the post-Reformation religious wars spelled destruction for many houses of nuns as soldiers recklessly raped, looted, sacked, and pillaged villages and monasteries. The Vannists accepted some monasteries of women, but the Maurists refused to aggregate any nuns. Cardinal Richelieu, Louis XIII's Premier and Catholic Primate of France, once ordered the Maurists to accept affiliation of the illustrious Abbey of Chelles. Only two other monasteries, Moulins and Nevers, former members of Chézal-Benoît, were also eventually aggregated. As Schmitz admits reluctantly, "this repugnance to concern themselves with their sisters seemed to have been common to the Benedictine monks of this epoch in France."[74] In 1634, Article VII of the Concordat of the short-lived union of Cluny and Saint Maur stipulated that the dependent monasteries of women organize their own congregation. The monks would take no other charge than that of giving them a triennial visitator. Monks were not to be chaplains, confessors, or ecclesiastical superiors of the nuns.[75]

In 1660 there were 18,000 Benedictine nuns in France alone—double the number there in 1600. St. Pierre at Montmartre led the seventeenth-century French reform of the women's monasteries. Some of the most remarkable women were part of that community. Abbess Marie de Bauvillier, who had been the King's appointment in 1598, was not only a prayerful nun but also brilliant, scholarly, and talented woman who received the profession of more than two hundred nuns and sent over fifty nuns to found other Benedictine monasteries of women. In less than three years, she restored regular discipline in her community and introduced reform in several other French monasteries. Her teachings were published in 1631 under the title, *Practice of Conformity to the Will of God* (*Exercice divin ou pratique de la conformité de notre volonté a celle de Dieu*). She also wrote, "on behalf of Benedictine monks and nuns," a commentary on the Rule of Benedict.[76]

One of Abbess Marie's illustrious protégés was Marguerite d'Arbouze (1580–1626), later abbess of Val-de-Grace in Paris. As a child, Marguerite's penchant was toward the Carmelites. Her parents, opposing this inclination, placed her with the Benedictines of St. Pierre at Lyons. In 1599, she professed her vows and received the name Mère St. Gertrude. (*Mother* is the appellation of all professed choir nuns in France.) Particularly fond of Teresa of Avila's mystical writings, she learned Italian and Spanish to read the current spiritual publications of her day. Mère St. Gertrude continued to nourish a vocation to a more contemplative community and unsuccessfully applied to the Carmelites, among others. When she heard of the new reform at Montmartre, she transferred there and made another novitiate, this time under the direction of Marie de Beauvillier. In 1619 the King appointed Mère St. Gertrude abbess of the royal abbey of Val-de-Grace. She reformed it and many other monasteries before her death in 1626. This abbess was known for her winning over nuns' hearts rather than dispensing terse commands in cases of obedience, yet she required them to spend two hours daily in mental prayer. To facilitate that experience, she composed and published a treatise on mental prayer and a series of daily spiritual exercises.[77] Her confessor published her biography within two years of her death.[78]

There were several mystics at Montmartre, including Marie Granger. She joined the community in 1617, directed the novices for several years, and in 1630 founded the community of Montargis, of which she became abbess. Marie deemphasized mystical states and extraordinary graces, assuming a method of prayer of the heart and liberty of the spirit in God. She was an early spiritual director for the controversial mystic Madam Jeanne Guyon, entrusted to her care at age four and later imprisoned on charges of Quietism.[79] The abbess was also one of the precursors of devotion to the Sacred Heart.[80]

Jeanne Deleloé (1604–1660), abbess of Poperinghe, was also an outstanding mystic and reformer.[81] She was born in 1604 in Artois where she joined the Benedictines at age sixteen. She was soon favored with the gift of contemplative prayer and other spiritual graces. After a frustrating period under incompetent superiors and confessors, she finally received Martin Gouffart (1607–1669), the abbot of St. Denis in Brocqueroye as spiritual director. Her progress became so rapid and profound—and her devotion to the Sacred Heart so like that of the medieval mystic of Helfta—that she has often been considered a modern St. Gertrude. Her autobiography, written at her director's behest, is valued as a masterpiece of religious psychology, and another of her works, *Communication*, related her mystical experiences. Jeanne died in 1660.

The Dutch and Belgians have special devotion to another reformer, though not a mystic, Dame Florence de Werquignoeul—the instrument of a splendid seventeenth-century renaissance in the houses of nuns in the Spanish Netherlands. She was a compassionate, sensitive leader, a woman of prayer and a promoter of austerity in monastic customs. In the name of the Peace of Our Lady she established monasteries for nuns at Douai, Arras, Namur, Liège, Bruges, Béthune at Hunneghem, and at St. Amand. When Dom Martene visited her monasteries, he compared her to St. Teresa of Avila.[82]

Among the Italian nuns who impacted the seventeenth century was another mystic, the beatified Venetian Abbess Jeanne-Marie Bonomo (1606–1670). Her ecstasies, often occurring during the communal recitation of the Liturgy of the Hours, were criticized and often misunderstood. She kept up a voluminous correspondence full of counsel and consolation. According to Schmitz, she had the gift of bilocation, and different persons recounted receiving her personal counsel simultaneously. Without leaving her cell, her biographers maintain, she attended Mass and communicated in distant churches. She is also alleged to have mysteriously appeared to several persons at Loretto, Rome, Assisi, and Jerusalem without leaving her Bassano monastery. She is the patroness of Bassano, where the citizens erected a statue of her. About forty different spiritual works of hers are still extant. One of these was titled *Meditations on the Passion of Our Lord*

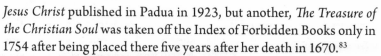

Jesus Christ published in Padua in 1923, but another, *The Treasure of the Christian Soul* was taken off the Index of Forbidden Books only in 1754 after being placed there five years after her death in 1670.[83]

Sicilians have their own beatified nun, Palermo's Venerable Marie Tommasi, daughter of Duke Julio of Palma. At age fourteen she took the veil at a monastery in Palma that she had convinced her father to build. She lived a life of prayer and penance. Her apostolic ardor was satisfied by an extensive correspondence with bishops, priests, monks, and lay Christians. She was favored with mystical phenomena and always identified with the devotion and love of the Sacred Heart. She died in 1699.[84]

The Trappists and Mechitarists

The seventeenth century saw new groups of Benedictines just as most of the previous centuries had. The Trappists, or Order of Cistercians of Strict Observance (OCSO), received papal approval in 1678. Led by Abbot de Rancé, their base was in France at La Trappe. The reform spread rapidly throughout France and Western Europe where religious orders were tolerated. Only on their expulsion during the Revolution would they cross to the British Isles. Eventually, they would establish monasteries throughout the world including Australia and several developing countries.[85]

Eastern Europe also witnessed the rise of a new group of Benedictines. Peter Manuk (1674–1749), an Armenian, established the Congregation of the Mechitarists that was finally approved in 1712. Manuk was a native of Sebaste. He joined an Eastern Orthodox monastery where he took the name Mechitar ("consoler"), but became Roman Catholic after meeting a Catholic missionary at Erzeroum. In 1696 a Catholic bishop at Adana ordained him priest. He went to Constantinople with the intention of founding an Armenian college, but local persecutions of the Armenian minority aborted that project. He disbanded the small community he had gathered about him and sought refuge in Modon, a Venetian possession in southwestern Greece where he built a monastery and church and reestablished a community. By 1703 it had a name, St. Anthony, and a constitution composed by Mechitar. When Rome was requested to approve the new monastic group, Pope Clement XI, referring to Trent's having decreed that no new orders be founded, recommended that the community adopt one of the earlier approved rules. Mechitar selected the Rule of Benedict, so his congregation became known officially as the Congregation of Antonian Benedictine Armenians, popularly as the Mechitarists. The appointment of the founder as the first abbot accompanied the approval.

Just two years after the community began its official existence, war broke out between Turkey and the Republic of Venice. Mechitar, with his eleven monks, was compelled to leave Modon for Venice, where he settled on the island of San Lazzaro, where he built a monastery of that name. It eventually became the head abbey of all European Mechitarist communities. During the first century of its existence, it was the congregation's only abbey. After Mechitar's death some of the monks left Venice to establish a house at Trieste, more in opposition to certain changes in Venice than to spread their observance. In 1810, these Mechitarists received authorization from the Austrian government to establish a monastery in Vienna where the Armenian rite was maintained. The Venetian and Viennese monasteries both had printing presses; the monks spent much of their time and effort translating manuscripts and disseminating information and spiritual literature to other Armenians.[86]

Seventeenth-Century Benedictine Prayer, Study, and Advancement to the New World

All the Benedictine branches—as well as the root branch of Black Benedictines, monks, and nuns following the Rule of Benedict—were affected by a decree published in 1616 by the Sacred Congregation of Rites. It prescribed for all Benedictine monks and nuns who had made solemn vows the *Monastic Breviary*, including the psalmody, antiphons, readings, and the like of the Divine Office, often called the Liturgy of the Hours. A commission of Roman procurators who represented all the Benedictine male congregations had revised it. A dominant influence on the work was the practice of the Rule and the customs of the Congregation of St. Justina, the Cassinese observance. A revised edition of the *Roman Missal* (the liturgy of the Eucharistic service as authorized by Trent) was published in 1624. Several feasts honoring Benedictines were added. The monks generally adopted this as the *Missale Monasticum.*[87]

Education was a notable feature of the seventeenth century as more schools were opened to Benedictines. In the first half of the century, Abbot Constantine Cajetani, custodian of the Vatican archives, conceived the project of establishing a Gregorian College at Rome, establishing it with the approval of Gregory XV at the church of San Benedetto in Piscinula in 1621. More of a hostel than a school at first, it housed Benedictines from all parts of the world who came to Rome on pilgrimage or to study at other Roman Colleges. The pope eventually opened a house of studies at San Benedetto, the historical origin of the College of the Propaganda. The University of Salzburg, founded on the recommendation of Marcus Sitticus, was placed in the Benedictines' hands when its doors opened in 1618. It was a public university with courses in philosophy, theology, law, the liberal arts, and medicine intermittently. Several abbeys agreed to maintain a house in which professors and students might lead monastic life while at the University. It eventually became the residence of many prominent monastics, scholars, and authors from Germany, Austria, and Switzerland before its suppression by the government in 1810 during the general secularization of the nineteenth century.[88]

Abbot Andrew Diodato of San Callisto opened a "Collegium Anselmianum" at the Benedictine abbey of St. Paul Outside the Walls in Rome in 1687 with Pope Innocent XI's approval. It was projected as a university for the young monks of the Cassinese Congregation who were to be engaged in the study of theology, philosophy, and canon law. The professors were selected by the definitors at the general chapters. Theology was taught according to the principles of St. Anselm. Although not of the caliber of the University of Salzburg, some professors received recognition and fame for their scholarship. In Spain, some Benedictines were called to be chairs in famous universities. The Congregation of Valladolid conducted a university in

Navarre for monastic students, where many of the priests working in underground missions in England received their education. Unfortunately all these educational institutions were limited to men. Nuns' education was strictly intramural.[89]

A Portuguese Congregation approved in 1566 eventually included twenty monasteries of monks. The first Benedictine monastery in Latin America was founded by this Union. Dom Placid de Villalobos, General of the Congregation, sent a contingent of monks to Bahia in 1581 where they organized the St. Sebastian community. Soon other foundations were made in Rio de Janeiro, Olinda, and São Paulo. Montserrat Abbey also opened monasteries in Lima, Peru, and Mexico before the end of the sixteenth century. They would expand throughout the seventeenth and into the eighteenth century.[90]

Persecution and secularization took over some of the Iberians and the Latin American foundations in the nineteenth century. Antedating them, however, was the great revolutionary upheaval of the late eighteenth century in France that would spread throughout the Christian world to affect monasticism in general almost everywhere in the eastern and western hemispheres. The eighteenth would be another century of change for most of the world's Benedictines, but especially for the French. ❀

CHAPTER 8

The French Revolution and Benedictine Monasticism

Eighteenth Century

As the Council of Trent responded to the overwhelming decline and suppression of monasteries following the Protestant Reformation, a springtime of spiritual and intellectual life invigorated monasteries. While Maurist and other Benedictine scholarship and theology began to demonstrate the very best of the sixteenth- and seventeenth-century Enlightenment's turn to reason, other less desirable forces exerted deleterious effects on French Catholicism, particularly on Benedictine monasticism.

Since France had remained predominantly Catholic, the effects of the Reformation were less significant in French monasticism than in other regions. English monks, nuns, and other monastic aspirants—driven from the British Isles by Protestant reformers— often established or joined monasteries in the measured stability of sixteenth- and seventeenth-century France. In the late eighteenth century, the roles were reversed: French and English monks and nuns, responding to the tumultuous and sometimes violent political climate, often fled to England for safety. Other monastics displaced by the French Revolution also sought refuge in Spain and the Netherlands. The French Revolution, begun in 1789, brought French monasticism to a temporary close as it spread its complex movement and ideas to other nations.

Revolutionary Roots and Contributors

In the minds of many European monarchs, the pressure of the Zeitgeist toward what later became the French Revolution's pervasive motto, "Liberty, Equality, Fraternity," determined a series of regrettable actions greatly affecting monasticism and Christianity as a whole. For many of the revolutionaries initiating the early nineteenth-century Republican movements, the church and political state were conceptually inseparable. French revolutionaries found defiance of the Catholic Church imperative since it supported the political structures they determined to overthrow. The long-held abuses of monasticism's link with political power thus reaped popular scorn and derision. The Church also threatened monarchs' absolute power and—once overthrown—that of the revolutionary leaders who succeeded them.

Consequently, the eighteenth and nineteenth centuries wreaked havoc with Continental monasticism. Despite the terror, the crises promoted new shoots that blossomed in other regions of continental Europe and the British Isles, and even across the sea to the Americas. While an adequate treatment of the complexity of causes, events, and outcomes of the French Revolution are well beyond the scope of this book, the global importance of this tumultuous era—and the difficulties it initially imposed on monasticism—remain a crucial backdrop to subsequent monastic development in the following centuries.[1]

A few French monasteries had disappeared during the seventeenth-century Huguenot wars, and some were dissolved when the paucity of members made them less than viable. As the French political philosophies supported an increasing measure of economic equality among citizens, large monastic property holdings—particularly when held by such diminished congregations—became untenable. Furthermore, a general anti-Christian sentiment was pervasive in eighteenth-century France during this Age of the Enlightenment.

Voltaire (1694–1778) popularized the then-new science of Isaac Newton and the empiricist philosophy of John Locke, circulating his view of the primacy of reason beyond mythological faith in his writings. Though initially urging religious toleration, suppression of his and others' works provoked Voltaire's angry response. He inveighed against Christianity with a vengeance, particularly condemning the monastic life as irrational and useless.[2] Along with a scathing critique of monasticism, Voltaire and his fellow philosophers generally condemned the Catholic Church as a whole: since the Church was the main support of a monarchy that had sinned against its people, the Church must suffer the same fate as the monarch—death.[3] Count Mirabeau (1749–1791), influential during the early Revolution, expressed this condemnation to the French patriots publicly: "If you wish for a revolution, you must banish the Catholic religion from France."[4] Despite the widespread anti-Christian antagonism, no general elimination of monastic houses took place before 1765.

An Incident of Imprudent Maurist Monks

The complex events leading up to the first anti-Benedictine movements remain debated among Benedictine scholars, but one episode is of particular interest. Initiated by a group of imprudent monks in 1765, the incident occurred at the headquarters of the Maurist Congregation, the famous Parisian monastery of Saint-Germain-des-Prés. Several monks, without proper authority, petitioned the king for some mitigation of the austerities stipulated in their current customary. The men, devoted to study and research, pointed out that they had scrupulously refrained from sacrificing religious regularity on the altar of scholarship. They were desirous only for some modification of their horarium to eliminate customs they felt vitiated the balance between scholarship and religious observance. Although they had been excused from the 2 a.m. rising for Matins, the monks asked that the hour of prayer be moved to 4 a.m. so they could attend. Certain changes of dress were also suggested, with the monks desiring to wear something less cumbersome than their regular garb, then a full cuculla choir habit with ample yards of pleated material and wide sleeves (remnants from the Middle Ages).

Seeking more names on their petition to the monarch, the monks—in true Machiavellian mode—signed in addition to their own the names of several who had died, as well as some of those who had declined their signature or had not been asked to sign. At least a third of the signatures were fraudulent. The monks whose signatures had been forged were indignant.

The substance of the demands and that the king—not the General Chapter—was the recipient of the petition was not a new phenomenon. Yet French monarchs were usually somewhat caesaro-papist; the monks knew that although several of the Parisian Maurist houses had discussed these issues among themselves, the response might be quicker and more in accordance with their desires if they petitioned the king. It appears that going to Rome never occurred to the French monks accustomed to a Gallican mentality that generally separated the French from Roman Catholicism.[5]

Although the monks of Blancs-Manteaux abbey had hoped for the same changes, because of the long-standing rivalry between the two abbeys (Saint Germain had replaced Blancs-Manteaux as the leader of the Maurists) most of the monks denounced the petition, convinced that no good could come from Saint Germain. They even accused some of the Germain monks of heresy, which the latter took pains to refute. The monks' imprudence in allowing this publication to be copied and circulated throughout the provinces, coupled with the Blancs-Manteaux members' jealousy, encouraged non-monastics to become judgmental about something they knew little about—or as Dom Anger states, who "judge things monastic as blind men."[6]

The Maurist Superior General and hundreds of Congregation members sought to nullify the original petition by submitting an opposing one to the king. The controversy quelled only when silence was strongly recommended to both parties by the General Chapter, but the friction between the abbeys spawned a Commission of Regulars by the French government that marked the opening of the general French dissolution of the monasteries.

Legislating Suppression

The National Assembly of the Clergy meeting in 1765—to forestall more state interference in Church matters—called for papal commissioners to investigate reports of irregularities in some religious houses. It had acted too late, and the king had already appointed his own commission to do just that. Five bishops and five royal councilors immediately drew up reform legislation without any papal authorization. A prelude to more extreme measures, the new civic regulations stipulated that profession of vows in French communities be limited to French citizens and be deferred for ten years after the candidates' entrance at houses of religious men or women.[7] All communities with fewer than fifteen members were to be suppressed. Consequently, between 1766 and 1788 over a thousand houses of men and women of various religious orders in France closed.

The work of the commission—considerably destructive to monasticism—was enacted principally by the duplicitous Archbishop of Toulouse, Lomenie de Brienne (1727–1794).[8] With a vengeance, de Brienne, as head of the Commission of Regulars, demanded implementation of the decree suppressing any house having fewer than nine members. Applications for admissions to religious orders plummeted in this insecure atmosphere. The Cluniac Congregation dropped from 671 monk-members in 1766 to 301 in 1790, just before its annihilation. The Maurists' numbers declined by almost 3,000.[9] The commission had suppressed outright a group of eleven exempted Benedictine houses. The fifty houses of the Cluniac Congregation of the Old Observance were also dissolved, but all the Vannist monasteries remained intact. Of the 410 Benedictine monasteries of men before 1765, only 122 remained. By 1790 the total population of the remnant houses had decreased by 24%. Over 45% of the members remaining were over age fifty.[10] Twenty-four Maurist houses ceased to exist. The Commission's decisions, then, further aggravated the decrease in monastery numbers they purported to correct. Ironically, the decree had little relation to the original petition of the Saint Germain Abbey monks who must have pondered and regretted the magnitude of its effects.

De Brienne subsequently used his ample ecclesiastical connections to succeed in getting himself raised to the cardinalate though he was later expelled from the prestigious College of Cardinals by Pope Pius VI for taking the Constitutional Oath of the Clergy. Although threatened by the scaffold, because of his noble birth de

Brienne was imprisoned and died in his cell, perhaps taking his own life. But the damage had been done, and some congregations ceased to exist altogether.

The parallels between the French and Wolsey's English commissions are remarkable. Catholic leaders inspired both, and they eventually set the stage for the radical and systematic suppression of all the houses of vowed men and women in the nation. The English Reformation had left no monasteries in the British Isles; the French Revolution eliminated all monasteries in France.

Charles Maurice de Talleyrand-Périgord (1754–1838), originally the Roman Catholic Bishop of Autun, was excommunicated in 1791 after making the oath to the Civil Constitution that subjected the French Church to the government rather than the Pope. As self-appointed spokesman, he urged the General Assembly to seek the national confiscation of all property of the church and its affiliated institutions to alleviate France's indebtedness.[11] After making the motion, he argued that the nation possessed extensive power so it had the right "to destroy, if not the whole, at all events, portions of the ecclesiastical body, if they are considered hurtful, or even useless, and that this right over their existence necessarily carries with it an extensive right over the disposal of its property."[12] Talleyrand called for surrender to the government of both the persons and fortunes of the Church. He rationalized the extremity of this measure by insisting that such a move would silence criticism of ecclesiastical opulence; he promised the country would never forget this kind of generosity.[13]

Count Mirabeau (whose father allegedly had him committed to prison to keep him from accruing more debts) proposed another motion to make Talleyrand's more palatable. It provided that all the clergy's wealth become the nation's property, which would then be charged with providing for the expenses of worship and the livelihood of the dispossessed. Proponents of the legislation made extravagant estimates of the financial benefits to be derived by the state from the sale of confiscated property. It would, they claimed, endow the clergy, eliminate the national debt and the salt tax, and provide a surplus for a contingency fund.[14]

Anti-clerical members of the Assembly had a moment of triumph when several monks and lay brothers of the Clunisian Abbey of Saint-Martin-des-Champs sent a missive to them during the debates, voluntarily offering their monastic property to the nation. (An offer made without mandate or authority and immediately denounced by Maurist and other superiors.) That not all monastics were opposed to nationalization of their material goods fortified those in the Assembly lobbying for Mirabeau's motion. They encouraged the public to take, without any qualms of conscience, what the "patriotic" monks had offered. To compound the frustration, five more communities— Saint-Lew, Collège de Cluny, Mossac Abbey, Collège de Saint-Jerome-de-Dole, and the Abbey of Bec—eventually supported in writing the Saint Martin monks' offer.[15]

The Archbishop of Aix was more realistic. He urged the Assembly to consider the number of Frenchmen wealthy enough to purchase any of the hundreds of properties to be sold after the confiscation. He astutely noted that the government could never realize the amount of revenue on which the Assembly was basing its hopes, because most of the property would have to sell at ridiculously low prices, a prediction that eventually proved true. Mirabeau quelled some Assembly opposition by amending his own resolution to read: "the wealth of the clergy is at the disposal of the nation." He secured passage of the decree by a vote of 568–346 with 40 abstentions. His original resolution concerned only the property of the diocesan clergy, but shortly thereafter members devised statutes to cover nationalizing the assets of the properties belonging to all religious communities. The men's houses were seized in August 1790, and the confiscation of nuns' properties was legalized two years later. All the dispossessed were promised pensions.[16]

The national treasury issued assignats, a form of I.O.U. to pay some of the claims against it. These notes, bearing 5% interest, could be accepted as payment for church properties offered for sale. The new notes soon became quasi-legal tender negotiable by the banks of France. During one three-year span, forty-four million assignats were issued. They soon matched other French currency and suffered similar inflationary spikes, which regularly decreased the value of the notes.

Eventually, the bourgeoisie bought most of the monastic properties. Some constitutional clergy acquired a few of them. Friends and relatives of the religious often purchased what they could, hoping to restore their acquisitions to the former owners when they could safely reoccupy them. However, destitute peasants of some regions were proactive, sacking the properties before the auctions took place. They claimed that they had been informed that monastic property was at the nation's disposal so, reasoning that they were the nation so identified, they carried away whatever they could from the monastic premises. During the peasant uprisings, the monastery buildings were often burned or destroyed beyond repair.

The town near the renowned Abbey of Cluny purchased the monastery property, but the local townspeople gradually demolished most of that medieval abbey and church buildings. During the 1790s, Cluny's ruins provided shelter for fugitives from the law, whether a priest fleeing the guillotine or an occasional thief seeking refuge. Eventually a school was operated in buildings annexed to the historic ruins, which are now popular as a tourist attraction. Other French monasteries suffered a similar fate, though many were used for state and civil purposes.

Solignac Abbey became a prison for refractory priests who would not swear to the new Constitution of the Clergy. The men's monastery at Cambrai eventually became the archiepiscopal palace. Mont-Saint-Michel was restored as a national monument to serve as a popular tourist attraction, though some monks attempted to bring monastic life back there. Saint Bertin became a public park surrounding the monastery's ruins, Corbie an orphanage. The nuns' house at Doullens was turned into a city hall and prison. Saint Vanne served the nation as a military barracks. Moyenmoutier housed a spinning mill; Gorze Abbey was a workhouse. Saint-Gervais-et-Protais became a reformatory. The huge complex surrounding a cloister yard that belonged to the nuns of Saint Pierre at Lyons became a shopping mall where a gate opened onto a public courtyard frequented by shoppers and strollers. Moutons housed a theater with barracks attached. Valognes became a hospice and Val-de-Grace a military hospital. Bec was a health resort eventually reoccupied by Olivetan Benedictines.

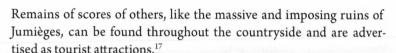

Remains of scores of others, like the massive and imposing ruins of Jumièges, can be found throughout the countryside and are advertised as tourist attractions.[17]

In addition to disposition of monastery properties, the French government dealt a blow to the monks and nuns residing on those properties. The *Moniteur*, the national gazette, printed many arguments concerning the destiny of the dispossessed religious in 1790. The winning argument claimed that religious communities were incompatible with the Revolution's foundational "Declaration of the Rights of Man and the Citizen of 1789" and with the needs of society, that they were "a nuisance to religion, and useless for all the other purposes to which one would wish to devote them."[18]

Monastic professions and all religious vows were declared invalid. Monks and nuns were told that they could leave their monasteries after making a declaration of departure before the officials of the locality. Those departing gracefully were promised a pension. Initially the religious under fifty years of age who renounced community life were to receive a minuscule sum of 900 livres annually; those aged fifty to seventy received 1000 livres, those over seventy 1200.[19]

The government organized "Houses of Reunion" where the religious who refused to renounce their vows were mixed with other orders (Carmelites, Dominicans, Benedictines, and Franciscans) and told to live, pray, and worship together. Men and women from different traditions found that almost impossible and many chose lay life to this alternative. Some group residences of nuns were subjected to mob raids during which the rioters attacked the cloistered nuns, often beating and raping them. In an attempt to discredit and degrade the women religious, some members of the Assembly hired a contingent of prostitutes garbed in religious habits to offer their services on the promenades of the Palais Royal in Paris. Subsequently even the religious garb—the habits of monks, nuns, and sisters—was officially proscribed.[20]

In August 1792, all religious were given fifteen days either to take the civil oath of loyalty or go into exile and become an émigré. Furthermore, the legislative assembly had passed the Civil Constitution of the Clergy bill, which set up a French National Catholic Church.

After lengthy deliberation about this schismatic move, the pope decreed the excommunication of all who upheld it. The French leaders then classified Catholics as juring (constitutional) those who swore the oath or non-juring or refractory (those who refused). Individuals who balked risked trial, often resulting in death at the guillotine. Non-juring priest-monks occasionally operated underground, holding clandestine services in private homes or parish churches served by the constitutional clergy. At Crespin, for example, there were two communities of the faithful: those meeting secretly with the monks of the abbey and those, a distinct minority, attending the services of the constitutional priest. In frustration and despair, one of the Crespin monks, Dom Romain Lemer, eventually left the church altogether.

The National Archives in Paris has preserved thousands of pages of records made by the agents of the Assembly sent to interrogate the monks and nuns. It was the English Reformation all over again. The papal authorities had already notified the religious in 1790 that those who believed they had a legitimate reason to leave their religious houses were canonically free to go. Many did so, hoping it was a temporary respite to be terminated when conditions changed and they could return. Some of these refugees emigrated to foreign houses or reassembled across French borders and reassumed community life elsewhere. On August 17, 1792, it was officially decreed that all religious houses, including those of "reunion" had to be vacated by October 1. This was liberty by force.

Fate of Individual Monks and Nuns

Some religious were unwilling the leave the area where they had lived most of their lives. Thus they, as far as circumstances permitted, sought shelter somewhere in the shadow of their former monastic homes. Others went to towns where they found a sympathetic group of officials, which attracted many monks and nuns to the Paris suburb of Saint Denis. Most of the Crespin monks went to Westphalia where they spent the next years in abject misery.

Imprisonment and Execution

Caunes, a Maurist abbey, numbered seven monks in 1789. Some of them emigrated while others returned to their families. The abbot, the sixty-fifth and last in line, was the aristocratic Dom Vernon, who died an émigré in Spain where he and another monk sought refuge. The Saint Vanne monks fled one night in April 1792. They were threatened by ill treatment or death at the hands of a battalion of volunteers of Mayenne-et-Loire then in garrison in the citadel of the town. When the foreign armies invaded and occupied the area, they permitted the monks to return and repossess their monastery. This lasted only until the French republican soldiers regained the area, after which several monks were arrested and convicted as traitors. The prior, Dom Ghislain Lefebvre, was sent to Paris for trial and execution.[21]

The nuns suffered similar fates. With the exception of the venerable old abbess who died a few months after their expulsion, the entire community of Saint-Laurent-de-Bourges (located about a hundred miles south of Paris) were all detained in prison at Aubusson while the Reign of Terror (1793–1794) ran its course. The nuns were released just a few days prior to their scheduled appointment with the guillotine. Among those was Mère Saint Scholastique who, on her return to Bourges, assembled several of the expelled religious and opened a private boarding school. In 1802 they relocated to a house on the Rue de Jour and reassumed their former community name, Saint Laurent.

Another community that suffered imprisonment was the Hospitaliers de Fécamp. They had remained as civil employees at their hospital until their eviction in May 1794. Only two days after taking up residence in a private home put at their disposal, they were arrested for having refused the oaths of allegiance to Liberty-Equality-Fraternity. After a few moments grace in which they gathered some clothing, they were transported with heavily armed guards in carriages to prison in Montivilliers, about fifteen miles away.

Other arrivals at the prison on that same day included seven Sisters of the Annunciation, two Montivilliers Benedictines, and four lay women. The eight Fécamp nuns were confined to a room where fresh air, space, and sanitation were lacking. Their daily ration was a pound of coarse black bread, occasionally soaked in thin gruel. They were allowed neither visitors nor letters, but they were blessed with an "informer." Once a month, Rose Malandain, a former servant girl at the nuns' house, walked to Montivilliers to loiter casually under the windows of the nuns' single room hoping to keep her beloved friends in touch with the current situation. Her mode of exchange was to engage the first street urchin who happened to pass in a lengthy one-sided conversation, while stuffing him with the delicacies she had brought. The nuns, meanwhile, listened attentively at their window as she related all the current news to the youngster. He was too busy gorging himself with treats to interrupt. If the youth ran off for any reason, the girl would accost another until all her news had been relayed. Thus the prisoners were kept *au courant* of the happenings in Fécamp and throughout France.

After seven months of incarceration, the women were released, returning to a house in Fécamp until 1802 when the town's commissioners pleaded with the nuns to return to the hospital where the administration, finances, and patient care had deteriorated in their absence. They returned immediately, and with the aid from well-wishers could again bring the institution to the standards it had achieved in the previous decade.[22]

The nuns at Saint Pierre, Montmartre, were expelled in 1792, having first occupied two houses in Saint Denis. The day after their departure, one of them returned to their monastic home where the district officials were occupied in transporting the chapel's silver and copper vessels to the mint. The nun demanded and received authorization to load four wagons with wine, brandy, oil, and several pieces of furniture for transportation to their exile. The sympathetic commissioners classified the lot as "articles of necessity" and permitted the courageous nun to leave with the supplies.

Having been reassured that they might in conscience do so, most the Montmartre nuns appeared before the permanent council of the Commune of Saint Denis to take the oath of allegiance to Liberty-Equality-Fraternity in June 1793. Thus, they obtained a certificate of citizenship entitling them to the continuation of payments of their meager pensions that were consistently less than those of the monks—usually between 500 and 700 livres—and seldom arriving as often and promptly as promised. Nevertheless, shortly thereafter, the abbess Marie-Louise de Montmorency-Laval (1723–1794) was executed. With her departure, the 600-year-old community of Montmartre seemed to end, but many years later the name would live on as other nuns reorganized as a Montmartre community.[23]

The community of Montmartre's daughter house, Montargis, remained united and left the country together. The thirty nuns were on their way to Brussels where they had been invited to join a group of English Benedictines, during what was planned as only a temporary stopover in England en route to Belgium. Welcomed by the British Prince Regent, he became their patron immediately upon their arrival. Well received, they decided to remain in England, settling at Princethorpe, Warwick. Much later they relocated at Fernham near Faringdon.[24]

Émigrés on the European Continent

Legislation passed by the French in June 1792 stipulated that any priest, curate, vicar, professor, teacher, preacher, lay brother, or cleric in minor orders who had not taken the loyalty oath was subject to deportation after being denounced by any six citizens. The threat of a ten-year imprisonment or deportation to the swamps of French Guiana hovered over those who did not voluntarily emigrate in time. Within a year, even the formality of citizen denunciation was unnecessary; a resolution mandating mass deportation of all nonjuring clerics who had declined the oath passed the Assembly. Throughout the Reign of Terror, all émigrés who returned to France were subject to the death penalty within twenty-four hours of their arrival on their native soil.

Ordained men over sixty were allowed to remain in France if they claimed exemption from implementation of the law and consented to be confined in designated houses in the capital city of each department, the new provincial organization of the Revolutionaries. Personal liberties at those houses depended upon the local officials who were in charge of surveillance. In October 1792, the local administrators were notified that they had ten days in which to deport the refractory priests to the French colonies. Anyone found on French soil after that was subject to the guillotine. Many monk-priests and other clerics attempted to take ships for Spain.

Some did not reach their destination. Even at the point of embar-kation men were often arrested as they boarded the escape ships. Still others were forced off ships to be drowned at sea while en route. Scores of prisoners boarded only to be massacred. Some escaped across the Pyrenees on foot or found carts to take them into Spain or Portugal. Others went to Swiss or German towns, Belgium and Luxembourg, or the Papal States or other Italian city-states. Although the refugee monks drained the finances of their host abbeys, they found Benedictine hospitality whenever they arrived at monastic houses in Einsiedeln, Fribourg, Saint Gall, or Montserrat. The Belgian diocese of Tournai was hosting more religious than it could sustain financially. At least a hundred monks from the abbeys of Northern France settled there. Another hundred Maurists from Toulouse migrated to Spain.

The monks who remained soon discovered that, as the French troops poured over their own borders into neighboring countries, they brought with them Revolutionary anti-clericalism. As a result, thousands of monastics trekked to Brussels, Swabia, Poland, and on to Moravia. Others crossed to England and, if they survived until 1805, often returned to France where they lived quietly as individ-uals, seldom attempting any community life. The émigrés did not always escape being killed. Two members of the community of the Cistercian abbey of Casamari in Italy were killed by French troops when they arrived. One of these was a former Maurist of Saint Faro at Meaux, Prior Simeon Cardon.[25]

The Prison Ships

Some of the monks, herded aboard ships, expected to be trans-ported to the colonies but soon realized that they were on a floating prison for an undetermined length of time. Some spent up to nine months aboard these floating torture chambers unless death relieved their agony. A few survivors of ordeals aboard two Rochefort prison ships, the *Washington* and the *Deux-Associes*, left graphic tales of life and death aboard the vessels. The *Deux Associes*, a ship with an ordinary capacity of 250, took on four hundred priests in the summer of 1794. When on deck, they could neither walk nor sit for lack of space. At night they were confined in airless steerage, with bare planks for beds. There was no linen, no change of clothing. Old and young, sick and well, even living and dead, lay side by side. Portholes were not open, and sanitation facilities were not provided. The miasmatic vapor would be almost opaque by morning.[26]

A doctor was permitted aboard when disease became rampant. He descended into the hold and returned a moment later, gasping for breath. "If four hundred dogs were put down there for only one night," he angrily informed the crew, "they would be dead or mad the next morning."[27] He recommended a drastic cut in numbers of prisoners, which the death of 112 men had already begun. Eighty-seven invalids were shuttled to two badly equipped hospital ships where conditions were little better. Aboard the *Deux Associes*, the dead soon numbered 245. Finally, at the end of the summer, a little more humane treatment began and the sick were permitted to land on an island. Simple joys greeted them—the sight of a tree, the song of birds, and the timid salute of the fishermen along the shore, and a certain relaxation of surveillance that gave them some liberty to pray. Two monks died aboard the *Deux Associes* though three survived the *Washington*, a ship named in honor of the famous general in and then president of the new free republic so admired by the French.[28]

Marriage or Military Enlistment

Though numerous monastics underwent similar persecutions, another survival option for monk-priests became available after November 1793. The Convention, the French legislative body which succeeded the Assembly, decreed that all refractory priests who married would not be liable to deportation. A former Benedictine was informed that he had three alternatives: "Marry or be a soldier, otherwise you risk being sent to the tribunal of Lebon."[29] The religious caught in the Revolutionary terror often sought means to avoid martyrdom, and there are countless records of monks and nuns who hid when pursued, ministered underground to others when the possibility arose, and survived even into the 1830s. There were also some Benedictine monks who accepted the new Constitutional church and served it as priests, bishops, or hospital chaplains. With the allowance of 1793, many married, thereby avoiding the punishments inflicted upon those refusing military consignment or matrimony.[30]

Uncertain Victims

The title of Christian martyr usually denotes one who has suffered and died for his or her faith. During the French Revolution, many Benedictine men and women who perished were straightforward martyrs who died defending their faith, though others died only as a result of the political quagmire. Like all things related to this complicated time, history leaves little clarity about detailed circumstances surrounding the events. Among the uncertain victims were several who had taken the Constitutional Oath and conformed to the national laws, but then became embroiled on the wrong side in the series of political coups that frequently occurred before Napoleon assumed personal control in 1799. One of these was Dom Estenssant, former professor of rhetoric at the College of Cluny, who was condemned to the guillotine in 1793 as a counter-revolutionary at Lyons. He had been president of the Liberty Committee in that city before his arrest.[31]

Uncertainty also remains over the motivation for the execution of Dom Etienne Mauger of Caen. A former professor of philosophy and theology at Saint Etienne, he accepted a position as curé at Villy-Bocage and later in the town of Saint Wandrille. Entirely absorbed in the new philosophies and a leader of the Jacobin club, he also acted as the village mayor. Mauger was denounced by a former monk of Saint Wandrille, who listed a series of fraudulent charges against him, including association with other former monks. Hoping to survive, the former priest-monk renounced all his ecclesiastical functions and gave an account of all of his actions after 1789. Those who searched his presbytery for incriminating evidence found only empty bottles. Nevertheless, associated with the federalist revolt, he was transferred to Paris and convicted for "conspiring against the indivisibility of the Republic." His greatest political mistake seems to have been writing a tract against the Montagnards, the powerful political faction of the moment. He was guillotined in 1704.[32]

Benedictine historians claim incarceration of between forty and fifty monks during the Terror. After some relaxation of the persecutions, a second wave ensued in 1798 when four Vannists were deported to Devil's Island on the South American coast of French Guiana. Prisoners there fought for survival against floods, mosquitoes, fever, brutality, destitution, and starvation. Others were sent to island prisons off the French coast—all preferable to Devil's Island—such as the penal colony on the Island of Ré, a half-hour by sea from La Rochelle. At one time, there were thirty-one Benedictine monks there, ranging in age from the mid-thirties to the late sixties, representing every French Congregation. Most of the monks incarcerated at Ré in 1798 were released two years later. With obstinate determination the monks could eventually work and pray together. Eighteen Benedictines, including three Vannists, were on the prison Island of Oleron. Their lot was somewhat worse than that of the prisoners on Ré.[33]

The number of actual deaths ranged somewhere between twenty and sixty. Historians claim that perhaps 10 to 28 were Clunisians and between 16 and 40 Maurists. It is certain that fourteen monks died in prison; 62 were deported and over 1,000 were expelled from France. Eighteen nuns died at the scaffold.[34] Outstanding among the martyred monks were the three presidents-general of the Congregations: Dom C. Chevreux of the Maurists (who died in the September Massacres), Vannist Dom Nicholas de Bras (from exhaustion and starvation on a public road), and Dom Jean-Baptiste Courtin, the Cluniac (who was executed at the scaffold). The seventy-nine-year-old president of the Congregation of Cluny was accompanied to his death by two of his confreres. He was convicted of having continued to celebrate Mass and administer the Catholic sacraments in the environs of Saint-Martin-des-Champs, their former abbey in Paris, where they were guillotined.

Another courageous monastic was Dom Benedict Lempereur, former prior of the exempt abbey of Maroilles in the diocese of Cambrai. He spent his last years with the underground clergy ministering to a large number of the Catholic faithful in northern France. He baptized, officiated at marriages, and buried many Catholics during the era when such activity was considered criminal. In 1797, refusing to take the oath of hate against royalty, Lempereur was transferred between prisons until a final incarceration at Douai. He was fifty when he was shot, the legal death penalty for a returned émigré (he had briefly gone to Belgium).

Dom Etton Larivière from the community at Liessies, and Dom Benedict Selosse of Masnon, were also guillotined for illegally exercising their priestly ministry.[35] Dom Pierre Moncomble, a seventy-five-year-old monk of Saint Vaast, had also been in the underground ministry. He was one of five members his community lost to the scaffold. Another, Dom Barthelemy Laignel, exempt from deportation because of his infirmities, was guillotined in 1794 for "attachment to fanaticism." The eighty-four-year-old prior of Benvière, a cell of Saint Vaast's, Dom Maximilian Ansart, was executed for his "incendiary" writings and his refusal to take the oath.[36] Dom Pontois of Saint Vaast acted as parish priest in Mons in 1792 while the Austrians occupied the city. When the French returned, he was convicted as an émigré, exercising ministry under the protection of the enemy. He went to the scaffold encouraging his companions to chant the *Te Deum* with him. A Vannist, forty-five-year-old Dom Joseph Baudet, had publicly retracted his Constitutional Oath after acting for some years as a curé. In a moving sermon he informed his parishioners that he intended to live and die a Catholic; because he encouraged them to follow his example, in 1794 he was charged with and guillotined for "inciting civil war" by "superstition and fanaticism."[37]

Officials discovered the Maurist, Dom Chabanel, former prior of Angers, concealed in a three-foot hole covered with boards. The three young ladies who had hidden him were accused as accomplices and condemned to accompany him to the scaffold in Angers in 1794. Another Maurist, Dom Henri de Noyelle, a former army officer, was forced to flee to Rouen from Paris, and then to Dieppe, Havre, Fécamp, Abbéville, and several other towns. He was finally arrested in Amiens, transferred to Tours, and guillotined there in 1794.[38] A monk of Blanc-Manteaux, Dom Pierre Deforis, scholarly editor of the works of Bossuet, was imprisoned at the Conciergerie and guillotined during the Terror. His request that he might be last to place his head on the guillotine so he could encourage his companions was kindly granted. Dom Etton La Rivière, on the other hand, wanted to be first at the scaffold, perhaps to show how one could die courageously. He asked for the privilege from his companions in the cart on the way to the scaffold after they had chanted the *Te Deum* together. An older Recollect priest, however, argued that, because of his seniority, he should be allowed to die first. Dom La Rivière acceded to his request and to the pleas of the others that he go last. He did, courageously.

The September Massacres

Three Benedictines were among the 191 priests beatified in 1926, some for giving their lives during the French Revolution, by Pope Pius XI. One was the Maurist Superior General, Dom Augustine Chevreux. He had been an elected delegate to the Estates General but had refused to take any of the Revolutionary oaths. He publicly denounced the abuses of the radical officials. Imprisoned at the former Carmelite monastery (Les Carmes) in Paris, he was one of the victims; a monk of Saint Florent was another victim and Chevreux's nephew, Dom Louis de la Touche, was the prisoner's third Benedictine victim of the September Massacres. These were so deplorable that Napoleon himself later called the tragic events the Saint Bartholomew Massacre of the Revolution.[39]

On September 2, 1792, the clerical prisoners were reciting vespers in the cloister prison garden at the former Parisian Carmelite monastery. A band of thirty mercenaries, followed by an armed mob, began assaulting the men at prayer. After killing the Archbishop of Arles and wounding the Bishop of Beauvais, they started pursing the priests around the garden. To save time and facilitate the massacre, the commandant ordered the condemned into the prison church where a tribunal was set up to charge them with the specious crime of treason.

Summoned two at a time to appear before the judges to take the oath to the Civil Constitution, all refused. Then, without exception, they were sentenced to death. While others waiting to be called to "trial" recited the prayers for the dying, the condemned proceeded down the stone stairs where they had been sent and where their executioners met them. Armed with pikes, the assassins stationed themselves at three points, the top of the stairs, half way down, and at the bottom. If the victim was spared at the first level, he met his doom at the second or third. Each execution took about a minute. Among the victims were the three Benedictine monks.[40]

Leaving the Carmelite prison, the mob proceeded to another former monastery—the famous Benedictine Abbey of Saint Germain, former home of Mabillon and the Maurist scholars—where other clerics were being held prisoner. They began a mass execution in the Abbey's courtyard. Though only one monk was on the premises, a Clunisian had arrived at the scene with fifteen other priests, charged with leaving to fraternize with the enemy, who had been arrested at the gates of Paris. As the Benedictine entered the abbey-prison, he noticed, among the civic officials, an acquaintance he had met at the home of a common friend. The friend had confided the large sum of 40,000 livres to the monk, which the latter hoped to return by handing it over to the commissioner for delivery to their mutual friend.

The official, who recognized the monk, devised a scheme to save his life. He conducted him into the office where the clerks were drawing up the records of the day's executions even as they were taking place. Having had no opportunity to explain his strategy, the official placed the monk at a table and loudly bade him write. When the perplexed victim asked what he should write, the commissioner assumed a severe reprimanding tone and commanded, "write what I ordered you and let it be ready for my return." The monk understood his tactics at this point and proceeded to assume a very busy attitude as other officials and clerks mingled around him.

When the ruffians participating in the bloodshed in the courtyard came into the office to complain that one of the sixteen latest arrivals had somehow slipped through the net, they had no idea that their lost prey was the obscure clerk at the end of the table ostensibly preoccupied in copying lists of the condemned. The commissioner-friend of the monk watched for a favorable moment to return, examined the

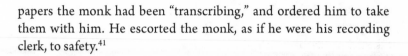

papers the monk had been "transcribing," and ordered him to take them with him. He escorted the monk, as if he were his recording clerk, to safety.[41]

Nuns Who Sacrificed Their Lives

The most famous of the women beatified by Pope Pius XI in 1925 was Marie-Rose de Loye, a member of the Benedictines of Caderousse. She had spent thirty years in that community before its suppression. Arrested at her family home in Sérignan, she was taken to Orange in 1794. There she refused the loyalty oath and courageously took her place among the twenty-nine nuns and sisters already at La Cure prison. For some time the religious women lived a modified community life within the prison, but that soon came to an end. Marie-Rose was charged with being an enemy of liberty, of trying to destroy the Republic by fanaticism and superstition. On July 6, she was tried and convicted of "tending to incite civil war," and guillotined the same day.[42]

Execution of fifteen other Benedictine nuns occurred in Paris, Angers, Cambrai, Arras, Lyons, and Poitiers. The *Moniteur,* a Parisian newspaper, listed among the reports of those guillotined in 1794 a forty-year old Benedictine nun, "J. N. Saint-Sebert."[43] Mère Saint-Cecile, recorded on the lists as Dame Rosalie du Verier de la Sorinière, was forty-nine when she died at the scaffold during the Reign of Terror. Other martyrs include Dame Rosalie Grousseau (68) and Dame Therese Lesage (50) who attempted to evade arrest by hiding in the grotto of Saint Benedict in the garden of their Poitiers abbey when the officials invaded the monastery. The agents discovered them and ordered the nuns to leave their sanctuary. When they refused, the officials killed them.

The eighty-year-old abbess of Saint-Ausône at Angoulême, Madame Marie de Civrac, was the great-aunt of the general of the insurgent Vendean armies who were fighting a civil war against the Republican revolutionaries. She accepted her grandnephew's offer of refuge at his chateau near Bressuire. She then followed the fleeing Vendean army to Angers where she was captured and shot. Another

Benedictine, Mère Marie de Courbeau, was hiding in Lyons after being evicted from Saint Pierre. Because she consistently refused to take the prescribed oath, she was also executed. The noble abbess of Montmartre, Marie Louise Montmorency de Laval, was imprisoned at the Lazare in Paris. Bribed by the officials to betray her, three prisoners reported that the abbess was one of a group planning to escape. After the usual farcical Revolutionary trial, the aristocratic abbess was condemned and executed.[44]

English Monks and Nuns Return to Their Island Home

The first decrees concerning the nationalization of property and invalidation of vows had not been applied to the English monks and nuns residing in monasteries in France. It was in the midst of the Reign of Terror that the Convention finally decided that the English monastics should be arrested as enemy aliens and their property confiscated. Following the decision, the prior and two monks of Saint Laurent escaped as a force of 400 men invaded their monastery one night in October 1793. Four monks were caught, imprisoned, but later released to rejoin the restored community that had migrated across the Channel. Its permanent reestablishment took place at Ampleforth, eventually achieving great prominence in the twentieth century.[45]

During the eighteenth century, the Parisian monastery of Saint Edmund had frequently hosted the American statesman Benjamin Franklin when he was residing in Paris between 1766 and 1784. Though lacking documentation, an anecdote speaks of his reception of a copy of this Benedictine congregation's constitutions, some features of which he later incorporated into the American Constitution. During the French Revolution, this monastery was converted into a prison for French and English monks. They were among the few fortunate prisoners. After fourteen months of imprisonment, they all were released.

The Saint Edmund's community moved to Flanders in 1818 where they occupied the monastery vacated by the Douai monks who had left in 1794 for England. In 1903, Saint Edmund's left Douai for England and permanently settled at Woolhampton near Reading where they retained the Douai name. The original Douai community, which had occupied the site since its foundation in 1607, left England in 1794 to take up final residence near Bath where, as Downside Abbey, it shares leadership of the English Congregation with Ampleforth. In 1897 Downside sent Benedictine monks to Ealing near London.[46]

During the Revolution, Dunkirk was seized by French troops after their victory over the Duke of York. The nuns' monastery was first converted into a soldiers' club, then a hospital, while for some months the nuns remained confined to one part of the building constantly subjected to harassment by the soldiers. The French then put the nuns on a prison ship, destination unknown to the passengers. At one point, they overheard a guard proposing to the ship's captain that they drown the lot of them and save themselves a great deal of trouble.

To the relief of the eavesdroppers, the humane captain refused to dispose of the prisoners in that manner. Most survived the floating prison to endure another long ordeal of incarceration at Gravelines where they were imprisoned for eighteen months. The Reign of Terror ended just before they were to mount the scaffold. The nuns left for England where they were given the historic Mary Ward Convent at Hammersmith. In 1863, they moved to Teignmouth in Devon until a remnant of five moved to Buckfastleigh, also in Devon.[47]

The Cambrai nuns of Our Lady of Good Hope Foundation settled at Colwich in England in 1795. The other Cambrai nuns from the Abbey of Our Lady of Consolation—that in the last century had numbered among its famous Dames Gascoigne and Gertrude More (and had been involved in the Augustine Baker controversy)—returned to England only after a narrow escape from the guillotine. Dame Ann Teresa Partington (1744–1820), a Lancashire woman, had joined the community in France in 1773. When all the nuns in her monastery were arrested, she was the official cellarer and appears to have been the calmest of the community, then led by Dame Lucy Blyde. With her encouragement and some artifice, the nuns took other objects in addition to the small bundle of clothing they were permitted to assemble. The women were subjected to a five-day journey in open carts guarded by Hussars. They faced constant heckling from the menacing crowds until they reached Compiègne. There they were lodged with thirty-two other prisoners in a former Visitation convent.

A month later the two monk-chaplains, arrested with them, were admitted to another area of the convent-prison but were forbidden any communication with the nuns. One of them, Dom Walker, died early in 1794 of a fever which also claimed the lives of many nuns, four of them dying within two weeks of the chaplain's death. Food became even scarcer and treatment by the guards harsher as they harassed the women in a most degrading manner. Early in June, sixteen Carmelite nuns arrived at the prison in street clothes. The Benedictines still wore the remnants of the habits in which they had been arrested. The Carmelites, wearing their religious habits, were laundering their street clothing when they were unexpectedly hurried off to the scaffold on July 17, an event Gertrude von LeFort later immortalized them in her drama, "Song at the Scaffold."[48]

A few days after the Carmelites' execution the Mayor of Compiègne—presuming that the Benedictines would also be scheduled shortly for the scaffold and not wishing to have them wearing their religious garb to the guillotine—ordered the Benedictines to wear the street clothes the Carmelites had left behind. The Benedictine nuns were spared, however. Two weeks after the death of the Carmelites, the Reign of Terror ended with the execution of Robespierre, yet prison life and hardship continued. Food was no longer issued in the prison and the winter of 1794–1795 was so cold that few of the nuns expected to survive. Finally in April 1795 they were released and allowed to go home to England. A Danish vessel landed on the shores of Dover on May 2, 1795, and a sorry sight of sixteen starving, prematurely aged women, clad in tattered French peasant dresses, disembarked. With no visible means of support nor any hope of shelter in sight the nuns traveled to London where the Marchioness of Buckingham and her Anglican chaplain, informed of the women's plight, offered to house them temporarily. They gave them what comfort they could. After two weeks, the nuns were asked to undertake the management of a school at Woolton near Liverpool. Thus, after twenty years, Dame Ann Teresa Partington (1744–1820) and her blood sister, Dame Benedicta Partington (d. 1783), found themselves back in their native Lancashire.

English law still forbade wearing religious garb, so the nuns bought some black material for dresses. They added white neckerchiefs and hoods, completing their understated ensemble with blue cloaks, purple shawls, and black silk bonnets. They began the education of young English ladies. Dame Lucy Blyde (elected abbess in 1792) became Mrs. Blyde in the English press, which reported the reopening of the Woolton School. Despite donations of food and money and a small government pension paid by the English from French indemnities, the nuns' struggle was heroic during their twelve years at Woolton. They next moved to Abbot's Salford and in 1838 to their permanent residence at Stanbrook where they again lived in strict enclosure. Their abbey became one of the most prominent women's houses in modern England. George Bernard Shaw, the great English dramatist, was a close friend of one of Stanbrook's abbesses; some of their correspondence has been published.[49] The reception of the monks and nuns by the English continued to provide the most open and surprising welcome, even to the point of supporting the French religious with token pensions collected from public, private, and Church of England donors. The country that had exiled its religious to France during the English Reformation now received them back with open arms.[50]

Secularization Beyond France

The spread of Revolutionary principles was also disastrous for the Benedictines outside France. All the Habsburg imperial and prince abbeys were suppressed in German lands between 1802 and 1810. The Irish monastery of Saint James in Regensburg, eventually suppressed in 1862, was spared dissolution in the eighteenth century because foreigners occupied it. Saint Mary's at Fulda, a monastery of nuns, also evaded suppression. In Bavaria, the German secularization resulted in the eviction of about 3,000 monks and 2,000 nuns.

The Abbey at Eichstätt has a particular history. Although temporarily suppressed, a few of the pensioner nuns were allowed to remain in the building. When the King of Bavaria received jurisdiction over the city of Eichstätt, the nuns were allowed to resume community life. King Ludwig insisted that the nuns staff the girls' school and reopen their brewery. The monastics acted on the academic offer but begged off the brewery enterprise. They maintained that there were already enough breweries in Eichstâtt. In Austria, following a general secularization, the ancient, venerable monastery of nuns at Nonnberg in Salzburg was first to renew itself. Frauenwörth in Chiemsee and the nuns of Tettenweis in Bavaria also reassembled with renewed vitality.[51]

Switzerland lost Saint Gall—never to be restored except as a national museum—and most of its other abbeys, at least temporarily. The Einsiedeln community had fled before the French invasion but could return after four years. Engelberg was pillaged in 1802; valuable manuscripts were carried off and the house was subjected to heavy financial levies. In 1803, however, novices were again admitted to the community.

Montserrat in northeastern Spain, the largest of the fourteen Spanish monasteries of monks at that time and a viable monastery today, was used as an ammunition depot. The monks had gone to Majorca to escape the invading French armies. The Spanish and Portuguese had to undergo three more periods of monastic dissolution: 1808, 1812, and 1834–1835. The worst was not over for the Iberian monks when that century closed. On July 2, 1936, all of the 250 monks at Montserrat were compelled to leave—and some were shot—during the insurrection that began the Spanish Civil War. Spanish nuns had twenty-eight monasteries and suffered similarly.

Italians lost most of their monasteries between 1798 and 1810. Monte Cassino was pillaged in 1798 and all but two monks fled the mountain. They returned in 1801 when peace seemed possible. Then, Joseph Bonaparte, despite assurances to Abbot Visconti, unscrupulously confiscated the Abbey and all its possessions in 1806. The house was nationalized, and the fifty monks were designated state custodians of an art museum for tourists. After Napoleon's exile in 1815, the Monte Cassino monks resumed their garb and communal life. King Ferdinand I of Naples accorded each of them a minimal annual income of 14,000 ducats. Monasteries were suppressed in the Netherlands in 1796 and much of Hungary between 1810 and

1815. Poland's monasteries were suppressed in 1835. Of more than a thousand monastic houses of men only a few dozen were restored later in the nineteenth century. The nuns fared just a bit better, but they had also lost hundreds of monasteries.

The Napoleonic Era

Although Napoleon seized power in 1799, monastics were not free to reestablish their communities. Even before Napoleon and Pope Pius VII—the former Benedictine abbot of Saint Paul Outside the Walls—signed the Concordat in 1801 regularizing the position of the Roman Catholic Church in France, some nuns were gradually emerging from seclusion. A few could resume their ministry of education and other works of charity and mercy. Some monasteries, which had not yet been sold by 1799, were returned to the former owners. A few nuns had remained together secretly in small groups in the same town as their monastery and were ready to reoccupy what had been taken from them years before. Others acquired their former homes by gift from those who had purchased them in the hopes that they could be returned to the nuns. With the support of the local people, restorations of the dilapidated buildings were begun promptly. The public had missed the nuns' ministry, and those who had earlier benefited from their presence —whether materially or spiritually—were happy to see them return to their work among the townspeople.[52]

Napoleon considered the religious women a social force par excellence, so—although the restoration of communities of nuns was not wholeheartedly supported—they were at least openly tolerated. The pragmatic government had no use for the contemplative communities, but the teaching and nursing sisters could soon acquire legal status. Those not engaged in a social service apostolate could exist only where the officials were willing to ignore them as they reconstituted their communities. The contemplative, strictly cloistered nuns were legally not permitted to admit new members. On the other hand, apostolic organizations were, at times, promoted, as in the case of the Fécamp nuns who were requested to reassume the management of their former hospital in that city.

The Calais community—numbering twenty-five at the time of its secularization—could reassemble quite early, having quietly sat out the Revolution in two private residences. In 1796 they opened a day school and resumed their communal lifestyle. They had managed somehow to survive under the Directorate and rejoiced when they were given the freedom to exist openly under Napoleon's Consulate. Similarly, the nuns at Bourges opened a school shortly after the Napoleonic concordat negotiations began and by 1806 were in permanent residence. Their former dwellings had been divided into lots and sold, so they were not able to reoccupy it. Though thirteen former religious comprised the community, other women interested in monastic life were not long in coming. In 1827 they could resume the monastic habit. Later they affiliated with other houses in the Congregation of Perpetual Adoration.[53]

Several of the former religious of Montmartre, Confians, and Saint-Paul-de-Nancy joined the nuns of Saint Genevieve who resumed conventual life in Paris in 1802. The Caen nuns eventually relocated near Bayeux, after they repossessed their monastery in 1804 but later lost it to the bombardments of Normandy in World War II. A former nun of Lyons, Madame de Bavoz, founded a community at Pradines that took the lead in establishing and restoring many other French monasteries of nuns including Jouarre in 1837. In 1853, at the request of the Bishop of Moulins, the Pradines community sent nuns to occupy the former priory of Chantelle in Allier. These nuns, for financial reasons, set up workshops where they produced colognes and other fragrances still popular in the French markets. Pradines and its dependencies eventually joined to form the Congregation of the Immaculate Heart of Mary (Très-Pur-Coeur-de-Marie). By 1824, two more houses—La Rochette and Saint Jean d'Angély near Orléans—affiliated with the union.[54]

Rise and Fall of New Beginnings

While the nuns were resuming their lives and renovating or reconstructing their monastic buildings, the monks were making several unsuccessful ventures to restore their communities. Dom

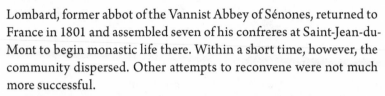

Lombard, former abbot of the Vannist Abbey of Sénones, returned to France in 1801 and assembled seven of his confreres at Saint-Jean-du-Mont to begin monastic life there. Within a short time, however, the community dispersed. Other attempts to reconvene were not much more successful.

Dom Marquet and six former Maurists established a college at Senlis. They sent notices to many ex-Maurists of the intention to revive the Congregation. The government doomed the project when the Commission of Instruction refused to incorporate the college to the university; the college was then closed, and the monks dispersed.

Similarly, several Clunisians vainly attempted community life at Saint-Martin-des-Champs in Paris, but few young men were interested in supporting a general restoration of monasticism. The former priest-monks had become members of the diocesan clergy that assured them of more security as pastors than as monks in a monastery that could not get legal approbation. Many of the former monastics were unwilling to abandon their good positions and run the risk of dissolution in the unstable political environment.

Some monks sought to regularize their life as laymen outside a community by seeking dispensations from vows. Jean Thouvenin, a former Clunisian professed in 1788, wrote to the Cardinal Legate in Paris for a dispensation from his vows and clerical orders. Since he was only thirty-seven, he also wanted permission to marry. The Cardinal informed him of his dispensation from stability and obedience, but that he could not be absolved from perpetual chastity. Many former monks shared this dilemma.[55]

The conceptual unity of church and state in eighteenth-century France provoked political movements against monarchies throughout Europe that often evolved into hostile movements against Christianity. Due to the historically central position of monasticism in the Roman Catholic Church, political oppression usually began with movements against monastics. Since the church was viewed as a powerful collaborator with the monarchial status quo, elimination of the monarchy equaled suppression of its clerical and monastic support. Especially in Europe, the life of the Church deeply depended on the great abbeys and other monasteries whose antiquity represented the continuity of both Christianity and rulers supporting it. Both needed some purification.

The effects of the French Revolution offered Christian monasticism a new beginning. Not only would non-nobles now be able to be bishops in the post-Revolution church, but also monastics would no longer be subject to the *commende* as a general practice. In this regard, perhaps the dissolution was somewhat a blessing in disguise. Monarchs and officials, especially clergy with illegitimate children, would no longer be imposing their sons and daughters on monasteries. Restorations brought a new spirit and vision of monasticism.

Yet there was much to be regretted as well. Many of the great abbeys of the past would never be restored, and the former monastic glory seemed to disappear forever. Much, however, can be learned from this pivotal epoch, and there is hope as one pursues the evolution of monastic life. The undulating rise and fall of monasteries throughout history resumed its cyclic course with the nineteenth-century restoration of monasticism. ✳

CHAPTER 9

Benedictine Restoration, Renewal, Expulsions, and Expansion

Nineteenth and Early Twentieth Centuries

After the havoc wrought by the French Revolution, the Napoleonic period—through the Restoration of the French Monarchy into the late nineteenth century—brought Benedictine monasteries renewed efforts of reform and expansion. The early twentieth century experienced more oppression and secularization in some regions but continued successful efforts in others. In the wake of the French Revolution, monastic restoration and renewal began a new wave of expansion.

Prosper Guéranger Restores the Abbey of Solesmes

The English monks who had returned to their homeland were able to regain their monastic foothold in their country and abroad. The French nuns had succeeded in founding new congregations, but the monks—many of them now pastors in diocesan ministry—had been unable to regroup as early as the nuns did.[1] As Cluniac monasticism and French political philosophy had transformed the European continent, so the influence of French monasticism would be unparalleled once the ancient medieval abbey of Solesmes was restored and revitalized by its first three abbots. Renowned as a model of renewal, Solesmes would influence Eastern and Western Europe, as well as impact the new monastic foundations of North and Latin America, Oceania, and eventually Asia and Africa.[2]

Guéranger's Background

A French diocesan priest from the small village of Sablé just out-side Paris, Père Prosper Guéranger (1805–1875), had absorbed from childhood the traditions surrounding the old priory of Solesmes, just a mile from his home. In 1833, six years after his ordination to the priesthood, Guéranger purchased the old buildings at Solesmes. Prior to its suppression during the French Revolution, the monastery had once housed a thriving community of monks, but it was now only inhabited by transient wanderers. Determined to restore monasticism for men in France, he gathered a small community of men (no former French monks applied), refurbished the old abbey, and went to Rome to seek canonical approval.

At age thirty-two, Guéranger underwent a distinct and brief novi-tiate in 1837. Awaiting permission for the restoration of Solesmes and the appointment of himself as its abbot, he spent ten days at Saint Paul Outside the Walls, a renowned monastery and church built and restored on the site of Saint Paul's execution. Granted permission to restore the monastery, he immediately returned to France and launched the Congregation of France, or simply "Solesmes" as it more commonly came to be known. In hopes of its prominence, the Holy See honored the congregation with all the privileges of the pre-Revolution reform congregations of St. Maur, Saint Vanne, and Cluny even while it was a single, newly restored abbey. The deter-mined Guéranger became the first abbot and president; laymen and priests soon arrived at the monastery seeking admission. French monks again became an influential factor in French Catholicism and European monasticism.[3]

Guéranger was an intellectual, steeped in the Fathers of the Church and passionately attached to the medieval Roman liturgy as the Golden Age of Monasticism. Desiring to restore these ancient traditions to the monasticism of his time, he sought to recapture the glory of the High Middle Ages. He purposed to retrieve the influen-tial force of monasticism's past, reviving at Solesmes the image of the medieval Church, especially medieval Benedictine life. His constitu-tions, customary, and general interpretation of the Rule of Benedict and its applications continued to reflect that premise. Because these became models for new foundations, reform, and renewal throughout Europe and America in the nineteenth and into the twentieth century, the influence of the first Abbot of Solesmes is inestimable.[4]

The Liturgical Restoration of Solesmes

During his tenure as abbot, he published significant multi-volume treatises on the liturgy while initiating the restoration of the medieval Gregorian chant melodies in their purity.[5] In 1865, he commissioned two monks to research and collect the plain chant manuscripts extant in European libraries; the studies were published by Joseph Pothier in 1883 and later revised and expanded by André Mocquereau.[6] Solesmes published the volumes describing detailed historical introductions and reproductions of the principal plain chant manuscripts after 1889. Mocquereau, Pothier's successor as director of the liturgy at the abbey, found in these texts the rules of chant interpretation and reintroduced the ancient rhythms of the Gregorian chant.[7] In 1934, Mocquereau spearheaded the publication of an updated edition of the chants used for daily monastic prayer.[8] Dom Guéranger's liturgical influence is somewhat ironic. His restorative work was coupled with suspicions of liberalism during his lifetime, and he became a controversial figure in mid-nineteenth century in religious and political circles. An early associate of the famous Catholic liberals Lammenais, Lacordaire, and Montalembert, he eventually distanced himself and assumed leadership of the conservative *ultramontaines* devoted to Pius IX. More recently, the liturgical reforms of the Second Vatican Council of the mid-twentieth century—often rejected by Roman Catholic traditionalists—owe much of their impetus to Guéranger's restoration.

The membership of Solesmes Abbey soared, allowing the monastery to make two foundations during Guéranger's lifetime. The Solesmes monks first reoccupied the oldest Western European monastery at Ligugé, allegedly founded during the fourth century by Martin of Tours, in 1853. Through a friend's mediation, Solesmes also acquired property in Marseilles in 1865. The monastery, Sainte-Marie-Madeleine, relocated to Hautecombe in Savoy in 1922. It had been a pre-Revolution Cistercian house, where the royalty of Savoy were often interred. Before the end of the century the Congregation established five more monasteries: St. Paul at Wisques (1889); a house of studies in Paris, Sainte-Marie (1893); St. Anne at Kergonan in Brittany (1897); the ancient abbey of Glanfeuil (reoccupied in 1894); the medieval Fontenelle, St. Wandrille (restored in 1894).[9]

Nuns of Solesmes

Abbot Guéranger initiated another project in the 1860s: the establishment of a monastery of nuns at Solesmes. A small group of devout laywomen, assembled at a local residence in the village, followed the leadership of Guéranger's intelligent, twenty-one-year-old protégé, Cécile Bruyère (1845–1909). The abbot himself instructed this group of postulants about the basics of Benedictine life. Within three years, Cécile made her profession of vows and was installed as abbess two years later. Abbess Cécile proved an outstanding spiritual and intellectual leader among the Benedictine nuns in France. She researched and contributed to Delatte's biography of Guéranger and other Solesmes publications. Within the next twenty-eight years, the women's abbey, named Sainte-Cécile, established two foundations to accompany those of the Solesmes monks: at Wisques (Notre Dame) and Kergonan (Saint-Michel). They all became part of the Congregation of Solesmes, though the women had limited rights and privileges.[10]

Another group of women, non-cloistered active nuns, were closely affiliated with the Congregation of France. In contrast to the contemplative life under strict enclosure lived by the nuns related to Solesmes (most French nuns spoke to visitors through the grille in the parlors) these women dedicated their lives to the care of the poor, offering a range of services. Their founder, Dom Camille Leduc of Solesmes (1819–1895), called them Servants of the Poor and established their motherhouse at Angers. They lived and worked among the neediest, operating dispensaries at various centers in large cities and going out alone to tend to the sick and poor in their homes. The members of the Congregation took simple vows, rather than the solemn vows solely permitted cloistered nuns.[11] Additionally, five more

French monasteries of nuns eventually adopted the constitutions Dom Guéranger wrote for the nuns in Solesmes, though they were never part of the Congregation of France (Solesmes).[12]

The French Foundation at Pierre-Qui-Vire

Another French diocesan priest-founder was Jean-Baptiste Muard (1809–1854). In 1850 he brought a Trappist spirit to his French foundation at Pierre-qui-Vire, a monastery destined to head the French province of the Congregation of Subiaco. Muard and his first companions made their novitiate at the Trappist Abbey of Aiquebelle. They admired and absorbed the spirit there and adopted it when they organized their own community.[13] At Pierre-qui-Vire the monks combined their contemplative lifestyle with biblical studies and parish ministry, maintaining an atmosphere of rigorous asceticism in both. Muard died prematurely at forty-five, perhaps exhausted by his austere life and energetic labors. Since Rome judged that the Trappist customs at Pierre-qui-Vire were incompatible with their active ministry, Muard's successor was unable to receive approval for the constitutions Muard had written for the monastery.

The Abbey solved this dilemma in 1859 by aggregating to the new Cassinese Congregation of Primitive Observance, presently called the Congregation of Subiaco. Pierre-qui-Vire received approval after adopting its statutes. That same year they could open another house, Saint-Pierre in Oise at Béthisy, and several more daughterhouses eventually joined the Province. In 1865 three monks were sent to serve the parish church of the great medieval abbey of Saint-Benoît-sur-Loire where they began a modified monastic life with their parish ministry.[14]

Several nuns' communities also associated with the monks of the Subiaco Congregation. These monasteries were under the jurisdiction of the neighboring abbots, who in lieu of the bishops acted as the nuns' ecclesiastical superiors and usually presided over the elections of the community superiors. Before the close of the eighteenth century, forty-three monasteries of Benedictine women had been restored or newly founded. Most belonged to the Congregations of Solesmes, Subiaco, or the Servants of the Poor. Flavigny,

Fécamp, Mantes, and Igoville were under the jurisdiction of the diocesan bishops.

Political Instability and the French Monasteries

France became a haven for refugees during Europe's general secularization in the latter part of the century. Among these were Swiss monks expelled from Mariastein by the anti-clerical cantonal government of Soleure in the diocese of Basel. The community settled at Delle in the Belfort prefecture.[15] The sixteen French monasteries restored or newly founded in nineteenth-century France always maintained something of an extra-legal existence. The government never authorized the congregations, which was a statutory requirement, though they were openly tolerated until 1880. Some of the men's apostolic orders engaging in educational endeavors outside their own houses were authorized.

Similarly, Napoleon I had authorized 265 houses of sisters and nuns of various orders before 1815, considering them useful as educators and nurses. Regardless of their civil authorization, religious communities survived and expanded in the midst of France's unstable political system.[16]

Napoleon III's Minister of Cults, a member of the monarch's inner council, attempted to stem the expansion of religious communities. He claimed that Rome was aiming to dominate France through the clergy and religious men and women. The political climate affecting the monasteries worsened after the Empire fell. The French Senate and Chamber of Deputies of the Third Republic seated a majority of anti-clericals in its chambers in 1876 and 1877. To the radical Republicans, clericalism was a designated enemy. The Church was seen as pro-monarchical and therefore anti-Republican, a concern heightened after attempts had been made to put descendants of the Restoration monarchs back on the throne.

There was a call to arms against the threat of a theocracy. Throughout this tumultuous era, church officials were not blameless. Although some leading Catholic statesmen were vocal in defense of religious communities, many bishops, priests, and some of the religious still

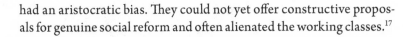

had an aristocratic bias. They could not yet offer constructive proposals for genuine social reform and often alienated the working classes.[17]

The French Laic Laws, 1880–1905

Overt political moves against the educational influence of religious orders began after the elections of 1879 during the premiership of Jules Ferry. The Premier proposed a bill that would curtail religious control of education; a provision stipulated that no member of any legally unauthorized congregation would be allowed to teach students at any level. The reaction was immediate, with almost two million citizens signing petitions advocating rejection of the bill. For a short time, even the monarchists and Bonapartists forgot their differences to join the defense of the 100,000 women and 9,000 men affected by the legislation. The Chamber, however, bowed to the popular pressure and that of the executive: it passed the entire bill except the article concerning the religious teachers. The remnant became law in March 1880. The law limited the conferring of degrees to the state, making students in private institutions take state examinations to obtain their degrees. To avoid confusion with the state schools, private institutions of higher learning could no longer use the title "university." Therefore the Catholic University of Paris became and remains known as the Institut Catholique.[18]

Religious suppression that could not be done by legislation was accomplished by executive decree. The Premier, with questionable legality, decreed suppression of the Jesuits and all congregations that did not apply for authorization.[19] In response, forty-five superiors and delegates from the various male communities met at the Oratory in Paris to determine their course of action. They resolved unanimously to remain united in a common refusal to seek authorization. Also in protest, there were mass resignations of lay officials in the courts and law enforcement agencies. Many others simply refused to enforce the mandates against the religious.[20]

Ninety civil suits were initiated within three months. The Jesuits, however, were expelled immediately. Eventually over five thousand men from twenty-six communities of various orders were expelled from their religious houses. The government did not yet suppress the congregations of women, most likely due to their popularity.[21]

The Solesmes Expulsion

The Solesmes monks were among those expelled. The religious drama seemed to be combined with a bit of theater, according to one biographer.[22] Abbot Charles Couturier, Guéranger's immediate successor, led the community at the time of this first post-Revolution expulsion. According to a Parisian news report on November 19, 1880, in *Le Temps*, a detachment of 200 men arrived at the abbey at 4 a.m. Like a full-scale police exercise, six brigades of gendarmes were simultaneously stationed on the roads leading to the abbey to detour the traffic. Not until 6:15 a.m., however, did the subprefect and secretary general finally demand that the monks open the main entrance. Abbot Couturier refused the request. By 8 a.m. the officials had forced the first door and made inroads on the piles of stone and planks behind it. A second door also was forced open before the invaders could enter the abbey proper. The first monk they encountered resisted, so the police carried him out. The same scene was repeated as they forcibly evicted the occupants of fifteen of the monks' cells.

It was noon when those engaged in the assault realized that sixty-seven more monks were somewhere in the abbey needing transport off the premises. They eventually discovered all but six of them in the chapel chanting psalms as the Solesmes and Sainte-Cécile abbey pealed the tocsin. It took another hour and a half to break down the barricades and door to the chapel to reach the men seated in the choir stalls. Several women—including a benefactress, the Duchess of Chevreuse—were also present in the chapel. It took twenty-five gendarmes to free the subprefect from the women who had launched an assault against him. Apparently, these women did not have the same commitment as the monks to passive, nonviolent, resistance.

After subdual of the women, the abbot read the formula of excommunication to the intruders; undaunted, the agents of the law proceeded to follow their orders. The women were evicted first, and then the monks were carried out individually. It was 3:30 p.m. when the abbot, carrying the Blessed Sacrament, appeared at the door of the monastery. Ironically the troops, following the Concordat of 1801 to the letter, rendered military honors as the abbot passed through their ranks with the Eucharist.

The officials then returned to expelling the last of the monks. Some monks were still barricaded in the bell tower, having destroyed several steps of the staircase behind them to make the assault more difficult. After three more doors and a trap door were all forced, all monks were on the street. It was about fourteen hours after the arrival of the first officials on the monastery grounds. Some of the nonviolent resisters continued their efforts, with about eight monks prostrating themselves across the path of the officers saying they would have to pass over their bodies. Ultimately, all the Benedictines were forcibly removed. The officials affixed state seals on the abbey doors and left amid abusive shouts of onlookers sympathetic to the monks.[23]

After the expulsion, the monks dispersed to homes of friends and relatives in and near the monastery. Several remained to serve as chaplains and to assist the nuns of Sainte-Cécile. At one point the monks were in twenty-two different shelters, eating in three separate dining rooms, and meeting at the parish church for Matins at 4:30 each morning, daily Mass, and evening vespers. The abbey buildings stood empty until about twenty monks (including those individuals listed as legal proprietors of the monastic property), the ill, the librarians, and several lay brothers soon reoccupied the older part of the monastery. The wax seals placed on the property melted away in a suspiciously short time, and by March 1882 all the monks had quietly resumed domicile in the monastery only to be expelled anew before the end of the month. After filtering back in again, they underwent a third expulsion in June 1885. At that point, the government undertook the costly process of reinforcing with iron the 160 wax seals on the doors and furniture. Five gendarmes and a brigadier took up residence to prevent the return of the monks.[24]

Abbot Delatte, who had succeeded Couturier, took advantage of a more tolerant milieu in 1894, petitioning sympathetic local officials if he might build a residence for the refugee monks adjoining the old wing of the abbey. The scheme led eventually to reoccupation of the old *and* new monastery wings. Making room for the monks, the gendarmes were gradually shifted into smaller and smaller quarters until they gave up in disgust and left the premises.[25] New members continued to petition, be accepted, and make monastic profession, swelling the ranks of the congregation despite the unstable situation at the abbey. There were enough men to honor the request of the former Empress Eugénie, widow of Napoleon III, who asked for monks to form a community at an English monastery built for the tombs of her husband and son. At the site of the ancient Farnborough Abbey near Portsmouth, French Premonstratensian Canons had first been entrusted with the mausoleum, but in 1895 the monks of Solesmes replaced them.[26]

With a bit less resistance, all the monks in France were evicted in the 1880s. In some cases this promoted monastic expansion abroad. Ligugé restored the tenth-century abbey of Silos in Spain to use as a refuge. Though most of those monks eventually returned to France before 1900, the nucleus of a permanent foundation was left behind. Located near Burgos, the Solesmes Congregation abbey of Silos opened a dependent daughter-house priory housing nine monks in Madrid.[27] In 1882, the novices of the abbey of Pierre-qui-Vire were sent to reoccupy the pre-Reformation Cistercian abbey of Buckfast in England. Most of them returned in 1890 to France, but some remained and new members assured its permanence. The monks of Belloc were evacuated for one night only. The day after their expulsion they reentered the monastery by crawling back through the windows. By 1895, expelled French monks had reoccupied all their abbeys and were living in relative peace, which would be shattered again within a decade.[28]

Taxation and Secularization

Taxation imposed a significant burden on French monasteries of the nineteenth century. Even the authorized monasteries of nuns were affected by tax legislation passed in December 1880. Not only were all taxes for everyone raised a percentage point, but an additional complex inheritance tax specifically aimed at members of religious orders was also newly legislated. Upon the death of any member of a religious community, a tax was to be computed on that member's presumed proportional share in the community's property. The government reasoned all should be subject to inheritance tax after the dead member's goods were distributed to other occupants of the house. The national levy was set at 5% of gross value; if one of a fifty-member monastery died, 1/50th of appraised value of the total assets was to be taxed at 5%. After the next member died, it would be 1/49th of the total gross value, and so on. The levy was prohibitive for all monastics. Furthermore, it involved meticulous calculation and was complicated to collect. An overwhelming number of appeals for exemption from payment soon plagued the courts. After five frustrating years, the tax was converted in to a regular annual levy. This amounted to 2% of an arbitrary revenue figure. Being unable to pay, the majority of the houses successfully ignored the legislation.[29]

Other legislation burdened religious orders in France. Between 1882 and 1901, the government secularized hundreds of private Catholic schools where religious women comprised a majority of the instructors. After 1882 all private schools were denied the state subsidies on which they had depended for much of their financing. Instead of crippling the schools, however, the anti-clericals watched in consternation as the system continued to expand at an unprecedented rate. In Paris alone, donations from the public supported the opening of 126 additional schools for 50,000 children. Similar events occurred in the provinces.[30] The Vatican protested the nationalization of the French schools, but its worst fears were soon realized as a new premier assumed power in 1899. The cabinet became dominated by anti-clerical Republicans fearing the church's power to restore the monarchy. Some legislators felt the only remedy would be to curb the church's influence entirely. Thus, the stage was set for legislation that would ultimately lead to the twentieth century's complete separation of church and state in France.

Nineteenth Century Reforms in Italy

The Italian Cassinese Superior General, Peter Francis Casaretto

(1810–1878), viewed reform of the Italian monasteries in his congregation as his primary goal. Encouraged by Pope Gregory XVI—who had appointed him abbot—he wanted to reestablish the communal life in a more traditionally monastic mode while still being involved in the missionary apostolate. Casaretto's renewal observance was characterized by fiscal reforms dealing with more communal sharing, banning the customary peculium (individual spending money). Daily life was also to be renewed by making choral office obligatory day and night. Monks were to abstain from eating meat. He addressed other aspects of daily life and tightened restrictions in the monastic lifestyle.

Resistance and Political Ferment

Initially Monte Cassino and Subiaco—then led by Abbot Casaretto—were united in the effort to restore strict observance, though ultimately they charted different courses. Casaretto met a great deal of hostility from some monastics as he pushed his reforms. In the Piedmont, it almost amounted to persecution. When monasteries in Flanders, France, and Spain joined the congregation, what became an inevitable separation of Subiaco from the Cassinese took place. The division completed in 1867 when the monasteries that followed Subiaco's new reform were organized into four provinces (French, Italian, Spanish, and Anglo-Belgian) in a new Congregation of Primitive Observance, later known as the Subiaco Congregation. Structure was changed in the new congregation. Superiors of abbeys were to be named for three-year terms by the general chapter. Priories had no elections; the provincial chapter appointed the priors. Since each province was to have a house of studies, the monastery of St. Ambrose in Rome opened its doors after 1861 to the congregation's student monks attending Roman universities.

Pius XI approved the constitutions of the congregation in 1872. The political crises in Italy, the national unification of the peninsula in 1861 under Cavour, and the occupation of Rome in 1870 hastened the approval. It was just in time. Many of the congregations' monasteries were closed two years later. The political situation and internal dissension prompted Casaretto to resign in 1875, with his disciple, Raphael Testa, named as successor. Shortly thereafter, a commission of cardinals was charged to investigate internal problems in the congregation's houses, particularly related to the concentration of authority at Subiaco. The commission president, Cardinal Franzelin, presided over a general chapter in 1880 that amended the constitutions of 1867. The changes stipulated that abbots were to be elected for life by their communities. Monks were to promise stability in their own houses rather than to the entire congregation, and visitators and consultors were to be elected by the provincial chapters, not the general chapter. The Holy See approved the new constitutions in December 1880.[32]

The Italian Laic Laws

Following the unification of Italy by the Kingdom of Sardinia, the new government moved against the monasteries. By 1861, laic laws attempted to eliminate all religious houses, and all houses of men and women religious were forbidden to receive novices in 1876. The Italian women suffered more suppressions than the men. At times some of the nuns were allowed to remain on a small pension in a restricted area of their monasteries, but the majority were suppressed or remained threatened by future suppression. The only houses that expanded and flourished were those of nuns who had come from France to seek refuge in Italy after 1880, such as the Congregation of the Blessed Sacrament in Milan, which became a thriving house of study under Catherine Lavizzari (1867–1931). With numerous foundations made throughout Italy, this French congregation organized a strictly Italian federation of the Blessed Sacrament.

The women's monastery Arpino in the province of Frosinone exemplifies many of these 1860s and 1870s Italian houses. When the monastery was ordered to be suppressed in 1861, there were twenty-seven nuns. Of these twenty-two were choir nuns, four were lay sisters, and three were externs, those who did the monastery business and dealt with people outside the walls. These three classifications were prevalent in the nineteenth and twentieth centuries in most continental monasteries of cloistered Benedictine nuns, while the monks simply had ordained choir monks and lay brothers. The choir nuns expelled from Arpino all received the same pension, the lay and externs half that of the choir nuns.

The difference was rationalized in that the choir nuns generally brought dowries to the monasteries on their entrance, whereas the others did not. Seven nuns and the abbess of Arpino immediately opted for lay life. When only five nuns remained in the suppressed monastery, the Civil Commune listed the house for sale. Some of the nuns' friends bought it at a modest sum and returned it to the previous owners. Communal life, however, was not fully restored until 1908. About seventy other houses of Benedictines and other orders eventually reopened in Italy, though only five of these had over thirty members. Most of the nuns were constantly faced with destitution for decades, some for a century thereafter.[32]

Secularization in Spain and Portugal

After the expulsion of Napoleon's brother and French troops, Spanish national and political instability created an anti-monastic climate. The Cortes (national parliament) passed legislation mandating suppression of all religious orders in 1820. The Nuncio notified the monks and nuns that their vows were dispensed if they wished to laicize, though Ferdinand VII abrogated the law three years later. Then, in 1835, a new decree promoted by the Minister of Finance, Juan de Mendizabal, again called for the dissolution of all houses of religious communities.

A year later the Cortes restricted this mandate to houses that had fewer than twenty members. Local officials ignored or enforced the legislation at will. Another revolution in 1868, which dethroned Queen Isabella II, spelled a rash of temporary closures. With meager pensions the nuns particularly were condemned to live on a subsistence level.

In Portugal the closures came in 1834. Religious men and women—including those of the famous abbey of Montserrat—were deprived of their monasteries and possessions. Most houses would never be restored; a few would reappear only a century later just in time to suffer the expulsions and executions during the Spanish Civil War.

Expansion of German-Language Monasteries

The German-speaking Bavarian, Austrian, and Swiss monks and nuns would be most successful in Benedictine expansion in Europe and, subsequently, in the Americas, Asia, and Africa. With the accession to the Bavarian throne of King Ludwig I in 1825, the Benedictines gained a friend and a protector. The first abbey reoccupied was Metten. In 1803, Count Pronath had purchased the buildings constructed in the seventeenth and eighteen centuries (fire had destroyed the medieval structures). He gave them to Ludwig in 1830, hoping that he would sponsor their restoration. However, the king's minister questioned the "usefulness" of monks dedicated to asceticism and prayer. After a visit to Metten, he recommended to his King that the monks be encouraged to establish a school so they would be of more benefit to Bavaria. The king was amenable since Benedictines had a long and renowned history as educators.[33] The king was also aware that the Benedictines had brought faith and learning to the German lands in the Middle Ages. Education, he realized, was a proper, traditional ministry of Benedictine monks and nuns. The royal ministers then proposed to restore another abbey, St. Stephen in Augsburg, and there reinstitute the college the monks had staffed before the 1803 suppression. In 1834, the Metten monks made St. Stephen's a dependency and began administration of Ottobeuren, which had gained prestige for its rich collection of art treasures.

In 1838, again at the request of King Ludwig I, Metten undertook the restoration of monastic life at the twelfth-century abbey of Scheyern. This community opened a college and flourished so rapidly that the archdiocese of Munich-Freising confided to it part of the episcopal minor seminary. Scheyern was also a pilgrimage center as it claimed a relic of the Holy Cross. Like Metten, it soon acquired pastoral ministry responsibilities that helped support the works of education. Metten assisted the foundation of St. Boniface in Munich in 1835 and then acquired another donation of Ludwig's, the dependent priory at Andechs (still famous for its brewery). St. Boniface was raised to abbey rank in 1859. In 1866 Ludwig began the restoration of the medieval abbey of Schäftlarn—the Bavarian government had in 1803 looted its priceless manuscripts and music-scripts—that he had purchased a year earlier. There, a secondary school with boarders became the monks' main labor. This priory was eventually raised to abbatial rank and other foundations followed. In 1842, the Metten monks restored the monastery of Weltenburg on the Danube, founded in the seventh century by the monks of Luxeuil. Pius IX approved the Bavarian Congregation in 1858 after it had expanded overseas to the North American continent.[34]

Beuron Abbey

Five years after the approval of the Bavarian Congregation of Metten and its foundations, another was being organized—the Beuronese. Beuron Abbey was a medieval foundation of the Augustinian Canons. After being almost destroyed in the Thirty Years War, it was rebuilt in the eighteenth century, but the Augustinian community was evicted in 1802. The buildings passed into the hands of Princess Catherine of Hohenzollern-Sigmaringen, who aided another diocesan priest-turned-monk, Maurus Wolter (1825–1890)—a German Guéranger—in its reestablishment. Wolter restored the monastery and organized a Benedictine community to occupy it.

Maurus Wolter and his brother Placid were natives of Bonn. After ordination as a diocesan priest, Wolter and his brother became monks at Saint Paul Outside the Walls in Rome. Encouraged by Pius IX, and in response to the urging of Princess Catherine, the two brothers left Rome in 1860. They visited Solesmes where they became disciples of Dom Guéranger, seeking his counsel and benefiting from his experience in the organization and structure of the French Congregation. Especially impressed by the abbot's devotion to the restoration of the chant and the Benedictine liturgy, the brothers took up residence in Beuron in 1863 determined to achieve their goal: the renewal of monastic life in the spirit of the Middle Ages. This, they were convinced, could be accomplished only by the cultivation of an intense liturgical life.[35]

According to Knowles, Beuron translated Solesmes "into the German mode."[36] With great intensity, the monks undertook the study of the liturgy and the monastic life. Within the next two decades, Abbot Maurus Wolter succeeded in publishing a five-volume commentary on the psalms and a study of the principles of monastic life.[37] Although the Beuronese Congregation was organized in 1878 it received final approval of its constitutions only in 1894.

The *Kulturkampf,* Chancellor Bismarck's anti-Catholic movement designed to subject church to state, expanded the congregation by exiling the monks to places they could flourish. Several monks were welcomed in England at Erdington by the Benedictine bishop of Birmingham, Monsignor Ullathorne. The majority went to Prague in 1880 where they restored the ancient abbey of Emmaüs.

Others sojourned at Seckau in Styria, Austria in 1883. Still others began the restoration of the German medieval abbey of Maria Laach in 1892. This picturesque Rhineland abbey was destined to become another leader of the liturgical movement when Abbot Ildefonse Herwegen (1874–1946) led the community during its zenith in the twentieth century.[38]

After the foundation in Belgium at Maredsous by the monk Hildebard de Hemptinne and the return of the community to Beuron, with its spiritual, scholarly, and administrative resources it seemed destined—with footholds in Rome, England, and Brazil—to take in the modern world something of the place that Cluny had taken in an earlier age.[39]

Saint Ottilien Abbey

A Swiss-born Beuronese monk, Andrew Amrhein (1844–1927), felt that he was called to a different ministry—the mission apostolate. He left Beuron to begin a community at the Abbey of Reichenbach in the Upper Palatinate of Bavaria. After three years he transferred his small contingent of monks to an old estate in Emming, the site of a pilgrimage chapel honoring Saint Odilia (also known as Saint Ottilien). Thus the congregation that recognized Amrhein as founder organized under the patronage of a woman other than Mary the mother of Jesus, honored in the title of several congregations of monks.

Saint Ottilien was designated a priory in 1896, the same year that Amrhein resigned its leadership, then to abbey in 1902.[40] In 1887, it had been entrusted with a vast territory in Africa, almost a third of the southern German East Africa (present Tanzania). After a temporary expulsion from the African mission, the monks returned there under British domination in 1922, also when the St. Ottilien monks accepted a mission in South Africa, Eshowe in Zululand, which later became an abbey.[41]

German-Speaking Nuns

The German-speaking nuns fared similarly. The members of the ancient abbey of Nonnberg in Salzburg, who had been in a Bavarian exile, were able to return to Austria in 1816. The community was fortunate to have a succession of remarkable abbesses. Probably the most notable was Frau Magdalen Klotz (1876–1890). She was firmly attached to the Beuronese model of observance and dedication to the liturgy. In 1888 she assisted in a new foundation for nuns at Saint-Gabriel in Prague. The nuns had to leave Prague in 1920, so they transferred the community to Bertholdstein in Styria where they prospered.

A second attempt to make a new foundation, this time at Gurk, did not succeed. Under the *Kulturkampf* of Bismarck, Saint Mary's at Fulda was suppressed in 1875. The nuns restored it again as a priory in 1887, and by 1898 it was again an abbey. The next year Frauenwörth Abbey established a priory in Bavaria at Tettenweiss that was raised to abbatial rank in 1924.[42]

Between 1854 and 1898, several German communities of Perpetual Adoration were also established. These included Trier, Osnabrüch, Bonn Endenich, and Cologne-Raderberg. Another house opened in Johannisberg in 1907. The nuns there observed strict enclosure and attracted many vocations.

The greatest numbers of German women, however, sought out a different congregation dedicated to foreign missionary service, where they were not subject to strict enclosure. These German missionary Benedictine nuns also owe their origin to the founder of St. Ottilien, Andrew Amrhein. He brought women monastics to Reichenbach when he established his monks there. They also transferred to St. Ottilien, but left shortly thereafter for their own permanent priory at Tutzing. The expansion of the Missionary Benedictine Congregation of Saint Ottilien into North America, Asia, and Africa took place in the twentieth century.

Other European Benedictines

Switzerland had several houses of Benedictine women under the direct jurisdiction of a neighboring Benedictine abbot. Among these were Fahr in canton Zurich and Seedorf in canton Uri, both dependent upon the abbot of Einsiedeln. Sarnen in canton Obwald was supervised by the abbot of Engelberg, as was Maria Reichenbach, a newly founded group of Benedictine oblate sisters dedicated to educating girls. It was built atop a mountain, along the road to the abbey of Engelberg. Claro in Tessin and Münster in Canton Grisons came under episcopal jurisdiction. Like other European communities, the Swiss monastics' future was not always secure. Between 1841 and 1843, Fahr was temporarily suppressed. Some houses began to search for possible refuges. Others, like Maria Reichenbach, hedged their future by permitting a good number of the Sisters to immigrate to the United States to open new houses. The following chapter tells that story.

Eastern European Monastics

Federations of houses of monks and nuns in Eastern Europe were long restricted by civil and episcopal bodies. They reorganized late in the nineteenth century in the Hapsburg domains of Austria-Hungary. Only one house of Benedictine nuns was dissolved in 1782 under Joseph II. The pragmatic government considered the women useful as they were involved in education. Exploitation by the state, however, led to severe impoverishment in all the monasteries, nuns as well as monks. By 1889, through the intervention of Leo XIII, eleven abbeys in Austrian Styria, Carinthia, and Bohemia were allowed to form a Congregation under the patronage of the Immaculate Conception. Several houses in the Tyrol, Moravia, and Salzburg united under the patronage of Saint Joseph. They generally worked in teaching and parochial ministry.

A new Hungarian Congregation of five abbeys also engaged in education and pastoral ministry following the return of the Benedictines to Hungary in 1901. The Archabbot of Pannonhalma was always Abbot General. After consultation with the general chapter, he named the abbots of the other houses subject to confirmation by the Hapsburg monarch. Priors were named by the archabbot from a list of three names presented by the community. Centralization was complete with a novitiate and scholasticate for philosophy and theology at Pannonhalma. Two of the Pannonhalma abbots were eventually named Cardinal-Archbishops and Primates of Hungary: Chrysostom Kruez (1865–1885) and Claude Vaszary (1885–1891) were appointed by Popes Pius IX and Leo XIII, respectively.

Poland was absorbed by neighboring Russia, Prussia, and Austria, which completed its division among themselves in 1795. Prussian Polish monasteries became nationalized properties, and the monastics were given a small pension and forbidden to accept applicants to the monastic life. In 1836 there was only one house of nuns in Prussian Poland. Most Russian Polish monasteries succumbed to open persecution. The nuns in Lithuania founded a congregation that was gradually suppressed during the early nineteenth century. The last monastery, Krozé, was dissolved in 1893.

The Polish insurrection of 1863 had worsened the situation for the remaining religious men and women. The nuns' priory in Warsaw lost 50% of its members in twenty-five years. A 1905 edict of tolerance provided some surcease for the Russian controlled monasteries. After restoration of Poland as an independent nation occurred in 1918, monasteries of Perpetual Adoration for nuns spread rapidly. The Warsaw monastery reached a membership of sixty by 1935. Other houses usually averaged about forty women, a large number for central Europe at that period.

Belgian Monastics

The survival of some fervently individualistic eighteenth-century monks and the support of Beuron resulted in the revival of two Belgian unions—the Flemish province of the Subiaco Congregation and Maredsous's Congregation of the Annunciation of Our Lady (approved in 1920). After 1837, monks also regrouped at Dendermonde, an old Capuchin monastery destined to remain home to Benedictines through that century and thereafter. In 1870 the monks bought back the eleventh-century monastery of Afflighem, where only a small structure remained after the Revolutionary demolitions. Monks then were sent, nine years later, to Steenbrugge to open a monastery on land gifted them by a pastor there who had erected a church, presbytery, and school. By 1896 the monastery had abbey status.

The Desclée family of Tournai had long projected the construction of a monastery on their vast estate between the Sambre and Meuse at Maredsous. The Desclées appealed to Beuron. That monastery responded with an outstanding group of monks in 1872. Placid Wolter (1828–1908)—one of the famous brothers who had made a lasting impression on the Beuronese Congregation—was elected its first abbot in 1878. The man who would be the first Abbot Primate of the Benedictine Order, Hildebrand de Hemptinne (1849–1913), succeeded Abbot Placid in 1890. He was able to turn Maredsous over to the renowned spiritual director and writer, Columba Marmion (1858–1923), who held abbatial office from 1909–1923. In 1899 Maredsous established a house of studies at Louvain on Mont César. In 1927 the Maredsous monks restored Black Benedictinism to their single monastery in Ireland at an old castle at Glenstal in County Limerick.

Maredsous and its daughter-houses naturally became the center of much intellectual and liturgical activity. The monks published a missal and a liturgical periodical, *Revue Liturgique et monastique.* Dom Ursmer Berlière initiated another periodical, the *Revue Bénédictine*, internationally acclaimed for its articles on patristics, liturgy, and exegesis. The Maredsous monks Berlière and Philibert Schmitz were both outstanding French-language Benedictine historians who began another periodical, *Bulletin d'histoire Bénédictine*, in 1895.

In the late twentieth century, ethnic strife in Belgium affected the abbeys in that country. Louvain became Flemish Leuven; the abbey was renamed Keizersberg. Forty of the French-speaking monks left for Walloon (French-speaking) Belgian monasteries. In 1995 only eight monks resided at Leuven, but it had a brilliant past. Earlier the abbey could boast of a number of great liturgists and intellectuals. One of the outstanding members was the famous ecumenist, Lambert Beauduin (1873–1960), who later founded a monastery at Chevetogne. He also initiated two French periodicals dedicated to questions on the liturgy.[43] At Saint-André in Bruges, the monks were also dedicated to the liturgical apostolate. Gaspard Lefebvre (1880–1966) edited a popular daily missal and vesperal. It was the first of many editions, eventually translated into at least six languages. Called the *Saint Andrew Daily Missal*, the liturgical book was well known throughout the world.[44]

Saint-André monks were also involved in missionary work and were one of the first congregations to send monks to Africa and Asia. Their monastery sent missionaries to China until the Communists there imprisoned or exiled them; in 1955 they then sought refuge in California at Valyermo. That monastery was raised to the rank of abbey and elected its first abbot in 1992.[45]

In 1893 Belgian nuns founded a monastery at Maredret, near Maredsous, which became famous for its miniaturists and eventually affiliated with the monks in the Belgian Congregation. Luxembourg's Grand Duke also wanted nuns in his duchy, so he established a monastery of Perpetual Adoration for them at Peppange in 1883. This house joined the Congregation of the Blessed Sacrament founded earlier in France and regionalized into federations in 1957.

Throughout the nineteenth century, Benedictine monks and nuns continued to flourish even in the midst of oppression and political upheaval. Restorations and new congregations exerted a lasting impact beyond the monasteries to affect Roman Catholicism as a whole. Suppressions gave way to growth as many communities expanded, eventually bringing the Rule of Benedict's presence westward to the New World. ✽

CHAPTER 10

Benedictine Roots in North America

Nineteenth Century

The influence and rapid expansion of monasteries in the nineteenth century, despite many governments' attempts at suppression, had a lasting effect well beyond their European origins. By the twentieth century, Benedictine monasticism was no longer limited to either hemisphere as foundations in the Americas and Australia flourished. Asian, African, and European monastic houses also fostered new foundations despite—and in some cases, because of—political suppression. The Benedictine way of life was to become a worldwide phenomenon and see much change—especially for American Benedictine women.

Early American Ventures

Although foundations in colonial Latin America dated from the sixteenth century, no permanent settlement of Benedictines was made in the United States until the early nineteenth century.[1] A few individuals following the Rule of Benedict had migrated to North America, but when colonial Maryland Catholics wished to become Benedictines, they traveled to the continent to join English or Spanish monasteries. For example, Richard Chandler, after attending school at Douai, remained to join that community, making profession in 1705. Seven Maryland women, including three sisters from the Semmes family, also went to Europe for schooling in the eighteenth century, subsequently joining the English nuns exiled in Paris, Ghent, Brussels, and Pontoise.[2] Another Marylander, John Carroll—originally a Jesuit, though the order had been dissolved worldwide in 1773—appreciated the work of Benedictines. Named the first bishop of the United States, Carroll was consecrated in England in 1789 by the Benedictine Vicar Apostolic of the Western District of England Charles Walmesley.[3] After Carroll's return from Europe, he desired to commit American Catholic education to the Benedictines. Nonetheless, Benedictines arrived much later in the United States than he had anticipated. The Jesuit Order was restored in 1814 allowing it to take charge of Carroll's Georgetown University and much of the higher education in the country. Though Benedictines would be trusted later with a multiplicity of American schools, lack of personnel diminished the possibilities of their dominance. Regardless, Benedictines became highly influential in elementary, secondary, and post-secondary education in America.

Individuals following the Benedictine Rule made some early ventures to America, and several White Benedictine Trappists fleeing the French Revolution arrived in the States about 1803. For a very brief period, another group of Trappists and a Trappistine nun emigrated from France in 1812. Hoping to establish an American house, all returned to Europe in a few years, although the nun had received several American postulants. Finally, in 1848, a permanent Trappist monastery was established in Gethsemani, Kentucky.[4]

Benedictines *may* have visited North America even before they migrated there in the late-eighteenth and nineteenth centuries. A non-documented tradition claims that monks and nuns had established monasteries in Greenland after the arrival there of the Scandinavians in the thirteenth century.[5] Permanent foundations in North America would come centuries later. Some maintain that there was a Benedictine monk on one of Columbus's later voyages and others that the only Black Benedictine in the United States before Boniface Wimmer was a French monk, Pierre Joseph Didier (d. 1826), who fled the Revolution to spend the rest of his life in pastoral work in Ohio and Missouri.[6] Another monk of Saint Peter's in Salzburg, Austria, arrived in 1836 and ministered to the German immigrants in Pennsylvania assisting his countryman, Stephen Raffeiner.[7] The Benedictine Nicholas Balleis (d. 1891) also spent his first years in and around Philadelphia, moving to Saint Mary's parish in Newark, New Jersey, in 1838 where Boniface

Wimmer, the American Benedictine Founder, sought his advice. Balleis later served as pastor at Saint Francis Church in Brooklyn, where he died in 1891. By 1846, Wimmer had landed in New York.[8]

Boniface Wimmer: From Metten to Pennsylvania

In 1831, five young German priests from the diocese of Regensberg entered the novitiate at the restored Bavarian abbey of Metten. Among them was Leonard Scherre, who received the name Gregory. Elected abbot eight years later, he eventually became Archbishop of Munich where, among other duties, he excommunicated the famous church historian and writer, the Reverend Dr. Ignaz von Döllinger, in in 1871. Döllinger was Wimmer's former history professor; he could not publicly support the papal infallibility doctrine of Vatican I.[9] Another of these priest-novices later became the first abbot of Scheyern, Metten's daughterhouse, and the third reintroduced Benedictine life into the ancient abbey of Weltenburg. Finally there was Sebastian Wimmer (1809–1887), who became Boniface as a monk, in honor of the Dean of Regensburg, Boniface Urban. Wimmer was later compared with another Boniface, his patron Saint and the apostle of Germany discussed earlier in this book. Due to the extensive efforts of this nineteenth-century Boniface, Benedictine life spread throughout the United States and expanded into areas of Latin America, Canada, Asia, and Africa.

Wimmer's Background

Wimmer's background gave little indication that he would later be venerated as the founder of American Benedictine monasticism. He was the son of a tavern keeper of Thälmassing, a village near Ratisbon. Later, when he evaluated his own gifts in comparison with those of his fellow novices, Wimmer seemed quite humble, a virtue some felt he lacked once he landed in America. He considered himself least in stature, the "trouble-maker and visionary" of the class.[10] Despite his self-depreciation, he professed his solemn vows of stability, conversion of morals, and obedience at Metten in December 1833 at age twenty-four, two years following his ordination as a diocesan priest. He had entered the monastery, he said, because he felt called to a monastic rather than a parochial vocation. Ironically, his first assignment was to assist the pastor at Edenstätten, a village near Metten. Wimmer spent almost two years serving those village parishioners.

In October 1835, several monks from Metten, including Boniface Wimmer, were sent as professors to Saint Stephen's Monastery in Augsburg. These monks feared that if they transferred their vow of stability to the Augsburg house, lack of personnel at Metten would threaten its existence. The monks sent to Augsburg consequently insisted on remaining Metten monks by not transferring their stability since the smaller Metten abbey was made a dependent house of Saint Stephen's, these most recent arrivals soon received a mandate to submit themselves to the Bishop of Augsburg and the Abbot of Saint Stephen's. Lacking confidence in the monastic future of Saint Stephen's, they all refused to sign the transfer papers. Wimmer had already complained about the diminished quality of monastic observance at Augsburg, reporting repeated violations of the enclosure and that women sometimes frequented the monks' corridors and cells. Despite a two-hour verbal debate with the bishop, the Metten monks remained adamant. As leader and spokesman, Wimmer had another two-hour dialogue with the abbot of Saint Stephen's, explaining all the objections the Metten monks had to the transfer. The monks would sign the transfer document on the condition that they could return to Metten if that house regained its independence. Appeals and lobbying maneuvers were then set in motion to convince the king that Metten should regain its independence.

Through an intercessor, Wimmer encouraged the king to expand Metten to include more of the former monastic buildings and support a school on the monastery grounds. Knowing that the Metten prior did not have King Ludwig's confidence, Wimmer also suggested his replacement. The king agreed that Metten could become independent again when it had the means to do so, and a competent superior would then be elected to replace the prior. Wimmer began to campaign for a free election by the monks of a new superior. Within a year the monks were back at Metten, and Ludwig had granted its independence, allowing it to receive novices and giving the monks the right of free election of their superior. In 1837, Rupert Leiss, a novitiate confrère of Wimmer's, was elected prior for a three-year term. Wimmer was pleased. He began to speak often of plans to open a Latin school and eventually a *gymnasium* (a secondary school for boys) at the monastery.

In addition to his active participation in the Metten–Saint Stephen's decision making, Wimmer had some procurator duties for a year. When King Ludwig I established a *gymnasium* and a state college with a boarding school in Munich, he requested the abbot staff the new institutions. Abbot Gregory (Metten now had abbatial status) assigned five monks to Munich, including Boniface, who became prefect-in-residence at the boarding school while teaching Latin and Greek to the secondary students. In the meantime, another altercation was on the horizon. In 1842, Weltenburg abbey was chosen for restoration rather than Mellersdorf, which Wimmer favored. The abbot of Metten and the king had grave reservations about Mallersdorf's viability. Wimmer objected to their opposition and sent a scathing letter to the abbot denouncing him personally for not favoring Mallersdorf's restoration. In that letter he used a phrase that would often appear in his speech and writings in his later communications to Europe: "He who is not with me is against me."[11]

Wimmer the "project maker," as his fellow monks had dubbed him, began to be concerned with those emigrating from Bavaria and other German lands to America. There were mission societies to assist such emigrants such as the Propagation of the Faith of Paris-Lyons, founded in 1822, and the Leopoldine Foundation of Vienna of 1829. Both disbursed financial aid to American bishops whose dioceses were almost daily receiving European immigrants. In 1838, in response to the urging of Bishop Frederick Rese of Detroit and others, King Ludwig founded the *Ludwig-Missionsverein* with the stated purpose of propagating the Catholic faith in Asia and North America and to support the churches, educational institutions, and the missionaries in their endeavors.[12]

After July 1844, Ludwig and the Foundation director changed the policy that had allowed the Paris-Lyons society to determine expenditures in the missions. Because of complaints that the German

Catholics in America were being neglected, they ordered the funds sent to Rome to be distributed by the Sacred Congregation for the Propagation of the Faith. Much of the correspondence from America, however, went directly to Ludwig and his directors, who appear to have had a large part in determining its allocation.

Shortly after his hostile missive about the Mellersdorf situation arrived at Metten, Wimmer requested permission to emigrate to America to do mission work. The request was denied. Yet the abbot encouraged Wimmer, while residing in Munich, to devote what energy he could to helping his countrymen in America. The abbot also sent some Mass stipends to Wimmer to be forwarded to German priests in America. When the 1842–1843 school year ended, Wimmer again reminded the abbot about his concern for America. The monk maintained that since missionary work was not being fostered the Order was suffering, pointing out that "perhaps the fact that we are not making greater progress than we are is a sign from heaven that we are remiss in this work."[13] Then the priest Peter Lemke (1796–1882) arrived in Munich.

A Monastery in America

Lemke, a convert from Lutheranism, requested to be an assistant to the American missionary, Prince Demetrius Gallitzin (1770–1840), a Russian aristocrat. After the noble prince died, Lemke near single-handedly took on the apostolate to the German Catholics in Cambria County, Pennsylvania. When the diocese of Pittsburgh was created in 1843, Bishop Michael O'Connor agreed to Lemke's proposal that he travel to Europe to seek aid for the new diocese. Lemke informed Wimmer—who had expressed great interest in his work—that he could offer the Benedictines some land for a monastery and also intimated that he personally might be willing to join the community.

Wimmer wrote his abbot, reporting his plan to establish a monastery in America where the monks could staff a seminary to prepare German immigrant sons for the ministry in American missions. Wimmer offered to lead an expedition of monk-missionaries to fulfill this dream. The monk also informed the abbot that he had written the papal nuncio and had included a request to be relayed to the Propagation in Rome for permission to travel to the States as a missionary. He had explained to the nuncio his plans to purchase the property offered by Lemke noting that several young men who wished to become Benedictine brothers and five clerical students were willing to accompany him. He concluded his letter to his abbot, "I am sure that my departure from Metten will be more a gain than a loss. The blessing of God will be with us; more priests will enter our Order, and the unforgettable Mallersdorf affair will prove a success."[14]

In June 1845, one of Ludwig Mission Society's directors secured an audience for Wimmer with the king in Munich, Bavaria's capital. Wimmer told the abbot that the king had listened sympathetically and that he and the coadjutor archbishop of Munich, Karl August von Reisach (1800–1869), thought that Benedictines were best suited for the work. Within ten days of the audience, Lemke had a document for Wimmer from Bishop O'Connor that authorized the monk to travel to Pittsburgh to open a monastery. By the end of the same month, Father Boniface informed the abbot that his plans for departure to America were on schedule and that he was only awaiting some reply from the Vatican concerning his request.

This request was also denied. Cardinal Fransoni, Prefect of the Propagation, responded that his petition would not be honored because Wimmer was more needed in his own community than in the missions in America. Wimmer insisted to his abbot that Fransoni had been misinformed, but the abbot then also revoked permission to apply for the American missions. Wimmer obeyed, but not long after—hoping that Abbot Scherr would rescind his ban on the mission sojourn—informed him that he was submitting another petition to the papal nuncio to be forwarded to Rome. Wimmer, now thirty-six, was more than ever determined to cross the ocean to serve the German immigrants and would go alone if necessary.

Wimmer next wrote an anonymous editorial for the Augsburg *Postzeitung* (November 8, 1845) calling for a Benedictine response to the needs of the American missions. He posed such signature questions as, "What religious order is most adapted for the American missions, not to convert the native Indians but to provide for the spiritual necessities of German immigrants?" He then responded to his own question with historical references, pointing out how the Benedictines had converted England, Germany, Denmark, Sweden, Hungary, and Poland. His arguments tended, at times, to appear Machiavellian. He promoted the attractive material advantages for young German-Americans, the security of community life, where the priest would be "better dressed and better housed than the ordinary settler." Hundreds, he wrote, "would prefer to spend their lives in well regulated monasteries in suitable and reasonable occupations, than to gain a meager livelihood by incessant hard labor in forest regions."[15]

In the editorial, Wimmer claimed there were several Bavarian Benedictine Fathers and brothers eager to go on to the mission. The anonymous author reassured his readers that the necessary funds could be secured from the Mission Society to which Bavarians contributed 100,000 florins annually. Also appealing to German nationalism, he informed the newspaper's readers that German emigrants to America had a tendency to lose their national character and language in the second and third generation. He predicted that America would repay the German people just as England, converted by the Benedictines, repaid Europe (by sending missionaries, the readers might assume).

After King Ludwig discovered the editorial writer's identity he openly supported Wimmer's proposal. The Apostolic Nuncio eventually authorized the project as well. The Mission Society, supported by Ferdinand Josef Müller (Court Chaplain and Director of the Mission—Wimmer's perennial defender), finally approved the plan and offered 6000 florins to fund the venture. The exultant Wimmer was on his way to the New World, and on July 25, 1846, the man destined to be the patriarch of American abbots left Munich for America, accompanied by four clerical students and fourteen young lay brother candidates. At the time of their departure, Wimmer was the only one professed or ordained.

Two months later, the group arrived in New York where two of them became ill and were left there. The rest of the party proceeded to Carroltown to the Lemke property, which Wimmer immediately realized was far from an ideal site. The land was poor; a monastery and school could not survive there. Consequently, he accepted Bishop O'Connor's offer of Mount Saint Vincent in Westmoreland County, forty miles east of Pittsburgh. The bishop gave Wimmer 315 acres of land and a parish of Irish and German Catholics then being served by an Irish priest. A year later Pius IX granted monastic status to the small colony of missionaries at Saint Vincent's.

The community inhabited a small two-room building that had been a schoolhouse. The men spent freezing nights on thin, straw-sack beds in the attic. Wimmer soon invested his four young clerics and twelve brother candidates with the Benedictine habit (which had to be circulated during the ceremony since only six garments were available). The community fortunately included men of diverse talents: such as carpenter, farmer, blacksmith, stonemason, cook, teamster, tanner, miller, locksmith, and baker. Nonetheless, the daily regime of a traditional European monastic schedule was taxing. Those preparing for the priesthood rose at 3:45 a.m. daily for Matins and Lauds in the church's organ loft. The brothers recited the rosary in the nave. Meditation at 5 a.m. was followed by Prime at 6 a.m. Mass and breakfast. Then the young men had periods of work and study interspersed at intervals with the prayers of the Liturgy of the Hours. The members chanted Vespers at 3 p.m. Two hours later they had a conference on the Rule followed by dinner, accompanied by a monk's reading aloud while they ate. Recreation was permitted after dinner until 7:30 p.m. when the monks prayed Compline and the rosary. Their day ended at 9:30 p.m.

New Arrivals and Expansion

Back in Europe, Müller continued trying to recruit Bavarian monks for the American foundation. Wimmer was delighted when the Revered Peter Lechner came from the Sheyern abbey. Like Bernard at Citeaux centuries earlier, he brought not only a doctorate in theology but also sixteen Benedictine brother candidates. Another ordained Benedictine came from Metten and one from Augsburg. Wimmer's friend, Cardinal Archbishop von Reisach, president of the Mission Society, pledged 2000 florins annually for twenty years to assist the monastic endeavors. Other financial sponsors included the Benedictine Bishop of Linz, Gregory Ziegler, the king, and the abbots of Metten and Scheyern.

As more priests were ordained Wimmer included the Czech, Polish, Slovak, and Irish Catholics as well as the Germans in pastoral services. Several monks lived at mission stations while others traveled many miles in the Allegheny Mountains to serve small colonies of immigrants. More land was purchased at Saint Mary's, Pennsylvania, and some at Carrolltown, Indiana, with a view to possible monastic expansion. The seminary soon was filled to capacity with students for the diocesan priesthood and monks. There were five professors and twenty-five students, almost all Bavarians. Two German laymen assisted in teaching mathematics and music. Wimmer's philosophy of education, as explained to the directors of the Mission Society, was that students be educated in "first what is necessary, then what is useful, and finally what is beautiful and will contribute to their refinement."[16]

It was not long before English-speaking students were accepted, along with other young men intent on receiving a liberal arts education in preparation for professions in the lay state. Thirteen students from ten to eighteen years old were admitted in 1849; they had no intention of entering the ranks of the priesthood but were poor German youths from Saint Mary's who desired a classical education. The seminarians occupied separate quarters and had separate classes but attended liberal arts classes with the other students. Wimmer also felt that labor was good for the students and seminarians. They were required to work the fields, make hay, and plant corn—also a necessity when there were people and livestock to feed. Wimmer wrote about the practical aspects of the school's curriculum when he explained the most important subjects at that time were "English for the German boys and German for the English." Greek, he said, was taken "less thoroughly." Some of the beginners, Wimmer wrote, were becoming adept at declining interesting Latin nouns—such as *mensa* and *mensae* (table)—or conjugating the popular verb, *love* (*amo*).[17]

Wimmer was having second thoughts about the place of the fine arts in the curriculum. The academic program began to accent the artistic and cultural heritage of Bavarian Catholicism, especially in music and painting. Even after Lechner, Brunner, and Zugtriegal returned to Europe because of "disagreements with the superior" Wimmer sustained the rich cultural milieu that characterized the environment at Saint Vincent's in the 1850s. He wrote about this change of heart: "I am absolutely persuaded that a monastic school that does not give just as much attention to art as to knowledge and religion is a very imperfect one and that a deficiency in scholarship at the beginning can be more readily excused than a neglect of art."[18]

As the monastery counted more numbers and the school was flourishing, Wimmer continued to work for his community's autonomy. He petitioned the Holy See in 1848 for priory status. Rather undiplomatically, he bypassed Bishop O'Connor and used the services of Archbishop Henni of Milwaukee to relay his petition to Rome. When Bishop O'Connor received the affirmative response to Wimmer's request to elevate the community to a canonical priory, he refused to act because of the "tavern controversy."

To Brew or Not to Brew: The Tavern Controversy

One of Wimmer's nephews left Bavaria for the United States carrying $800 he had received from Chaplain Müller to relay to Wimmer at Saint Vincent's. The nephew appropriated a considerable portion of the money to his personal use. To recoup the loss and repay the community through anticipated profits, he requested that his uncle purchase a tavern and brewery for him in Indiana, Pennsylvania, about thirty-five miles from Saint Vincent's. Wimmer agreed to the project but kept the purchased property in his own name. As the son of a tavern-keeper in Germany, and knowing that the common drink—beer—would be acceptable to the Germans, Wimmer felt no qualms about this enterprise.

Wimmer explained to Bishop O'Connor and the others who questioned him that it was an ancient practice for Bavarian monasteries to brew and sell beer just as the French monks generally cultivated vineyards and produced wines. Bishop O'Connor, who was advocating temperance, demanded that the brewery be shut down. Wimmer agreed to close the tavern section but informed the bishop that the adjacent brewery had to remain open until payment of the accrued debts. O'Connor retaliated with refusal to raise the monastery to the rank of a priory. Wimmer, deeply concerned about this episcopal intervention, left for Europe to see what could be done on behalf of his petition for an autonomous American monastery.

Wimmer arrived in Munich on Christmas Eve 1850. After seeking the support of the directors of the Mission Society, he drafted a second petition that was submitted to the Propagation in January. The Prefect replied that they would make no decision until an official report had been received from Bishop O'Connor of Pittsburgh. He pointed out that some of those close to Propaganda, acquainted with American popular opinion, were concerned that the brewing of beer under monastic aegis could easily create scandal. Bishop O'Connor strongly complained about the "nice kettle of fish" two priests had handed him—one owning a "tavern in full blast," while another suspended "for drunkenness" was rooming at another tavern across town and "to his drunken frolics" adding "others more grievous." He closed with the hope that, when Wimmer got to Rome "instead of a mitre and crozier he will get what he wants much more badly a good lesson on the shameful manner in which he has acted, disregarding all I could say to him."[19]

One of O'Connor's correspondents was a Benedictine, Dr. Bernard Smith, a fellow Irishman living in Rome. Smith had been sent to complete his studies at the Irish College; he then obtained a doctorate at the Jesuit University, followed by ordination to the priesthood in 1839. He made solemn profession at Monte Cassino in 1847 but sought secularization following the Italian government's hostility toward him after the 1848 Revolution. He became Vice-Rector of the Irish College in Rome, but in 1857 he again received the Benedictine habit at Saint Paul Outside the Walls.[20] Bishop O'Connor wrote Smith on November 20, 1851, questioning Wimmer's leadership:

> Proofs grow upon me that the present superior is unfit for his position and the interests of the Community and the diocese alike require that there should be a change. I forwarded some evidence of this to the Cardinal not long ago....Bishop Henni of Milwaukee (himself a German) gave me his opinion a few

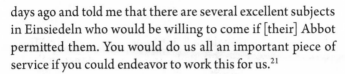

days ago and told me that there are several excellent subjects in Einsiedeln who would be willing to come if [their] Abbot permitted them. You would do us all an important piece of service if you could endeavor to work this for us.[21]

By the time Smith received the letter, Wimmer was back in Pennsylvania. He was forced to bring the matter of the brewery to a speedy resolution. He had rented it to a parishioner who, he later complained, "deceived me even more than my nephew and caused me greater losses." Fortunately for Wimmer, the parishioner also owned a farm he could sell at a reduced rate to make up for the financial losses. Wimmer also reported that the tavern had been changed into a residence for the priest of the parish that he had organized in the town. "The brewery will not be opened again," he said, "unless I find a good manager. In any case, we will only brew for wholesale deliveries and even the bishop is not against that business."[22]

For the moment, the controversy over the brewery had subsided. Nine years later, however, after O'Connor had resigned his See, Wimmer opened another brewery in the Latrobe monastery itself with the product labeled "Saint Vincent's Beer." Years later, temperance advocates criticized the Benedictines and claimed that the initials O.S.B. really meant "Order of Sacred Brewers." The monastery closed the brewery in 1920.[23]

O'Connor's questioning Wimmer's suitability as superior may well have been, in part, the influence of Father Peter Lechner who was in Pittsburgh teaching in the bishop's seminary while the brewery and canonical status were being debated. Lechner had earlier expressed his concern about the value of the monastic life at Saint Vincent's in letters to the abbots of Scheyern and Metten. He was back in Bavaria at Scheyern by the time the rescript elevating the monastery to the rank of priory arrived.[24]

In July 1852, Bishop O'Connor officially promulgated the document that raised the monastery to the priory rank but did not exempt it from the bishop's jurisdiction. Boniface was named prior and irremovable pastor of the local parish. The monastery was also granted the privilege of brewing beer for wholesale distribution only. By that time Wimmer's attention had turned elsewhere.

Benedictine Nuns Arrive in the United States

Sister Grace McDonald of Saint Benedict's Priory in Minnesota tells of the inauguration of Benedictine nuns' presence in the United States. One day in April 1852,

> the peace of St. Walburga's in Eichstätt was disturbed when a traveler from America knocked at its portals. But his loud and determined knock could not have disturbed the conventual silence as much as did his message. Father Boniface Wimmer, O.S.B., the stranger at the door had come to apply for sisters to teach the German immigrants in Pennsylvania.[25]

The nuns were filled with consternation at this proposition so foreign to their life under strict enclosure. There were educators in the community, but the school was limited to girls who dwelt with them at the monastery site. Wimmer, however, won the sisters over with a dramatic account of the great loss of faith among children of German immigrants and the urgent need for Catholic schools. He promised that they could keep the rules of enclosure and would teach only girls. The American convent would remain a dependency of Saint Walburga's. The Bishop of Eichstätt approved, so Wimmer was promised teachers.[26] The prioress of the forty-two member Eichstätt was Mother Edwarda Schnitzer (in office 1849–1898). To defray the cost of the first contingent to leave for America—only three sisters—Mother Edwarda requested and received help from the Mission Society.

The designated superior was twenty-seven year old Benedicta Riepp (1825–1862). A choir nun, forty-eight year old Walburga Dietrich and a lay sister, Maura Flieger, age thirty accompanied her.[27] The three arrived on the *Washington* from Bremen on July 4, 1852, greeted by the strange and alarming sounds of fireworks and Independence Day celebrations. They were a strong and intrepid lot though Mother Benedicta was young and of slight, delicate build with fragile health (she died after only ten years in America). A Swabian, she had been at Saint Walburga's only eight years working as a teacher and novice directress before her assignment to the States. Mother Walburga was the daughter of a German businessman; Sister Maura was a farmer's daughter from Heilig Kreuz and had spent only five years in the Eichstätt priory. These two women had taught needle-work to schoolgirls.

The Foundation at Saint Mary's

Curiously, no one met the nuns at the docks in New York despite communications with both Bishop O'Connor and Wimmer, who had been informed of their departure plans. Father Boniface failed to have someone greet them in New York to guide them to Saint Vincent's, though with the help of good Samaritans, they reached Latrobe five days later. An anecdote about this arrival relates that when the horse-drawn wagon carrying the women and their luggage neared Saint Vincent's, it was sighted by a lay brother in the fields who ran to report to Prior Boniface that a "wagonload of trouble" was coming down the road. A biographer of Wimmer cynically remarks, "if the story is true, it was one of the most prophetic statements made by a Benedictine monk in the New World."[28]

The nuns remained at Saint Vincent's awaiting approbation from the bishop before proceeding to Saint Mary's where Wimmer planned to open a school for girls. On July 15, 1852, O'Connor wrote Wimmer from Youngstown:

> I hereby certify that it was with my permission that you took the preparatory measures to establish the community of German Sisters in St. Marytown, Elk Co. I expected, though, to have the matter prepared more formally and documents accordingly issued containing everything necessary for such a purpose. Feeling confident, however, that no difficulty will arise in framing these so as to be satisfactory to all, I have no objection to see the institution commenced....I will remark merely, that until the community is incorporated, I will require that the property which the sisters may possess shall be held in trust for them by the bishop of the diocese so that their position here will be such as to enable to bishop to make sure of the promotion of discipline and to feel satisfied that what is commenced shall not be easily abandoned nor without proper cause.[29]

Obviously the bishop considered the sisters diocesan, under his jurisdiction, not Wimmer's. Later, this matter became a tense debate.

As a prolific correspondent, Wimmer described the plight of
the sisters in letters to three German abbots. He reported that they
were even poorer "than we ourselves—in a wretched frame building,
with only $100 in money which they brought with them. My monks
furnish them with flour, etc., they need. I bought them a cow.... Next
year we want to get a stone house for them, to be attached to the new
(not yet completed) church."[30] He was elated about the numbers of
new candidates arriving to join the nuns. Of the first twelve, one was
Bavarian, the others all Americans by birth. He intimated that there
was already some consternation at Saint Walburga's about the Americans opening a novitiate when they were still a dependency.

The Beginning of Tensions

Former King Ludwig wrote Mother Benedicta from Munich,
informing her that, at his request, Müller was sending 8000 florin or
gülden to her from the Society's funds. Mother Edwarda at Eichstätt
wrote a note of gratitude to Ludwig for the generous gift for "the
erection of the first convent of our Order in Saint Mary's." Another
missive came from Benedicta in January 1853 acknowledging that
the finances "for the construction of a new convent in Saint Marys-
town" were indicated in a document relayed to her through Wimmer
who also remarked that 4000 florins of the promised amount was
already in his hands.[31]

The nuns, however, never saw the 8000 florins. No construction
was begun on the promised convent. Wimmer diverted the money
to his own projects. When called to task, he explained that he had
appropriated it as a "loan" to construct a new building and mill at
Saint Vincent's. Defending this action in a letter to Ludwig on July 4,
1853, he stated "the sisters were prepared to lend me the money, since
they were not in a position to use it at once."[32] Wimmer explained that
the lower story of the nuns' frame building was being used as a church,
and the upper story and nearby buildings provided living quarters and classrooms. He conjectured that it would be the following

spring before preparations could begin for a new convent, bricks obtained, and so on. He presumed that it would take all summer for "my masons, carpenters, and cabinet builders to complete the building."[33] In actuality, it took Wimmer eight more years to begin the shelter for the sisters.

The nuns were living on a combined salary of $35 a month. The young children were poor and often came to school with only a piece of black bread for lunch. Their teachers fared little better. Bread was portioned out to each of the nuns daily. The bulk of their meals consisted of potatoes and buckwheat cakes. A red-letter day was one in which an extra plum, a full bowl of mush, or a few dried berries were added to the menu. One Christmas a large kettle of mush was cooked and the nuns were told that each might eat until her hunger was satisfied. The chronicler remarked, "the great treat was to be able to get filled up."[34] Soon there were even more women who needed to share the little available.

Near the end of 1853, a second contingent of nuns arrived from Eichstätt: a choir nun, Mother Scholastica Burkhardt; two lay sisters, Alexia Lechner (later foundress of several convents) and Sister Lidwina Uhl; along with one postulant. When Boniface went to Eichstätt on his next trip to Europe, he recruited five more sisters. Two of these would be very significant. One was Willibalda Scherbauer (1831–1914), the future superior of the Minnesota pioneers; the other was Emmerana Bader (1829–1902) who, as later events suggest, might have fared more favorably had she never left her native land.

Benedicta Riepp and the Challenges of Pioneering

Wimmer invested a group of novices with their religious habits—despite his awareness that these ceremonies lacked the approval of the Eichstätt superior—at Saint Mary's in 1853, then two groups in 1854, and another in 1855. Wimmer wrote to the Metten abbot that he knew better what was needed in America than the nuns in Eichstätt. He also wrote of his high regard for the American pioneer, Mother Benedicta. "The superior, M. Benedicta, is a very wise and pious woman, energetic and yet pleasant and helpful toward her subjects.

The children in the school as well as the candidates…are attached to her with deep affection."[35] However, Wimmer's opinion of Mother Benedicta soon underwent a drastic change.

The sisters' school for girls and boys was very popular. Mother Benedicta taught elementary subjects in German while a lay woman taught the English classes to the girls and a man was hired to teach the boys. Mother Walburga taught needlework. Most of the students were of German heritage until the railroad arrived; then, Irish children also began to matriculate and it was not long before there were almost seventy students. One allocation of money from the Mission Society was sent directly to Benedicta. It consisted of 1,000 florins that she used to furnish the house and school. In her letter of gratitude to the Society in December 1853, Benedicta wrote with vision toward the future: "The Americans…look with approval on the growth of Orders of women, because in the vicinity of every convent there arises a school for the higher education of young women."[36]

Promising their support and protection, Wimmer also tried to recruit Dominican sisters from Germany for schools in Pennsylvania. When Mother Benedicta Bauer of Regensburg sent four sisters in May 1853, they were also left to fend for themselves in New York. Wimmer had delegated the task of meeting them to Father Nicholas Balleis, the Benedictine pastor of Saint Mary's church in Newark who failed to meet them. Although the sisters had anticipated working with the monks at Carrolltown, Pennsylvania, Wimmer decided that they should settle near some Midwestern Dominican priests. Because Müller had thoughtfully given them letters of introduction to the Redemptorist priests in New York City, they sought temporary shelter there. Father Balleis eventually arrived and took two of the sisters back to Newark.

The others, after being "shuffled from place to place, without specific arrangements for permanent shelter or work…remained in their uprooted condition until Father John S. Raffeiner, vicar general for the archdiocese of New York…learned of their dilemma."[37] He eventually took them to his parish in Williamsburg, New York, and offered them what was to become their permanent home in America. Though Wimmer's promise to Mother Benedicta Bauer had fallen to others, he did take credit for their final placement after he arrived in New York and learned of the arrangements that had been made. He wrote their superior that the sisters were happy but that he suspected that Father Raffeiner took them only because he needed a cook and now he could save the cost of hiring one. He even encouraged her to send more nuns because "everything was so well ordered that one cannot help feeling that the will of God is being done."[38]

The Confusion of Debated Jurisdiction

The tension between Benedicta and Boniface erupted in 1856—a year after Saint Vincent's achieved abbatial rank. While securing his abbacy in Rome in 1855, he attempted to have the Saint Mary's convent declared independent of Eichstätt so that, as his biographer writes, "its dependence on his jurisdiction [would be] made all the greater."[39] He failed in this regard—at least for the time being—but the matter of whose jurisdiction the nuns were to follow would have extraordinary consequences in the years soon following.[40]

Wimmer responded unfavorably to another incident at Erie, Pennsylvania as well. When the diocese of Pittsburgh was divided in 1853, Bishop Josue Young was named to head Erie. Since Saint Mary's was located in the new diocese, the jurisdiction of the diocesan community of Benedictine sisters was transferred to him. Hence, when he visited Saint Mary's in 1854 he requested Mother Benedicta to send sisters to Erie to open a school. Two years later, without Wimmer's formal approval, four sisters were sent to Erie, the first Benedictine daughterhouse of nuns in America. Mother Benedicta took the nuns there personally. Wimmer shortly thereafter appointed the novice directress at Saint Mary's, Mother Scholastica Burkhardt, superior. Wimmer expressed his displeasure because he had not been consulted and complained that the sisters who had gone to Erie were not sufficiently prepared to take on the responsibilities of teaching. He accepted Scholastica from that judgment but said she was needed back at Saint Mary's to direct the novices. He also objected to Mother Benedicta's sending two novices to Erie, but for the time being held his peace. Eventually he determined "to end this feminine tyranny by deposing the Mother Superior and putting another in her place."[41] Circumstances would eventually allow that threat to be carried out.

Expansion from Pennsylvania to Minnesota

Wimmer had always been interested in expanding westward. He considered invitations from Bishop Henni of Milwaukee who had been requesting monks since 1846. Henni reminded Wimmer and the Swiss at Einsiedeln that the Benedictine could achieve their greatest potential only if they established themselves in what was still being considered the frontier west. Henni reminded Wimmer that Wisconsin was the real home of German culture and should be considered in the plans for German missions. The Milwaukee bishop cherished the idea of a seminary for educating priests to minister to the German immigrants in the Midwest. He promised land to Wimmer on one of the four Madison lakes, but Wimmer rejected that offer. The Swiss arrived in 1854, but decided to locate in southern Indiana. In 1856 Henni finally secured Jesuits for his Saint Francis seminary; he eventually founded the present Marquette University in Milwaukee.[42]

Wimmer chose to respond to the petition of Bishop Joseph Cretin of Saint Paul, Minnesota. This bishop had appealed to the Mission Society for German priests to serve the Catholic Germans in his diocese. At the first general chapter of the new American Cassinese Congregation held within a month after Wimmer's return from Rome in January 1856, the capitulars agreed to send monks west to Minnesota where the need seemed to be greatest. Wimmer, the Abbot President of the Congregation, was eager promote this Benedictine expansion westward.

Wimmer, who had the reputation of being too progressive, too reckless in accumulating debts accrued in land speculation, and too much influenced by the material values of the American populace was also considered an activist who neglected spiritual values. He was reported to Rome several times, even by his own monks. Müller admonished him more than once and urged him to go more slowly. The Archbishop of Munich was also displeased with his excessive activity. Lemke, who had finally professed vows at Saint Vincent's, called his abbot to task publicly in an article in the Augsburg *Postzeitung* (Wimmer had used the journal earlier to lobby for the American mission). Although exonerated in Rome, Wimmer would have to defend the charges again as a consequence of his Minnesota venture. This call of the missions, Wimmer wrote to Müller in his defense, "cannot have its limits and knows no rest....After the Benedictine Order awakens form this century-old lethargy," he advised, "it must become conscious of adapting itself to present conditions, to unfurl its banners in the field of battle, where one-half of the earth is the price of victory....The stream of immigration is tending westward. We must follow it."[43] He had to reply to the same objections many more times.

Demetrius Di Marogna and Companions Reach Saint Cloud

It took five days by train to reach Saint Paul, Minnesota, from Latrobe. Their leader was Demetrius di Marogna (1803–1869), who would make a significant contribution to the foundation. He was always a prior and never an abbot, yet this founding father of Saint John's cared a great deal about succeeding in the venture, although his ancestry and experience hardly prepared him for Minnesota.

Di Marogna was born in Trent on the German–Italian border in 1803 at the Villa Lagarina, property of the patrician family of Verona. As Count Carlo Guiseppe di Marogna, the young man served as a page at the court of the archduke of Tuscany in Florence. When he was six, his father moved the family to Trent where they were strongly attached to the Bavarian court.

The youth, however, entered the diocesan seminary of Mainz and was ordained for the diocese of Augsburg in 1826. After twenty-one years in German parishes, he was determined to go to the American missions, which he did in 1847. For five years he served Illinois parishes in Chicago, Germantown, and Hanover. His was soon a household name among the German Catholics of southern Illinois but he found himself in conflict with several Irish priests of the Chicago diocese over parochial jurisdiction.

Deciding to apply to the Latrobe novitiate, Wimmer gave him the religious name of Demetrius in honor of Prince Gallitzin, the well-known Pennsylvania priest. A few months after his profession, the Abbot appointed di Marogna prior of Saint Vincent's though Wimmer felt that he needed an older priest to assist him—especially during his absences in Rome—during those early critical years. Confirming the abbot's hesitation, di Marogna imprudently amassed debts by over-expanding construction at Saint Vincent's during Wimmer's absence. Bishop O'Connor had actually favored him when he was looking for a replacement for Wimmer, so di Marogna was quite eager to leave the area and the current tension to go west.

The *Minnesota Belle* arrived at Saint Paul via the Mississippi from Saint Louis on May 2, 1856. Di Marogna and his four Bavarian-born monk companions accepted Bishop Cretin's hospitality. Language was an immediate barrier. The clergy, church staff, and school teachers were all French; Irish people served the kitchen, stables, and chapel liturgy. The two young clerics—refusing to converse in anything but German—did not speak French, but di Marogna did. The contingent remained at the rectory for two weeks until the ordination of the two clerics when the new priests heard confessions, solemnized marriages, presided at a funeral, baptized the faithful, and attended Vespers and May devotions. The bishop jokingly regretted that no sick call had been requested so they could have that experience also.

The monks soon moved to the Saint Cloud area where they temporarily resided on some claims that they eventually discovered were not available to them. Father Bruno had sighted an area around Saint Joseph, acres of woodland and meadows near the Sagatagan, which Wimmer inspected and approved. The monks erected two claim shacks on two 360-acre plots. Father Bruno also claimed another 240 acres near Saint Joseph, which he envisioned as ideal for a convent of sisters.

Although the monks first supervised a small parish elementary school in Saint Cloud, Demetrius looked forward to establishing a liberal arts seminary and a school at the monastery. Through intensive lobbying, the prior received a charter for his educational endeavor and began the first Catholic educational institution for higher learning in Minnesota. Saint John's University opened late in 1857.[44]

Benedictine Sisters in Minnesota

The historian of Saint John's credits Prior Demetrius for the permanence of the nuns' foundation of Saint Benedict's, now in Saint Joseph, Minnesota. When speaking of the prior's determination to resign his office, Colman Barry wrote: "He performed one last service to the establishment of Benedictinism in the West. It was his support, at times in opposition to a hostile abbot, of the Minnesota nuns' foundation."[45] While the Minnesota foundation of monks was getting a firm footing, Wimmer was at Saint Mary's Convent in March 1857 to receive several nuns' profession of vows. There he became aware that several sisters were chafing under the rule of Mother Benedicta.[46] The nuns petitioned the abbot to allow them to go to Minnesota to respond to the call of di Marogna to come to teach in the Saint Cloud school. The prior wrote to the abbot about the need of and plans for the sisters in Minnesota. He spoke of fencing in lots for the "proper observance of enclosure."

Mother Benedicta wrote to the Mission Society mentioning di Marogna's request and asked for financial support to assist her in responding affirmatively. She did not anticipate that Wimmer would promise the Minnesota assignment to the dissatisfied sisters at Saint Mary's (whom he, often over the objections of the nuns' chapter, had allowed to be admitted to and later professed). Mother Benedicta and her close friend, Sister Willibalda, had hoped that they might go themselves; the nuns' superior apparently felt she needed to put more distance between herself and the abbot. Benedicta firmly maintained that it was her prerogative to determine who would go to Minnesota, not the abbot's.

However, Wimmer sent a small group of sisters to Indiana, Pennsylvania, to be prepared for the Minnesota mission by Prior Ulric Spoettl. This contingent never went west; they were shortly thereafter sent to teach in Newark, New Jersey. Benedicta wrote to Wimmer while he was in Newark, pleading with him to approve her going to

Minnesota because of her health (she died there three years later of tuberculosis). Father Rupert Seidenbusch warned Wimmer that Benedicta was proceeding with her own plans for the Minnesota mission although "she has nothing to say here anymore."[47] In the face of such formidable opposition from two powerful monastics, Benedicta courageously continued to implement her agenda. She accompanied the group of volunteers she had approved as far as Erie, where they were to continue on to Minnesota. She informed di Marogna of their impending arrival. The prior then alerted the abbot that he was not yet ready for them. Unfortunately, Mother Benedicta inadvertently neglected to inform Bishop Thomas Grace of Saint Paul about the sisters' proposed mission in his diocese.[48]

Four young nuns and two postulants went on to Minnesota under the leadership of Sister Willibalda Scherbauer. The superior was the daughter of a Bavarian Count, and had been placed at an early age with the nuns at Eichstätt. She has been described as "a dominating personality, more forcible than gentle or sweet in character."[49] Two of the Sisters were Bavarian, two American. One postulant, Prisca Meier, was Prussian. The nuns first lodged at the hospital in Saint Paul with the Sisters of Saint Joseph until Prior Demetrius coincidentally arrived in the city at the same time to get citizenship papers for one of his monks. The prior took the sisters back to Saint Cloud and greatly supported them, defending them in letters to the abbot who continued to voice his objections to their going to Minnesota without his approval.

Legislative Complexities Foment More Conflict

Wimmer was most upset, however, when he discovered that Mother Benedicta had left Erie too, but not for Minnesota. Accompanied by Sister Augustine, Mother Benedicta went to Europe to try settling jurisdictional problems between Wimmer and herself. In response, Wimmer successfully received the collaboration of Bishop Young whom he requested to detain the other nuns who had not yet left for Minnesota. Eventually they became members of the Pennsylvania, not the Minnesota, community. The bishop had, however, approved

Mother Benedicta's going abroad ostensibly to collect funds for the schools and the sisters' sustenance. In a letter to Wimmer on July 4, 1857, Bishop Young indicated that he was aware of their departure for Europe. He also expressed his confidence in Wimmer, adding that Benedicta had said "nothing of her proposed appeal to some authority to discover the extent mutually of her authority and yours. Till she arrived here," he wrote, "I was unaware of the existence of any difficulty." He regretted that Wimmer had not made him aware of the tension between the two. He added "she seemed willing to be deposed for the sake of peace and discipline" and the bishop claimed no jurisdiction in the matter. He conceded all his power "to you as my vicar general," he informed Wimmer. He added that Sister Scholastica Burkhardt had told him that she was also scheduled to go to Minnesota and asked Wimmer if he should detain her in Erie.[50]

The irreparable break was not long in coming, and Wimmer and Mother Benedicta were never to see each other again. As Jerome Oetgen mused, "Mother Benedicta had obviously had enough of Wimmer's rigid control." Wimmer continued to argue that Benedicta's sending sisters to Erie without his permission or the bishop's formal approval had occasioned their first rift. He maintained that the sisters and monks had gotten along well in Saint Mary's, and that the sisters taught school and helped the monks by washing, mending, and baking for them. The monks supplied the nuns with firewood and coal and drove their cattle to pasture and home again, plowed their fields, and acted as their confessors. Yet he added, "If I were not given the right to rule the Sisters, their monastic regiment would become disrupted and I would end up with a group of women to feed, who are good for nothing and who would just make trouble for me."[51]

Benedicta perceived the crisis differently. She remembered the appropriation of the sisters' funds earmarked for convent construction and remained concerned that Wimmer considered himself the immediate superior of all the Benedictine nuns in America. At will he had changed their daily horarium, mandating them to follow the order of Saint Vincent's spiritual exercises—to rise at 3:30 a.m. to recite the Divine Office and adopt a grueling daily schedule. She disagreed with his choosing who should be admitted and who should be professed among the applicants to the nuns' communities.[52]

A cursory survey of how each of these adversaries signed some of their letters indicates how they viewed their own position in relation to the other. Boniface Wimmer, especially in the first few years in the States, followed his signature with "Superior of the Benedictines in North America." In an 1853 letter to Ludwig, Wimmer was less pretentious, titling himself "Abbot Superior of the Bavarian Benedictine Mission." After 1855, his signature was most often accompanied by the designation as president, "Praeses of the American Cassinese Congregation." Benedicta also varied her titles. When she signed a letter to Ludwig, she added the phrase "Superior of the Bavarian Benedictine Sisters of North America." To the Society in December 1853, she wrote: "Superior in North America." In the same letter she described Father Boniface, however, as "Superior of the Benedictines in North America." After 1855 she was signing simply, "Superior, O.S.B." Two years later she signed letters to the Mission Society as "Superior of the Benedictine Sisters of North America."[53]

Di Marogna posed the jurisdictional problem to his abbot in August 1857. "I have read to Sister Willibalda the conditions mentioned in your letter. She assured me that the Mother Superior, as well as herself and the other Sisters, are agreed that they had no one else in mind as superior for the Minnesota foundation than myself, or if need be, yourself or your successor. The Mother Superior and the Sisters are very willing to have a superior in accordance with the prescriptions of their statutes." Then he relayed that the Sisters told him that Benedicta had gone off to Europe to petition for "definite norms and rules of conduct, which are to govern the relations between a superior (priest) and the Sisters' convent with its Mother Superior."[54] He also asked Wimmer to reconsider his order to have him laicize Maryanna Wolters. The Prior not only intimated that he had confidential information from her that would change Wimmer's mind, but also that "it would be manifestly quite impossible now to find a place for her to stay, or to find a suitable husband for her. And even if the right kind of man could be found for her, because looked for, would we not have to fear the jibe and mockery of the Yankees and the bad Catholics?" He reminded Wimmer that he had once written, "I in the first place, and you, if necessary, had the right to decide in the reception of novices and their profession."[55]

Demetrius informed the sisters in Minnesota of Wimmer's disapproval of their foundation. Wimmer insisted that Mother Willibalda, whom Benedicta had appointed, resign in favor of Mother Evangelista Kremeter and that she leave the Benedictines. Willibalda wrote a pair of long, pleading letters to Wimmer asking forgiveness for whatever she may have done wrong and begging him to tell her what that was. From our historical vantage point, could it have been that Benedicta—not the abbot—had appointed her was at issue? Speculation aside, he never replied to her letters, but did—several months later—allow her to remain.[56]

Benedicta Riepp's Visit to Europe

The bishop of Eichstätt had not approved Benedicta's coming to Europe either. After requesting authorization from him, he replied that instead of making the journey she should send him a written report of her complaints and petitions and that he would then direct her. She ventured to Europe despite this reply. Nor was her arrival at Saint Walburga's a pleasant homecoming. Although she had informed Mother Edwarda of her journey, she was coldly received, partially resulting from novices having been received in America without proper authorization from Eichstätt.

Mother Benedicta and her companion were placed in an isolated wing of the convent throughout her ten-month stay in Bavaria, and they were rarely in communication with the other nuns of Saint Walburga's. Since she felt personally rejected by Mother Edwarda, she appealed to the Bishop of Eichstätt to take her cause to Rome. He was unsympathetic, again recommending that she write a conscientious, articulate, but short account of her petitions, grievances, and questions.

Realizing that she could get no help from the Eichstätt church leaders, Benedicta traveled to Munich—Ludwig was also in residence—to seek the aid of Archbishop Karl August. The bishop of

Eichstätt, however, undercut that visit also. He wrote Müller to indicate his displeasure and asked him prevent Benedicta from presenting herself to Ludwig. He rationalized that he would be "unspeakably distressed" if Benedicta were to annoy the king by repeating what he saw as her groundless and unjustifiable complaints.

Wimmer was sure that Benedicta would not attempt to go to Rome, at least while the abbot was there. He also wrote to the Archbishop of Munich saying that he intended to bring the matter to Rome in person. Furthermore, Wimmer complained to Müller that he based his displeasure with Benedicta on the premise that "she is too self-willed, does not take advice, and still does not perform her duty satisfactorily. I never took it upon myself to rule the sisters. But I thought myself *justified* and *obliged* to see to it that they obey the Holy Rule properly, and follow it according to our own Statutes as much as possible." He quoted canon law in his defense: "According to the *jus canonicum* the sisters always enjoy the same privileges as the monks do; they would, therefore, be exempt here and the President of the Congregation at the time would be their highest superior, as I have considered myself to be."[57] He maintained that the bishop is too far away to govern the nuns and that he "does not understand much about our Order." He also stated quite emphatically that the prioress of Saint Walburg also could not be their superior because she was too far away and did not understand "American conditions." He wrote "the sisters were invited by and were sent to me; I provided a place for a convent for them, gave them the necessary buildings, made many long and expensive trips, spent very much money for them, brought many of the sisters to the convent, supplied confessors for them."[58]

Wimmer defended his actions in the same letter. "Because of proximity to my brothers, I am justified and obliged to be solicitous that they [the nuns] be genuine good Benedictines and also good teachers. Otherwise, the sisters could bring prejudice, disgrace, and scandal upon my priests and brothers." He expressed his hope to his correspondent that there should be appointed one abbess "under the leadership of the president and General Chapter, for which I hoped to get approval from Rome easily," again citing canon law and the bishop's right of visitation that would then be reserved to the

Congregation president. He appealed for sympathy on grounds that "Pastor Hartmann, of course, did everything he could for the Sisters, but he too, is not a hen-pecked hero." He related that when he tried to replace Father Benedict Haindl with Rupert Seidenbusch as the nuns' confessor, they seldom called for him to come to Saint Mary's but continued to contact Father Benedict who "was pursued with letters which contained secrets of confession about the Superior and Willibalda until I put an end to it."[59] One wonders how he knew about private letters to the nuns' chosen confessor.

Wimmer complained to Müller that spiritual exercises at the convent had been disturbed by the cries of the abandoned one-year-old girl the superior had taken in. The nuns even wasted time preparing the child's Christmas surprises. They could have used the time to work for the fair where the sale of their handwork and other crafts would profit the convent. Since they were working until midnight, they slept late—until 6 a.m.—so prayers in choir were often, if not "completely," neglected.[60] Wimmer maintains, despite penitential confidence, that he knows the truth of his charges because "in the confessional there were general complaints about this as well as in reports and letters." He cited the case of the "persecuted" Emmerana who had reported disorders to Seidenbusch.[61]

Wimmer explained to Müller in the same lengthy letter how he had deposed Mother Benedicta during her absence from the Pennsylvania monastery. "I had to return to Saint Mary's, restore order, and declare Mother Benedicta banished, once and for all from Saint Mary's." He confirmed Mother Teresia as prioress for the interim and appointed Walburga as subprioress and Edwarda as novice mistress. He had the child "removed from the convent, restored the choir and daily order."[62] Wimmer complained that he had trouble and annoyance, had lost money and time, and that the two women in Rome had gone to complain "that I assume sovereign authority over them to which I have no right: I should be good enough to pay, but I should not say anything? We will see who is master! Just now, I still am....[F]or such tramps as Benedicta and Willibalda I will not do anything."[63]

The written report of complaints Benedicta took to Europe were eventually sent to Pius IX who, in May 1858, through Cardinal

Barnabo (Prefect of the Propagation of the Faith), relayed the report
to Wimmer. When the bishops of Pittsburgh, Erie, and Eichstätt and
the Minnesota monastery prior were asked to express their views on
the statements of disagreement, they generally favored Wimmer on
all points. When Wimmer responded to the complaints Mother Benedicta had outlined, he reported that in his opinion he was an "exempt
abbot" and felt he owed the bishops no explanation. He maintained in
his correspondence that this was a legal, not a private, affair. He was
sure that he was "right *on all points*" and that Benedicta could never
again be admitted to any American priory. In response to Mother
Benedicta's charge that the sisters were neglected—that within the
past year four had died of malnutrition and more than two-thirds
were ailing because they had nothing but cornbread, soup, and noo-
dles made from rye flour or salted and half-spoiled beef (and even not
enough of that)—Wimmer countered that the sisters never had to
suffer from hunger. He insisted that he sent hundreds of bushels of
rye and forty bushels of wheat and that they had fattened and killed
hogs, bought meat from the butcher, and received lard from him. That
most of the sisters died from tuberculosis (then labeled "consumption") was, he maintained, because they were too young; the superior
had admitted them at 14, and she probably contracted the disease
"through much praying and singing in choir!"[64]

Wimmer argued that the students he had brought (ages 12
and 14) were "both paid for." He maintained that he never let the
sisters suffer necessity anywhere, and the trouble was that Benedicta opened daughterhouses without his approval. He reminded
his correspondent that he still planned to build that convent for
which he had been given the 8000 florins but since they (monks and
nuns) were "all as children of one house" he felt justified in taking
something that was not needed somewhere and using it where it was
needed.[65] Wimmer considered Benedicta inferior compared to his
monks. Ironically, he wrote: "each of my priests is naturally better
schooled in monastic life than Sister Benedicta. Yes, there is the
difficulty. *She thought herself smarter than I and all my brothers.* For
that reason Father Prior Rupert Seidenbusch was not allowed in the
house except to hear confession. Why does one need a priest when

one is so smart oneself."[66] He continued to pen his complaint well past the point of redundancy.

Wimmer petitioned Cardinal Barnabo that Rome incorporate the convents in Erie and Newark into the American congregation of monks and be placed under his jurisdiction. He also requested that the sisters be allowed to make solemn vows without being held to the customary strict enclosure and that they be permitted to teach in the public schools. He also asked Rome that they be permitted to substitute the Little Office of the Blessed Virgin for the monastic Divine Office. Neither he nor anyone else, it seems, ever consulted the sisters about this question. Wimmer was later informed that his cause was in the hands of the Congregation of Bishops and Regulars, since the controversy concerned not only the points of difference but also the question of solemn vows then taken by the Benedictine nuns in America. Rome found no record of Wimmer's having asked for dispensation from strict enclosure for the American nuns. The final disposition was only made in 1864 by the Congregation and reinforced by decree from the Council of Baltimore in 1866. It forbade the profession of solemn vows by American sisters except by special permission and under particular circumstances.[67] Henceforth all American sisters who were not under strict enclosure were denied solemn vows. However, in 1917 Canon Law allowed that those belonging to "ancient orders" could be considered nuns even if engaged in apostolic works.[68]

The Return to America

Mother Benedicta and Sister Augustina returned to America on money given them by the community of Saint Walburga's. Mother Edwarda also declared that community would now have nothing more to do with the nuns in America.[69] That attitude would change as Mother Edwarda, Mother Willibalda, and Prioress Carolina Korisz corresponded amicably later with their American foundations. Sister Augustina, welcomed to return to Saint Mary's, later joined the pioneers to Atchison, Kansas, where she eventually directed the academy for fourteen years. She died at another foundation in Kentucky in

1902.[70] In late summer 1858, Mother Benedicta and a companion left Erie for Minnesota. She was there in time to protest, in concert with Mother Willibalda, of a second misappropriation of funds. Wimmer again diverted funds (3000 florins) sent to the sisters, allegedly to purchase more land for the monks.

The Minnesota sisters and monks, for the most part, presently maintain that the nuns have been more than repaid for this misappropriation, yet as part of the historical record this incident warrants mention. Mother Benedicta informed Cardinal Barnabo in January 1859 that she readily agreed "the Reverend Prelate in every respect understands better than I do how to direct our whole Order." Her qualifying statement followed: "In respect to our sisters, however, Your Eminence will agree with me, I am sure, that much, and especially what concerns the internal direction of the convent, should not always be left to men." As yet, there is no located correspondence to indicate the Cardinal's response.

Wimmer wrote to Ludwig in December 1858, thanking him for the money sent to the Kansas monks and Minnesota sisters. Although Wimmer had requested money specifically for the Minnesota sisters in earlier correspondence with Müller, when funds arrived he justified his using it for the monks. He told the former king about the Minnesota sisters, but questioned whether they would be there much longer since a report had been directed to the Apostolic See and he was awaiting the answer. He wrote: "Under these circumstances, I thought it unwise to send them the 3000 fl., fearing that they would be squandered foolishly. And since I did not want them to be idle I bought eight so-called land warrants." He wrote that he had sent the land warrants immediately to Benedict Haindl, the first prior of Saint Cloud, with the request that the land held by the brothers, but not yet paid for, be paid with the money, "and so give the Monastery of Saint Ludwig [an honor he temporarily bestowed on his great benefactor] a solid foundation. For these eight warrants the prior gets 1280 acres of land or 2 sq. miles in one place a magnificent estate! Gratitude and love for your Majesty greatly urged me to build a lasting monument to your name and memory in the far West."[71] He could not, he concluded, give it in conscience "to the sisters and there is nothing lost because the land is worth ten times more and further we will also do all what we can for the sisters."[72]

Wimmer received acknowledgment from Ludwig that what he did with the 3000 florins destined for the sisters and diverted to land purchase was approved "under the conditions presently existing and which you described."[73] Mother Willibalda had also appealed to Ludwig, however. In May Müller questioned Wimmer's right to divert the funds and told him that he considered it an "injustice." He reminded Wimmer that it happened twice before—at Saint Mary's and in Newark and that he would soon "lose the good will of His Majesty." The money, he decreed, would have to be repaid by September 1. He strongly advised Wimmer "not to do the same in the future." He lauded the "great opportunities" of which Wimmer took advantage to use the money, but he reprimanded him for his Machiavellianism: "This does not, however, give you the right to take what was allotted to others, no matter how honestly you mean it."[74] Wimmer subsequently sent a receipt to the King from the Monastery of Saint Louis (Ludwig) and defended himself again, saying that he was "not so unsympathetic to the other sex that I would want to enrich the men at the expense of the women." The appropriation of funds, however, had brought extraordinary benefits to the brothers which could have been attained only "through the sacrifice of the sisters." If it had been used as allocated, Wimmer added, "[i]t would be very probable that little or nothing of lasting worth would have come from Your Highness' gift."[75]

In later correspondence Wimmer continued to maintain that the sisters would have misused the money, though he admitted making a mistake in not getting approval to divert the funds from the Directors of the Mission Society. He also wrote Müller that he had exercised his "rights" and removed "tyranny of women" by deposing Benedicta. He had accepted Willibalda's apology on his last trip to Minnesota but had forbidden the nuns to receive any novices, since he would not encourage growth of an "undisciplined convent." He would not, he said, "support a crowd of insubordinate nuns near my young priests and brothers!" He knew the king was withholding 3000 florins from Wimmer's next allotment of funds, and that he was satisfied since if it were sent to the sisters, he would not be responsible. "But it is very probable that the money will be uselessly spent in traveling and employed in a wrong way."[76]

Again he promised to build the sisters a convent attached to the "now completed parish church" at Saint Mary's. He reminded the monarch that the monks were heavily in debt and "the heart of the Order is in Saint Vincent. Should the pulse stop here, it will stop everywhere."[77] Ludwig and Müller accepted Wimmer's lengthy defense of his actions.

Landmark Change for American Benedictine Women: Rome Responds in 1859

Benedicta Riepp's protestation of Wimmer's jurisdiction over the nuns resulted in a significant response from Rome dated December 6, 1859. Benedictine women were mandated to be supervised by the bishops of their respective dioceses rather than by the American Cassinese Congregation. Additionally, nuns no longer could make solemn profession due to their inability to remain cloistered in their apostolic work among immigrants. Only permitted to make simple vows, nuns were further ordered in 1866—following Boniface Wimmer's lead—to dispense with the Divine Office altogether, substituting the abbreviated Little Office for the Blessed Virgin Mary. The two decrees essentially removed the traditionally upheld rights of autonomy, solemn vows, and practice of the Divine Office characteristic of monasticism for American sisters.[78]

According to the 1859 Vatican decree, Wimmer had lost the right to being Benedictine nuns' superior. Nonetheless, he never accepted the transfer of jurisdiction to the bishops in reality, continuing to act as the sisters' superior whenever he felt justified in doing so. He did, however, recognize that he would have to use the bishops as intermediaries. He had sent a missive to Bishop Young of Erie requesting him to send Mother Benedicta back to Eichstätt during her sojourn in his diocese between Rome and Minnesota. Young had equivocated, reminding Wimmer that Mother Benedicta should be allowed to finish her days in Minnesota as it was obvious that she was terminally ill. Before any other efforts were made to remove her from Saint Cloud, she died of tuberculosis.

The *St. Cloud Democrat* of March 10, 1862, stated in her obituary that "the Mother Superior of the Sisters of the Benedictine Order died at the convent in this place on last Saturday morning," and the writer added, "The funeral was largely attended."[79] Her body was interred in Saint Cloud, but later removed to the sisters' cemetery at Saint Benedict's in Saint Joseph, where the nuns established their permanent residence in 1863. Mother Benedicta Riepp is revered as their foundress. The convent building at Saint Mary's was completed in February 1861, eight years after it was promised and the first funds for its construction had been put to other use.

Although the sisters were often economically destitute, their numbers continued to grow. At the time of Benedicta's death, there were seven monasteries of Benedictine nuns, all founded from Saint Mary's. Eventually its daughterhouses made their own foundations and America, especially the Midwest, was soon dotted with houses of nuns who traced their beginnings to that first foundation in Pennsylvania.[80]

Other American foundations and expansion continued throughout the nineteenth and twentieth centuries. All would be affected by the outcome of the conflict between Mother Benedicta Riepp and Abbot Boniface Wimmer. Matters of ministry, jurisdiction and authority affecting American nuns resulted in an unprecedented change in women monastics' status and future. While this new horizon dawned, Benedictine monasticism spread westward in America, continuing to exemplify the spiritual and cultural adaptability of Benedict's sixth-century Rule. ❊

CHAPTER 11

North American Expansion and Indian Missions

Nineteenth Century

The unprecedented changes wrought by the nineteenth century American monastic experience remained scarcely perceptible in subsequent Benedictine missionary growth and expansion. Foundations continued to attract candidates of both men and women, and American monasticism was well on its way to becoming a significant force and presence in the American religious landscape.

Initial ministry focused on German immigrants shifted as monastics from Switzerland arrived. Their vision for missions on the American frontier, particularly among the Indian populations, began a new wave of missionary endeavors.

Benedictine Expansion to Kansas

Before the American Civil War, Abbot Boniface Wimmer was preoccupied with the fact that many of his monks felt compelled to join the military—some serving the Confederacy, others the Union—as medics and chaplains. As a consequence of his preoccupation, Peter Lemke—now Father Henry—left Saint Vincent's without leave, ending his westward excursion at Doniphan, Kansas. Wimmer eventually sent two monks to join him, but when passed over as prior, Lemke left for Kansas in 1857—this time with permission—though Wimmer did not plan the move into Kansas.

When the community there was organized and recognized, Lemke—who had earlier hoped to become prior at Carrolltown—was again passed over as superior and travelled to Europe for a three-year sojourn. He collected funds and arranged for the biography of Prince Gallitzin.[1] On his return to the States in 1861, he became a pastor in Elizabeth, New Jersey, where he established a convent of Benedictine nuns whom he recruited from the Newark foundation. In 1878 he left New Jersey to retire in Carrolltown. He died there at the age of eighty-six, but the work he had begun in Kansas had a significant future.

The Benedictine monks' community in Doniphon later relocated to Atchison, Kansas, and sisters were soon called to assist them. The monastery had received priory status in 1858, and abbatial in 1876. Prior Augustine had favored the move to Atchison because the donated land seemed better adapted to the opening of an educational institution. The college on the monks' compound was founded in 1859.[2]

In 1863, when Prior Augustine was building a grade school for the Atchison children, he consulted Mother Willibalda. She and the sisters agreed that the Minnesota foundation would send missionaries, and seven of the twelve sisters at Saint Cloud were allowed to go to Kansas. Their selection was made by drawing straws in contrast with the former Wimmer-dominated appointments. The lot fell to Sister Evangelista, appointed superior of the band by Mother Willibalda.

Arriving in November 1863, the sisters found the nine-year-old Atchison village unnerved by the vicissitudes of the Civil War and plagued by horse-thieves. A convent building was prepared for them, so by early December, Saint Scholastica's Academy "for young ladies" was in session. As was typical on the eager frontier, the first postulant was admitted almost immediately—before the end of the same month.[3] The roots of the Atchison monks and nuns were stabilized here, eventually expanding into several monasteries and significantly influencing Benedictines and the American public throughout the twentieth century.

Saint Vincent's and Saint Mary's Foundations Multiply

Abbot Boniface Wimmer's monks had established a priory at Newark in 1857. He lived to see it receive abbey status in 1884, the same year as the southern monastery at Belmont, South Carolina, which dates its foundation to 1876 and became an abbey nullius with quasi-episcopal jurisdiction by the monastic abbot in 1910.[4] In 1886, a year before his death, Wimmer also sent monks to Pueblo, Colorado, who eventually relocated to Cañon City, Colorado, in 1923. Nuns were in Covington, Kentucky, by 1869 and five years later a house opened in Bristow, Virginia. The Kentucky nuns sent a group to New Orleans in 1870 where courageous sisters opened integrated schools—though eventually they were forced to segregate racially—and moved across Lake Pontchartrain to Covington, Louisiana. This house was closed in 1988 after long years of service by the nuns in Louisiana.[5]

The flourishing eastern and Midwestern communities continued to make new foundations in their areas and the south, southwest, and on the west coast throughout the later nineteenth and early twentieth centuries. Nuns from Erie established Saint Scholastica's Priory in Chicago in 1861. A monastery designed to minister to the Czech and Slovak immigrants was also founded in Chicago in 1885 but moved to Lisle in the Joliet diocese in 1914, where nuns from Saint Mary's had preceded them in 1895. Carrolltown, Pennsylvania, nuns planted a daughterhouse in Creston, Iowa, which eventually relocated, first to Guthrie, Oklahoma, and then to Tulsa where in the post-Vatican II period it separated into two groups, one now located at Red Plains Priory in Oklahoma City. Florida received both monks and nuns in 1889 at Saint Leo's.

Monks were present in Washington state by 1895. Other houses followed at intervals especially throughout the first half of the twentieth century. Nuns came finally to Boerne, Texas, after they had first settled in Cuba in 1911 and then relocated to San Antonio. Cullman, Alabama, received monks and nuns in 1891 and 1892. Many of these also established communities in foreign lands. The Saint Joseph, Minnesota, nuns had so many daughterhouses that they were able to organize these into a congregation in 1947. That federation (Saint Benedict) eventually included motherhouses in Wisconsin (Eau Claire), Washington (Lacey), Illinois (Nauvoo), North Dakota (Bismarck), and Minnesota (at Duluth and Saint Paul), as well as foreign monasteries in Japan (Sapporo) and Taiwan (Taipei). The Saint Benedict Monastery at Saint Joseph has three dependent priories: in the Bahamas at Nassau, Humacao, and in Ogden, Utah. Since the revision of canon law, many Benedictine motherhouses of nuns have reclaimed the title "monastery" instead of "convent" for their main monastic dwelling. The federations of American nuns have generally made this optional, so it varies depending on the decisions of the nuns of the different communities.

By the dawn of the twenty-first century, twenty-two American Cassinese monasteries included an archabbey (Latrobe, Pennsylvania), twenty abbeys with three American dependent priories, and foundations also in Brazil, Taiwan, Japan, and the Bahamas. At the same time the nuns of both Saint Scholastica Federation and that of Saint Benedict's (which include most of the communities traced back to Eichstätt) had also expanded to include monasteries throughout North America.[6] Benedicta Riepp and Boniface Wimmer, despite their differences, had succeeded in building a successful, significant, and flourishing monastic system of Benedictine communities of men and women whose influence has become world-wide. Benedicta and Boniface were founders, individuals of tremendous vision and courage.

The Swiss Foundations in the United States

Other American congregations of monks were in their embryonic state while Mother Benedicta and Abbot Boniface were contesting the limits of their jurisdictions. Just two years after Benedicta stepped on American soil, a Swiss monastery took root in southern Indiana. The language was German (Swiss speak German, French, Italian, depending on which is a border country, or Romansh in the canton of Graubünden), but the general culture and heritage was Swiss. The roots were at monasteries of men at Einsiedeln and Engelberg for monks, and women's communities at Maria-Reichenbach (Niederrickenbach), Sarnen, and Melchtal in that diminutive country (the area of Switzerland is one-fifth that of the state of South Dakota). Despite its size, the nation's monastics made a significant impact on American Benedictinism.

Maria-Einsiedeln Abbey in the canton of Schwyz dates from the tenth century erection of a monastery at the hermitage of the martyr-monk, Saint Meinrad, who had perished at the hands of brigands a century earlier. The Abbey had taken a leading role in the founding of the Swiss Congregation in 1602. Left in ruins in 1798, it was finally restored in the early nineteenth century. The future there remained uncertain, as in most European abbeys. Because of anti-clerical movements and the political instability, many began to found communities abroad in case of displacement. The political climate in nineteenth-century Switzerland deeply concerned Abbot Heinrich Schmid von Baar (1846–1874). There were unjust exactions leveled in consequence of the Sonderbund War that had drained the monastery's financial resources. Further aggravation resulted when the monks were expelled from the school in Bellinzona in the canton of Ticino in 1852. A blessing in disguise, this made several monks available for an American foundation.[7]

Another request for Swiss monks came from the bishop of Vincennes, Indiana, Maurice de Saint Palais (1811–1877), who had been a pastor in the diocese under its first bishop, Simon Bruté (1779–1839). Saint Palais had served the surrounding parishes of Saint Mary's in Davis County. He could visit the more than fifty settlers in the Catholic German immigrant towns of Evansville and Jasper only once every three months. Because he was unable to converse in German, he felt that he was not a quality minister to those needing spiritual leadership in these growing settlements. Joseph Kundek (1810–1857), a Croatian missionary, had arrived from his home archdiocese of Agram. He was immediately assigned to the Jasper–Evansville area where he conceived the project of encouraging wide-scale German immigration.[8]

Ferdinand, Indiana

Subsequently, Kundek claimed 1440 acres of land, located mostly in the southern part of Dubois County. He paid for much of it with allotments from the Leopoldine Society of Vienna that had originally sponsored his relocation to the American missions. Later, for a moderate price, Kundek resold the land to Catholic settlers whom he attracted by advertising in German Catholic papers in Ohio and points east. Kundek founded the town of Ferdinand in 1840 along the Troy-Jasper road and the nearby town of Celestine three years later. There were soon too many parishioners for one priest. Kundek, as the bishop's vicar general, traveled to Europe to recruit German-speaking priests from Einsiedeln Abbey.

The abbot ultimately promised him monks—but could spare only two. Abbot Henry envisioned a new foundation and impressed Kundek with the fact that it would be a dependent mission of Einsiedeln and must remain perpetually affiliated with the founding Swiss abbey. Henry stipulated that pastoral work might be its first commitment, but that a seminary for students interested in the priesthood would soon have to follow—as numbers permitted.[9] Kundek agreed that the Ferdinand parish could be assigned to the Benedictines immediately upon arrival while they looked for an appropriate site for a dependent priory. He pledged continued support to the monastic project.

When a delegate from Einsiedeln presented the project to Pius IX in a private audience in Rome, the proposal asked approbation for a "so-called daughterhouse, connected with it and dependent on it, and for that very reason dependent on the Holy See."[10] The pope blessed the undertaking and even suggested that the whole faculty expelled from the Bellizona School be transferred at once to the United States. Kundek, however, was not always of the same mind—at least on all points.

The diocesan vicar-general, also in Rome with the Einsiedeln delegate, Gall Morel (1803–1872), expressed to him the hope that as soon as the new monastery had twelve priest-monks it could gain its independence from Einsiedeln and have its own abbot. Father Gall disapprovingly repeated Kundek's conversation to his abbot, who did not change his plans. Two men left the abbey for America, not dubbed as "founders" but "explorers" charged with locating a site for the new priory. A Swiss native, Ulrich Christen (then 38), was put in charge of the expedition. His companion was Bede O'Connor, taken when he was fourteen to Einsiedeln to take advantage of the free education provided to economically deprived youth.

At Einsiedeln, he learned not only the classical languages but also how to read and write German as perfectly as his native English. He also spoke some Italian and French. Ordained the year before he left for the States, he was twelve years younger than the sometimes opinionated Ulrich. O'Connor was reputed to have a "Celtic temper," a genuine sense of humor, a gifted oratorical style, and a serious physical impairment—a significant hearing loss. These then were to work together for the good of the people in Indiana and the future of Swiss-American Benedictinism, although there would be some personality clashes.

The farewell program in Einsiedeln for the missionaries assigned two student-speakers who would become intimately connected with the American mission's future. They were Martin Marty, later the new monastery's first abbot, and Johann Mundwiler, its second. The cost of travel was defrayed by the Society of the Propagation of the Faith at Lyons, which also donated several thousand francs to the project. After attempts to leave a stormy England where they had gone to visit Bede's mother and sister in London, the monks landed in New York on January 31, 1853. Before they traveled west, the bishop offered them a thousand acres in Philadelphia. They spent five days at Saint Vincent's, where Wimmer mapped out more of their future than they were ready for at that time. After several mishaps, they arrived at Vincennes, Indiana. Conversation with the bishop did not flow freely even after trials with French, German, English, and Latin. Nevertheless, the bishop pledged full support and encouraged them to "look for the best place in the diocese."[11]

Ulrich wrote optimistic letters back to the abbot asking for more monks, while Bede reported that the anti-Catholic and anti-immigrant Know-Nothing Party was inciting a gullible public against Catholics. Priests and members of religious orders were their chief targets. Bede wrote the abbot that the Protestant women were especially fearful, but that some had attended his English language sermons marveling that he was not thoroughly German, nor did he have "horns and goat's feet."[12] There was no immediate stability for the priests. They frequently spent a great deal of time in the saddle and wagons circuit riding between parishes while residing, for the most part, at the Ferdinand rectory. The pastor there was not enthusiastic about the monks'

presence and eventually circulated a petition against any proposed Benedictine monastery in the area.

The monks were eager to get their own land. Father Ulrich subsequently found some to his liking in Spencer county about six miles south of Ferdinand. The monk bought 2400 acres that purportedly covered coal, sandstone, limestone, and even iron. There were two farms with log houses, barns, a gristmill, and sawmill that also had to be purchased. Henry Denning, the owner, offered one of the farms at the inflated price of $2700. In a "gentleman's agreement" Ulrich made a down payment of $1250 and promised to remit the balance by March 1, 1854. The total purchase cost of land and buildings totaled $12,000, of which he had to borrow almost $4,000 from the bishop to hold in an informal contract for deed. The monk wrote the abbot requesting more money and more men.

Correspondence laden with admonitions, misunderstandings, and evidence of tensions between the monastic pioneers and the Einsiedeln chapter led to requests that the monks progress more slowly and provide more documentation flowed to and from Switzerland. However, Abbot Henry wrote the bishop that he could spare two more priests for the Indiana mission. These were Jerome Bachmann, who would be the community superior, and Eugene Schwerzmann, who would be accompanied by some hired lay people. Both monks had been professors, and Bachmann had done some pastoral work but spent many of his recent years as house superior and business manager at the abbey.

These recruits, except for Eugene who had stayed behind in Cincinnati tracing their lost luggage, arrived at Ferdinand in October 1853. The lay persons accompanying them were two women housekeeper-designates and two men. Jerome approved of Ulrich's purchase after he inspected the property, but he and his abbot were both utterly dismayed when they discovered that they needed another $12,000 loan to buy the whole tract. The abbot sent $4,000 that he had sequestered secretly as a pleasant surprise for his successor, but he willingly sacrificed it for the new foundation. In January 1854, Abbot Henry designated the foundation as a dependent priory and named Father Jerome its prior.

Saint Meinrad

In March, the move to the new farm—named Saint Meinrad's by Abbot Henry—was made by wagon caravan from Ferdinand. A brother candidate who arrived a month before brought simple furnishings and household utensils, as well as Oblates Sales and Kälin. One of the housekeepers and Gertrude Kälin rode horseback to the small, crowded quarters where they lived in extreme poverty. Mosquitoes and insects plagued everyone in the house while snakes—including poisonous ones —met them in the fields. Humidity and rain in summer (prompting them to take umbrellas to their leaky bedrooms nightly) and fierce cold and snow in winter tormented them. Meals were more than frugal, and the perennial staple was cornbread.[13] The school occupied a lean-to attached to the log monastery. The low-ceilinged small rooms were converted into two bedrooms, Father Eugene's office, a dormitory, and a classroom. There were only two students in 1854. When Father Eugene died, the school was closed.[14]

Drought brought disappointment and scarcity in the grain harvest and orchards. The pastures and meadows burned out, and the few animals had to be fed sparingly. Nothing could be paid on the debt. Despite—or perhaps because of—this state of affairs, Prior Jerome decided that the gristmill and sawmill might bring some profit. He purchased both and 166 more acres of land in March for another $2800. Disaster struck again when fire destroyed all the surrounding frame buildings and over 300 feet of fence in April 1855.The mills began to lose profits as the people in the area presumed that the Benedictine owners could grind their grain and saw their logs *gratis.* Eventually the mills were leased, then sold, but reclaimed when the purchasers defaulted.

All was not well on the diocesan level either. The bishop, himself a Frenchman, had apparently received some pressure from the influential pioneer French clergy who were intimidated by the preponderance of German immigrants and German-language priests. Consequently the bishop refused to sign an agreement with Abbot Henry similar to those he had with Swiss bishops whose parishes were served by the monks. The abbot threatened to withdraw his monk-priests from the parishes they served so that they might concentrate on community

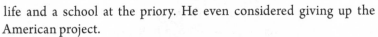
life and a school at the priory. He even considered giving up the American project.

The Indiana priory chapter of four, however, saved the day by drawing up a new contract acceptable to the bishop. The monks urged the abbot to sign the document and come in person to inspect the American mission. Abbot Henry accepted the agreement with one condition—that, at his own discretion, he could deprive any of his monks of their priestly faculties. When the bishop again asked for more priests, the abbot declined on the basis of lack of personnel and the Swiss government's objection to missionaries making land purchases abroad. Abbot Henry feared the loss of passports of those already in Indiana and the inability to get approval for more monks to emigrate to the fledgling American monastery.

Assistance soon came from unexpected sources. Seven young men from German Swabia (Württemberg) had read newspaper reports about the abbey's American mission and resolved to cast their lot with the Indiana foundation. Einsiedeln, to avoid more trouble with the Swiss government, informed them that they had to travel at their own risk and expense, make their novitiate and vows as lay brothers at Saint Meinrad's, and be monks of that community—not Einsiedeln's. The young men agreed, arriving at the American priory on July 4, 1855, to bring the number of brother candidates to ten. They had a rigorous daily schedule under the supervision of Father Jerome, their prior and formation director. At first they had devotional prayers including the rosary, but eventually they were given the English Little Office of the Blessed Virgin since only the priest-monks prayed the breviary, the Divine Office. Sudden deaths, in the span of only four months, decimated the monks. Forty-four-year-old Father Eugene, after a brief one-week illness, died in August. Two months later Oblate Kälin, victim of malaria and other fevers, followed him. One of the Swabian brothers succumbed to tuberculosis just a month later. Things did not improve.

Jerome's leadership had been constantly questioned. Bede had complained that he was not mission-oriented, and related that he had even told the bishop he had come not to preach but to plow. Finally in October, the Abbot replaced Jerome as prior with Bede, who apparently did not feel qualified to be superior. When he arrived from his parish at Cannelton, he found $25 in the cash box and debts of over $7,000, of which almost $2,000 was coming due. He traveled to Cincinnati where, for three weeks, he knocked on many doors and raised $1776. Father Jerome returned to Switzerland with reports about the mission that led to more recriminating letters from the Swiss abbot to the new American community.

Abbot Henry decided to send a new superior to Indiana, Athanasius Tschopp (d. 1882), who requested that Father Jerome return with him to supervise the manual labor. After the usual obstacles on the voyage (this time a thirteen-hour delay on a sandbar off Nova Scotia) the three monks arrived to ringing bells and shotgun salvos at their new home. Father Chrysostom Foffa (d. 1899), who eventually became the most significant of the three, was described as a Goliath with an exuberance proportionate to his size, large of mind and heart. However, he also could be brusque and explosive, and he detested being tied to schedules. His failures he usually blamed on someone else but when needed most, he would be there; it was he who later volunteered to accompany Marty to the Dakota Indian missions.

Father Bede left for the parish at Fulda in September, accompanied by Gertrude Kälin, whom he had requested for housekeeping duties. Father Athanasius succumbed to typhoid fever and became so ill that Abbot Henry began to feel that he was getting signs that the project should be abandoned. "It is my firm resolution," he wrote, "that if Father Superior does not fully recover, to sell our whole possession over there as soon as possible or to hand it over to Father Boniface Wimmer, inasmuch as most likely no one of us would any longer care to take it over at his own risk and responsibility."[15] Even after the prior recovered, the abbot told him that, at his discretion, he had the liberty to liquidate the property and return with his monks to Einsiedeln where all would be welcomed with open arms.

The mission would not be abandoned, and the harvest of 1855 was better. Even wild grapes of excellent quality ripened in abundance. The outcroppings of sandstone on the acreage further promised materials for future construction. Yet the prior, after a second attack of fever, left in August 1856 for his native climate with Jerome, who had never endeared himself to the community, accompanying him. Chrysostom was confirmed as vicar for the prior. He soon had a frame dwelling added to the cramped quarters and found a well with clear water. Bede was usually serving in parishes, and Chrysostom occasionally helped priests in parochial duties for additional income. Often the priory housed only brother novices and candidates, with no resident professed monk.

Chrysostom began to suffer bouts of malaria. He was told to sterilize his drinking water with some liquor, then a popular hygienic precaution. There was often a danger, however, that he would become too voluble and indiscreet in speech after trying to quell his fever attacks with such "medicine." However, Chrysostom could invest five more candidates with the habit in January 1847 and reopen the school. Two of the ten students began to study Latin in preparation for ordination to the priesthood, along with two of the monastic novices who assisted in the instruction of the students during their seminary days. This marked the inauguration of Saint Meinrad's seminary, which would be one of the monks' main ministries.

Another Swiss missionary came to augment the numbers. Father Isidor Hobi arrived from Einsiedeln to join the school staff in April 1857. He retrieved the discarded violin of the late Father Eugene, taught himself to play, and provided the only musical accompaniment at Mass, Vespers, Compline, and the Little Hours on great feasts of the church year. Isidor was appointed prior. He supervised the building of a frame church where monks and students worshipped for several decades.

The problems, demands, debts, and obstacles were still so great that the four priests wrote a joint letter to Abbot Henry in April 1858 recommending either partial or total liquidation. They preferred partial, but it meant that the abbot had to determine if the house was to be a monastery with a school, a monastery without a school, a school without a monastery, a mission house without a monastery, or a school from which the priests went to neighboring parishes to serve as pastors. The monks agreed, however, that "a school without a monastery is an institute foreign to our Order."[17]

If a buyer was found, the abbot preferred total liquidation. He also felt that immediate independence from the Swiss house was imperative. The property was transferred to Father Isidor's name in 1859, followed by application to the Holy See for approval of the separation. When the bishop did not agree with the monks' plans, Father Isidor proposed that Einsiedeln salvage the mission by sending a capable man to assume full authority. He recommended Father Martin Marty. The Abbot accepted the recommendation and made what he considered a temporary appointment. In August the abbot informed Saint Meinrad that Fathers Martin and Fintan were soon to pay a visit to inform them verbally of their commission.

Beginnings of the Swiss American Congregation

Recruited to become the struggling Saint Meinrad's trouble-shooter, Martin Marty (1834–1896) was credited with saving the pioneering monastery from extinction. Like Wimmer, he ultimately founded a new congregation of monks—the Swiss American, approved in 1881. Like Wimmer, Marty's native language was German, yet there the similarity seems to stop. Marty is known best as another Pierre Jean DeSmet (1801–1873), the pioneering mid-nineteenth century Jesuit "apostle to the Indians."[18] Marty's beginning at the Indiana monastery initiated his becoming the first bishop of a Dakota diocese and the third of one in Minnesota. Ironically as the Ordinary of the diocese of Saint Cloud, Marty's jurisdiction included Wimmer's foundation—Saint John's Abbey, formerly named Saint Louis after its principal patron.[19]

Martin Marty's Background

Marty was a native-born Swiss from Schwyz. He was the first child, oldest of eleven born to a former servant and a shoemaker who do ubled as church sexton. He was baptized Alois in Saint Martin's church in Schwyz. All four boys who survived to adulthood eventually became priests. The untimely death of one of his sisters, when Marty was young, affected him deeply; his grief almost led to his death in an accidental fall down one of the Alpine mountains. After an initial rejection of his 1850 application for admission to the Einsiedeln monastery—apparently because of his independent and assertive temperament—Marty was accepted for reapplication four years later. The monks had left for America just a year before and had now moved into their first log-house monastery at Saint Meinrad.

Marty took as his monastic name Martin in honor of the great fourth-century priest-missionary of Gaul, Martin of Tours. Little did he know then how closely his destiny would emulate his patron's. Marty professed vows in 1855 and was ordained priest a year later. For the next five years he taught in the *gymnasium* at Einsiedeln where he had once been a student. Meanwhile he contributed articles to several publications dealing with the history of Benedictine education and the value of student associations in Catholic boarding schools. He was twenty-six when he was sent to America on temporary assignment to make the priory viable or to dissolve it.

Marty in Indiana

His first task in Indiana was to reduce the monastery's debt. This he did through the sale of monastery property to settlers who then charted the town of Saint Meinrad on the former monastic lands. With increased farm production and astute financing, Marty made substantial payments on the monastery's loans. He expended most of his energy, however, reopening the seminary (it was closed temporarily for want of instructors) in which he taught not only philosophy and homiletics but also aesthetics, violin, and organ.[20] He attended the Provincial Council in Cincinnati in 1861 and also the Second Plenary Council of Baltimore in 1866.

Marty soon became attached to the new land, and despite being very close to his family and community in Switzerland, he soon applied for and received the abbot's reluctant permission to remain in America. In 1865, he built ten parish churches and a year later expanded the college building when the Bishop of Vincennes sent all his seminarians to Saint Meinrad's to prepare for the priesthood.

As usual, the monks saw the need for nuns to assist them in the parishes and schools. In 1867 the Covington, Kentucky, Benedictines acceded to the request of Father Chrysostom for sisters to teach religion in the Ferdinand parish. These same sisters had, a year earlier, requested permission from Marty to build a priory on the abbey's property, a short distance from the monastery at a spot called "Monte Cassino." Abbot Henry, who still had final authority, rejected that project, so the women established a community mother-house a few miles away in the small town of Ferdinand.[21]

Boniface Wimmer soon encouraged Marty to apply to Rome for abbatial rank. Wimmer likely hoped that the Swiss monastery would join the Bavarian Americans (American Cassinese) Congregation of which he was the *Praeses* (president). That, however, was not to be. When Marty returned to Einsiedeln for a personal visit with the abbot and some necessary chapter decisions, the monks voted to allow the American priory to apply for abbatial rank on condition that it remain in the Swiss Congregation. They also stipulated that the monks who had professed vows at Einsiedeln forfeit all rights of membership at the mother abbey, unless someone chose to return. Another condition stated that all the members of the new American priory have the same rights and obligations—observances, constitutions and customs—as the Einsiedeln monks.[22]

Pius IX approved the request for abbatial rank in September 1870, just before the invasion of Rome by the new republic's army that had earlier necessitated cessation of Vatican I. When notified, the monks proceeded to elect Marty as abbot, unaware that Rome had reserved the appointment to itself. The Vatican document finally also arrived, naming Marty abbot to every one's relief.

Among those present at the new abbot's installation was Boniface Wimmer. Now, Marty was in a position to fully implement what he had written earlier to a confrère at Einsiedeln about his vision of the Benedictine mission in America: "Now we can live in accord with our vocation and with showing ourselves to others for what we are to be called to be—religious, Benedictines, educators and missionaries."[23] He had no idea, then, just how far away from his Indiana monastery his sense of mission would eventually take him.

New Fields of American Benedictine Endeavors

Before the end of 1873, a new abbey building was completed. The seminary seemed to be a viable institution, and the parishes operated smoothly. Monastic candidates came by the dozens. Marty was ready for new fields of endeavor. Even he must have been surprised, however, at the turn fate took him.

Indian missionary work had long been a dream of the young abbot's. He had once met the famous Jesuit missionary to the Native Americans, Father Pierre Jean DeSmet, when the Belgian priest had lectured at Einsiedeln during Marty's student days. He was, thus, not unacquainted with the needs of the Sioux tribes in the Dakotas where DeSmet—while traveling between Saint Louis and the Jesuit missions in Montana—often paused to celebrate the Eucharist or baptize and catechize the Indians. DeSmet had stayed days, weeks, or even as much as four months along the route, especially in the western area near the Black Hills.

DeSmet had ministered to many Native Americans and white settlers. Although he had not organized permanent missions, DeSmet was known and respected by many of the Indians. Dubbed "Blackrobe" by the Native Americans, he paved the way for Marty, who established permanent Catholic mission churches and reservation schools. Marty would have had a longer and harder time of it had not the personable Jesuit laid the groundwork for his success among the Sioux.

Having heard from several women interested in Indian missionary work that the Benedictines were also willing to undertake Native American ministry, Father J. B. Brouillet, Director of the Catholic Indian Mission Bureau, wrote to Abbot Marty at Saint Meinrad's in 1876. He relayed to him the need for priests at Standing Rock Reservation in the Dakota Territory. He also wrote Prior Frowin, who had come from Engelberg to establish a monastery in Missouri at Conception. This letter reflected the tenor of the time regarding Indian conversion and education:

> The education of several generations is unthinkable without stability, and the family life of a genuine Benedictine family, embracing the material as well as the spiritual progress, is the

exemplar and ideal of the Christian family life, upon which the welfare of the individual and of society rests. The ora et labora is today still the only remedy for healing the children of Adam and neither the one nor the other can be taught in words alone.[24]

Marty informed his friend, James A. McMaster (editor of the New York *Freeman's Journal*), that it seemed God's will that Benedictines should be the missionaries to unbaptized Native Americans. Marty told him that *he* planned to go see "what could be done."[25]

Marty soon discovered that the Indians were virtually prisoners on their reservations, and that their means of livelihood had been taken away. The politically appointed agents supervised a weekly doling of meager rations of flour and meat. They received some items of clothing—annually. These U. S. agents often placed their self-interest above the needs of the Indian people; some were guilty of outright theft and fraud. They tended to be greedy men who profited illegally by their position. Not without great effort, Marty helped change that situation somewhat. At least some conditions were bettered on the reservations as he tried to alleviate what prevalent injustices he could.[26]

The Dakota Territory Missions

When Abbot Marty was reading the letter of request for Indian missionaries to Father Chrysostom, who had just returned from a sabbatical year at the Swiss abbey, the monk interrupted to ask Marty to send him to Dakota. Abbot Marty acquiesced and then immediately added that he would be the second priest to respond to the call—an unprecedented move on the part of a monastic abbot. The two monks from Indiana arrived in Dakota Territory in 1876, shortly after the Sioux Indians lost the Black Hills where the discovery of gold had prompted mass invasions by whites. The Indians had just bested Custer and his troops at Little Big Horn and the surviving Native American leaders, including Sitting Bull, were evading the troops sent after them or exiling themselves across the Canadian border.

Sitting Bull and American Policy

At first, as he was establishing the missions on Standing Rock, Marty dealt with the Hunkpapas, Blackfoot, and the Yanktonais Sioux. Before long, however, his ministry extended to all the Sioux tribes. Marty explained his observations of the Indians' dilemma, which was fairly common to missionaries, in an article for a Munich newspaper:

> Less than 20 years ago this territory was crossed by innumerable herds of buffalo which the Indians followed every summer with bow and arrow. With them they roamed the immense prairies and gathered their winter supplies which they consumed in snug comfort and peace in the tree-lined shores of the streams during the cold part of the year. The tents and clothing fashioned from buffalo skins kept them warm. The trees protected them from the storms, and provided fuel for their tent fires. Unfortunately all this has changed. The Dakota Indians are freezing and famine stricken. With powder and lead the Whites have destroyed the herds for the sake of the hides thousands were killed and there were not enough wolves and fox, hawks and eagles to consume the meat. Uselessly the brave Dakotas attempted to defend their source of supplies against the avaricious intruders. Numerical superiority of the Whites and their use of deception made the original inhabitants prisoners who are not allowed to leave their Reservations without a pass from a military of civil functionary. Forts have been erected where several companies of soldiers now guard the defenseless Dakotas.[27]

After Marty had the Standing Rock mission organized, he wrote the Director of the Bureau of Catholic Indian Missions for authorization to visit Sitting Bull in his Canadian exile. He hoped that he could convince him to return peacefully to the reservation before all the Sioux died of starvation.

On March 12, 1877, the War Department extended permission for Marty to travel at his own risk *not* as an emissary of the United

States but as an individual who would in no way alter, modify, or delay military operations in progress. The Commissioner of Indian Affairs spoke for the Department of the Interior in a memorandum addressed to the government agent at Standing Rock. Marty could go at his personal expense and take as escorts a few of the Indians from the Agency. Return to the reservations, then, would mean that the Indians would not starve, but they would be prisoners of war and had to surrender their arms and horses. Marty saw no alternative for the Native Americans. For him, it was that or complete extinction of the bands that had fled north after Little Big Horn.

The abbot set out to track Sitting Bull, who had more than 2,000 Sioux with him in western Canada. Marty felt compelled to do this because, as he expressed himself later in 1879, "I must first save their lives if I shall save their souls."[28] At Fort Peck the Benedictine priest obtained a horse and secured the services of eight Indians as companions and scouts. William Halsey, a mixed-blood interpreter, also accompanied the band. It was May 26 by the time they arrived at Sitting Bull's camp. The Hunkpapa Teton Sioux leader may have admitted Marty to his presence; if so, it was likely because he was a *Sina Sapa* (Blackrobe). In respect for Marty's predecessor DeSmet, Sitting Bull was willing to listen to the Benedictine. After greeting him, he led Abbot Marty to his lodge where the priest reminded him and the leaders with him that they would not be permanently welcomed in Canada. They were free to return in safety to the reservation before their food sources were completely gone. Sitting Bull replied that as long as the hunting was good, they would be able to remain. They would not consider leaving until absolutely necessary.[29]

Two years later Marty made another unsuccessful attempt to lure the leader back to the States. Sitting Bull had just had a rewarding buffalo kill, so the tribal leaders were not interested in the government terms Marty brought with him. Ultimately, however, the priest's prophecy that the whites would destroy too many of the buffalo— including those in Canada—to enable the Indian to continue his nomadic ways was unfortunately fulfilled.

Chief Spotted Eagle, Sitting Bull, and 1300 Native Americans chose to return to the reservations in 1881 to avoid starvation. Marty was on hand to assist but could not at that point prevent the sort of tent-arrest Sitting Bull endured at Fort Randall.[30] Marty and Agent James McLaughlin of Standing Rock then worked diligently and successfully to secure permission for Sitting Bull's return to his home territory on the Standing Rock reservation. He remained there the rest of his life, except for the tours he made with Buffalo Bill's Wild West Show which even took him to England. The great leader was killed in 1890 when he attempted resistance to move to another reservation during the "agitation" which would eventually climax in the Wounded Knee Massacre.

In order to be more effective, Marty realized that he had to learn the Sioux languages—Dakota, Lakota, and Nakota—for use in teaching and preaching. At one point, Marty excused his inability to master them, especially Lakota, by saying it was nearly impossible for any white person over thirty to learn.[31] He could make himself understood, however, in day-to-day conversation. He often used bilingual Indians or another missionary to translate when he had official conversations and occasionally when he gave sermons during Mass. He encouraged English and tribal bilingualism (he had mastered English so well that few could trace more than a slight German accent). After Marty had discovered a Sioux grammar, he had it reprinted at Saint Meinrad's. To that he added a dictionary, a catechism, and a few religious hymns. These he mastered and taught. He also instructed the Sioux how to sing the liturgical Gregorian chant and the Latin responses in exchange for tutoring in Lakota.

The Native American Schools

As was customary for his times' pioneering civil and missionary workers, Marty believed that the best way to reach the adults was through the children, and that education was the only way the Native Americans could survive in a white-dominated culture. In this context, he set about establishing a strong mission school system. He envisioned opening elementary schools on all the Dakota reservations, a move favored by the federal Indian Bureau but not always financially supported and, when it was, only to a point. The government allowed every child a fixed subsidy for board and tuition at schools of religious denominations eventually assigned to particular tribes. The missionaries were expected to furnish the school and dormitory buildings.

As time went on, however, missionaries—like Marty—often convinced the agents to turn over little-used agency structures for use as schools, trading their use for the buildings' upkeep.[32] The Standing Rock Reservation population was most concentrated at Fort Yates, where two schools opened with more following. The first was in a former soldiers' kitchen and warehouse that had once been a theater and storeroom. It was makeshift but adequate. The Kenel Farm School and the Fort Yates School endured long after Marty's demise. Eventually the Benedictine sisters opened a small hospital there.

Marty realized the critical need for religious women to teach and nurse. In 1878 he recruited the first Benedictine nuns from the Ferdinand, Indiana, community, but eventually let it be known that religious from any Benedictine houses were welcome. The need for additional priests, however, was even more critical but less easily filled. Red Cloud, Chief of the Oglala Sioux tribe at Pine Ridge in the southern part of the Territory, sent Marty a request for Roman Catholic priests for his people, although Episcopalian clergy had been assigned to the reservation under Grant's religious policy of peacekeeping by dividing reservations among the major Christian denominations. Chief Spotted Tail of Rosebud also requested priests for the Brule Teton Sioux recently relocated at Rosebud Creek.

To assess the needs of each reservation the Benedictine missionary visited them all personally spending long hours—regardless of weather—on horseback or in wagons. Many times his life was in jeopardy from rain and snowstorms as he doggedly made his rounds. When his requests for the assistance of more Benedictine monk-priests and Brothers from his own monastery or Conception, Missouri, were denied he recruited exiled German Jesuits. They eventually took pastoral charge of the Pine Ridge and Rosebud reservations, where they served throughout the rest of the nineteenth and the whole of the twentieth century.

Marty as Bishop of Dakota Territory

In 1879, Pope Leo XIII named Marty bishop and Vicar Apostolic of the Dakota Territory. He had charge of 150,000 square miles of country, occupied by thousands of Indian people and a diverse mix of white farmers, traders, land speculators, gold diggers, saloon-keepers, and their families. The new bishop chose the capital of the Dakota Territory, Yankton, as his home base, eventually building a modest residence on the hill at the western edge of the river-city, soon known as Mount Marty.

The Sisters of Mercy, whom Marty had asked to open a school in Yankton, moved their small girls' academy into a new stone structure on the hill. When a local scandal broke that lost their credibility (a Sister left the community to marry a Russian who had settled in Yankton), Marty requested that the Mercy community return to Omaha. Their school became an Indian boys' school until government policy required that Indian schools be on a reservation to get funding. After the boys had been moved to the Stephan mission near Fort Thompson, Marty invited the Benedictine nuns—then two hundred miles north at Zell—to take over the house (and the debt) that eventually became their permanent motherhouse.[33]

Marty eventually had to give up his dream of establishing a monastery of Benedictine monks with a seminary in the Dakotas. Bishop O'Connor once offered him territory in Knox County, Nebraska, just across the Missouri from Yankton, but that had not seemed feasible at that time. Only when Saint Meinrad opened a daughterhouse in the Milbank area of South Dakota in 1950 was his dream of a monastic foundation posthumously realized. Blue Cloud Abbey, though never a seminary, endured sixty years there before its closure due to lack of candidates. However, the nuns Marty brought to Yankton in 1887 remain there. The Bishop Marty Memorial Chapel, constructed in the bishop's honor, dominates their monastery. Their college, Mount Marty, is also named for the monk-bishop who first brought Benedictine nuns to the Dakotas.[34]

By 1880 Marty had fourteen Benedictines from Saint Meinrad's and Conception abbeys in his Territory. He sent two Native American men to Saint Meinrad to study for the priesthood, but the lifestyle at the seminary and their homesickness for their Native American culture and family brought them back laicized to Dakota. The shortage of clergy often led Marty to accept wandering priests who came without too much recommendation and often became troublesome individuals. His fellow abbots and bishops were not always pleased with his taking their rejects or discontents for his widespread missions. But Marty needed priests, and he needed money, which he had to seek abroad in personal fundraising visits to Switzerland, Austria, Germany, Ireland, and England.

After his trip to Rome to report to Pope Leo, Marty was named to a select committee for the promotion of the Catholic University of America in Washington, D.C. While in the capital city he spent time with Father Joseph Stephan, the new director of the Bureau of Catholic Indian Missions. Together they went to Philadelphia to request funds from Katharine Drexel, inheritor of much of the Drexel/Morgan banking fortune. In response to this and later appeals, the young woman—later founder and leader of the Blessed Sacrament Sisters—channeled a considerable part of her inheritance to the Dakota missions even after Marty's death. Marty Mission opened near Wagner where her sisters and eventually the Benedictine-oriented Oblate Sisters of the Blessed Sacrament continued the education and boarding of Indian children for more than a century after Marty's death.

When the Dakota Territory divided into the states of North and South Dakota in 1889 (with some land added to neighboring states), Marty was appointed first Bishop of the new Diocese of Sioux Falls.[35] Another bishop was appointed for North Dakota, first at Jamestown; the See was moved later to Bismarck. Four years after erection of the North Dakota diocese, another Einsiedeln monk, Vincent Wehrle, began a monastery at Devils Lake. In 1889 he moved that community to Richardton where he began to erect what would later be known as Assumption Abbey. The community was dedicated to ministering to the German-Russian and Hungarian immigrants who were arriving almost daily in the area. Wehrle was elected abbot in 1903. Seven years later he brought nuns from Saint Mary's, Pennsylvania, to the state.[35]

Marty was then responsible for half of the territory that had been under his jurisdiction. He was a man of vision and energy and continued to supervise closely the growth of the missions and the number of parishes as the population of South Dakota grew steadily. He was constantly in demand—confirming hundreds in small German, Irish, Bohemian, and mixed ethnic parishes and on the reservation missions.

In 1889 he accepted President Benjamin Harrison's appointment to a special commission to negotiate with the Chippewa Indians of Minnesota about ceding most of their reservation lands. Marty, who always seemed to follow his conscience unequivocally, felt then that the cession was just. Later, however, he championed the Chippewas against the government. He lodged a complaint that on the unceded reservation the Native Americans were being cheated by the sale of timber.

During the 1890s, Martin Marty faced a series of crises. The Wounded Knee Massacre on the Pine Ridge Reservation saddened him deeply. The Panic of 1893, which brought a temporary economic depression, and the searing drought of the summer of 1894 brought financial failure to many of the white settlers. He had never cared much about his health, either. The Bishop of Jamestown commented on Marty's peregrinations over the state: sod houses, bug-ridden beds, no privies, and long wagon rides of eighty and ninety miles, with few breaks in his travels. No wonder, the bishop mused, that his stomach, liver, kidney, nerves, brain, and everything else went to pieces.

The deterioration of Marty's "human machinery" necessitated a change to a less stressful environment when he passed age sixty. After five years in Sioux Falls, he was transferred to the St. Cloud, Minnesota, diocese, where he served only eighteen months before his death in September 1896. His body remains interred in Calvary Cemetery near his last See city, where he had been its third bishop.

Overall, historical documentation about Marty evidences that he was an idealist with a very practical streak of character. He was sensitive to cultural differences, but he occasionally treated the Indians and nuns condescendingly. He was generous, yet could be manipulative. He appears to have been guided by his conscience and principles and worked tirelessly for his beloved Sioux. (He even gave up his favorite German drink, beer, to show the Indians how they, too, could refrain from alcohol.) His lasting impact in South Dakota—educationally and ecclesiastically—and his championing of the Sioux make him one of the most prominent Benedictines of the late nineteenth century in the Northern Plains.[36]

Martin Marty's efforts in Dakota Territory again demonstrate the adaptability of the Benedictine Rule to new and challenging situations. The monastic presence continued to expand in America with the addition of Swiss nuns for ministry in Missouri and on the Dakota Plains. In the midst of the American missions, other Benedictines were simultaneously pioneering regions beyond North America. ❋

CHAPTER 12

American Expansion and the Benedictines of Australia

Nineteenth and Twentieth Centuries

B y the end of the nineteenth century, Benedictine ministry to Native Americans and German immigrants had brought the foundation of monasteries, schools, and seminaries across the American landscape. More developments would bring additional monastics to the United States while large numbers of American and immigrant members continued to join the German and Swiss congregations. Benedictine outreach to the frontier had not been wlimited to the North American continent, however. Monks also arrived in Australia during the nineteenth century, likewise establishing a Benedictine presence in another new world.

Swiss Roots: American Benedictine Nuns

Almost every motherhouse of Benedictine nuns and Presentation sisters in North and South Dakota owes its origin to an invitation of Bishop Marty. The Benedictines, especially, came in response to the monk's call to assist him in the education of the Sioux and the white settlers, most of whom were immigrants or children of immigrants. Fortunately, the Marty and Leupi relationship was far different from that of the Wimmer and Riepp drama. Marty was very different from Wimmer, and Mother Gertrude did not have the same characteristics as the pioneer Mother Benedicta.

Despite their distinctions, they had two things in common: they were born in the same year (1825) and, like Benedicta, Gertrude was considered the founder of many monasteries of nuns. Most Swiss-connected American communities claim her as the original founder: Sacred Heart Monastery in Yankton; its daughterhouse, Mother of God in Watertown; Sisters of Perpetual Adoration originating at Clyde, Missouri; Olivetan nuns in Jonesboro, Arkansas (originally at Clyde); the Madison, Wisconsin, Benedictines; and those in Mount Angel, Oregon. They all began on an Alpine mountaintop called Maria-Rickenbach in Switzerland.

Mother Gertrude Leupi

Gertrude Leupi (1825–1904) was baptized Josephine in the parish church at Reiden, although she was raised at Wikon in Switzerland. Later she recalled that she had a mystical experience at age three. She claimed a lovely child appeared in her room. He responded to her question about his identity by saying, "I am who am." At age nine, she received another visit—this time, allegedly, from the Blessed Mother. She also admitted to severe temptations against purity, vanity, and even her faith. Being a lively, attractive young lady, she was often tempted to respond affirmatively to the many suitors and to invitations to partake of the many social gatherings of the fun-loving Swiss youths.

Conscious of a call to serve God as a vowed religious, Josephine urged her family to move to Lucerne while still in her teens. There, she found a Jesuit confessor and spiritual director. When he advised her to enter a cloistered convent in Switzerland, her father refused to part with her so soon after the deaths of her mother and sister. She then cared for a young woman suffering from a contagious disease. Consequently Josephine, too, became critically ill. She begged her father to allow her to join a religious community on her recovery, but again he refused. With a bit of subterfuge, she managed to convince him that she was merely learning the profession of teaching when she joined a small community of women at Baldegg Institute who lived together, taught teachers and other students, and made annual vows of dedication to the praise of God and service of those in need.[1]

When political events necessitated relocation, several of the Baldegg community responded to the call of the monks of Engelberg to help staff the poorhouse, orphanage, and girls' school. They needed a permanent base, however. This finally evolved on the site of the pilgrimage shrine to Our Lady on top of the mountain at Maria-Rickenbach just a short distance from Engelberg. In 1857, Gertrude Leupi and Vincentia Gretener, with whom she helped select the site and who preceded her for a short time as prioress, were able to call Maria-Rickenbach's small, vacant wood structure home. Gertrude had made her vows at Engelberg as a "regular" Benedictine Oblate, not as a cloistered nun with solemn vows as was common in Germany. The "regular" term indicated she and Sister Vincentia, who had made her profession at Maria-Einsiedeln, were committed to living in community according to the Rule of Saint Benedict, but were not canonically enclosed as the contemplative, cloistered nuns were. Eventually the small community of Sisters could occupy new wood buildings with a small chapel atop the mountain, under the leadership of Gertrude who replaced Vincentia. By 1864 a boarding school for thirty to forty children had been added to the mountain complex, attained only by cable car unless one attempted the mountain path, which took hours.

Although Gertrude is revered as the real founder of Maria-Rickenbach, the sisters themselves, in their centennial publication called Abbot Anselm Villager their first superior ("*erster Superior*").[2] It was he who drew up their first statutes and their revised ones that regulated every aspect of the nuns' lives at Maria-Rickenbach. Although he kept for himself the supreme authority as visitator and official ecclesiastical superior, he allowed them a confessor-chaplain other than himself. Since Anselm was elected abbot at Engelberg after he had become the nuns' mentor, another monk was needed on site to lead them in the Benedictine way of life.

The Sisters' Statutes and Regulations

Abbot Anselm addressed the statutes he composed to his "beloved daughters of Perpetual Adoration." He offered them the observances that he hoped "contain nothing, in any way opposing the rule of Saint Benedict." He reserved for himself, however, the final decisions concerning "the admission of the novices, the erection of new buildings, greater purchases or sales." His power was almost unlimited as he stipulated that nothing could be changed without his consent, and above all he admonished them that all the Sisters should render him, their spiritual superior, "love and obedience." He could remove any official from her position, shorten or lengthen the three-year term of the prioress, and regulate how much cloister they had to observe:

> Although the Sisters do not oblige themselves by any vow to clausura and it is not canonically established among them, as they are but a simple religious Congregation [sic], nevertheless their Institute would necessarily in a short time, be brought to moral ruin, and discipline and regularity would decay, if the sisters would not cling to it with perseverant tenacity....We ordain the following regulations. 1. That except the sisters, novices, candidates and maid-servants, to no one else [may enter] the clausura....2. That without the express consent of the Visitator no layman...except the Physician and the eventually necessary workmen.[3]

Cloister was to be respected and enforced as observed in solely contemplative nuns' monasteries. The Abbot-legislator imposed a grille composed of a metal grate through which the Sister could see and speak to others living outside the cloister. Perhaps because of the school, the grille did not endure long at Maria-Rickenbach in the twentieth century.

The public, the Abbot wrote in the statutes, was not to be entertained freely, nor were the sisters to go out in public, even to visit family and relatives. They were to "cut off as much as possible all communication with the world, and no sister shall importune the Superior with petitions to visit her relations or acquaintances; on the contrary, everyone shall earnestly strive to forget the world with all it contains."[4] In this, the abbot appeared to reinstate the Romanticism modeled by Solesmes and Beuron rather than the more ancient, open apostolic-contemplative tradition of the Benedictines' earlier tradition.

The Abbot also advocated that the sisters were to be conscious of their own "unworthiness" and apparent daily temptations. To preserve chastity, he advised that when the Sisters rise and go to rest, "they should reflect on the all-seeing eye of God and dress and undress themselves with all possible modesty." He regulated the times the Sisters could receive communion. The senior professed Sisters communicated daily, but novices only on Saturdays, Sundays, Tuesdays, and all higher feasts—unless the confessor felt that he must withhold the sacrament for an individual to punish her for failing to give up certain faults or "favorite inclinations."[5]

The Statutes regulated their horarium and prayer to the last detail. He stipulated that they pray shorter and regular versions of the Liturgy of the Hours, naming Matins, Prime, Tierce, Sext, None, Vespers, and Compline. He referred to the term "Divine Office" constantly, a point especially notable because of the later controversy in America about the content of nuns' Liturgy of the Hours. Perpetual adoration of the Blessed Sacrament, however, was to have priority. Sisters were to rotate hourly night and day, in prayer before the Blessed Sacrament. They were to make annual (not perpetual) and only simple vows (as opposed to the solemn vows enclosed nuns were privileged to profess). These vows, however, were to be renewed annually and kept intact until "their last breath." The sisters promised obedience, poverty, and chastity, but no mention is made of the Benedictine vows of stability and commitment to the monastic way of life. Fortunately, perpetual vows have now replaced the annual ones, and solemn vows are more widely professed in this century.

Diet was prescribed with the same detail. Although the sisters were to have savory well-cooked meals, not too rich but "digestible as is required for a manner of life without much exercise" the hired men were to have "heavier and richer meats" than those prepared for the members of the community. Rank and etiquette were spelled out for the claustral superior, who was always to be ranked at the guest table *after* priests (other than the confessor). Monthly manifestation of conscience was to be made to the prioress and father confessor. The sisters were to disclose to one or both, separately, "their struggles, temptations, inclinations, passions."[6] Later, the American

Swiss Sisters did not adhere to these policies, but adopted their own constitutions and customary that governed their lives differently.

Abbot Anselm appointed Father Frowin Conrad as chaplain to ensure that the new community followed the Rule. Frowin and Adelhelm Odermatt were later appointed by Anselm to journey to Missouri to seek a possible refuge when the revision of the civil constitution of the Confederation of Switzerland (1872) again threatened the existence of monks and nuns in the Swiss Republic. Frowin alerted Mother Gertrude concerning the Bishop of Missouri's recommendation that the monks take up residence in his diocese, advising her to consider following them as soon as possible to ensure an American exile.

Benedictine Monks in Missouri

When the Engelberg monks arrived in Missouri in 1873, they first ministered to an Irish colony of refugees from the potato famine and to a scattering of German settlers. The monks then received an invitation to settle in the village of Conception, after Latrobe and Saint Meinrad's had rejected the offer. Martin Marty had corresponded with his friend, Father Frowin, prompting the Engelberg abbot to submit the recommendation to his monastic community for its consideration. En route to America the monks visited at Einsiedeln and the German abbey of Beuron. There Abbot Maurus Wolter supplied them with a copy of the Constitution of Beuron, a novice-master's handbook, and a copy of the Beuron ceremonials (much of which was patterned after Guéranger's). Frowin had not taken similar materials with him from Engelberg. Both Wolter brothers were friends of Frowin; Placid was at that time Abbot of Maredsous in Belgium, but their correspondence would flow across the Atlantic at frequent intervals.[7]

Frowin was determined to build a Beuronese model monastery at Conception, with little or no involvement in pastoral or other apostolic mission work since all monks were to report for choir daily. Novices were to be admitted immediately, so plans forged ahead and building plans were completed. Agreements were signed and sealed with Engelberg. A small frame church graced the hillside dominating the little colony where some thirty-five Irish, sixty-five German Catholic, and two Protestant families had settled. Frowin first occupied the parish rectory, acting in the interim as pastor. His cook and housekeeper was seventy-year-old John Brassil, a man well loved but whose dishwashing technique may have been common on the frontier: he reportedly spat on the silver and dishes and wiped them off with a rag.[8]

Candidates soon arrived from Switzerland in October, two weeks after Frowin had settled at Conception. These novices soon were scattered in several homes in Maryville (about sixteen miles away) where he instructed him that learning English took priority. Full monastic life began on Christmas Day 1873, when the completed building could house all the monks. The parish church was the only chapel they could use, however. The horarium was demanding, the labor hard, and the meals simple. Frowin purposed that Conception become the center for the liturgical movement in the United States as Beuron and Solesmes were for Europe; he was also dedicated to having the community render Gregorian chant as perfectly as possible in a monastery that highly valued learning.[9]

Swiss Nuns: From the Alps to Missouri and the Dakota Plains

In November 1873, Father Frowin indicated in his correspondence with Abbot Anselm that there had been several requests for primary instruction for illiterate young people up to age twenty. He stressed the need for sisters from Maria-Rickenbach to teach the younger children, disclosing his plans for convents in Conception and Maryville. With the abbot's approval, he hoped to welcome the Sisters in the spring. When word spread in Switzerland that Mother Gertrude was considering an American mission, so many candidates appeared that she had to turn some away due to lack of space.

Frowin was delighted that the sisters were planning a mission in Missouri but warned them that they could not expect too much in the way of material accommodations and goods. "I hope that their zeal is greater than their expectations," he wrote his abbot.[10] His preparation for their arrival consisted in his engaging a sister from the Indiana community—whom Marty had recommended—to teach English to the German-speaking Swiss sisters. She could also introduce them to American educational methods.

Arrival in America

Abbot Anselm and Mother Gertrude then went about selecting missionaries from all those who wanted to go to America. They picked five: Sisters Anselma (superior), Adele (the only experienced teacher), Agnes, Beatrix, and Augustine. They arrived in New York where they entrained for Maryville, reaching their destination on September 5, 1874. Father Adelhelm, the pastor there, had not received the telegram sent from New York by the sisters' traveling companions. A kind, German-speaking immigrant brought them by wagon from the train to the rectory on their arrival, which was a surprise to Father Adelhelm. With no little trepidation and much misgiving they accepted that their temporary home would be the upper floor of the rectory where two rooms were cleared for them.

Father Frowin, concerned about the propriety of this arrangement, consulted Abbot Marty, who admonished Adelhelm: "the Sisters should not live under the same roof with you. In such matters one has to be very cautious." Frowin then got a second opinion from Abbot Placid Wolter in Belgium: "Regarding the Rickenbach sisters, I hesitate to give an answer since I have had little experience in such matters and I do not know all the circumstances." He went on to say what worried him most was their lack of cloister. "Benedictine Sisters living without a clausura? All innovations in any sphere are repugnant to me but especially innovations in the sphere of religious life." He conceded, however, that Frowin was nearer the problem: "you are in a better position to make a decision on the matter since you are on the spot and know the circumstances."[11]

Since Anselm had made such a point of the recitation of the Divine Office in his statutes, the controversy that arose about the type of prayer the sisters should chant or recite appears inconsistent and is not easily understood. When Sister Rose Chapelle of Ferdinand resided with the sisters to teach them English, she spoke no German. Marty suggested that they pray the Latin Little Office of the Blessed Virgin together instead of the German texts of some of the Exercises of Saint Gertrude, changed from the recitation of the full Divine Office Anselm had prescribed for the sisters at Maria-Rickenbach.

Frowin consulted Anselm at Engelberg, who was insistent that the sisters retain the Exercises since he said they were obligated to perpetual adoration, not a liturgical prayer life. He wrote that since they were a "Congregation of the Third Order of Saint Benedict," they were not to be classified with the "regular Benedictine Sisters previously established in America."[12] This ended that debate for a time, but controversies about their ecclesial status continued to interest monastics and ecclesiastical superiors for a century to come.[13]

Ministry and Growth

By February 1875, the Sisters were teaching German, sewing, and embroidery in Maryville, where the church housed the classes. Tuition was one dollar monthly, payable in advance. By December a small convent building near the Conception monastery was ready for occupancy, and three sisters left Maryville for the new residence. Young women soon came to be admitted as candidates and two more sisters arrived from Switzerland. By 1877, it became apparent that a rift had developed that would eventually lead to two separate congregations of Swiss communities, and one that would become Olivetan Benedictine.

Anselm finally gave up trying to govern women across the Atlantic and turned over the charge to Father Frowin. The sisters were able to leave the Maryville rectory at this time for a freestanding, small convent building. In correspondence indicative of the sisters' daily work, the pastor had objected to this move and wrote Frowin that if the sisters left the rectory he could not make ends meet and would have to engage a housekeeper, stable-boy, and others to replace them. Nevertheless, he let them move.

Meanwhile at Maria-Rickenbach, Mother Gertrude, after twenty years as superior, declined reelection. She received Abbot Anselm's authorization to go to America where both feared Mother Anselma, the superior, was critically ill. He was most unwilling to leave the direction of the community to Americans, a common fear of European monastics who felt that the monastic tradition had been transplanted most precariously. Although Frowin objected to Abbot Anselm's insistence that Mother Gertrude be superior of the Maryville convent (called New Rickenbach) and the one at Clyde (Perpetual Adoration), he finally acquiesced. The fifty-five-year-old Swiss superior arrived at Maryville on November 1, 1880, with four sisters from Maria-Rickenbach.

Later Beatrix Renggli, one of the original pioneers, characterized the end of the rift and the permanent division of the Clyde/Maryville nuns as one of rejection of the authority of Mother Gertrude. She came to Clyde from Maryville and "asked the surrender of the Convent and Community to her jurisdiction, which the American Sisters stoutly refused."[14] The three remaining Europeans then returned to Maryville. Four candidates were invested with the Benedictine habit later that month on the feast of Saint Gertrude, opening the Maryville novitiate. This date would be observed as the beginning of Sacred Heart Monastery in Dakota where many Maryville sisters would finally take up permanent residence.

The Indian Missions

Marty requested teaching assistance for the Standing Rock Reservation from Maryville community. The young Sisters in the novitiate moved to Zell, South Dakota, first to be nearer the Indian missionary sisters and later to Yankton under Bishop Marty's and Mother Gertrude's leadership. Mother Gertrude, accustomed to continually operating under an abbot's leadership, returned to Switzerland when Marty became bishop of Sioux Falls. The woman who had founded Maria-Rickenbach and stabilized the American community began another on her return, at the Castle of Wikon near her birthplace, ostensibly to recruit candidates for the American house at Yankton. Five arrived in South Dakota, but soon the Wikon house became a permanent independent foundation called Marienberg, where Mother Gertrude died in 1904.[15]

Another Sister, Gertrude McDermott, founded a community after she left Standing Rock in 1901, after what was termed a "disagreement." After a sojourn in Elkton and other points in South Dakota, she organized a community in Sioux City, Iowa, which eventually sponsored a hospital. The community administration moved to Madison, Wisconsin, in 1953, where a retreat house became the primary ministry. In time, it became an ecumenical monastery affiliated with the Saint Gertrude Congregation. Sisters from the Missouri groups also settled near the monks who had made a foundation in Oregon (Mount Angel).[120] Other nuns went to Jonesboro, Arkansas, and remained outside the two unions under the jurisdiction of the bishop, eventually becoming Olivetans, who fell under the local bishop's authority. Nuns from Sarnen, a cloistered community, responded to Father Adelhelm's call and settled finally in Cottonwood, Idaho, under Mother Johanna Zumstein's leadership.

In 1888 Melchtal sisters, led by Mother Angela Arnes, spent a year in the Yankton community studying English and then proceeded to the Black Hills. At Sturgis, South Dakota, they first took up residence in a former wayside tavern. They opened Saint Martin's Academy eventually, moved it and the motherhouse to Rapid City in 1962, and closed the Academy before 1990. These all united in the Federation of Saint Gertrude, approved in the 1930s. The Clyde nuns first organized the Congregation of Perpetual Adoration into a centralized, Cluny-like system though later had prioresses to head them and have gained a bit more autonomy.[16] Eventually, headquarters moved to St. Louis, though a priory remained at Clyde. Five of their members opened a hermitage complex at Sand Springs, Oklahoma, in 1978, Osage Monastery, modeled on Bede Griffith's ashram in India.

Benedictines in the Southern Missions

Benedictine foundations of monks and nuns were not limited to the East, Midwest, or Northwest, but they also extended into the southern states after the Civil War. Abbot Marty accepted an invitation to come to Arkansas and sent the subprior of Saint Meinrad's, Wolfgang Schlumpf, to select a site for both monks and nuns. Marty had secured the approval of the Ferdinand Sisters for a foundation in Arkansas as well. Since Wolfgang's recent surgery did not permit him to travel at the time, Isidor Hobi did the initial site selection. When he returned to Indiana, Isidor somewhat exaggerated the description of the new site he and the railroad had agreed would make an ideal monastic setting, "a paradise fallen from heaven."[17] When the first abbot was elected in 1891, it was not Wolfgang but Ignatius Conrad (1846–1926), brother of the Abbot of Conception. In 1893, Wolfgang returned to Switzerland where he died in 1904. The nuns first lived at Shoal Creek, then moved to Fort Smith, eventually opening a daughterhouse in Columbia.

Wimmer was concerned about the South as well. Already in 1865, just after the war, his monks were ministering to the black population in northern Alabama. It was twenty-six years, however, before five Benedictine priests stationed in Alabama acceded to the request of the Bishop of Mobile for a monastery in his diocese. They settled at Cullman in 1892 and opened Saint Bernard's. The Cullman sisters came ten years later.[18] Wimmer also accepted the challenge to begin a monastery in North Carolina, so the monks finally established a house at Belmont that became an abbey in 1884. The dependent missions at Richmond, Virginia, at Skidaway on the Isle of Hope, and those in Savannah, Georgia (where monks had ministered for decades), came under Belmont's jurisdiction. Leo Haid (1849–1924), who was abbot from 1885 to 1904, and was named Vicar Apostolic of North Carolina in 1887, then consecrated Titular bishop of Messene a year later. Belmont was an abbey nullius—a monastery with episcopal jurisdiction.[19]

Belmont monks were being sent to Florida as early as 1889 to minister to the needs of the German immigrants. Saint Leo Abbey dates its foundation from that year, raised to abbatial status in 1902. Nuns also located in Saint Leo as well as in Covington, Louisiana, where they preceded the monks—a unique situation. The Covington, Kentucky, nuns sent missionaries to Louisiana to teach the youth in New Orleans in 1870. They moved across Lake Pontchartrain to Covington, and the monks came from Saint Meinrad to Covington in 1902. A year later Saint Joseph's, the men's monastery, received abbatial status.[20]

There was one exception to the nineteenth-century German and Swiss monastic foundations. The French also sought haven in America. Pierre-qui-Vire, Muard's foundation, sent three priests in 1877 to take possession of Sacred Heart Mission in Indian Territory (Oklahoma). This became the monastery of the Sacred Heart that later moved to Shawnee. In 1882 five more émigrés arrived from France exiled by the laic laws of 1880. After 1893, the central core of French monks came from Belloc in the Basque region, a daughter-house of Pierre-qui-Vire. Nuns also came to Oklahoma, but from the German-American priories rather than from France. They settled first at Guthrie in 1879, and later in Tulsa.[21]

Before the twentieth century, Benedictine houses dotted every point of the compass in the United States. Benedictinism was firmly established and would continue to be a significant factor in the growth and development of the American Catholic Church. Near the same time that American Benedictine monasteries were being founded, another continent and hemisphere would realize an English Catholic's Benedictine dream in Australia.

Another New World: Benedictines in Australia

Although Australian and American Benedictines were missionary pioneers of the same stamp, they were only somewhat similar. There were some major differences in the nineteenth-century beginnings of monastic life, not only in motivation but also particularly in process.

English Monk William Ullathorne

Among Benedictines with a missionary dream, two monks of England's Downside Abbey, William B. Ullathorne (1806–1889), and the man who had inspired him, Bede Polding (1794–1877) are of particular importance, especially to Australia. Ullathorne, a direct descendant of the martyred Benedictine oblate Saint Thomas More, was born into a family engaged in the drapery business. His father's ancestors had been yeoman farmers who had remained Catholic during the long period of the English Penal Laws. His mother, a Longstaff, was a convert to Catholicism.[22] After some years as a seaman, the young Ullathorne joined Downside in 1823.

When William Morris, a monk of Downside, was consecrated bishop and appointed Vicar Apostolic of Australia and its oceanic environs, he asked for assistance from the Downside community. He specifically requested Ullathorne to aid him at the mission in New South Wales, still regarded as a penal colony. Although many ex-convicts settled there, Irish immigrant farmers and traders had also settled in the area. The President of the English Congregation gave Ullathorne permission to accept the invitation to collaborate with Bishop Morris.

A scholar as well as a monk, Ullathorne was first concerned about the books needed in his mission, so he gathered about a thousand volumes of works of theology, the Church Fathers, canon law, and "sacred literature" in every language of which he had command.[23] He was twenty-seven when he sailed from England in 1832 for ten memorable years in the Australian mission. Before he had embarked his position had been changed, and he arrived as the Vicar General for Australia with residence in Sydney. He received a stipend from the English nation for his official position as Government Catholic Chaplain of Australia. After a five-month voyage, he landed in Sydney in February 1833. It was thirteen years after the first two Irish Catholic chaplains, and forty-three after the first Catholic convicts (the consequence of an Irish uprising in 1798), had arrived in Australia.[24]

One of the ex-convicts remaining in Australia, an Irish blacksmith who had been a political prisoner (having made pikes for the insurgents in the 1798 rebellion), had resumed his trade and became affluent enough to donate his house and garden in Sydney for the site of a new Saint Patrick's church, also providing a convent for the Sisters of Charity at Parramatta in 1839. Although the Irish Catholics often supported the English Benedictines, the Irish clergy in Australia were less willing to accept leadership from nationals whose presence represented to them centuries of British religious suppression, even if they were Catholic and Benedictine. That ethnic division was never resolved and ultimately spelled the demise of the original Benedictine dream for the region.[25]

The Australian Foundation

When Ullathorne arrived there were only three priests in Australia, including John Joseph Therry (1790–1864), considered the "founder of the Catholic church in Australia."[26] In 1829, the English Act of Catholic Emancipation had made a radical difference in the legal status of Catholics, so Catholic laymen could now hold high official positions. The Governor General of Australia, Sir Richard Burke, nephew of the non-Catholic political theorist Edmund Burke, had relatives who were sympathetic to the needs and claims of the Catholic colony in Australia. It was not the end, however, of the friction between Catholic, Anglican, and Protestant leadership.

When Father Ullathorne occupied the parish house at the yet unfinished Saint Mary's Church in Sydney,[27] there were already Australian Catholic schools in Parramatta and Campbelltown. Irish Christian Brothers had come in 1842, but there was always a dearth of religious teachers. Ullathorne soon joined Therry and any clergy available as circuit riders—preaching, attending the sick, celebrating the Eucharistic liturgy, and traveling forty to fifty miles round-trip with horses or horse-drawn rigs on Sundays and holidays as they ministered to three or four different village-parishes. Some convicts in neighboring towns had to be spiritually prepared for execution. Others, who were servants and day laborers held in quasi-slavery status by English families, had to be released by the priests to attend Mass and receive the sacraments. The priests, though already overextended, were also expected to be military chaplains.[28]

It soon became obvious to Ullathorne that, in addition to the need for more priests, Australia needed a bishop. He recommended that his former novice master at Downside, Father Bede Polding—who had originally inspired in him a desire for the Australian Mission—be considered as Australia's first bishop. Polding had been offered an episcopacy and Vicariate in India (Madras) but declined, seemingly in part because his heart was in the Australian mission for years. The other reason was his health, which a physician determined would deteriorate in the Indian climate. Subsequently, Polding was consecrated Vicar of New Holland (New South Wales) and Van Diemen's Land (Tasmania) and sailed from Liverpool in 1835 for his new diocese.

Bede Polding

Polding was born in Liverpool in 1794. He was the son of a German descendant and a mother whose brother had been the President General of the English Benedictine Congregation from 1799 to 1822. Both parents died while Polding was young, so his Benedictine uncle had taken charge of him. When he was only eight, John was sent to day school to the nuns who had come from Cambrai, temporarily at Woolton, before their move to Stanbrook. At eleven he was with the Benedictines of Saint Gregory's then in charge of the school at Acton Burnell, Shropshire. Polding joined the community in 1811 at age seventeen, entering the same novitiate class as the later Bishop Morris. Bede moved with the community after his profession in 1812 to their permanent home at Downside, where he resided for the next twenty years.

Bede had been novice master and subprior at the monastery. As prefect of the school he was credited by the Irish students as having identified with them in their concern for their country subjugated to a nation that denied their human rights, particularly free practice of their religion. He was invited to preside at the Irish monks' festive supper on Saint Patrick's Day—an honor for a Lancashire man. He prepared well for his mission to the Australian church, which was then predominantly Irish. With him he took a monk-priest, three Benedictine subdeacons, two catechists, two diocesan clergy, and funds he had collected for the mission. On his arrival in Sydney, Polding soon began what was to be a career of extraordinary missionary work, extending over forty years that won for him, according to Butler, "his recognized place among the greatest missioners of modern times."[29]

Ministry and Challenges

Though characterized by Bishop Morris as an energetic and intelligent man, Polding failed in fulfilling his dream of dotting Australia with Benedictine cathedral-monasteries as Augustine had done in England. His greatest concern was to attend to the spiritual and material needs of the convict population. One day he erected his altar in a jail, another in the convicts' barracks. He ministered at the penal settlement on Goat Island, the huge house of correction for women, and the reformatory for juveniles. When prison ships arrived, with government permission, he could have all the Catholics under his command for the first few days. They were supervised at the church a greater part of the day and, after brief instructions on the sacraments and the ministry available to them, they went off to their various destinations in the penal settlements.

Ullathorne was named Polding's Vicar General. The bishop asked him to return to Europe in 1836 to recruit more priests. Italy and England refused to release any clergy, so Ullathorne went to Ireland where he met the bishops assembled at Maynooth. Consequently, he had two contingents of recruits comprising eleven priests and several seminarians and schoolteachers. Three priests, five seminarians, and five nuns from the newly founded Institute of Irish Sisters of Charity accompanied him on his return to Sydney in late 1838.

Polding's proposal to consider Australia a missionary province and receive regularly assigned monks was rejected by the General Chapter of the English Congregation. With four from the Congregation having come to Australia, Polding nevertheless continued his plans to establish a Benedictine monastery at Saint Mary's, Sydney, under his jurisdiction. The monks there would then educate priest-monks and diocesan clergy. Monastic life began, but it lasted only a few decades although there were candidates and profession of vows by several monks (one of them, a Dublin ex-convict).[30] To Polding's further dismay, when Ullathorne returned to Australia, his health had been broken. Ullathorne had to suffer more when vilified by the press almost daily for six months. He was criticized for lecturing and writing in Europe about the abuses of the Anglo-Australian convict system, especially the practice of allowing private individuals and concerns to use prisoners as slave labor.

Although Ullathorne continued to love and respect Polding, he was aggravated by the bishop's deplorable lack of organization, his poor financial administration, and his inept handling of the government's bureaucracy. When it became intolerable, Ullathorne asked to be relieved of his Vicar Generalate and sought permission to leave Australia. In response to the request, Polding surrendered the administrative duties of the diocese and charge of the seminary to his Vicar General. That temporary treatment did not endure for long, however.

In the meantime, the Sisters of Charity resided at their house in Parramatta, where there was a house of correction for women some fifteen miles from Sydney. At times a thousand or more women prisoners—a third of whom were Catholic—were incarcerated. Ullathorne was asked to reside in Parramatta and commute into Sydney weekly. Not finding this challenge any more satisfying, he renewed his original resignation and again requested that he be allowed to return to England. At the end of 1840, he left for his native land. Polding, who felt the need to spend time in Europe recruiting more missionaries, accompanied him. After they landed in 1841, Ullathorne traveled to Ireland to seek more priest-recruits. Polding joined him there later, and they separated only on their return to England.

Ullathorne did not rejoin the monks at Downside, however. He was first given charge of the Coventry mission, then appointed Vicar Apostolic of the Western District of England. During this time he began a life-long friendship with the influential John Henry Newman (1801–1890), dedicating his last book to him. In 1850, the former Australian missionary became the first bishop of Birmingham, where he resided, administered, preached, and wrote copiously despite the chronic ill health that precipitated his resignation in 1888. During his attendance at Vatican I, his correspondence served as the base for Butler's history of the Council. Ullathorne died on the feast of Saint Benedict in 1889, leaving an unfinished letter to another distinguished colleague, the Benedictine Cardinal Gasquet (1874–1929).

The Australian mission had its peaks and troughs. Charles Henry Davis (1815–1854), a Benedictine monk, arrived in 1848 to be Polding's coadjutor. Although there were thirty-two members at the small monastery of Saint Mary's in Sydney in 1851, the monks were beginning to favor turning over the Australian mission to the diocesan clergy, so great did they feel the antipathy of the Irish Catholics and clergy. Nor had Polding chosen well when he placed Henry Gregory in the position of vicar general and monastic superior, since the monks perceived him as arrogant. Several lay brothers left in 1851; a professed monk eloped with the housekeeper, and others departed for various reasons.

The colony's journalists judged the Benedictines unfit to lead, so they adroitly exposed the monks' departure from what they considered appropriate behavior. During the diocesan meeting in 1858, the clergy had opted for new parishes and dioceses, but with Irish bishops. The social gulf was too great to be bridged. The Irish clergy regarded the English Benedictines as arrogant and not understanding the real work of the mission. The ethnic clash was a mix of parochial/intellectual antagonism, theory vs. practice, and irreconcilable, historically antagonistic nationalist and ethnic loyalties. In 1860 Abbot Gregory was recalled to England where he died in 1877. In 1865 fire destroyed what had been the monastic Cathedral at Saint Mary's, and by 1874 there were only twelve monks left.[31] Closure of the Academy (Lyndhurst) took place in 1877. The Benedictine dream of Ullathorne and Polding had disintegrated.[32]

The Irish bishops and priests maintained their leadership in the control and expansion of parochial life and education in Australia. Polding died in 1877 to be succeeded (against the wishes of the Irish) by another Benedictine, Roger Vaughan (1834–1883), second son of an English Catholic squire. This second and last English Benedictine Archbishop of Sydney died at forty-nine, just six years after his appointment.[33] Cardinal Patrick Francis Moran (1830–1911), the first of a succession of Irish archbishops of Sydney, succeeded him. Before Polding died, however, the Benedictine monks from Spain were in Western Australia and nuns, contemplative and active, were increasing in membership throughout the island-continent.

In 1846 two Spanish monks arrived in Western Australia from Saint Martin's Compostella, committed to working with the Bishop of Perth in the Australian mission. These two monks, Joseph Serra (1810–1886) and Rosendo Salvado (1814–1900), baptized and preached among the aborigines and European settlers. They established a Benedictine monastery in the Perth diocese at a lonely spot many miles from the city, naming the complex New Norcia and dedicating it to the Holy Trinity. From 1867 to 1982, the monastery was an abbey nullius. In 1908, Abbot Fulgentius Torres (1861–1914) founded the mission of Kalumburu in the far north of Western Australia, which the Diocese of Broome took over in 1981.[34] Two secondary schools, one for boys and one for girls, were opened at New Norcia between 1908 and 1913. They were amalgamated in 1974 and renamed Salvado College. Although four Good Samaritan Benedictine Sisters remained in charge, Perth's Catholic Education Office have had jurisdiction over the school since 1986. Monks taught religion and art and filled the chaplaincy. The monastery eventually was committed to retreats and hospitality to guests as well as caring for the pastoral needs of neighboring parishes.

There are other houses of monks who follow the Rule in Australia: Sylvestrines in Arcadia N.S.W. (since 1961); Cistercians/Trappists in the Diocese of Melbourne at Tarrawarra Abbey (since 1954); and Anglican monks in Victoria (founded in 1975, adopted the Rule of Benedict in 1979.) Although there was an extraordinary Italian Benedictine in New Zealand from 1879 to 1887, Felice Vaggioli—who served in Gisorne, then in Coromandel—no viable abbey of the Cassinese or Subiaco Congregation opened there. The greatest contribution the Italian monk made was a published study about the history of New Zealand's Christians and Maori natives.[35] Additionally, another monastery remains vital in the twenty-first century: the Cistercians at Southern Star Abbey, Hawkes Bay, founded in 1954 by the Irish monks from New Melleray.

Benedictine Nuns in Australia

Bede Polding succeeded in establishing permanent houses of Benedictine nuns. On his first visit to Europe two young ladies volunteered to go to Australia to begin monasticism for women there. One was Abbot Gregory's sister, a former student of the Stanbrook Benedictines whom Polding had known since she was a child. Having made their novitiate at Princethorpe, when Polding failed to keep in touch with the novices, they also made profession of vows there. However, Dame Scholastica Gregory had made vows conditionally with the understanding that if Polding still wanted her presence in Australia, she would be free to go there. After Polding found another woman interested in the Australian mission, Dame Magdalen LeClerc, the two traveled together to his diocese. Before the end of 1849, three other young women joined them.

The novitiate opened in February 1849 and recital of the Divine Office began at the estate house purchased by Archbishop Polding for the nuns' use, The Vineyard at Rydalmere, about three miles from Parramatta and fifteen from Sydney. They immediately dubbed it "Subiaco." Dame Magdalen had charge of the spiritual matters, and Dame Scholastica of the material—as co-superiors (a short-lived Polding innovation) though the archbishop reserved the supreme authority to himself, however. Until they could open a school and sustain themselves, the nuns were engaged in washing the altar linens used at the Cathedral, sewing, mending, and laundering the monks' clothing. The tasks were so demanding that thirty-three-year-old Scholastica died of tuberculosis in 1850. In fact, that disease of the "overworked and underfed" claimed many of the nuns' lives, most of them dying before age 40.[36]

The community, in imitation of those in England (except for the constitutions, which were modeled on the Beuronese), was divided into two classes. The choir nuns, usually the educated and daughters of well-to-do parents, were separated from the lay sisters who made simple vows, seldom were educated and were generally Irish or English women who had come over as domestics. The title, Dame, was allotted to the choir nuns while the women without solemn vows were called Sister. They ate together but prayed and recreated separately. In contrast to the European model, the community levied no dowry, so poor women could enter. Much of the servile work, however (the monks' laundry came down the Parramatta River on specific days), was abandoned when Dame Magdalen, then sole superior, opened the school on the monastery grounds at Subiaco nine years after their arrival in Australia.

The nuns elected their first prioress in 1864. Up to that time, the archbishop had appointed the superior or superiors. Unfortunately, the monastery finances were not separated from the archbishop's. The procurator of the monks at Saint Mary's received the income and paid the bills for the nuns and their school, though the nuns' archivist maintained that actually the archbishop's coffers received and disbursed the income. After the arrival of three more Princethorpe nuns, in 1856 the new business-minded subprioress convinced Polding that the nuns could manage their own affairs.

Australian nuns bought an area in West Pennant Hills (then well outside Sydney) in 1957, after part of their acreage was sold and the school had been closed due to encroachment by nearby industry. In 1988, when West Pennant Hills also became part of the suburbia of Sydney and privacy was difficult to maintain, the community moved again—to Jamberoo, still in New South Wales, in the diocese of Wollongong, south of Sydney. The nuns also maintained two dependent houses. Some members lived at Croydon, Victoria (near Melbourne), under the superiorship of Dame Marie Gregory Foster, who has now rejoined the community at Jamberoo (near Melbourne).[37] Others were at Lammermoor Beach in Queensland. In 1982, the community received abbatial status. The first abbess, Dame Benedicta Philips, heads the community at Jamberoo.

The Good Samaritan Benedictine Sisters

A greater number of women, however, chose affiliation with the Good Samaritan nuns who also follow the Rule of Benedict.[38] Their beginnings were hardly auspicious. When Polding returned from a visit to England in 1856, he brought back with him a young woman, Mary Anne Adamson of Manchester, a family connection who was interested in religious life. The bishop sent her to the nuns at Subiaco near Parramatta to learn the basics of Benedictine observance.

Mother Scholastica, a Sister of Charity and former superior of a small number in charge of a refuge for "penitent" young women, was now the only Sister left there. Polding thus put her in charge of the five women—two Clarke sisters, Miss Adamson, Miss Byrne and Miss Hart—to begin his Institute as an apostolic branch of Benedictines. They were admitted to the postulancy early in 1857 and to the novitiate on the Solemnity of Saint Benedict the same year. A year later, all five made profession of vows, and other young women came to seek admission regularly. In March 1866, when Archbishop Polding was in Rome getting approval for this religious community, he was advised not to use the name Benedictine even if the women followed that Rule, as they would then be subject to enclosure inconsistent with the active apostolate. Thus, he chose to call them Good Samaritans. Because they were following a well established rule and observance, there was no difficulty getting approval, which was granted the following year. By that time there were forty sisters.

Originally engaged in social work, the community soon branched into the educational field especially when the government withdrew state aid from parochial schools in 1880. Nine years after the approval of the Good Samaritans, the Sisters of Charity superior, who had kept her own observance while heading the Benedictine community, resigned in favor of an elected superior.

That new superior was Mother Adamson, whom Polding had brought with him from England. As Mother General she had charge of all the sisters now being scattered throughout the cities and the countryside in small convents near parish schools and orphanages, among other places. The Good Samaritans of Saint Benedict retained that style of structure, eventually dividing into provinces, ultimately restructuring more along traditional Benedictine lines. Even with this provincial structure, one Mother-General continued to exercise overall jurisdiction from Glebe Point in Sydney. The sisters reside in Australia, Japan, the Philippines, the Republic of Kiribati, and Timor Leste.[39]

As the former English colonies—the United States and the Australian continent—received the Rule of Saint Benedict from the European monks and nuns, they influenced the vast lands once known as the "missions" or the "frontier" in varied ways. Their influence remains significant in the history of both the United States and Australia. Through profound difficulties and conflict, pioneering monastics established a network of monastic schools and ministries that greatly impacted the people they served and indelibly transformed Benedictine life itself. ✳

CHAPTER 13

Benedictines Face Challenges in the Modern Era

Early- to Mid-Twentieth Century

The Benedictine legacy had endured centuries of cultural and political change. As nations had become subject to the challenges of their times, so had monastic men and women borne the struggles of their varied regions. Overcoming a vast measure of conflicts, suppressions, and seemingly insurmountable obstacles, Benedictines continued to adapt and change while expanding their vision into new and unknown worlds.

As the twentieth century opened, the Benedictines were reorganizing in several European countries, enjoying relative peace in others, and steadily expanding in the Americas. Some countries were still without Benedictines as the century opened; others were on the verge of again legislating them into exile. Benedictines continued to be multifaceted and live diverse lifestyles in both secure and insecure environments as monasteries opened and closed. Some survived and prospered, others barely subsisted. The twentieth century brought significant changes to monastic life that continued to stretch, form, and relocate the Benedictine way of life.

France Issues the Law of Associations

At the close of the nineteenth century, France seemed to have temporarily given up trying to curb the power of the church by efforts to suppress monastic men and women and their communities. Many of the monastics in exile had returned, and monasteries were admitting new members while ignoring the prohibitive taxation laws levied earlier. Monks and nuns generally went about their daily *ora et labora* in relative peace. It did not last.

Within a year after the turn of the century, the French Republicans, who had found anti-clericalism to be good politics, won new legislation in the parliamentary halls of the Third Republic. After much debate, another anti-religious laic law passed the Chamber and Senate, and under the title "Law of Associations" was signed by the French President in July 1901.[1] According to the new law, all congregations of religious who failed to apply for and secure authorization from the legislature were subject to dissolution. Schools under the direction of or staffed by members of unauthorized groups were subject to closure. Violators could be fined from sixteen to as high as five thousand francs and sentenced from six days to a year in prison. (The guillotine, fortunately, was no longer in use.) Anyone renting property for use by members of religious orders in violation of the law was subject to the same penalty.

Liquidation of Monasteries

The law's Article 15 required that each congregation requesting authorization send the Minister of Cults a list of receipts and expenses, an inventory of all movable and immovable property, and a complete roster of its members including surnames, religious names, nationality, age, place of birth, and date of entrance. Perpetrators of false reports would be subject to substantial penalties. Unless the unauthorized congregation applied for authorization within three months, it would be shut down.

The property of the dissolved communities would be at the disposal of a tribunal that would name an official liquidator. Donors of property, or their legitimate heirs, could reclaim their gifts of land, money, or movable property. Appeals to the courts against the liquidators would be honored, however. Provision of some form of pension and medical care for the ill would result from the proceeds of the property sale. A ministerial decree published simultaneously with the legislation included a clause requiring that a copy of the community's or congregation's constitutions and statutes accompany all applications for authorization. The document was to specify explicitly that the group be under the direct jurisdiction of the bishop of the diocese.

Reaction to the Law of Associations was immediate. The Catholic hierarchy and press strongly condemned the legislation. Few militant Catholics agreed with the position of the Parisian newspaper *Le Temps* that, after condemning the law as contrary to the principle of liberty editorialized resignedly, "but the law is the law; there is nothing to do but conform."[2] All eyes turned toward Rome to see how the Holy See would react and what course it would advise. A memorandum marked "very confidential" informed the Minister of Cults on July 5 that Rome was planning to recall the papal nuncio to protest the passage of the Law, a move the nuncio had earlier warned Théophile Delcassé that the pope planned to make if the bill passed.[3]

Leo XIII sent a letter of sympathy to the superiors general of the French congregations on July 6. It was a supportive note encouraging resignation, confidence, and trust. The pope counseled compassion and dignity instead of indignation, suggesting that the victims render good for evil.[4] There was no definite guidance about the course they should take—namely, whether to apply for authorization or wait for expulsion. Correspondents in Rome told the French press that the pontiff preferred not to recommend a specific action. The superiors could determine what was in the best interests of the church and the individual congregation. They were to weigh the possibilities of success or failure, and then act accordingly. Most of them presumed, however, that the pope preferred that they apply for authorization.[5]

A letter from the Sacred Congregation of Religious on July 10 confirmed this presumption but left other questions unanswered. There was still the call for exemption from episcopal jurisdiction. Cardinal Gotti's cover letter listed the two conditions under which the religious "to avoid grave consequences and avert the total extinction of the congregations in France," might ask authorization.[6] The congregations were to present only an abridged, edited copy of their constitutions and statutes (approved by the bishop); also, submission to that bishop must conform to the character of each institute (e.g., referral for faculties and certain permissions, but not complete surrender of papal jurisdiction).

Most of the monasteries saw the irreconcilable differences immediately and decided that they would not seek authorization—especially Solesmes' congregation. The Chapter unanimously called for exile rather than a dishonorable vassalage to the state and a precarious future existence.[7] The Abbot General, Dom Delatte of Solesmes, anonymously published an "Examination of Conscience of a Religious" cynically picturing the French premier and his ministers judging the Rule of Saint Benedict and the statutes of the Jesuits. He warned that after the religious, the church would be placed under the yoke of the state. He defended his refusal to ask authorization because, at the price of his dignity, he would not seek "the right of being, of living and of acting" from the secular power.[8]

Resistance and Refuge

As several congregations opting for exile began to investigate possible refuges, the French government informed other European governments that it highly disapproved of any foreign nations accepting these exiles. Bishop Heylen of the Namur diocese disregarded the intimidation and welcomed them all to his diocese on the condition that they be self-supporting and not solicit financial aid from Belgian Catholics. He eventually was overwhelmed with the presence of 200 French communities of men and women. Germany agreed to respect the French government's wishes, with one exception. The newly installed Bishop of Metz, Abbot Willibrord Benzler of Maria Laach, received the emperor's permission to invite the Swiss Benedictines from Delle to settle in Lorraine. Holland and England adopted a more liberal attitude. Thousands seeking freedom from the laic laws crossed the Dutch borders and the English Channel to accept those nations' generosity.

Ministerial decrees flowed profusely from the corridors of the bureaucracy. Some were more notable than others. In September Monis, the Minister of Justice, reminded the court officials that those congregations within their jurisdiction who failed to submit an application for authorization by October 3 were to be dissolved immediately and their property forfeited. The *procureurs généraux* were also to investigate any initial "fraudulent sales" of the property to the detriment of the state coffers. In November the Premier directed the prefects to take particular note of the recruitment of the parochial clergy from non-authorized congregations. By early October, 64 houses of men and 543 of women had submitted requests for authorization, and almost 9500 did so by the end of that month.[9]

Abbot Delatte at Solesmes felt strongly that his leadership would have to be responsible. He explained to a reporter from *Le Matin* (August 21) that since the sons of St. Benedict were the eldest of the monks, they were obliged to give their confrères a good example. The government was a bit embarrassed by these Benedictines' choice of exile because of their popularity. Members of the Congregation of France had published works in theology, patrology, archaeology, church history, and especially chant and liturgy. To add to the embarrassment, on the eve of Solesmes' departure, the French Society of Architects gave one of its highest awards to Dom Julius Mellet, who had recently renovated and expanded the abbey church.[10] The peasants and workingmen of Solesmes and the neighboring towns petitioned their deputy to use his influence to keep the monks and nuns at Solesmes. They stated, "the suppression of the two abbeys of Solesmes is for us a matter of life or death," not a political or social question, the signers emphasized, but a question of bread.[11]

The burden of locating a refuge in England for the two Solesmes abbeys fell upon the shoulders of the procurator of Saint-Pierre, Dom Maurice Noetinger, and Prior Fernand Cabrol of Farnborough. By mid-August they had located two sites on the Isle of Wight in the diocese of Portsmouth. On August 19 the abbess of Sainte-Cécile, the prioress, and two nuns left for England to complete the negotiations for the property.

The monks negotiated for the former Benedictine priory, Appuldurcombe House, in the southern part of the island. Both appeared too small to be more than temporary, especially the monks' residence, since there was concern about space to store the 70,000-volume Solesmes library. Preparations for departure continued even as the monks found their abbey grounds overrun by newspaper correspondents taking one last look at life there and reporting their impressions and interviews. Most were sympathetic, but one criticized the abbot for his "imprudence" in excommunicating the subprefect of the Department (province) and his wife.[12]

Before their departure the mayor and municipal council of Solesmes and almost 250 of the abbey's neighbors (including officials, aristocracy, laborers, and peasants) sent joint communiqués of sympathy to the monastics.[13] The outpouring of support when the departure time arrived showed the high regard the people had for the Solesmes communities. They departed at intervals in small groups, but the most publicized evacuations took place on September 17, when twenty nuns left St. Cécile and the abbot and a group of monks left St. Pierre for England. At 6:30 a.m. as more than 200 relatives, friends, and reporters gathered around him, Abbot Delatte dramatically opened the cloister door of St. Cécile, greeted and blessed each nun individually, permitted them last embraces and farewells with their assembled relatives, and placed them in the carriages for the railroad station in Sablé. Shortly after 10 a.m. the monks left in a torrential rain as more than 400 persons silently gathered at the abbey entrance to bid them adieu. An estimated 1500 more (though Solesmes is a small village) lined the streets as the cortege of carriages passed to the depot where hundreds more awaited the emigrants. After doleful farewells, the crowd accompanied the departure of the train with shouts of "Vivent les Péres, vivent les Bénédictins, vive le Père Abbé."[14]

The French religious fascinated the Church of England members and English Roman Catholics, as none had been able to live openly since the dissolutions legislated by Henry VIII. Church of England adherents regularly filled the French monastics' abbey chapels, primarily to hear the impeccable rendition of the Gregorian chant sung by the monks and nuns who had escaped the consequences of the late nineteenth and early twentieth century French laic laws. The king's sister, Princess Beatrix, the governor of the Island, visited the French nuns who had taken refuge in the Isle of Wight as did the reigning queen of England. She conversed with the nuns in the refectory when she came to see the former Duchess of Bragance, Mère Adelaide

(French nuns were titled "Mother," English nuns, on their return, were called "Dame").

On a second visit, the Princess brought King Edward VII who "reviewed" and greeted the standing nuns again in the dining room, toured the chapel and gardens, and talked with the Abbess and Mother Adelaide. Both abbeys moved to more spacious buildings when they became available, but still remained on the Isle of Wight. In 1906, the St. Cécile community moved to Ryde, which continued to house some nuns while others returned later to Solesmes, resulting in another English Benedictine foundation. The monks reoccupied the site of the twelfth-century Cistercian monastery, Quarr Abbey, in 1908. They soon began building a permanent church and residence wing that continued to serve as a monastery for the remnant the abbey left behind when some of them returned to restore St. Pierre after the war.[15]

When the monks of Ligugé left France, attention revolved around writers and scholars rather than superiors and royalty. Two renowned historians (Doms François Chamard and Jean Besse) and a famous oblate layman (the novelist Joris-Karl Huysmans, a Catholic convert) got most of the press. At Solesmes under Guéranger, Dom Chamard began publication of a score of his works on ecclesiastical history. He was prior of Glanfeuil for five years and, after 1897, of Ligugé. When his community went into exile, the French Academy of Political and Moral Sciences made a vain attempt to keep the historian in France. When he left Ligugé, Dom Chamard remarked to a reporter that his greatest consolation was in the discovery that the library was transported in 63 crates in 1880, whereas it required 260 boxes to hold the 25,000 volumes in 1901. He died at the abbey's Belgian retreat in 1908, a year after publication of his last book.[16] Dom Besse, his colleague and founder of the scholarly *Revue Mabillon*, was no less famous, but both received comparably less attention than Huysmans. After his conversion to Catholicism, the novelist was attracted to the liturgy as celebrated in Benedictine monasteries. In *En Route* he immortalized the nuns of St. Louis in Paris. In *L'Oblate* (which he was writing in 1901), he did the same for the abbot of Ligugé, Dom Bourigaud, and his close friend, Dom Chamard. The novel was being written in a little home the writer had built near the abbey in 1898. When the monks were exiled, the novelist reluctantly returned to Paris where he died in 1907. Reporters lionized him during his last days at Ligugé and his first in Paris, where he temporarily occupied the guest quarters of the monastery of the Benedictine nuns on the rue Monsieur.[17]

Most of the local villagers regretted that Ligugé monks left in small groups, since at least a third of them depended on the abbey for their income. The community settled in Belgium near Nonnay in the province of Limbourg. In 1903 they transferred to Chevetogne, in the religious-congested diocese of Namur. Ligugé's house of studies in Paris, Sainte-Marie, opted for dispersion rather than attempt to finance an exile. The monks chose to be incardinated into the diocesan priesthood or joined the Benedictines already exiled in Belgium and Italy. The prior and three monks returned to Paris when feasible to guard the property and continue their scholarly research. The French Academy continued to give monetary and prestigious awards to monks in exile for their contributions to French scholarship.[18] The reporter of a provincial paper was forcefully reminded by the monks that the Benedictines had a glorious past—namely, Benedictine popes and cardinals (200), archbishops (116), and bishops (4600), as well as the "innumerable writers and scholars" like Mabillon and Montfacon who had contributed to the church's leadership and scholarship throughout the medieval and modern periods.[19]

The monks of the Angevin abbey of Saint-Maur-de-Glanfeuil also stopped temporarily in Namur. The French nation missed the scholars when Solesmes and Ligugé went into exile, but viticulture also suffered when Glanfeuil's abbey left Anjou. Before the monks departed, the Mayor of Toureil, M. E. Roblin, had written the abbot expressing the local population's regrets. He emphasized that they all recognized the moral and material benefits the abbey had conferred upon the region's occupants since the restoration of the abbey eleven years before. For example, French agricultural societies had often recognized the experiments and achievements in the hundreds of acres of vineyards under cultivation by the abbey. The monks also produced four varieties of the highest-quality wines. The monks could leave Namur in 1909, thanks to the generosity of the former abbot's relatives. The gift was a newly constructed abbey overlooking the medieval town of Clervaux in the Grand Duchy of Luxembourg. The community never returned to France.[20]

The Kergonan monks remained in the Namur diocese throughout their exile, though the nuns chose England rather than Belgium and first resided at Blake Hall in Essex, near London. A group of Anglican nuns who joined the church in 1908 credited the nuns of St. Michel with the inspiration to become Roman Catholic. They had only one restriction in their exile: instead of the customary twenty to thirty times daily (each period of prayer had three signals), the bells were to be rung for services only twice, at 8 a.m. and 6 p.m. In October 1902, the nuns went to the Isle of Wight, where the priory was raised to the rank of abbey while in exile.[21] The monks of Saint-Paul-de-Wisques also settled temporarily in Belgium. In 1907 they occupied a newly constructed monastery at Oosterhout, a village in the Catholic section of northern Brabant in the Netherlands. The nuns of Notre-Dame-de-Wisques had already settled there six years previously. Thus Holland gained two Benedictine houses that remained permanently even after most of the French monks and nuns returned to France.

These monasteries, among every other community of the Congregation of France, were in exile shortly before the eviction date of October 1. Other Benedictines either asked for authorization or counted on their nineteenth-century charters to forestall their monasteries' dissolution. Some succeeded. For others, their hopes were dashed by enforcement of the 1901 or 1904 laws.

Subiaco and Foreign Congregations Leave France

Among those waiting hopefully were the monasteries of the French Province of Subiaco and other foreign congregations. The year 1902 brought changes in French officialdom and in the manner and scope of the anti-monastic movements. When the premier resigned, his radical anti-clerical Republican successor, Émile Combes, accepted the post on the condition he be given *carte blanche* to suppress the religious orders.[22] Successful in achieving this desire, the Combes cabinet was approved on June 7, 1902. Within weeks he put into motion the machinery needed to carry out his program of dissolution. His weapon was to be strict enforcement of the Law of Associations, first to destroy the Catholic educational system and then the religious congregations. On June 27, 1902, he issued a decree ordering the immediate closure of 125 schools staffed by religious. These, he claimed, had been opened in violation of the law after July 1, 1901. In mid-July a ministerial circular ordered the prefects to shut down in the next eight days another 2500 Catholic schools. In 1902 alone, 11,000 hospitals and schools staffed by members of religious communities were ordered closed.[23]

A deluge of protests descended upon the ministry from mayors, clergy, and thousands of citizens. Reports of riots in the provinces arrived in Paris daily. The Bretons especially resorted to violence in vain attempts to prevent closures. The mayors who had objected were frequently suspended for their "anti-government activities." Army officers faced suspensions and courts-martial if they objected to the duty of evicting nuns and brothers who were teaching in the schools.[24] The protests of Cardinal Richard of Paris and the bishops were to no avail. They soon had even more reason for concern. Requests for authorization were under study in the Chambers. When the episcopate submitted a common petition urging the Chambers to accept the applications for authorization, the Council of Ministers declared the petition an abuse of power.

The ministry kept strict tabs on the reaction of each member of the hierarchy to the school closures and the public protests some of the bishops generated against the treatment of the religious.[25] To facilitate the handling of the authorization requests, Combes set up several *en bloc* categories. The men's congregations were to be reviewed first—teaching (25 congregations), preaching (28), and "commerce" (only the Carthusians). He submitted those applications to the Chamber of Deputies and asked that the legislators reject them. He submitted five to the Senators for approval: Trappists, Brothers of St. John of God, Cistercians of Lérins, White Fathers, and African Missionaries of Lyon. The report submitted by the commission that studied the fifty-four congregations of men became available to the press during the final processing and rejections of the authorization applications. It became known as the *Rapport Rabier.*[26]

During April 1903 most of the congregations concerned received personal messages from Combes stating, "I have the honor of personally notifying you of the rejection of...establishment is dissolved and must be closed."[29] In vain the monks at Pierre-qui-Vire had modified the constitutions that had accompanied their request for authorization, renaming their community "The Benedictine Missionaries of Pierre-qui-Vire." They had opened a mission in American Indian Territory—eventually Shawnee—and had based their hopes for authorization on the fact that monks were staffing the Sanctuary of St. Jerome in Palestine given to them by the French government in 1900. Nevertheless, the Prefect of Yonne was informed on April 4 that the monks had received a closure notice, although for three years the monastery had received nothing but praise from the Minister for Foreign Affairs for their work in the Holy Land. The gendarmerie informed the monks that the monastery had to be evacuated by April 19.[30] Two elderly and infirm monks were left behind in the monastery. Within weeks they were charged with attempting to reconstitute the community and issued a warrant. The local press predicted that the charges would be invalidated or at least the fines would be minimal— about sixteen francs.

The monks of Béthisy-Saint-Pierre (Oise) joined the Pierre-qui-Vire community and the monks of Saint-Benoît-sur-Loire in their Belgian exile. They had all received favorable reports from their local officials who had tried to keep them in France. The monks of Belloc, however, were subject to an unfavorable evaluation according to the *Rapport Rabier.* The Prefect of Basses-Pyrénées stated that prayer, study, and preaching did not occupy all the monks' time and energy. They were also engaged in a vast agricultural enterprise and several commercial and industrial ventures ingeniously conceived and organized. They not only raised livestock but also had a mill, bakery, pastry shop, and chocolate factory. The most serious charge was the accusation that they had involved themselves in politics.

Their political involvement related to the election of three monks to the municipal council of the village of Urt. One monk, Donatien,

founder of the Institut Agricole near Pau, had supposedly intimidated all the merchants into supporting the political campaign of a M.
d'Ariste.[31] After the dissolution notice came the monks immediately
worked to *"sauve-qui-peut"* (save what you can). Friends who also took
in several of the monks stored the furniture. The liquidator's agent
moved into the empty abbey and denounced the monks still living
in the environs in defense against the villagers' scorn. The prior (who
had been staying at the nuns' monastery), the director of the mill, and
the monk-accountant were ordered to appear before the tribunal of
Bayonne on the charge of violation of the dissolution order. The mill
director was fined but the monk refused to appear at the court, saying
he preferred imprisonment. When the gendarmes arrived at the mill
to arrest him, the monks' workers, friends, and neighbors encircled
the accountant, yet this resistance was ineffective. The monk went to
prison and the rest of the community crossed into Spain, and boarding students, novices, and theology students went to Olza in Navarre.
In 1906 they transferred to Lazkao where there was sufficient space
to accommodate them and several of the monks who had remained
in France.[32]

The Prefect of Tarn had the same complaint against the monks
of d'En Calcat as his colleague had against Belloc. "Since they have
been in the region," he wrote, "the Congregation of Benedictines has
always taken part against the Republicans and devoted itself to the
most active propaganda in favor of reactionary candidates."[33] What
he did not know was that the monks had spent the whole night in
prayer in the chapel pleading for a happy outcome for those elections.
When a false alarm predicted imminent expulsion on December 8,
1902, the monks carried away all the movables that could be stored
in homes of friends. For months the monks slept on pallets, and when
the refectory tables were finally removed they ate off planks. On
Easter Sunday (April 12, 1903), while Abbot Dom Romain Banquet
chatted with friends in front of the church, an officer of the gendarmerie of Dourgne handed him the dissolution notice. The abbot
calmly took the paper and continued the conversation as if he had
been only slightly interrupted. His appeal to the tribunal of Castres to
extend the fifteen-day eviction date until after the close of the school

year was successful. However, that delay was rescinded on April 21 when another notice arrived. Four days later the abbot heard from the *procureur-général* that they had until July 31 to leave. Those who could not pass as students or teachers left for Spain.

On April 27, despite the latest notice to the abbot, the liquidator arrived to affix the seals on the property. He desisted when shown the court official's letter fixing the July eviction date. The community rented a summer resort called Parramon across the Pyrenees. Some rode and some walked into Spanish exile. In June, two brothers left on foot for the four-day march, followed shortly thereafter by the novices who hiked to their Spanish exile. When Dom Banquet arrived after dismissing school on June 24, he found the monks already engaged in renovating the seventy-room hotel. The monks had been astonished to find that there were no pipes, heating stoves, or chimneys in the cold, high altitude, and no door or window in the old building closed tightly. Readily improvising, they made the breakfast room into a chapel and the billiard room into the sacristy. They held their chapter meetings in the ballroom. Summer bathers who had never heard Gregorian chant began to frequent the chapel. When one of the monks received faculties to hear confessions of the laity, the porter complained that the procession was long enough to keep ten monks busy. In 1908, the community and twenty young students moved to their permanent monastery: a well-preserved twelfth-century abbey at Besalú in Catalonia, where they remained there until it was safe to return to France after World War I (WWI).[34]

Kerbénéat (Breton for "village of Benedict"), where the Prefect of Finistère (Brittany) had questioned their utility since the parish priest could minister to the Catholics in the area, received support from the municipal council of Plounéventer. The mayor informed the Council of the life of prayer and scholarship that was traditional in Benedictine monasteries, but added how economically beneficial the abbey was for the area. He pointed out that their agricultural and industrial enterprises were widely recognized, mentioning the dairy specifically where cheese was produced and sold in France and Algeria. "This industry," he said, "constitutes a very precious resource for the farmers who sell all the milk there that they can dispose of, resulting in an unprecedented affluence, especially in the small households."[35] The mayor pointed out that a fair amount of the profits of the monastery's enterprises were consecrated to works of charity and care of the poor. He described how the monks had made marshy land produce vegetables in abundance, especially large crops of asparagus. He said the priests were on call night and day for the sick and dying, noting also that the people would have much farther to go to chapel services if the monastery closed. The council concurred; members joined in the praise of the monks and their work, and by unanimous consent requested that they be allowed to remain. The departure, according to the Council, would constitute a general misfortune for the poor, the workers, and the peasants of the area.[36]

Despite these commendations, the monks considered it prudent to prepare for exile. The community was informed it had two weeks to evacuate on Good Friday, 1903. One aged monk could remain at the abbey to guard the property. Père Corentin was to remain in the infirmary section, celebrate Mass there only, and recite his Office alone. He could receive one person—the doctor. The official who had served the eviction notice had encountered a hostile reception from a crowd of laypersons when he visited the abbey, so he advised the prefect that any officials would need sufficient protection in the future. Three brigades, two horses and one infantry from the communes in the area, arrived only to be resisted by a group of hardy peasants who spent the night defending the monastery against incursion. The following day, only the pleas of the monks could move the women away from the door so the officials could enter. The inevitable happened: monks and peasants left the premises.[37] Lord Ashburnam, who put his Welsh country estate at their disposal, gave the monks provisional shelter. They resided in another provisional monastery for the next fifteen years.[38]

English and Swiss Monks Leave France

The Swiss monks at Delle in Belfort decided not to seek authorization. They left their school in the hands of diocesan priests and laymen and left for Austria in 1901. After several more moves, the community eventually settled at the Mariastein Shrine in Switzerland.[39] Authorization laws also affected the English Benedictines who conducted a seminary-college at Douai. The government's *Rapport Rabier*, determined to undermine the monastic structure, accused the monks of Douai of having only one objective—furthering the interests of the English. The report mendaciously stated that there was no relationship between the monks and the French people, and that the monastics left their grounds only on business or with their students. The abbey, however, requested authorization. The municipal council recommended unanimously that it be authorized. The ministry, however, placed the abbey in the "bad teaching" (*enseignment mauvais*), so the Chamber voted their dissolution. The officials came on April 4, 1903, to affix seals to their property but then granted a two-day delay when the abbot insisted that he had not received the dissolution notice. Subsequently they were given three months to close the school and evacuate the premises.

The monks had considered a transfer to England already in 1880 when threatened with the earlier laic law, saved through the intervention of the English ambassador. This time the embassy failed, probably, as one of the monks speculated, because the negotiations for an *Entente Cordial* between France and England were in process. Apparently the ambassador was not going to insist that a few Catholic subjects be allowed to remain on French soil. Bishop Cahill of the Portsmouth diocese offered the community the diocesan school of St. Mary's at Woolhampton, which they accepted. By June 18, 1903, all the monks and students were in England, where for the first time they could publicly educate young men in Catholic doctrine.[40]

The Diocesan Clergy Alternative

Some priest-monks who chose not to go with their communities into exile often attempted to be integrated into the diocesan clergy. These attempts were seldom successful. In a circular from Premier Waldeck-Rousseau to the prefects in November 1901, two conditions were decreed for acceptance into a diocese of former members of religious orders: (1) the priest could not belong to a congregation still in existence and (2) he was obliged to seek incardination into his native diocese, though not that where the monastic community had been located. All the rejections were then based on the first condition. In one case, the ministry informed the prefect at Dijon that he should advise the bishop that he could not admit a former Benedictine to the parochial clergy because the community he remained a member of was still in existence elsewhere in Europe.[41] A Belloc monk seeking to work as a diocesan priest faced the same charge, but successfully argued that since he was the only monk of his congregation officially incardinated in any diocese, his was a genuine transfer. He was canonically incardinated and never rejoined his former community.[42]

By summer 1903 no monastery of Benedictine monks remained in France. Along with England and Wales, several other countries—Belgium, Italy, Spain, Luxembourg, Holland, and Switzerland—harbored expelled communities. The nuns fared differently: none were expelled. Except for the women's' communities in the Congregation of France, who had followed the monks into exile, the nuns tenuously remained in their monasteries. Many had received authorization decades before as they generally were teachers or had a school at the monastery itself. Their fate was changed only by the passage of the laic law of 1904.

Suppression of All Catholic Schools

After the men in religious orders were expelled, Premier Combes turned his attention to the women's communities and those of the men who had been authorized to teach. For a year the premier had kept religious teachers under constant surveillance. He had given strict orders to the prefects of the departments to send him regular reports about the actions and attitudes of the religious men and women engaged in teaching. In December 1903, he presented a bill to the Chamber of Deputies that called for an end to academic instruction at all levels by all members of religious communities, authorized or unauthorized. The bill also provided that those communities authorized solely for teaching purposes be dissolved.[43] The Chamber studied the bill for six months. Objections arose when Deputy Millerand, losing patience with the premier's obsession with anti-clerical legislation, demanded consideration of certain social problems. Other officials were concerned about the cost of replacing the private schools. The Combes bill, however, had foreseen such objection. It stipulated that proceeds of the liquidations were to be used for public school construction.[44]

Cardinals Richard and Langénieux sent strongly worded letters of protest to the President of the Republic. Pope Pius X sent a confidential letter to the President Loubet in December in which he warned against the serious consequences to France's prestige abroad should the bill pass and publicly registered his indignation to the College of Cardinals in March 1904. The French government ordered its ambassador at the Vatican to relay its objections to this interference in the internal politics of the country. The French argued that since the Concordat of 1801 had not mentioned the religious orders, no violation had been involved.[45] The legislative committee reported to the Chamber on February 11, 1904. They theorized that citizens who were not free, as well as religious who had infeudated themselves to a high religious power, were incapable of educating free citizens. It also recommended that pensions be given to teachers left without means of sustenance. The estimate for replacement of the private system was set at 73 million francs. Despite vigorous attempts to stop Combes' measure, it was signed into law by a narrow margin on July 7, 1904. According to one French historian, "Many of the spouses of parliamentary members of the bloc had analogous reactions. It is difficult to understand the success of Combes' policies if one forgets that women did not have the vote."[46]

The Law stated all congregations were to be suppressed within ten years if authorized exclusively for teaching or to combine teaching with another social service. Mixed groups who were engaged in nursing, administration of orphanages, or homes for the aged were to cease educational activities but could continue their other charitable works with the revenue gained by the liquidation of the goods involved in their educational endeavors. Schools for the physically handicapped were exempted from closure. All novitiates of teaching institutes except those training members to staff foreign schools were to be closed. Novitiate membership was to be strictly limited to the needs of schools outside France. All statistics comparable to that exacted by the Law of Associations in 1901 were to be sent to the prefects to be relayed to the ministry immediately.[47]

Officials would notify the religious congregation concerned fifteen days before the end of the school year if its dissolution was decreed. The government would name liquidators, inventories would be taken, and administrators appointed to oversee the property of the dissolved communities. Proceeds not returned to donors or heirs were to be channeled for public school construction and expansion. Court action against the liquidator had to occur within six months after the date of the dissolution notice. The liquidator would then proceed to sell all movables and immovables, except those allocated by him as compensation for old and ill members of the communities. Beginning on July 10, three days after the signing of the bill, dissolution notices in the *Journal Officiel* were first published; they would be printed there throughout 1904 and 1905. Hundreds of dissolutions and partial closures were listed.[48]

The nuns faced the usual dilemma—what course of action to take. The options were court appeals, secularization of members, or exile abroad. Many, especially the bishops, favored laicization of the religious to keep the schools open and the costs down (hiring lay men and women at regular salaries would be prohibitive in many cases.) When some attempted this subterfuge two of the most radical newspapers, *Le Lanterne* (September 24, 1904) and *Le Siècle* (October 4 and November 3) kept their readers informed of the farce being played out in the private schools. They argued that they had been secularized only in one respect—the teachers no longer wore religious habits. On September 28, *Le Lanterne* argued that the best way for the so-called laicized religious to show their "good faith" (that they were sincerely secularized) and be above suspicion would be to marry.

Only a few weeks before the fall of Combes' cabinet in January 1905, two more major decrees were issued. The first detailed the administration of the law suppressing instruction; the second dealt exclusively with the legal aspects of the mixed communities' property. In December 1905, the Law of Separation of Church and State passed the legislature. General elections in 1906 gave sixty more seats to the

Radicals at the expense of the Conservatives. Radicals celebrated that their moves against the church obviously had popular approval of the male population of France.[49]

Benedictine Nuns Under the Law of 1904

Except for the nurses of the Fécamp community and the Servants of the Poor, the Benedictine nuns who had secured authorization in the post-Revolution era had been designated as teaching institutes only because they had a monastery school. They were, as a consequence of the new law, now subject to dissolution because of that school. The few unauthorized congregations found survival especially difficult.

The Congregation of the Most Pure Heart of Mary partially survived the blow. In 1904 it consisted of eight communities. One of these (Jouarre) had already left in 1903 for a sixteen-year exile. Two were definitively dissolved; the rest survived, often on a mere sustenance level. The Jouarre nuns, members of one of the most heavily endowed royal abbeys before the Revolution, were welcomed to Losange, Belgium, where they occupied a small hunting lodge.[50] In 1910, the Jouarre nuns moved to Thy-le-Chateau in Namur then migrated to northern Brabant. The nuns remained in Holland until their return to France in 1919, five years after the official date of their dissolution by the French government.[51] Le Sembel, another community of the Congregation of the Most Pure Heart of Mary, anticipated the Law of 1904 and dispersed. The monastery was never restored.[52] The newest foundation, Nîmes, also dispersed, never to be revived. It was legally dissolved on July 11, 1904; the nuns left for other communities in exile, or with families or friends.[53]

Pradines, the motherhouse, was one of the more fortunate, although its fate remained uncertain until 1914. The nuns were authorized in 1813 as Hospital Sisters of St. Charles, as its original affiliation had been with that group. Cardinal Fesch had purposely named the affiliation because those Sisters were being recognized as of "public utility" and could easily be authorized. The abbey applied for reauthorization under its own name after the 1901 Law of Associations. Throughout 1903, Parisian friends of the abbey attempted to secure the intercession of the president's wife to promote the reconfirmation of authorization. Although these efforts were valiant and eventually successful, the *Journal Officiel* published the notice of the closing of the school on July 11, 1904. The nuns were assured that although they could not operate a school, they could continue as nurses. In December 1914, the nuns were finally authorized. They had again found firm and influential friends in Pradines and Paris.[54]

Chantelle Abbey continued the search for a foreign refuge, but responses from abroad were discouraging. The Trappists in Brazil warned them of the difficulties involved in a long, expensive trip across the Atlantic and a change of climate, language, and environment. From England came two notes counseling secularization. The superior of the Marists in London advised against their settling in England. He predicted that their meager resources would be insufficient to sustain them across the Channel. From Italy came word that in Turin, because the religious were now so numerous, the archbishop had forbidden the nuns to appear in religious habits outside their houses. Although some Italian bishops welcomed French communities, the government expressly forbade foreign congregations to teach, so the French nuns had to resort to needlework or taking in laundry to sustain them in that already impoverished country.

The Chantelle nuns were warned not to consider Switzerland since the Carmelites and Carthusians who had settled there in 1901 were expelled two years later. Belgian refugees from France counseled the nuns to wait it out. Foreign congregations could not staff schools in Spain. The French Marists there reported back that there were already too many communities scattered between Barcelona and the French border, a favorite refuge for the congregations leaving France. The Spanish bishops of five dioceses had "absolutely and without mercy" refused to admit more communities of French nuns.[55] The nuns stayed and, inexplicably, the Chantelle community was neither authorized nor dissolved. Similarly, La Rochette Abbey received a favorable decision when the abbess resorted to the courts, though they prepared for dissolution and continued to exist extra-legally.

They were categorized as nursing nuns so the dissolution decree was ruled invalid in their case. The community at Saint Jean d'Angély was also officially suppressed in 1904. The courts, however, ruled in favor of their suit against the liquidator and were permitted to remain in their abbey.[56]

The Congregation of Perpetual Adoration had twelve authorized houses as educators. The nuns at Rue Tournefort in Paris had an 1826 authorization, but they closed its school in 1886. However, in July 1904 the priory appeared on the list of dissolutions. The response to their appeal was courteous but negative.[57] Eventually the community was being categorized as a nursing institution thanks to a phrase in the constitution and could thus continue to exist and reclaim its property. The nuns returned in 1907. Another community who appealed their dissolution was Saint-Louis-du-Temple, another Parisian community of the Congregation of Perpetual Adoration. When the liquidator arrived on July 27, 1904, the prioress refused to assist him on the grounds that their case was under litigation. When they lost in the courts and before the Council, the nuns continued appeals until 1938. In the end they lost their case and their monastery. The community moved to Limon, a town near Paris, where they constructed a new building.[58]

Craon, in Anjou, also appealed their dissolution notice in 1904. When the nuns received word in 1905 that they had been declared a "mixed" community, some nuns returned then and the following year, but the skeptical prioress and others remained in Belgium. The liquidator lost three court appeals against them. A benefactor left them a sizable legacy in 1908 that eased the financial situation. Finally in 1912 all the nuns returned to France—and more litigation.[59] When the government decided to enforce the ten-year clause of the Law of 1904, the community was shocked to find itself among the list of the communities proscribed by a decree of June 30, 1914. Within weeks after the beginning of World War I, the subprefect of Château-Gontier notified the mayor of Craon that Minister Malvy has suspended all decrees against the congregations. The war saved them.[60]

While the community of nuns from Toulouse was crossing into Spain, the Rouen nuns were accumulating juridical victories. They had maintained a boarding school only for fifteen years after their authorization in 1828. Bishop Fuzet was so influential in 1904 that, in his presence, the monastery's name was deleted from the list of communities to be liquidated. Yet a liquidator was named and then inventoried the nuns' possessions in August 1904. Suits and counter-suits were initiated in the courts while the nuns looked for shelter abroad. In October 1907, the appellate court at Caen rendered the final decision—in their favor. In 1908, they secured recognition as purely contemplative. The nuns sent to Holland to prepare the refuge for occupancy were recalled.[61]

The dissolution notice for the community of Arras came in July 1904. The nuns resorted to the courts, but the school closed in August. Despite appeals, the Douai tribunal ordered the liquidator to proceed with the inventory in December. The day after Christmas the police summoned the twelve oldest nuns to appear the next day before the Judge of Instruction. All were semi-invalids. He interrogated seven of them for over three hours, returning the next day to interview sixteen of the other nuns. On December 31, his last "visit," he kept all of the members, even those confined to the infirmary, at a long session. When he asked for the names of the students educated in the school, he met with stubborn refusals. In January the liquidator arrived to inventory their possessions.[62] In September 1904 the police informed the Arras nuns that they had until October 1 to evacuate, with more appeals ensuing. The bishop told them in November 1906 that all efforts to save them had failed, so he advised them to leave France as soon as possible. They never returned to Arras. In 1921 they moved back to France, to Tourcoing.[63]

Notre Dame d'Orient moved twenty-eight of their nuns to Spain after their dissolution in 1904. Six others remained as infirmarians in France, and seven returned to their families.[64] One of the largest boarding schools staffed by the Benedictine nuns of Perpetual Adoration was closed at Caen in July 1904. The community of eighty nuns was slated for dissolution but not forced to evacuate.[65] Other communities in the Congregation had similar experiences, still others were permanently destroyed.[66]

The community at Lisieux, where St. Therese had received her early education, was also scheduled for dissolution in July 1904. The nuns appealed on the grounds they, too, were "mixed." The liquidator reported that he found only nine aged women-boarders and no other evidence that the nuns were engaged in nursing. Their decree of dissolution was declared invalid, however, on the basis that their charters in 1816 and 1851 had indicated that education and care of the aged were its objectives. They remained in France, and several more communities of nuns survived liquidation decrees.[67]

The Lorraine Benedictines at Flavigny have a somewhat different story. They were advised not to resort to the courts but were encouraged in their objective of remaining until removed by force (*manu militari*). Some nuns left France to prepare an Italian exile. Refuge in Germany was ruled out, despite its proximity. Nuns there were required to don secular garb and forbidden to give private lessons, maintain schools, or engage in any commerce or industry. German nuns in the community who felt that they could not withstand the deprivations to come were sent home. In October, five nuns were sent to the United States to join the Benedictines in Atchison, Kansas. The aged and infirm nuns were evacuated to local hospices or to Sisters of the Poor at Nancy. At each request to evacuate the buildings, the nuns refused to leave. When a final move seemed imminent, three œinfluential friends arrived to dissuade any official action against the nuns. According to the monastic chronicler this time the "executors dared not march."[68]

When the nuns were again subpoenaed in November, the bishop represented them. Because their house had been denuded of furniture and space heaters since July, he was concerned that the thirty-four nuns still in residence would die of cold and hunger. When a commissioner arrived at their monastery later, he was again informed that they would not leave unless forced. Consequently, the final expulsion was by force on November 11, 1904; all members of the community were in the chapel when the military arrived to evict them.

Surrounded by chanting nuns, a pale and embarrassed commissioner approached the abbess to read the court order. Ignoring his presence, the nuns' chanting continued. In desperation he attempted to halt the singing, calling for silence until the abbess finally signaled for quiet and allowed him to read the court's decision. She then protested that their property rights and liberty were being violated.

Then she reminded him of the excommunication attached to this pro-
cedure and the warning of final judgment later at the eternal tribunal.
No one moved in response to the gendarmes' request that they leave
the chapel. While they sang the "Suscipe," the profession anthem,
the gendarmes bodily dragged them out. They were deposited in the
midst of a downpour into the center of a mounted cordon controlling
the sympathetic crowd that greeted the sisters as they arrived with
shouts of "Vive les soeurs! Vive la liberté." From across the street,
however, a different refrain came from the upper-story windows of a
café, "Vive la République."

The abbess and two companions were the last in choir to be
approached. They were chanting the "Ave Maris Stella" when a gen-
darme approached and begged the abbess not to force him to put his
hands on her. When she remained immobile, she was dragged out as
the others had been. The monastery seemed empty but still the bells
tolled. Ten gendarmes took up the search and shortly returned in triumph with their trophies, two lay sister–bell ringers from the tower.
The gendarmes allowed the curé to lead the expellees to the parish
church where they intoned the "Stabat Mater." The local families vied
for the privilege of sheltering the nuns until they eventually went to
Italy, where they lived a life of severe economic poverty.[69]

Fate of the Monastic Properties

Once monastic property had undergone the official liquidation
procedures, there were no restrictions on its use. The nuns could use
schools that were closed on property not liquidated for some charitable purpose—presumably nursing the ill or aged. (When WWI broke
out, most were used for the care of the wounded.) Limited pensions
were to provide for those expelled and certified as indigent. Dowries
and donations made by members or their families could be reclaimed.
The liquidator had charge of selling all movable and immovable property. Combes and the Ministry of Justice were constantly urging
more haste in the liquidation process throughout 1903 and 1904.[79]
By 1907 the liquidators were being asked which of their nationalized
properties would be suitable for reformatories for minors.

By the time the last dissolutions were ordered in July 1914, the general public had already long been revolted by the abuses that had accompanied the liquidations. Nor were the billion francs top officials had once predicted would be added to the state treasury realized. In actuality, only twenty-nine million francs had been netted from all the religious houses. Property, of course, could not be sold at full value and most of it went for a fraction of its worth. Adaptation to other uses and the fear of excommunication was held over the buyers accounted for much of the failure to realize more money—let alone the long and costly litigations. The press suggested that much of the "French Catholic money" went with the religious to foreign lands. The Solesmes monastics must have been amazed to read the charge in one of the newspapers that the monks and nuns carried at least twenty-six million francs away with them from Solesmes.[70]

Of the properties associated with Solesmes, twenty-nine of the fifty-nine Benedictine monastic properties were appropriated and sold by the state. Eight were purchased with the intention of returning them to the monks or nuns. The exiled communities kept three of their own homes through delegate buying. Seven were acquired by bishops or lay people who sold them back to the former occupants after the war. Eleven were never restored.

Though hardly calculable in terms of francs, the financial burden thrust upon the French Benedictines in the implementation of the laic laws was staggering and, in some cases, destructive. In addition to underwriting the high costs of shipping their necessary movable articles into exile, they sustained the loss of what they left behind— e.g., the abbey presses of Solesmes and Ligugé, and the latter's new organ. Thousands of francs were needed for the repurchase and renovation of their buildings, or for new construction. Furniture, printing presses, and chapel furnishings had to be repurchased. Total losses often included fields, orchards, vineyards, and gardens that had been auctioned. The material losses sustained by the French Benedictines between 1901 and 1914 contributed immeasurably to the lowering of the already frugal living standard of the nuns and monks. The results of the economic drain are incalculable.

World Wars I and II and Their Aftermath

World War I, ironically, not only saved many of the French communities destined for dissolution, but also wrought a complete change in the political atmosphere. The anti-clericalism so prevalent in the pre-war period was undermined. The thousands of clergy and monks who served along with the ordinary French peasant-soldier—living with and eating crusts alongside him in all the filth of the trenches and barracks, and being wounded and often killed in battle—engendered a new respect for the habit, the cassock, and the clerical biretta. After the war the Church was seen in a different guise as the men still recalled the image of the churchman in the ranks, crawling through No Man's Land to battle the enemy or give absolution to the dying. The soldiers and populace saw the nuns nursing the wounded in the hospitals and at dressing stations, and often in their own converted empty classroom buildings or former monasteries.[71]

Only France mobilized its clergy, seminarians, and members of religious orders into the ranks as combatants. Until 1889 French law had respected canonical immunity exempting priests from the obligation of bearing arms and shedding blood even in defensive wars. But where the Revolution feared to tread, the Third Republic boldly trampled. National legislation in 1889, 1906, and 1913 eliminated these exemptions. In 1914 it was necessary for the Holy See, in the case of the French draftees, to suspend the canonical penalties imposed on any priest who "inflicts a wound or causes death" resulting in his loss of the right to perform "ecclesiastical functions."[72] About 45,000 clergy and religious directly served the French war effort. Of these, 30,000 were priests, and over 5000 lost their lives in this service. Many who were too old for regular military service often volunteered as military chaplains and served without pay. About 10,000 were able to be non-combatant stretcher-bearers or medics (Pierre Teilhard de Chardin the famous Jesuit, was one of these). Many monasteries were converted to military purposes. The valor and sacrifices of these men were duly noted by awards of over 1000 military medals.[73]

The nuns were also actively involved throughout the war. Two of the outstanding military institutions for the care of the wounded were at the vacated monasteries of Craon and Jouarre. At Craon, where the hospice received high commendation from officials, the staff consisted of formerly cloistered nuns and one local doctor. While the Jouarre community in its Dutch exile was caring for twenty-eight refugee children from occupied areas, the abbey in France was converted into a military hospital. When word of its having been requisitioned reached the exiled nuns, the community sent back three choir nuns and a lay sister to aid in the nursing and laundry duties. They performed so well that a medal was awarded to one of the nursing nuns for outstanding devotion to duty in the care of the wounded.

In view of the heroism and the service to the country of the men and women religious, there could be no official objection to the reconstitution of religious community life on the soil where so many had served so well and for which so many had died in its defense. Throughout the early twenties, the government merely winked at the reestablishment of religious communities and the reopening of their houses in France. In many cases, local officials not only placed no obstacles in the way of the communities' revival but also often gave them overt support. During the war and immediately after the armistice, leading French statesmen recognized that it would be "morally impossible to tell the members of the congregations who had returned to France to fight that they had to go back into exile if they wished to live according to their vows of religion."[74]

Although the monks had returned to France, there was still a great gap resulting from the loss of candidates during the period of the laic laws of 1901 and 1904, the Law of Separation of Church and State in 1905, and WWI. Among those ordained for the priesthood, French monks and friars had numbered 15,000 in 1900 (of a total 56,000 clerics). By 1913 the number of regular clerics had dropped to about 11,000. In 1929, numbers increased sufficiently, so regulars comprised 20% of the ordained men, still short of the 1900 ratio. By 1949 the French had only 42,500 clerics, far short of its pre-twentieth century numbers.[75] In 1898 there were 546 Benedictine monks in France, including the Swiss and English. Numbers actually increased during the exile—to 616 in 1905.

Yet, after the war, only 446 French monks were in French communities in 1920. The difference reflected the war casualties, the loss of the Swiss and English communities, and the monks left at Quarr, Oosterhout, and Lazkao to make the refuges permanent when the exiles returned. There was also the new foundation, a newly constructed abbey at Clervaux in Luxembourg (not to be confused with Bernard's French Clairvaux), for the entire Glanfeuil community. There had been no decline in numbers of professions before the war in the Congregation of France. In fact, monks' membership in the Congregation increased. Solesmes and Ligugé also added members. As the third decade of the twentieth century dawned, the monks of the Congregation of France seemed thriving and prospering.[76]

The nuns had been somewhat successful in recruiting new members while exiled, with the exception of Jouarre Abbey, which left behind 54 graves in Belgium and Holland. Ten Dutch women entered the community, but only seven left their country for France after the abbey's restoration there. Because they had assisted so valiantly in the abbey-military hospital during the war, the villagers viewed them differently when they returned. There had seemed little regret on their part when forced into exile, but the mayor, curé, and local school children were all on hand to welcome them back.[77] Other monasteries of women—such as the Arras, Orient, and the Erbalunga house on the Corsica island—never fully recovered from the expulsion and confiscation.[78]

After their return to France the nuns and monks lived in comparative peace, quietly resuming their monastic life. They were more than disturbed in 1924, however, when a resurgence of anticlericalism again threatened their existence. Their nemesis then was M. Poincaré, who had addressed a secret circular to the prefects of the departments urging them strictly to enforce the unrepealed laws against the congregations. Furthermore, the 1924 elections returned a majority of anticlerical to the Chamber and Senate. Premier Herriot announced to his Council of Ministers that it was time to send the monastics on their travels again. The rumor that the religious congregations were to be dissolved again spread rapidly.

Steadfast Catholics, the clergy, and returned servicemen among the religious and those who had fought beside them, immediately organized to stave off the enforcement of the laic laws. Clerical veterans, under the leadership of a Ligugé monk, Dom F. J. Moreau, organized DRAC (Droit de Religieux Ancien Combattants) that held rallies, published pamphlets, and loudly proclaimed that former religious had the right to remain in their homeland. Paul Doncoeur, a Jesuit veteran wounded at the Somme, wrote an open letter to the premier that was published in almost every French newspaper and placarded over hundreds of walls to be read by the general public. He pointed out that they would not leave because they did not want a Belgian, Englishman, American, or any other foreigner to meet them far from home and ask them questions to which they would be forced to reply that France had driven them out again. For the honor of France, he said, they would not say such a thing to a foreigner and therefore they would stay.[79]

The Parisians read the letter on the front page of *Paris Soi*, as Premier Herriot must have as well. At the next meeting of his Council he concentrated on the recent uprising in Morocco. The anti-clerical reaction died out and the religious lived on, marginally legal but usually peaceful. Pro-religious pressure became so strong that when the budget of 1929 came under consideration, public opinion forced the government to introduce an article proposing the authorization of missionary congregations. It was adopted, after somewhat bitter debate, in March 1929, authorizing nine specific missionary congregations (none of which were Benedictine).

Several deputies attempted to secure the abrogation of the laic laws in 1927 and 1931, but were unsuccessful. Only after the German army again occupied the Republic in 1940 did the Vichy government under Pétain finally take the laic laws off the books. By that time, the monks and nuns were again committed to the service of their country in whatever way they could help. Some, like the Kergonan nuns, even had to put up with German soldiers as co-occupants of their monastery. A law passed in April 1942 permitted authorization by decree. Unauthorized congregations, though not legal, would no longer be illicit. The Benedictines, however, did not hasten to be authorized. Though women could own property under the law of 1825, monks' assets were still best left in the hands of lay societies as the law of 1942 was still insufficient juridically to allow the men to possess their own property.

The religious remained in France, not illicitly but, for the most part, extra-legally. The Benedictine Order in France may have been damaged, but not destroyed. They lived on in France on the margins of the law, contributing as they had in the past to the social, economic, and religious life of the country as true French citizens.[80] Through these events, Benedictine monasticism was once again challenged and changed by events of the first half of the twentieth century. The French Laws of Association had dispersed congregations and their properties. While two world wars had shifted political attention, they had exerted their own extraordinary toll on the Benedictine men and women enduring—with their compatriots—devastation. The second half of the twentieth century would bring new challenges and new hope for restoration and renewal. Coming events would again call Benedictines to exercise the extraordinary adaptability of the Rule.❈

CHAPTER 14

Continuing Change and Contemporary Perspectives

Mid-Twentieth Century and Beyond

B enedictine monasticism has experienced both exhilarating heights and abysmal valleys across its centuries. The twentieth century sustained this historical pattern, manifesting undulations of change as the second millennium came to its close. After the depths of dispersal and war, phenomenal twentieth-century expansion of monastic houses marked a highpoint. More men and women—especially throughout the old and new nations of Asia and Africa—sought to enter communities based on Benedict's Rule. This trend, however, did not endure.

The Second Vatican Council (1962–1965) brought renewal and reform accompanied by major upheavals in the 1960s and 1970s, while scores of worldwide revolutions took their toll throughout the century. Overall, Benedictine lives were radically changed and sometimes sacrificed; monasteries were both built and destroyed. Nonetheless, the Rule of Benedict has continued steadily to guide an increasing number of those who seek to apply its wisdom worldwide.

The Aftermath of World War II

Early in the century, two devastating wars affected monasteries in Europe and the British Isles. Among those monasteries that had to face destruction again in the twentieth century was Monte Cassino, the cradle of Benedictine monasticism. During World War II, the battle for Cassino brought American bombers—erroneously suspecting German military had been harbored there—that nearly demolished the great monastery. Like monasticism itself, it would not remain in a state of ruins. Today the archabbey, rebuilt and still owned by the Italian government, is considered a national treasure. It is a favorite tourist stop while remaining an *abbey nullius*. The abbey library holds more than 100,000 volumes, and the archives, most of which were preserved by German-led evacuation teams during World War II, continue to be an invaluable source of Benedictine history.[1] The nearby nuns' abbey of St. Scholastica, claimed by its inhabitants to have been founded in 530 by Scholastica, Benedict's sister, was also in ruins after the bombing of Monte Cassino. The abbey has been rebuilt and restored.

German monasteries were not generally established in the cities, so they were spared widespread destruction in the bombing raids of World War II. However, several did sustain damage and some quite extensively. Saint Boniface in Munich and the French monasteries in Normandy suffered the most damage, especially the nuns at Lisieux, Valognes, and Argentan. After the Irish nuns' abbey at Ypres was demolished by bombing, they relocated in Ireland and are now at their monastery (a former manor house) at Kylemore.

Numerous other monasteries were damaged or obliterated during the war, and monastics dispersed or relocated until rebuilding began. European Benedictines faced these vicissitudes courageously and, in general, survived. Sometimes their numbers increased, sometimes perceptibly decreased. While the peregrinations prompted by legislation of the French laic laws and the rise and fall of Communism closed many monasteries and dispersed monks and nuns, the two world wars and many national revolutions had shaken monastic life to its foundation. Widespread economic and social shifts in both developed and developing nations also impacted the Benedictine way of life, influencing growth or diminishment of monastic communities. Furthermore, the storm following the Second Vatican Council's (Vatican II) mid-century call for renewal profoundly affected life in the world's Benedictine monasteries.

The Second Vatican Council

The Second Vatican Council, announced by Pope John XXIII in 1959, impacted mid-twentieth century monastic life extensively. Not only were religious communities called to return to the spirit of the founder, but the Council also called for adaptation in modes of living, praying, and working to the physical and psychological environment of the twentieth century.[2] Customs and costumes were reexamined and generally modified by the nuns during the first years after the close of the Council in 1965. However, in neither men's nor women's monasteries was the call to update accepted universally, let alone instantaneously. Nor did it succeed without serious and occasionally permanent polarization in some communities where strong attachments to what had been considered traditional conflicted with the mandate for renewal and reform.

Analyzing the change in customs of most monasteries of men and women between the 1950s and the 1990s—probably most markedly those in the Americas—shows the radical impact of Vatican II. In 1962, before such renewal, Cardinal Suenens of Belgium issued women religious a prophetic call to update their lifestyles and ministries in his *The Nun in the World*.[3] Additionally, as social demands for justice and solidarity took hold across the globe, monastic women initiated varied ministries of justice and service. In light of momentous cultural shifts of the time, some communities of women had already requested and received permission to use the vernacular instead of Latin at the Liturgy of the Hours. Vatican II made that linguistic change normative.

The greatest, and often most difficult, challenge for some of the monks and their leaders was the mandate that priest-monks and brother-monks (those not ordained) no longer be separated in choir during recitation of the Divine Office or in rank and recreation. American nuns had few lay sisters among the predominant choir nuns, but the European nuns—who had choir sisters, lay sisters, and externs in their communities—had less difficulty than the monks in unifying the different groups. Choir sisters usually outnumbered lay but the latter were quite easily assimilated.[4] However, it soon became evident that external changes in garb (especially for women), the daily horarium, use of the vernacular in the Liturgy of the Hours, and radical revisions of the customary were often easier to adapt than interior reform of monastics' inner life and spirit. Regardless, the Council profoundly affected monastic life in its relationship to the world.

Vatican II's reforms and reformers, however, were not always genuinely accepted. Hundreds of monks and nuns reexamined their motives for joining communities and chose to change their lifestyles drastically—to leave monastic life and be dispensed from their commitment. Others remained through the period of reform and renewal, which lasted several decades. The process of dispensation from vows for those who felt that the renewal effort was going too rapidly or too slowly was modified to limit bureaucratic hurdles. Those who decided to return to lay life also discovered that the stigma accompanying their leaving the cloister had lessened. Some met and married others who had also been dispensed from their vows or simply left their monasteries.

The Worldwide Reach of Post-Conciliar Benedictine Monasticism

Those who remained in monastic orders after Vatican II included monastics committed to mission life in the developing nations of the Eastern Hemisphere and Latin America. Although there were many foundations in Asia and Africa throughout the nineteenth-century colonial period, the greatest impetus for foreign missions followed Vatican II. All able communities were urged by the papacy to expend up to ten percent of their membership in the mission apostolate. Consequently, many Benedictines attempted to make some inroads among the non-Christian populations of Asia and Africa, with varying degrees of success.

Wherever Benedictines were or are sent out as foreign missionaries, dependent monasteries are initially erected. These provide the base for the monastics engaged in evangelization or education of those in the environs, much as the early medieval monks and nuns impacted

Europe. They constitute the only permanent missions in Asia, Africa, and Latin America. The monastic charism—reemphasized by Vatican II—continues to be, as it has been historically, one of mission: of being sent to those in need.[5] The number of global Benedictine mission houses increased significantly in the twentieth century in particular. While an extensive overview of each particular foundation, mission house, or dependent monastery exceeds the scope of this chapter, a basic overview of the worldwide presence of Benedictine monasticism offers a glimpse of its continuing spirit.[6]

Benedictines in Latin America

Christianity had been introduced in Latin America during the sixteenth-century European invasions, but Vatican II's call to increased missionary service meant extending varied apostolates to supplement the insufficient numbers of indigenous clergy. As in other nations, bringing the Christian gospel to Central and South America involved education, health care, translating and publishing, as well as working directly to bring justice to the economically deprived classes, particularly the Indian and mixed ethnic groups. In addition to issues of social justice, communities of nuns work in a variety of apostolates: extending hospitality, translating documents, creating art, baking altar breads, running bakeries, and sewing liturgical vestments. Much monastic work avoids scrutiny or censure from military or other governments by remaining quietly situated on the margins of the political milieu, focusing on social change through service of the poor. Many Benedictine houses often have a mix of local and European members, though an abundance of entirely indigenous congregations exist.[7]

African Nations

Benedictine monks and nuns also minister in many African countries, and several African states hold Cistercian monasteries. Since French colonialism in West Africa favored Catholic missions, former colonies of the French and Belgians retained a considerably higher number of monastics than nations that gained independence from British control. Religio-political tensions in Morocco, Algeria, and other countries have had intense periods when Christian monasteries have been diminished or suppressed, often accused of promoting the colonial Christian European culture in opposition to the African or Muslim one. Many monasteries incorporate African culture, music, and dance into their celebrations and liturgies.[8]

Asian Foundations

Asia has over forty monasteries of Cassinese monks and nuns, and at least fifteen Cistercian houses. The Philippines—still a Spanish colony in 1895 when the Montserrat monks began monastic life in Manila— boast the largest number. Monastics of Vietnam and Korea were forced to relocate during the prolonged mid-century wars involving their nations, and some monastics endured long political imprisonments and expulsion. Several monasteries of both men and women now thrive in these nations.

In pre-Communist China, in 1936, the monks of a Lisle, Illinois, foundation were imprisoned and then expelled during the Communist takeover. These monks eventually resettled in Taiwan, along with monks of the Wimmer Priory (Hsin Chuang) in Latrobe, Pennsylvania (founded in 1964). Though Japan has few Benedictines, there are several foundations of monks and nuns representing German, American, and Australian congregations whose membership has extended to the Japanese.[9]

The Indian Subcontinent

Numerous Benedictine congregations minister in health care, education and spirituality throughout India, including one founded in 1970 by an Indian-born founder, Abbess Teresita D'Silva.[10] Of particular note is the monastery-ashram of Shantivanam, founded by two French priests, Abbé J. Monchanin and Dom Henri le Saux (Abhishiktananda) and led by Bede Griffiths, an English Benedictine who affiliated his ashram with the Camaldolese Benedictines before his death in 1993. In these monasteries, there is a profound embrace of Indian culture and Asian—especially Hindu—spirituality demonstrated throughout their communal celebrations, liturgy, and architecture.[11]

Monasteries in Israel

The Holy Land, especially the Jerusalem-Bethlehem area, provides a fascinating study of the diversity within Benedictinism. No two houses have any similarity except in location and the following of the Rule. Each represents its European cultural roots and local Israeli environment. The oldest house, founded in 1896 on the Mount of Olives, operated an orphanage for Greek Orthodox children in hopes of fostering church unity. In 1977, the orphanage became a hostel for pilgrims but it, too, soon closed. The religious make rosaries and paint icons to support their cloistered contemplative life. Dormition Abbey in Jerusalem, founded by Beuron monks in 1906, is dedicated to ecumenical dialogue, archeological research, social work, and a theological institute for German students. In 1952 this abbey founded Weston Priory in the United States. Additionally, members of a small Melkite Greek monastery reside near Bethlehem.[12]

New Foundations in Australia

As previously noted, Australia received its first Benedictine missionaries in the nineteenth century. Those originating efforts were furthered by Spanish monks who founded Holy Trinity Abbey in Western Australia.[13] Along with the aforementioned Good Samaritan Benedictines—active in Japan and the Philippines—contemplative nuns also live in a number of houses. Good Samaritan sisters are educators, social workers, and pastoral ministers.[14] A cloistered contemplative community, Adorers of the Sacred Heart of Jesus, was founded in 1956 in North Sydney, maintaining a novitiate for Australia and the Pacific. Along with their spiritual practice, contemplative nuns in Australia are usually engaged in making altar breads, vestments, and giving retreats.[15]

The Twenty-First Century Horizon: Exploring the Future of Benedictine Monasticism

Numbers of admissions to religious orders throughout history rise and fall as cycles of politics, values, economics, and other factors militate for or against numbers joining communities of men and women dedicated to life under the Rule of Benedict. Despite prophecies of doom and many closings and amalgamations in the last decades of the century, the total numbers of Benedictine monks worldwide who made profession or oblation showed modest increases. Nonetheless, numbers of Benedictine women, including those classified as "moniales" (cloistered nuns), decreased slightly. Women monastics not restricted by constitutional, diocesan, or papal enclosure also lost total members. As the century ended, an abbot primate elected by the monks' congregational delegates and residing in Rome acts as the spiritual leader and liaison with the Roman Curia for over 9,000 monks and almost 20,000 nuns worldwide.

Global Benedictines depend on an abbot primate who can see the trends and patterns shaping the order's future. Being aware of the diverse situations, lifestyles, cultures, and individuals that influence monastery openings and closings worldwide allows a measure of predictive insight toward the future. Just months before his untimely death in 1995, an interview with the Order's former American Abbot Primate, Jerome Theisen, disclosed the complexities of planning for the rapidly changing future of the twenty-first century Benedictines.

Although the landscape shifts rapidly, he indicated that the trend of more new monasteries arising in Africa, Asia, and Latin America than in Europe and North America will likely continue. Furthermore, restoration of some monasteries of Eastern Europe will continue, especially the Czech Republic where four monasteries including Prague and Emmaüs were being restored, with more opening in Hungary and Poland. A small priory of nuns in Croatia may presage other foundations and the Missionary Sisters of Tutzing have a house in Romania.

Abbot Primate Jerome also predicted there will probably be less expansion in the Ukraine and other republics no longer tied to Russia, but the St. Ottilien Congregation and the American Cassinese were then discussing possible restorations in China in the mid-1990s. The Tutzing Sisters had already opened a small priory and hospital in northern China. He also saw Latin American houses continuing at their present level but significant numerical expansion in Korea, the Philippines, and Africa. He also saw the European cultural model giving way to structures, prayer, mission, and lifestyles more closely reflecting the developing world cultures. He was optimistic about the future, and closed his comments with a promise: "It [Benedictine life] will continue in some form."[16]

Changing Structures

Like Christianity, Benedictine monasticism has many divergent facets requiring different kinds of organizational groups and systems. The structure of the Benedictine houses, with the exception of the Cistercians and Trappists, are ordinarily united in a common membership in or affiliation with the Confederation. Most of the congregations (or federations, as some are titled) of Benedictine men and women comprised ten or more communities. Some, especially of women, have fewer. Varying degrees of centralization occur; some are centralized with a generalate and dependent houses in different localities with some had very little central administration. The monastics in general chapters determine their structure, compose their constitutions, and submit them to Rome for approval. The character of each house's autonomy depends on what authority the constitutions give the local and the congregational superiors.

Most congregations of men title their presidents as *pareses*. The nuns generally use *president, superior,* or *Mother General* to designate congregational or federation leadership Benedictines, throughout history, have been elected to the papacy and appointed to the episcopacy. As bishops they reside in their dioceses (or Rome if members of the Curia) and are released from obedience to their abbots and priors. Though working in particular dioceses in service to the whole Church of their region, they remain Benedictine monks.

Changing Distinctions

Another distinction is between monks who are priests or brothers. The twentieth century saw a majority of Benedictine monks ordained as priests, with fewer brother monks making profession. One perennial tension in Christianity that categorizes Benedictine women involves the distinction between the strictly contemplative, cloistered, or semi-cloistered nun, and her active counterpart, working in the midst of the world. Throughout the century, more women entered active houses that integrate an active apostolate with contemplation than cloistered and semi-cloistered houses, but both gained novices regularly.[17] Houses of contemplative nuns existed worldwide in most countries with Benedictine foundations.

The Benedictine Federation continues to classify those actively engaged in varied ministries—those not strictly cloistered—as "sisters," despite many of these former convents of nuns recently having renamed their communities as monasteries to reclaim their traditional monastic nomenclature. This distinction—"sister" for active and "nun" for contemplative woman—results from a nineteenth-century canonical ruling dividing nuns into two classes.[18] Furthermore, contemplative cloistered nun's superiors are "abbesses" and apostolic monasteries who elect their head is usually called a "prioress." Because the contemplative tradition is vital to both, active "sisters" are also nuns in Rule and practice, even when they engage in interreligious education, nursing, social and pastoral work, care of the aged and disadvantaged. These sister-nuns are organized into over thirty different congregations, serving the Church and all faiths in their diverse ministries. The largest congregations are all in the United States, headed by an elected American nun/sister, usually a prioress or former prioress.[19]

Emerging Congregations

As new political landscapes, organizational structures, and role distinctions continue to develop, unions of old and new monastic congregations may expand and enrich the Benedictine tradition. In the last decades of the twentieth century, other congregations that traditionally followed the Rule of Benedict affiliated with the Benedictine Confederation. In 1960, the Olivetan Congregation, founded in 1319 by Bernard Tolomei, joined this organization. There are more than twenty of their monasteries in Italy, although some elsewhere include houses of men and women, with a few like the early double monasteries. Olivetans are in France, Israel, and the United States. Similarly, the Vallombrosians, founded in 1039 by John Gualbert, joined the Benedictine Confederation in 1966. There are a modest number of these monks in independent monasteries and four houses dependent on the Abbot General. All are in Italy except for one small Brazilian community of eight established in 1967. Another group that joined the Benedictine confederation in 1966, the Camaldolese Congregation, was founded in 980 by St. Romuald. Monks and nuns made several American foundations on both the east and west coasts during the middle of the twentieth century. Three Italian houses are dependent on the General Council. Because of its hermitage mission, the late Dom Bede Griffith's East Indian monastery in Tamil Nadu gained affiliation with the Benedictine Confederation as Camaldolese, although Bede had been professed in the English Congregation. The distinct lifestyles and charisms of other congregations will doubtless continue to form and draw from the Benedictine Rule and its wisdom.

Conclusion

Benedictine monasticism is rooted in the ancient traditions of the desert mothers and fathers. It evolved in varied ways through the Pachomian, Cassian, and Basilian movements. Culminating in a global organization claiming fifteen centuries of history, Benedictines were not able to make a worldwide impact without overcoming a great deal of internal and external strife. Their history is not without pain, nor is it without glory. The expansion of the Christian Church was often the result of the expansion of monasticism. While the monks and nuns evangelized and Christianized, educated, nursed, and fed those in need, they demonstrated the power of their way of life all over the world. Eventually, Benedictines would include houses on every continent with the exception of Antarctica and in almost every country that has allowed a modicum of religious freedom. Wherever they went, Benedictine monks and nuns gained not only respect, but also power, prestige, wealth and real estate. These benefits often aided in fulfillment of their mission, but it also led to abuses of power by some church and monastic leaders that undermined fulfilment of monasticism's original vision.

Even the earliest Christian writers did not ignore the prophetic charge to care for the needs of the world. Notable among these writers was Augustine of Hippo who, a century before Benedict's birth, warned against non-involvement in society when he admonished his monks to balance monasticism with social needs. "Do not prefer your own monastic leisure to the needs of the Church," he wrote to his monks.[20] Ideally, monastic history would perpetually fulfill this prophetic mission. Yet, this has not always been the case, and some monastics failed to practice Gospel values—peace, justice, respect for the lowly, caring for the least—plunging their venerable tradition to its nadir. No longer prophetic voices, they became ineffective, "noisy gongs and clanging symbols"[21] when they failed to respond to the needs of the world around them and neglected those whom their mission originally sought to reach. In consequence, monasticism stagnated, declining in commitment and numbers. Inevitably, others—those who had authentically maintained the traditional objectives of Benedictine life—brought reform and renewal. Integrative adaptation of the culturally changing natures of prayer and work, rather an exclusive focus on one or the other, has repeatedly renewed monastic life.

Since its beginning, monastic communities have endured when rooted in a commonly held commitment and vision. They have defined their ministry and means of achieving their goals collectively, and then have sought to live their lives accordingly. The perennial tension between the emphasis on contemplation or its active counterpart—contemplation in action—remains a challenge to the monastic way upholding the simultaneous preeminence of both. Thomas Merton argued that contemplative life is an instrument of social reform through its fullest expression as action, and that action is always fed, directed, and enriched by contemplation.[22] Particular ways of achieving this balance continue to inspire much debate throughout monasticism.

Additionally, there has always been controversy concerning how the Rule itself should be interpreted. Some argue for a literal interpretation in keeping with the Anglo-Saxon interpretation that allowed for few exceptions. Others seek to take a more flexible "spirit of the law" approach, one more consistent with Roman practice that made adaptation and exception the rule. History demonstrates that the spirit of Benedict's Rule has often been lost in the attempt to interpret literally what he advised for a sixth-century community and patriarchal environment. Yet, most of the Rule enunciates such enduring values it can be exercised in spirit by everyone—not only monastics—including ordinary men and women.

Active involvement in responding to others' needs was the practice of Benedict and his followers, male and female, for the first three centuries. It was only in the tenth century and thereafter that Benedictines became predominantly contemplative, and in the case of nuns, often strictly cloistered contemplatives. Strict interpreters of the Rule, epitomized by Benedict of Aniane, led monasticism to focus its efforts on the otherworldly by constant prayer and liturgical celebration. Benedict of Aniane's mode of centralization and institutional restructuring set the stage for the Cluniac, then Cistercian, and later Trappist movements. His retracting of apostolic ventures—the efforts that had spread Christianity to most of Europe—eventually became further modified to eliminate involvement of monastics outside their own cloistered monasteries. This was this medieval ideal that the nineteenth-century Dom Prosper Guéranger reintroduced to European, American, and missionary monasticism, greatly influencing its further development.

Cataclysmic events like the Reformation and the French Revolution were disastrous for Benedictines and other religious orders, but there were some salutary effects. In the aftermath, the State no longer dominated the Church and monasticism as it once had. Religious and political upheaval during the centuries also meant that exiles from Europe spread their monasticism into Latin America, North America, Asia, and Africa. Political events also spearheaded the colonization of

Australia, where monasticism also spread. Historically, monastic exile and threatened dissolution has often resulted in greater expansion, necessary purification, and deeper commitment to the Benedictine way of life than ever before.

Throughout monastic history, whenever monasteries of men and women were dissolved and even destroyed, they arose elsewhere. When vocations to monastic life seemed few and secularization seemed imminent, change of life or locale could reform, renew, or simply relocate congregations so profoundly they burgeoned in effectiveness if not numbers. Such resilience is characteristic of Benedictine monasticism. Congregations generally thrived when they expanded to other countries, opened new missions, or served particular needs monks and nuns could address. Monasticism has flourished despite the historical vicissitudes that remain its legacy and challenge.

Benedictine life offers the world a definite force for good. As the future unfolds, monasticism will continue to exert a spiritual *and* social influence throughout a rapidly changing planet, affecting Christian and non-Christian lives. At present, many people seek a form of community to replace the impersonal alienation of societies emphasizing individualism. Whether Catholic, non-Catholic, or interreligious laypersons, priests, or vowed religious, many look to Benedictine monastics for direction about incorporating the Rule into their own lives, often through personal spiritual direction or retreats led by monastics. The Benedictine Oblate movement also accommodates single or married men and women who wish to live the Benedictine Rule more intentionally in their homes and at their occupations. Men and women of many professions, occupations, and dispositions throughout the world observe the Benedictine Rule in various ways. The Benedictine influence will remain in the forefront of some of the most vital social and ecclesial issues of the day, whether through monastics themselves or by others influenced by their longstanding legacy.[23]

As the future of Benedictine monasticism unfolds, changes will and should take place. Very small houses of few members and financially non-viable monasteries that have failed to attract new members may have to consolidate, seeking affiliation with more vital communities. Vast grounds and buildings may cease to be landmarks of monastic areas, but the value of community may be evident in the future in smaller, more obscure dwellings only slightly removed from contemporary urban and rural lifestyles. There will be fewer communities that number hundreds of members, and most may number under fifty members. The spirit of these communities could be firmer and more influential as their radical lifestyles deeply impact their societies. Their ministries in education, healthcare, administration, scientific research, social service and every other facet of daily life will continue in some form. Perhaps the Benedictines of the future will impact the coming ages as greatly as their monastic forebears have influenced the past fifteen hundred years.

As long as individuals seek to live the Gospel according to the Rule in community, the Benedictine monastic movement and way of life is not in jeopardy. Perhaps future structures will be more open, allowing for more participation by lay groups of single men and women as well as families. Monastic scholars, researchers, writers, and ecclesiastical leaders will continue to make significant contributions to Christianity and the world. As the existence of some new associations and lay communities suggest, perhaps the remainder of the twenty-first century will see a revival of the double monastery concept—men and women on the same compound working together under a common superior—a phenomenon already evident and expanding in North America, Asia, and Europe.

The fifteen-hundred-year history of Benedictinism has been an evolutionary, and sometimes a revolutionary, one. As we have seen, it is the story of an institution that has survived periods of destruction, reform, renewal, and revivification in recurring cycles. Benedictine history is replete with individuals who have had common human weaknesses but also men and women of indomitable courage. Like their original founder, many of the monks and nuns—whether cloistered or non-cloistered—have proven to be exemplars across the twenty-first century threshold. Many also hold lessons of wisdom gained through difficulty, trial, and occasional mistakes. While prophets remain "those who comfort the disturbed and disturb the comfortable," Benedictine values—like the teachings of Jesus—offer

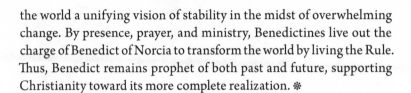

the world a unifying vision of stability in the midst of overwhelming change. By presence, prayer, and ministry, Benedictines live out the charge of Benedict of Norcia to transform the world by living the Rule. Thus, Benedict remains prophet of both past and future, supporting Christianity toward its more complete realization. ✼

NOTES

CHAPTER 1
Benedict and Scholastica: Their Predecessors and Contemporaries

[1] For a comparative overview of monasticism in varied world religions, see Mayeul Dreuille, *From East to West: A History of Monasticism* (New York: Crossroad, 1999). The expansive *Encyclopedia of Monasticism* includes wide-ranging articles on Buddhism. See William Johnston, ed., *Encyclopedia of Monasticism* (Chicago: Fitzroy Dearborn, 2000). Many other sources on specific religions are available for the interested reader.

[2] For the complexities of interpretation of first-century Palestinian monastic movements, see John Collins, "The Site of Qumran and the Sectarian Communities in the Dead Sea Scrolls," in Craig Evans, ed., *The World of Jesus and the Early Church: Identity and Interpretation in Early Communities of Faith* (Peabody, MA: Hendrickson Publishers, 2011), 9–22. For one perspective on Jesus' possible Essene influence, see James Charlesworth, "Research on the Historical Jesus Today: Jesus and the Pseudepigrapha, the Dead Sea Scrolls, the Nag Hammadi Codices, Josephus, and Archeology," in *The Historical Jesus*, ed. Craig Evans (New York: Routledge, 2004), 355–374.

[3] Luke Eberle, ed., *The Rule of the Master: Regula Magistri* (Kalamazoo, MI: Cistercian Publications, 1977).

[4] See David Knowles, *Christian Monasticism* (New York: McGraw Hill, 1969), 9ff. Vincent Desprez of Ligugé authored a series of articles on early monastic history in his abbey's newsletter, *Lettre de Ligugé*, some translated for the December and March 1990 and March 1991 issues of the *American Benedictine Review* (cited hereafter as *ABR*). M. Basil Pennington, ed., *Rule and Life: An Interdisciplinary Symposium*, ed. (Spencer, MA: Cistercian Publications, 1971). The Symposium is reviewed by S. Imogene Baker in *Benedictines* 26 (Fall–Winter 1971), 88.

[5] See Timothy Fry, et al., eds., *RB 1980* (Collegeville, MN: Liturgical Press, 1981), 157–297 (cited hereafter as *RB 1980*).

[6] Patrice Cousin, *Précis d'Histoire Monastique* (Paris: Bloud et Gay, 1956), 5; *RB 1980*, 3–34, 321.

[7] For an introduction to these first Christian monastic women, see Laura L. Swan, *The Forgotten Desert Mothers: Sayings, Lives, and Stories of Early Christian Women* (New York: Paulist Press, 2001).

[8] See William Harmless, *Desert Christians: An Introduction to the Literature of Early Monasticism* (New York: Oxford, 2004); and Helen Waddell, *The Desert Fathers: Translations from the Latin with an Introduction* (London: Constable & Co Ltd., 1936).

[9] See Terrence Kardong, *Pillars of Community: Four Rules of Pre-Benedictine Monastic Life* (Collegeville, MN: Liturgical Press, 2010).

[10] Garcia M. Colombas, *San Benito Su Vida: y Su Regula* (Madrid: Biblioteca de Autores Christianos, 1954), 13–16. See also Athanasius, *The Life of Saint Anthony*, Ancient Christian Writers (Westminster, MD, 1950).

[11] Cousin, 37–39.

[12] Philobert Schmitz, *Histoire de l'Ordre de Saint-Benot* (Maredsous: Editions de Maredsous, 1949), 7:5.

[13] See Philip Rousseau, *Pachomius: The Making of a Community in Fourth-Century Egypt* (Berkeley: University of California Press, 1999); and Armand Veilleux, *Pachomian Koinonia* (Kalamazoo, MI: Cistercian Publications, 1996).

[14] Cousin, 52–53. See also Palladius, *Lausiac History*, Ancient Christian Writers, trans. Robert Meyer (New York: Newman Press, 1964), 92–95.

[15] Basil of Caesarea, *The Rule of St. Basil in Latin and English: A Revised Critical Edition*, trans. Anna Silvas (Collegeville, MN: Liturgical Press, 2013).

[16] Cousin, 53–72. See also *Saint Basil: Ascetical Works*, Fathers of the Church, vol. 9, trans. S. Monica Wagner (Washington, DC: Catholic University Press, 1950).

[17] John Bamburger, "Introduction," in *Evagrius Ponticus: The Praktikos and Chapters on Prayer*, Cistercian Studies Series 4 (Spencer, MA: Cistercian Publications, 1970); Julia Konstantinovsky, *Evagrius Ponticus: The Making of a Gnostic* (Burlington, VT: Ashgate, 2009).

[18] Palladius, *The Lausiac History*, Ancient Christian Writers, 34, trans. and annotated Robert T. Meyer (New York: Newman Press, 1964), 200n337.

[19] Evagrius, *The Praktikos and Chapters on Prayer*, trans. John Bamburger (Kalamazoo, MI: Cistercian Publications, 1978); Evagrius, *Evagrius of Pontus: The Greek Ascetic Corpus*, trans. R. E. Sinkewicz, (Oxford: Oxford University Press, 2003).

[20] See Migne, Jacques-Paul, *Patrologiae Cursus Completus Series Graeca* (Parisiis: Garnier, 1857), 1093–1233 (cited hereafter as *PG*) and *The Lausiac History*, no. 38.

[21] Stephanus Hilpisch, *History of Benedictine Nuns* (Collegeville, MN: St. John's Abbey Press, 1956), 5; Joanne Turpin, *Women in Church History* (Cincinnati: St. Anthony Messenger Press, 1990), 29–36; Ruth Albrecht, *Das Leben der heiligen Makrina auf den Mintergrund der Thekla-Traditionem* (Göttingen: Vandenhoeck and Ruprecht, 1986). Gregory of Nyssa's *Vita Macrinae Junioris* (Migne, *PG* 46, 960*ff.*) is the original biography on which most of the others are based. It has been translated by Virginia Woods Callahan, *Gregory of Nyssa: Ascetical Works*, Fathers of the Church (Washington, DC: Catholic University Press, 1967), v. 58, 163–191. For Gregory's insightful dialogue with Macrina on the soul and resurrection, see 195–272.

[22] Schmitz 7:7; Cousin, 105.

[23] Palladius, 110–114; Rosemary Reuther, *Women of Spirit* (New York: Simon and Schuster, 1979), 83. Also see Timothy Barnes, *Early Christian Hagiography and Roman History* (Tübingen: Mohr Siebeck, 2010).

[24] See Lina Eckenstein, *Woman under Monasticism* (Cambridge, England: Cambridge University Press, 1896); George Lawless, *Augustine of Hippo and His Monastic Rule* (Oxford: Clarendon Press, 1987); Philip Schaff, ed., *A Select Library of the Nicene and Post-Nicene Fathers of the Christian Church* (Buffalo, NY: Christian Literature Co., 1986), 563–568; and *St. Augustine: Letters 204–270*, Fathers of the Church, trans. S. Wilfred Parsons, 32. George Lawless maintains that *Letter 211* was first written for monks, then "feminized."

[25] Marcel Sahler, *Les Grands Ordres Monastique des Origines 1949* (Auch: F. Cocharaux, 1949–1950), 1, 10. Pierre Gally, in a leading French newspaper, *La Croix*, June 30, 1961, "Ligugé, Berceau du Monachisme Occidental," maintains that the community first occupied abandoned barracks of a Gallo-Roman military company

and was organized on quasi-military lines with Martin as a pseudo-general. Dom Pierre Minard of Ligugé disagrees (*Lettre de Ligugé*, 1960), 84. There must, however, be some explanation for the ancient fourth-century Roman floors excavated at the site of the earliest chapel. If not an officers' barracks, then they may have once graced a room of an aristocratic estate. Martin may have tread them in his day (Interview, Ligugé, 1961).

²⁶ Jacques Hourlier, *A la recherche de Saint-Germaine-des-Pres* (Sablé-sur-Sarthe: Imprimerie E. Coconnier, 1957), 1–11.

²⁷ Jeffrey Hamburger & Susan Marti, eds., *Crown and Veil: Female Monasticism from the Fifth to the Fifteenth enturies* (New York: Columbia University Press, 2008).

²⁸ Archives, Sainte-Croix Monastery, Poitiers; Mary Bateson, "Origin and Early History of Double Monasteries," in *Transactions of the Royal Historical Society* (London: Longman's and Green, 1899), 13:146–149; Lina Eckenstein, *Women under Monasticism* (Cambridge: Cambridge University Press, 1896), *passim*; Joan Morris, *The Lady was a Bishop* (New York: Macmillan, 1973). According to Margaret Wade Labarge in *A Small Sound of the Trumpet: Women in Medieval Life* (Boston: Beacon Press, 1986), 6–7, Radegund's house was known as a literary center as she "followed the advice given by Cesarius of Arles in his rule for nuns. He felt that all nuns should not only learn to read and write but should also have access to a wide range of books and spend at least two hours a day in such studies." Deaconesses, like Radegund, were not at all rare during this period. There were also many Greek deaconesses during the fourth, fifth, and sixth centuries according to Roger Byron, *The Ministry of Women in the Early Church* (Collegeville, MN: Liturgical Press, 1976), 88–91.

²⁹ See Owen Chadwick, *John Cassian: A Study of Primitive Monasticism* (Cambridge: Cambridge University Press, 1950) and Schmitz 7:7; Colombas 32–35. Cassian's works include John Cassian, *The Conferences* (New York: Paulist Press, 1997) and John Cassian, *The Institutes* (New York: Newman Press, 2000).

³⁰ Dom Stephanus Hilpisch, 5–14. See Ludwig Bieler, *The Life and Legend of Saint Patrick* (Dublin, 1949).

³¹ Lawless, 60; Cousin, 159. Book Two of the *Dialogues* (chapter 9) tells of Benedict's prescription for missionary evangelization to win over the people of Cassino to Christianity. For a defense of this statement, see Matthias Neuman, O.S.B., "The Creative Charism of Benedictine Monasticism: A Reply to Francis Mannion," *American Benedictine Review* (*ABR*), 46, no.3 (Sept. 1995): 254–270. He traces the integration of apostolic and contemplative throughout Benedictine history.

³² See Timothy Joyce, O.S.B., *Celtic Christianity: Sacred Tradition, A Vision of Hope* (Maryknoll, NY: Orbis Books, 1998) and J. F. Denny, *The Sources for the Early History of Ireland* (New York, 1929), *passim*. Brigid is also mentioned in Bateson, 165–168. Brigid's foundation did not survive the Reformation but there have been attempts to bring back monasticism to Kildare. See also Thomas Cahill, *How the Irish Saved Civilization: The Untold Story of Ireland's Heroic Role from the Fall of Rome to the Rise of Medieval Europe* (New York: Doubleday, 1995), 246.

³³ Bateson, 167.

³⁴ Gregory the Great, *The Life of Saint Benedict*, trans. Terrence Kardong (Collegeville, MN: Liturgical Press, 2009); and *Gregory the Great: The Life of Saint*, trans. Adalbert de Vogüé, (Petersham, MA: St. Bede's Publications, 1993).

³⁵ Housekeepers, or "nurses" as some mistranslate, were generally sent with upper-class students who left their homes for their education in some city. Campus

dormitories were unheard of in Benedict's time and are still not too common in many European universities. Male students were not expected to do their own cooking.

[36] Lives of Benedict are available in every European and many Asian and African languages. The English studies include John Chapman, *Saint Benedict and the Sixth Century* (London, 1929); I. Herwegen, *Saint Benedict: A Character Study*, trans. P. Nugent (St. Louis, MO: Herder, 1924); Justin McCann, *Saint Benedict* (New York, 1937); T. Maynard, *Saint Benedict and His Monks* (New York: P. J. Kennedy, 1954). For French readers, a brief edition by Dom Léon Chaussin, *Saint Benoît de Nursia* (Paris: Editions de la Source, 1943) is highly recommended by this writer. Although the monks of Monte Cassino claim that two bodies discovered after the WWII bombings were those of Benedict and Scholastica (and they were backed up by experts in the field), the monks of Fleury still claim they have his bones, which had been transferred there in medieval times. At one time Subiaco also claimed relics, so all were assured Benedict did live—as there were no fewer than three bodies.

[37] Luke Eberle, *The Rule of the Master: Regula Magistri* (Kalamazoo, MI: Cistercian Publications, 1977).

[38] Numerous translations of the Rule exist. See Timothy Fry, et al., eds., *RB 1980: The Rule of St. Benedict in Latin and English with Notes* (Collegeville, MN: Liturgical Press, 1981); Terrence Kardong, *Benedict's Rule: A Translation and Commentary*. Collegeville, MN: Liturgical Press, 1996).

[39] *Vie de Saint Benoît: Grégoire le Grand: Dialogues, Livre Second*, Vie Monastique, no. 14 (Bégrolles-en-Mauges, Maine-et-Loire: Abbaye de Belle Fontaine, 1982), 185–189. It is available in English translation by Hilary Costello and Eoin de Bhaldraithe, *The Life of Saint Benedict: Gregory the Great, Commentary by Adalbert de Vogüe* (Petersham, MA: St. Bede's Publications, 1993). See also de Vogüé, *Cistercian Studies*, 18, 1983.

[40] Pius XII, *Fulgens Radiatur* (Vatican, 1947), http://www.vatican.va/holy_father/pius_xii/encyclicals/documents/hf_p-xii_enc_21031947_fulgens-radiatur_en.html.

[41] Cypriano Vaggagini, "La Posizione di San Benedetto nella questione semipelagiana," *Studia Anselmiana*, 18 (Rome, 1947): 17–84.

[42] Joel Rippinger, Madison, WI, Sesquimillenium Conference, 1980.

[43] In addition to *RB 1980*, other commentaries include an inclusive language edition by Joan Chittister, *Wisdom Distilled from the Daily: Living the Rule of Saint Benedict Today* (San Francisco: Harper and Row, 1990), and two of Esther de Waal's interpretations for the monastic and layperson *Seeking God: The Way of Saint Benedict* (Collegeville, MN: Liturgical Press, 1984), and *Living with Contradiction: Reflection on the Rule of Benedict* (New York: Harper and Row, 1989).

[44] In all 595 pages of Dom Cousin's work on Benedict and his monks, there is no mention of Scholastica. Dom Schmitz, who wrote six volumes on the monks and one on nuns (half of which is an index to the seven-volume work) like some does not question her existence. He refers to Gregory's statement that she was a sister of Benedict, dedicated to God from infancy. In contrast, Adalbert de Vogüé, one of the foremost Benedictine scholars, not only describes the famous meeting with her brother, but also twice calls Scholastica a religious (*religeuse*). In his commentary, he refers to her as a *moniale*, a nun.

[45] *Life of St. Benedict*, 161.

[46] See Jacques-Paul Migne, *Patrologia Latina Database*, ed. Thomas Patrick Halton (Cambridge: Chadwick Healey, 2006) 66: 125–204, http://pld.chadwyck.com/ (cited hereafter as *PL*).

[47] During post-WWII excavations in the Church of St. Scholastica in Norcia, a mural was discovered which pictured a young boy and an older woman (his mother?) waving farewell to what appears to be an older sister. Some conclude that it portrays Benedict and his mother saying goodbye to an older Scholastica who left home first, perhaps for a house of virgins.

[48] Cousin, 185; Chaussy et al., *Notre Dame de Jouarre* (Paris: Editions Guy Victor, 1961), 5–7.

[49] John Crean, ed., *The Altenburg Rule of St. Benedict: A 1505 High German Version Adapted for Nuns; Standard RSB Text Edition Annotated, Benedictine Abbey of Altenburg, Austria, Ms AB 15 E 6, fol. 119r–156v* (St. Ottilien: EOS Verlage, 1992).

[50] Chaussy et al., 33–47; R. M. Paule Greterin, Jouarre: *L'Age d'Or Merovingian* (Jouarre: Abbaye Notre-Dame, 1961), 14; Joan Morris, 32–33; Bateson, 154.

[51] Ignasi Fossas, ed., *Regla per als Monjos: Text Llatí/català*, Vol. 21 (Barcelona: Publicacions de l'Abadia de Montserrat, 1997).

[52] Walderbert, "Cujusdam Patris Regula ad virgines" in *PL* 88, 1053–1070.

[53] Bateson, 155–159. See also the study of double monasteries by Dom Stephanus Hilpisch, *Die Doppelkloster Enstehung und Organization* (Münster: Aschendorff, 1928).

[54] Chaussy at al., 33–47; R. M. Paule Greterin, *Jourre: L'Age d'Or Merovingian* (Jourre: Abbaye Notre-Dame, 1961), 14; Joan Morris, 32–33; Bateson, 154.

[55] Bateson, 161; Greterin, 20; Jane Tibbetts Schulenberg, "Women's Monastic Communities, 500–1100: Patterns of Expansion and Decline," *Sign: Journal of Women in Culture and Society* 14, no. 2 (Winter, 1989): 261–293.

CHAPTER 2
Early Benedictines in Europe

[1] Bede, *History of the English Church and People*, trans. Leo Sherley-Price (Baltimore: Penguin Books, 1965) Book I, Chap. 1. Because of the many translations of Bede, citations will be made to book and chapter. Bede describes four linguistically distinct groups—five languages including Latin—populating the region, giving clues to the sociological diversity of his time and place: the Angles spoke Old English, the British used Breton, the Scots (Celts and Irish) spoke Celtic (Gaelic), and the Picts had their own language. Britain was already organized into several kingdoms: Kent (land of the Jutes), Essex, Sussex, Wessex (Saxon areas), Northumbria, and East Anglia where the latest invaders, the Angles, surrounded Mercia. This Anglo-Saxon heptarchy endured with some variations until the Norman Conquest in 1066.

[2] Bede, Book I, Chaps. 23–33.

[3] Bede, Book I, Chaps. 5–6.

[4] Bede, Book III, Chap. 25; Turpin, 59.

[5] Primary accounts of Hilda include Bede's *Ecclesiastical History* and Stephen of Ripon's *Life of Wilfred*. J.F. Webb, ed., *Lives of the Saints: The Voyage of St. Brendan, Bede: Life of Cuthbert, Eddius Stephanus: Life of Wilfred* (New York: Penguin Books, 1965).

[6] There is no evidence, in contrast, that Hackness, another of Hilda's foundations from 680, was a double monastery of both men and women.

[7] Bede, Book IV, Chap. 24; Turpin, 57; Labarge, 9.

[8] G. P. Browne, *The Importance of Women in Anglo-Saxon Times*, Studies in Church History (New York: Macmillan, 1919), 7–26; Turpin, 53–57; Bede, Book IV, Chap. 23; Labarge (8–9) places Hilda at Chelles, where her mother had retired, when Bishop Aidan called her "back home."

[9] Schmitz 7:25.

[10] Bede, Book IV, Chap. 23; Cousin, 170; Turpin, 58–59; Labarge, 8–9.

[11] Eckenstein, 81–82, 93–95, 106; Eleanor Shipley Duckett, *Anglo-Saxon Saints and Scholars* (Hamden, CT: Archon Books, 1967), 134–214 (cited hereafter as Duckett, *Saints and Scholars*).

[12] The source of this designation is sixteenth century Georg Fabricius, who drew from the eleventh century Latin *Annals of Quedlinburg*.

[13] See Joan Morris, *The Lady was a Bishop. The History of Women with Clerical Ordination and the Jurisdiction of Bishops* (New York: Macmillan, 1973).

[14] Bede, Book IV, Chap. 19; Joan Morris, 225ff.; Duckett, *Saints and Scholars*, 153–154; Eckenstein, 96–99; Browne, 19.

[15] Bede, Book IV, Chap. 19.

[16] Gregory the Great, Epistola XII; PL. 77–78.

[17] Morris, 26; Peter Lechner, *A Benedictine Martyrology* (Collegeville, MN: St. John's Abbey, 1922), 182.

[18] Virgil R. Stallbaumer, "St. Benedict Biscop's Wearmouth-Jarrow Monastic School," *ABR* 17 (Summer, 1962): 3–11.

[19] Virgil R. Stallbaumer, "The Canterbury School of Saint Gregory's Disciples," *ABR* 6 (Winter 1955): 389–407; Cousin, 173.

[20] Schmitz 7:28.

[21] Browne, 28.

[22] For more about Tetta, see Deborah Hameling's "Tetta, 'Noble in Conduct,' and Thecla 'Shining Like a Light in a Dark Place," in Mariam Schmitt and Linda Kulzer, eds., *Medieval Women Monastics: Wisdom's Wellsprings* (Collegeville, MN: Liturgical Press, 1996), 99–114.

[23] Bateson, 174–175; Eckenstein, 113; Duckett, 190–191.

[24] Norman Tanner, ed., *Decrees of the Ecumenical Councils: Nicea I to Lateran V* (London: Sheed & Ward, 1990), Canon 20.

[25] Browne, 19; Eckenstein, 117–118; Francesca M. Steele, *The Life of Saint Walburga* (St. Louis: B. Herder, 1921), 64–65; Nuns of St. Walburg, *Spring and Harvest* (St. Meinrad, IN: Grail, 1952), 16–17.

[26] Cousin, 192–193; Stephanus Hilpisch, *Benedictinism through Changing Centuries*, trans. Leonard J. Doyle (Collegeville, MN: St. John's Abbey Press, 1958), 24 (cited hereafter as *Monks*).

[27] Monk of Douai Abbey, ed., *The High History of Saint Benedict and his Monks* (London: Sands and Co., 1945), 368–370; Cousin, 92.

[28] J. Lowrie, *Benedictine Monasticism: Its Formation and Development through the Twelfth Century* (New York: Sheed and Ward, 1965), 117–123; Cousin, 194–195.

[29] Saint Adalbert had also been aided by English nuns in the seventh-century evangelization of the Dutch coast, so Boniface was not the first to call for their assistance.

[30] Hilpisch and Schmitz say very little about Walburga, Lioba, or Thecla. There are several German biographies. English sources include the translation of the history of Eichstätt, by S. Gonzaga Engelhart, the Steele biography and the Rudolf sketch upon which the others are based (Talbot, ed.) See also Reuther, *Women of Spirit*, 103ff., and Labarge, 9.

[31] Talbot, ed., 205–226; Labarge, 9.

[32] Steele, 41, 92–93; *Spring and Harvest*, 15–16.

[33] *Spring and Harvest*, 19–22; Steele, 133–147. Some of Willibald's remains are in the church across the road from the nuns' monastery at Eichstätt. According to a member of the community who escorted this writer to the tomb of St. Walburga in the crypt at the monastery church, the Walburga oil flows only at specified times of the year. Tourists flock to her burial site. Non-monastics are also welcome in the monastery church where the nuns at the time of this writer's visit in 1982 prayed the Liturgy of the Hours and participated in the Mass in a gallery-loft at the back of the church. The baroque screen was opened when the Eucharistic liturgy was celebrated. A recent renovation has occurred which now enables the nuns also to occupy the main floor of the church for their liturgies.

[34] Bateson, 190.

[35] John Cassian, *The Conferences* (New York: Paulist Press, 1997).

[36] Schmitz 7:37; Abbé Orlandis, "La vie du perfection des laics dans visigoths," *Revue historique français et étranger*, Series 4, no. 32 (1954): 314–316.

[37] Lechner, 102. See also Verecke, "Fructuosus of Braga, St.," *New Catholic Encyclopedia* 6:213. Alexius Hoffmann, *A Benedictine Martyrology: Being a Revision of Rev. Peter Lechner's Ausfürliches Martyrologium des Benedictiner-Ordens und seiner Verzweigungen* (Collegeville, MN: St. John's Abbey, 1922). See also Maribel Dietz, *Wandering Monks, Virgins, and Pilgrims: Ascetic Travel in the Mediterranean World, A.D. 300–800* (University Park, PA: Pennsylvania State University Press, 2005).

[38] Bateson, 193–194; Orlandis, 314–316. The Rule is printed in its entirety in Migne, *Patrologia Latina* 87, C1099–1130.

[39] See James Halprin and Mark Vessey, eds., *Cassiodorus: Institutions of Divine and Secular Learning and On the Soul* (Liverpool: Liverpool University Press, 2003).

[40] White, 11–28, 123. At least one of the restorations appeared to be at the same site of one of Gregory's earlier foundations.

[41] See Arthur S. Napier, ed., *Enlarged Rule of Chrodegang: Capitula of Theodolf, Epitome of Benedict of Aniane* (London: Early English Text Society, 1916).

[42] See Jerome Bertram, *The Chrodegang Rules: The Rules for the Common Life of the Secular Clergy from the Eighth and Ninth Centuries* (Burlington, VT: Ashgate, 2005).

[43] Schmitz, 7:41–43.

[44] Schmitz, 7:41–43. See also Kevin Madigan and Carolyn Osiek, *Ordained Women in the Early Church: A Documentary History* (Baltimore, MD: Johns Hopkins University Press, 2005) and Gary Macy, *The Hidden History of Women's Ordination: Female Clergy in the Medieval West* (Oxford; New York: Oxford University Press, 2008).

[45] Schmitz 7:40–44.

[46] Schmitz 7:40–44.

CHAPTER 3
Carolingian and Cluniac Reforms

[1] Cousin, 199. See also James G. Clark, *The Benedictines in the Middle Ages* (Rochester, NY: Boydell Press, 2011).

[2] Jerome Bertram, ed., *The Chrodegang Rules: The Rules for the Common Life of the Secular Clergy from the Eighth and Ninth Centuries* (Burlington, VT: Ashgate, 2005).

[3] Cousin, 11. This author also reports of Gisela's and Rotrod's correspondence with Alcuin over "serious literary matters." He asked for their criticism on his unfinished commentary on John's Gospel and sent them Bede's works.

[4] Cousin, 220. Dom Schmitz recommends a study of the attitude of Charlemagne toward nuns (which is in need of translation): A. Stosiek, *Das Verhaltnis Karls des Grossen zur Klosterordnung mit besonderer Ruchsicht auf die Regula Benedicti* (Greifswald, 1909).

[5] Cousin, 220; Lechner, 124.

[6] See E. S. Duckett, *Alcuin, Friend of Charlemagne: His World and Work* (New York, 1951); L. Wallach, *Alcuin and Charlemagne: Studies in Carolingian History and Literature*, Cornell Studies in Classical Philology (Ithaca: Cornell University Press, 1959).

[7] See Smaragdus, *The Crown of Monks*, Vol. 245, trans. David Barry (Collegeville, MN: Cistercian Publications, Liturgical Press, 2013).

[8] Daly, 142–145; Cousin, 220–223.

[9] Daly 142–145; Cousin 220–223.

[10] See discussions of interpretation at Janneke Raaijmakers, *The Making of the Monastic Community of Fulda, c.744–c.900* (Cambridge: Cambridge University Press, 2012); and Santha Bhattacharji, Rowan Williams, and Dominic Mattos, eds., *Prayer and Thought in Monastic Tradition: Essays in Honour of Benedicta Ward SLG* (Edinburgh: T & T Clark, 2014).

[11] See the description of the empire's administrative capitularies in Rosamond McKitterick, "Charlemagne's Missi and Their Books," in *Early Medieval Studies in Memory of Patrick Wormald*, ed. Stephen Baxter (Burlington, VT: Ashgate, 2009), 253–282.

[12] Daly, 146–147; Cousin, 223; Hilpisch, *Monks* 33–39.

[13] Hilpisch, *Monks* 38–39; Schmitz 7:263.

[14] L. Palmer, *English Monasteries in the Middle Ages: An Outline of Monastic Architecture and Custom from the Conquest to the Suppression* (London: Constable, 1930) has floor plans of some of the English monastic houses built in this style.

[15] Hill Monastic Microfilm Library at St. John's, Collegeville, MN, has copies of thousands of the illuminated manuscripts still preserved in European monasteries and archives. The nuns' artistic achievements are credited by Schmitz 7:252–276.

[16] Recent scholarship on Cluny includes Giles Constable, *The Abbey of Cluny: A Collection of Essays to Mark the Eleven-hundredth Anniversary of its Foundation* (Piscataway, NJ: Verlag, Transaction Publishers, 2010).

[17] Some authors maintain that there was continuity in Carolingian and Cluniac spirituality but discontinuity in institutional forms according to Richard Sullivan, who reviewed *Benedictine Culture* by W. Lourdaux and D. Verhelst (Leuven: Leuven University Press, 1983) in the *Catholic Historical Review* 71 (Oct, 1985), 597–599.

[18] C. H. Lawrence, *Medieval Monasticism* (New York: Longman, 1984), 76–90;

Daly, 153; Knowles, *Christian Monasticism* 48–53; F. A. Ogg, *A Source Book of Mediaeval History* (New York: American Book Co., 1907), 247*ff.*

[19] Rev. Dr. Guy N. Hartcher, "Witness to an Alternative: Cluny and its World in the Year 1000," *Tjurunga*, 38 (May 1990): 13–21. Reverend Hartcher envisions the tenth century in which Cluny rose and prospered, alluding to the historical aspects of the environment that promoted dependence, growth, and expansion of the type of monasticism that Cluny cultivated and that thrived in the culture of the time.

[20] Lawrence, 76–80; Cousin, 231.

[21] Lawrence, 84; Hilpisch, *Monks* 48–49.

[22] Lawrence, 84–85.

[23] Cousin, 234.

[24] See more noteworthy Cluniac influences in Constable, *The Abbey of Cluny.*

[25] For an additional history of nuns, see Jo Ann McNamara, *Sisters in Arms: Catholic Nuns Through Two Millennia* (Cambridge, MA: Harvard University Press, 1996).

[26] Issues regarding this and other complexities during the Cluniac reforms were manifold. See Patrick Healy, *The Chronicle of Hugh of Flavigny: Reform and the Investiture Contest in the Late Eleventh Century* (Aldershot, England; Burlington, VT: Ashgate, 2006); Dominique Iogna-Prat, *Order & Exclusion: Cluny and Christendom Face Heresy, Judaism, and Islam, 1000–1150* (Ithaca, NY: Cornell University Press, 2002); Jane Schulenburg, "Gender, Celibacy, and Proscriptions of Sacred Space: Symbol and Practice," in Michael Frassetto, ed., *Medieval Purity and Piety: Essays on Medieval Clerical Celibacy and Religious Reform* (New York: Garland, 1998), 353–376.

[27] Schmitz 7:71–74; Jean de Hemptinne, *L'Ordre de Saint Benoît* (Maredsous: Editions de Maredsous, 1951), 84–87.

[28] Cousin, 234–236.

[29] Kenneth Conant, *Carolingian and Romanesque Architecture, 800 to 1200* (Baltimore, MD: Penguin Books, 1959).

[30] Labarge, 48.

[31] Schmitz 7:75. The documents are translated by Dom Thomas Symons in *The Monastic Agreement* (London: Nelson and Sons, 1953). See the same author's "The Regularis Concordia" in the *Downside Review* 40 (January 1922): 15*ff.* Mary Bateson discusses this also in "Rules for Monks," *English Historical Review* 9 (1894), 690–708. For an interesting perspective on medieval English obedience, see Katherine O'Brien O'Keeffe, *Stealing Obedience: Narratives of Agency and Identity in Later Anglo-Saxon England* (Buffalo, NY: University of Toronto Press, 2012).

[32] Verona (Ann) Kessler "The Effects of the Laic Laws of 1901 and 1904 on the Benedictines in France" (PhD Dissertation, University of Notre Dame, 1963), 80. Cited hereafter as "Laic Laws."

[33] Schmitz 7:79–81.

[34] New houses of nuns also appeared in Cortenberg, Messines, Ghistelles, Merchem, Florival, Bourbourg and Nonnenbosch. In 950, the nuns at Egmond transferred to Bennebroek.

[35] For historical breadth, see Joseph O'Callaghan, *A History of Medieval Spain* (Ithaca: Cornell University Press, 1975).

[36] See Mette Bruun, *The Cambridge Companion to the Cistercian Order* (Cambridge: Cambridge University Press, 2013).

[37] Pauline Matarasso, *The Cistercian World: Monastic Writings of the Twelfth Century* (New York: Penguin Books, 1993).

[38] Lawrence, 146–166; Schmitz 7:73–75; L. Lekai, *The White Monks* (Okauchee, WI: Our Lady of Spring Bank, 1953). See also Matarasso, *The Cistercian World*. For the Trappist story see Lekai's *The Rise of the Cistercian Strict Observance in Seventeenth Century France* (Washington, DC: Catholic University of America, 1966) and A. J. Krailsheimer, *Armand-Jean de Rancé, Abbot of La Trappe: His Influence in the Cloister and the World* (Oxford: Clarendon Press, 1974).

[39] See Anne Lester, *Creating Cistercian Nuns: The Women's Religious Movement and its Reform in Thirteenth-Century Champagne* (Ithaca: Cornell University Press, 2011); for an architectural analysis of these women's monasteries, see Meredith Lillich, *Cistercian Nuns and Their World* (Kalamazoo, MI: Cistercian Publications, 2005).

CHAPTER 4
European Reform and Mysticism

[1] Daly, 60; Cousin, 284–285.

[2] For the organizational structures, see Steven Vanderputten, *Monastic Reform as Process: Realities and Representations in Medieval Flanders, 900–1100* (Ithaca: Cornell University Press, 2013).

[3] Cousin, 286.

[4] Although still in existence at this date, these abbeys became public schools after the Revolution.

[5] For monastic reforms in Normandy, see Cassandra Potts, *Monastic Revival and Regional Identity in Early Normandy* (Rochester, NY: Boydell Press, 1997).

[6] See the introductory descriptions about Saint Victor in Hugh Feiss, ed., *On Love: A Selection of Works of Hugh, Adam, Achard, Richard, and Godfrey of St. Victor*, Victorine Texts in Translation 2 (New York: New City Press, 2012).

[7] Schmitz 7:220.

[8] Recent work on the history of women's ecclesial consecrations sheds much light on the often controversial subject. References from varied perspectives include Gary Macy, *The Hidden History of Women's Ordination: Female Clergy in the Medieval West* (New York: Oxford University Press, 2008); Kevin Madigan and Carolyn Osiek, *Ordained Women in the Early Church: A Documentary History* (Baltimore, MD: Johns Hopkins University Press, 2005); and less contemporary but still a valuable source, Joan Morris, *The Lady was a Bishop: The Hidden History of Women with Clerical Ordination and the Jurisdiction of Bishops* (New York: Macmillan, 1973).

[9] Schmitz 7:224. Migne (P.L. 216, c356) includes a letter from Pope Innocent III to the bishops of Burgos and Valencia commenting unfavorably on these practices.

[10] Derek G. Smith traces the history of claustral oblature and lay affiliation in his "Oblates in Western Monasticism," *Monastic Studies* 13 (Autumn, 1982): 47–72. He includes an excellent list of English, French, and German-language references in the notes, 48–50.

[11] Schmitz 7:254–255.

[12] Schmitz 7:87.

[13] For more on the complexities of canon law and women's cloister, see Elizabeth Makowski, *English Nuns and the Law in the Middle Ages: Cloistered Nuns and Their Law-*

yers, 1293–1540 (Woodbridge: Boydell, 2011); and Elizabeth Makowski, *Canon Law and Cloistered Women: Periculoso and its Commentators, 1298–1545* (Washington, DC: Catholic University of America Press, 1997).

[14] Caesarius, *The Rule for Nuns of St. Caesarius of Arles*, trans. Maria McCarthy (Washington: Catholic University of America Press, 1960).

[15] Labarge, 48. She had retired there, and her son, King Richard I, was also buried at Fontevrault.

[16] For the document, see Elizabeth Makowski, *Canon Law.*

[17] Schmitz 7:234–237. The complete decree and an English translation is in the appendices of Elizabeth Makowski, *Canon Law.* See 3n5 where she cites Sister Marie-Amélie Le Bourgoeis' article "Dieu aime-t-il les murs?" ("Does God love walls?").

[18] Although this writer was still wearing full religious habit while traveling from monastery to monastery throughout France in 1961, I was most often required to speak through grilles as they were still generally used in houses of nuns (monks' monasteries do not have them). Drawers, opened from both sides and placed below the grille section some 3–4 feet from the floor, were used more frequently than turnstiles. In the 1980s, however, the French, German, and English nuns spoke to me either through an aperture in the grille or in front of or beside it, explaining that it was used now only on certain public occasions.

[19] Cousin, 346; Schmitz 7:241.

[20] Eckenstein, 146–180; Labarge, 13. Labarge insists that Hrotsvitha is now believed to have been a canoness there, not a nun. She insists that there were two classes, the religious and the canonesses (who retained their property, had servants, and bought their own food). Not too many other writers support Labarge. Almost all concede that she was a professed monastic, a nun. Roswitha's plays have been revived and are now being staged again.

[21] See Frederick Paxton, *Anchoress and Abbess in Ninth-Century Saxony: The Lives of Liutbirga of Wendhausen and Hathumoda of Gandersheim* (Washington, DC: Catholic University of America Press, 2009).

[22] Elisabeth of Schönau, *Elisabeth of Schönau: The Complete Works*, trans. Anne Clark (New York: Paulist Press, 2000).

[23] They have also been republished in German editions by F. W. E. Roth, *Die Visionender hl. Elizabeth under die Schriften der Abte Ekbert u. Emecho von Schönau* (Brunn, 1894) and K. Koster, *Elizabeth von Schönau Wirk u. Wirkung im Spiegel der mittelalterlichen hanscriftlichen Uberlieferung in Archiv Mittelrh.* K.B. 3 (1951), 243–315.

[24] Hildegard of Bingen, *Scivias*, trans. Columba Hart and Jane Bishop (New York: Paulist Press, 1990). Miriam Schmitt, "Hildegard of Bingen: A Prophetic Sign for her Times" (*Benedictines*, 41:1 Spring–Summer 1960) provides an excellent introduction as well as a brilliant synthesis of Hildegard's life and influence. German biographies abound including Heinrich von Schipperges, *Hildegard von Bingen: Ein Zeichen für Unsere Zeit* (Frankfurt am Main: Joseph Knecht, 1981). Although the translation is faulty, the illustrations in Matthew Fox, *Illuminations of Hildegard of Bingen* (Sante Fe, NM: Bear & Company, 1985) and in the English translation by Adelgundis Fuhrkotter, *The Miniatures from the Book Scivias: Know the Ways* from the illuminated Rupertsberg Codes (Thurnhout, Belgium: Brepols, 1977) are outstanding. See also Peter Dronke, *Women Writers of the Middle Ages* (Cambridge: Cambridge University Press, 1984); Francesca Maria Steele. *The Life and Visions of St. Hildegard* (St. Louis: B. Herder,

1915); Rogatia Sohler, "Hildegard von Bingen," *Sisters Today* 51, no. 5 (January 1980): 291–296. Turpin has a short sketch (91–99).

[25] Examples include Hildegard and Richard Souther, *Vision: The Music of Hildegard von Bingen*, Angel B000002SL6, 1995, compact disc; Hildegard and Emma Kirkby, *A Feather on the Breath of God Sequences and Hymns*, Hyperion B000002ZGD, 1993, compact disc.

[26] Schmitt, 32–33.

[27] Schmitt, 33; Schmitz 7:292; Eckenstein, 277–279.

[28] For the Latin versions of her works, see Hildegardis Abbatissa, *Opera Omnia*, in Migne, *Patrologia Latina*. See also Nancy Fierro, *Hildegard of Bingen and Her Vision of the Feminine* (Kansas City, MO: Sheed and Ward, 1995).

[29] Eckenstein, 328–329.

[30] Additional information on Hildegard can be found in Anne King-Lenzmeier, *Hildegard of Bingen: An Integrated Vision* (Collegeville, MN: Liturgical Press, 2001). For the Latin versions of her works, see Hildegardis Abbatissa, *Opera Omnia* in Migne, *Patrologia Latina*. See also Nancy Fierro, *Hildegard of Bingen and Her Vision of the Feminine*.

[31] Eckenstein, 262–263.

[32] "Pope's Letter to Cardinal Volk, Bishop of Mainz," *L'Osservatore Romano* October 1, 1979, 10, cited by Schmitt, 32.

[33] The Cistercian abbots already in 1210 objected to the activities of the Spanish abbess of Las Huelgas. They reported to Innocent III that she not only held councils of abbesses and made visitations of her affiliated convents, but also blessed the nuns, read the gospel, preached publicly, and heard confessions. The Pope ordered the Spanish bishops to forbid these practices, explaining that although the Virgin Mary was "worthier and more excellent than all the apostles, it was still to them, and not to her, that Christ had committed the keys of the kingdom" (Labarge, 33).

[34] Schmitz 7:293. Caroline Walker Bynum, in *Jesus as Mother: Studies in the Spirituality of the High Middle Ages* (Berkeley: University of California Press, 1982), 174n, calls the controversy a "meaningless question." Some Benedictines, however, do not consider it meaningless at all.

[35] See Mechthild, *The Flowing Light of the Godhead*, trans. F. Tobin (Mahwah, NJ: Paulist Press, 1998).

[36] See Alberta Dieker, "Mechtild of Hackeborn: Song of Love," in Mariam Schmitt and Linda Kulzer, eds., *Medieval Women Monastics: Wisdom's Wellsprings* (Collegeville, MN: Liturgical Press, 2002), 231–242.

[37] Bynum, 210–217; Schmitz 7:297–298; Eckenstein, 347–351. One of the latest editions of the Exercises has been edited by a nun of Regina Laudis (Westminster, MD: Newman Press, 1956). The most recent edition of *The Herald* is edited by Margaret Winkworth, *Gertrude of Helfta: Herald of Divine Love*, Classics of Western Spirituality (Mahwah, NJ: Paulist Press, 1993). A three-volume series, *Medieval Religious Women*, concentrates on the Cistercians. The second volume, *Hidden Springs* (1987), explores the spirituality of medieval women. Alban Goodier's *The Love of the Sacred Heart Illustrated by Saint Gertrude* (London: Burns, Oates and Washbourne, 1921) has a good brief sketch (33–41) of her life, but both he and Guéranger confuse the two Gertrudes and call her an abbess. P. Doyere, "Gertrude (the Great), St." in the *New Catholic Encyclopedia* (6:451) is a capsule biography illustrated with a picture of a sixteenth-century

polychromed wooden statue in the Cadiz cathedral. The garb and crosier are those of an abbess, which is incorrect.

[38] Jack Lewis, ed., *Spiritual Exercises* (Kalamazoo, MI: Cistercian Publications, 1989).

[39] One example is the drama, Hélène Gingold, *Abelard and Heloise: A Tragedy in Five Acts [and in verse]* (London: Greening & Co., 1906).

[40] Although Augustine of Hippo seems to have been readily forgiven for his long affair with his mistress, the mother of his illegitimate child, the sin of Abelard and Heloise seems to have found less forgiveness from monastic historians of the medieval period.

[41] See the discussion by Sidney R. Packard, *12th Century Europe: An Interpretive Essay* (Amherst: University of Massachusetts Press, 1973), 183–189.

[42] Peter Abelard, *Yes and No: The Complete English translation of Peter Abelard's Sic et Non*, trans. Priscilla Throop (Charlotte, VT: MedievalMS, 2007).

[43] Henry Bellows, ed., *The Story of My Misfortunes (Historia Calamitatum): The Autobiography of Peter Abélard* (Glencoe, IL: Free Press, 1958).

[44] This autobiography is available in several translations. In it he admits he, not Heloise, was the seducer. The aforementioned (n43 above) 1922 English translation of the *Historia Calamitatum*, *The Story of My Misfortunes*, trans. by Henry Adams Bellows (Saint Paul: MN: Thomas A. Boyd), has been superseded by later editions, but the Bellows translation has an excellent introduction by Ralph A. Cram, which the others lack.

[45] Packard, 183–189.

[46] Labarge (101) writes that although Hildegard may have been the "most remarkable" nun, Heloise was the "most famous" of the most notable twelfth-century monastic women.

[47] Labarge, 184. Among the numerous biographies of Abelard and Heloise the best is probably Etienne Gilson's *Heloise and Abelard*, trans. L. K. Shook (Chicago: H. Regenery, 1951). See also Charles Charrier, *Heloise dans l'histoire et la legende* (Paris: 1933) and P. Guilloux, "Abelard et le couvent du Paraclet," in *Revue d'Histoire ecclesiastique* 2, no. 21 (1925): 455–478. Popular novels and films often dwell on the romance rather than the intellectual gifts of the couple and the influence Heloise had on women monastics.

[48] Constant Mews, "Heloise and Hildegard: Re-visioning Religious Life in the Twelfth Century," *Tjurunga* 44 (May 1993): 20–29, writes that the nuns were "two of the most articulate women of the 12th century." He also insists that Abelard's Rule for the Paraclete was never implemented there (26). Another article, also in *Tjurunga* 37, Dr. Deirdre Stone, "Heloise: La Trés Sage Abbess of the Paraclete" (20–31), not only defends the monastic influence on the learning of the great abbess, but also annotates and analyses most of the scholarly discussions of Abelard and Heloise.

[49] Peter Abelard and Héloïse, *The Letters and Other Writings*, ed. William Levitan (Indianapolis: Hackett, 2007). Those letters which have been verified as genuine indicate that Heloise had a harder time separating herself from Abelard than he did, and may have indicated, at times, that she did not feel she had a true religious vocation. They also show how she began to reconcile herself to becoming the model Abbess that Abelard was urging her to be and she strove for the holiness monastic life called her to. Most letters purported to be those of the couple should be perused with a great deal of skepticism.

[50] These letters are in Migne, P.L. 178, Letters 7 and 9 especially. Schmitz (7:91) cannot refrain from editorializing that since garrulity ("bavardage") was a "common fault of women" special attention to the observance of silence was necessary.

[51] Schmitz 7:91.

[52] Packard, 188. Dom Schmitz (7:89–93) does some justice in his capsule biography of Heloise. The historians of RB 1980, however, neglect both Abelard and Heloise. An interesting brief section questioning the authenticity of the lovers' correspondence and comments about Heloise is in Dom Jean Leclercq's *Monks and Love in Twelfth-Century France* (Oxford: Clarendon Press, 1979), 119–121. See also P. Dronke, *Abelard and Heloise in Medieval Testimonies* (Glasgow: University of Glascow Press, 1976).

CHAPTER 5
Rise and Fall of English Benedictines

[1] Thomas Symons, ed., *The Monastic Agreement of the Monks and Nuns of the English Nation: Regularis Concordia Anglicae Nationis Monachorum Sanctimonialiumque* (New York: Oxford University Press, 1953).

[2] John Morris, Frank Thorn, and Caroline Thorn, eds., *Domesday Book* (Chichester: Phillimore, 1986).

[3] Knowles, *Monastic Orders,* 74–81.

[4] Twentieth-century English monastic historian David Knowles, a major source for the original version of chapter, remains a significant contributor to the history of English monasticism. Aware of what he called effects of the "siren voice of romanticism" on written accounts, he counseled care that the "enchantress"—wielding power over writers and readers of medieval history—not scatter "the golden mist of the unreal over the generations of the past," David Knowles, *The Monastic Order in England: A History of Its Development From the Times of Saint Dunstan to the Fourth Lateran Council* (Cambridge: Cambridge University Press, 1949), 691–693 (abbreviated herein as *Monastic Orders*). See Joan Greatrex, "After Knowles: Recent Perspectives on Monastic History," in *The Religious Orders in Pre-Reformation England,* ed. James Clark (Rochester, NY: Boydell & Brewer, 2002), 35–50. For more recent scholarship on English monastic history, see James Clark, ed., *The Culture of Medieval English Monasticism* (Rochester, NY: Boydell Press, 2007); Janet Burton and Karen Stöber, eds., *Monasteries and Society in the British Isles in the Later Middle Ages* (Rochester, NY: Boydell Press, 2008); Martin Heale, *The Dependent Priories of Medieval English Monasteries* (Rochester, NY: Boydell Press, 2004); and the other essays in James Clark, ed., *The Religious Orders in Pre-Reformation England* (Rochester, NY: Boydell & Brewer, 2002).

[5] Knowles, *Monastic Orders,* 103–106.

[6] Knowles, *Monastic Orders,* 127–129.

[7] Knowles, *Monastic Orders,* 128–129.

[8] Knowles, *Monastic Orders,* 82–88.

[9] Knowles, *Monastic Orders,* 87–89.

[10] For further discussion of Lanfranc, Anselm, and the influence of Bec, see entries in William Johnston, ed., *Encyclopedia of Monasticism* (Chicago: Fitzroy Dearborn, 2000).

[11] He was even a distant model for Guèranger's revival of French monasticism in the nineteenth century.

[12] See David Knowles, Christopher Brooke, and Lawrence Nugent, eds., *The Monastic Constitutions of Lanfranc* (New York: Oxford University Press, 2002). Helen Clover and Margaret Gibson, eds., *The Letters of Lanfranc, Archbishop of Canterbury* (New York, Clarendon Press, 1979); Lanfranc, *On the Body and Blood of the Lord*, ed. Mark Vaillancourt (Washington, DC: Catholic University of America Press, 2009).

[13] David Knowles, *The Monastic Constitution of Lanfranc* (New York: Thomas Nelson and Sons, 1951), x–xi.

[14] Knowles, *Lanfranc*, xii.

[15] Knowles, *Lanfranc*, xii–xiii.

[16] Knowles, *Lanfranc, passim*.

[17] Knowles, *Monastic Orders*, 110–111.

[18] Knowles, *Monastic Orders*, 96.

[19] "Analecta Monastica," *Studia Anselmiana* 20 (1948): 15–16.

[20] Knowles, *Monastic Orders*, 138–139.

[21] Knowles, *Monastic Orders*, 172.

[22] Knowles, *Monastic Orders*, 177–180.

[23] For more on the political context of this century, see Thomas Bisson, *The Crisis of the Twelfth Century: Power, Lordship, and the Origins of European Government* (Princeton, NJ: Princeton University Press, 2009).

[24] Mercenary warfare was not uncommon in this era. See Donald Kagay and Andrew Villalon, *The Circle of War in the Middle Ages: Essays on Medieval Military and Naval History* (Rochester, NY: Boydell Press, 1999).

[25] Knowles, *Monastic Orders*, 270.

[26] Eckenstein, 204. Ian C. Hannah, *Christian Monasticism: A Great Force in History* (New York: Macmillan, 1925), 21, sees a debatable relationship between monastic practices in the Middle Ages and the later Puritan policies maintaining—erroneously—that it was "medievalism that inspired the noblest of all the writings of early Puritanism, which in its general atmosphere still preserves much of the old monastic point of view."

[27] For extensive background and to view illustrated manuscripts on Saint Albans, see the University of Aberdeen's Web site, "The St. Albans Psalter," last modified 2003, http://www.abdn.ac.uk/stalbanspsalter/english/.

[28] Find additional background on twelfth-century manuscript illuminations in Nigel Morgan, *Early Gothic Manuscripts* (New York: Oxford University Press, 1982). For a frequently reprinted mid-twentieth century biography of Paris' life and writings, see Richard Vaughan, *Matthew Paris* (Cambridge: Cambridge University Press, 1958); for a richly illustrated example of his illuminations see Richard Vaughn, *Illustrated Chronicles of Matthew Paris: Observations of Thirteenth-Century Life* (Stroud, Gloucestershire: A. Sutton, 1994).

[29] David Knowles, *The Religious Orders in England* (Cambridge: University Press, 1959), 294.

[30] For an illustrated context of Christina's life, see J. Geddes, *The St. Albans Psalter: A Book for Christina of Markyate* (London: British Library, 2005). The St. Albans Psalter Web site was constructed in response to interest in Christina of Markyate's life. See "The Debate: Developing Theories and Observations About the Psalter," St. Albans Psalter, last modified 2003, http://www.abdn.ac.uk/stalbanspsalter/english/essays/debate.shtml. For an earlier discussion of the influence of her life and mysticism on the St. Albans Psalter, see C. Holdsworth, "Christina of Markyate," in *Medieval Women*, Studies in Church History Subsidia 1, ed. D. Barker (Oxford: Blackwell, 1978), 193–195.

[31] For a scholarly feminist interpretation of Christina's legendary context, see Sheri Horner, *The Discourse of Enclosure Representing Women in Old English Literature* (Albany: State University of New York Press, 2001).

[32] See the narrative in C H. Talbot, ed. and trans., *The Life of Christina of Markyate* (Oxford: Clarendon Press, 1959).

[33] Knowles, *Monastic Orders*, 188–189.

[34] Knowles, *Religious Orders*, 41–45. See also James Clark, ed., "Mare, Thomas de la (c. 1309–1396)" in *Oxford Dictionary of National Biography* (Oxford: Oxford University Press, 2004). Retrieved from http://www.oxforddnb.com/view/article/18039.

[35] Like other English mystics Julian was rediscovered by the English Benedictines of the seventeenth century. In 1670 Dom Serenus Cressy printed the text that is now in Paris at the B. N. (Fonds anglais 40). It was reprinted again the 19th and often in the 20th century (David Knowles, *The English Mystical Tradition*, New York: Harper, 1961, 120n2). See Alexandra Barrat, "Julian of Norwich and Her Children Today: Editions, Translations, and Versions of her Revelations," in *Julian of Norwich's Legacy: Medieval Mysticism and Post-Medieval Reception*, eds. Sarah Salith and Denise Baker (New York: Palgrave Macmillan, 2006), 13–28.

[36] For analysis of Julian in iconography, see Sarah Salith, "Julian in Norwich: Heritage and Iconography," in *Julian of Norwich's Legacy: Medieval Mysticism and Post-Medieval Reception*, eds. Sarah Salith and Denise Baker (New York: Palgrave Macmillan, 2006), 153–172.

[37] *Julian of Norwich: The Teachings of a 14th Century English Mystic* (New York: Longmans, Green and Co., 1958), 8–10. After a visit to Norwich Cathedral, the Carrow area and Julian's reconstructed cell, the writer is convinced that Julian was Benedictine. Not only is Julian portrayed with prominent Benedictine saints in the Norwich Cathedral window commemorating the Benedictine origins of Norwich Cathedral (now Anglican) but also the argument that her document of profession at Carrow is not extant can hardly be proof when so many others have also been lost—probably destroyed in the 500 not-so-peaceful years of English monastic history.

[38] Knowles, *The English Mystical Tradition*, 120–121. Knowles surmises that she could have been a Carrow nun, but states that he is convinced that she was still living at home when her mystical visions took place in 1373, when she was about thirty.

[39] Schmitz 7:56, 305.

[40] Knowles, *The English Mystical Tradition*, 120–121.

[41] Short and long versions of her manuscript survived, both indicating the composition around 1393; *Julian of Norwich: Showings*, trans. Edmund Colledge and James Walsh (New York: Paulist Press, 1978).

[42] Quoted in Knowles, *The English Mystical Tradition*, 132.

[43] For example, Denys Turner describes her as a culturally innovative, systematic theologian. See Denys Turner, *Julian of Norwich, Theologian* (New Haven: Yale University Press, 2011).

[44] *Julian of Norwich: Showings*, 3–11.

[45] *Julian of Norwich: Showings*, 237.

[46] See Thomas Bisson, *The Crisis of the Twelfth Century: Power, Lordship, and the Origins of European Government* (Princeton, NJ: Princeton University Press, 2009).

[47] For background and details on both sides of the controversy, see Richard Huscroft, *Ruling England, 1042–1217* (New York: Pearson/Longman, 2005).

[48] Knowles, *Monastic Orders*, 277.

⁴⁹ Knowles, *Monastic Orders,* 678–681. Eckenstein's nineteenth-century work estimated that in France, as a result of the Merovingian donations to monasteries and churches, almost two-thirds of the land was at one time in the hands of the bishops, priests, monastic communities, or individual religious. See Lina Eckenstein, *Women Under Monasticism* (Cambridge: University Press, 1896), 74.

⁵⁰ Knowles, *Monastic Orders,* 680.

⁵¹ Knowles, *Monastic Orders,* 680–681.

⁵² Knowles, *Religious Orders,* 5–18.

⁵³ Knowles, *Religious Orders,* 18–20.

⁵⁴ Knowles, *Religious Orders,* 283.

⁵⁵ For more on the liturgical use of secular music, see Tess Knighton and David Fallows, eds., *Companion to Medieval and Renaissance Music* (Berkeley, CA: University of California Press, 1997).

⁵⁶ Anthony Emery, *Greater Medieval Houses of England and Wales, 1300–1500* (Cambridge: Cambridge University Press, 1996), vol. 3.

⁵⁷ Knowles, *Religious Orders,* 22–26.

⁵⁸ One example of the popular romanticization of this period is Walsh's early twentieth-century high school textbook: James Walsh, *The Thirteenth, Greatest of Centuries* (New York: Fordham University Press, 1952).

⁵⁹ The impact of these multiple calamities on daily monastic life are discussed in Barbara Harvey, *Living and Dying in England: 1100–1540, The Monastic Experience* (Oxford: Clarendon Press, 2002). See also Joëlle Rollo-Koster and Thomas Izbicki, *A Companion to the Great Western Schism (1378–1417)* (Boston: Brill, 2009).

⁶⁰ For the Black Death's effect on English women generally, see Mavis Mate, *Daughters, Wives, and Widows after the Black Death: Women in Sussex, 1350–1535* (Rochester, NY: Boydell Press, 1998).

⁶¹ Eileen Powers, *Medieval English Nunneries, 1275–1535* (Cambridge: Cambridge University Press, 1922), 62–65, 230–232.

⁶² *Reg. Ep. J. Peckham,* 2: 247; cited in Powers, 348.

⁶³ Powers, 349–359.

⁶⁴ Powers, 386.

⁶⁵ Powers, 464.

⁶⁶ Powers, 456–468.

⁶⁷ Powers, 244–245.

⁶⁸ *Reg. Ep. J. Peckham,* 3:8847 cited in Powers, 586.

⁶⁹ Schmitz 7:133–135.

CHAPTER 6
Autumn and Winter of Monasticism: Decline and Suppression

¹ For one history of heresy in the Middle Ages, see R. Moore, *The Birth of Popular Heresy* (Toronto: University of Toronto Press, 1995).

² For more extensive considerations of Peter the Venerable, see "Commemoration and Confraternity at Cluny during the Abbacy of Peter the Venerable," in Giles Constable, *The Abbey of Cluny,* Chapter 20.

³ See Thomas Sullivan, *Benedictine Monks at the University of Paris, A.D. 1229–1500: A Biographical Register* (New York: E.J. Brill, 1995). This is the published

edition of a doctoral dissertation by a Conception Abbey monk, Brother Thomas Sullivan, *Studium Monastica: Benedictines at the University of Paris in the Late Middle Ages, 1260–1500* (Madison: University of Wisconsin Press, 1982).

[4] For a thorough overview of the Lateran Council's contexts, see Stephen Bowd, *Reform Before the Reformation: Vincenzo Querini and the Religious Renaissance in Italy* (Leiden; Boston: Brill, 2002).

[5] For detailed background on the periods' religious socioeconomics see Susan Wood, *The Proprietary Church in the Medieval West* (New York: Oxford University Press, 2006).

[6] Cousin, 364–370. For an exacting report of these legislation's effects on Cistercian life, see the richly illustrated Terryl Kinder, *Cistercian Europe: Architecture of Contemplation* (Grand Rapids, MI: W.B. Eerdmans, 2002).

[7] The social complexities attributing to monastic decline are further discussed in Patricia Wittberg, *The Rise and Decline of Catholic Religious Orders: A Social Movement Perspective* (Albany: State University of New York Press, 1994).

[8] See Anne Curry, *The Hundred Years' War: 1337–1453* (Oxford: Osprey, 2002); Desmond Seward, *The Hundred Years War: The English in France, 1337–1453* (London: Robinson, 2003).

[9] See Sullivan, *Benedictine Monks, passim.* Other colleges were also founded in Paris for Benedictine monks.

[10] Cousin, 373–374.

[11] Phillip Stump, "The Council of Constance (1414–18) and the End of the Schism," in *A Companion to the Great Western Schism 1378–1417*, eds. Joëlle Rollo-Koster & Thomas Izbicki (Boston: Brill, 2009), 395–442.

[12] Cousin, 396–397.

[13] Barry Collett, *Italian Benedictine Scholars and the Reformation: The Congregation of Santa Giustina of Padua* (Oxford: Clarendon Press, 1985), 2–8. Cousin and Collett do not always agree on dates, names, sequence, and numbers, but Collett's research is more concentrated on Italian sources and is probably more accurate. Collett also concentrates on the scholarly endeavors of the Cassinese monks during the sixteenth century—and they were many and highly commendatory.

[14] This, the oldest of present Congregations in the Benedictine Confederation (thus listed first in *Catalogus 2000*, 17), then had no monastery with more than 30 monks.

[15] Benjamin Paul, *Nuns and Reform Art in Early Modern Venice: The Architecture of Santi Cosma e Damiano and its Decoration from Tintoretto to Tiepolo* (Burlington, VT: Ashgate, 2012).

[16] Schmitz 7:127.

[17] C.H. Lawrence, *Medieval Monasticism: Forms of Religious Life in Western Europe in the Middle Ages* (New York: Longman Group Ltd., 1984), 226.

[18] For overall context, see Stephen Wessley, *Joachim of Fiore and Monastic Reform* (New York: P. Lang, 1990). For Joachim's theology and its effects, see Warwick Gould and Marjorie Reeves, *Joachim of Fiore and the Myth of the Eternal Evangel in the Nineteenth and Twentieth Centuries* (New York: Clarendon Press, 2001).

[19] Scott Montgomery, "Melk," in *Medieval Germany: An Encyclopedia*, ed. John Jeep (New York: Garland, 2001), 517–518.

[20] Hirsau's adaptation of Cluniac observance is detailed in Phyllis Jestice, *Wayward Monks and the Religious Revolution of the Eleventh Century* (New York: E.J. Brill, 1997).

[21] Cousin, 397. Peter of Rosenheim's *Roseum memorial* used illuminations for memorization of texts. See Mary Carruthers and Jan Ziolkowski, *The Medieval Craft of Memory: An Anthology of Texts and Pictures* (Philadelphia, PA: University of Pennsylvania Press, 2002).

[22] For context and history of Basel and the other councils of the Middle Ages, see Christopher Bellitto, *The General Councils: A History of the Twenty-One General Councils from Nicaea to Vatican II* (New York: Paulist Press, 2002).

[23] Cousin, 398. Also see Kevin Kavenagh, "Congregations, Benedictine," in *Encyclopedia of Monasticism*, ed. William Johnston (Chicago: Fitzroy Dearborn, 2000), 322–327.

[24] See Christopher Bellitto, Thomas Izbicki, and Gerald Christianson, eds., *Introducing Nicholas of Cusa: A Guide to a Renaissance Man* (New York: Paulist Press, 2004); Nicholas of Cusa, *Selected Spiritual Writings*, ed. Lawrence Bond (New York: Paulist Press, 1997).

[25] Hilpisch, *Nuns* 52.

[26] *Studien und Mitteilungen, OSB* 38, 1917, 232*ff.*, cited in Hilpisch, *Nuns* 52–53.

[27] By 1500, at least sixty-six monasteries of women had adopted the Bursfeld reform, among them: Oberwerth at Coblenz, Burtscheid at Aachen, Willebadessen, St. Mauritius, a monastery of Machabees in Cologne, and a number of important royal abbeys, most of whom had limited their membership to nobility.

[28] *Studien und Mitteilungen, OSB* 38, 1917, 232*ff.* cited in Hilpisch, 53–55.

[29] Trithemius influenced medieval magic and modern occultism. For fascinating accounts of his life and work, see Noel Brann, *Trithemius and Magical Theology: A Chapter in the Controversy over Occult Studies in Early Modern Europe* (Albany: State University of New York Press, 1999); and Noel Brann, *The Abbot Trithemius (1462–1516): The Renaissance of Monastic Humanism* (Leiden: Brill, 1981).

[30] Heinrich Floss, *Das Kloster Rolandswerth bei Bonn* (Köln: Annalen des historischen Vereins für den Neiderrhein 1868).

[31] Jean Leclercq et al., *La Spiritualite du Moyen Age* (Aubier: Editions Montaigne, Belgium, 1961), 512–641. For one translation, see Dennis Billy, ed., *The Imitation of Christ: Thomas à Kempis: A Spiritual Commentary and Reader's Guide* (Notre Dame, IN: Christian Classics, 2005).

[32] See John Van Engen, *Sisters and Brothers of the Common Life: The Devotio Moderna and the World of the Later Middle Ages* (Philadelphia: University of Pennsylvania Press, 2008).

[33] Leclercq et al., *La Spiritualité du Moyen Age*, 640–641. The Cisneros Exercises have been translated by E. Allison Peers (*The Book of Exercises for the Spiritual Life*, Montserrat, 1929).

[34] George Ganss, *The Spiritual Exercises of Saint Ignatius: A Translation and Commentary* (Chicago: Loyola Press, 1992).

[35] For the effects of this legislation on nuns, see Sharon Strocchia, *Nuns and Nunneries in Renaissance Florence* (Baltimore, MD: Johns Hopkins University Press, 2009). For the political association of Portugal with Italy, see K. Lowe, *Cultural Links Between Portugal and Italy in the Renaissance* (New York: Oxford University Press, 2000).

[36] Cousin, 400–403.

[37] Cousin, 402. Montserrat Abbey, on a serrated mountain (from which it derives its name), sits high above the countryside a few miles from Barcelona. It is still a prom-

inent shrine and community that attracts thousands annually. The Lady statue is above the High Altar and now enclosed in glass. Candle smoke long ago blackened her face and that of the child, as at other famous shrines—e.g., Einsiedeln in Switzerland.

[38] Schmitz 7:129.

[39] See Kavenagh, "Congregations."

[40] Schmitz 7:132

[41] Cousin, 401; See also Pál Engel, *The Realm of St. Stephen: A History of Medieval Hungary, 895–1526* (New York: I.B. Tauris, 2001).

[42] See Susan Kerr, "Frances of Rome: Patron of Benedictine Oblates," in *Benedict in the World: Portraits of Monastic Oblates*, eds. Linda Kulzer & Roberta Bondi (Collegeville, MN: Liturgical Press, 2002), 79–86.

[43] For Clare, see Regis Armstrong, ed., *The Lady: Clare of Assisi: Early Documents* (New York: New City Press, 2006).

[44] Lawrence, 214–215. See also Elizabeth Makowski, "Monasticism, Women's: Papal Policy," in *Women and Gender in Medieval Europe: An Encyclopedia*, ed. M. Schaus (New York: Routledge, 2006), 587–589.

[45] Schmitz 7:122–124.

[46] Schmitz 7:125 ("*Mais a quoi bon continuer?*").

[47] See Eamon Duffy, *Saints & Sinners: A History of the Popes* (New Haven, CT: Yale University Press, 1997).

[48] For one introduction to Luther, see Bernhard Lohse, *Martin Luther: An Introduction to his Life and Work* (Edinburgh: Clark, 1993).

[49] The Benedictines were also involved in Renaissance literary efforts. The monks of Subiaco introduced into the Italian peninsula the printing press (developed by the Germans, although the Chinese had it centuries before). See John Henry Newman, *Historical Sketches* (New York: Longmans, Green, 1912), 2:419.

[50] Knowles, *Religious Orders* 3:165–167.

[51] Hilpisch, *Nuns* 58–59.

[52] Hilpisch, *Monks* 100–101.

[53] Knowles, *Religious Orders* 3, 167–170.

[54] Fifteen nuns reside at Aasebakken after three years in Copenhagen.

[55] Knowles, *Religious Orders*, 3:149–150.

[56] Knowles, *Religious Orders*, 3:64–65.

[57] Barry Collett, "Here Begynneth the Rule of Seynt Benet: Richard Fox's Translation of the Benedictine Rule for Women, 1517," *Tjurunga* 36 (May 1989), 10–25. Anecdotes circulated in modern English-speaking monasteries relate how the monks who read the Rule during table-reading (still a convention in many monasteries) accent or emphasize the last three words of the familiar title of Chapter 2, "What the Abbot Ought to Be."

[58] Knowles, *Religious Orders*, 3:93.

[59] Knowles, *Religious Orders*, 3: 94–97.

[60] Not all of More's biographers agree on the time, degree of involvement, or manner of his relationship with the Carthusians. Although there is general agreement that he never made profession, some maintain he was a novice, others that he was a long-term guest. Still others question that he resided there, but that is a minority opinion. See Bernard Basset, S.J., *Born for Friendship: The Spirit of Sir Thomas More* (London: Burns and Oates, 1965), 15–35. Basset maintains that More's father

threatened to disown him unless he studied law (15) and also that between the time More resigned and his imprisonment, he spent most of it at Chelsea at a small hermitage on his estate "leading his Carthusian life again" (201). See also Elizabeth Rogers, *The Correspondence of Sir Thomas More* (Princeton: Princeton University Press, 1947), especially 439*ff.* Most biographers rely heavily on the life written by his son-in-law William Roper and Nicholas Harpsfield, *Lives of Saint Thomas More* (Dent: Everyman's, 1963). A more recent work is J.A. Guy, *Thomas More* (New York: Oxford University Press, 2000).

[61] Knowles, *Religious Orders*, 3:157; Schmitz 7:138; Knowles, *Religious Orders* 3:167–170.

[62] Knowles, *Religious Orders*, 3:157–161.

[63] Knowles, *Religious Orders*, 3:176–179.

[64] Barton's story is related in almost every study of the English Reformation but is most accurately detailed in Knowles, *Religious Orders*, 3:182–195 and by Cardinal Gasquet, who is considered less accurate in his apologetic for the Benedictines in the very dated *Henry VIII and the English Monasteries* (London: John C. Nimmo, 1899), 35–44. Gasquet sometimes sacrifices truth in his partiality toward his own Order. He was a Downside Abbey monk-historian who is prominently interred in their church.

[65] Knowles, *Religious Orders* 3:182–186.

[66] James Gairdner and R. Brodie, eds., *Letters and Papers, Foreign and Domestic, of the Reign of Henry VIII*, Volume 15 (Burlington, ON: Tanner Ritchie Pub. in collaboration with the Library and Information Services of the University of St. Andrews, 2006), 43.

[67] Knowles, *Religious Orders*, 3:190–191, 204.

[68] According to Knowles, Lord Tregonwell asked for a house of nuns.

[69] Gasquet, *Henry VIII*, 203*ff.* See also Geoffrey Baskerville, *English Monks and the Suppression of the Monasteries* (London: Jonathan Cape, 1937), 218–227. He is biased against the nuns, so these two writers have opposing points of view about the value of monastics as they discuss the dissolution.

[70] Gasquet, *Henry VIII* 307–360.

[71] Baskerville 207, 218–226.

[72] J. C. Dickinson, *Monastic Life in Medieval England* (Westport, CT: Greenwood Press, 1961), 139–141.

[73] Dickinson, 126.

[74] Dickinson, 132–133.

[75] Michael Barrett, *The Scottish Monasteries of Old* (Edinburgh: Otto Schulze, 1913), 25–27.

[76] Barrett, 115–118.

[77] Barrett, 118–120.

CHAPTER 7
Benedictine Spring: The Catholic Counter-Reformation

[1] For the full text of the Council see Henry Schroeder, ed., *Canons and Decrees of the Council of Trent* (St. Louis: B. Herder, 1941); for historical context and contemporary interpretation, see John O'Malley, *Trent: What Happened at the Council* (Cambridge: Harvard University Press, 2013). Anne Schutte discusses the effects of

Tridentine decrees on early European culture and monastic life in her *By Force and Fear: Taking and Breaking Monastic Vows in Early Modern Europe* (Ithaca: Cornell University Press, 2011).

[2] See Schutte, *By Force and Fear*, for greater elaboration.

[3] Schmitz 7:152–153.

[4] Cousin, 403; Schmitz 4:3–7, 152–154.

[5] For a mid-twentieth century overview of this era, see Charles Montalembert, Aurélien Courson, and Francis Gasquet, *The Monks of the West from St. Benedict to St. Bernard* (New York: AMS Press, 1966).

[6] Cousin, 436–437.

[7] For broader context, see Joseph Patrouch, "The Investiture Controversy Revisited: Religious Reform, Emperor Maximilian II, and the Klosterrat," *Austrian History Yearbook*, 25 (1994): 59–77. doi:10.1017/S0067237800006317.

[8] Cousin, 435–436.

[9] See a general discussion of the era in Ulrich Lehner and Michael Printy, eds., *A Companion to the Catholic Enlightenment in Europe* (Boston: Brill, 2010), and an older narrative by J. Sowerby, *The Forest Cantons of Switzerland: Lucerne, Schwyz, Uri, Unterwalden* (London: Percival & Co., 1892).

[10] Cousin, 437.

[11] Robert Sayr entered Monte Cassino; Ansel Beach, St. Justina; and Anthony Martin, Cava. Mark Barkworth left the seminary at Douai for Valladolid and then set out for the English mission in 1599. On the way, he stopped at the Spanish abbey of Yrache where he made promises as a Benedictine Oblate though he was hanged at Tyburn in 1601.

[12] See Bede Camm, *A Benedictine Martyr in England: Being the Life and Times of the Venerable Servant of God, Dom John Roberts, OSB* (London: Burns, Oates and Washbourne, 1931).

[13] Ethelred Taunton, *The English Black Monks of St. Benedict* (New York: Longmans, Green, 1898), 2:173.

[14] For varied perspectives on Baker's history and spirituality, see Hugh Feiss, "Baker, Augustine," in *Encyclopedia of Monasticism* vol. 1, ed. William Johnston (Chicago: Fitzroy Dearborn, 2000), 114; and Gordon Mursell, *English Spirituality* (Louisville, KY: SPCK/Westminster John Knox Press, 2001).

[15] James Gaffney, "Biographical Preliminaries for a Life of Dom Augustine Baker," *American Benedictine Review* 19, no. 4 (December, 1968): 524.

[16] Benedictines of Stanbrook, *In a Great Tradition: Tribute to Dame Laurentia McLachlan, Abbess of Stanbrook* (London: John Murray, 1946), 4. This monastery eventually transferred to Stanbrook in England during the French Revolution.

[17] Teachings are collected in Augustine Baker, *Holy Wisdom: Or, Directions for Prayer of Contemplation Extracted Out of More than Forty Treatises*, ed. S. Casey (New York: Benziger, 1890).

[18] Benedictines of Stanbrook, 4–5.

[19] Catherine preferred the Douai community to Brussels, the motherhouse of the Cambrai monastery established in 1597 by Lady Mary Percy, the daughter of the martyred Earl of Northumberland, Blessed Thomas Percy. The Brussels house had also sent nuns to Ghent who also later returned to England where they relocated at Oulton. The nuns from Brussels transferred to England in 1794, but had to be evacuated during

World War II. They settled temporarily at Haslemere in Surrey but because of reduced numbers disbanded in 1976. The remnant of twelve joined seven other English communities. Benedictines of Stanbrook, 6–7, 124–125.

[20] Benedictines of Stanbrook, 8, 11–12; Gaffney, 515. See Dom Benedict Weld-Brundell, *The Inner Life and Writings of Dame Gertrude More*, 2 vols. (London: R. T. Washbourne, 1910–1911) and "Records of the English Benedictine Nuns at Cambrai (1620–1793)," *Publications of the Catholic Record Society* (London, 1913), 13:39. Benedictines of Stanbrook, 12–14; Gaffney, 525–526.

[21] Benedictines of Stanbrook, 11–12; Gaffney, 515; "Records of the English Benedictine Nuns at Cambrai (1620–1793)," 13:39*ff*.

[22] Betty Travitsky, Anne Prescott, and Arthur Marotti, eds., *Gertrude More* (Burlington, VT: Ashgate, 2009).

[23] Benedictines of Stanbrook, 12–14; Gaffney, 525–526.

[24] Gaffney, 527.

[25] Benedictines of Stanbrook, 17–18; Gaffney, 528.

[26] Gaffney, 529.

[27] There is an extant manuscript some claim to be Baker's autobiography. Published sources include: McCann, *Confessions of Venerable Father Augustine Baker, O.S.B.*, (London, 1922); McCann and Connolly, eds., "Memorials of Father Augustine Baker and Other Documents Relating to the English Benedictines," *Publications of the Catholic Record Society*, 33:3. The same volume includes the biography by Leander Prichard written about 1643. McCann also edits Salvin-Cressy's *The Life of Father Augustine Baker, OSB* (London, 1933) incorporating two works by the authors. Salvin wrote in 1646, Cressy about 1657 (cited in Gaffney, 515–535). When I asked Matthias Neuman, OSB, author of an exceptional article, "Monk-Chaplain for Communities of Monastic Women: Some Landmarks of a Neglected History" (*American Benedictine Review*, 53, no. 1 (March 2002): 74–89, why Dom Baker was not included in his study, he replied that Baker had not really been the chaplain, but the nuns' spiritual director—which was certainly the case. The article is unique for its balanced treatment of a subject about which very little was written.

[28] Benedictines of Stanbrook, 23.

[29] Benedictines of Stanbrook, 23.

[30] Benedictines of Stanbrook, 23–25.

[31] Benedictines of Stanbrook, 25.

[32] Benedictines of Stanbrook, 26–27.

[33] Benedictines of Stanbrook, 29.

[34] Archives and interviews, Colwich Monastery, 1982; Beattie, 122. The Cambrai nuns were in financial difficulty by 1651, so to decrease their numbers they sent three of their nuns to make a foundation in Paris. With the beneficence of the French Queen, Henrietta Maria, the community of Our Lady of Good Hope was established. In 1657, the Archbishop of Paris assumed jurisdiction of these nuns who remained in Paris until the Revolution. They moved to England where they went from Dorset to Somerset and finally to Colwich. See Bantoft, A., *The Gascoigne Family and the Catholic Church in the 17th and 18th Centuries: Part 1. The Gascoigne Nuns at Cambrai and Paris*. http://www.barwickinelmethistoricalsociety.com/bhs.html.

[35] Helen Smith, *'Grossly Material Things': Women and Book Production in Early Modern England* (Oxford: Oxford University Press, 2012), 30.

[36] See Tobie Matthew, *The Life of Lady Lucy Knatchbull* (London: Sheed and Ward, 1931); Bennet Weldon, *Pax: Chronological Notes Containing the Rise, Growth and Present State of the English Congregation of the Order of St. Benedict* (Stanbrook: J. Hodges, 1881), 38. A primary document for the Ghent nuns is Lady Abbess and Community, *Obituary Notices of the English Benedictine Abbey of Ghent in Flanders 1627–1811* (1917), 19, http://www2.history.qmul.ac.uk/wwtn/the_project.html; Caroline Bowden, "Knatchbull, Elizabeth (1584–1629)," in *Oxford Dictionary of National Biography* (Oxford: Oxford University Press), http://www.oxforddnb.com/view/article/66981.

[37] The community's story is in *A History of the Benedictine Nuns of Dunkirk* (London: Catholic Book Club, 1957). The abbey is now a favorite tourist stop (Interview, Kylemore, June, 1982). See T. Moody, F. Martin, and F. Byrne, *A New History of Ireland*, III (Oxford: Oxford University Press, 2009); Patrick Nolan, *The Irish Dames of Ypres: Being a History of the Royal Irish Abbey of Ypres Founded A.D. 1665 and Still Flourishing: And Some Account of Irish Jacobitism, With a Portrait of James II and Stuart Letters Hitherto Unpublished* (Dublin: Browne and Nolan, 1908); Martin Browne and Colmán Ó Clabaigh, *The Irish Benedictines: A History* (Blackrock, Co. Dublin: The Columba Press, 2005).

[38] Kathleen Villiers-Tuthill, *History of Kylemore Castle & Abbey* (Connemara, Co Galway: Kylemore Abbey Publications, 2002).

[39] See the entry for "Sarnen" in Leo Schelbert, *Historical Dictionary of Switzerland* (Lanham, MD: Scarecrow Press, 2007), 301-302.

[40] See Ulrich Lehner and Michael Printy, eds., *A Companion to the Catholic Enlightenment in Europe* (Boston: Brill, 2010).

[41] Jean François, *Bibliothèque Générale des Ecrivains de l'Ordre de Saint Benoit, Patriarche des Moines d'Occident* (Bouillon: Société typographique, 1777).

[42] Charles Chardon, *Histoire des sacrements, ou de la Manière dont ils ont été célébrés et administrés dans l'Église et de l'usage qu'on en a fait depuis le temps des apôtres jusqu'à présent, par le R. P. Dom C. Chardon* (Paris: G. Desprez, 1745); Cousin, 424–426.

[43] Daniel-Odon Hurel, "The Benedictines of the Congregation of St. Maur and the Church Fathers," in *The Reception of the Church Fathers in the West: From the Carolingians to the Maurists*, ed. D. Backus (New York: E.J. Brill, 1997), 1009–1038; John McClintock, *Cyclopaedia of Biblical, Theological, and Ecclesiastical Literature*, Reprint of the 1871–1881 ed., vol. 5 (New York: Arno Press, 1969).

[44] E. Bishop, "Richelieu and the Maurists," *Downside Review* 30 (1911), 271–290. Cardinal Richelieu had appointed himself commendatory abbot of Cluny and subsequently attempted to unite that congregation with the Maurists. The union lasted only four years and was dissolved by mutual consent in 1644, two years after Richelieu's death.

[45] David Knowles, *Great Historical Enterprises: Problems in Monastic History* (New York: Nelson, 1963), 38.

[46] Knowles, *Great Historical Enterprises*, 41.

[47] G. Gooch, *History and Historians in the Nineteenth Century* (New York, Longman's, Green, 1952), 4–5.

[48] Knowles, *Great Historical Enterprises* 42–43. The Maurist centuries are characterized by four distinct phases. According to David Knowles, the pre-Mabillon period of individual and undirected effort marks the first phase (1640–1665) begun with the emergence of the single great figure of Dom Luc d'Archery (1609–1685),

who organized programs and proposed methods. The Age of Mabillon (1665–1707) followed, dominated by the greatest of the scholars, his disciples and companions. The third phase (1708–1741) was that of Edmond Martène and Bernard Montfaucon. Lesser-known men closed the final phase (1742–1817), continuing the works of their predecessors, reflecting the earlier models.

[49] Joseph Urban Bergkamp, *Dom Jean Mabillon and the Benedictine Historical School of Saint-Maur* (Washington, DC: Catholic University, 1928), 18–20.

[50] Bergkamp, *Dom Jean Mabillon*, 18–20.

[51] See David Knowles's discussion of Mabillon's works in Chapter 10 of Knowles, *The Historian and Character, and Other Essays* (Cambridge: Cambridge University Press, 2008).

[52] Knowles, *Great Historical Enterprises* 46–47.

[53] Bergkamp, 72–84 treats the "Traité des Etudes Monastiques" at length.

[54] Jadart, *Travaux de l'Académie de Reims*, LXIV, 100, cited in Bergkamp, 84.

[55] Bergkamp, 1.

[56] Jean Mabillon, *De re diplomatica libri vi, in quibus quidquid ad veterum instrumentorum antiquitatem, materiam, scripturam, & stilum, quidquid ad sigilla, monogrammata, subscriptiones, ac notas chronologicas, quidquid inde ad antiquariam, historicam, forensemque disciplinam pertinet, explicatur & illustrator* (Palma: Luteciae-Parisiorum, 1709).

[57] Mabillon's study of St. Bernard was superseded only in the twentieth century by the publications of the late Dom Jean Leclercq of Clervaux, Luxembourg (Knowles, *Historical Enterprises* 46). A work of note is Jean Mabillon, *Museum italicum, sev Collectio veterum scriptorum ex bibliothecis italicis* (Lutetiae Parisiorum: E. Martin, J. Boudot & S. Martin, 1687).

[58] J. Besse and Société Mabillon, eds., *Archives de la France monastique* (Abbaye Saint-Martin, 1907).

[59] See especially *Revue Mabillon*, 4 (May, 1908).

[60] Knowles, *Great Historical Enterprises*, 48–49.

[61] Ruinary's biography of Mabillon, *Abregé de la vie de Dom Jean Mabillon, prêtre & religieux benedictin de la Congregation de Saint Maur*.was published the year of the author's death in 1709.

[62] Jean Mabillon, Edmond Martene, and René Massuet, *Annales Ordinis S. Benedicti Occidentalium Monachorum Patriarchæ. In quibus non modo res monasticæ, sed etiam ecclesiasticæ historiæ non minima pars continetur. Auctore J.M. [The fifth volume edited, with additions, after the author's death, by R. Massuet, and the sixth by E. Martène.]* (Paris: Luteciæ Parisiorum, 1703).

[63] One volume of his remarkable corpus is Bernard Montfaucon, *The Antiquities of Italy: Being the Travels of the Learned and Reverend Bernard de Montfaucon, from Paris through Italy, in the Years 1698 and 1699* (London: J. Darby, A. Bettesworth, F. Fayram, 1725).

[64] Knowles, *Great Historical Enterprises*, 62. See also David Knowles, "A Preface of Mabillon," *Downside Review* 38 (1919), 53–57. An incomplete list of the publications of the "Twentieth century Maurist," Dom Knowles, fills seven pages in his biography written by another Downside monk, Dom Adrian Morey, *David Knowles: A Memoir* (London: Barton, Longman and Todd, 1979).

[65] Msgr. Nicola Fusco, *Elena Lucrezia Cornaro Piscopia*, 1646–1684 (Pittsburgh:

University of Pittsburgh, n.d.), 21–23, 34. See the 1999 publication by Jane Howard Guernsey, *The Lady Cornaro: Pride and Prodigy of Venice* (Clinton Corners, NY: College Avenue Press). A shorter version of her life is authored by S. Ann Kessler in a chapter in *Benedict in the World: Portraits of Monastic Oblates,* edited by S. Linda Kulzer and Roberta Bondi (Liturgical Press, 2002). There is no longer any debate about her being the first woman to receive any degree from a university.

[66] Fusco, 45. *Kappa Gamma Pi Newsletter* (November, 1974) headlined its tribute to Elena "Patron Saint of Educated Women."

[67] Every source indicated in 50n and most of the articles in some 300 periodicals and newspapers highlight the oral exam. A genealogical chart of the Cornaros is at www.boglewood.com/cornaro/xfamily.html.

[68] Mathilde Pynsent, *The Life of Helen Lucretia Coronaro Piscopia, Oblate of the Order of St. Benedict and Doctor in the University of Padua* (Roma: St. Benedict's, 1896).

[69] Nicola Fusco, *Elena Lucrezia Cornaro Piscopia, 1646–1684* (Pittsburgh: United States Committee for the Elena Lucrezia Cornaro Piscopia Tercentenary, 1975).

[70] Francesco Maschietto, *Elena Lucrezia Cornaro Piscopia, 1646–1684: Prima Donna Laureata nel Mondo,* vol. 10 (Padova: Antenore, 1978); translated as Francesco Maschietto, *Elena Lucrezia Cornaro Piscopia (1646–1684): The First Woman in the World to Earn a University Degree,* trans. Jan Vairo & William Crochetiere (Philadelphia: Saint Joseph's University Press, 2007). Jane Howard Guernsey published an English book-length biography, *The Lady Cornaro: Pride and Prodigy of Venice* (Clinton Corners, NY: College Avenue Press, 1999). The present author contributed a chapter on Elena in a compendium of oblate biographies, Ann Kessler, "Oblate and Heroine: Elena Lucrezia Scholastica Cornaro Piscopia," in *Benedict in the World: Portraits of Monastic Oblates,* eds. Linda Kulzer & Roberta Bondi (Collegeville, MN: Liturgical Press, 2002), 19–30. Numerous other articles have now brought her name to public notice.

[71] A group of moderates adapted the Feuillant label, including the Marquis de Lafayette, who met in the unoccupied monastery during the early days of the French Revolution. It remains the name of a stop of the Paris Metro.

[72] Alexius Hoffmann, "History of the Order" Ms. Ch. 7:20–24. (Collegeville, MN: St. John's Abbey Archives).

[73] For context, see Natalie Davis, *Society and Culture in Early Modern France: Eight Essays* (Stanford: Stanford University Press, 1975).

[74] Schmitz, 7:159.

[75] Schmitz, 7:159. The text of the Concordat is in P. Denis, *Le Cardinal de Richelieu* (Paris, 1913), 457–462

[76] Schmitz, 7:310–311.

[77] A new edition of her treatise was published in 1934 at Maredsous by S. Sodar, *Traité de l'oraison mentale par la Mère Marguerite d'Arbouze,* followed by several extracts from the *Traité de l'Exercice journalier de M. d'Arbouze* (cited in Schmitz 7:312).

[78] Schmitz 7:311–312.

[79] Marie-Florine Bruneau, *Women Mystics Confront the Modern World: Marie de l'Incarnation (1599–1672) and Madame Guyon (1648–1717)* (Albany: State University of New York Press, 1998).

[80] Schmitz 7:314–315.

[81] Her biography is also the work of B. Sodar, *Une Mystique bénédictine du XVIIe siècle: La Mère Jeanne Deleloé* (Maredsous, 1925).

[82] See Parenty, *Histoire de Florence de Werquignoeul* (Lille, 1846) and P. Delmer, "Florence de Werquignoeul et sa réforme," 23 (1937–1938), 221–229, cited in Schmitz 7:324.

[83] Schmitz 7:326–328 includes the citation of her two-volume biography by an Italian, L. Bracco: *Vita della B. Giovanna Maria Bonomo* (Rome, 1883) and one by a Frenchman A. du Bourg, *La B. Jeanne-Marie Bonomo, moniale bénédictine, 1606–1670* (Paris, 1910).

[84] Schmitz 7:330–331. Manuscript study of Benedictine women saints (Collegeville: St. John's Abbey Archives), 241–242.

[85] See A. Krailsheimer, *Armand-Jean de Rancé, Abbot of La Trappe* (Oxford: Clarendon Press, 1974).

[86] Alexius Hoffmann, Ms. Chap 7 (Collegeville: St. John's Abbey Archives), 24–27.

[87] Hoffmann, "History of the Order," 28–29. Also see Alexius Hoffmann, *A Benedictine Maryrology* (Collegeville, MN: St. John's Abbey, 1922).

[88] Hoffmann, "History of the Order," 31–32.

[89] Hoffmann, "History of the Order," 32–35.

[90] Cousin, 418. The Brazilian Congregation was approved in 1827 by Pope Leo XII when the monasteries separated from the Portuguese Congregation of Lusitania. (See *Catalogus Monasteriorum OSB* 2000.) Various American and European Benedictine monasteries of monks and nuns have founded—and continue to support—dependent and independent priories in Brazil and many other Latin American nations.

CHAPTER 8
The French Revolution and Benedictine Monasticism

[1] An immense corpus of scholarly and popular work about the background, causes, events, and outcomes of the French Revolution exists from multiple points of view. One accessible resource addressing the interwoven extent of the Revolution with England and the United States is David Andress, *1789: The Threshold of the Modern Age* (New York: Farrar, Straus and Giroux, 2009). For a detailed survey, see William Doyle, *The Oxford History of the French Revolution* (New York: Oxford University Press, 2002).

[2] Voltaire criticized the church in many of his works including the satire, *Candide* (1759) and the *Treatise on Tolerance* (1769). See Voltaire, *Candide and Related Texts*, trans. David Wootton (Indianapolis: Hackett, 2000); and Voltaire, *Treatise on Tolerance*, ed. Harvey Simon and trans. Brian Masters (New York: Cambridge University Press, 2000).

[3] Donald Sullivan, "Critiques of Western Christian Monasticism," in *Encyclopedia of Monasticism*, ed. William Johnston (Chicago: Fitzroy Dearborn, 2000), 337–341.

[4] Abbé Barruel, *The History of the Clergy during the French Revolution* (Dublin: H. Fitzpatrick, 1794), 2.

[5] Gallicanism, originating in France, emphasized the independence of the French church over papal control. For one study, see Jotham Parsons, *The Church in the Republic: Gallicanism & Political Ideology in Renaissance France* (Washington, DC: Catholic University of America Press, 2004).

[6] Dom P. Anger, "Les Mitigations demandées par les moines de Saint-Germain-des-Pès in 1765," *Revue Mabillon* 4 (1908), 203–231.

[7] It was modified in 1778 to permit profession by men over twenty-one and women over eighteen.

[8] Later, when nominated to be Archbishop of Paris, the king (who had final veto over all recommendations) was by then suspicious of his character and refused to confirm the appointment of the former royal commissioner, saying it was necessary that at least the Archbishop of Paris believe in God. Schmitz 4:69; Alexius Hoffmann, "History of the Order," Chapter 8, 2. Saint John's Abbey Archives, cited hereafter as SJAA.

[9] François Rousseau, *Moines Bénédictins martyrs et confesseurs de la foi pendant la Révolution* (Paris: Desclée de Brouwer, 1926), 8.

[10] Schmitz 4:72–73.

[11] For the effects of the Revolution on the Benedictines, see S. Verona (Ann) Kessler, "The Suppression of the Benedictine Order in France during the Revolution," (MA thesis, Creighton University, 1957).

[12] Wallace Willard Taylor, "The Confiscation of Church Property in France in 1789" (PhD dissertation, University of Iowa, 1941), 52–60.

[13] Taylor, 62–63; G. Lacour-Gayet, *Talleyrand, 1754–1838* (Paris: Payot, 1928), I:121. Crane Brinton, *The Lives of Talleyrand* (New York: W. W. Norton, 1936).

[14] Pierre de la Gorce, *Histoire religieuse de la Révolution Français* (Paris: Plon-Nourrit, 1922), I:143; Clement L. Benson, "The French Revolution and the Church Property: The First Phase" (MA thesis, University of Nebraska, 1921), 11.

[15] *Procès-Verbal* of the National Assembly, October 10, 1789, 17.

[16] Benson, 63.

[17] The status of the monasteries is recorded by a "Moine Bénédictine" in *Les Abbayes de France au Moyen Age et en 1947* (Paris: G. Durassie, 1947) 81*ff*.

[18] See *Le Moniteur (Reimpression)* (Paris: René et Cie, 1841), February 13, 1790, and subsequent issues. For an analysis of historical context and ideological complexities of the 1789 declaration of rights, see Thomas Kaiser, "Property, Sovereignty, the Declaration of the Rights of Man, and the Tradition of French Jurisprudence," in *French Idea of Freedom: The Old Regime and the Declaration of Rights of 1789*, ed. Dale Van Kley, (Stanford, CA: Stanford University Press, 1994). The French Declaration is companioned with the American Bill of Rights in *The French Declaration of the Rights of Man and of the Citizen and the American Bill of Rights: A Bicentennial Commemoration Issued Pursuant to S.J. Res. 317, 100th Congress* (Washington, DC: U.S. Congress, Senate, 1989).

[19] *Procès-Verbal*, February 19, 1790. A copy of the *Procès-Verbal* was selling for six livres in 1790.

[20] H. M. Delsart, *La Dernière Abbesse de Montmartre: Marie-Louise de Montmorency-Laval, 1723–1794* (Paris: P. Lethielleux, 1921), 76.

[21] Em. Trelcat, *Histoire de l'Abbaye de Crespin: Ordre de Saint Benoît* (Paris: Librairie Générale Catholique, n.d.), 2:206; Louis Béziot, *Histoire de l'Abbaye de Caunes* (Paris: A. Claudin, 1858), 223; François Rousseau, 59.

[22] Gaston Lecroq, *L'hôpital de Fécamp et sa communauté des bénédictines hospitalières: contribution à l'histoire de l'hôpital (XIe–XXe s.)* (Caen: Société d'impression de Basse-Normandie, 1939), 277, 284, 309–310.

[23] Delsart, *passim*.

[24] Basil Whelan, *Historic English Convents* (London: Burns, Oates and Washbourne, 1936), 155; Beattie, ed., 126.

[25] Ursmer Berlière, "Un des derniers moines de Marchiennes (Nord)," *Revue Liturgique et Monastique* 16, 1931, 240; Romanos Rios, *Benedictines of Today* (Worcester: Stanbrook Abbey Press, 1946), 27–28.

[26] Gorce 3:402–403.

[27] Gorce 3:409.

[28] G. Charvin, "La Fin de l'Ordre de Cluny (1789–1791)," *Revue Mabillon* 40 (1950): 39.

[29] Gorce 3:409. See also Kessler, "Suppression," 144. Gorce 3:49, 366–367.

[30] Names of some of the monks are recorded in Schmitz 4:82*ff.*; Rousseau, 88*ff.*; and Lecroq 287*ff.*

[31] A. Mâcon, "Société des arts, belles-lettres, et agriculture de Saône-et-Loire," *Annales de l'Académie de Mâcon* (Saône-et-Loire: L'Académie, 1910).

[32] Paul Hanson, *The Jacobin Republic Under Fire: The Federalist Revolt in the French Revolution* (University Park, PA: Pennsylvania State University Press, 2003).

[33] Rousseau, 296–353; Schmitz 4:82.

[34] Rios, 19; Schmitz 4:82.

[35] Rios, 21; Rousseau, 92, 107, 149; Charvin, 40; D. B. Becker, "Causes de beatification dans l'ordre de Saint Benoît," *Revue Liturgique et Monastique*, Advent, 1938, 24–34.

[36] Rios, 27.

[37] Rousseau, 149–150, 154–155.

[38] Rousseau, 138–145.

[39] Rios, 20; Abbé de Salamon, *Mémoires inédits de l'Internonce à Paris pendant la Révolution, 1790–1801*, Abbé Bridier, ed. (Paris: Plon-Nourrit, 1903), xxxi. For additional narratives, see also Edwin Bannon, *Refractory Men, Fanatical Women: Fidelity to Conscience During the French Revolution*. Leominster: Gracewing, 1992).

[40] Gorce, 3: 260–294. Theodore Maynard, *Saint Benedict and His Monks* (New York: P. J. Kenedy and Sons, 1954) claims that thirty Maurists died at Les Carmes. No other historian supports that statement. The September Massacres are also mentioned briefly by the famous French historian of the Revolution, Albert Mathiez in *After Robespierre: The Thermidorian Reaction*, trans. Catherine Alison Phillips (New York: Alfred A. Knopf, 1931), 200.

[41] Barruel, 300.

[42] Guilio Meritan, *Vita delle Trentadue Beate Religiose Ghigliottinate ad Orange in Odio della Fede* (Rome: Scuola Tiprografica Pio X, 1925), 169–172.

[43] *Le Moniteur (Reimpression)* 21:48.

[44] Rousseau, 126–128; Delsart, 101–108.

[45] Rousseau, 77; Ethelred L. Taunton, *The English Black Monks of St. Benedict* (New York: Longmans, Green, 1898), 2:291. Ampleforth had 96 monks, including 10 in temporary vows in 2000 (*Catalogus*, 29–33). Ampleforth was the monastery of twentieth-century Catholic Archbishop of Westminster Cathedral, Cardinal Basil Hume (d. 1999).

[46] Beattie, 76. For the interview at Downside, see the Abbey's scholarly publication, *The Downside Review*. The Ealing story is told by René Kollar, "The Return of the Benedictines to London," *Tjurunga* 37 (September 1989): 36–51.

[47] Whelan, 161–178; Beattie, 127.

[48] Gertrude Le Fort, *The Song at the Scaffold*, trans. O. Marx (Kirkwood, MO: Catholic Authors Press, 1954).

[49] Beattie, 118; Benedictines of Stanbrook 37*ff.*; interviews and archives, Stanbrook Abbey.

[50] Schmitz 4:80; Rousseau, 70–77; Gorce 3:269–270; Trelcat, 154; Barruel, 378.

[51] Hilpisch, *Nuns* 83–84; Nuns of St. Walburg, *Spring and Harvest*, 34–36; Abtei St. Walburg, *900 Jahre in Wort und Bild 1035–1935* (St. Walburg, Eichstätt, 1934), 45–55; Regina Baska, *The Benedictine Congregation of Saint Scholastica: Its Foundation and Development (1852–1930)* (Washington, DC: Catholic University of America, 1935), 4–8; Hilpisch, *Monks* 118–121.

[52] Léon Deries, *Les Congrégations religieuses au temps de Napoléon* (Paris: Librairie Félix Alcan, 1929), 194–198.

[53] Deries, 191; Ursmer Berlière, "La Congrégation Bénédictine de Chézal-Benoît," *Revue Bénédictine*, 18 (1901): 19.

[54] Archives and interviews at French monasteries of La Rochette, Pradines, Chantelle, Jouarre, and Bouaké in the Ivory Coast. See Dom D. Buenner's biography and history of the congregation, *Madame de Bavoz: Abbesse de Pradines* (Paris, 1961).

[55] Schmitz 4:175; Académie de Macon, *Millénaire de Cluny* (Macon: Protat Frères, 1910), 137–139.

CHAPTER 9
Benedictine Restoration, Renewal, Expulsions, and Expansion

[1] Eventually the English Congregation expanded to the United States—a Scottish monastery (former twelfth-century abbey relocated at Lambscring in 1645 then Fort Augustus in 1876) founded two American houses, St. Anselm's in Washington, DC, and St. Gregory's in Portsmouth, Rhode Island. Saint Louis Abbey in Missouri was established by Ampleforth in 1955.

[2] For extended context of the Benedictine congregations discussed herein, see Terence Kavenagh, "Congregations, Benedictine," in *Encyclopedia of Monasticism* (Chicago: Fitzroy Dearborn, 2000), 322–326.

[3] John Higgens, "Dom Guéranger and the Founding of Solesmes," *ABR* 6 (Spring, 1955), 53–57. Dom Paul Delatte, third abbot of Solesmes, in collaboration with Mother Cécile, wrote the French biography of his predecessor, *Dom Guéranger: Abbé de Solesmes*, 2 vols. (Paris: Plon, 1910 and 1950), under anonymous authorship ("Moine Bénédictin"). See also the abbey's brief historical sketch, *Le Monastère Saint-Pierre de Solesmes* (Sablé, 1955). For a later twentieth-century biography, see Louis Soltner, *Solesmes and Dom Guéranger, 1805–1875* (Orleans, MA: Paraclete Press, 1995). A twenty-first century study of Solesmes' liturgical influence is found in Pierre Combe, *The Restoration of Gregorian Chant: Solesmes and the Vatican Edition* (Washington, DC: Catholic University of America Press, 2003).

[4] See Abbot Delatte's commentary on the Rule in Paul-Henri Delatte, *The Rule of St. Benedict: A Commentary*, trans. Justin McCann, (Latrobe PA: Archabbey Press, 1959). This commentary and earlier editions were the main source for the study of the Rule in many nuns' novitiates and a few monks' in pre-Vatican II days. Delatte, disciple of Guéranger, put into writing what his mentor, the first abbot, taught earlier. It was definitely the Rule according to Guéranger. Those novices among the monks and nuns who were formed by Dom Maurus Wolter's publication, *The Principles of Monasticism* (St. Louis, MO: Herder, 1962) were also formed à la Solesmes as Wolter took more than

one page from the Solesmes abbot's life and works during their long years of monastic alliance. It is more difficult to find which monastic leader or group was *not* influenced by him.

⁵ Prosper Guéranger, *The Liturgical Year*, trans. James Shepherd (New York: Benziger Bros., 1897); also Guéranger's, *Institutions liturgiques* (Mans; Paris: Fleuriot Débecourt, 1840).

⁶ Joseph Pothier, *Du liber gradualis et de la manière d'en interpréter la notation* (Solesmes: Imprimerie saint-Pierre, 1892); André Mocquereau, *Le nombre musical grégorien, ou Rhythmique grégorienne, théorie et pratique* (Paris: Société Saint Jean l'Évangéliste Desclée, 1908), among other manuscripts.

⁷ André Mocquereau, *Paléographie musicale: les principaux manuscrits de chant grégorien, ambrosien, mozarabe, gallican* (Solesmes, France: Solesmes, 1969).

⁸ Pierre Combe has several articles on the reform and restoration of the chant in *Etudes Grégoriennes* 6:185–234 and 8:137–198. He maintains that the initial move came from the Bishop of Le Mans who invited Guéranger to participate in a commission to edit liturgical and chant books for the diocese. Dom Guéranger carried "great weight" on this commission (6:191) The curator of the Sacred Music Resources Center, at the Benedictine Monastery in Yankton, SD, Sister Jane Klimisch OSB, has printed "A Cumulative Index of Gregorian Chant Resources." See also Ralph S. March, "Dom Joseph Pothier, OSB *Sacred Music*" March 1973, 8–12. Also see Pierre Combe, *The Restoration of Gregorian Chant: Solesmes and the Vatican Edition* (Washington, DC: Catholic University of America Press, 2003).

⁹ Sahler 1:10–20; 2:75–76. Archives and interviews at Solesmes, Sainte-Marie (Paris), Kergonan, Liguge, and St. Wandrille.

¹⁰ See Delatte's biography of Guéranger, and archival research and interviews at Ste. Cécile and St. Pierre, Solesmes, Notre Dame at Wisques, and Saint-Michel at Kergonan. The nuns are represented at the general chapters only when their monasteries are under discussion. They do not share in decisions affecting general policies or those of individual monasteries of men. The monks, however, share in making the decisions concerning the nuns.

¹¹ Archives of the Servantes-des-Pauvres, Angers: Gabriel Meunier, *Dom Leduc, Moine de Solesmes et l'oeuvre des oblates Servantes des Pauvres* (Angers, 1923). The Servants of the Poor (in 2000) had almost 200 members in fourteen dependent houses in France, Belgium, and Senegal (Keur Moussa and Dakar), *Catalogus 2000*. Since 1928 the Congregation has been pontifical. They and all non-papal enclosed Benedictine women are listed as "Sorores" (Sisters) in contrast to the cloistered "Moniales." When this writer asked Abbot Primate Jerome if this categorization would continue in July 1995 at his home abbey at St. John's, Collegeville (there is no longer a distinction between simple and solemn vows), he responded that there would probably be a study of monastic enclosure of monks and nuns—which could, by implication, break down the distinction. Monks have enclosure, but are classified according to the amount of it as compared to those who are more active contemplatives. He did not live to supervise the publication of the *Catalogus 2000*, but at least the nuns now have a volume of their own.

¹² Archival research and interviews at Argentan, Poitiers. The monasteries include the restored medieval communities of the Holy Cross at Poitiers, Notre-Dame at Argentan and Notre-Dame-du-Pré at Lisieux (where St. Therese received her pri-

mary education). The reestablished seventeenth-century monasteries at Verneuil-sur-Avre and Estaires also adopted the Guéranger constitutions.

[13] See Ann Kessler's PhD dissertation, "The Effects of the Laic Laws of 1901 and 1904 on the Benedictines in France" (University of Notre Dame, 1963), 14–15; Gaetan Bernoville, *Un Moine Apôtre: Le Père Muard* (Paris, 1938) and Denis Huerre, *Jean Baptiste Muard* (Saint-Leger-Vauban, 1950). When I requested use of the monastic archives at Pierre-qui-Vire in 1961, I was told that my topic (dealing with the twentieth century laic laws) was still too controversial. I had to be satisfied with an interview and published materials or those gleaned from other French monastic archives.

[14] Cousin, 493–497; archives and interviews at Landévennec, Saint-Benoît-sur-Loire, Belloc, and d'En Calcat.

[15] Mariastein was eventually reoccupied in the twentieth century. See Jules Joachim *Histoire du Collège Saint Benoît à Delle, 1875–1901* (Colmar, n.d.) and Kessler, "Laic Laws", 10, 15.

[16] The Napoleonic era and the restoration of the monarchy gave way to a Second Republic (when Louis Napoleon became president), then to a Second Empire (Napoleon III) in 1852 when the Republican President won a plebiscite allowing him to reestablish an Empire in imitation of his uncle (Napoleon I).

[17] Evelyn Acomb, *The French Laic Laws, 1879–1889* (New York, 1941), 249; Kessler, "Laic Laws", 20–23.

[18] Jules Affray, *Les Expulsés devant les tribunaux* (Paris, 1881), i; Abbé A. Boulenger, *Histoire Générale de l'Eglise*, 3rd. ed. (Paris, Emmanual Vite, 1950), 9:638.

[19] *Journal Officiel de la République Française*, March 30, 1880, 1673–1675. This is the French equivalent of the *Congressional Record* of the U. S. Congress. Cited hereafter as *J.O.*

[20] Boulenger 9:289; P. Rimbault, *Histoire politique des Congrégations religieuses françaises, 1790–1914* (Paris, 1926), 156.

[21] Rimbault, 157; Paul Nourrison, *Histoire légale des congrégations religieuses in France depuis 1789*, 2:234.

[22] Augustin Savaton, *Dom Paul Delatte, Abbé de Solesmes* (Paris, 1954), 71.

[23] For a fuller account of all the expulsions see Kessler, "Laic Laws," 29*ff.*

[24] For the next ten years, the anecdotes surrounding this "occupation" of the abbey were collected by the monks. This irreverent manuscript poking fun at these monastery "custodians" (labeled the "Opus Gendarmicum") is still preserved in manuscript in the Solesmes Abbey archives.

[25] Savaton, 139.

[26] *Catalogus 2000* lists eight monks at Farnborough. The monastery at the site became an independent abbey in 1903. The Prinknash monks of the Subiaco Congregation succeeded the French in 1947. It was raised to abbey status in 1990 and remains in the Subiaco Congregation.

[27] This is the Silos monastery that marketed a Gregorian chant audio recording (1994–1995) that hit the top of the charts in most of Europe and then in North America. Silos, of course, might be considered a grand-daughter of Solesmes—so that monastery's revival of chant was again resurrected, this time for a popular, not a monastic or Roman Catholic, constituency; *Catalogus 2000*, 128–130.

[28] Kessler, "Laic Laws," 29–34; Buckfast is now in the English Congregation. There were 34 Buckfast Abbey monks in 2000 (*Catalogus 2000*, 40–41).

²⁹ According to a memorandum in the Solesmes Abbey archives, the exaction amounted to seven times that of the levy on civil corporations and three times that on individuals. See Kessler, "Laic Laws," 33–34.

³⁰ Charles Poulet, *Histoire de l'Eglise de France* (Paris: P. Lethielleux, n.d.), 3:333.

³¹ Cousin, 497–498

³² David Knowles, *Christian Monasticism* (New York: McGraw-Hill, 1969), 174–175.

³³ See S. Marielle Frigge, *Schola Christi: Benedictine Insight for Theological Education* (PhD dissertation, Boston College, 1992).

³⁴ Interviews at St. Boniface and St. Ottilien. Cousin, 499–500; *Pax* (Abbaye de Landévennec) 23 (January, 1963, 13–14; Jerome Oetgen, *An American Abbot: Boniface Wimmer, O.S. B., 1809–1887* (Latrobe, PA: Archabbey Press, 1976), 23–30; Benedict Kominiak, ed., *Loci Ubi Deus Quaeritur: The Benedictine Abbeys of the Entire World* (St. Ottilien: Eos Verlag 1980). This is a publication with pictures and brief sketches in English and German, French, or Italian, of most of the abbeys of monks. This Newton, New Jersey, monk was beginning a similar volume on the nuns when he died in October 1991 during a sojourn at Sant'Anselmo. He was buried at St. Ottilien where he had spent most of his last years when he was not working in Rome. This writer was able to interview him in Munich in 1982.

³⁵ Cousin, 499–500. See also the Beuronese centenary history, *Festschrift zum hundertjahrigen Bestehen der Erzabtei St. Martin* published by the abbey in 1963.

³⁶ David Knowles, *Christian Monasticism* (New York: McGraw Hill, 1969), 174–175.

³⁷ Maurus Wolter, *Praecipua ordinis monastici elementa* (Brugis: Desclée, De Brouwer et Soc., 1880). The abridged English translation is Maurus Wolter, *The Principles of Monasticism*, ed. and trans. Bernard Sause (St. Louis: Herder, 1962).

³⁸ Knowles, *Christian Monasticism*, 174–175.

³⁹ Knowles, *Christian Monasticism*, 175. The Beuronese also significantly influenced Latin American monasticism. The Portuguese foundation at Bahia and monasteries founded two decades later, including Rio de Janeiro, Olinda, and São Paulo organized a separate Brazilian Congregation in 1827. Later, after near annihilation by an anti-clerical government, Beuronese monks from Maredsous at Saint-André (before the Belgian Congregation was organized) in 1895 restored the Brazilian Congregation. See Oliver Kapsner, "The Benedictines in Brazil," *ABR* 28 (1977), 113–132. See also *RB 1980*, 136 and Kominiak, 472–480.

⁴⁰ A longstanding oral account, though not confirmed in my interviews, credits the resignation as result of a scandal involving himself and a nun of whom he was mentor and spiritual director.

⁴¹ Kominiak, 100. The life of Amrhein and his search for an apostolic, yet monastic, community is best told in the *Festschrift* published by Beuron, 1863–1963, in the section by H. Brechter (231–267). The abbey's history was written by Frumentius Renner, *St. Ottilien: Sein Werden und Werken* (St. Ottilien, Eos Verlag, 1976). An English sketch by Justin Dzikowicz, Abbot Emeritus of St. Paul's (Newton, NJ), a daughterhouse of St. Ottilien, is available in the Newton Abbey archives. (This monastery was transferred to the monks of the Congregation's house in Waegwan, Korea, in January 2002. The ten remaining Newton monks were transferring stability to other American Benedictine abbeys.) The scandal involving Amrhein is not generally in print, but oral history carries it. As stated in n40, it was

not repeated to this writer at St. Ottilien when interviews were conducted there.

⁴² Schmitz 7:199. At one point on this page, Dom Schmitz confuses Ludwig I and II. *Catalogus 2000*, 711, lists 40 members at Tettenweiss.

⁴³ Interviews at Keizersberg, Leuven, 1982. It was Beauduin whom John XXIII credited with the idea of a council to promote ecumenism. They had been friends and correspondents when John was a Cardinal-Archbishop. Another unconfirmed oral account tells that Beauduin (who was promoting dialog with the Eastern Orthodox Christians) had said to Cardinal Roncalli (who took it as a jest), "When you become Pope, call a Council." So John did. He always credited Beauduin with motivating him to focus on ecumenism. See Sonya Quitsland, *Beauduin, A Prophet Vindicated* (New York: Newman Press, 1973).

⁴⁴ Gaspar Lefebvre, *Saint Andrew Daily Missal* (St. Paul, MN: E.M. Lohmann Co., 1937).

⁴⁵ Interview, Luke Dysinger OSB, St. Andrew's Abbey, Valyermo, CA.

CHAPTER 10
Benedictine Roots in North America

¹ A writer in *The Catholic Church in the United States of America* Volume 1 (New York: Catholic Edition Co., 1914), 34, claims that historical societies of Copenhagen and Rhode Island, as well as individual researchers, have concluded that some Benedictines came with the first Normans to Iceland and Greenland where monasteries were established and that Benedictine bishops accompanied the missionaries farther west. Church and cloister archaeological discoveries in New England are supposed to attest to this monastic tradition. Abbot Justin Dzikowiz speaking at the 1995 Monastic Institute at St. John's recalled the tradition that a Benedictine did accompany Columbus on one of his four voyages to the New World.

² M. Hall, "Colonial American Benedictines," *St. Anselm's Abbey Newsletter* (Washington, DC, Spring 1980) cited in Fry, et al., eds., *RB 1980*, 136.

³ Adrian Morey in *David Knowles, A Memoir* (London: Darton, Longman and Todd, 1979), 5, calls the Benedictine Charles; others name him Arthur. He had been a student at Douai and had become a onk of St. Edmund's, Paris. As a Fellow of the Royal Society of England, he was instrumental in the English government's adoption of the Gregorian calendar.

⁴ See Mary Ewens, *The Role of the Nun in Nineteenth Century America* (New York: Arno Press, 1978). Thomas Merton, *The Waters of Siloe* (New York: Harcourt Brace, 1949) relates the story of the early Trappists in America.

⁵ See n1 above.

⁶ John Rothensteiner, "Paul de St. Pierre: The First German-American Priest of the West," in *The Catholic Historical Review*, ed. American Catholic Historical Association (Washington, DC: Catholic University of America Press, 1920), 195–222.

⁷ See Mary Benedict, *The Patriarch of German Missionaries: Father Stephen Raffeiner* (Collegeville, MN: Saint John's University, 1940).

⁸ T. O'Connor, "A Benedictine in Frontier America," *Downside Review* 3 (1952): 23–26; Colman J. Barry, *Worship and Work* (Collegeville MN: Saint John's Abbey, 1956), 9.

[9] For one perspective on the background and context of this controversy in the United States, see John Ford, "Country, Church and Conscience: John Henry Newman Versus William Ewart Gladstone," in *Religion and Political Structures: From Fundamentalism to Public Service*, eds. John Ford, R. Destro and C. Dechert (Washington, DC: Council for Research in Values and Philosophy, 2005), 85–100.

[10] Felix Fellner, "Abbot Boniface and His Monks," ms. in Saint Vincent Abbey Archives, vol. 1, 6–17.

[11] Oetgen, *An American Abbot*, 26–35. Several of Wimmer's letters have also been reprinted in vols. 22–25 of the *American Benedictine Review*, cited hereafter as SVAA. See also Joel Rippinger, *The Benedictine Order in the United States: An Interpretive History* (Collegeville, MN: Liturgical Press, 1990).

[12] Theodore Roemer, *The Ludwig-Missionsverein and the Church in the United States, 1838–1918* (Washington, DC: Catholic University, 1933), 10–11.

[13] Oetgen, *American Abbot*, 36–37; Fellner, 1:22.

[14] Oetgen, *American Abbot*, 40–43; Fellner, 1:22.

[15] Barry, *Worship and Work*, 345–351; John Tracy Ellis, ed., *Documents of American Catholic History* (Milwaukee, WI: Bruce, 1962), Document 86, 279–288.

[16] Oetgen, *American Abbot*, 8–11.

[17] Oetgen, *American Abbot*, 85. See also Joel Rippinger, *The Benedictine Order*.

[18] Oetgen, *American Abbot*, 85.

[19] O'Connor to Dr. H. Kirby, August 13, 1851, copy in Saint John's Abbey Archives, cited hereafter as SJAA.

[20] Obituary notice of Abbot Bernard Smith, copy (undated), SJAA.

[21] File A.S.A.C. (2), B.I. (4) SJAA. The Abbot Smith letters are on microfilm and in typescript, copies of the originals in Saint Paul Outside the Walls (Rome) archives.

[22] Oetgen, *American Abbot*, 92–93

[23] Barry, 130n15; Oetgen, *American Abbot*, 94.

[24] This is the Peter Lechner who authored the *Martyrologium de Benedictines Ordens*, trans. Alexius Hoffmann (*The Benedictine Martyrology*, Collegeville, MN: Saint John's Abbey, 1922).

[25] Grace McDonald, *With Lamps Burning* (St. Joseph, MN: St. Benedict's Priory Press, 1957), 7.

[26] McDonald, 8.

[27] M. Incarnata Girgen, *Behind the Beginnings: Benedictine Women in America* (St. Paul, MN: North Central Publishing, 1981), 13.

[28] Oetgen, *American Abbot*, 99. See also Judith Sutera, *True Daughters: Monastic Identity and American Benedictine Women's History* (Atchison, KS: Mount St. Scholastica, 1987).

Editor's note: The difficult—and fascinating—story of Boniface Wimmer and the first American Benedictine women remains a sensitive matter even between contemporary nuns who vary in its interpretation. This narrative demonstrates, as in all retellings of history, Sister Ann Kessler's particular perspective and approach. While Abbot Boniface Wimmer's voluminous correspondence was preserved, only a few documents remain from Mother Benedicta Riepp to fill in the many interpretive gaps that remain. Regardless, these nineteenth–century American events profoundly changed the history of Benedictine nuns.

[29] Girgen, 16.

[30] Girgen, 17–18.

[31] Girgen, 20–26.

[32] Girgen, 20–26.

[33] Girgen, 28–29.

[34] Chronicle manuscript (Saint Joseph's Convent archives at Saint Mary's, PA), cited in McDonald, 11.

[35] Girgen, 30.

[36] Girgen, 35–36.

[37] Oetgen, *American Abbot*, 95–97.

[38] Oetgen, *American Abbot*, 97–98.

[39] Oetgen, *American Abbot*, 152.

[40] Additional aspects of Boniface Wimmer's desire and reasoning to unify the legislation of the men's and women monasteries is discussed more fully in Judith Sutera's *True Daughters* (Atchison, KS: Mt. St. Scholastica, 1987), Chapter 4.

[41] Mary Louis Morkin and Mary Theophane Siegel, *Wind in the Wheat* (Erie: McCarty Printing, 1956), 54; Oetgen, 152–154.

[42] Barry, *Worship and Work*, 16–17. Colman Barry, a Benedictine of Saint John's, was also the author of *The Catholic Church and German Americans* (Milwaukee: Bruce, 1953). Benedictines did relate later to Henni; Martin Marty later wrote the bishop's biography.

[43] Barry, *Worship and Work*, 18.

[44] Barry, *Worship and Work*, 26–49

[45] Barry, *Worship and Work*, 52.

[46] Girgen relates these complaints issuing from the sisters' perceived neglect of adequate attention from their superiors Mother Benedicta and novice mistress Willibalda, as well as complaints regarding the altered horarium, presumably related to delay of the 3:45 am rising and prayer. See Girgen's "A Theory About Internal Strife," 115–119.

[47] Girgen, 59–67.

[48] Girgen, 67–68.

[49] McDonald, 20.

[50] Girgen, 69–70.

[51] Oetgen, 155–157.

[52] Oetgen, 156–157.

[53] Girgen, 27, 35–48, 55–63.

[54] Girgen, 74–75.

[55] Girgen, 74–75.

[56] Girgen, 77–79.

[57] Boniface Wimmer quoted in Girgen, 87. Wimmer's entire letter to Müller is quoted in Girgen, 86–99.

The implications of Wimmer's desire for the nuns' jurisdiction included their ability to remain solemnly vowed. Most American missionary sisters were required to take simple vows due to their active apostolate. See Wimmer's address of this in his letter to Alessandro Barnabo dated July 4, 1858, found in Jerome Oetgen, ed., *Boniface Wimmer: Letters of an American Abbot* (Latrobe, PA: Saint Vincent Archabbey, 2008), 201–222; and the discussion regarding "Legislation" in Sutera, *True Daughters*, 38–44.

[58] Boniface Wimmer quoted in Girgen, 87.

[59] Boniface Wimmer quoted in Girgen, 89.

[60] Boniface Wimmer quoted in Girgen, 90.

[61] Boniface Wimmer quoted in Girgen, 90. Emmerana left America in 1892, went to Eichstätt but was not accepted. She finally joined Chiemsee monastery, where she died in 1902.

[62] Boniface Wimmer quoted in Girgen, 90.

[63] Boniface Wimmer quoted in Girgen, 90. Wimmer apparently had trouble not only with the nuns but also with his own monks. His correspondence includes other letters describing varied issues arising among them as well.

[64] Boniface Wimmer quoted in Girgen, 110–121. Benedicta's "Points on Which I Cannot Agree" is three pages long. Wimmer's response is nine.

[65] Boniface Wimmer quoted in Girgen, 117.

[66] Boniface Wimmer quoted in Girgen, 118

[67] *Catalogus* 2000 still spoke of two categories of nuns: *sorores* and *moniales*.

[68] *Codex iuris canonici* (1917). Intratext website. Retrieved from http://www.intratext.com/IXT/LAT0813/_P1D.HTM . Canon 488.

[69] Saint Walburga Abbey Archives, cited in Girgen, 125.

[70] Faith Schuster, *The Meaning of the Mountain* (Baltimore, MD: Helicon, 1963), 47, 70–75.

[71] Boniface Wimmer quoted in Girgen, 133–134.

[72] Boniface Wimmer quoted in Girgen, 134.

[73] Boniface Wimmer quoted in Girgen, 139.

[74] Ludwig to Boniface Wimmer quoted in Girgen, 140–141.

[75] Boniface Wimmer to Ludwig quoted in Girgen, 141–142.

[76] Boniface Wimmer quoted in Girgen, 142–150.

[77] Boniface Wimmer quoted in Girgen, 148–150.

[78] See Conference of American Benedictine Prioresees, *Upon This Tradition*, "Introduction, Historical Background," http://www.msb.net/Community_About_UTT_Historical_Bkgrnd.html.

[79] McDonald, 49.

[80] See Ephrem Hollermann, *American Benedictine Women, 1852–1881* (St. Joseph, MN: Sisters of St. Benedict, 1994) and Sutera, *True Daughters*.

CHAPTER 11
North American Expansion and Indian Missions

[1] Peter Lemcke, *Leben und Wirken des Prinzen Demetrius Augustin Gallitzin : ein Beitrag zur Geschichte der katholischen Missionen in Nordamerika* (Münster: In Commission der Coppenrath'schen Buch-und Kunsthandlung, 1861).

[2] Fellner, ms. 347–353 SVAA; Peter Beckman, *Kansas Monks: A History of St. Benedict's Abbey* (Atchison, KS: Abbey Student Press, 1956), 4–45; Stephanie Campbell, *Chosen for Peace: The History of the Benedictine Sisters of Elizabeth, New Jersey* (Paterson, NJ: St. Anthony Guild Press, 1968), 3–40.

[3] Schuster, 22–39.

[4] The monastery officially transferred to Morristown, NJ, in 1956. The Newark contingent that remained to staff a secondary school for poor black and white students in what became a black ghetto, eventually became independent of Morristown. It was named an abbey in its own right in 1968. They are both in the American Cassinese

Congregation. In 2000 Morristown numbered 55 monks, Newark and its dependent priory in Indianapolis, 28 (*Catalogus*, 156). In 1989 Newark accepted as a dependent priory Saint Maur in Indianapolis, which had been founded in 1947 and gained its independence in 1963. In 1995 it had 7 monks. Archives and interviews at Belmont, Morristown, and Newark; Pascal Baumstein, *My Lord of Belmont: A Biography of Leo Haid* (Belmont, NC: Belmont Abbey, 1985).

[5] The archives of the Louisiana sisters were very valuable when this writer search them in 1981 before the convent's dissolution.

[6] *Catalogus 2000*; interviews and/or archives of Benedictines in Boerne, Lisle, St. Joseph (MN), Tulsa, St. Paul, and Nauvoo. See also Rippinger, *The Benedictine Order in the United States* and Sutera, *True Daughters* on the juridical aspects of the American monastic foundations.

[7] Albert Kleber, *History of St. Meinrad Archabbey, 1854–1954* (St. Meinrad, IN: Grail Press, 1954) details the story of Einsiedeln (which the Swiss pronounce *Ine-seed-len*) and the Indiana foundations, 1–78. See also Rippinger's, *The Benedictine Order in the United States* and "The Swiss-American Congregation: A Centennial Survey" in *American Benedictine Review* 32:2 (June, 1981), 87–99.

[8] See Dunstan McAndrews, *Father Joseph Kundek, 1810–1857: A Missionary Priest of the Diocese of Vincennes* (St. Meinrad, IN: St. Meinrad Archabbey, 1954).

[9] Kleber, 30–31.

[10] Kleber, 31.

[11] Kleber, 34–43.

[12] Kleber, 44–47.

[13] Kleber, 47–69.

[14] Kleber, 69–76.

[15] Kleber, 98–104.

[16] Kleber, 98–104.

[17] Kleber, 122.

[18] The complex history of the interwoven relationships between the United States government, Protestant and Catholic missionary schools, and North American Indian tribes are well beyond the scope of this book. However, the regrettable indignities sometimes suffered by Native Americans at the hands of Christian missionaries must be addressed as a profoundly regrettable episode in the history of Christianity. While recognizing that American Christian missionaries were embedded in a cultural structure that influenced—or even determined—their attitudes and valorized their actions, admittance of the deleterious effects of aspects of American Indian Christianization is an essential step toward reconciliation. For divergent perspectives, see Joel Martin and Mark Nicholas, eds., *Native Americans, Christianity, and the Reshaping of the American Religious Landscape* (Chapel Hill: University of North Carolina Press, 2010); and George Tinker, *Missionary Conquest: The Gospel and Native American Cultural Genocide* (Minneapolis: Fortress Press, 1993).

[19] Kleber, 15–16. A popular biography written to celebrate the centennial of a monastery of nuns who trace their beginnings to Marty's influence is Robert Karolevitz, *Bishop Martin Marty: The Black Robe Lean Chief* (Yankton, SD: Sacred Heart Monastery, 1980). It is based on a scholarly study of Marty's career by Ildefons Betschart, *Der Apostel der Siouxindianer* (Einsiedeln: Benziger 1934), trans. Sister Stanislaus Van Well. The manuscript is in Sacred Heart Monastery Archives, Yankton. Marquette

University Archives, to which the Catholic Bureau of Indian Missions archives have been relocated, holds a great deal of material dealing with Marty's life among the Sioux. Karolevitz, Kleber, and Betschart all deal with the work of Martin Marty. See also Assenmacher's and Malone's histories of New Subiaco and Conception abbey. Einsiedeln, Saint Meinrad, Saint John's, and the Sisters of the Blessed Sacrament, Cornwall Heights, all have some of Marty's letters or copies and other documents in their archives. Marquette University archives have acquired the Catholic Indian Mission Bureau archival material including Marty's correspondence. Sister Ann Kessler, O.S.B., has used these sources in the chapter, "First Catholic Bishop of Dakota: Martin Marty, the Blackrobe Lean Chief," in *South Dakota Leaders*, ed. Herbert Hoover (Vermillion, SD: University of South Dakota Press, 1989), 107–125. Joel Rippinger's, "Martin Marty: Monk, Abbot, Missionary and Bishop," I and II, *American Benedictine Review* (*ABR*) 33, no. 3 (September 1982): 223–240 and 33, no. 4 (December 1982): 376–393, as well as his *The Benedictine Order in the United States* are good sources of Marty's life history.

[20] Rippinger, "Marty I," *ABR* 33, no. 3: 227–228.

[21] Betschart and Rippinger relate the request but do not include the rejection. It can be found in Fredericka Dudine, *The Castle on the Hill* (Milwaukee, WI: Bruce, 1967), 5–9.

[22] Betschart, trans. S. Stanislaus van Well, ms., 42–43.

[23] Marty to Father Gall, October 26, 1864, cited in Rippinger, *ABR* 33:3, 39; Karolevitz 51; Kleber, 213–219.

[24] Kleber, 267; Karolevitz, 63. Contemporary concern about the attitudes, goals, and activity of the early missionaries to North America continues to generate a significant body of popular and scholarly literature confronting the issues from varied perspectives. As an historical account, this chapter presents missionaries' viewpoints as they appear in original documentation and events. See n18 above.

[25] Kleber, 267–268. A great deal of the Marty-McMaster correspondence is available in Notre Dame's Catholic Church History Archives.

[26] American Indian theologian George E. Tinker discusses the often well-meaning intentions of missionaries while challenging the admittance of their mistakes. See his *Missionary Conquest*.

[27] "Das Apostolische Vikariat Dakota" in the Munchener Fremdenblatt, 1885, trans. Louis Pfaller, Assumption Abbey Archives, Richardton, ND.

[28] Karolevitz, 65.

[29] Louis Pfaller, *James McLaughlin: The Man with an Indian Heart* (New York: Vantage Press, 1978), 94–95; Kessler, *South Dakota Leaders* 115–117.

[30] Crazy Horse had died in September 1877.

[31] Pervasive loss of Native languages —sometimes imposed—later became an unfortunate result of missionary and government intervention.

[32] For one comprehensive educational history, see Jon Reyhner and Jeanne Eder, *American Indian Education: A History* (Norman: University of Oklahoma Press, 2004).

[33] Kessler, *South Dakota Leaders* 115–117.

[34] Karolevetz, 58–71. In a letter to Katherine Drexel (April 6, 1889) he suggested that she begin her new religious community, Sisters of the Blessed Sacrament, at a site near his See City, then Sioux Falls. In the same letter he expressed the hope that one day he could begin a "Benedictine community of fathers and brothers" in the same area (copy, Sacred Heart Monastery Archives, Yankton, SD. Saint John's Abbey archives

have some letters and documents, especially Marty's report card and naturalization papers. The over-zealous housekeeper is reported to have cleaned out too much of his archival material after his death in Saint Cloud. It is also argued that every time he moved—Yankton to Sioux Falls to Saint Cloud—he destroyed quantities of letters and other materials. Saint Meinrad Abbey archives has copies of Marty's letters in German script, written to and from Einsiedeln Abbey and a few personal ones in English which show some apparent condescension but also some warmth. See Kessler's earlier work on Marty in Hoover, ed., *South Dakota Leaders*, 115–118.

[35] The documents of Marty's major promotions and the Catholic newspapers he initiated to keep his priests and parishioners informed are in the Sioux Falls Cathedral Diocesan Archives, Sioux Falls, SD.

[35] Two communities of nuns reside (1992) in North Dakota—one at Richardton—previously at Garrison and Minot; and another in Bismarck. See Kominiak for the Assumption Abbey sketch.

[36] Kessler in Hoover, ed., *South Dakota Leaders*, 117–123. Marty's short term in Saint Cloud and his relationship with the first bishop there, Zardetti, are included in Vincent Yzermans, *Frontier Bishop of St. Cloud* (Waite Park, MN: Park Press, 1988).

CHAPTER 12
American Expansion and the Benedictines of Australia

[1] A manuscript copy translation of a life of Gertrude by Alexander J. Luetkemeyer, *Schwester Gertrude Leupi* (Kanisius Verlag) is in SHMAY. See also Claudia Duratschek, *Under the Shadow of His Wings* (Yankton, SD: Sacred Heart Monastery, 1971), which makes use of the same material in her history of the Yankton community. German Swiss biographies are also included in publications of Maria-Rickenbach's history, *Verschlossener Garten* (Stans: Paul von Matt, 1956); Ida Luthold-Minder, *Maria Rickenbach* (Sarnen: Landenberg, 1968); the collectively authored *Benediktinerinnen von Maria Rickenbach* (Niederrickenbach, Schweiz: Kloster der Benediktinerinnen Maria Rickenbach, 2003); Konstantin Dopinger, *Maria Rickenbach: Kurze Wallfahrtsgeschichte* (Stans: Paul von Matt, 1946); and Anita Baumann and Beatrix Thum, ed., *Schweizer Benediktinerinnen* (Einsiedeln: Benziger, 1980).

[2] *Verschlossener Garten.*

[3] "Statutes 1866," translated, ms. handwritten copy in Sacred Heart Monastery Archives Yankton (SHMAY).

[4] "Statutes 1866." One modern monk argues this kind of separation is a misinterpretation of Benedictine tradition, Matthias Neuman, "The Creative Charism of Benedictine Monasticism: A Reply to Francis Mannion," *ABR* 46:3 (September 1995), 254–270.

[5] "Statutes 1866," SHMAY.

[6] "Statutes 1866," SHMAY.

[7] See Edward E. Malone, *Conception* (Omaha, NE: Interstate Publishing Co., 1971), 1–54. Conception Abbey archives has the correspondence between Placid Wolter and Frowin Conrad.

[8] Malone, 65.

[9] Malone, 41, 62–69. In 1909 a monk was sent from Oklahoma to "hear the execution of the Gregorian Chant" at Conception, and a monk was requested to go to

Oklahoma from Conception to instruct the members there in the rendition of the chant (Abbot Leo to Abbot Frowin, Sec 23, 1909, Conception Abbey Archives).

[10] Malone, 78.

[11] Malone, 83.

[12] Malone, 83.

[13] The Swiss abbot won the case in point about the sisters' prayers, though eventually the Little Office or the Exercises of Saint Gertrude became the norm for the Swiss-founded convents until the full Latin monastic Divine Office was adopted. It would be revised into English and abbreviated into morning, noon, and evening prayers at most houses of the union called the Federation of Saint Gertrude, most of whom traced their ancestry to Switzerland. For the history of the Federation see Jane Klimisch, *Women Gathering: The Story of the Federation of St. Gertrude* (Toronto: Peregrina, 1993).

[14] Duratschek, 63.

[15] Beatrix Renggle, Jonesboro, to Sister Stanislaus Van Well, 1934, SHMAY; Chronicles, SHMAY. Eventually the Yankton nuns acquired a house across the road from the Einsiedeln abbey (Marienheim) as a base to recruit European candidates and prepare them while they operated a hostel for the American mission. It was sold in 1935; its proceeds helped build Mount Marty College. See Sister Ann Kessler's "Founded on Courage, Inspired with Vision: Mount Marty College," in Hoover, ed., *From Idea to Institution*, (Vermillion, SD: University of South Dakota Press, 1989), 193–203). See Kessler and Susan Peterson, "Valiant Religious Women: Mothers Superior Joseph Butler, Raphael McCarthy, and Jerome Schmitt" in Hoover, ed., *South Dakota Leaders*, 125–143 for more of the Yankton history under Mother Jerome Schmitt and the Aberdeen Presentations, originally brought to the Dakotas by Marty. Since the revision of Canon Law, the Yankton and some of the other Saint Gertrude Federation houses (now under papal jurisdiction) no longer distinguish between simple and solemn vows; they have also changed their titles from "convent" to "monastery" to recall their monastic Benedictine heritage.

[16] See Dolores Dowling, *In Your Midst* (1988).

[17] Hugh Assenmacher, *A Place Called Subiaco: A History of the Benedictine Monks in Arkansas*, tells the story of the foundation and its subsequent history. The "paradise" quote is on p. 12.

[18] Archives, Saint Bernard's Abbey and Sacred Heart Convent, Cullman; Kominiak, 434.

[19] Belmont Abbey archives and interviews at Belmont. See the archival history by Paschal Baumstein, *My Lord of Belmont: A Biography of Leo Haid*, Belmont, NC: Belmont Abbey, 1985.

[20] Interviews and archives at Covington and Saint Benedict, Louisiana (Saint Scholastica's and Saint Joseph's) February 15–28, 1981; Kominiak, 436–437. Covington had closed by 1988. After over twelve years without novices, the nuns eventually transferred to other communities.

[21] Joseph Murphy, *Tenacious Monks: Oklahoma Benedictines 1875–1975* (Shawnee, OK: Benedictine College, 1974); Archives and interviews, Tulsa, 1981.

[22] Ullathorne's autobiography has been reprinted: *From Cabin Boy to Archbishop: The Autobiography of Archbishop Ullathorne* (London: Burns Oates, 1941). Cuthbert Butler, *Life and Times of Bishop Ullathorne, 1806–1889* (London: Burns, Oates & Washbourne, 1926) is another early source for Ullathorne and Polding. General sources

include Cardinal Moran's *History of the Catholic Church in Australasia* (Sydney, n.d.) published late in the nineteenth century.

[23] Most of these were sold by him later to his successor, Archbishop Polding. See Frank Carleton, "Monastic Books: The Sydney Benedictine Collection," *Tjurunga* 44 (May 1993): 87–91.

[24] Patrick O'Farrell, *The Catholic Church and Community in Australia: A History* (West Melbourne: Thomas Nelson, 1977), 19. Convicts had formerly been taken to the American colonies as indentured servants, but after 1776, a new place of exile had to be found.

[25] For a comprehensive history of Australia see F. Clarke, *The History of Australia* (Westport, CT: Greenwood Press, 2002).

[26] Butler, 31–37; Henry Norbert Birt, *Benedictine Pioneers in Australia* (Melbourne: Polding Press, 1970), 168–169. See the Australasian Benedictine Review, *Tjurunga*, for several articles on Ullathorne, Polding, the Good Samaritan Sisters, and the Cistercians. Therry's biography was written by Eric M. O'Brien, *Life and Letters of Archpriest John Joseph Therry, Founder of the Catholic Church in Australia* (Sydney, 1922). The writer, Birt, is the subject of a controversy explored in *Tjurunga* 47 (December 1994): 45–62, by Sylvestrine Terence Kavenagh.

[27] The present Cathedral of St. Mary's in Sydney replaced the first Saint Mary's, which was destroyed by fire in 1865. A stone column outside the eastern door is all that remains of the building. A historical window in the Cathedral commemorates the laying of the foundation stone by Governor Macquarie in 1821. Polding is commemorated in another historical window. Archbishop Vaughan, also Benedictine, dedicated the new cathedral in 1882 and is commemorated in a historical window. The Cathedral was completed in 1928.

[28] See Frances O'Donohue, *The Bishop of Botany Bay: The Life of John Bede Polding, Australia's First Catholic Archbishop* (Sydney, 1982); Butler, 48–50; Birt, 180–187.

[29] Butler, 51.

[30] O'Farrell, 44; Butler, 61; Terence Kavenagh, "Aspects of Monastic Observance at Old St. Mary's," *Tjurunga*, 27, 59–78. Polding returned to Sydney in February 1856 from a lengthy stay in Europe with new constitutions for his community approved by Rome. Earlier "Rules" had been approved by Pius IX in 1847, although monks had lived community life since 1843 when Polding clothed the first five novices. Ten monks professed vows in 1845. See Graeme Walker and Terence Kavenagh, "The 1855 Monastic Declarations of St. Mary's, Sydney: Adapting 'RB' to Colonial Australia?," *Tjurunga* 34: 65–74; *Tjurunga* 35: 44–80; *Tjurunga* 36: 73–80; *Tjurunga* 37: 80–87; *Tjurunga* 38: 88–96; *Tjurunga* 39: 114–126. Kavenagh also gives us a portrait of a feisty Dublin-born monk who survived even the closing of Lyndhurst in 1877 ("Michael Jerome Duffy, The Last Brother of Old St. Mary's," *Tjurunga* 31: 79–80).

[31] In six issues of *Tjurunga*, vols. 34–39 (May 1988 to September 1990), Kavenagh and Walker discuss "The 1855 Monastic Declarations of St Mary's, Sydney: Adapting 'RB' to Colonial Australia?" They finish this series, which includes a great deal of other documentation, with the statement, "Unfortunately, it seems clear that, in the end, the enormous amount of time and skill which had been invested in the St. Mary's Declarations, produced nothing of lasting significance."

[32] O'Farrell, 44–80, 90–172.

[33] Frank Carleton, "Roger Bede Vaughan OSB, Archbishop of Sydney: Some Private Papers and a Book," *Tjurunga* 47 (December 1994): 63–73 and "Some Archives

of Benedictine Provenance at St. Mary's Sydney" 37: 62–77.

[34] Biographies of Salvado and Torres are available. Among them are *The Salvado Memoirs,* reprinted by the University of Western Australia Press in 1978; the *Torres Diaries* edited by Rosemary Pratt and Dr. John Millinton (Perth: Artlook Books, 1986) and George Russo, *The Life and Times of Bishop Salvado.* The New Norcia archives were mined by the writer in 1988, with the generous assistance of a committed lay archivist, Tony James. Holy Trinity Abbey's Prior Administrator from Ampleforth (Placid Spearritt) was elected its abbot in 1997. The Benedictines of Australia, monks and nuns, are members of the Benedictine Union of Australia and New Zealand.

[35] Felice Vaggioli, *History of New Zealand and Its Inhabitants,* trans. J. Crockett (Dunedin, New Zealand: University of Otago Press, 2000).

[36] Birt, 399–401.

[37] Sister Gregory Forster was one of the founding nuns. The nuns' history is related in a series of articles in *Tjurunga* 29–32 (1985–1987) by Marie-Thérèse Malone, O.S.B., "An Obit List and Brief History of the Nuns of 'Subiaco': Rydalmere, and the Benedictine Abbey, Pennant Hills."

[38] Marilyn Kelleher, *Annals of the Sisters of the Good Samaritan of the Order of Saint Benedict,* Vol. 1–3 (Australia: Sisters of the Good Samaritan, n.d.).

[39] The early history of the nuns is the 137-page publication by S. Dominica McEwan, S.G.S., *A Living Stream: Resource Book, Sisters of the Good Samaritan, 1857–1924* (Glebe Point, N.S.W.: Good Samaritan Generalate) and "The Growth of a Religious Institute: Some Lists and Statistics Relating to the History of the Good Samaritan Sisters O.S.B., 1857–1937"—a historical overview by Marie Gerard McGlynn SGS, *Tjurunga* 39: 90–111. Another *Tjurunga* article deals with the nuns and Polding's relationships with them (Moira M. K. O'Sullivan, "Religious in Polding's Sydney Early Connections between the Benedictine Nuns and the Sisters of Charity" (November 2001): 45–77. A centennial story was written anonymously in 1957, *The Wheeling Years: The Sisters of the Good Samaritan* (Sydney: Sisters of the Good Samaritan, 1956). The most recent history is by Margaret Walsh, *The Good Sims: Sisters of the Good Samaritan 1857–1969* (Mulgrave: John Garrett, 2001). These nuns affiliated with the Benedictine Federation in 1975. They are listed in the *Catalogus* as *sorores* (non-cloistered). See their vision statement and the report of their 1993 chapter in *Tjurunga* 45, "Ngirramini": 94–96, and "The Good Samaritan Contribution to Catholic Education" *Tjurunga* 29: 26–36. For one of their mission stories see Sonia Wagner, "Good Samaritan Life and Mission in Kiribati Celebrates Ten Years," *AM Bulletin* 74 (2002): 80–81.

CHAPTER 13
Benedictines Face Challenges in the Modern Era

[1] *Journal Officiel,* July 2, 1901, 4025–4027, cited hereafter as *J.O.* This is the French equivalent of the U.S. *Congressional Record.*

[2] July 3, 1901. *Le Temps* (The Times) probably had the largest circulation among Parisian newspapers.

[3] "Le Rappel du Nonce," Unsigned memorandum, July 5, 1901, F19.6268 (Archives Nationales, Paris, cited hereafter as A. N.).

[4] "Le Pape et les Congrégations," *Semaine Religieuse du diocèse d'Angers,* July 14, 1901, 748–753. *Le Temps* printed the letter on July 7.

412 Notes to Chapter 13

La Croix, July 9, 1901. Dom Boniface Natter of Buckfast Abbey wrote from Rome to the Abbot of d'En Calcat (September 2, 1901) that the Holy See was insisting the monks retain their exemption from episcopal control. Confusion reigned because at the same time he confirmed his earlier correspondence from Subiaco (August 1 & 28) that they felt that the pope favored application for authorization (d'En Calcat Abbey Archives, Natter Corr. DD1603, 1904, 1605).

[6] The letter was published in the *Semaine Religieuse du diocèse d'Angers*, July 21, 1901, 7791–7792.

[7] Memorandum, St. Pierre, Solesmes Abbey Archives; Savaton, 206.

[8] The Solesmes archives indicate that Delatte was the author. *La Vérité Française* printed the long "Examen" in three parts, July 24, August 7 and August 23. These were later reprinted at Solesmes in a sixteen-page booklet and sold at quantity prices. The *Journal de Sablé* (August 11, 1901) printed a large section of it. It was widely debated in the Catholic and public press.

[9] *Le Figaro*, September 29, 1901; *Le Soleil*, September 30, 1901; *Journal des Débats*, October 6, 1901; *Le Temps*, October 1, 1901. The Premier's instruction to the prefects is in A.N. F19.6268. The Carthusians requested authorization, but the application was rejected and the monks exiled. Many Benedictine houses, especially of nuns, did seek authorization. Justine Redmond, *Laicism in the Schools of France* (Washington, DC: Catholic University of America Press, 1932) imprecisely states, "it is to the glory of the Benedictines that rather than seek legal authorization they chose exile and dispersion." She could mean only the Solesmes Congregation of monks and nuns and a few others.

[10] See the *Bibliographie de Bénédictins de Congrégation de France* (Paris, 1906), and *Semaine Religieuse de Paris*, February 22, 1902, 484–485.

[11] *Journal Flêchois*, June 26, 1901.

[12] *Le Matin*, August 21, 1901, devoted three columns to pictures and text. *Le Figaro*, August 29, 1901, and *La Vérité Française*, September 4, 1901, also had lengthy features.

[13] St. Pierre Abbey Archives, St. Cécile Abbey Archives, Solesmes. The letters were noted or published in the *Journal de Sablé*, September 8, 1901; *Journal des Débats*, September 14, 1901; *Gazette de France* September 14, 1901.

[14] Detailed (and sometimes very sentimental) reports of these departures occurred in *Le Figaro*, September 19; *La Libre Parole*, September 18; and *Le Matin*, September 18, 1901, as well as most of the other Parisian and some local newspapers. Although the newspaper reports all estimated the numbers a bit differently, some counted thousands, a nobleman writing to his son, a monk already in England, told him that 500 train platform tickets had been sold (Memorandum, Archives St. Pierre, Solesmes). Dom Hubert Van Zeller (*The Benedictine Idea*, London, 1959, 192) erroneously reports that the departures took place in 1903.

[15] There was no objection to their appearance in habits outside the monasteries, but children often found it irresistible to refrain from transposing the new term, "monks," to "monkeys." This and the royal visits are recorded in the archives, St. Pierre, Solesmes. The *Gazette de France* published a series by Joseph Thirion (January 15, 22, 29, February 5, 1902) about the French religious in England ("Les Religieux Français sur la terre d'exil"). London's *Daily Mail* (April 1, 1904) explained to its readers the meaning of the monastic life and included a discussion of the liturgical chant and a line of music—the solemn "Ite missa est" under the headline "Island Exiles: The Strange Tenants of an English Country House." Both Quarr and the Ryde abbeys are both still

on the Island over a century later.

[16] Correspondence of Wehrle to Picot of the Academy, Paris, July 14, 1901 (Abbey archives, Ligugé); *Journal de l'Ouest*, July 30, 1901; *Echo de Paris*, September 26, 1901.

[17] In 1920 Dom Besse founded the Missionary Benedictines of St. Bathilde, a group of Sisters at Vanves, a Paris suburb (Interview, Vanves).

[18] Dom Besse (1861–1920), who had already published six volumes on abbeys and priories of medieval France received the Prix du Baron de Courcel award of 2400 francs in 1907 for his publication, *Les Moines de l'ancienne France*.

[19] *Le Courrier de la Vienne et des Deux Svrèes*, September 19, 1901.

[20] *Gazette de France*, November 20, 1901; Archives: L'Abbaye Saint-Maurice-et-Saint-Maur de Clervaux (Luxembourg, 1961). The abbot's letter and posters marketing the wine are among the treasures in the archives. The writer was fortunate to be able to interview Frère Joseph Plumejeau (1877–1963) at Clervaux two years before his death—then still able to discuss at length the history of the abbey. Abbot Henri-de-Sainte-Marie was also generous with his time there and later in Rome in 1982 where he was prior at the house of biblical studies. He died in 1989.

[21] *Progrès Catholique de Namur*, September 8, 1901; "Annales," Archives, St. Michel Abbey, Kergonan; Interviews, St. Michel, St. Anne Abbeys.

[22] Émile Combes, *Mon Ministère: Memoires, 1902–1905* (Paris, 1956), iii–iv, xiv, 22ff.

[23] The speeches, legislation, and ministerial decrees are in two volumes: Emile Combes, *Une Campagne Laïque, 1902–1903* (Paris, 1904) and *Une deuxième Campagne laïque: Vers la Séparation* (Paris, 1905). A biography of Combes was published in Paris already in 1904 (Geraud-Bastet, *Monsieur Combes et les siens*). Waldeck-Rousseau had never applied the law to schools; none were closed during his ministry. The Combes decree was written into formal law, December 4, 1902 (*J.O.*, December 5, 1902, 7901).

[24] A.N. F19.6082, 6085 and 6087 files include scores of these protests signed by officials and indignant parents. In files F19.6079 are ministerial reports from the Prefect of Finistère who described in detail the manifestations of support for the schools and the religious teachers in his department. The Pradines Abbey archivist (1961) informed the writer that her father, an army officer, left military service because he could not in conscience take part in the evictions of the nuns.

[25] The letters of Cardinal Richard and his bishops to the President of the Republic on July 19 are in A. N. F1.6275.

[26] The full name was the *Rapport de M. Fernand Rabier* (Paris, 1903) cited hereafter as *Rapport Rabier*. The 389-page publication includes 100 devoted to the discussions in the Chamber (*J.O.*, January 21, 1901) when the Law of Associations was debated. Statistics about each congregation were listed and so were adverse reports from the prefects. *Le Temps* (March 12, 1903) noted a glaring error that challenged that the Benedictines of Soulac—a dentifrice trademark—were not categorized as commercial. The paper printed the letter from the mayor of Soulac to Brisson, the writer of the preface, informing him that the congregation was non-existent. The dentifrice factory was owned by a widow whose husband had purchased the trademark from Olivetan Benedictines about 1867.

[29] Minister for Religious Affairs to Superiors, April 1903; A.N. F19. 6268; *Liberal de l'Yonne* (Sens), April 4, 1903.

[30] A.N. F19. 6270.

[31] *Rapport Rabier,* 292–293.

[32] In 1904, according to a memo, "Religieux vivante hors de la Communaute," in the Belloc Abbey archives, there were 18 priests and 10 brothers who were not in the Spanish exile. Two were in military service (monks were not exempt), three still cared for the sick in the home for the aged at Saint-Leon, and several had returned to their families. The Lazkao monastery became an independent priory in 1943 when it aggregated to the Spanish Province of Subiaco. In 1967 it was elevated to an abbey. Some monks returned to Belloc when feasible and continued monastic life there also. In 1990 Lazkao had a dozen Spanish monks, Belloc about 40—with mixed nationalities—French, Spanish, African, and native Basque (*Catalogus 2000,* 216–217).

[33] D'En Calcat Abbey archives.

[34] D'En Calcat Abbey archives.

[35] Interviews and archives, Landévennec Abbey. From July 1954 through April 1956, historians of Landévennec Abbey (the former Kerbénéat community) published their history "Petite histoire de Kerbénéat," in a series of articles in *Pax,* their community's scholarly bulletin.

[36] When the monks left France, the farmers had no markets for their milk, so they sold most of their cows (*Pax,* July 1954, 14, Archives Landévennec).

[37] *Le Temps,* April 26, 1903; *Liberal de l'Yonne,* April 28, 1903; *Pax,* July 1954, 15–17, Landévennec Abbey archives.

[38] Procès-verbaux. "Extraits des Annales de Buckfast Abbey," Landévennec Abbey archives.

[39] Jules Joachim, *Histoire du Collège Saint-Benoît à Delle, 1875–1906* (n.p., n.d.), 49–53; interview, Paul Keller, Mariastein Abbey.

[40] A.N. F19.6270 includes lists on which the English Benedictine abbey appears, and the Chamber of Deputies report; *Le Temps* April 4 and 8, 1903, notes the process as does the brief community history, *Douai Abbey.* The Commission's "report" is in *Rabier,* 148.

[41] A.N. F19.6271, 6272. Dom Grégoire is listed with the Belloc community members in the *Catalogus,* 1905, 1910, and 1920. Another circular (undated but "1902" is written in the margin) from the Department of Justice to the *procureurs generaux* reported the legalistic subterfuges the religious might use to gain access to the diocesan ranks and added those the officials could resort to in return (A.N. BB30.1614). R. P. [Edouard] Lecanuet (*L'Eglise de France sous la Troisième République,* Paris: Félix Alcan, 1930, I, 306 n.1) mentions two Benedictine monks who were in the diocese, but were forbidden by the bishop to celebrate Mass. They were monks of Solesmes (Maurice Noetinger and R. de la Messeliere) who were not seeking diocesan incardination, but were there for business purposes. The bishop asked that they refrain from wearing their habits in their diocese.

[42] A. N. F19.6272. Archives and interviews, Belloc Abbey. Claudeville's name does not appear in the Catalogus after 1905.

[43] A.N. F19.6214; A. Debidour, *L'Eglise catholique et l'Etat sous la Troisième République, 1870–1906* (Paris: Félix Alcan, 1909), vol. II, 383. *Le Temps,* January 13, 1904, chided the premier for his preoccupation with the religious orders. In a report of his speech before the Committee of Commerce and Industry the paper commented that his treatment of the financial and international situation concerned "problems that had not been discussed for a long time."

[44] Debidour II: 383–385; Jacques Chastenet, *Histoire de la Troisième République*,III, 239–240; A.Boulenger, *Histoire générale de l'Eglise* (Paris: Emmanuel Vitte, 1950), vol. IX, 360; A.N. F19.6275.

[45] Debidour, II:387; A.N. F19.6275.

[46] Debidour II:387. The debates are in *J.O.* March to July 1904 and the signing is noted July 8, 4129–4130.

[47] The entire bill is printed in *J.O.* July 8, 1904, 4129–4130.

[48] Benedictines were listed especially on July 9–11, 1904, January 18, May 4, and July 11, 1905. A. N. F196214 includes documentation concerning the instructions to the prefects to enclose reports of the notification and accounts of any incidents relative to the dissolutions.

[49] *J.O.*, January 2–3, 1905; *Conseil d'Etat*, No. 1402, January 7, 1905; A.N. F19.6214.

[50] A. N. F19.6268; *Le Temps*, November 9, 1901; Memorandum, Jouarre Abbey archives.

[51] For the full history of the community see Y. Chaussy and others, *L'Abbaye Royale: Notre-Dame de Jouarre* (Paris: Editions Guy Victor, 1961).

[52] Pradines Abbey archives.

[53] Pradines Abbey archives.

[54] Chambre des Députés. No. 3556, Annexe au procès-verbal de la 2e séance du 17 fevrier, 1914, p. 13; A.N. F19.6268; Pradines Abbey archives. These archives have several files of copies of the correspondence between the nuns and their Parisian benefactresses, Sister Felicité's correspondence with her "bien cher Cousin" in the Chamber of Deputies, and the letters from the deputies and senator to the abbess assuring her of their efforts on the monastery's behalf.

[55] Chantelle Abbey archives.

[56] Annales, 1901, LaRochette Abbey archives; interview (1961) with Madame l'Abbesse Bernard Lepine of Saint-Marie de Maumont (Juignac) where the abbey of St. Jean was transferred in 1959. Fire destroyed most of their archives.

[57] Minister for Religious Affairs to Superior, Mère Stanislaus Kostka, August 23, 1904, Priory archives, rue Tournefort, Paris (1961). The story of this Perpetual Adoration priory was gleaned wholly from the monastery's archives.

[58] Their story is told briefly in *Les Bénédictines de la rue Monsieur*. The nineteenth century authorization is in the *Bulletin des Lois*, no. 863, Loi 9688, 409. *Le Matin*, August 11, 1904 reports the early moves against liquidation. The Limon Abbey archives are a legal gold mine with documentation and correspondence detailing the decades of court battles. Of special note is the letter of Combes to the Superior, February 13, 1905. It appears that heirs of some of the donors of the Parisian property were keeping the court battle going in order to claim their "shares" under the 1904 law.

[59] "Annales," and correspondence, Craon Priory archives; *Gazette de Chateau-Gontier* (Mayenne), July 28, 1904.

[60] *J.O.*, July 4, 1914, 5850; "Annales," Craon Priory archives. *L'Autorité*, July 1, 1914, listed the dissolved communities under the headline, "La dernière charrette" and referred to the "guillotine seche" (the dry guillotine) when deriding this belated move against the communities.

[61] The community returned to Breda itself in 1922 to make a foundation that transferred to Baarle-Nassau in the same diocese in 1989. Other daughterhouses were

founded in the Netherlands in Valkenburg in 1942 and at Heesch in 1952. In 1960 they began a mission in Uganda, which became an independent priory in Tororo in 1966. (Interview, Father C. Damen at St. Paul's Abbey, Oosterhout; *Catalogus* 2000.) The nuns from Toulouse who had gone to Spain returned to France in 1921 where twenty-four nuns occupy a priory at Mas-Grenier (Interviews and archives, Mas-Grenier).

⁶² "Annales," Tourcoing Priory archives.

⁶³ Turcoing Priory archives. *Catalogus 2000* did not list a house at Turcoing.

⁶⁴ The "supposed" proprietorship is indicated in the report of the Superintendent of Police from the Ville de Millan, July 15, 1904 (A.N. F19.7935). According to the ministry's list of personnel (A.N. F19.7935) there were thirty-six nuns at the priory. The archivists reported that there were actually forty-two (interviews and archives, Notre Dame d'Orient).

⁶⁵ The monastic archives were destroyed in the battle for Caen in WWII. In the Archives Nationales only one script note mentions the community at this time (A.N. F19.6268). There is a note in the margin, "pas de liquidation" (no liquidation).

⁶⁶ A. N. F19.7980.

⁶⁷ *J.O.*, July 10, 1904, p. 4180; *Procès-Verbal*, No. 175, July 12, 1904; "Congrégations religieuses, loi du 1er Juillet, 1901," "Bénédictines du Saint-Desir de Lisieux," Archives Departmentales du Calvados, Caen. The Lisieux monastery archives were incinerated and twenty nuns lost their lives during the Allied invasion of Normandy in World War II (Interviews, Lisieux).

⁶⁸ "Annales de Flavigny," Archives, Poyanne abbey (where the Flavigny nuns eventually moved).

⁶⁹ *Le Liberal*, November 13, 1904; News clippings and "Annales de Flavigny," Archives Poyanne.

⁷⁰ *Le Temps*, January 10, 1901; *Le Matin*, April 6, 1910; A.N. BB30.1614.

⁷¹ Alfred F. Schnepp, "The Decline of French Anticlericalism," *Catholic World*, March 1939, 664–667; E.E.Y. Hales, *The Catholic Church in the Modern World* (Garden City NY, 1958), 249.

⁷² Jules A. Baisnée, "The French Clergy in the War," *Catholic World*, March 1940, 660; Adrien Dansette, *Religious History of Modern France* (New York: Herder and Herder, 1961), II:331. According to Schnepp, p. 666, "Priests by the hundreds were in the trenches, not as chaplains, but as ordinary poilus. This is corroborated by most French historians contrary to popular American writers who claim that the priests were not combatants, but only hospital attendants. Teilhard de Chardin was a stretcher-bearer, not a combatant, but that was an exception.

⁷³ Dansette, II, 331–332. He also remarks, "their opportunities of performing their priestly functions and of exercising spiritual influence over the wounded were all too frequent." See also Charles L. Souvay, "The Church in Contemporary France," Chapter III of *The Catholic Church in Contemporary Europe, 1919–1931* (New York, 1932), 103.

⁷⁴ Adrien Dansette, "Contemporary French Catholicism," in Waldemar Gurian and M. A. Fitzsimmons eds., *The Catholic Church in World Affairs* (Notre Dame: University Press, 1954), 244.

⁷⁵ Dansette, II, 429; Dansette in *The Catholic Church in World Affairs*, 260.

⁷⁶ Landévennec Abbey archives; *Catalogus 1905, 1910, 1920, 1990*. *Catalogus 1920* listed thirteen monks so the secularizations were apparently still in process.

[77] Archives, St. Michel, Kergonan and Jouarre; *Catalogus* 1905, 1910, 1920.

[78] Reports of archivists, interviews and monastic archives—Erbalunga, Jouarre, and Mas-Grenier; and archives, Tourcoing and Notre-Dame-d'Orient; *Catalogus, 1905, 1910, 1920.*

[79] Auguste Rivet, *Traité des congrégations religieuses,* 1789–1943 (Paris: Editions Spes, 1944), 41; Dansette, II, 348.

[80] Rivet, 45, 333–334; 448–449; Dansette, II, 436. The missionary congregations authorized included the Christian Brothers, the nuns of the Child Jesus of Puy, the Marists, some Franciscans, and several groups dedicated to missions in Africa and the Levant (*J.O.,* Chambre des Députés, March 14, 1929, 979–983).

CHAPTER 14
Continuing Change and Contemporary Perspectives

[1] Father Agostino Saccomano, monk-survivor of the destruction, was interviewed by this writer at Monte Cassino in 1956 after a personal tour of much of the abbey undergoing rebuilding—areas restricted to monks and denied to tourists. He insisted that there were no Germans in the monastery itself when the Americans bombed it. He admitted, however, that they were dug in almost up to the top of the mountainside. In the inner courtyard were bomb cases unearthed during the reconstruction, which was then still in process. The WWII destruction is the subject of Fred Majdalany's *The Battle of Cassino* (Boston: Houghton Mifflin, 1957) and *The Monastery* (Boston: Houghton Mifflin, 1946). These record a British soldier's viewpoint. David Hapgood and David Richardson have another point of view in *Monte Cassino* (New York: Congdon and Weed, 1984). They also speak of the treasures the Germans failed to return. In the courtyard, the statue of St. Benedict stood tall and almost totally undamaged. That of St. Scholastica lost its head and has been replaced. The bombing also unearthed the tombs of Benedict and Scholastica, which have been reinterred behind the high altar. A concrete slab indicating Benedict's cell was also a quarried treasure. As the architectural plans were rescued before the bombing, the restoration was on the same lines—very baroque. Monks are still there to welcome tourists (and see that they are properly attired—even men are not permitted in shorts) and sell them souvenirs. While a popular tourist attraction, the clausura is always closed to outsiders.

[2] Second Vatican Council, *Perfectae Caritatis: The Decree on the Adaptation and Renewal of Religious Life* (1965), http://www.vatican.va/archive/hist_councils/ii_vatican_council/documents/vat-ii_decree_19651028_perfectae-caritatis_en.html.

[3] Leon Suenens, *The Nun in the World: New Dimensions in the Modern Apostolate,* trans. G. Stevens (London: Burns & Oates, 1963).

[4] Some Abbots of European as well as American monasteries shared their frustration with this writer as they recounted the problems involved in the transition from choir monks who recited the Office in Latin and lay brothers who recited the rosary generally at the same or different hours. The sharing of both groups at recreation periods and the placing of lay brothers in rank according to seniority made for some uncomfortable situations. Even in the 1990s, however, an abbot elected by his community had to be ordained before his installation if he was not yet a priest.

[5] An excellent analysis of the mission tradition, of joining the active with contemplative apostolate (the emphasis on *labora* as integrated with *ora*) is that of Matthias

Neuman, "The Creative Charism of Benedictine Monasticism: A Reply to Francis Mannion," *ABR*, 46, no. 3 (September 1995): 254–270. This article is integral for those who
seek to understand why the tradition of the active apostolate has been submerged into
the later medieval aspect and some present studies emphasizing only what has been
known as the "fuga mundi" (flight from the world) aspect of monasticism. Both active
and contemplative charisms are active in Benedictine communities. At the turn of the
twenty-first century, cloistered and semi-cloistered houses of Benedictine women live
worldwide, including European countries such as England, France, Spain, and Ireland.
Italy has more monasteries of cloistered Benedictine monastic women than any other
country—123 small communities at the turn of the twenty-first century. France houses
over forty cloistered monasteries, Great Britain and Poland, thirteen; the Netherlands,
six; and Switzerland eight. Malta, Luxembourg, and some countries of the former
Soviet Union and the Eastern Bloc struggle to maintain one or two. Four houses in
America are considered contemplative nuns by the Confederation: Regina Laudis, a
Jouarre foundation in Bethlehem, CT; its daughter-house Our Lady of the Rock on
Shaw Island, WA; and the Eichstätt foundation of Saint Walburga in Boulder, CO.
St. Emma in Greensburg, PA, began as a place of retirement for former nun domestic
workers at the Latrobe monastery of monks. Eleven of Africa's houses are contempla-
tive; three in Canada and one in Martinique, one on Saint Lucia in the Caribbean and
one in Mexico. In Latin America, there are five houses in Argentina, two in Brazil and
one in Uruguay. Australia has two houses, India, one, Jerusalem two, and one in the
Philippines and Sri Lanka.

⁶ See the first edition of this book for more detailed information about specific
congregations.

⁷ Interviews at Mineiros, 1982; Brazilian missionary Sisters at Atchison, 1984;
Blue Cloud Abbey and Federation newsletters. The Yankton Benedictines were in San
Pedro Carchá from 1965 until 1972.

⁸ Interview, Dom Dominique Hermant, at Bouaké, 1982.

⁹ Interviews at Seoul and Pusan (Busan), Korea, 1972, and with Korean stu-
dent-sisters, Mount Marty College, Yankton, SD, 1992–1994. See also n4.

¹⁰ Interview, Abbess Teresita at her Indian ashram, 1971. Later she recounted the
story of her years at the priory in "Benedictine Life in India: Notes on Community and
Leadership" (*Benedictines*, Spring-Summer, 1989: 12-21). Another article "A View from
India," *Benedictines* (Winter, 1993–1994): 74–80, is a publication of the paper she read
at the 1993 Symposium of Benedictine Women at Sant'Anselmo, Rome. The paper is a
brief and very clear encapsulation of the similarities between Hindu and Benedictine
spirituality. She calls India "the cradle of monasticism" (75). She is pictured in the
AIM Bulletin 74 (2002): 96, at Shanti Nilayam Abbey with four Burmese novices. Also,
Abbess Teresita to S. Pascaline Coff cited in *AIM Bulletin*.

¹¹ Interview, Bangalore Asirvanam, 1971. Le Saux is the subject of two *Tjurunga*
articles (31 and 32) "Abhishiktananda: The Benedictine Swami" by Robert A. Stephens.
There are many books by and about Dom Bede Griffiths. His autobiography is *The
Golden String* (Springfield, IL: Templegate, 1980). One of his earlier books is *Return
to the Center* (1976). When I visited him at his ashram in India, he gave me a tour and
even took me to see his own hermitage hut, a rare privilege. He then gave me two books
about the earlier missionaries who had called him to the Indian mission: *Swami Parama
Arubi Anandam: Fr. J. Monchanin, 1895-1957* (Tiruchirappalli, 1958) and Monchanin

and Dom Henri Le Saux, O.S.B., *A Benedictine Ashram* (Douglas, England: Times Press, 1964). Like Matteo Ricci, honored with the title, "the Wise Man from the West" who adapted Catholicism to Chinese culture, Dom Bede made every attempt to do the same. When I met him he was still wearing a Benedictine traditional cut habit of the saffron color of the local Buddhist Hindu monks, not black or white as the European and American monks are garbed. Unfortunately, it was not a universal effort. When I attended the Eucharistic liturgy in Bombay, the presider railed against any accommodation to the "pagan" culture in art, architecture, or whatever. As he and a layman transported me to the airport, and he continued speaking about his life and work, I could only reflect that I was in the presence of a saint.

[12] Interview, Dormition Abbey, 1982, Abu Gosh Monastery, 1982, and Emmanuel Monastery, Bethlehem, 1982.

[13] Archives and interviews, New Norcia Abbey, W. Australia, 1988.

[14] Archives and interviews, Good Samaritan Benedictines, Australia, 1988.

[15] Interview, Tyburn monastery, England, 1982.

[16] Interview at St. John's Abbey, July 3, 1995, where Abbot Primate Jerome was taking a brief respite from the Roman summer just three months before his death.

[17] Interview, Kylemore Abbey, Ireland, June 1982. Cloistered and semi-cloistered houses of Benedictine women can be found in such European countries as England, France, Spain, and Ireland, including the Irish Dames of Ypres who moved onto an estate in County Galway in 1920 after two centuries in Flanders.

[18] See also Margaret McGuinness, *Called to Serve: A History of Nuns in America* (New York: New York University Press, 2013).

[19] See the history of the American federations and congregations of women which have been published in various volumes since the 1930s. One of these is S. Jane Klimisch O.S.B., *Women Gathering: The Story of the Federation of St. Gertrude* (Toronto, Ontario: Peregrina Publishers, 1993).

[20] Ep. 48.2 CSEL34.138 AD 393: *"nec uestrum otium necessitatibus ecclesiae praeponatis."* Cited in Lawless, 60.

[21] 1 Cor 13:1 New Revised Standard Version: Catholic Edition.

[22] Thomas Merton, *Contemplation in a World of Action* (Garden City, NY: Doubleday, 1971).

[23] Esther de Waal's books and commentaries encourage laymen and women to live out, as much as possible, the monastic values as enunciated by Benedict. Another non-Catholic Oblate, Kathleen Norris, relates her spiritual journey toward lay monasticism in *Dakota: A Spiritual Geography* (New York: Ticknor and Fields, 1993) and *The Cloister Walk* (New York: Riverhead Books, 1996).

BIBLIOGRAPHY

Abelard, Peter. *Historia Calamitatum: The Story of My Misfortune*. Translated by Henry Adams Bellows. Saint Paul, MN: Thomas A. Boyd, 1922.

——— . *Yes and No: The Complete English Translation of Peter Abelard's Sic et Non*. Translated by Priscilla Throop. Charlotte, VT: MedievalMS, 2007.

Abelard, Peter and Héloïse. *The Letters and Other Writings*. Indianapolis: Hackett 2007.

Aberdeen, University of, "The St. Albans Psalter." Last modified 2003. https://www.abdn.ac.uk/stalbanspsalter/english/.

Acomb, Evelyn M. *The French Laic Laws (1875–1889)*. "Studies in History, Economics, and Public Law." No. 486. New York: Columbia University Press, 1941.

Ahern, Patrick H., ed. *Catholic Heritage in Minnesota, North Dakota, South Dakota*. St. Paul, MN: H. M. Smyth Co., 1964.

Albertson, C. *Anglo-Saxon Saints and Heroes*. New York: Fordham University Press, 1967.

Andress, David. *1789: The Threshold of the Modern Age*. New York: Farrar, Straus and Giroux, 2009.

Anson, Peter F. "Anglican Benedictines." *American Benedictine Review* 23, no. 1 (1971): 21–28.

——— . *The Religious Orders and Congregations of Great Britain and Ireland*. Worcester: Stanbrook Abbey, 1949.

Armstrong, Regis J., ed. *The Lady: Clare of Assisi: Early Documents*. New York: New City Press, 2006.

Aspenleiter, F. J. "Cluniac Women," *Historical Bulletin*, 24 (November, 1945): 9–10.

Assenmacher, Hugh. *A Place Called Subiaco: A History of the Benedictine Monks in Arkansas*. Little Rock, AR: Rose Publishing Co., 1977.

Athanasius. *The Life of Saint Antony*. Ancient Christian Writers. Westminster, MD: Newman Press, 1950.

Backes, Pia. *Her Days Unfolded*. Translated by Bernadine Michel. St. Benedict, OR: Benedictine Press, 1953.

Backus, Irena Dorota. *The Reception of the Church Fathers in the West: From the Carolingians to the Maurists*. New York: E. J. Brill, 1997.

Backhouse, Janet L. *The Lindisfarne Gospels*. Ithaca, NY: Cornell University Press, 1981.

Baker, Augustine David. *The Confessions of Venerable Father Augustine Baker, O.S.B.* New York: Benziger Bros., 1922.

Baker, Augustine. *Holy Wisdom*. Edited by Abbot Sweeney. London: 1948.

Baldwin, Summerfield. "Benedictine Historical Monographs." In *The Catholic Negotiation*. Washington, DC: St. Anselm's Priory, 1926.

Bamburger, John Eudes. "Introduction to Evagrius Ponticus' The Praktikos and Chapters on Prayer." In *Evagrius Ponticus' The Praktikos and Chapters on Prayer* 4, xxiii–xciv. Spencer, MA: Cistercian Publications, 1970.

Bannon, Edwin. *Refractory Men, Fanatical Women: Fidelity to Conscience During the French Revolution*. Leominster: Gracewing, 1992.

Bantoft, Arthur. "The Gascoigne Family and the Catholic Church in the 17th and 18th Centuries: Part 1. The Gascoigne Nuns at Cambrai and Paris." Barwick-in-Elmet Historical Society. Last modified March 2003. http://www.barwickinelmethistoricalsociety.com/6908.html.

Barnes, Timothy David. *Early Christian Hagiography and Roman History*. Tübingen: Mohr Siebeck, 2010.

Barrat, Alexandra. "Julian of Norwich and Her Children Today: Editions, Translations, and Versions of Her Revelations." In *Julian of Norwich's Legacy: Medieval Mysticism and Post-Medieval Reception*, edited by Sarah Salih and Denise Nowakowski Baker, 13–28. New York: Palgrave Macmillan, 2006.

Barrett, Michael. *The Scottish Monasteries of Old*. Edinburgh: Otto Schulze, 1913.

Barrow, G.W.S. *The Kingdom of the Scots*. New York: St Martin's Press, 1973.

Barry, Colman J. *A Sense of Place: Saint John's of Collegeville*. Collegeville, MN: Liturgical Press, 1987.

———. "Boniface Wimmer, Pioneer of American Benedictines." *Catholic Historical Review* 41 (1955): 272–288.

———. *Worship and Work*. St. Paul, MN: Central Publishing Co., 1956.

———. *The Catholic Church and German Americans*. Milwaukee, WI: Bruce Publishing Company, 1953.

———. *Upon These Rocks*. Collegeville, MN: St. John's Abbey Press, 1983.

Baska, Regina. *The Benedictine Congregation of St. Scholastica: Its Foundation and Development*. Washington, DC: Catholic University, 1935.

Baskerville, Geoffrey. *English Monks and the Suppression of the Monasteries*. London: Jonathan Cape, 1937.

———. "Married Clergy and Pensioned Religious in Norwicsh Diocese, 1555 Part II." English Historical Review 48, no. 190 (April 1933): 199–228.

Basil of Caesarea. *The Rule of St.s Basil in Latin and English: A Revised Critical Edition*. Rev. ed. Translated by Anna Silvas. Collegeville, MN: Liturgical Press, 2013.

Bateson, Mary. "Origin and Early History of Double Monasteries." *Transactions of the Royal Historical Society*, 13 (1899): 137–398.

Baudier, Roger. *The Catholic Church in Louisiana*. New Orleans: A.W. Hyatt, 1939.

Baumstein, Paschal. *My Lord of Belmont: A Biography of Leo Haid*. Belmont, NC: Belmont Abbey, 1985.

Beach, Peter and William Dunphy. *Benedictine and Moor: A Christian Adventure in Moslem Morocco*. New York: Holt, Rinehart, and Winston, 1960.

Beattie, Gordon, ed. *The Benedictine Yearbook 1981*. York, England: Ampleforth Abbey, 1981.

Beckman, Peter. *Kansas Monks: A History of St. Benedict's*. Atchison, KS: Abbey Student Press, 1957.

Bede. *History of the English Church and People*. Translated by Leo Sherley-Price. Baltimore, MD: Penguin, 1965.

Behrens, Lilian Boys. *Battle Abbey Under Thirty-Nine Kings*. London: St. Catherine Press, 1937.

Bellitto, Christopher M. *The General Councils: A History of the Twenty-One General Councils from Nicaea to Vatican II.* New York: Paulist Press, 2002.

Bellitto, Christopher M., Thomas M. Izbicki and Gerald Christianson, eds. *Introducing Nicholas of Cusa: A Guide to a Renaissance Man.* New York: Paulist Press, 2004.

Bellows, Henry Adams, ed. *The Story of My Misfortunes (Historia Calamitatum): The Autobiography of Peter Abélard.* Glencoe, IL: Free Press, 1958.

Benedict, Mary. *The Patriarch of German Missionaries: Father Stephen Raffeiner.* Collegeville, MN: St. John's University, 1940.

Benedictus. *The Altenburg Rule of St. Benedict: A 1505 High German Version Adapted for Nuns; Standard RSB Text Edition Annotated, Benedictine Abbey of Altenburg, Austria, Ms Ab 15 E 6, Fol. 119r–156v.* St. Ottilien: EOS Verlage, 1992.

Benedictine Nun of Regina Laudis, ed. *The Exercises of Saint Gertrude.* Westminster: Newman Press, 1956.

Benedictines of Stanbrook, eds. *Any Saint to Any Nun.* New York: P.J. Kennedy and Sons, 1946.

————. *In a Great Tradition: Tribute to Dame Laurentia McLachlan, Abbess of Stanbrook.* London: John Murray, 1956.

————, eds. *Letters from the Saints.* New York: Hawthorne Books, 1964.

Betschart, Father Ildefons, *Bishop Martin Marty, O.S.B., Apostle of the Sioux, 1834–1896.* Einsiedeln, Switzerland: Benziger, 1934. Translated by Sister M. Stanislaus Van Well. Sacred Heart Monastery Archives, Yankton, SD.

Bergkamp, Joseph Urban. *Dom Jean Mabillon, and the Benedictine Historical School of Saint-Maur.* Washington, DC: Catholic University of America Press, 1928.

Besse, J.M. and Société Mabillon, eds. *Archives De La France Monastique*: Abbaye Saint-Martin, 1907.

Bhattacharji, Santha , Dominic Mattos, Rowan Williams, et al. *Prayer and Thought in Monastic Tradition: Essays in Honour of Benedicta Ward SLG.* Edinburgh: T & T Clark, 2014.

Bieler, Ludwig. *The Life and Legend of St. Patrick: Problems of Modern Scholarship.* London: Burns Oates & Washburn, 1949.

Billy, Dennis Joseph, ed. *The Imitation of Christ: Thomas À Kempis: A Spiritual Commentary and Reader's Guide.* Notre Dame, IN: Christian Classics, 2005.

Birch, Una. *Secret Societies and the French Revolution.* London: John Lane, 1911.

Birt, Henry Norbert. *Benedictine Pioneers in Australia.* Melbourne, Australia: Polding Press, 1970.

Bishko, Charles Julian. *Spanish and Portuguese Monastic History, 600–1300.* London: Variorum Reprints, 1984.

Bisson, Thomas N. *The Crisis of the Twelfth Century: Power, Lordship, and the Origins of European Government.* Princeton, NJ: Princeton University Press, 2009.

de Blois, Georges. *A Benedictine of the Sixteenth Century (Blosius).* Translated by Lady Lovat. Dublin: M.H. Gill and Son, 1878.

Boggis, R.J.E. *A History of St. Augustine Monastery.* Canterbury: Cross & Jackman, 1901.

Bosworth, William. *Catholicism and Crisis in Modern France: French Catholic Groups at the Threshold of the Fifth Republic*. Princeton, NJ: Princeton University Press, 1962.

Boulding, Maria. *A Touch of God: Eight Monastic Journeys*. London: S.P.C.K., 1982.

Bowd, Stephen D. *Reform before the Reformation: Vincenzo Querini and the Religious Renaissance in Italy*. Boston: Brill, 2002.

———. "Knatchbull, Elizabeth (1584–1629)." In *Oxford Dictionary of National Biography*. Oxford: Oxford University Press, 2004.

Brann, Noel L. *Trithemius and Magical Theology: A Chapter in the Controversy over Occult Studies in Early Modern Europe*. Albany: State University of New York Press, 1999.

Brennan, Robert J. "Benedictines in Virginia." *American Benedictine Review* 23, no. 1 (1962): 25–40.

Brittain, Alfred. *Woman In all Ages and in all Countries*. Vol. 2 of *Roman Women*. Philadelphia, PA: George Barrie, 1907.

Brodhead, Jane M.N. *The Religious Persecution in France, 1900–1906*. London: Kegan, Paul, Trench, Trubner and Co., 1907.

Brooke, Christopher. *The Monastic World, 1000–1300*. New York: Random House, 1974.

Browne, G.F. *The Importance of Women in Anglo-Saxon Times*. Studies in Church History. New York: Macmillan, 1919.

Browne, Martin and Colmán N. Ó Clabaigh. *The Irish Benedictines: A History*. Blackrock, Co. Dublin: The Columba Press, 2005.

Bruneau, Marie-Florine. *Women Mystics Confront the Modern World: Marie De l'Incarnation (1599–1672) and Madame Guyon (1648–1717)*. Albany: State University of New York Press, 1998.

Bruun, Mette Birkedal. *The Cambridge Companion to the Cistercian Order*. Cambridge: Cambridge University Press, 2013.

Burne, Martin. "First Episcopal Abbot in America." *American Benedictine Review* 20, no. 4 (1969): 572–577.

Burrows, Aelred. *Ampleforth Abbey and College*. Norwich, England: Jarrold and Sons, 1978.

Burton, Janet E., and Karen Stöber, eds. *Monasteries and Society in the British Isles in the Later Middle Ages*. Rochester, NY: Boydell Press, 2008.

Burton, Katherine. *The Golden Door: The Life of Katherine Drexel*. New York: P.J. Kennedy & Sons, 1957.

Butler, E. Cuthbert. *Benedictine Monachism: Studies in Benedictine Life and Rule*. New York: Barnes and Noble, 1962.

———. "Dame Gertrude More." Review of *The Inner Life and the Writings of Dame Gertrude More*. 2 vols. London: Washbourne, 1910–1911.

———. *The Life and Times of Bishop Ullathorne, 1806–1889*. 2 vols. London: Burns, Oates, & Washburn, 1926.

Caesarius. *The Rule for Nuns of St. Caesarius of Arles*. Translated by Maria Caritas McCarthy. Washington, DC: Catholic University of America Press, 1960.

Campbell, Stephanie. *Chosen for Peace: The History of the Benedictine Sisters of Elizabeth, New Jersey.* Paterson, NJ: Saint Anthony Guild Press, 1968.

Camm, Bede. *A Benedictine Martyr in England: Being the Life and Times of the Venerable Servant of God, Dom John Roberts, O.S.B.* London: Bliss, Sands, 1897.

————. *Nine Martyr Monks: The Lives of the English Benedictine Martyrs Beatified in 1929.* London: Burns, Oates, & Washburn, 1931.

Capps, Walter. *The Monastic Impulse.* New York: Crossroad Publishing, 1983.

Carruthers, Mary J. and Jan M. Ziolkowski. *The Medieval Craft of Memory: An Anthology of Texts and Pictures.* Philadelphia, PA: University of Pennsylvania Press, 2002.

Cary-Elwes, Columba. *Monastic Renewal.* New York: Herder and Herder, 1967.

————. "Report from Africa." *American Benedictine Review* 20, no. 4 (1969): 578–582.

Cassian, John. *The Conferences.* Ancient Christian Writers, edited by Boniface Ramsey. New York: Paulist Press, 1997.

————. *The Institutes.* Ancient Christian Writers, edited by Boniface Ramsey. New York, NY: Newman Press, 2000.

Casper, Henry W. *History of the Catholic Church in Nebraska.* (Vol. II). Milwaukee, WI: Bruce Publishing Company, 1966.

Cassiodorus. *Cassiodorus: Institutions of Divine and Secular Learning and on the Soul.* Translated by James Halprin. Liverpool: Liverpool University Press, 2003.

Catalogus Monasteriorum O.S.B.: Monachorum. Edition 14. Rome: Centro Studi S. Anselmo, 2000.

Catalogus Monasteriorum O.S.B.: Sororum et monialium. Edition 1. Rome, Centro Studi S. Anselmo, 2000.

The Catholic Church in the United States of America. Vol. 3, *The Religious Communities of Women.* New York: Catholic Editing Co., 1914.

Chadwick, Owen. *John Cassian: A Study in Primitive Monasticism.* Cambridge: Cambridge University Press, 1950.

Chambers, P. Franklin. *Juliana of Norwich: An Introductory Appreciation and an Interpretative Anthology.* New York: Harper, 1955.

Champney, Elizabeth Williams. *Romance of the French Abbeys.* New York: Putnam's 1905.

Chapman, John. *Saint Benedict and the Sixth Century.* New York: Longman, Green, 1929.

Chardon, Charles-Mathias. *Histoire des sacrements, ou de la Manière dont ils ont été célébrés et administrés dans l'Église et de l'usage qu'on en a fait depuis le temps des apôtres jusqu'à présent, par le R. P. Dom C. Chardon.* Paris: G. Desprez, 1745.

Charlesworth, James H. "Research on the Historical Jesus Today: Jesus and the Pseudepigrapha, the Dead Sea Scrolls, the Nag Hammadi Codices, Josephus, and Archeology." In *The Historical Jesus,* edited by C.A. Evans, 355–374. New York: Routledge, 2004.

Chittister, Joan. *Wisdom Distilled from the Daily: Living the Rule of Saint Benedict Today.* San Francisco: Harper & Row, 1990.

————, ed. *Climb Along the Cutting Edge: An Analysis of Change in Religious Life.* New York: Paulist Press, 1977.

Chrodegang. *The Chrodegang Rules: The Rules for the Common Life of the Secular Clergy from the Eighth and Ninth Centuries.* Translated by Jerome Bertram. Burlington, VT: Ashgate, 2005.

Chrodegang, Saint, Bishop of Metz. *The Old English Version of the Enlarged Rule of Chrodegang Together with the Latin Original.* London: Paul, Trench, Trubner & Co., 1916.

Clark, James Midgley. *The Abbey of St. Gall as a Centre of Literature and Art.* Cambridge, England: The University Press, 1926.

Clark, James G. "Mare, Thomas De La (C. 1309–1396)." In *Oxford Dictionary of National Biography.* Oxford: Oxford University Press, 2004.

————. *The Benedictines in the Middle Ages.* Rochester, NY: Boydell Press, 2011.

————, ed. *The Religious Orders in Pre-Reformation England.* Rochester, NY: Boydell & Brewer, 2002.

————. *The Culture of Medieval English Monasticism.* Rochester, NY: Boydell Press, 2007.

Clarke, F. G. *The History of Australia.* Westport, CT: Greenwood Press, 2002.

Clover, V. Helen and Margaret T. Gibson, eds. *The Letters of Lanfranc, Archbishop of Canterbury.* New York: Oxford University Press, 1979.

Collett, Barry. *Italian Benedictine Scholars and the Reformation: The Congregation of Santa Giustina of Padua.* Oxford: Clarendon Press, 1985.

————, ed. *Female Monastic Life in Early Tudor England: With an Edition of Richard Fox's Translation of the Benedictine Rule for Women, 1517.* Burlington, VT: Ashgate, 2002.

Collins, John J. "The Site of Qumran and the Sectarian Communities in the Dead Sea Scrolls." In *The World of Jesus and the Early Church: Identity and Interpretation in Early Communities of Faith,* edited by Craig A. Evans, 9–22. Peabody, MA: Hendrickson Publishers, 2011.

Combe, Pierre. *The Restoration of Gregorian Chant: Solesmes and the Vatican Edition.* Washington, DC: Catholic University of America Press, 2003.

Conant, Kenneth John. *Carolingian and Romanesque Architecture, 800 to 1200.* Baltimore, MD: Penguin Books, 1959.

Connolly, R. Hugh, Justin McCann, and Augustine Baker. *Memorials of Father Augustine Baker and Other Documents Relating to the English Benedictines.* London: Catholic Record Society, 1933.

Constable, Giles. *The Abbey of Cluny: A Collection of Essays to Mark the Eleven-Hundredth Anniversary of Its Foundation.* Piscataway, NJ: Verlag/Transaction Publishers, 2010.

Corless, Roger. "The Androgynous Mysticism of Julian of Norwich." *Magistra: A Journal of Women's Spirituality in History* 1, no.1 (Summer 1995): 55–71.

Council, Second Vatican. *Perfectae Caritatis: The Decree on the Adaptation and Renewal of Religious Life.* Vatican website (1965). http://www.vatican.va/archive/hist_councils/ii_vatican_council/documents/vat-ii_decree_19651028_perfectae-caritatis_en.html.

Cousin, Patrice. *Précis D'histoire monastique*. Paris: Bloud & Gay, 1959.

Cowdrey, H.E.J. *The Cluniacs and the Gregorian Reform*, New York: Oxford University Press, 1970.

Cram, Ralph Adams. *The Great Thousand Years*. Francetown, NH: Marshall Jones, 1944.

Crean, John, Jr. "Benedict in Berlin: Another Feminine Voice." *Magistra: A Journal of Women's Spirituality in History* 1, no. 1 (Summer 1995): 172–190.

Cressy, Serenus, Justin McCann, and Peter Salvin. *The Life of Father Augustine Baker, O.S.B. (1575–1641)*. Vol. 20 of Salzburg English and American Studies. Salzburg: Universität Salzburg, Inst. f. Anglistik und Amerikanistik, 1997.

Craine, Renate. *Hildegard: Prophet of the Cosmic Christ*. New York: Crossroad, 1998.

Cruden, Stewart. *Scottish Abbeys: An Introduction to the Medieval Abbeys and Priories of Scotland*. Edinburgh: Her Majesty's Stationery Office, 1960.

Cummings, Charles. *Monastic Practices*. Kalamazoo, MI: Cistercian Publications, 1986.

Currier, Charles Warren. *History of Religious Orders*. New York: Murphy & McCarthy, 1894.

Curry, Anne. *The Hundred Years' War: 1337–1453*. Oxford: Osprey, 2002.

Daly, Lowrie J. *Benedictine Monasticism*. New York: Sheed and Ward, 1965.

Dansette, A. *Religious History of Modern France*. 2 vols. Translated by John Dingle. New York: Herder, 1961.

Davis, Natalie Zemon. *Society and Culture in Early Modern France: Eight Essays*. Stanford, CA: Stanford University Press, 1975.

Decarreaux, Jean. *Monks and Civilization: From the Barbarian Invasions to the Reign of Charlemagne*. Translated by Charlotte Haldane. Garden City, NY: Doubleday, 1964.

Dehey, Elinor Tong. *Religious Orders of Women in the United States*. Hammond, IN: W. B. Conkey Company, 1930.

De Vogüé, Adalbert. *Community and Abbot in the Rule of St. Benedict*. Translated by Charles Philipi. Kalamazoo, MI: Cistercian Publications, 1979.

———. *The Life of Saint Benedict*. Translated by Hilary Costello and Eoin de Bhaldraithe. Petersham, MA: St. Bede's Publications, 1993.

De Waal, Esther. *Seeking God: The Way of St. Benedict*. Collegeville, MN: Liturgical Press, 1984.

———. *Living with Contradiction: Reflection on the Rule of Benedict*. New York: Harper & Row, 1989.

Delatte, Paul-Henri. *The Rule of St. Benedict: A Commentary*. Translated by Justin McCann. Latrobe, P: Archabbey Press, 1959.

Deleloë, Jeanne. *Une mystique Bénédictine du XVIIe siècle, La Mère Jeanne Deleloë. vie, correspondance et communications spirituelles*. Bruges (Belgique): Desclée, De Brouwer et Cie, 1929.

Destree, Bruno. *The Benedictines*. Translated by a Benedictine of Princethorpe Priory. London: Burns, Oates, & Washburn, 1923.

Dickinson, J.C. *Monastic Life in Medieval England*. Westport, CT: Greenwood, 1961.

Dieker, Alberta. "Mechtild of Hackeborn: Song of Love." In *Medieval Women Monastics: Wisdom's Wellsprings*, edited by Miriam Schmitt and Linda Kulzer, 231–242. Collegeville, MN: Liturgical Press, 1996.

Dietz, Maribel. *Wandering Monks, Virgins, and Pilgrims: Ascetic Travel in the Mediterranean World, A.D. 300/800.* University Park, PA: Pennsylvania State University Press, 2005.

Doyle, William. *The Oxford History of the French Revolution.* New York: Oxford University Press, 2002.

Dowling, Dolores. *In Your Midst: The Story of the Benedictine Sisters of Perpetual Adoration.* Clyde, MO: Perpetual Adoration Convent, 1988.

Dressman, Aloysius. *Saint Leo Golden Jubilee, 1890–1940.* St. Leo, FL: Abbey Press, 1940.

Dreuille, Mayeul de. *From East to West: A History of Monasticism.* New York: Crossroad, 1999.

Dronke, Peter. *Abelard and Heloise in Medieval Testimonies.* Glasgow: The University of Glascow Press, 1976.

Duckett, Eleanor Shipley. *Alcuin, Friend of Charlemagne: His World and His Work.* New York: Macmillan, 1951

——— . *Anglo-Saxon Saints and Scholars.* Hamden, CT: Archon Books, 1967.

——— . *Carolingian Portraits: A Study in the Ninth Century.* Ann Arbor, MI: University of Michagan Press, 1962.

——— . *The Gateway to the Middle Ages.* New York: Macmillan, 1938.

——— . *Medieval Portraits from East and West.* Ann Arbor, MI: University of Michigan Press, 1972.

——— . *Saint Dunstan of Canterbury: A Study of Monastic Reform in the Tenth Century.* New York: W.W. Norton, 1955.

——— . *The Wandering Saints of the Early Middle Ages.* New York: W.W. Norton, 1964.

Dudine, M. Frederica. *The Castle on the Hill: Centennial History of the Convent of the Immaculate Conception, Ferdinand, Indiana: 1867–1967.* Milwaukee, WI: The Bruce Publishing Co., 1967.

Duffy, Eamon. *Saints & Sinners: A History of the Popes.* New Haven, CT: Yale University Press, 1997.

Duratschek, M. Claudia. *Crusading Along Sioux Trails.* St. Meinrad, IN: Grail, 1947.

——— . *Under the Shadow of His Wings.* Yankton, SD: Sacred Heart Monastery, 1971.

——— . *Builders of God's Kingdom: The History of the Catholic Church in SD.* Yankton, SD: Sacred Heart Convent, 1985.

Duratschek, M. Claudia, and Klimisch, M. Jane. *Travelers on the Way of Peace.* Yankton, SD: Sacred Heart Convent, 1955.

Dysinger, Luke. "Are We Contemplatives? What is Our Future? In *The Proceedings of the American Benedictine Academy Convention,* August 8-11, 1990, Yankton, SD, 49–58. Edited by Renee Branigan. Mott, ND: Eido Printing, 1991.

Dzikowicz, Justin. "Quiet Riddle: Monasticism for the Church of Tomorrow." In *The Proceedings of the American Benedictine Academy Convention,* August 8-11, 1990, Yankton, SD, 75–80. Edited by Renee Branigan. Mott, ND: Eido Printing, 1991.

Eaton, Robert Ormston. *The Benedictines of Colwich, 1829–1929.* London: Sands, 1929.

Eberle, Luke. "Hildebrand de Hemptinne: First Abbot Primate." *American Benedictine Review* 9, no. 3 (1958): 164–178.

——. *The Rule of the Master: Regula Magistri.* Kalamazoo, MI: Cistercian Publications, 1977.

Eckenstein, Lina. *Woman Under Monasticism.* Cambridge, England: University Press, 1896.

Egeria. *Diary of a Pilgrimage.* Translated by George E Gingras. Ancient Christian Writers 38. New York: Newman Press, 1970.

Egler, Raymond Othmar. *St. Benedict's Rule Adapted to American Conditions.* Notre Dame, IN: University of Notre Dame Press, 1936.

Elisabeth of Schönau. *Elisabeth of Schönau: The Complete Works; Translated and Introduced by Anne L. Clark; Preface by Barbara Newman.* Translated by Anne L. Clark. Classics of Western Spirituality. New York: Paulist Press, 2000.

Ellis, Thomas Peter. *The Welsh Benedictines of the Terror.* Newton, GB: Welsh Outlook, 1936.

Ellspermann, Gerard, trans. *Saint Walburga: Her Life and Heritage.* 2nd ed., rev. Eichstätt, Germany: Abtei St. Walburga, 1985.

Emery, Anthony. *Greater Medieval Houses of England and Wales, 1300–1500.* 3 vols. Cambridge: Cambridge University Press, 1996.

Engel, Pál. *The Realm of St. Stephen: A History of Medieval Hungary, 895–1526.* New York: I.B. Tauris, 2001.

Ernsdorff, Bede P. "Niels Stenson and the Benedictines." *American Benedictine Review* 13, no.3 (1962): 324–337.

Evagrius. *Evagrius of Pontus: The Greek Ascetic Corpus.* Translated by Robert E. Sinkewicz. Oxford: Oxford University Press, 2003.

Evagrius of Ponticus. *The Praktikos and Chapters on Prayer.* Translated by John Bamburger. Cistercian Studies Series 4. Kalamazoo, MI: Cistercian, 1978.

Evans, Joan. *Monastic Life at Cluny, 910–1157.* London: Oxford University Press, 1931.

Ewens, Mary. *The Role of the Nun in Nineteenth-Century America.* New York: Arno Press, 1978.

Farmer, D.H., ed. *Benedict's Disciples.* Leominster, Herefordshire, UK: Fowler Wright Books, 1980.

Father of Gethsemani, KY. *Compendium of the History of the Cistercian Order.* Order of the Cistercians of the Strict Observance, 1944.

Feiss, Hugh. "A Poet Abbess from Notre Dame de Saintes." *Magistra: A Journal of Women's Spirituality in History* 1, no. 1 (Summer 1995): 38–54.

——. "Baker, Augustine." In *Encyclopedia of Monasticism,* edited by William M. Johnston, 1, 114. Chicago: Fitzroy Dearborn, 2000.

——, ed. *On Love: A Selection of Works of Hugh, Adam, Achard, Richard, and Godfrey of St. Victor.* Vol. 2, Victorine Texts in Translation. New York: New City Press, 2012.

Fierro, Nancy. *Hildegard of Bingen and Her Vision of the Feminine.* Kansas City, MO: Sheed and Ward, 1995.

Finnegan, Mary Jeremy. *The Women of Helfta: Scholars and Mystics.* Athens, GA: University of Georgia Press, 1991.

Fiske, Adele M. *Friends and Friendship in the Monastic Tradition.* Cuernavaca, Mexico: Centro Intercultural de Documentacion, 1970.

Fitzgerald, Sister Mary Clement, "Bishop Marty and His Sioux Missions, 1876–1896." In *SD Historical Collections.* Vol. 20. Pierre, SD: State Historical Society, 1940.

Flanagan, M. Raymond. *Burnt-Out Incense.* New York: P. J. Kennedy, 1949.

Floss, Heinrich Joseph. *Das Kloster Rolandswerth Bei Bonn.* Köln: Annalen des historischen Vereins für den Neiderrhein, 1868.

Ford, John T. "Country, Church and Conscience: John Henry Newman Versus William Ewart Gladstone." In *Religion and Political Structures: From Fundamentalism to Public Service,* edited by J.T. Ford, R.A. Destro and C.R. Dechert, 85–100. Washington, DC: Council for Research in Values and Philosophy, 2005.

Forster, Ignatius. "Bishop Martin Marty, O.S.B., Apostle of the Sioux." *The Indian Sentinel* 2, no. 1 (January 1920): 7–10.

Fossas, Ignasi M., ed. *Regla Per Als Monjos: Text Llatí/Català.* Vol. 21, Subsidia Monastica. Barcelona: Publicacions de l'Abadia de Montserrat, 1997.

Fox, Matthew. *Illumination of Hildegard of Bingen.* Santa Fe, NM: Bear & Co., 1985.

Fowler, John Clement. *The Benedictines in Bath During a Thousand Years.* London: Western Chronicle, 1895.

Frances Clare, ed. *The Life and Revelations of Saint Gertrude: Virgin and Abbess of the Order of St. Benedict.* Westminster, MD: Newman Press, 1952.

François, Jean. *Bibliothèque générale des écrivains de l'ordre de Saint Benoit, patriarche des moines d'occident.* Bouillon: Société typographique, 1777.

Frigge, Marielle. "Schola Christi: Benedictine Insight for Theological Education." PhD diss., Boston College, 1992. Ann Arbor, MI: UMI Dissertation Information Service.

Fry, Timothy, Imogene Baker, Timothy Horner, Augusta Raabe and Mark Sheridan, eds. *RB 1980: The Rule of St. Benedict in Latin and English with Notes.* Collegeville, MN: Liturgical Press, 1981.

Fruth, Allan. *A Century of Missionary Work Among the Red Lake Chippewa Indians, 1858–1958.* Red Lake, MN: St. Mary's Mission, 1958.

Fusco, Nicole. *Elena Lucrezia Cornaro Piscopia, 1646–1684.* Pittsburgh, PA: United States Committee for Elena Lucrezia Cornaro Piscopia Tercentenary, 1975.

Gaffney, James. "Biographical Preliminaries for a Life of Dom Augustine Baker." *American Benedictine Review* 19, no. 4 (1968): 515–535.

Gairdner, James and R. H. Brodie, eds. *Letters and Papers, Foreign and Domestic, of the Reign of Henry VIII.* Vol. 15. Burlington, ON: Tanner Ritchie Pub. in collaboration with the Library and Information Services of the University of St. Andrews, 2006.

Ganss, George E. *The Spiritual Exercises of Saint Ignatius: A Translation and Commentary.* Chicago: Loyola Press, 1992.

Gassner, Jerome. "Mariazell, the National Shrine of Austria." *American Benedictine Review* 8, no. 4 (1957): 313–323.

Gasquet, Francis Aidan. *The Eve of the Reformation*. London: George Bell and Sons, 1905.

———. *Henry VIII and the English Monasteries*. London: John C. Nimmo, 1899.

———. *The Last Abbot of Glastonbury and His Companions: An Historical Sketch*. London: Simpkin, Marshall, Hamilton, Kent, 1895.

———. *Monastic Life in the Middle Ages*. London: G. Bell and Sons, 1922.

Geddes, J. *The St. Albans Psalter: A Book for Christina of Markyate*. London: British Library, 2005.

Gertrude the Great of Helfta. Spiritual Exercises. Translated by Gertrud Jaron Lewis and Jack Lewis. Kalamazoo, MI: Cistercian Publications, 1989.

Gertrude of Helfta. *Herald of Divine Love*. Translated by M. Winkworth. Mahwah, NJ: Paulist Press, 1993.

Gilson, Etienne Henry. *Heloise and Abelard*. Translated by L.K. Shook. Chicago: Regnery, 1951.

Gingold, Hélène. *Abelard and Heloise: A Tragedy in Five Acts [and in Verse]*. London: Greening & Co., 1906.

Girgen, Incarnata. *Behind the Beginnings: Benedictine Women in America*. Saint Paul, MN: North Central Publishing, 1981.

Gleason, Philip. *The Conservative Reformers: German-American Catholics and the Social Order* Notre Dame, IN: University of Notre Dame Press, 1968.

Gooch, G. P. *History and Historians in the Nineteenth Century*. New York: Longmans, Green, and Co., 1952.

Goodier, Alban. *The Love of the Sacred Heart*. London: Burns, Oates, Washbourne, 1921.

Gould, Warwick and Reeves Marjorie. *Joachim of Fiore and the Myth of the Eternal Evangel in the Nineteenth and Twentieth Centuries*. New York: Clarendon Press/Oxford University Press, 2001.

Goyau, Georges. *Histoire De La Nation Française* Paris: Soc. de l'Histoire Nat., 1922.

Graf, Ernest. *Anscar Vonier, Abbot of Buckfast*. Westminster, MD: Newman Press, 1957.

Graham, Rose. *English Ecclesiastical Studies*. New York: Macmillan, 1929.

Gregory The Great. *Life and Miracles of St. Benedict: Book Two of the Dialogues*. Translated by Odo J. Zimmerman and Benedict R. Avery. Collegeville, MN: St. John's Abbey Press, 1949.

Griffiths, Bede. *The Golden String: An Autobiography*. Springfield, IL: Templegate, 1980.

———. *Return to the Center*. Springfield, IL: Templegate, 1976.

Greatrex, Joan. "After Knowles: Recent Perspectives on Monastic History." In *The Religious Orders in Pre-Reformation England*, edited by James G. Clark, 35–50. Rochester, NY: Boydell & Brewer, 2002.

Guéranger, Prosper. *Institutions Liturgiques*. Paris: Débecourt, 1840.

———. *The Liturgical Year*. Translated by James Laurence Shepherd. New York: Benziger Bros., 1897.

Guernsey, Jane Howard. *The Lady Cornaro: Pride and Prodigy of Venice.* Clinton Corners, NY: College Avenue Press, 1999.

Guy, J. A. *Thomas More.* New York: Oxford University Press, 2000.

Hall, Jeremy. "Benedictines and the Mission Vocation." *American Benedictine Review* 15, no. 1 (1964): 14–45.

Hamburger, Jeffrey F., and Susan Hamburger Marti, eds. *Crown and Veil: Female Monasticism from the Fifth to the Fifteenth Centuries.* New York: Columbia University Press, 2008.

Hanson, Paul R. *The Jacobin Republic Under Fire: The Federalist Revolt in the French Revolution.* University Park, PA: Pennsylvania State University Press, 2003.

Hapgood, David, and Richardson, David. *Montecassino.* New York: Congdon and Weed, 1984.

Harkness, Georgia Elma. *Women in Church and Society: A Historical and Theological Inquiry.* Nashville, TN: Abingdon Press, 1972.

Harksen, Sibylle. *Women in the Middle Ages.* Translated by Marianne Herzfeld. Revised by George Shepperson. New York: Schram, 1975.

Harmless, William. *Desert Christians: An Introduction to the Literature of Early Monasticism.* New York: Oxford, 2004.

Harp, Alice Marie. *A Song in the Pines: The History of Benet Hill Community.* Erie, PA: Benet Press, 1975.

Hart, Mother Columba, ed. and trans. *Hadewijch: Complete Works.* New York: Paulist Press, 1980.

Harvey, Barbara F. *Living and Dying in England 1100–1540: The Monastic Experience.* Reprinted ed. Oxford: Clarendon Press, 2002.

Heale, Martin. *The Dependent Priories of Medieval English Monasteries.* Rochester, NY: Boydell Press, 2004.

Healy, Patrick. *The Chronicle of Hugh of Flavigny: Reform and the Investiture Contest in the Late Eleventh Century.* Burlington, VT: Ashgate, 2006.

Henderson, J. Frank. "Feminizing the Rule of Benedict in Medieval England." *Magistra: A Journal of Women's Spirituality in History* 1, no. 1 (Summer 1995): 9–38.

Henry, Desmond Paul. *The Logic of Saint Anselm.* Oxford, England: Clarendon, 1967.

Herwegen, I. *St. Benedict: A Character Study.* Translated by P. Nugent. St. Louis, MO: Herder, 1924.

Higgens, John. "Dom Gueranger and the Founding of Solesmes." *American Benedictine Review* 6 (1955): 53–75.

Hildegard of Bingen. *Scivias.* Translated by Bruce Hozesky. Santa Fe, NM: Bear & Co., 1986.

——— . *Scivias.* Translated by Mother Columba Hart and Jane Bishop. Classics of Western Spirituality. New York: Paulist Press, 1990.

Hilpisch, Stephanus. *History of Benedictine Nuns.* Translated by M. Joanne Muggli. Edited by Leonard J. Doyle. Collegeville, MN: St. John's Abbey Press, 1958.

——— . *Benedictinism Through Changing Centuries.* Translated by Leonard J. Doyle. Collegeville, MN: St. John's Abbey Press, 1958.

Hodes, Ursula. *The History of Mount Angel, Oregon, 1848–1912*. Eugene, OR: 1940.

Hoffmann, Alexius. *A Benedictine Martyrology*. Collegeville, MN: St. John's Abbey, 1922.

———. *A Benedictine Martyrology: Being a Revision of Rev. Peter Lechner's Ausfürliches Martyrologium Des Benedictiner-Ordens Und Seiner Verzweigungen.* Collegeville, MN: St. John's Abbey, 1922.

Hoffman, Mathias M. *Arms and the Monk: The Trappist Saga in Mid-America.* Dubuque, IA: William C. Brown, 1952.

Holdsworth, C.J. "Christina of Markyate." In *Medieval Women*, edited by D. Barker, 193–195. Oxford: Blackwell, 1978.

Hollermann, Ephrem. *American Benedictine Women, 1852–1881.* St. Joseph, MN: Sisters of the Order of St. Benedict, 1994.

———. *The Reshaping of a Tradition: American Benedictine Women, 1852–1881.* Saint Joseph, MN: Sisters of the Order of Saint Benedict, 1994.

Hollis, Stephanie. *Anglo-Saxon Women and the Church: Sharing a Common Fate.* Rochester, NY: Boydell Press, 1992.

Hoover, Herbert T., ed. *From Idea to Institution: Higher Education in South Dakota.* Vermillion, SD: University of South Dakota Press, 1989.

Hoover, Herbert T., and Larry J. Zimmerman, eds. *SD Leaders: From Pierre Chouteau, Jr., to Oscar Howe.* Vermillion, SD: University of South Dakota Press, 1989.

Horner, Shari. *The Discourse of Enclosure Representing Women in Old English Literature.* Albany: State University of New York Press, 2001.

Hughes, Kathleen, and Hamlin, Ann. *Celtic Monasticism.* New York: Seabury, 1981.

Hume, Basil. *Searching for God.* New York: Paulist Press, 1978.

Hurel, Daniel-Odon. "The Benedictines of the Congregation of St. Maur and the Church Fathers." In *The Reception of the Church Fathers in the West: From the Carolingians to the Maurists*, edited by Irena Dorota Backus, 1009–1038. New York: E.J. Brill, 1997.

Huscroft, Richard. *Ruling England, 1042–1217.* New York: Pearson/Longman, 2005.

Iogna-Prat, Dominique. *Order & Exclusion: Cluny and Christendom Face Heresy, Judaism, and Islam, 1000–1150.* Translated by Graham Robert Edwards. Ithaca, NY: Cornell University Press, 2002.

Ingulph, Abbot of Croyland. *Ingulph's Chronicle of the Abbey of Croyland.* Translated by Henry T. Riley. London: Henry G. Bohn, 1854.

Jacobs, Margaret D., *White Mother to a Dark Race: Settler Colonialism, Maternalism, and the Removal of Indigenous Children in the American West and Australia, 1880–1940.* Lincoln, NE: University of Nebraska Press, 2009.

Jäger, Moritz. *Sister Gertrude Leupi, 1825–1904.* Translated by Alexander Luetkemeyer. Fribourg, Switzerland: Kanisius Verlag, 1974.

James, Janet Wilson, ed. *Women in American Religion.* Philadelphia: University of Pennsylvania Press, 1980.

Janssen, Hans. "Bishop Martin Marty in the Dakotas." *The American German Review* 27 (June-July, 1961): 21–25.

Jestice, Phyllis G. *Wayward Monks and the Religious Revolution of the Eleventh Century.* New York: E.J. Brill, 1997.

Johnson, William, ed. *Encyclopedia of Monasticism*. 2 vols. Chicago: Fitzroy Dearborn, 2000.

Johnston, Helen. *The Fruit of His Works: A History of the Benedictine Sisters of St. Benedict's Convent, Bristow*. Bristow, VA: Linton Hall Press, 1954.

Jones, L.W. "The Scriptorium at Corbie: I. The Library." *Speculum* 22, no. 2 (April, 1947): 191–204.

———. "The Scriptorium at Corbie: II. The Script and the Problems." *Speculum* 22, no. 3 (July, 1947): 375–394.

Joyce, Timothy. *Celtic Christianity: Sacred Tradition, a Vision of Hope*. Maryknoll, NY: Orbis, 1998.

Julian of Norwich. *Showings*. Translated by Edmund Colledge and James Walsh. New York: Paulist Press, 1978.

Kagay, Donald J., and L. J. Andrew Villalon. *The Circle of War in the Middle Ages: Essays on Medieval Military and Naval History*. Rochester, NY: Boydell Press, 1999.

Kaiser, Thomas E. "Property, Sovereignty, the Declaration of the Rights of Man, and the Tradition of French Jurisprudence." In *The French Idea of Freedom: The Old Regime and the Declaration of Rights of 1789*, edited by Dale K. Van Kley. Stanford, CA: Stanford University Press, 1994.

Kardong, Terrence Benedict. *Benedict's Rule: A Translation and Commentary*. Collegeville, MN: Liturgical Press, 1996.

Kardong, Terrence. *The Benedictines*. Wilmington, DE: Michael Glazier, 1988.

Kardong, Terrence. *Pillars of Community: Four Rules of Pre-Benedictine Monastic Life*. Collegeville, MN: Liturgical Press, 2010.

———. *Together Unto Life Everlasting: An Introduction to the Rule of Benedict*. Richardton, ND: Assumption Abbey Press, 1984.

Karolevitz, Robert F. *Bishop Martin Marty: The Black Robe Lean Chief*. Yankton, SD: Benedictine Sisters of Sacred Heart Convent, 1980.

———. *Challenge: The South Dakota Story*. Sioux Falls, SD: Brevet Press, 1975.

———. *Pioneer Church in a Pioneer City*. Aberdeen, SD: North Plains Press, 1971.

———. *Yankton: A Pioneer Past*. Aberdeen, SD: North Plains Press, 1972.

Kavenagh, Terence. "Congregations, Benedictine." In *Encyclopedia of Monasticism*, edited by William M. Johnston, 322–327. Chicago: Fitzroy Dearborn, 2000.

Kelleher, Marilyn. *Annals of the Sisters of the Good Samaritan of the Order of Saint Benedict*. 3 vols. Good Samaritan of the Order of Saint Benedict, n.d.

Kerr, Susan Anderson. "Frances of Rome: Patron of Benedictine Oblates." In *Benedict in the World: Portraits of Monastic Oblates*, edited by Linda Kulzer and Bondi Roberta C., 79–86. Collegeville, MN: Liturgical Press, 2002.

Kessler, Ann. "Assimilating the Contemplative II." *Benedictines* 38 (Fall-Winter 1983–84): 16–27.

———. "Benedictine Mission and Ministry: The Historical Tradition." *Benedictines* 40 (Spring-Summer, 1985): 31–42.

———. "The Effects of the Laic Laws of 1901 and 1904 on the Benedictines in France." PhD diss., University of Notre Dame, 1963.

———. "Feminine Monasticism and a Ray of Hope" in *The Proceedings of the American Benedictine Academy Convention*, August 8-11, 1990, Yankton, SD, 41–48. Edited by Renee Branigan. Mott, ND: Eido Printing, 1991.

———. "First Catholic Bishop of Dakota: The Black Robe Lean Chief." In *South Dakota Leaders*, edited by Herbert T. Hoover and Larry J. Zimmerman. Vermillion, SD: University Press, 1989.

———. "French Benedictines under Stress." *American Benedictine Review* 27, no. 3 (1966): 314–335.

———. "Founded on Courage, Inspired with Vision: Mount Marty College." In *From Idea to Institution: Higher Education in South Dakota*. Edited by Herbert T. Hoover. Vermillion, SD: University of South Dakota Press, 1989.

———. "Oblate and Heroine: Elena Lucrezia Scholastica Cornaro Piscopia." In *Benedict in the World: Portraits of Monastic Oblates*, edited by Linda Kulzer and Roberta C. Bondi, 19–30. Collegeville, MN: Liturgical Press, 2002.

———. "Political Legacy to the Religious in France: The Laic Laws of the Third Republic." *American Benedictine Review* 20, no. 4 (1969): 559–572.

———. "Post-Revolution Restoration of French Monasteries." *South Dakota Social Science Journal* 7 (Autumn, 1977): 111–120.

———. "The Suppression of the Benedictine Order in France during the Revolution." Master of Arts thesis, Creighton University, 1957.

———, and Susan Peterson. "Valiant Religious Women: Mothers Superior Joseph Butler, Raphael McCarthy, and Jerome Schmitt." In *SD Leaders: From Pierre Chouteau, Jr., to Oscar Howe*, edited by Herbert T. Hoover and Larry J. Zimmerman, 125–143. Vermillion, SD: University of South Dakota Press, 1989.

Kinder, Terryl N. *Cistercian Europe: Architecture of Contemplation*. Grand Rapids, MI: W.B. Eerdmans, 2002.

King, Archdale A. *Citeaux and Her Elder Daughters*. London: Burns and Oates, 1954.

King-Lenzmeier, Anne H. *Hildegard of Bingen: An Integrated Vision*. Collegeville, MN: Liturgical Press, 2001.

Kingsbury, George W. *History of Dakota Territory*. Chicago: S.J. Clarke, 1915.

Kleber, Albert. *History of St. Meinrad Archabbey, 1854–1954*. St. Meinrad: Grail, 1954.

Klimisch, Jane. *Women Gathering: The Story of the Benedictine Federation of St. Gertrude*. Toronto: Peregrina, 1993.

Knighton, Tess, and David Fallows, eds. *Companion to Medieval and Renaissance Music*. Berkeley, CA: University of California Press, 1997.

Knowles, David. *Christian Monasticism*. New York: McGraw-Hill, 1969.

———. *The English Mystical Tradition*. New York: Harper, 1961.

———. *From Pachomius to Ignatius*. Oxford, England: Clarendon Press, 1966.

———. *Great Historical Enterprises: Problems in Monastic History*. New York: Nelson, 1964.

———. *The Historian and Character, and Other Essays*. Reprint ed. Cambridge: Cambridge University Press, 2008.

———. *The Monastic Constitution of Lanfranc*. New York: Thomas Nelson and Sons, 1951.

———. *The Monastic Order in England: A History of its Development from the Times of St. Dunstan to the Fourth Lateran Council, 943–1216*. Cambridge: Cambridge University Press, 1949.

———. *The Religious Orders in England*. 3 vols. Vol. II. *The End of the Middle Ages*. Vol. III. *The Tudor Age*. Cambridge, England: Cambridge University Press, 1959.

———. *What is Mysticism?*. London: Sheed and Ward, 1966.

Knowles, David, Christopher Brooke and Lawrence Nugent, eds. *The Monastic Constitutions of Lanfranc*. New York: Oxford University Press, 2002.

Knowles, David, and Hadcock, R. Neville. *Medieval Religious Houses: England and Wales*. New York: Longmans, Green, 1953.

Kolmer, Elizabeth. *Religious Women in the United States: A Survey of the Influential Literature from 1950 to 1983*. Wilmington, DE: Michael Glazier, 1984.

Kominiak, P. Benedict. *Loci Ubi Deus Quaeritur: The Benedictine Abbeys of the Entire World*. St. Ottilien, Germany: EOS/Verlag, 1980.

Konstantinovsky, Julia. *Evagrius Ponticus: The Making of a Gnostic*. Burlington, VT: Ashgate, 2009.

Korte, Alexander. "The University of Salzburg." *American Benedictine Review* 9, no. 3 (1958): 209–226.

Kulzer, Linda, and Roberta Bondi, eds. *Benedict in the World: Portraits of Monastic Oblates*. Collegeville, MN: Liturgical Press, 2002.

Kurth, G. *Saint Boniface*. Translated by F. S. Batten. Milwaukee, WI: Bruce Publishing Company, 1935.

Labarge, Margaret Wade. *A Small Sound of the Trumpet: Women in Medieval Life*. Boston: Beacon Press, 1986.

Lackner, Bede K. *The Eleventh Century Background of Citeaux*. Washington, DC: Cistercian Publications, 1972.

Lady Abbess, and Community, . "Obituary Notices of the English Benedictine Abbey of Ghent in Flanders 1627–1811." *Catholic Record Society* 11, no. 19, (1917). http://wwtn.history.qmul.ac.uk/publications/pdfs/ObituaryGhentBenedictinesFiinal.pdf Lanfranc. *On the Body and Blood of the Lord*. Washington, DC: Catholic University of America Press, 2009.

Larkin, Georgia. *Chief Blue Cloud*. Marvin, SD: Blue Cloud Abbey, 1964.

Lawson, Frederick Robert. *A Short Hand-book of the Abbey Church of Pershore and the Church of St. Andrew*. Pershore, Worcester, England: Fearnside and Martin, 1915.

Lawless, George. *Augustine of Hippo and His Monastic Rule*. Oxford: Clarendon, 1987.

Lawrence, C. H. *Medieval Monasticism*. New York: Longman 1984.

Le Fort, Gertrud *The Song at the Scaffold*. Translated by Olga Marx. Kirkwood, MO: Catholic Authors Press, 1954.

Leach, A. F. *The Schools of Medieval England*. New York: Barnes and Noble, 1969.

Leckner, Peter. *A Benedictine Martyrology.* Collegeville, MN: St. John's Abbey, 1922.

Leclerq, Jean. *A Study of Monastic Culture.* Translated by Catherine Misrahi. New York: Fordham University Press, 1961.

———. *Alone with God.* New York: Farrar, Straus, Cudahy, 1961.

———. *Aspects of Monasticism.* Translated by Mary Dodd. Kalamazoo, MI: Cistercian Publications, 1978.

———. *The Love of Learning and the Desire for God: A Study of Monastic Culture.* New York: Fordham University Press, 1982.

———. "Liturgy and Mental Prayer in the Life of St. Gertrude." *Sponsa Regis* (1960): 1–5.

———. "The Monastic Tradition of Culture and Studies." *American Benedictine Review* 11 (1960): 99–131.

———. *Monks and Love in the Twelfth-Century France: Psycho-Historical Essays.* Oxford, England: Clarendon Press, 1979.

———. *Monks on Marriage: A Twelfth-Century View.* New York: Seabury, 1982.

Leclercq, J., F. Vandenbroucke, and L. Bouyer. *The Spirituality of the Middle Ages.* London: Burns, 1968.

Lecroq, Gaston. *L'hôpital se Fécamp et sa Communauté des Bénédictines hospitalières: Contribution a l'histoire de l'hôpital (Xie-Xxe S.).* Caen: Société d'impression de Basse-Normandie, 1939.

Lefebvre, Gaspar and Abbaye de Saint-André-lez-Bruges. *Saint Andrew Daily Missal.* St. Paul, MN: E.M. Lohmann Co., 1937.

Lefebvre, Georges. *The Coming of the French Revolution.* New York: Vintage, 1957.

Lehane, Brendan. *The Quest of Three Abbots.* New York: Viking Press, 1968.

Lehner, Ulrich L., and Michael O. Printy, eds. *A Companion to the Catholic Enlightenment in Europe.* Boston: Brill, 2010.

Lekai, Louis J. *The Cistercians: Ideals and Reality.* Kent, OH: Kent State University Press, 1977.

———. *The White Monks: A History of the Cistercian Order.* Our Lady of Spring Books, Okaucheu, WI: 1953.

———. *The Rise of the Cistercian Strict Observance in Seventeenth Century France.* Washington, DC: Catholic University of America Press, 1966.

Lennon, Stephen. *The Story of New Norcia.* New Norcia, Australia: Benedictine Community, 1977.

Lester, Anne Elisabeth. *Creating Cistercian Nuns: The Women's Religious Movement and Its Reform in Thirteenth-Century Champagne.* Ithaca: Cornell University Press, 2011.

Letters of Abelard and Heloise. Translated by Betty Radice. New York: Penguin Books, 1974.

Life of Christina of Markyate, A Twelfth-Century Recluse. Translated and edited by C. H. Talbot. Oxford: Clarendon Press, 1959.

Ligugé, Abbaye Saint-Martin de. *Revue Mabillon: Archives De La France Monastique.* Vol. 4: Abbaye Saint-Martin, 1908.

Lillich, Meredith Parsons. *Cistercian Nuns and Their World.* Kalamazoo, MI: Cistercian Publications, 2005.

Lindstrom, Mary D. "Julian of Norwich and the Motherhood of God." *Sisters Today* 54, no. 4 (December, 1982): 203–211.

Lohse, Bernhard. *Martin Luther: An Introduction to His Life and Work.* Edinburgh: Clark, 1993.

Louth, Andrew. "The Image of Heloise in English Literature." *Downside Review* (January, 1993): 45–65.

Lowe, K. J. P. *Cultural Links between Portugal and Italy in the Renaissance.* New York: Oxford University Press, 2000.

Low, Anthony. *Augustine Baker.* New York: Twayne Publishers, 1970.

Lowry, Cynthia. *The Biography of Benedictine Hospital.* Monroe, NY: Library Research Associates, 1976.

Lunn, David. *The English Benedictines, 1540–1688: From Reformation to Revolution.* New York: Barnes & Noble, 1980.

Mabillon, Jean. *De re diplomatica libri VI. in quibus quidquid ad veterum instrumentorum antiquitatem, materiam, scripturam, & stilum; quidquid ad sigilla, monogrammata, subscriptiones, ac notas chronologicas; quidquid inde ad antiquariam, historicam, forensemque disciplinam pertinet, explicatur & illustratur.* Palma: Luteciae-Parisiorum, 1709.

Mabillon, Jean, Edmond Martene and René Massuet. *Annales Ordinis S. Benedicti Occidentalium Monachorum Patriarchæ. In quibus non modo res monasticæ, sed etiam ecclesiasticæ historiæ non minima pars continetur.* Luteciæ Parisiorum, 1703.

Mabillon, Jean and Germain Michel. *Museum italicum, sev Collectio veterum scriptorum ex bibliothecis italicis.* Lutetiae Parisiorum: E. Martin, J. Boudot & S. Martin, 1687.

Mâcon, Academie de and sciences Société des arts, belles-lettres, et agriculture de Saône-et-Loire. *Annales De L'académie De Mâcon.* Saône-et-Loire: L'Académie, 1910.

Macy, Gary. *The Hidden History of Women's Ordination: Female Clergy in the Medieval West.* New York: Oxford University Press, 2008.

Madigan, Kevin, and Carolyn Osiek. *Ordained Women in the Early Church: A Documentary History.* Baltimore, MD: Johns Hopkins University Press, 2005.

Makowski, Elizabeth M. *Canon Law and Cloistered Women: Periculoso and its Commentators, 1298–1545.* Washington, DC: Catholic University of America Press, 1997.

Makowski, Elizabeth M. *English Nuns and the Law in the Middle Ages: Cloistered Nuns and Their Lawyers, 1293–1540.* Woodbridge: Boydell, 2011.

Makowski, Elizabeth M. *Canon Law and Cloistered Women: Periculoso and Its Commentators, 1298–1545.* Washington, DC: Catholic University of America Press, 1997.

Makowski, Elizabeth M. "Monasticism, Women's: Papal Policy." In *Women and Gender in Medieval Europe: An Encyclopedia,* edited by M. Schaus, 587–589. New York: Routledge, 2002.

Majdalany, F. *The Monastery.* Boston, MA: Houghton Mifflin, 1946.

———. *The Battle of Cassino*. Boston, MA: Houghton Mifflin, 1946.

Malone, Edward E. *A History of Conception Colony, Abbey, and Schools*. Omaha, NE: Interstate Printing Company, 1971.

Maredsous, Abbaye de. "Revue Bénédictine." *Revue bénédictine*, (1890).

———. "Bulletin D'histoire Bénédictine." *Bulletin d'histoire bénédictine* (1907).

———. "Revue Liturgique & Monastique." *Revue liturgique & monastique* (1919).

Marmion, Columba. *Christ the Ideal of the Monk*. St. Louis, MO: Herder, 1925.

Martin, Aquinata. *The Catholic Church on the Nebraska Frontier, 1885–1954*. Washington, DC: Catholic University of America Press, 1937.

Martin, Joel W. and Mark A. Nicholas, eds. *Native Americans, Christianity, and the Reshaping of the American Religious Landscape*. Chapel Hill: University of North Carolina Press, 2010.

Martin, Kathleen J., ed. *Indigenous Symbols and Practices in the Catholic Church: Visual Culture, Missionization, and Appropriation*. Burlington, VT: Ashgate, 2010.

Maschietto, Francesco Ludovico. *Elena Lucrezia Cornaro Piscopia (1646–1684): The First Woman in the World to Earn a University Degree*. Translated by Jan Vairo and William Crochetiere. Philadelphia: Saint Joseph's University Press, 2007.

Matarasso, Pauline Maud. *The Cistercian World: Monastic Writings of the Twelfth Century*. New York: Penguin Books, 1993.

Mate, Mavis E. *Daughters, Wives, and Widows after the Black Death: Women in Sussex, 1350–1535*. Rochester, NY: Boydell Press, 1998.

Marty, Bishop Martin. *Dr. Johann Martin Henni, First Bishop and Archbishop of Milwaukee*. Milwaukee, WI: Benziger Brothers, 1888.

Marx, Paul B. *Virgil Michel and the Liturgical Movement*. Collegeville, MN: Liturgical Press, 1957.

Matthew, Tobie. *The Life of Lady Lucy Knatchbull*. London: Sheed and Ward, 1931.

Maynard, Theodore. *Saint Benedict and His Monks*. New York: P.J. Kennedy, 1954.

McAndrews, Dunstan. *Father Joseph Kundek, 1810–1857: A Missionary Priest of the Diocese of Vincennes*. St. Meinrad, IN: St. Meinrad Archabbey, 1954.

McCann, Justin. *Ampleforth Abbey and College*. York, England: Ampleforth Abbey, 1975.

———. *The Life of Father Augustine Baker, O.S.B.* London: Burns, Oates, 1933.

McCarthy, Charles. *Lives of the Principal Benedictine Writers of the Congregation of St. Maur*. London: Burns, Oates, 1868.

McClintock, John Strong James. *Cyclopaedia of Biblical, Theological, and Ecclesiastical Literature*, reprint of the 1871–1881 ed. 10 vols. New York: Arno Press, 1969.

McDonald, Grace. *With Lamps Burning*. Saint Joseph, MN: Saint Benedict's Priory, 1957.

McDonnell, Ernest W. *The Bequines and Beghards in Medieval Culture*. New Brunswick, NJ: Rutgers University Press, 1954.

McGuinness, Margaret M. *Called to Serve: A History of Nuns in America*. New York: New York University Press, 2013.

McKee, J.R. *Dame Elizabeth Barton, O.S.B.: The Holy Maid of Kent.* New York: Benziger, 1925.

McKitterick, Rosamond. "Charlemagne's *Missi* and Their Books." In *Early Medieval Studies in Memory of Patrick Wormald.* Edited by Stephen David Baxter, 253–282. Burlington, VT: Ashgate, 2009.

McLeod, Enid. *Héloise: A Biography.* London: Chatto & Windus, 1971.

McNamara, Jo Ann. *Sisters in Arms: Catholic Nuns through Two Millennia.* Cambridge, MA: Harvard University Press, 1996.

Meade, Davis. "From Turmoil to Solidarity: The Emergence of the Vallumbrosian Monastic Congregation." *American Benedictine Review* 19 (1968): 323–357.

Mechthild. *The Flowing Light of the Godhead.* Mahwah, NJ: Paulist Press, 1998.

Melling, Leonard. *Abelard and Heloise.* London: Regency Press, 1970.

Melville, Annabelle M. *John Carroll of Baltimore: Founder of the American Catholic Hierarchy.* New York: Scribner, 1955.

Merton, Thomas. *Contemplation in a World of Action.* New York: Doubleday, 1973.

——. *The Waters of Siloe.* New York: Harcourt, Brace, 1949.

Milliken, E.K. *English Monasticism: Yesterday and Today.* London: George G. Harrap, 1967.

Mocquereau, André. *Le nombre musical Grégorien, ou rhythmique Grégorienne, théorie et pratique.* Paris: Société Saint Jean l' Évangéliste Desclée, 1908.

——. *Paléographie musicale: les principaux manuscrits de chant Grégorien, Ambrosien, Mozarabe, Gallican.* Solesmes, France: Solesmes, 1969.

Mohler, James A. *The Heresy of Monasticism: The Christian Monks, Types and Antitypes: An Historical Survey.* New York: Alba House, 1971.

Molinari, Paul. *Julian of Norwich: The Teaching of a Fourteenth Century English Mystic.* New York: Longmans, Green, 1958.

Monchanin, J. and Lesaux, Henri. *A Benedictine Ashram.* Isle of Man: Times Press, 1964.

Monk of Douai Abbey, ed. *The High History of Saint Benedict and His Monks.* London: Sands, 1945.

Montalembert, Count de. *The Monks of the West.* 2 vols. Boston: Thomas B. Noonan, 1860.

Montfaucon, Bernard de Henley John. *The Antiquities of Italy: Being the Travels of the Learned and Reverend Bernard De Montfaucon, from Paris through Italy, in the Years 1698 and 1699.* London: J. Darby, A. Bettesworth, F. Fayram, 1725.

Montgomery, Scott Bradford. "Melk." In *Medieval Germany: An Encyclopedia*, edited by John M. Jeep, 517–518. New York: Garland 2001.

Moody, T. W., F. X. Martin, and F. J. Byrne. *A New History of Ireland.* Oxford: Oxford University Press, 2009.

Moore, R. I. *The Birth of Popular Heresy.* Toronto: University of Toronto Press in association with the Medieval Academy of America, 1995.

Morey, Adrian. *David Knowles: A Memoir.* London: Darton, Longman and Todd, 1979.

Morgan, Marjorie McCallum. *The English Lords of the Abbey of Bec.* London: Oxford, 1946.

Morgan, Nigel J. *Early Gothic Manuscripts.* New York: Oxford University Press, 1982.

Morkin, M. Louis, and Seigel, M. Theophane. *Wind in the Wheat: A Century of Prayer and Work in Erie, The Sisters of Saint Benedict, 1856–1956.* Erie, PA: McCarty Printing, 1956.

Morris, Joan. *The Lady Was a Bishop: The Hidden History of Women with Clerical Ordination and the Jurisdiction of Bishops.* New York: Macmillan, 1973.

Morris, John, Frank Thorn, and Caroline Thorn, eds. *Domesday Book.* Chichester: Phillimore, 1986.

Morton, James, ed. *The Nun's Rule: Being the Ancren Riwle Modernized.* New York: Cooper Square Publishers, 1966.

Mould, Daphne. *The Monasteries of Ireland: An Introduction.* London: B.T. Batsford, 1976.

Muehlenbein, Wibora. *Benedictine Mission to China.* St. Joseph, MN: St. Benedict's Convent, 1980.

Murphy, Joseph F. *Tenacious Monks: The Oklahoma Benedictines, 1875–1975.* Shawnee, OK: Benedictine College Press, 1974.

Murphy, Margaret Gertrude. *St. Basil and Monasticism.* New York: A.M.S. Press, 1971.

Murray, Albert Victor. *Abelard and St. Bernard: A Study in Twelfth-Century "Modernism."* New York: Barnes and Noble, 1967.

Mursell, Gordon. *English Spirituality.* Louisville, KY: SPCK/Westminster John Knox Press, 2001.

Napier, Arthur S. *Enlarged Rule of Chrodegang; Capitula of Theodulf; Epitome of Benedict of Aniane.* London: Kegan, Paul, Trench, Trubner, 1916.

Neuman, Matthias. "Benedictine Spirituality and the Challenge of Pluralism Today." *Benedictines* 35, no. 2, (1980): 13–26.

———. "The Creative Charism of Benedictine Monasticism: A Reply to Francis Mannion." *American Benedictine Review* 46, no. 3 (1995): 254–270.

Newman, Barbara. *Sister of Wisdom: St. Hildegard's Theology of the Feminine.* Berkeley: University of California Press, 1987.

Newman, John Henry Cardinal. *The Mission of the Benedictine Order.* London: Long, 1908.

———. *Historical Sketches.* New York: Longmans, Green, 1912.

Nicholas of Cusa. "Selected Spiritual Writings." Edited by H. Lawrence Bond. New York: Paulist Press, 1997.

Nichols, John A. "Cistercian Monastic Women: An Introduction to Hidden Springs." *Cistercian Studies Quarterly* 28, no. 1 (1993): 59–73.

———. *Medieval Religious Women.* 3 vols. Kalamazoo, MI: Cistercian 1984–93.

Nolan, Patrick. *The Irish Dames of Ypres: Being a History of the Royal Irish Abbey of Ypres Founded A.D. 1665 and Still Flourishing: And Some Account of Irish Jacobitism, with a Portrait of James II and Stuart Letters Hitherto Unpublished.* Dublin: Browne and Nolan, 1908.

Norris, Kathleen. *The Cloister Walk.* New York: Riverhead Books, 1996.

———. *Dakota: A Spiritual Geography.* New York: Ticknor and Fields, 1993.

———. "What I Do Not See I Do Not Know: Hildegard and the Poetic Way of Knowing." *American Benedictine Review* 46, no. 2 (1995): 183–194.

Nuns of Stanbrook. *Stanbrook Abbey: A Sketch of Its History.* London: Burns, Oates, & Washburn, 1925.

Nuns of St. Walburg. *Spring and Harvest.* Translated by Gonzaga Englehart. St. Meinrad, IN: Grail, 1952.

Obbard, Elizabeth Ruth, ed. *Medieval Women Mystics: Selected Spiritual Writings*. Hyde Park, NY: New City Press, 2002.

Oer, Sebastian von. *A Day in the Cloister*. New York: Benziger Brothers, 1906.

Oetgen, Jerome. *An American Abbot: Boniface Wimmer, O.S.B., 1809–1887*. Latrobe, PA: Archabbey Press, 1976.

———. "Benedictine Women in Nineteenth-Century America." *American Benedictine Review* 34, no. 4 (1983): 396–424.

———, ed. *Boniface Wimmer: Letters of an American Abbot*. Latrobe, PA: Saint Vincent Archabbey Publications, 2008.

O'Brien O'Keeffe, Katherine. *Stealing Obedience: Narratives of Agency and Identity in Later Anglo-Saxon England*. Toronto, ON: University of Toronto Press, 2012.

O'Callaghan, Joseph F. *A History of Medieval Spain*. Ithaca: Cornell University Press, 1975.

O'Farrell, Patrick. *The Catholic Church and Community in Australia: A History*. West Melbourne: Thomas Nelson, 1977.

O'Malley, John W. *Trent: What Happened at the Council*. Cambridge: Harvard University Press/Belknap Press, 2013.

O'Sullivan Moira M. K. "Religious in Polding's Sydney: Early Connections between the Benedictine Nuns and the Sisters of Charity." *Tjurunga* (November 2001): 45–77.

Oury, Guy-Marie. *Saint Benedict, Blessed by God*. Translated by John A. Otto. Collegeville, MN: Liturgical Press, 1980.

Packard, Sidney R. *12th Century Europe: An Interpretative Essay*. Amherst: University of Massachusetts Press, 1973.

Paor, Liam de, ed. *Saint Patrick's World: The Christian Culture of Ireland's Apostolic Age*. Notre Dame, IN: University of Notre Dame Press, 1993.

Palladius. *The Lausiac History*. Translated by Robert T. Meyer. Ancient Christian Writers. New York: Newman, 1964.

Palmer, R. L. *English Monasteries in the Middle Ages: An Outline of Monastic Architecture and Custom from the Conquest to the Suppression*. London: Constable, 1930.

Panikkar, Raimundo. *Blessed Simplicity: The Monk as Universal Archetype*. New York: Seabury Press, 1982.

Paris, Matthew, and Richard Vaughan. *Illustrated Chronicles of Matthew Paris: Observations of Thirteenth-Century Life*. Stroud, Gloucestershire: A. Sutton, 1994.

Parsons, Jotham. *The Church in the Republic: Gallicanism & Political Ideology in Renaissance France*. Washington, DC: Catholic University of America Press, 2004.

Patrouch, Joseph F. "The Investiture Controversy Revisited: Religious Reform, Emperor Maximilian II, and the Klosterrat." *Austrian History Yearbook* 25 (1994): 59–77.

Paul, Benjamin. *Nuns and Reform Art in Early Modern Venice: The Architecture of Santi Cosma E Damiano and Its Decoration from Tintoretto to Tiepolo*. Burlington, VT: Ashgate, 2012.

Paxton, Frederick S. Liutbirg Hathumoda. *Anchoress and Abbess in Ninth-Century Saxony: The Lives of Liutbirga of Wendhausen and Hathumoda of Gandersheim.* Washington, DC: Catholic University of America Press, 2009.

Peers, E. Allison. *Spain, The Church and the Orders.* London: Eyre and Spottiswoode, 1939.

Peifer, Claude. *Monastic Spirituality.* New York: Sheed and Ward, 1966.

Pennington, M. Basil, ed. *Contemplative Community: An Interdisciplinary Symposium.* Washington, DC: Cistercian Publications, Consortium Press, 1972.

——— . *Monastery.* San Francisco: Harper and Row, 1983.

Petroff, Elizabeth Alvilda, ed. *Medieval Women's Visionary Literature.* New York: Oxford, 1986.

Pfaller, Louis L. *The Catholic Church in Western North Dakota, 1738–1960.* Mandan, ND: Diocese of Bismarck, 1960.

Pinto, Gaspar A. *The Benedictines in India.* Dindigul, India: Mission Literature Stores, 1941.

Pius XII. *Fulgens Radiatur.* Vatican, 1947. Vatican website http://www. vatican.va/holy_father/pius_xii/encyclicals/documents/ hf_p-xii_enc_21031947_fulgens-radiatur_en.html.

Pothier, Joseph. *Du liber gradualiset de la manière d'en interpréter la notation.* Solesmes: Imprimerie Saint-Pierre, 1892.

Potts, Cassandra. *Monastic Revival and Regional Identity in Early Normandy.* Rochester, NY: Boydell Press, 1997.

Power, Eileen. *Medieval English Nunneries c. 1275 to 1535.* Cambridge: Cambridge University Press, 2010.

——— . *Medieval Women.* Cambridge, England: Cambridge University Press, 1975.

Prioresses, Conference of American Benedictine. "Upon This Tradition: Introduction, Historical Background." *Conference of American Benedictine Prioresses* (n.d.). http://www.msb.net/Community_About_UTT_Historical_Bkgrnd.html.

Putnam, Johnette. *Women in Medieval Monasticism: Appropriating Our Tradition.* St. John's Monastic Institute, Collegeville, MN: 1980.

Pynsent, Mathilde. *The Life of Helen Lucretia Coronaro Piscopia, Oblate of the Order of St. Benedict and Doctor in the University of Padua.* Roma: St. Benedict's, 1896.

Quarr Abbey. London: Matthews, Drew and Shelbourne, 1960.

Quitslund, Sonya A. *Beauduin, A Prophet Vindicated.* New York: Newman Press, 1973.

Raaijmakers, Janneke. *The Making of the Monastic Community of Fulda, c. 744–c. 900.* Cambridge: Cambridge University Press, 2012.

Rader, Rosemary. *Breaking Boundaries.* New York: Paulist Press, 1983.

Raftis, J. Ambrose. *The Estates of Ramsey Abbey.* Toronto, Canada: Pontifical Institute of Medieval Studies, 1957.

Ranek, Jeanne. "Monastic Community: Ongoing Evolution and Survival. In *The Proceedings of the American Benedictine Academy Convention,* August 8-11, 1990, Yankton, SD, 59–64. Edited by Renee Branigan. Mott, ND: Eido Printing, 1991.

Rasmussen, Douglas James. *A Time to Be Born: The First Catholic Church in Dakota.* Vermillion, SD: Pax Book Bar, 1975.

Reardon, James Michael, P.A. *The Catholic Church in the Diocese of St. Paul.* St. Paul, MN: North Central Publishing Company, 1952.

Redmond, M. Justine. *Laicism in the Schools of France.* Washington, DC: Catholic University of America Press, 1932.

Reuther, Rosemary, ed. *Religion and Sexism: Images of Woman in the Jewish and Christian Traditions.* New York: Simon and Schuster, 1974.

Reuther, Rosemary, and Eleanor McLaughlin, eds. *Women of Spirit.* New York: Simon and Schuster, 1979.

Revelations of Divine Love of Julian of Norwich. Translated by James Walsh. New York: Harper and Brothers, 1961.

Reyhner, Jon Allan, and Jeanne M. Oyawin Eder. *American Indian Education: A History.* Norman: University of Oklahoma Press, 2004.

Rios, Romanus. *Benedictines of Today.* Worcester, England: Stanbrook Abbey, 1946.

Rippinger, Joel. "Assimilating the Contemplative I." *Benedictines* 38, no. 1 (1983): 37–44.

——— . *The Benedictine Order in the United States: An Interpretive History.* Collegeville, MN: Liturgical Press, 1990.

——— . "Some Historical Determinants of American Benedictine Monasticism, 1846–1900." *American Benedictine Review* 27 (1976): 63–85.

——— . *Marmion Abbey Sesquimillennium Essays on Monasticism.* Aurora, IL: The Abbey, 1980.

——— . "Martin Marty: Monk, Abbot, Missionary and Bishop I." *American Benedictine Review* 33, no. 3 (1982): 223–240.

——— . "Martin Marty: Monk, Abbot, Missionary and Bishop II." *American Benedictine Review* 33, no. 4 (1982): 376–393.

Roberts, Augustine. "Spiritual Methods in Benedictine Life, Yesterday and Today." *Cistercian Studies* 10 (1975): 207–233.

Robertson, Durante Waite. *Abelard and Heloise.* New York: Dial Press, 1972.

Robinson, Elwyn B. *History of North Dakota.* Lincoln, NE: University of Nebraska Press, 1966.

Roche, Aloysius. *The First Monks and Nuns.* London: Burns and Oates, 1942.

Roemer, Theodore. *The Ludwig-Missionsverein and the Church in the United States (1838–1918).* Washington, DC: Catholic University of America Press, 1933.

Rollo-Koster, Joëlle and Thomas M. Izbicki. *A Companion to the Great Western Schism (1378–1417).* Boston: Brill, 2009.

Rothensteiner, John. "Paul De Saint Pierre: The First German-American Priest of the West." In *The Catholic Historical Review,* edited by American Catholic Historical Association, 195–222. Washington, DC: Catholic University of America Press, 1920.

Rousseau, Philip. *Pachomius: The Making of a Community in Fourth-Century Egypt.* Berkeley: University of California Press, 1999.

Rudloff, Leo and Hammond, John. "The Weston Story: An Interview." *American Benedictine Review* 13, no. 3 (1962): 390–400.

Ruinart, Thierry. *Abregé de la vie de Dom Jean Mabillon, prêtre & religieux Benedictin de la Congregation De Saint Maur*. Paris: Chez la veuve François Muguet et Charles Robustel, 1709.

Salih, Sarah. "Julian in Norwich: Heritage and Iconography." In *Julian of Norwich's Legacy: Medieval Mysticism and Post-Medieval Reception*, edited by Sarah Salith and Denise Nowakowski Baker, 153–172. New York Palgrave Macmillan, 2006.

Salih, Sarah and Denise Nowakowski Baker. "Julian of Norwich's Legacy: Medieval Mysticism and Post-Medieval Reception." In *New Chaucer Society Congress*. New York: Palgrave Macmillan, 2006.

Sargent, Leonard. *Pictures and Persons*. Washington, DC: St. Anselm's Priory, 1931.

Schaus, Margaret. *Women and Gender in Medieval Europe: An Encyclopedia*. New York: Routledge, 2006.

Schelbert, Leo. *Historical Dictionary of Switzerland*. Lanham, MD: Scarecrow Press, 2007.

Schell, Herbert S. *History of SD*. Lincoln, NE: University of Nebraska Press, 1961.

Schmitt, Miriam, and Kulzer Linda. *Medieval Women Monastics: Wisdom's Wellsprings*. Collegeville, MN: Liturgical Press, 1996.

Schmitz, Philibert. *Histoire de l'ordre de Saint Benoit*. 7 vols. Paris: Les éditions de Maredsous, 1942.

Schoenbechler, Roger. "Anglo-Saxon Monastic Women." *Magistra: A Journal of Women's Spirituality in History* 1, no. 1 (Summer 19995): 138–171.

Schneider, Edouard. *The Benedictines*. New York: Greenberg, 1926.

Schroeder, Henry Joseph, ed. *Canons and Decrees of the Council of Trent*. St. Louis, MO: B. Herder Book Co., 1941.

Schulenburg, Jane Tibbets. "Gender, Celibacy, and Proscriptions of Sacred Space: Symbol and Practice." In *Medieval Purity and Piety: Essays on Medieval Clerical Celibacy and Religious Reform*, edited by Michael Frassetto, 353–376. New York: Garland 1998.

Schuster, Ildephonse. *Saint Benedict and His Times*. Translated by Gregory J. Roettger. St. Louis, MO: Herder, 1953.

Schutte, Anne Jacobson. *By Force and Fear: Taking and Breaking Monastic Vows in Early Modern Europe*. Ithaca: Cornell University Press, 2011.

Senate, United States. *The French Declaration of the Rights of Man and of the Citizen and the American Bill of Rights: A Bicentennial Commemoration Issued Pursuant to S.J. Res. 317, 100th Congress*. Washington, DC: U.S. Congress, Senate, 1989.

Seward, Desmond. *The Hundred Years War: The English in France, 1337–1453*. London: Robinson, 2003.

Shanahan, Mary Margaret. *Out of Time, Out of Place: Henry Gregory and the Benedictine Order in Colonial Australia*. Canberra: National University Press, 1970.

Sharum, Elizabeth Louise. *Write the Vision Down: A History of St. Scholastica Convent. Fort Smith, Arkansas 1879–1979*. Fort Smith, AR: American Printing and Lithography, 1979.

Sikes, J. G. *Peter Abelard*. New York: Russell and Russell, 1965.

Sisters of the Good Samaritan. *The Wheeling Years: Sisters of the Good Samaritan, 1857–1957*. Sydney: Sisters of the Good Samaritan, 1956.

Sisters of St. Benedict. *One Hundredth Anniversary of the Benedictine Sisters, 1852–1952*. St. Mary's, PA: St. Joseph Convent, n.d.

Sisters of St. Benedict of Crookston. *With Gladdened Heart, 1919–1969*. Crookston, MN: Mt. St. Benedict Priory, 1969.

Skudlarek, William, ed. *The Continuing Quest for God: Monastic Spirituality in Tradition and Transition*. Collegeville, MN: Liturgical Press, 1982.

Smaragdus. *The Crown of Monks*. Translated by David Barry. Vol. 245, Cistercian Studies Series. Collegeville, MN: Cistercian Publications/Liturgical Press, 2013.

Smith, E. D. *The Battles for Cassino*. New York: Scribner, 1975.

Smith, Derek. "Oblates in Western Monasticism." *Monastic Studies* 13 (Autumn, 1982): 47–72.

Smith, Helen. *'Grossly Material Things': Women and Book Production in Early Modern England*. Oxford: Oxford University Press, 2012.

Smith, L. M. *Cluny in the Eleventh and Twelfth Centuries*. London: Sheed and Ward, 1958.

Smith, R. "The Early Community of St. Andrew at Rochester, 604–1000." *The English Historical Review* 60 (September, 1945): 289–299.

Sohler, Rogatia. "Hildegard von Bingen." *Sisters Today* 51, no. 5 (January, 1980): 291–296.

Sola, Ferdinand. "The Martyrs of Montserrat." *Downside Review* (April, 1940): 143–149.

Soltner, Louis. *Solesmes and Dom Guéranger, 1805–1875*. Orleans, MA: Paraclete Press, 1995.

Southern, R. W. *Western Society and the Church in the Middle Ages*. NY: Penguin, 1970.

Southern, R.W., and F.S. Schmitt, eds. *Memorials of St. Anselm*. London: Oxford, 1969.

Sowerby, J. *The Forest Cantons of Switzerland: Lucerne, Schwyz, Uri, Unterwalden*. London: Percival & Co, 1892.

Stanbrook Abbey. *In a Great Tradition: Tribute to Dame Laurentia McLaclan, Abbess of Stanbrook Abbey*. London: John Murray, 1956.

Stallbaumber, Virgil R. "The Canterbury School of St. Gregory's Disciples." *American Benedictine Review* 6, no. 4 (1955): 389–407.

———. "The Canterbury School of Theodore and Hadrian." *American Benedictine Review* 22, no. 1 (1971): 46–63.

Strocchia, Sharon T. *Nuns and Nunneries in Renaissance Florence*. Baltimore, MD: Johns Hopkins University Press, 2009.

Stump, Phillip H. "The Council of Constance (1414–18) and the End of the Schism." In *A Companion to the Great Western Schism, 1378–1417*, edited by Joëlle Rollo-Koster and Thomas M. Izbicki, 395–442. Boston: Brill, 2009.

Steele, Francesca M. *Anchoresses of the West*. St. Louis, MO: B. Herder Book Co., 1903.

———. *Life and Visions of St. Hildegarde*. London: Heath, Cranton, and Ousely, 1914.

———. *The Life of Saint Walburga*. St. Louis, MO: B. Herder Book Co., 1921.

Stenton, F.M. *Anglo-Saxon England*. 2nd. ed. Oxford, Great Britain: Clarendon Press, 1947.

Stormon, E. J., ed. *The Salvado Memoirs*. Perth: University of Western Australia, 1977.

Stuard, Susan Mosher, ed. *Women in Medieval History and Historiography*. Philadelphia: University of Pennsylvania, Press, 1987.

——— . *Women in Medieval Society*. Philadelphia: University of Pennsylvania Press, 1976.

Suenens, Leon Joseph. *The Nuns in the World: New Dimensions in the Modern Apostolate*. Westminster, MD: Newman Press, 1962.

Sullivan, Donald D. "Critiques of Western Christian Monasticism." In *Encyclopedia of Monasticism*, edited by William M. Johnston, 337–341. Chicago: Fitzroy Dearborn, 2000.

Sullivan, Thomas. *Benedictine Monks at the University of Paris, A.D. 1229–1500: A Biographical Register*. New York: E.J. Brill, 1995.

——— . "Studium Monastica: Benedictines at the University of Paris in the Late Middle Ages, 1260–1500." PhD diss., University of Wisconsin, 1982.

Sutera, Judith. *True Daughters: Monastic Identity and American Benedictine Women's History*. Atchison, KS: Mount St. Scholastica, 1987.

Swan, Laura. *The Forgotten Desert Mothers: Sayings, Lives, and Stories of Early Christian Women*. New York, NY: Paulist Press, 2001.

——— . *History of North American Benedictine Women: A Bibliography*. Lincoln, NE: Writers Club Press, 2001.

Symons, Thomas, ed. *The Monastic Agreement of the Monks and Nuns of the English Nation: Regularis Concordia Anglicae Nationis Monachorum Sanctimonialiumque*. New York: Oxford University Press, 1953.

Szarmach, Paul, ed. *An Introduction to the Medieval Mystics of Europe*. Albany, NY: State University of New York Press, 1984.

Talbot, C. H. *The Life of Christina of Markyate, a Twelfth Century Recluse*. Oxford: Clarendon Press, 1959.

——— , ed. *The Anglo-Saxon Missionaries in Germany*. New York: Sheed, Ward, 1954.

Tanner, Norman P. *Decrees of the Ecumenical Councils. Nicea I to Lateran V*. London: Sheed & Ward, 1990.

Taunton, Ethelred. *The English Black Monks of St. Benedict*. NY: Longmans, Green, 1898.

Theisen, Jerome, "Benedictine Monasticism in the Church of Today." *American Benedictine Review* 46, no. 4 (1995): 409–418.

Thimmesh, Hilary. "American Benedictines and Higher Education." *American Benedictine Review* 46, no. 2 (1995): 121–131.

Thompson, James Westfall. "The Age of Mabillon and Montfaucon." *American Historical Review* 47 (January, 1942): 225–244.

Tinker, George E. *Missionary Conquest: The Gospel and Native American Cultural Genocide*. Minneapolis, MN: Fortress Press, 1993.

Tosti, Abbot. *Saint Benedict: An Historical Discourse on His Life*. Translated by William Romuald Canon Woods. New York: Benziger Brothers, 1896.

Travitsky, Betty, Anne Lake Prescott and Arthur F. Marotti, eds. *Gertrude More*. Burlington, VT: Ashgate, 2009.

Trenholme, Edward. *The Story of Iona*. Edinburgh, Scotland: Douglas, 1909.

Tunink, Wilfrid. *Vision of Peace: A Study of Benedictine Monastic Life.* New York: Farrar, Strauss, 1963.

Turner, D.H. *The Benedictines in Britain.* New York: George Braziller, 1980.

Turner, Denys. *Julian of Norwich, Theologian.* New Haven, CT: Yale University Press, 2011.

Vaggioli, Felice. *History of New Zealand and Its Inhabitants.* Translated by John Crockett. Dunedin, New Zealand: University of Otago Press, 2000.

Valentine, Mary Hester. *Saints for Contemporary Women.* Chicago: Thomas More, 1987.

Van Damme, Jean Baptiste. *The Three Founders of Citeaux.* Kalamazoo, MI: Cistercian Press, 1998.

Van Engen, John H. *Sisters and Brothers of the Common Life: The Devotio Moderna and the World of the Later Middle Ages.* Philadelphia: University of Pennsylvania Press, 2008.

Van Kley, Dale K. *The French Idea of Freedom: The Old Regime and the Declaration of Rights of 1789.* Stanford, CA: Stanford University Press, 1994.

Van Zeller, Hubert. *The Benedictine Idea.* London: Burns & Oates, 1959.

Vanderputten, Steven. *Monastic Reform as Process Realities and Representations in Medieval Flanders, 900–1100.* Ithaca, NY: Cornell University Press, 2013.

Vaughan, Richard. *Matthew Paris.* Cambridge: Cambridge University Press, 1958.

Veilleux, Armand. *Pachomian Koinonia.* Kalamazoo, MI: Cistercian Publications, 1996.

Vestal, Stanley. *Sitting Bull, Champion of the Sioux.* Boston: Houghton Mifflin, 1932.

Villiers-Tuthill, Kathleen. *History of Kylemore Castle & Abbey.* Connemara, Co Galway: Kylemore Abbey Publications, Kylemore Abbey, 2002.

Vogüé, Adalbert de. *Reading Saint Benedict: Reflections on the Rule.* Translated by Colette Friedlander OCSO. Kalamazoo, MI: Cistercian Publications, 1994.

———. "The Rule of St. Benedict." *Cistercian Studies* 12 (1977): 243–249.

Voltaire. *Candide and Related Texts.* Translated by David Wootton. Indianapolis, IN: Hackett Pub. Co., 2000.

Voltaire. *Treatise on Tolerance.* Translated by Brian Masters. New York: Cambridge University Press, 2000.

Voth, M. Agnes. *Green Olive Branch.* Chicago: Franciscan Herald, 1973.

Waddell, Helen. *The Desert Fathers: Translations from the Latin with an Introduction.* London: Constable & Co Ltd., 1936.

Walderbert. "Regula Cujusdam Patris Ad Virgines." In *Patrologiae Cursus Completus. Series Latina (Patrologia Latina),* 88, 1053–1070. Paris, 6th Century.

Walsh, Henry H. *The Concordat of 1801.* New York: Columbia University Press, 1933.

Walsh, James J. *The Thirteenth, Greatest of Centuries.* New York: Fordham University, 1952.

Walter, Bernita. *Sustained by God's Faithfulness: The Missionary Benedictine Sisters of Tutzing.* Vol I. Translated by Matilda Handl. St. Ottilien, Germany: Eos Verlag, 1987.

Ward, Benedicta, ed. *The Desert Christian: Sayings of the Desert Fathers.* New York: Macmillan Co., 1975.

———. *Miracles and the Medieval Mind: Theory, Record and Event, 1000–1215*. Philadelphia: University of Pennsylvania Press, 1982.

Wathen, Ambrose. "Benedict of Nursia: Patron of Europe, 480–1980." *Cistercian Studies* 15 (1980): 105–125.

———. "Monasticism: Qumran and Christian." *Benedictines* 28, no. 3–4 (Fall-Winter 1973): 58–68.

Webb, J. F., ed. *Lives of the Saints: The Voyage of St. Brendan, Bede: Life of Cuthbert, Eddius Stephanus: Life of Wilfred*. New York: Penguin Books, 1965.

Weldon, Bennet. *Pax; Chronological Notes Containing the Rise, Growth and Present State of the English Congregation of the Order of St. Benedict*. Stanbrook: J. Hodges, 1881.

Welt, Hugh. "Saint Vincent Archabbey and China." *Benedictine Confluence*, 6 (Winter 1972): 31–39.

Wemple, Suzanne Fonay. *Women in Frankish Society: Marriage and the Cloister 500–900*. Philadelphia: University of Pennsylvania Press, 1981.

Wessley, Stephen E. *Joachim of Fiore and Monastic Reform*. New York: P. Lang, 1990.

Whelan, Basil. *The Annals of the English Congregation of the Black Monks of St. Benedict (1850–1900)*. 2 vols. Unpublished manuscript, 1932.

———. *The History of Belmont Abbey* (England). London: Bloomsbury Publishing Co., 1959.

———. *Historic English Convents of Today: The Story of the English Cloisters in France and Flanders in Penal Times*. London: Burns, Oates, & Washburn, 1936.

White, Lynn Townsend, Jr., *Latin Monasticism in Norman Sicily*, Cambridge, MA: The Mediaeval Academy of America, 1938.

Windschiegl, Peter. *A Brief History of the Order of Saint Benedict in the Abbacy Nullius of Saint Peter*. Muenster, Saskatchewan, 1952.

Winkworth, Margaret, ed. & trans. *Gertrude of Helfta: Herald of Divine Love*. Classics of Western Spirituality. Mahwah, NJ: Paulist Press, 1993.

Wispelwey, Berend. *Biographical Index of the Middle Ages*. 2 vols. Verlag, München Saur/Walter de Gruyter, 2008.

Wittberg, Patricia. *The Rise and Decline of Catholic Religious Orders: A Social Movement Perspective*. Albany: State University of New York Press, 1994.

Wolter, Maurus Benedict. *Praecipua Ordinis Monastici Elementa*. Brugis: Desclée, De Brouwer et Soc., 1880.

———. *The Principles of Monasticism*. St. Louis, MO: Herder, 1962.

Wood, Susan. *The Proprietary Church in the Medieval West*. New York: Oxford University Press, 2006.

Wormald, Francis. *The Benedictional of St. Ethelwold*. The Library of Illuminated Manuscripts. New York: T. Yoseloff, 1960.

Yzermans, Vincent. *Frontier Bishop of Saint Cloud*. Waite Park, MN: Park Press, 1988.

Zehringer, William C. "The Sound of Praise and Bliss of Life: The Place of Music in the Visionary Art of Hildegard of Bingen." *American Benedictine Review* 46, no. 2 (1995): 194–206.

GENERAL INDEX

ABOUT THE AUTHORS

SISTER ANN KESSLER, O.S.B., PH.D., joined the
Benedictines of Sacred Heart Monastery, in Yankton, South Dakota, in 1945, and
professed her religious vows in 1947. Given the name Sister Verona upon entrance to
the novitiate, she received her Bachelor of Arts degree from Mount Marty College,
a Master of Arts from Creighton University, and a Doctor of Philosophy in history
from the University of Notre Dame. After the Second Vatican Council, her baptismal name was restored, and she spent the rest of her forty-five year teaching career
as Sister Ann.

Sister Ann began teaching history and political science at Mount Marty College in 1962, also serving an interval as visiting professor at Marquette University.
During her tenure, she was appointed academic dean from 1962 to 1965, initiated
a new major in criminal justice, created the college's first endowed alumni scholarship with the Alumni Council, and received numerous grants and awards. In 2010,
she was named to Mount Marty College's Lancer Hall of Fame and received an
honorary Doctor of Humane Letters. She was also inducted into Aberdeen, South
Dakota's Central High School Hall of Fame in 2012.

Contributing to numerous books and writing articles for several publications
while teaching full time, she was also an active advocate of social justice, co-founding
a local rehabilitation center for juvenile legal offenders and another for psychiatric
clients needing continued care after their institutional dismissal.

Beyond the lecture hall, Sister Ann has applied her political acumen to South
Dakota state policy, serving as chair of the Governor's Council on the Aging, and as
co-chair of the Citizens' Committee for Study of Correctional Institutions. Three
governors appointed or maintained her service on the Governor's Task Force on
Correctional Policy and the State Criminal Justice Commission. In addition to
these appointments, she has served on two executive boards of the South Dakota's
Humanities Council.

Research tours on all five inhabited continents over a span of decades preceded
the publication of the first edition of this book, fulfilling the requests of many formation directors, oblates, historians, monastics, and other academics wishing for
an inclusive and comprehensive Benedictine history in a single volume. Sister Ann
continues her legacy of inspiring others' love of world and monastic history with this
new revision.

NEVILLE ANN (NEV) KELLY, D.MIN., PH.D., is an
independent scholar and spiritual practitioner. She has served as a spiritual director,
organizational founder, and assistant, visiting, and adjunct professor of religious
studies, philosophy, and theology at Mount Marty College. Previously leading
members of a lay, new monastic community, she & her husband continue in lifelong
pursuit of wisdom deeply embedded in Christian monastic and spiritual traditions.

❋

Benedictine Men and Women of Courage: Roots and History
was designed in Arno, Matrix II, and Trajan Pro
by Cheryl Finbow and Neville Ann Kelly,
and typeset by Lean Scholar Press,
Seattle, Washington.

Cheryl Finbow designed the cover
in Matrix II, P22Cezanne, and Trajan typefaces.

CPSIA information can be obtained
at www.ICGtesting.com
Printed in the USA
LVHW042145071222
734804LV00028B/490